T0181941

Communications in Computer and Information Science 1566

More information about this series at https://link.springer.com/bookseries/7899

Linqiang Pan · Zhihua Cui · Jianghui Cai ·
Lianghao Li (Eds.)

Bio-Inspired Computing: Theories and Applications

16th International Conference, BIC-TA 2021
Taiyuan, China, December 17–19, 2021
Revised Selected Papers, Part II

 Springer

Editors
Linqiang Pan 🄳
Huazhong University of Science
and Technology
Wuhan, China

Zhihua Cui 🄳
Taiyuan University of Science
and Technology
Taiyuan, China

Jianghui Cai 🄳
Taiyuan University of Science
and Technology
Taiyuan, China

Lianghao Li 🄳
Huazhong University of Science
and Technology
Wuhan, China

ISSN 1865-0929 ISSN 1865-0937 (electronic)
Communications in Computer and Information Science
ISBN 978-981-19-1252-8 ISBN 978-981-19-1253-5 (eBook)
https://doi.org/10.1007/978-981-19-1253-5

This Springer imprint is published by the registered company Springer Nature Singapore Pte Ltd.
The registered company address is: 152 Beach Road, #21-01/04 Gateway East, Singapore 189721, Singapore

Preface

Bio-inspired computing is a field of study that abstracts computing ideas (data structures, operations with data, ways to control operations, computing models, artificial intelligence, multisource data-driven methods and analysis, etc.) from living phenomena or biological systems such as cells, tissue, the brain, neural networks, the immune system, ant colonies, evolution, etc. The areas of bio-inspired computing include neural networks, brain-inspired computing, neuromorphic computing and architectures, cellular automata and cellular neural networks, evolutionary computing, swarm intelligence, fuzzy logic and systems, DNA and molecular computing, membrane computing, and artificial intelligence and its application in other disciplines such as machine learning, deep learning, image processing, computer science, cybernetics, etc. The Bio-Inspired Computing: Theories and Applications (BIC-TA) conference series aims to bring together researchers working in the main areas of bio-inspired computing, to present their recent results, exchange ideas, and foster cooperation in a friendly framework.

Since 2006, the conference has taken place in Wuhan (2006), Zhengzhou (2007), Adelaide (2008), Beijing (2009), Liverpool and Changsha (2010), Penang (2011), Gwalior (2012), Anhui (2013), Wuhan (2014), Anhui (2015), Xi'an (2016), Harbin (2017), Beijing (2018), Zhengzhou (2019), and Qingdao (2020). Following the success of previous editions, the 16th International Conference on Bio-Inspired Computing: Theories and Applications (BIC-TA 2021) was held in Taiyuan, China, during December 17–19, 2021, which was organized by the Taiyuan University of Science and Technology with the support of the Operations Research Society of Hubei.

We would like to thank the keynote speakers for their excellent presentations: Mingyong Han (Tianjin University, China), Chengde Mao (Purdue University, USA), Ling Wang (Tsinghua University, China), Rui Wang (National University of Defense Technology, China), and Wensheng Zhang (Chinese Academy of Sciences, China). Thanks are also given to the tutorial speakers for their informative presentations: Weigang Chen (Tianjin University, China), Cheng He (Southern University of Science and Technology, China), Tingfang Wu (Soochow University, China), and Gexiang Zhang (Chengdu University of Information Technology, China).

A special mention is given to Honorable Chair Gang Xie for his guidance and support to the conference.

We gratefully thank Xingjuan Cai, Yihao Cao, Guotong Chen, Weigang Chen, Tian Fan, Wanwan Guo, Yang Lan, Zhuoxuan Lan, Jie Wen, Lijie Xie, Linxia Yan, Huan Zhang, Jingbo Zhang, Zhixia Zhang, and Lihong Zhao for their contribution in organizing the conference. We also gratefully thank Shi Cheng, Weian Guo, Yinan Guo, Chaoli Sun, and Hui Wang for hosting the meetings.

Although BIC-TA 2021 was affected by COVID-19, we still received 211 submissions on various aspects of bio-inspired computing, and 67 papers were selected for this volume of Communications in Computer and Information Science. We are grateful to all the authors for submitting their interesting research work. The warmest thanks should be given to the external referees for their careful and efficient work in the reviewing process.

We thank Jianqing Lin and Guotong Chen for their help in collecting the final files of the papers and editing the volume. We thank Lianghao Li and Lianlang Duan for their contribution in maintaining the website of BIC-TA 2021 (http://2021.bicta.org/). We also thank all the other volunteers, whose efforts ensured the smooth running of the conference.

Special thanks are due to Springer for their skilled cooperation in the timely production of these volumes.

January 2022

Linqiang Pan
Zhihua Cui
Jianghui Cai
Lianghao Li

Organization

Steering Committee

Xiaochun Cheng	Middlesex University London, UK
Guangzhao Cui	Zhengzhou University of Light Industry, China
Kalyanmoy Deb	Michigan State University, USA
Miki Hirabayashi	National Institute of Information and Communications Technology, Japan
Joshua Knowles	University of Manchester, UK
Thom LaBean	North Carolina State University, USA
Jiuyong Li	University of South Australia, Australia
Kenli Li	University of Hunan, China
Giancarlo Mauri	Università di Milano-Bicocca, Italy
Yongli Mi	Hong Kong University of Science and Technology, Hong Kong
Atulya K. Nagar	Liverpool Hope University, UK
Linqiang Pan (Chair)	Huazhong University of Science and Technology, China
Gheorghe Paun	Romanian Academy, Romania
Mario J. Perez-Jimenez	University of Seville, Spain
K. G. Subramanian	Liverpool Hope University, UK
Robinson Thamburaj	Madras Christian College, India
Jin Xu	Peking University, China
Hao Yan	Arizona State University, USA

Honorable Chairs

Zhiguo Gui	Taiyuan University, China
Jiye Liang	Shanxi University, China
Gang Xie	Taiyuan University of Science and Technology, China
Jianchao Zeng	North University of China, China

General Chair

Jianghui Cai	North University of China, China

Program Committee Chairs

Zhihua Cui   Taiyuan University of Science and Technology,
                              China
Linqiang Pan   Huazhong University of Science and Technology,
                              China

Special Session Chair

Yan Qiang   Taiyuan University of Technology, China

Tutorial Chair

Weigang Chen   Tianjin University, China

Publication Chairs

Lianghao Li   Huazhong University of Science and Technology,
                              China
Gaige Wang   Ocean University of China, China
Qingshan Zhao   Xinzhou Teachers University, China

Publicity Chair

Haifeng Yang   Taiyuan University of Science and Technology,
                              China

Local Chair

Chaoli Sun   Taiyuan University of Science and Technology,
                              China

Registration Chair

Libo Yang   Taiyuan University, China

Program Committee

Muhammad Abulaish   South Asian University, India
Andy Adamatzky   University of the West of England, UK
Chang Wook Ahn   Gwangju Institute of Science and Technology,
                              South Korea
Adel Al-Jumaily   University of Technology Sydney, Australia
Bin Cao   Hebei University of Technology, China

Junfeng Chen	Hohai University, China
Wei-Neng Chen	Sun Yat-sen University, China
Shi Cheng	Shaanxi Normal University, China
Xiaochun Cheng	Middlesex University London, UK
Tsung-Che Chiang	National Taiwan Normal University, China
Sung-Bae Cho	Yonsei University, South Korea
Zhihua Cui	Taiyuan University of Science and Technology, China
Kejie Dai	Pingdingshan University, China
Ciprian Dobre	Politehnica University of Bucharest, Romania
Bei Dong	Shanxi Normal University, China
Xin Du	Fujian Normal University, China
Carlos Fernandez-Llatas	Universitat Politecnica de Valencia, Spain
Shangce Gao	University of Toyama, Japan
Marian Gheorghe	University of Bradford, UK
Wenyin Gong	China University of Geosciences, China
Shivaprasad Gundibail	Manipal Academy of Higher Education, India
Ping Guo	Beijing Normal University, China
Yinan Guo	China University of Mining and Technology, China
Guosheng Hao	Jiangsu Normal University, China
Cheng He	Southern University of Science and Technology, China
Shan He	University of Birmingham, UK
Tzung-Pei Hong	National Univesity of Kaohsiung, China
Florentin Ipate	University of Bucharest, Romania
Sunil Kumar Jha	Banaras Hindu University, India
He Jiang	Dalian University of Technology, China
Qiaoyong Jiang	Xi'an University of Technology, China
Licheng Jiao	Xidian University, China
Liangjun Ke	Xian Jiaotong University, China
Ashwani Kush	Kurukshetra University, India
Hui Li	Xi'an Jiaotong University, China
Kenli Li	Hunan University, China
Lianghao Li	Huazhong University of Science and Technology, China
Yangyang Li	Xidian University, China
Zhihui Li	Zhengzhou University, China
Jing Liang	Zhengzhou University, China
Jerry Chun-Wei Lin	Western Norway University of Applied Sciences, Norway
Qunfeng Liu	Dongguan University of Technology, China

Xiaobo Liu	China University of Geosciences, China
Wenjian Luo	University of Science and Technology of China, China
Lianbo Ma	Northeastern University, China
Wanli Ma	University of Canberra, Australia
Xiaoliang Ma	Shenzhen University, China
Francesco Marcelloni	University of Pisa, Italy
Efrén Mezura-Montes	University of Veracruz, Mexico
Hongwei Mo	Harbin Engineering University, China
Chilukuri Mohan	Syracuse University, USA
Abdulqader Mohsen	University of Science and Technology Yemen, Yemen
Holger Morgenstern	Albstadt-Sigmaringen University, Germany
Andres Muñoz	Universidad Católica San Antonio de Murcia, Spain
G. R. S. Murthy	Lendi Institute of Engineering and Technology, India
Akila Muthuramalingam	KPR Institute of Engineering and Technology, India
Yusuke Nojima	Osaka Prefecture University, Japan
Linqiang Pan	Huazhong University of Science and Technology, China
Andrei Paun	University of Bucharest, Romania
Gheorghe Paun	Romanian Academy, Romania
Xingguang Peng	Northwestern Polytechnical University, China
Chao Qian	University of Science and Technology of China, China
Balwinder Raj	NITTTR, India
Rawya Rizk	Port Said University, Egypt
Rajesh Sanghvi	G. H. Patel College of Engineering and Technology, India
Ronghua Shang	Xidian University, China
Zhigang Shang	Zhengzhou University, China
Ravi Shankar	Florida Atlantic University, USA
V. Ravi Sankar	GITAM University, India
Bosheng Song	Hunan University, China
Tao Song	China University of Petroleum, China
Jianyong Sun	University of Nottingham, UK
Yifei Sun	Shaanxi Normal University, China
Handing Wang	Xidian University, China
Yong Wang	Central South University, China
Hui Wang	Nanchang Institute of Technology, China
Hui Wang	South China Agricultural University, China

Gaige Wang	Ocean University of China, China
Sudhir Warier	IIT Bombay, India
Slawomir T. Wierzchon	Polish Academy of Sciences, Poland
Zhou Wu	Chongqing University, China
Xiuli Wu	University of Science and Technology Beijing, China
Bin Xin	Beijing Institute of Technology, China
Gang Xu	Nanchang University, China
Yingjie Yang	De Montfort University, UK
Zhile Yang	Shenzhen Institute of Advanced Technology, Chinese Academy of Sciences, China
Kunjie Yu	Zhengzhou University, China
Xiaowei Zhang	University of Science and Technology of China, China
Jie Zhang	Newcastle University, UK
Gexiang Zhang	Chengdu University of Technology, China
Defu Zhang	Xiamen University, China
Peng Zhang	Beijing University of Posts and Telecommunications, China
Weiwei Zhang	Zhengzhou University of Light Industry, China
Yong Zhang	China University of Mining and Technology, China
Xinchao Zhao	Beijing University of Posts and Telecommunications, China
Yujun Zheng	Zhejiang University of Technology, China
Aimin Zhou	East China Normal University, China
Fengqun Zhou	Pingdingshan University, China
Xinjian Zhuo	Beijing University of Posts and Telecommunications, China
Shang-Ming Zhou	Swansea University, UK
Dexuan Zou	Jiangsu Normal University, China
Xingquan Zuo	Beijing University of Posts and Telecommunications, China

Contents – Part II

Machine Learning and Computer Vision

Contents – Part I

DNA and Molecular Computing

Machine Learning and Computer Vision

Point Clouds Registration Algorithm Based on Spatial Structure Similarity of Visual Keypoints

Yingshuo Gao, Jie Ma[✉], Bingli Wu, Tianxiang Zhang, and Yu Yang

National Key Laboratory of Multispectral Information Processing Technology, School of Artificial Intelligence and Automation, Huazhong University of Science and Technology, Wuhan 430074, China
majie@hust.edu.cn

Abstract. In autonomous driving technology, vehicles use LiDAR to accomplish various tasks. Issues are that the point cloud collected by the LiDAR is too sparse and some objects are mutilated, which is a great challenge for tasks such as detection and recognition. It is necessary to merge multiple frames of point clouds with registration algorithm to make data complete and dense. Previous point cloud registration methods run slowly and have low accuracy when dealing with autopilot field point clouds. It is difficult to find the correspondence of different point clouds. While humans can easily find the exact corresponding through the visual information received by eyes, as it contains color and texture. The visual images acquired by optical cameras can simulate the human eyes well. Therefore, we propose to use visual image assisted point cloud registration. Firstly, we extract the keypoints of visual images, then we obtain their depth by depth completion algorithm and back-project them into 3D space as 3D keypoints. Finally, we screen 3D keypoint pairs by spatial structure similarity to estimate the rigid transformation parameters. After experiments, it is proved that our method achieves substantial improvement in both speed and accuracy.

Keywords: Point clouds registration · LiDAR · Image

1 Introduction

High sparsity of point clouds and view limitations constrain the widespread use of LiDAR in autonomous driving [1], as shown in Fig. 1(a), the objects in the box are mutilated or have too few points. By merging multi-frame point clouds, data densification and completeness can be achieved, thus improving the accuracy of target detection and recognition. Due to the different reference coordinate systems of different viewpoint point clouds, the objects in two frames of point clouds are misaligned, as shown in Fig. 1(b), the registration method is needed to merge the point clouds.

Previous point cloud registration algorithms require that the point clouds have low initial errors or simple structures, which are not suitable for point clouds in autonomous driving scenarios, and the speed of registration cannot meet the real-time requirements

© Springer Nature Singapore Pte Ltd. 2022
L. Pan et al. (Eds.): BIC-TA 2021, CCIS 1566, pp. 3–11, 2022.
https://doi.org/10.1007/978-981-19-1253-5_1

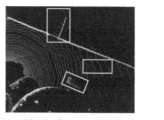 

(a)   Single-frame point cloud   (b)   multi-frame point clouds

Fig. 1. Single-frame/multi-frame point clouds.

of autonomous driving. Thus, we proposes a point cloud registration algorithm based on the spatial structure similarity of visual keypoints, which is fast and has much higher accuracy than the classical algorithm. The registration process is shown in Fig. 2.

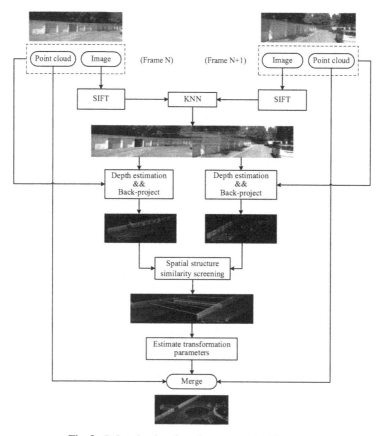

Fig. 2. Point cloud registration process in this paper.

2   Method

In this section, we introduce the main steps of the point cloud registration algorithm. Firstly, we illustrate the extraction and screening method of visual image keypoints, then we introduce the depth completion algorithm based on virtual normal guidance; subsequently, we investigate the 3D keypoint screening algorithm based on spatial structure similarity and test the screening performance, and finally the calculation method of transformation parameters is introduced.

2.1   2D Visual Keypoints

The SIFT feature descriptor algorithm [2] is used to extract 2D visual image feature points. SIFT operator has scale and rotation invariance. The coordinate system relationship between point clouds is a rigid transformation, SIFT operator is very suitable for this situation. After getting the keypoints and their descriptors, KNN algorithm is used to match the keypoints. The idea of this algorithm is as follow, for a keypoint, calculate the Euclidean distance between its descriptor and the descriptors of other keypoints, and take the two keypoints with the smallest distance after sorting, and record the nearest distance d_1 and the next closest distance d_2, if the nearest distance and the next closest distance satisfy $d_1 < ratio \cdot d_2$, then accept the pair of matching points, otherwise reject the keypoint. We take $ratio = 0.6$ (Figs. 3 and 4).

Fig. 3. SIFT 2D keypoints.

Fig. 4. 2D keypoint pairs after KNN.

2.2   Depth Completion and Back-Project

After obtaining the 2D keypoint pairs, there will be large errors in calculating the transformation parameters directly, so it is necessary to obtain their depth information and back-project them to 3D space as 3D keypoint pairs. Subject to the sparsity of the point cloud, most of the 2D keypoints do not have corresponding depth pixel, so it is necessary to estimate the depth of the 2D keypoints to obtain their positions in 3D space. We propose a depth completion algorithm based on virtual normal [3] guidance, which uses virtual normals instead of visual information for guidance. The virtual normal reflects the orientation information of a point, and the points located in the region similar to the center point tend to have similar surface orientation, while the surface orientation of the points crossing the bulge will obviously be more influenced by the bulge. Using the inner product of normals as one of the conditions to measure the similarity of neighboring points, the weights of the virtual normal bootstrap term are calculated as follows.

(1) Collect 8 neighborhood points uniformly in the vicinity of the point to be estimated, calculate the virtual normal of the center point according to the depth, and use the same way to calculate the virtual normal for each neighborhood point.
(2) Depth calculation by bilateral filter [4] as Eq. (1).

$$\tilde{D}_p = \frac{\sum\limits_{q \in \Omega} f(\|p - q\|) g\left(\|I_p - I_q\|\right) \bullet D_q}{\sum\limits_{q \in \Omega} f(\|p - q\|) g\left(\|I_p - I_q\|\right)} \tag{1}$$

$$g\left(\|I_p - I_q\|\right) = I_p \bullet I_q \bullet \sigma_n \tag{2}$$

$$f(\|p - q\|) = \frac{\sigma_r}{\|p - q\|^2} \tag{3}$$

Where p and q represent the pixel coordinates, $\tilde{D}_p$ is the completion depth, D_q is the depth of the neighboring points, Ω is the space domain window of the filter. g and f are the spatial filter kernel and the range filter kernel, respectively, which are used to calculate the weights of the neighboring points. I_p and I_q represent the virtual normal vectors. The distance term weights are adopted as euclidean distances, and the empirical values of the parameters σ_n and σ_r are 10 and 2, respectively.

The 2D keypoints are back-projected to 3D space by their depth values and coordinates, as shown in Fig. 5, where the blue points represent the keypoints.

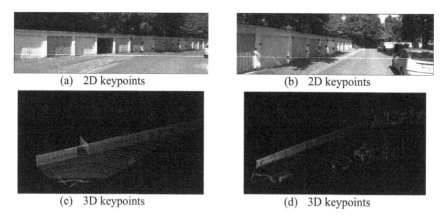

| (a) 2D keypoints | (b) 2D keypoints |
| (c) 3D keypoints | (d) 3D keypoints |

Fig. 5. 2D keypoints are back-projected to 3D space as 3D keypoints.

2.3   Screening 3D Keypoints

Although the KNN algorithm was used to do the initial screening of 2D keypoint pairs, there are still many mismatch pairs, and after conversion to 3D key points, the mismatch relationship still exists, thus further screening is needed. We proposed a screening algorithm of 3D keypoint pairs based on spatial structural similarity.

Under the premise of rigid transformation, the relative positions of the 3D keypoints that are correctly matched are invariant in their respective scenes. The relative positions of the keypoints in the source point cloud and other keypoints are still consistent after passing the rigid transformation, as shown in Fig. 6.

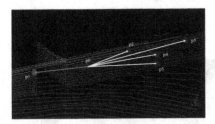   

(a)   Source keypoints spatial structure   (b)   Target keypoints spatial structure

Fig. 6. Comparison of spatial structure of source and target keypoints.

Each pair of keypoints is scored based on spatial structural similarity, and the best matching pairs can be selected. The specific steps are as follows.

(1)   Calculate the distance and direction between keypoints. Select a keypoint pair as the center point of the two point clouds, calculate the Euclidean distances and direction vectors from other keypoints to the center point.

$$L_{p_i} = \sqrt{(p_i(x) - p_0(x))^2 + (p_i(y) - p_0(y))^2 + (p_i(z) - p_0(z))^2}$$
$$L_{q_i} = \sqrt{(q_i(x) - q_0(x))^2 + (q_i(y) - q_0(y))^2 + (q_i(z) - q_0(z))^2} \tag{4}$$

$$N_{p_i} = \frac{\overrightarrow{p_0 p_i}}{L_{p_i}} \ , \ \ N_{q_i} = \frac{\overrightarrow{q_0 q_i}}{L_{q_i}} \tag{5}$$

$p_0(x, y, z)$ and $q_0(x, y, z)$ are the selected center pair, $p_i(x, y, z)$ and $q_i(x, y, z)$ are the other pairs. L_{p_i} represents the 3D Euclidean distance from point pi to point p0, and N_{p_i} represents the unit direction vector from point p0 to point pi.

(2)   Calculate the scores of other keypoint pairs. It can be seen that the distance and direction of the mis-matching pair (p_1, q_1) and the centroid of the respective scene will produce relatively obvious changes in characteristics, while the other keypoints will basically maintain their structural characteristics. The score of the jth keypoint pair is calculated by Eq. (6). To ensure the robustness of the score, each keypoint pair is set as the center point, and the scores are calculated and accumulated

$$score_j = \sum_{i}^{n-1} \frac{N_{p_i} \bullet N_{q_i} + 1}{|L_{p_i} - L_{q_i}| + 0.1} \tag{6}$$

(3) Keep the 8 keypoint pairs with the highest scores, and remove other keypoints. As can be seen from the Table 1, the screening algorithm based on spatial structural similarity has high pairing accuracy and is very fast (Fig. 7).

Table 1. Results of spatial structure similarity screening.

Number of remaining pairs	Matching success rate	Time consuming/s
20	98.33%	0.026
10	100%	0.025

Fig. 7. Results of spatial structure similarity screening.

2.4   Rigid Transformation Parameter Estimation

Estimate the rigid transformation parameters R and T based on the remaining 8 keypoint pairs after screening: the source point cloud keypoints $P = \{p_1, p_2, ..., p_8\}$ and the corresponding keypoints $Q = \{q_1, q_2, ..., q_8\}$ of the target point cloud. The process is as follows.

(1) Construct a model that requires the minimum distance between the corresponding keypoints after the transformation [5], as seen in Eq. (7).

$$(R, T) = argmin \sum_{i=1}^{8} w_i \|(Rp_i + T) - q_i\|^2 \tag{7}$$

(2) The two keypoint sets are decentered to obtain the new point sets X and Y, denoted as Eqs. (8) and (9). The model is then transformed into Eq. (10).

$$\hat{p} = \frac{\sum_{i=1}^{8} w_i p_i}{\sum_{i=1}^{8} w_i} \ , \ \hat{q} = \frac{\sum_{i=1}^{8} w_i q_i}{\sum_{i=1}^{8} w_i} \tag{8}$$

$$x_i = p_i - \hat{p} \ , \ y_i = q_i - \hat{q} \tag{9}$$

$$R = argmin \sum_{i=1}^{8} w_i \|Rx_i - y_i\|^2 \tag{10}$$

(3) In order to achieve the maximum value of $tr(\sum V^T RU)$, let $I = V^T RU$, simplify and obtain $R = VU^T$. Then the translation matrix T is obtained according to $T = \hat{q} - R\hat{p}$.

After the steps, the rigid transformation parameters R and T are applied to the source point cloud to finish the registration.

3 Experiment

3.1 Data and Metrics

The experimental data are point clouds and visual images from KITTI dataset [6]. Point cloud obtained from the LiDAR at a moment is set as the source point cloud, and the point cloud obtained after a period of time is set as the target point cloud. The corresponding visual images are acquired by the optical camera at the same time.

After registration, calculate the closest distance from each point in the point cloud to the other point cloud, and the points whose distance is greater than three times the average are removed to reduce the interference of noise. The average of the remaining points distance is used as the evaluation metrics, as seen in Eq. (11).

$$d = \frac{1}{n} \sum_{i=1}^{n} \|p_i - q_i\|^2 \tag{11}$$

3.2 Experiment and Comparison

We choose two mainstream point cloud registration methods for comparison. The first one is the Iterative Closest Point (ICP) algorithm [7], which sets the maximum number of iterations to 50 and the target error to 0.2 m. The second method is an registration method based on FPFH descriptors [8] of keypoints: firstly, the ISS (Intrinsic Shape Signatures) feature point detection algorithm [9] is used to extract the appropriate number of keypoints from the source and target point clouds respectively, then the FPFH feature vectors are calculated and keypoints are matched, finally the RANSAC algorithm [10] is used to iteratively eliminate the wrong point pairs and continuously optimize the transformation matrix. The number of RANSAC iterations is set to 1000. The experimental results are shown in Table 2.

As can be seen in Table 2, the algorithm based on the spatial structure similarity of visual keypoints can complete the complex scene point cloud registration within 1.5 s, which is sufficient to complete the Merge within the acquisition interval of adjacent frames. The average registration error is within 0.2 m, which can meet the requirements of vision tasks such as target detection and recognition in outdoor scenes.

As is shown in Fig. 8, the registration effect of ICP algorithm is unstable, as ICP algorithm is sensitive to the initial error. the FPFH-based registration algorithm fails in some cases because objects with similar structures can greatly mislead the matching of local keypoints. Our method performs better and is highly robust, which is applicable not only to regular inner-city roads but also to suburban areas filled with a lot of natural vegetation.

Table 2. Comparison of the registration results.

Method	Number of points	Error/m		Time consuming/s
		Before registraion	After registraion	
ICP [7]	120587	0.725	0.606	27.5
FPFH [8]			0.434	15.2
Ours			**0.240**	**1.5**

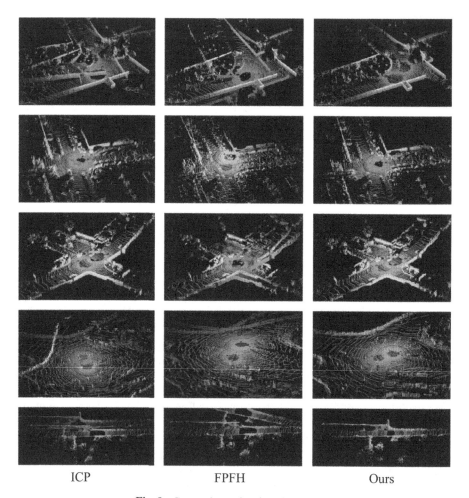

| ICP | FPFH | Ours |

Fig. 8. Comparison of registration results.

4 Conclusion

We propose a point cloud registration algorithm based on the spatial structure similarity of visual keypoints, which greatly improves the registration speed and accuracy of point clouds in autonomous driving scenarios.

We use SIFT descriptor algorithm and KNN algorithm for 2D keypoints extraction and matching, and then obtain 3D keypoint pairs by virtual normal guided depth completion algorithm and spatial structure similarity screening algorithm. Finally, we calculate rigid transformation parameters and finish the registration of point clouds. Experiments show that our method achieves the best results with high robustness.

However, our algorithm sometimes has the problem of registration failure, generally because (i) the number of correct matching pairs is insufficient, (ii) the depth calculation error is too large. This problem can be solved by using other visual feature descriptors or replacing the depth completion method.

References

1. Chen, S., Liu, B., Feng, C., et al.: 3D Point cloud processing and learning for autonomous driving: impacting map creation, localization, and perception. IEEE Signal Process. Mag. **38**(1), 68–86 (2021)
2. Lowe, D.G.: Distinctive image features from scale-invariant keypoints. Int. J. Comput. Vis. **60**(2), 91–110 (2004)
3. Yin, W., Liu, Y., Shen, C., et al.: Enforcing geometric constraints of virtual normal for depth prediction. In: Proceedings of the IEEE/CVF International Conference on Computer Vision, Seoul, South Korea, pp. 5684–5693 (2019)
4. He, K., Sun, J., Tang, X.: Guided image filtering. In: European Conference on Computer Vision, Crete, Greece, pp. 1–14 (2010)
5. Umeyama, S.: Least-squares estimation of transformation parameters between two point patterns. IEEE Trans. Pattern Anal. Mach. Intell. **13**(4), 376–380 (1991)
6. Geiger, A., Lenz, P., Urtasun, R.: Are we ready for autonomous driving? The kitti vision benchmark suite. In: 2012 IEEE Conference on Computer Vision and Pattern Recognition, Providence, USA, pp. 3354–3361 (2012)
7. Besl, P.J., Mckay, H.D.: A method for registration of 3-D shapes. IEEE Trans. Pattern Anal. Mach. Intell. **14**(2), 239–256 (1992)
8. Rusu, R.B., Blodow, N., Beetz, M.: Fast point feature histograms (FPFH) for 3D registration. In: IEEE International Conference on Robotics and Automation, Kobe, Japan, pp. 3212–3217 (2009)
9. Zhong, Y.: Intrinsic shape signatures: a shape descriptor for 3d object recognition. In: IEEE 12th International Conference on Computer Vision Workshops, ICCV Workshops, Kyoto, Japan, pp. 689–696 (2009)
10. Chen, C.S., Hung, Y.P., Cheng, J.B.: RANSAC-based DARCES: a new approach to fast automatic registration of partially overlapping range images. IEEE Trans. Pattern Anal. Mach. Intell. **21**(11), 1229–1234 (2002)

Software Defect Prediction Based on SMOTE-Tomek and XGBoost

Haotian Yang[1,2] and Min Li[1,2(✉)]

[1] School of Information Engineering, Nanchang Institute of Technology, Jiangxi 330099,
People's Republic of China
liminghuadi@hotmail.com
[2] Jiangxi Province Key Laboratory of Water Information Cooperative Sensing and Intelligent
Processing, Jiangxi 330099, People's Republic of China

Abstract. The use of machine learning techniques to predict software defects has received extensive attention over the years. In practice, there are far fewer defective software samples than non-defective software samples, resulting in a high imbalance of sample categories. The problem of imbalanced data classification is a hotspot and difficulty in machine learning and data mining. In order to effectively solve the problem of software defect prediction, we introduce a classification model that combines SMOTE-Tomek sampling and ensemble learning algorithm XGBoost. Our initial experimental results on ten NASA software defect datasets indicate a clear superiority of the proposed techniques when compared to other hybrid model regarding various assessment metrics, such Accuracy, F-Measure, and AUC.

Keywords: Software defect prediction · Imbalanced dataset · Combined sampling · Ensemble learning · XGBoost

1 Introduction

Software defects are errors in the software process caused by incorrect programming logic, misunderstanding of requirements, lack of coding experience, etc. Software defect detection is an important subject of software engineering. Researches in last two decades have focused on different statistical and machine learning methods to solve the software defect prediction problem, including Support Vector Machine (SVM) [1], Decision Trees (DT) [2], K-Nearest Neighbor (KNN) [3], Logistic Regression (LR) [4], and Naive Bayes (NB) [5]. However, software defect dataset suffers from the unbalanced distribution problems of defective and non-defective modules. For the problem of software defect prediction, defective module is more important from a learning point of view because it implies a great cost when it is misclassified. In fact, the training process of traditional classifiers generally follows the principle of minimizing the number of misclassified instances and thereby maximize the prediction accuracy for future samples. For imbalanced classification problem, the classification is biased towards the majority class, so the final model has poor classification performance for the minority class. In extreme

L. Pan et al. (Eds.): BIC-TA 2021, CCIS 1566, pp. 12–31, 2022.
https://doi.org/10.1007/978-981-19-1253-5_2

cases, the classification model is even completely invalid. Software defect prediction is a typical of class imbalance problems, which refers to the large difference in the number of samples of different classes in the training data, and the number of samples of some categories is much smaller than the number of samples of other categories. The imbalance of training samples makes it difficult for most classifiers to obtain ideal recognition performance for small categories of samples. Class imbalance problems exist widely in real applications. The algorithms to solve these problems are called class imbalance learning algorithms. Class imbalance learning has always been one of the research hot spots and difficulties in the field of machine learning and data mining. The objective of the imbalanced learning algorithm can be simply described as obtaining a classifier that can provide high accuracy for the minority class without severely jeopardizing the accuracy of the majority class. At present, many types of imbalanced learning technologies have been proposed, which can be roughly divided into data layer processing technologies [6], built-in technologies [7], and hybrid technologies [8]. For example, Razavi et al. [9] proposed a method of applying the idea of missing value filling to data over-sampling. In this method, missing values are estimated and updated by the expected value maximization method, which effectively realizes the generation of fault datasets. Chawla et al. [10] presents an approach named SMOTEBoost for improving prediction of the minority class. Unlike standard boosting where all misclassified examples are given equal weights, it creates synthetic examples from the rare or minority class, thus indirectly changing the updating weights and compensating for skewed distributions. Recently, Yang et al. [11] propose a hybrid optimal ensemble classifier framework that combines density-based under-sampling and cost-effective methods through exploring state-of-the-art solutions using multi-objective optimization algorithm.

In order to effectively improve the performance of software defect prediction, we introduce a novel hybrid proposal named STX that combines sampling technique of SMOTE-Tomek [12] and ensemble learning of XGBoost [13]. The processes of STX primarily includes two steps: firstly, it rebalanced a training dataset and filtering out noise samples of software defect prediction by SMOTE-Tomek; and next, the balanced train dataset is used to train XGBoost classifier for constructing a classification model. In order to evaluate the effectiveness of the proposed classification model, we conducted extensive comparative experiments using ten NASA software defect data sets [14]. The experimental results verify the superiority of the proposed model in solving the software defect prediction problem.

The rest of this article is organized as follows. In Sect. 2, we briefly introduce the most relevant works. In Sect. 3, we describe the proposed STX model. In Sect. 4, the experimental setup, results and analysis of this paper are introduced. Finally, the fifth part gives the final conclusion and outlines the future research direction.

2   Related Work

This section briefly reviews the work on sampling techniques and integrated learning. In Sect. 2.1, some most popular and relevant sampling methods are presented. Then, in Sect. 2.2, we present some common ensemble learning algorithm used in software defect prediction domains.

2.1 Sampling Technique

Sampling techniques mainly include under-sampling and over-sampling, which respectively obtain a new dataset with relatively balanced distribution by reducing the majority class samples and increasing the minority class samples. Under-sampling methods include: RUS [15], NearMiss-1 [16], NearMiss-2 [17], NearMiss-3 [18] and TOME-Links [19], etc. Random Under-sampling (RUS) balances the data by randomly selecting a subset of the data for the target category. The main contents of the three Near-Miss methods are as follows:

- NearMiss-1 selects the positive (generally mean minority class) samples for which the average distance to the N closest samples of the negative class (generally mean majority) is the smallest.
- NearMiss-2 selects the positive samples for which the average distance to the N farthest samples of the negative class is the smallest.
- NearMiss-3 is a 2-steps algorithm. First, for each negative sample, their M nearest-neighbors will be kept. Then, the positive samples selected are the one for which the average distance to the N nearest-neighbors is the largest.

TOME-Links calculates the distance between two instances x_i and x_j belonging to different classes: denoted by $d(x_i, x_j)$. The relationship between x_i and x_j is a Tomek Link if there is no other sample x in the dataset that satisfies $d(x_i, x) < d(x_i, x_j)$. If x_i and x_j are judged to be Tomek Links, either one of them is noise data or both located on the boundary. By looking for all TOMEK Links, Under-sampling can be achieved by deleting noisy and boundary data in majority classes.

In order to provide a visual comparison of the data Under-sampling mechanism mentioned above, we take the CM1 dataset (derived from NASA datasets) as an example. We performed respectively five different types of Under-sampling on CM1 dataset. After that, the PCA (principal component analysis) is used to reduce the original dimension space to a two-dimensional plane. The final results are show in Fig. 1. In Fig. 1 the red symbols (MA) represent the majority of the class samples, and the bule symbols (MI) represent the minority of the class samples. Figure 1(a) shows the original data distribution of CM1; Fig. 1(b) and (c) represent the data distribution after Under-sampling with Tomek Links and RUS (random Under-sampling), respectively; Fig. 1(d)–(f) show the data distribution after Under-sampling with NearMiss-1, NearMiss-2, and NearMiss-3, respectively.

Under-sampling is not suitable for the case when the total number of samples is too small. Over-sampling is usually applied to datasets with small sample sizes or too few samples of the minority class sample. Over-sampling methods add minority class samples to an imbalanced data set, so that the minority and majority class samples are balanced. Over-sampling methods mainly include ROS [8, 19, 20] (Random Over-sampling), ADASYN [20], SMOTE [21], etc. ROS is a method of balancing datasets by randomly increasing the number of samples from the minority class, which can increase the risk of over-fitting. Accordingly, SMOTE technique was proposed by generating artificial samples based on feature space similarities between existing minority samples. Specifically, the method synthesizes a new minority sample by linear interpolation

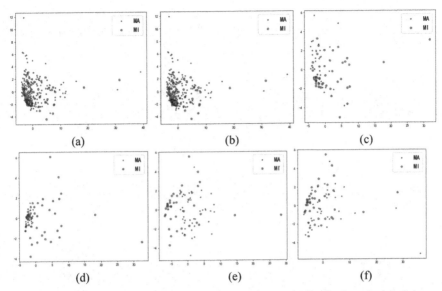

Fig. 1. Comparison of Under-sampling mechanisms. (a) Sample distribution of original data set. (b) Sample distribution after Under-sampling with Tomek Links; (c) Sample distribution after RUS; (d) Sample distribution after Under-sampling with NearMiss-1; (e) Sample distribution after with NearMiss-2; (f) Sample distribution after Under-sampling with NearMiss-3.

between a minority sample and its k intra-class nearest neighbors. Let x is a minority sample and x_i is one of its k intra-class nearest neighbor. The new synthesized minority sample x_{new} is created according to Formula (1).

$$x_{new} = x + rand(0, 1) \times (x - x_i), \tag{1}$$

where, $rand(0, 1)$ represents a random number between 0 and 1; All synthesized new samples are combined with the original training sample set into a new training sample set. To provide an intuitive comparison of the data Over-sampling mechanism mentioned above, we take the CM1 dataset (is derived from NASA datasets) as an example again. We performed respectively three different types of Over-sampling on CM1 dataset. After that, the PCA (principal component analysis) is used to reduce the original dimension space to a two-dimensional plane. The final results are show in Fig. 2. In Fig. 2 the red symbols (MA) represent the majority of the class samples, and the bule symbols (MI) represent the minority of the class samples. Figure 2 (a) shows the original data distribution of CM1; Fig. 2(b) and (c) show the data distribution after random Over-sampling and ADASYN, respectively; Fig. 2(d) shows the data distribution after Over-sampling with SMOTE.

2.2 Cost-Sensitive Learning

To solve the classification error problem of traditional machine learning algorithms, a cost-sensitive learning method is proposed. Cost-sensitive learning methods directly

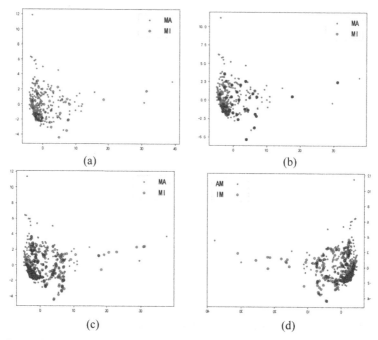

Fig. 2. Comparison of Over-sampling mechanisms. (a) Sample distribution of original data set; (b) Sample distribution after Over-sampling with random Over-sampling; (c) Sample distribution after Over-sampling with ADASYN; (d) Sample distribution after Over-sampling with SMOTE. (Color figure online)

assign distinct costs to misclassification of examples from different classes. Zadrozny et al. [22] fed the cost proportionate based weights to classification algorithm to enhance the performance. Hamed et al. [23] extended the hinge loss to the cost-sensitive setting, and derived the optimal cost-sensitive learning algorithm to find the minimizer of the associated risk. Liu et al. [24] decomposed F-measure optimization into a series of cost-sensitive classification problems, and investigated the cost-sensitive feature selection by generating and assigning different costs to each class. Chen et al. [25] applied different misclassification costs to different categories in PU classification to solve the problem of biased classifiers due to class imbalance of PU learning methods.

However, threshold determination and weight estimation in cost sensitive learning are difficult in practical applications. Therefore, an ensemble learning method is developed to train multiple classifiers and obtain better results by using voting or other techniques.

2.3 Ensample Learning Algorithm

In machine learning algorithm, ensemble learning integrates multiple weak classifiers to obtain a strong classifier, so as to improve the classification effect. In order to alleviate class imbalance problems, Sun [26] proposed a coding-based ensemble learning method which change imbalanced classes dataset into multiple balanced classes datasets. Aleem et al. [27] implemented experiments on 15 NASA datasets from the PROMISE repository to compare the performance of eleven types of machine learning methods. The results showed that in most datasets, Bagging and SVMs performed well in accuracy and recall. Alsaeedi et al. [28] compared many supervised machine learning approaches and ensemble classifiers on 10 NASA datasets. The experimental results show that, in most cases, random forest is the best classifier for software defect prediction. Laradji et al. [29] combine a selective ensemble learning model with efficient feature selection to address data imbalance and feature redundancy and mitigate their impact on defect classification performance. Furthermore, Ibrahim et al. [30] proposed a classification model by using feature selection and the Random Forest algorithm (RF) for the software defect prediction.

The above research did not specifically discuss the advantages of the combination of sampling technology and ensemble learning. This article refers to the above conclusions, adopts the SMOTE-Tomek algorithm, combined with the integrated classification algorithm, to effectively solve the software defect prediction.

3 The Proposed Model

In this section, a software defective prediction mode based on over-and-under fusion sampling SMOTE-Tomek and extreme gradient boosting decision tree (XGBoost) is proposed.

3.1 SMOTE-Tomek

In software defect prediction, the number of defective modules is much smaller than that of none-defective modules, which makes difficult to obtain ideal classification performance by using general classification model. As mentioned above, class imbalanced problem can be alleviated by over-sampling or under-sampling methods. However, both of the over-sampling or under-sampling methods have their disadvantages. On the one hand, the major disadvantage of under-sampling methods is the loss of potentially useful information that may be important to prediction, on the other hand, over-sampling methods can increase the risk of overfitting.

SMOTE sampling method expands the sample space of minority class so as to balance the distribution of training dataset. As a result, the space originally belonging to the majority class is occupied by the minority class sample, resulting in excessive bias of classification plane. Considering that, in our proposed model of software defect prediction, SMOTE-Tomek sampling is adopted. The process of SMOTE-Tomek includes two steps. First, the imbalanced dataset is balanced by SMOTE over-sampling. Next, TOME-Links under-sampling is used to remove noise and borders. Therefore, SMOTE-Tomek is fusion sampling technique, and it inherits the advantages of SMOTE over-sampling and TOME-Links under-sampling.

We take the CM1 dataset as an example again. We performed SMOTE-Tomek on CM1 dataset, which means the dataset was rebalanced by SMOTE over-sampling and then TOME-Links under-sampling is used to remove noise and borders. After that, the PCA is used to reduce the original dimension space to a two-dimensional plane. Figure 3(b) shows the data distribution after SMOTE-Tomek.

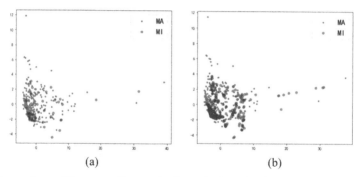

Fig. 3. Comparison of Over-sampling mechanisms. (a) Sample distribution of original data set; (b) Sample distribution after Over-sampling with SMOTE-Tomek.

3.2 XGBoost

XGBoost [31] (Extreme Gradient Boosting) is an optimized distributed gradient boosting algorithm. It provides a parallel tree boosting (also known as GBDT, GBM) that solves many data science problems with a fast and accurate way. The main idea of XGBoost is to select some samples and features to generate a simple model (such as a decision tree) as the basic classifier. When generating a new model, it learns the residuals of the previous model and minimize the objective function. The process is repeated until the specified number of linear or tree models are generated. Finally, all generated tree models are combined into a comprehensive model with high accuracy. The key step of XGBoost algorithm is that the new model is established in the direction of the corresponding loss function gradient to correct the residual while controlling the complexity.

XGBoost learning obtains gradient promotion-based regression tree with the same decision rules as the decision tree. In the regression tree, the inside nodes represent values of attributes test and the leaf nodes with scores represent a predicted value. The result of the prediction is the sum of the scores predicted by K trees, as shown in Formula 2.

$$\hat{y}_i = \sum_{k=1}^{K} f_k(x_i), f_k \in F \tag{2}$$

Where x_i is the i-th training sample, $f_k(x_i)$ is the score for the k-th tree and F is the space of functions containing all the regression trees. Compared with the gradient tree boosting algorithm, XGBoost improves the regularized objective. The regularization objective optimization formula is shown as Formula 3.

$$Obj = \sum_{i=1}^{n} l(y_i, \hat{y}_i) + \sum_{k=1}^{K} \Omega(f_k) \tag{3}$$

In the Formula 3, Obj is the objective function of the XGBoost learning model. The first term on the right-hand side of the equation is a differentiable loss function, and the second term is a term that penalizes model complexity. As the complexity of the model increases, the corresponding score is deducted. The purpose of this item is to avoid over-fitting of the model. The formula that penalizes the complexity of the model is denoted as Formula 4.

$$\Omega(f_t) = \gamma T + \frac{1}{2}\lambda \sum_{j=1}^{T} \omega_j^2 \tag{4}$$

Where γ and λ are constant coefficients, T is the total number of leaves, and ω is the score of each leaf. Gradient boosting includes gradient descent and boosting algorithm, which are often used in machine learning. The main idea is to add a new tree in each iteration, and the final score is the sum of the score of the previous tree and the score of the new tree. The process of gradient boosting optimizes the loss function by second order Taylor expansion. The derivation process and final result of the objective function are shown in Formula 5.

$$Obj^{(t)} \approx \sum_{i=1}^{n} [(g_i f_t(x_i) + \frac{1}{2} h_i f_t^2(x_i)] + \Omega(f_t)$$

$$= \sum_{i=1}^{n} \left[\left(\sum_{i \in I_j} g_i \right) \omega_j + \frac{1}{2} \left(\sum_{i \in I_j} h_i + \lambda \right) \omega_j^2 \right] + \gamma T + \frac{1}{2}\lambda \sum_{j=1}^{T} \omega_j^2$$

$$= \sum_{j=1}^{T} \left[\left(\sum_{i \in I_j} g_i \right) \omega_j + \frac{1}{2} \left(\sum_{i \in I_j} h_i + \lambda \right) \omega_j^2 \right] + \gamma T \tag{5}$$

Where $g_i = \partial_{\hat{y}^{t-1}} l\left(y_i, \hat{y}_i^{(t-1)}\right)$ is the first order derivative which is the gradient at current prediction and $h_i = \partial^2_{\hat{y}^{t-1}} l\left(y_i, \hat{y}_i^{(t-1)}\right)$ is the second order derivative. Let $G_j = \sum_{i \in I_j} g_i$, $H_j = \sum_{i \in I_j} h_i$, $G_L = \sum_{i \in I_L} g_i$, $G_R = \sum_{i \in I_R} g_i$. The structure of the tree is determined. In order to minimize the objective function, its derivative can be set to 0, and the optimal prediction fraction of each leaf node can be solved, as shown in Formula 6. Substituting ω_j^* into the objective function, the minimum loss is solved as shown in Formula 7.

$$\omega_j^* = -\frac{G_j}{H_j + \lambda} \tag{6}$$

$$\overset{\sim}{\mathcal{L}}^{(t)}(q) = -\frac{1}{2} \sum_{j=1}^{T} \frac{G_j^2}{H_j + \lambda} + \gamma T \tag{7}$$

The gain calculation of continuous leaf node splitting is shown in Formula 8.

$$\mathcal{L}_{split} = \frac{1}{2} \left[\frac{G_L^2}{H_j + \lambda} + \frac{G_R^2}{H_j + \lambda} - \frac{(G_L^2 + G_R^2)^2}{H_j + \lambda} \right] - \gamma \tag{8}$$

3.3 STX Model

In this section, we present a combined classification model named STX (SMOTE TOME-Links and XGBoost) for software defect prediction. The model primarily includes three phases: first, it rebalances an imbalanced train data set by SMOTE and TOME-Links process; next, an ensemble learning algorithm (XGBoost) is trained on the balanced training data set to obtain a prediction model; finally, the obtained prediction model is used to classify unknown samples.

During the data sampling stage, select a minority sample in the data sample set randomly, then find k minority samples close to it. Then one of the k samples is randomly selected to be connected to it, and a new sample is randomly generated on the connection. After smote sampling, Tomek-Links find the next two majority and minority samples and delete the majority of them. After the above sampling is repeated many times, a new sample set is finally generated. Through the serialization of n decision trees, the new data set constantly updates the weights and regularization terms, and finally trains a powerful classification model. The overall flow of the proposed model is shown in Fig. 4.

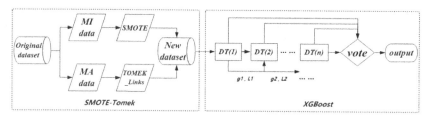

Fig. 4. STX model

4   Experiments

To evaluate the effectiveness of the proposed mode for software defect prediction, we conduct extensive comparative experiments on 10 NASA software defective prediction datasets. All datasets, performance measurements, and the results and discussions of experiment are presented subsequently.

4.1   Datasets

NASA Software Defective Prediction [32] data set is commonly used as a benchmarking dataset for software defect prediction problem. These software projects were developed in C/C++ language for satellite flight control, storage management for ground data, and spacecraft instrumentation. Ten of the most used datasets from this repository are used in this study. Each dataset consists of several software modules with quality metrics as input. Each module includes an output label of defective or non-defective, which indicates if any bugs were found in respective modules. Labeling of a module is done manually after a testing phase. Table 1 outlines the characteristics of the datasets, including number of modules, number of features, number of none defective, number of defective, and imbalanced ratio. The percentage of defective modules shows an imbalanced distribution of dataset varying from 8.65% to 35.20%.

Table 1. Software defect dataset of NASA

Dataset	Number of modules	Feature	None defective	Defective	Imbalanced ratio/%
CM1	327	38	285	42	12.84
JM1	7782	22	6107	1672	21.49
KC1	1183	22	869	314	26.54
KC3	194	40	158	36	18.56
MC2	125	40	81	44	35.20
MW1	253	38	226	27	10.67
PC1	705	38	644	61	8.65
PC3	1077	38	943	134	12.44
PC4	1287	38	1110	177	13.75
PC5	1711	39	1240	471	27.53

4.2 Performance Measures

Considering a two-class classification problem, we can always label one class as a positive and another one class as a negative. Given a testing data set with any one sample is labeled positive or negative. Assigning a class label to each sample is the primary work of the classification model. Four possible outcomes can be obtained by the classification work: true positives (TP, the number of labeled positive and classified as positive), true negative (TN, the number of labeled negative and classified as negative), false positive (FP, the number of labeled negative but classified as positive), false negative (FN, the number of labeled positive but classified as negative). All four possible outcomes form a confusion matrix as shown in Table 2.

Table 2. Confusion matrix

	True class	
Classifier output	Positive	Negative
Positive	TP	FP
Negative	FN	TN

On such basis, the performance measures of *Accuracy*, *Precision*, *Recall*, and $F_{measure}$ are calculated as Formulas (9)–(12) respectively. Among of these, *Accuracy* is not an ideal evaluation index to evaluate a classification model when the test data set is imbalanced. A good classifier should have both higher *Precision* and *Recall*, but both of the two indices inhibit each other. $F_{measure}$ combines *Precision* and *Recall* for maximizing the performance on a single class. Hence, it is used for measuring the performance of the classifier on the minority class samples. Another very popular measure is the area under the Receiver Operating Characteristics (*ROC*) graph, usually known as *AUC*. *AUC* is not sensitive to the distribution of the positive class and negative class samples, thus it is a reliable performance measure and it has been widely used to evaluate classifier performance.

$$Accuracy = \frac{TP + TN}{TP + TN + FP + FN} \tag{9}$$

$$Precision = \frac{TP}{TP + FP} \tag{10}$$

$$Recall = \frac{TP}{TP + FN} \tag{11}$$

$$F_{measure} = \frac{2 \times Precision \times Recall}{Precision + Recall} \tag{12}$$

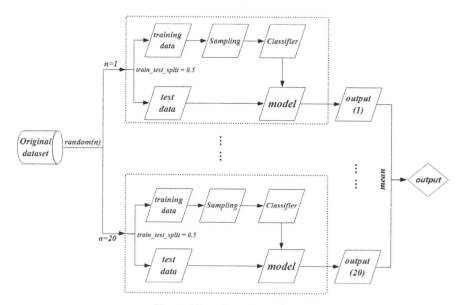

Fig. 5. Flow chart of experiment

4.3   Results and Discussion

STX model is a combination of SMOTE-Tomek and XGBoost, so it has both advantages of sampling technique of SMOTE-Tomek and XGBoost learning. In order to verify the performance of STX model, two groups of experiment are performed. Each one group includes various combination of sampling and learning algorithms.

- Different sampling techniques and XGBoost learning are combined to form various classification models which are used for comparison with STX.
- SMOTE-Tomek sampling is combined with different learning algorithms to form various classification models which are used for comparison with STX.

In our experiments, we randomly divided each dataset into half for training and the half for testing. We perform 20 consecutive random experiments according to the framework as shown in Fig. 5 to evaluate the generalization performance of all compared models.

4.3.1 Comparison with Different Sampling Techniques

In this group experiment, all comparison models use XGBoost learning, but these models use different sampling methods. Four widely used under-sampling methods of RUS, NearMiss-1, NearMiss-2, NearMiss-3, and four widely over-sampling methods of ROS, ADASYN [33], SMOTE, SMOTE-Tomek (used in STX) are used.

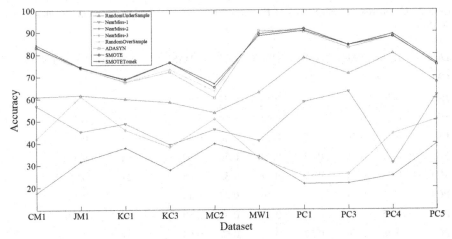

Fig. 6. Accuracy of different sampling techniques combined with XGBoost

For class imbalance problem, although the accuracy is not the ideal index to evaluate classification model, we still present results of accuracy for references. Figure 6 shows the accuracy of different sampling techniques combined with XGBoost learning on ten NASA software defect datasets. Figure 6 clearly shows that the models of XGBoost with over-sampling generally outperforms the models of XGBoost with under-sampling. The proposed model STX (SMOTE-Tomek with XGBoost) has the best accuracy except for MW1 dataset.

We further compare $F_{measure}$ and AUC values of each combination model. Tables 3 and 4 respectively show the $F_{measure}$ and AUC of each combination model for 10 NASA datasets. For each dataset, the best results are highlighted in bold. The direction comparison of all compared model can be obtained by checking the mean values in the last row in Tables 3 and 4. The mean value is defined as each model's value for a specific dataset, which is averaged over the 10 datasets.

Table 3 shows that STX (SMOTE-Tomek with XGBoost) obtains the highest $F_{measure}$ 4 times (one time identical with other model); the model of SMOTE (with XGBoost) obtains the highest $F_{measure}$ 3 times (two times identical with other models); the model of ADASYN (with XGBoost) obtains the highest $F_{measure}$ 3 times (one time identical with other model); the model of ROS (with XGBoost) obtains the highest $F_{measure}$ 3 times (one time identical with other model); the models of RUS (with XGBoost) and NM-1 (with XGBoost) respectively obtains the highest $F_{measure}$ one time; and the models of NM-2 (with XGBoost) and NM-3 (with XGBoost) respectively obtains the highest $F_{measure}$ zero time. Although STX model not obtains absolute advantage for all dataset, it obtains quite stable and super $F_{measure}$ on all datasets. In contrast, the results of other models show unstable. Taking ROS as an example, it has the best F-measure on MW1, but its result of CM1 is not satisfactory. The last row shows STX obtains the highest mean $F_{measure}$.

Table 3. Comparison mean values of F-measure between eight sampling methods with using XGBoost

Dataset	RUS	NM-1	NM-2	NM-3	ROS	ADASYN	SMOTE	SMOTETomek
CM1	0.27	0.23	0.21	0.21	0.23	0.35	0.31	**0.36**
JM1	0.39	0.39	0.34	0.35	0.37	0.37	0.40	0.40
KC1	0.43	0.45	0.41	0.42	0.36	0.41	0.44	0.45
KC3	0.27	0.26	0.26	0.27	0.40	0.40	0.35	0.37
MC2	0.49	0.47	0.52	0.50	0.50	0.49	**0.54**	0.51
MW1	0.23	0.17	0.17	0.17	**0.33**	0.25	0.21	0.25
PC1	0.29	0.21	0.17	0.16	0.47	0.40	0.37	0.40
PC3	**0.45**	0.30	0.24	0.24	0.32	0.30	0.34	0.40
PC4	0.48	0.30	0.27	0.32	0.57	**0.63**	0.61	0.62
PC5	0.55	0.50	0.41	0.44	0.53	0.56	0.56	0.56
MEAN	0.39	0.33	0.30	0.31	0.41	0.42	0.41	**0.43**

Table 4 shows that STX (SMOTE-Tomek with XGBoost) obtains the highest AUC 5 times (two time identical with other models); the model of SMOTE (with XGBoost) obtains the highest AUC 3 times (two times identical with other models); the model of ADASYN (with XGBoost) obtains the highest AUC 4 times (three time identical with other model); the model of ROS (with XGBoost) obtains the highest AUC 2 times (one time identical with other model); the model of RUS (with XGBoost) obtains the

Table 4. Comparison of AUC between eight sampling methods with using XGBoost

Dataset	RUS	NM-1	NM-2	NM-3	ROS	ADASYN	SMOTE	SMOTE-Tomek
CM1	0.63	0.53	0.48	0.48	0.56	0.63	0.64	**0.69**
JM1	0.57	0.58	0.49	0.51	**0.60**	**0.60**	**0.60**	**0.60**
KC1	0.55	0.57	0.50	0.52	0.57	0.59	0.59	**0.60**
KC3	0.58	0.55	0.55	0.57	0.68	0.71	0.70	**0.72**
MC2	0.58	0.46	0.53	0.49	0.60	0.59	0.57	0.53
MW1	0.62	0.56	0.53	0.53	0.62	**0.73**	0.59	0.65
PC1	**0.75**	0.61	0.50	0.48	0.66	0.69	0.69	0.70
PC3	**0.78**	0.64	0.51	0.51	0.60	0.59	0.63	0.68
PC4	0.80	0.58	0.53	0.63	0.74	**0.84**	**0.84**	0.83
PC5	0.70	0.65	0.52	0.57	0.68	**0.71**	**0.71**	**0.71**
MEAN	0.66	0.57	0.51	0.53	0.63	0.67	0.66	**0.67**

highest AUC two times; and the models of NM-1, NM-2, and NM-3 (with XGBoost) respectively obtains the highest AUC zero time. In brief, STX obtains quite stable and super AUC on all datasets. The last row shows STX obtains the highest mean value of AUC.

4.3.2 Comparison with Different Learning Algorithms

In this group experiment, all comparison models use SMOTE-Tomek sampling, but these models use different learning algorithms. Four competitive used (single) classifiers of SVM (support vector machine), naive Bayes, logistic regression, KNN (k = 5), decision tree classifiers (Cart), and four popular ensemble classifiers of Random Forest, Bagging, AdaBoost, and XGBoost (used in STX) are used. Among them, the basic learners of all ensemble learning mentioned above are all CART trees.

For the group experiment, we also present results of accuracy for references. Figure 7 shows the accuracy of different learning algorithms combined with SMOTE-Tomek sampling on ten NASA software defect datasets. Figure 7 clearly shows that the models of SMOTE-Tomek sampling with ensemble learning generally outperforms the models of SMOTE-Tomek sampling with single classifier. The proposed model STX obtains the stable and reliable results.

Tables 5 and 6 respectively list $F_{measure}$ and AUC values of each combination model. Table 5 shows that STX obtains the highest $F_{measure}$ 5 times (two times identical with other model); the model STAB (SMOTE-Tomek with XGBoost) obtains the highest $F_{measure}$ 3 times (one time identical with other models); the model STRF (SMOTE-Tomek with Random Forest) obtains the highest $F_{measure}$ 2 times; the model STSVM (SMOTE-Tomek with SVM) and STNB (SMOTE-Tomek with NB) respectively obtains the highest $F_{measure}$ 1 time; the other four models respectively obtains the highest $F_{measure}$ zero time. Although STX model not obtains absolute advantage for all datasets, it obtains

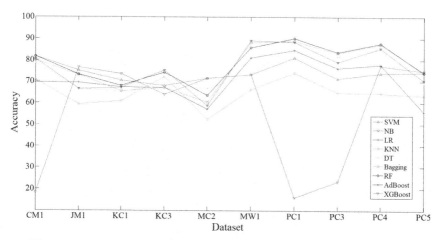

Fig. 7. Accuracy of SMOTE-Tomek combined with different learning algorithms

Table 5. Comparison of F-measure between nine learning algorithms with using SMOTE-Tomek

Dataset	STSVM	STNB	STLR	STKNN	STDT	STBagging	STRF	STAB	STX
CM1	**0.40**	0.17	0.35	0.35	0.20	0.11	0.17	0.20	0.36
JM1	0.37	0.20	0.40	0.35	0.33	0.37	0.40	**0.42**	0.40
KC1	0.43	0.30	**0.45**	0.43	0.44	0.39	0.41	0.44	**0.45**
KC3	0.16	0.26	0.2	0.34	0.25	0.24	0.24	**0.37**	**0.37**
MC2	0.44	0.44	0.47	0.42	0.45	0.49	0.48	0.45	**0.51**
MW1	0.26	0.15	0.40	0.22	0.19	0.30	0.36	**0.46**	0.25
PC1	0.25	0.17	0.31	0.23	0.46	0.34	**0.41**	0.35	0.40
PC3	0.32	0.24	0.43	0.29	0.31	0.32	**0.41**	0.29	0.40
PC4	0.27	0.24	0.50	0.29	0.54	0.62	0.61	0.59	**0.62**
PC5	0.32	0.25	0.47	0.47	0.50	0.53	0.55	0.50	**0.56**
MEAN	0.32	0.24	0.40	0.34	0.37	0.37	0.40	0.41	**0.43**

quite stable and super $F_{measure}$ on all datasets. The last row shows STX obtains the highest mean $F_{measure}$.

Table 6 shows that STX obtains highest AUC 4 times; the model STAB (SMOTE-Tomek with AdaBoost) obtains highest AUC 3 times; the model STSVM (SMOTE-Tomek with SVM) and the model STLR (SMOTE-Tomek with LR) respectively obtains highest AUC 2 times; the model STNB(SMOTE-Tomek with NB), the model STKNN(SMOTE-Tomek with KNN), and the model STBagging (SMOTE-Tomek with Bagging) respectively obtains highest AUC 1 times; the model STRF (SMOTE-Tomek with RF) obtains highest AUC zero time. In brief, STX obtains quite stable and super AUC on all datasets. The last row shows STX obtains the highest mean value of AUC.

Table 6. Comparison of AUC between nine learning algorithms with using SMOTE-Tomek

Dataset	STSVM	STNB	STLR	STKNN	STDT	STBagging	STRF	STAB	STX
CM1	0.68	0.41	**0.75**	0.68	0.54	0.54	0.50	0.54	0.69
JM1	0.60	0.54	0.62	0.56	0.56	0.60	0.62	**0.63**	0.60
KC1	**0.61**	0.57	0.61	0.59	0.60	0.60	0.60	**0.61**	0.60
KC3	0.49	0.56	0.52	0.64	0.55	0.55	0.56	0.66	**0.72**
MC2	**0.62**	**0.62**	0.57	0.52	**0.62**	**0.62**	0.60	0.57	0.53
MW1	0.65	0.52	0.77	0.61	0.57	0.57	0.72	**0.73**	0.65
PC1	0.60	0.51	0.63	0.60	0.68	0.68	0.66	0.64	**0.70**
PC3	0.63	0.50	**0.72**	0.60	0.62	0.62	0.68	0.59	0.68
PC4	0.57	0.55	0.77	0.58	0.74	0.74	0.77	0.79	**0.83**
PC5	0.58	0.56	0.62	0.63	0.67	0.67	0.70	0.66	**0.71**
MEAN	0.60	0.53	0.66	0.60	0.62	0.62	0.64	0.64	**0.67**

4.4 Statistical Comparison of Software Defect Predictors

In this section, Wilcoxon singed-rank test [34] was further used to assess whether the differences between the two comparison models were statistically significant.

The findings of experimental results are supported by Wilcoxon singed rank which is a nonparametric statistical hypothesis approach. Wilcoxon signed rank test performs pairwise comparison of two approaches used for software defect prediction and analyzes the differences between their performances on each dataset. The rank is assigned to the differences according to their absolute values from the smallest to the largest and average ranks which are given in the case of ties. Wilcoxon signed rank stores the sum of rank in $+$ and $-$ where $+$ stores the sum of ranks for the datasets on which STX has shown better performance over the compared model and $-$ stores the sum of ranks for the opposite. Owing to space limitations, we only take $F_{measure}$ for comparison. We have performed pairwise comparison according to the results of Tables 3 and 5. The results obtained from Wilcoxon signed rank test is shown in Tables 7 and 8 respectively. It is observed from the Tables 7 and 8 that the p value is less than 0.05 in most of the cases; that is, the proposed STF model outperforms most them with high degree of confidence in most case.

In summary, all experimental results illustrate the superiority of STX model. The Wilcoxon signed rank test demonstrates the strong competitiveness of STX model against other comparative model for software defect prediction.

Table 7. Summary of Wilcoxon signed rank test according to Table 3

Pairwise	R^+	R^-	p value
STX vs RUS_XGB	49	6	0.027
STX vs NM1_XGB	55	0	0.008
STX vs NM2_XGB	54	1	0.004
STX vs NM3_XGB	55	0	0.002
STX vs ROS_XGB	40	15	0.322
STX vs SMOTE_XGB	49	6	0.175
STX vs ADASYN_XGB	48	7	0.058

Table 8. Summary of Wilcoxon signed rank test according to Table 5

Pairwise	R^+	R^-	p value
STX vs STSVM	50	5	0.020
STX vs STNB	55	0	0.002
STX vs STLR	42	13	0.208
STX vs STKNN	55	0	0.002
STX vs STDT	53	2	0.010
STX vs STBagging	50	5	0.028
STX vs STRF	42	13	0.138
STX vs STAB	42	13	0.173

5 Conclusion

In software defect prediction, classification model suffers from the unbalanced distribution problems of defective and non-defective modules. For the problem of software defect prediction, defective modules are more important from a learning point of view because it implies a great cost when it is misclassified.

In order to effectively improve the performance of software defect prediction, we introduce a novel hybrid proposal named STX that combines sampling technique of SMOTE-Tomek and ensemble learning of XGBoost. The processes of STX primarily includes two steps: firstly, it rebalanced a training dataset and filtering out noise samples of software defect prediction by SMOTE-Tomek; and next, the balanced train dataset is used to train XGBoost classifier for constructing a classification model. STX model inherits both advantages of SMOTE-Tomek sampling and XGBoost learning. In order to evaluate the effectiveness of STX, we conducted extensive comparative experiments using ten NASA software defect datasets. The experimental results verify the superiority of STX in solving the software defect prediction problem.

Next, we will intend to investigate the effect of STX model in other imbalanced classification problems. In addition, we plan to extend STX model to multi-class imbalanced problems. Such research efforts are expected to promote development of techniques for classification of imbalanced problems.

Acknowledgements. Research on this work was partially supported by the grants from Jiangxi Education Department of China (No. GJJ201917, No. GJJ1611096), and National Science Foundation of China (No. 61562061).

References

1. Ahlawat, S., Choudhary, A.: hybrid CNN-SVM classifier for handwritten digit recognition. Proc. Comput. Sci. **167**, 2554–2560 (2020). https://doi.org/10.1016/j.procs.2020.03.309
2. Amir, F.S., Majid, Z., Ahmed, B.M.: To ameliorate classification accuracy using ensemble distributed decision tree (DDT) vote approach: an empirical discourse of geographical data mining. Proc. Comput. Sci. (2021). https://doi.org/10.1016/J.PRO-CS.2021.03.116
3. Hu, J., Peng, H., Wang, J., Yu, W.: KNN-P: a KNN classifier optimized by P systems. Theoret. Comput. Sci. **817**, 55–65 (2020). https://doi.org/10.1016/j.tcs.2020.01.001
4. Song, X, Liu, X., Liu, F., Wang, C.: Comparison of machine learning and logistic regression models in predicting acute kidney injury: a systematic review and meta-analysis. Int. J. Med. Inf. (2021). https://doi.org/10.1016/J.IJME-DINF.2021.104484
5. Jackins, V., Vimal, S., Kaliappan, M., Lee, M.Y.: AI-based smart prediction of clinical disease using random forest classifier and Naive Bayes. J. Supercomput. **77**(5), 5198–5219 (2020). https://doi.org/10.1007/s11227-020-03481-x
6. Deng, X., Xu, Y., Chen, L., Zhong, W., Jolfaei, A., Zheng, X.: Dynamic clustering method for imbalanced learning based on AdaBoost. J. Supercomput. **76**(12), 9716–9738 (2020). https://doi.org/10.1007/s11227-020-03211-3
7. Li, M., Xiong, A., Wang, L., Deng, S., Ye, J.: ACO resampling: enhancing the performance of oversampling methods for class imbalance classification. Knowl. Based Syst. **196**, 105818 (2020). https://doi.org/10.1016/j.knosys.2020.105818
8. Qi, W.: Hybrid fuzzy support vector classifier machine and modified genetic algorithm for automatic car assembly fault diagnosis. Exp. Syst. Appl. **38**(3), 1457–1463 (2011). https://doi.org/10.1016/j.eswa.2010.07.052
9. Razavi-Far, R., Farajzadeh-Zanjani, M., Saif, M.: An integrated class-imbalanced learning scheme for diagnosing bearing defects in induction motors. IEEE Trans. Indust. Inf. **13**(6), 2758–2769 (2017)
10. Chawla, N.V., Lazarevic, A., Hall, L.O., et al.: SMOTEBoost: improving prediction of the minority class in boosting. Eur. Conf. Knowl. Discov. Datab: Pkdd 107–119 (2003)
11. Yang, K., Yu, Z., Wen, X., et al.: Hybrid classifier ensemble for imbalanced data. IEEE Trans. Neural Netw. Learn. Syst. (99), 1–14 (2019)
12. Wang, Z., Chunhua, W., Zheng, K., et al.: SMOTETomek-based resampling for personality recognition. IEEE Access **7**, 129678–129689 (2019)
13. Chawla, N.V., Bowyer, K.W., Hall, L.O., et al.: SMOTE: synthetic minority over-sampling technique. J. Artif. Intell. Res. **16**(1), 321–357 (2002)
14. Yedida, R., Menzies, T.: On the value of oversampling for deep learning in software defect prediction. IEEE Trans. Softw. Eng. (99), 1 (2021)

15. Liu, B., Tsoumakas, G.: Dealing with class imbalance in classifier chains via random under-sampling. Knowl. Based Syst. **192**, 105292 (2020). https://doi.org/10.1016/j.knosys.2019. 105292
16. Ghaderyan, P., Abbasi, A., Sedaaghi, M.H.: An efficient seizure prediction method using KNN-based undersampling and linear frequency measures. J. Neurosci. Methods **232**, 134–142 (2014). https://doi.org/10.1016/j.jneumeth.2014.05.019
17. Kang, Q., Chen, X., Li, S., Zhou, M.: A noise-filtered under-sampling scheme for imbalanced classification. IEEE Trans. Cybern. **47**(12), 4263–4274 (2017). https://doi.org/10.1109/ TCYB.2016.2606104
18. Lübeck, T., Helmholz, H., Arend, J.M., et al.: Perceptual evaluation of mitigation approaches of impairments due to spatial undersampling in binaural rendering of spherical microphone array data. J. Audio Eng. Soc. **68**(6), 428–440 (2020)
19. Zhou, H., Yu, K.-M., Chen, Y.-C., Hsu, H.-P.: A hybrid feature selection method RFSTL for manufacturing quality prediction based on a high dimensional imbalanced dataset. IEEE Access **9**, 29719–29735 (2021)
20. Sedighi-Maman, Z., Mondello, A.: A two-stage modeling approach for breast cancer survivability prediction. Int. J. Med. Inf. **149**, 104438 (2021). https://doi.org/10.1016/j.ijmedinf. 2021.104438
21. Lin, W.-C., Tsai, C.-F., Hu, Y.-H., Jhang, J.-S.: Clustering-based undersampling in class-imbalanced data. Inf. Sci. **409–410**, 17–26 (2017). https://doi.org/10.1016/j.ins.2017.05.008
22. Zadrozny, B., Langford, J., Abe, N.: Cost-sensitive learning by cost-proportionate example weighting. IEEE Int. Conf. Data Mining (2003)
23. Masnadi-Shirazi, H., Vasconcelos, N.: Risk minimization, probability elicitation, and cost-sensitive SVMs. Int. Conf. Mach. Learn. DBLP (2010)
24. Liu, M., Chang, X., Luo, Y., Chao, X., Wen, Y., Tao, D.: Cost-sensitive feature selection by optimizing F-measures. IEEE Trans. Image Process. **27**(3), 1323–1335 (2018). https://doi. org/10.1109/TIP.2017.2781298
25. Chen, X., Gong, C., Yang, J.: Cost-sensitive positive and unlabeled learning. Inf. Sci. (2021). https://doi.org/10.1016/J.INS.2021.0-1.002
26. Sun, Z., Song, Q., Zhu, X.: Using coding-based ensemble learning to improve software defect prediction. IEEE Trans. Syst. Man Cybern. C **42**(6), 1806–1817 (2012)
27. Aleem, S., Capretz, L.F., Ahmed, F.: Benchmarking machine learning techniques for software defect detection. Int. J. Softw. Eng. Appl. **6**(3), 11–23 (2015). https://doi.org/10.5121/ijsea. 2015.6302
28. Alsaeedi, A., Khan, M.Z.: Software defect prediction using supervised machine learning and ensemble techniques: a comparative study. J. Softw. Eng. Appl. **12**(05), 85–100 (2019). https://doi.org/10.4236/jsea.2019.125007
29. Laradji, I.H., Alshayeb, M., Ghouti, L.: Software defect prediction using ensemble learning on selected features. Inf. Softw. Technol. **58**, 388–402 (2015). https://doi.org/10.1016/j.inf sof.2014.07.005
30. Ibrahim, D.R., Ghnemat, R., Hudaib, A.: Software defect prediction using feature selection and random forest algorithm. In: 2017 International Conference on New Trends in Computing Sciences (ICTCS), pp. 252–257. IEEE (2017)
31. Guo, F., Liu, Z., Hu, W., Tan, J.: Gain prediction and compensation for subarray antenna with assembling errors based on improved XGBoost and transfer learning. IET Microw. Anten. Propagat. **14**(6), 551–558 (2020). https://doi.org/10.1049/iet-map.2019.0182
32. Douzas, G., Bacao, F., Last, F.: Improving imbalanced learning through a heuristic oversampling method based on k-means and SMOTE. Inf. Sci. **465**, 1–20 (2018). https://doi.org/10. 1016/j.ins.2018.06.056

33. Zhang, Y., Qiao, S., Ji, S., Han, N., Liu, D., Zhou, J.: Identification of DNA–protein binding sites by bootstrap multiple convolutional neural networks on sequence information. Eng. Appl. Artif. Intell. **79**, 58–66 (2019)
34. Rosner, B., Glynn, R.J., Lee, M.-L.T.: The Wilcoxon signed rank test for paired comparisons of clustered data. Biometrics **62**(1), 185–192 (2006). https://doi.org/10.1111/j.1541-0420.2005.00389.x

Imbalance Classification Based on Deep Learning and Fuzzy Support Vector Machine

Kefan Wang[1], Jing An[1], Xianghua Ma[1(✉)], Chao Ma[1], and Hanqiu Bao[2]

[1] School of Electrical and Electronic Engineering, Shanghai Institute of Technology, Shanghai 201418, China
xhuam@sit.edu.cn

[2] Department of Control Science and Engineering, Tongji University, Shanghai 201804, China

Abstract. Imbalanced data is widespread in the fields of medical diagnosis, information security and industrial production. Traditional classification methods can handle balanced data very well. However, when dealing with imbalanced classification, it will favor majority classes, which results in low classification performance. This paper proposes an imbalanced classification method based on deep feature representation, named DL-FSVM. DL-FSVM extracts feature information in the input space using a deep neural network (DNN) to ensure similarity within class and improve the separation between different classes. After obtaining the feature representation, oversampling is performed in this embedding space based on the center distance to enhance the balance of the data distribution. Fuzzy Support Vector Machine (FSVM) is used as the final classifier. Assigning higher misclassification costs to minority class samples through cost-sensitive learning. Experiments were performed on six real-world datasets. The experimental results show that DL-FSVM achieves promising classification performance in three evaluation metrics: G-means, F1-score and AUC.

Keywords: Imbalance classification · Deep neural network · Fuzzy support vector machine

1 Introduction

In many fields, the data are imbalance. There are significant quantitative differences between the samples of different classes. For example, in disease diagnosis [1], most of the data is healthy, and it is difficult to obtain data on diseases. The class that is easily available and more numerous is referred to as majority class, and the class with less data due to the natural frequency of occurrence or data collection is called minority class. The imbalanced data distribution is also exist in the fields of fraud detection [2], computer security [3] and image recognition [4]. In machine learning, there are many well-established classification methods, but they are based on the setting of uniform data distribution and have overall accuracy as the optimization goal. When traditional classification methods are used to deal with imbalanced classification, the result are more in favor of the majority class. Although the overall accuracy is relatively high, the minority class data with important information cannot be accurately identified.

© Springer Nature Singapore Pte Ltd. 2022
L. Pan et al. (Eds.): BIC-TA 2021, CCIS 1566, pp. 32–44, 2022.
https://doi.org/10.1007/978-981-19-1253-5_3

Many imbalance classification algorithms have been proposed in recent decades. These algorithms in general can be grouped into two types: data-level and algorithm-level [5]. The data-level approaches first bring the original imbalanced dataset to balanced distribution by some sampling processing, and then classify it using a traditional classifier. The algorithm-level approaches attempt to improve traditional models by reducing their favoring for the majority class data, and thus adapt to imbalanced data distribution.

In this paper, a novel imbalance classification method based on deep feature representation is proposed, named DL-FSVM. First, from the perspective of data features, embedding space features are obtained by deep neural networks. Appropriate feature representation can lead to better classification quality, and it also enhances the differentiation of features of different classes and the similarity of feature areas of the same class. In addition, it will provide a basis for effective recognition of samples. The deep neural network has a complex nonlinear network structure, which can effectively extract the deep features of samples. When training the network, a triplet loss function [6] is used to enable the network to separate minority class and majority class features. Additionally, Gumbel distribution function [7] is applied as an activation function in the activation layer. This function is continuously differentiable, and it can be easily used as an activation function in stochastic gradient descent optimization neural networks. The original input samples are mapped to the same embedding space after feature extraction. In the embedding space, a new minority class sample is randomly generated based on the distance between the sample and the center of the class, which makes the data distribution balanced. After obtaining the embedding features of samples, FSVM [8] classifies the samples. FSVM introduces membership values (MVs) in the objective function of traditional support vector machine, and it sets different misclassification costs for different classes samples. Misclassification costs are higher for minority class than for majority class. FSVM is a cost-sensitive learning strategy that is effective in improving the recognition of the minority class samples. Traditional classification methods use accuracy as classifier evaluation metrics, but classifiers with accuracy as evaluation metrics tend to ignore the importance of minority class samples. Moreover, accuracy limits the effect of minority class samples on classification performance. Therefore, this paper uses G-means, F1-score and AUC values to evaluate the results more comprehensively.

2 Related Work

Research on imbalanced classification can be grouped into two levels: data-level, and algorithm-level.

2.1 Data-Level

Data resampling is the most important method of data-level, which reduces the imbalance rate (IR) by changing the data distribution. The under-sampling algorithm reduces the bias of model to the majority class samples by decreasing the number of them. Random under-sampling randomly selects and deletes parts of the sample. Some heuristic algorithms are proposed to compensate the limitations of the above non-heuristic method, such as neighborhood cleaning rule (NCL) [9]. Kang et al. added a noise filter to the under-sampling process [10]. In addition, Kang et al. also proposed a weighted under-sampling algorithm (WU-SVM) [11] based on the geometric distance of the data input space. Oversampling increases the number of minority class samples to make the data balanced. The most representative method, the Small Sample Synthetic Oversampling Technique (SMOTE), was proposed by Chawla et al. [12]. SMOTE randomly selects the k nearest neighbors in the same class of the minority class sample and generates new minority class samples between them using linear interpolation. In addition, Borderline-SMOTE (BSMOTE) [13] and adaptive synthetic sampling approach (ADASYN) [14] are also popular oversampling methods. Matthew et al. proposed the kernel-SMOTE algorithm [15] and weighted K-SMOTE [16] for sampling in the embedding space obtained by SVM.

2.2 Algorithm-Level

Algorithm-level methods use some methods to make appropriate improvements to existing algorithms, such as cost-sensitive learning and ensemble learning methods. As a cost-sensitive algorithm, the fuzzy membership values (MVs) in fuzzy support vector machine (FSVM) [8] reflects the importance of the sample. FSVM differs from the traditional support vector machine in that FSVM introduces the MVs of the sample in the objective function. Batuwita et al. [17] proposed the FSVM-CIL algorithm. FSVM-CIL works in the original data space and calculates the membership values based on the distance between samples. Yu et al. [18] design the membership functions (MFs) based on the relative density within and between classes. This approach makes up for the shortcomings of the distance-based membership values calculation method. ACFSVM [19] based on affinity and class probabilities was proposed by Tao et al. Dealing with imbalance problems using ensemble learning is generally a combination of the standard ensemble methods with the existing methods for classifying imbalanced data, such as SMOTEBagging [20] and SMOTEBoost [21].

The DL-FSVM method proposed in this paper uses FSVM as the base classifier and use data sampling method to obtain balanced data distribution. The new samples generated after oversampling still belong to the minority class, and the use of FSVM can further improve the model's focus on the minority class. In addition, deep neural networks are used to obtain more discriminative feature information, which convenience subsequent classification.

3 Proposed Method

3.1 Feature Extraction with Deep Learning

With the growth of data and the improvement of computing power, the powerful feature extraction capability of deep learning has attracted widespread attention in academia and industry. Deep neural networks (DNNs) have succeeded in significantly improving the best recognition rate of each previous problem by increasing the network depth or changing the structure of the model [22, 23]. Feature representation has a key role in classification quality, so this paper applies the classification method to the embedding space after feature extraction.

For this paper, a DNN is used for the feature extractor because it can learn advanced feature representations from samples [24]. Once training is complete, the hidden feature representations can be used as embedding features to reveal interesting structures in the data. To enhance the differentiation of features from different classes and reduce the differentiation of features from samples in the same class, a triplet loss [6] is used to train the network model, and bring samples in the same class closer and to further separate samples in different classes. Each sample can be converted into a differentiated feature space based on the trained model. The triple loss is based on anchor points, making the features in the embedding space more differentiated. It is defined as:

$$L_{triplet} = \left(D_{a,min} - D_{a,maj} + r\right)_+ \tag{1}$$

where r is the margin and set to 0.2 in experiments. D is the function used to calculate the Euclidean distance of samples in the embedding space. a is the anchor point belonging to the minority class, min is the minority class samples, and maj is the majority class samples. $(\cdot)_+$ indicates the value is taken as loss if it is greater than 0. If it is less than 0, the loss is 0.

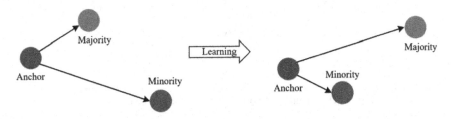

Fig. 1. Optimization result using triple loss function

Figure 1 shows the results and geometric significance of optimization using triple loss. Triplet loss tries to learn an embedding space in which anchor is nearer to the minority class samples, and the anchor is further away from the majority class samples. The advantage of triplet loss is detail differentiation, i.e., triplet loss is able to better model the details when the two inputs are similar. This allows better feature representation to be learned.

Gumbel distribution [7] is used as the activation function in DNN. The Gumbel distribution is widely used to design the distribution of extreme value samples of various distributions. The cumulative distribution function (CDF) is defined as:

$$\sigma(x) = e^{-e^{-x}} \tag{2}$$

As shown in Fig. 2, the Gumbel distribution function is continuously differentiable, so it can be easily used as an activation function with optimization in a neural network. Finally, the whole DNN framework used for feature extraction is shown in Fig. 3.

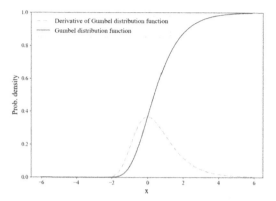

Fig. 2. The curves of CDF and derivatives of Gumbel functions

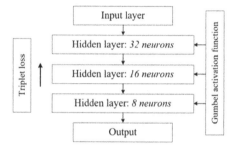

Fig. 3. Deep neural network framework for feature extraction

3.2 Random Feature Oversampling Based on Center Distance

After obtaining the embedding space representation of samples, the data distribution is still imbalanced. The dataset in the embedding space is $X = \{x_1, x_2, \cdots, x_n\}$, n is the total number of samples, $x_i = \left[f_i^1, f_i^2, \cdots, f_i^p\right] \in \mathbb{R}^p$, $i \in 1, 2, \ldots, n$. f_i^j is the feature of sample x_i on the j-th dimension, $j \in 1, 2, \ldots, p$. For the minority class samples, the set of features in each dimension is denoted as $F = \{F^1, F^2, \cdots, F^p\}$, where $F^j = \left\{f_1^j, f_2^j, \cdots, f_{n\_min}^j\right\}, j \in 1, 2, \ldots, p$. n_min is the number of the minority class samples. F^j is the set of values of all minority class samples on the j-th dimension feature. The feature of each dimension of the new synthetic sample is randomly selected from the corresponding feature set, $x_{syn} = \left[f_{syn}^1 \in F^1, f_{syn}^2 \in F^2, \cdots, f_{syn}^p \in F^p\right]$.

This method of randomly generated features can increase the diversity of the minority class samples and avoid overfitting. However, the method generates some outliers and noise, so a constraint based on class center distance is used to filter the synthetic samples. As shown in Fig. 4, in the embedding space, the majority class is centered on C_{maj}, the minority class is centered on C_{min}, and the whole data is centered on C_{all}. By calculating the distance between each center and the synthetic sample to determine whether the following equation is satisfied:

$$d\left(x_{syn}, C_{maj}\right) > d\left(x_{syn}, C_{all}\right) > d\left(x_{syn}, C_{min}\right) \tag{3}$$

where $d(\cdot)$ is the distance function. If the synthesized sample fits this condition, it will be kept, otherwise, it will be deleted. In this paper, the influence of irregular data distribution is avoided by calculating the class centers in the embedding space. The number of synthesized samples is set to achieve balanced data distribution.

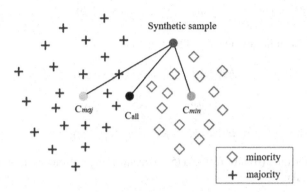

Fig. 4. Validation of the new synthetic feature vector

3.3 Fuzzy Support Vector Machine

In many practical situations, each sample has a different level of importance. For imbalanced data problems, the minority class tends to contain more important information. To improve the quality of classification, each sample needs to be assigned a corresponding weight according to its importance. In this paper, a fuzzy support vector machine (FSVM) [8] is used as the classifier to achieve the assignment of different weights.

The data after sampling as $X = \{x_1, x_2, \cdots, x_n\}$, n is the number of samples including all synthetic samples, $x_i \in \mathbb{R}^p$, $i \in 1, 2, \ldots, n$. p is the feature dimension. Assuming that the dataset is $D = \{(x_1, y_1), (x_2, y_2), \cdots, (x_n, y_n)\}$. $y_i \in [1, -1]$ is the label of the corresponding sample. FSVM adds an attribute to each sample to expand the original data set to $D = \{(x_1, y_1, s_1), (x_2, y_2, s_2), \cdots, (x_n, y_n, s_n)\}$, s_i represents the fuzzy membership value (MV) corresponding to different samples. The value of s reflects the importance level and the misclassification cost of the sample. In this way, the optimization function of FSVM can be written as:

$$min : \frac{1}{2}\|w\|^2 + C \sum_{i=1}^{n} s_i \varepsilon_i$$
$$s.t. y_i(w * \phi(x_i) + b) \geq 1 - \varepsilon_i \tag{4}$$
$$\varepsilon_i \geq 0$$

where $\|w\|^2$ represents the margin ratio of the generalization ability of the learning model. The slack variable ε_i represents the acceptable training error degree of the corresponding instance x_i. $C > 0$ is called the penalty parameter, it is a parameter that weighs the size of the separation interval and the number of misclassified points, as well as a trade-off between learning model accuracy and generalization ability. $\phi(\cdot)$ is the mapping of high-dimensional feature space. The fuzzy membership value s_i can adjust the punishment degree of the corresponding sample. In order to solve this optimization problem, firstly, formula (4) is transformed into an unconstrained problem using the Lagrangian function:

$$L(w, b, \alpha, \beta) = \tfrac{1}{2}w^2 + C \sum_{i=1}^{n} s_i\varepsilon_i - \sum_{i=1}^{n} \alpha_i(y_i(w*x_i + b) - 1 + \varepsilon_i) - \sum_{i=1}^{n} \beta_i\varepsilon_i \qquad (5)$$

The above formula satisfies the following conditions:

$$\begin{aligned}
\tfrac{\partial L(w,b,\alpha,\beta)}{\partial w} &= w - \sum_{i=1}^{n} \alpha_i y_i x_i = 0 \\
\tfrac{\partial L(w,b,\alpha,\beta)}{\partial b} &= -\sum_{i=1}^{n} \alpha_i y_i = 0 \\
\tfrac{\partial L(w,b,\alpha,\beta)}{\partial \varepsilon_i} &= \varepsilon_i C - \alpha_i - \beta_i = 0
\end{aligned} \qquad (6)$$

Introduce formula (6) into formula (5). Transforming optimization problem into the following formula:

$$\begin{aligned}
min : &-\sum_{i=1}^{n} \alpha_i + \tfrac{1}{2} \sum_{i=1}^{n} \sum_{j=1}^{n} y_i y_j \alpha_i \alpha_j \phi(x_i)\phi(x_j) \\
s.t. &\sum_{i=1}^{n} y_i \alpha_i = 0, \forall i : 0 \le \alpha_i \le s_i C
\end{aligned} \qquad (7)$$

where α_i is the Lagrangian multiplier corresponding to x_i, and it must also meet the KKT condition:

$$\begin{aligned}
\forall i : &\alpha_i(y_i(w*\phi(x_i) + b) - 1 + \varepsilon_i) = 0 \\
\forall i : &(s_i C - \alpha_i)\varepsilon_i = 0
\end{aligned} \qquad (8)$$

In this way, the value of α_i can be calculated. Then, according to formula (9), we can calculate w:

$$w = \sum_{j=1}^{n} \alpha_i \beta_j \phi(x_i) \qquad (9)$$

After that, the value of b can be calculated by formula (8). The sample of $\alpha_i > 0$ is called a support vector. When $0 < \alpha_i < s_i C$, the support vector is located on the boundary of the interval. When $\alpha_i = s_i C$, the sample is located between the boundary of the interval and the separation hyperplane or on the side of the separation hyperplane that is misclassified. The biggest difference between traditional SVM and FSVM is that even though two samples have the same value of α_i, the different values of fuzzy membership values s_i can also lead to two samples belonging to different types of support vectors. Under normal circumstances, a smaller s_i is assigned to the majority class to reduce the impact of the numerical advantage of the majority class on the classification results. Finally, the decision function of the optimal separating hyperplane can be expressed as:

$$f(x) = sign(w*\phi(x_i) + b) = sign\left(\sum_{j=1}^{n} \alpha_i y_i \phi(x_i)\phi(x) + b \right) \qquad (10)$$

4   Experiments and Results

4.1   Evaluation Metrics and Datasets

Evaluating the imbalanced classification effect of the model with overall accuracy can cause the model to be biased in favor of the majority class. The overall classification accuracy tends to guarantee the classification effect of only the majority class and ignore the effect of the minority class, which makes the classification effectiveness of the minority class become poor. In this paper, G-mean, F-score and AUC values are used to comprehensively evaluate the classification quality.

Sen is the sensitivity of minority class sample: TP/(TP + FN). *Pre* is the precision of the minority class sample: TP/(TP + FP). *Spe* is the specificity of the majority class sample: TN/(TN + FP). Based on the above definition, G-mean and F-score can be further defined:

$$G - mean = \sqrt{Sen*Spe} \tag{11}$$

$$F - score = 2*Sen*Pre/(Sen + Pre) \tag{12}$$

AUC is area under curve. It is defined based on the receiver operating characteristic curve (ROC) and its value is less than 1. The algorithm was tested on several datasets from the Keel database, as shown in Table 1.

Table 1. Description of the datasets

Name	Attributes	Data size	Imbalance ratio
ecoli3	7	336	8.6
haberman	3	306	2.78
pima	8	786	1.87
poker-8_vs_6	10	1477	85.88
yeast3	8	1484	8.1
yeast4	8	1484	28.1

4.2   Experiment Settings

In data feature processing, a deep neural network with four fully connected layers is be used. When using fuzzy support vector machine for classification operation, the Gaussian kernel is the kernel function. For FSVM classifier, penalty constant C and the width of Gaussian kernel σ are selected by gird search method from the set $\{10^{-3}, 10^{-2}, 10^{-1}, 1, 10^1, 10^2, 10^3, 10^4\}$ and $\{2^{-5}, 2^{-4}, 2^{-3}, 2^{-2}, 2^{-1}, 1, 2^1, 2^2, 2^3, 2^4\}$. The fuzzy membership value of the minority samples is set to the imbalanced ratio (IR):

$$IR = num_{maj}/num_{min} \tag{13}$$

where num_{min} is the number of the minority class samples, and the minority class is also the positive class. num_{maj} is the number of data of the majority class samples, corresponding to the negative class. For the fuzzy membership value of the majority class, set it to 1. In order to eliminate the randomness, five cross validation is applied, and the algorithms are executed for 5 independent runs.

4.3 Results and Analysis

To compare the classification quality of the proposed algorithm, four baseline methods are used. SMOTE [12] method uses linear interpolation to generate synthetic samples, and finally uses SVM as a classifier. ADASYN [14] assigns the sampling weights of different minority samples based on the number of majority classes in the nearest neighbors. DSVM sets different penalty coefficients C for different classes, the minority class is set to imbalance ratio (IR), and the majority class is set to 1. ACFSVM [19] is a FSVM algorithm combined with sample affinity. The experimental results are shown in Table 2.

In order to observe the table more intuitively, bold the best classification result. It can be seen that DL-FSVM has achieved better classification quality on all three evaluation indicators. On the ecoli3 dataset, DL-FSVM has an increase of 0.1041 in G-mean compared to SMOTE, and the F1-score also reached an increase of 0.1086. In addition, on other datasets, the classification results of DL-FSVM are better than the baseline SMOTE method. However, on the poker-8_vs_6 dataset, the baseline SMOTE and ADASYN achieved the best results on the AUC, but its classification performance on G-mean and F1-score was poor.

Compared with the two methods using cost-sensitive learning, the method proposed in this paper has better classification performance. On the pima dataset, the fuzzy support vector machine based on sample affinity achieved the best result on F1-score. The result of DL-FSVM is worse than ACFSVM, which is 0.6502. On the ecoli3 dataset, the G-mean and F1 of DL-FSVM are increased by 0.0201 and 0.0575 respectively compared with the ACFSVM method. The average ranking of algorithm under different evaluation metrics is shown in Fig. 5. It can be seen that the classification performance of DL-FSVM is the best. The imbalanced classification method based on DNN and FSVM proposed in this paper has good robustness and can be used for different types of imbalanced data.

Table 2. Results of different imbalanced classification methods on datasets

Dataset	ecoli3		
Algorithm	G-mean	F-score	AUC
SMOTE	0.7750 ± 0.0545	0.5186 ± 0.0878	0.9100 ± 0.0085
ADASYN	0.7619 ± 0.0134	0.5460 ± 0.0022	0.9042 ± 0.0112
DSVM	0.8317 ± 0.0069	0.5579 ± 0.0269	0.9233 ± 0.0061
ACFSVM	0.8590 ± 0.0671	0.5697 ± 0.0843	0.9368 ± 0.0371
DL-FSVM	**0.8791 ± 0.0712**	**0.6272 ± 0.1263**	**0.9552 ± 0.0587**
Dataset	**haberman**		
Algorithm	G-mean	F-score	AUC
SMOTE	0.5466 ± 0.0152	0.3342 ± 0.0111	0.5536 ± 0.0385
ADASYN	0.5580 ± 0.0124	0.4267 ± 0.0138	0.6116 ± 0.0080
DSVM	0.5666 ± 0.0052	0.4458 ± 0.0066	0.6303 ± 0.0120
ACFSVM	0.6176 ± 0.0535	0.5439 ± 0.0502	0.6794 ± 0.0542
DL-FSVM	**0.6354 ± 0.1442**	**0.5898 ± 0.0579**	**0.6945 ± 0.0595**
Dataset	**pima**		
Algorithm	G-mean	F-score	AUC
SMOTE	0.6880 ± 0.0059	0.6023 ± 0.0072	0.7586 ± 0.0130
ADASYN	0.6672 ± 0.0207	0.5770 ± 0.0247	0.7343 ± 0.0188
DSVM	0.7183 ± 0.0036	0.6541 ± 0.0049	0.7634 ± 0.0014
ACFSVM	0.7305 ± 0.0388	**0.6614 ± 0.0597**	0.8017 ± 0.0467
DL-FSVM	**0.7374 ± 0.0259**	0.6502 ± 0.0351	**0.8152 ± 0.0248**
Dataset	**poker-8_vs_6**		
Algorithm	G-mean	F-score	AUC
SMOTE	0.8487 ± 0.0260	0.8276 ± 0.0281	**1.0000 ± 0.0000**
ADASYN	0.8630 ± 0.0171	0.8133 ± 0.0189	**1.0000 ± 0.0000**
DSVM	0.8932 ± 0.0015	0.7905 ± 0.0642	0.9998 ± 0.0002
ACFSVM	0.8953 ± 0.0970	0.7830 ± 0.2871	0.9861 ± 0.0147
DL-FSVM	**0.9045 ± 0.0737**	**0.8313 ± 0.1115**	0.9976 ± 0.0057
Dataset	**yeast3**		
Algorithm	G-mean	F-score	AUC
SMOTE	0.8143 ± 0.0024	0.5544 ± 0.0063	0.9269 ± 0.0028
ADASYN	0.8161 ± 0.0028	0.6193 ± 0.0012	0.9199 ± 0.0011
DSVM	0.9081 ± 0.0057	0.6396 ± 0.0084	0.9687 ± 0.0032

(continued)

Table 2. (*continued*)

Dataset	ecoli3		
Algorithm	G-mean	F-score	AUC
ACFSVM	0.8987 ± 0.0223	0.6316 ± 0.0421	0.9660 ± 0.0072
DL-FSVM	**0.9106 ± 0.0236**	**0.6875 ± 0.0309**	**0.9718 ± 0.0187**
Dataset	**yeast4**		
Algorithm	G-mean	F-score	AUC
SMOTE	0.5742 ± 0.0047	0.3069 ± 0.0091	0.8586 ± 0.0010
ADASYN	0.5697 ± 0.0082	0.2971 ± 0.0073	0.8587 ± 0.0007
DSVM	0.8259 ± 0.0125	0.2976 ± 0.0178	0.8914 ± 0.0003
ACFSVM	0.8326 ± 0.0386	0.2391 ± 0.0415	0.9017 ± 0.0312
DL-FSVM	**0.8412 ± 0.0927**	**0.3391 ± 0.0746**	**0.9158 ± 0.0549**

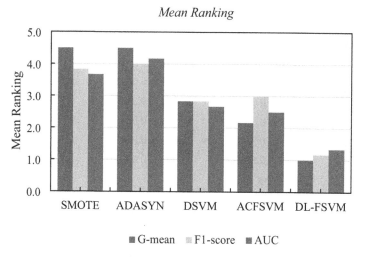

Fig. 5. Mean ranking of all compared algorithms on datasets

5   Conclusion

This paper proposes an imbalanced classification method combined with DNN, DL-FSVM. In order to obtain features with intra-class similarity and inter-class discrimination, DNN is trained using triplet loss function and Gumbel activation function to obtain the deep feature representation. To balance the data distribution, a random feature sampling algorithm based on the center of class is used in the minority samples to maintain the diversity of the minority class samples. Fuzzy support vector machine (FSVM) has provided a higher misclassification loss for the minority class, and it enhanced the classification quality of the algorithm for the minority class. Through the experimental results, it can be found that the proposed DL-FSVM has good classification results on evaluation metrics: G-means, F1-score, and AUC. In future work, more robust feature extractors can be used to provide effective measures for imbalanced classification.

Acknowledgements. This work was supported in part by the National Natural Science Foundation of China (61703279), in part by the Shanghai Municipal Science and Technology Major Project (2021SHZDZX0100) and the Fundamental Research Funds for the Central Universities.

References

1. Bhattacharya, S., Rajan, V., Shrivastava, H.: ICU mortality prediction: a classification algorithm for imbalanced datasets. In: The AAAI Conference on Artificial Intelligence, pp.1288–1294 (2017)
2. Li, H., Wong M.: Financial fraud detection by using grammar-based multi-objective genetic programming with ensemble learning. In: IEEE Congress on Evolutionary Computation (CEC), pp. 1113–1120 (2015)
3. Wang, S., Yao, X.: Using class imbalance learning for software defect prediction. IEEE Trans. Reliab. **62**(2), 434–443 (2013)
4. Romani, M., et al.: Face memory and face recognition in children and adolescents with attention deficit hyperactivity disorder: a systematic review. Neurosci. Biobehav. Rev. **89**, 1–12 (2018)
5. Tao, X., et al.: Affinity and class probability-based fuzzy support vector machine for imbalanced data sets. Neural Netw. **122**, 289–307 (2020)
6. Schroff, F., Kalenichenko, D., Philbin, J.: Facenet: a unified embedding for face recognition and clustering. In: The IEEE Conference on Computer Vision and Pattern Recognition, pp. 815–823 (2015)
7. Cooray, K.: Generalized gumbel distribution. J. Appl. Stat. **37**(1), 171–179 (2010)
8. Lin, C.F., Wang, S.D.: Fuzzy support vector machines. IEEE Trans. Neural Netw. **13**(2), 464–471 (2002)
9. Laurikkala, J.: Improving identification of difficult small classes by balancing class distribution. In: Quaglini, S., Barahona, P., Andreassen, S. (eds.) AIME 2001. LNCS (LNAI), vol. 2101, pp. 63–66. Springer, Heidelberg (2001). https://doi.org/10.1007/3-540-48229-6_9
10. Kang, Q., Chen, X., Li, S., Zhou, M.: A noise-filtered under-sampling scheme for imbalanced classification. IEEE Trans. Cybern. **47**(12), 4263–4274 (2016)
11. Kang, Q., Shi, L., Zhou, M., Wang, X., Wu, Q., Wei, Z.: A distance-based weighted under-sampling scheme for support vector machines and its application to imbalanced classification. IEEE Trans. Neural Netw. Learn. Syst. **29**(9), 4152–4165 (2017)
12. Chawla, N.V., Bowyer, K.W., Hall, L.O., Kegelmeyer, W.P.: SMOTE: synthetic minority over-sampling technique. J. Artif. Intell. Res. **16**, 321–357 (2002)
13. Han, H., Wang, W.-Y., Mao, B.-H.: Borderline-SMOTE: a new over-sampling method in imbalanced data sets learning. In: Huang, D.-S., Zhang, X.-P., Huang, G.-B. (eds.) ICIC 2005. LNCS, vol. 3644, pp. 878–887. Springer, Heidelberg (2005). https://doi.org/10.1007/11538059_91
14. He, H., Bai, Y., Garcia, E.A., Li, S.: ADASYN: adaptive synthetic sampling approach for imbalanced learning. In: IEEE International Joint Conference on Neural Networks (IEEE World Congress on Computational Intelligence), pp. 1322–1328. IEEE (2008)
15. Mathew, J., Luo, M., Pang, C.K., Chan, H.L.: Kernel-based SMOTE for SVM classification of imbalanced datasets. In: 41st Annual Conference of the IEEE Industrial Electronics Society (IECON 2015), pp. 1127–1132. IEEE (2015)

16. Mathew, J., Pang, C.K., Luo, M., Leong, W.H.: Classification of imbalanced data by over-sampling in kernel space of support vector machines. IEEE Trans. Neural Netw. Learn. Syst. **29**(9), 4065–4076 (2017)

17. Batuwita, R., Palade, V.: FSVM-CIL: fuzzy support vector machines for class imbalance learning. IEEE Trans. Fuzzy Syst. **18**(3), 558–571 (2010)

18. Yu, H., Sun, C., Yang, X., Zheng, S., Zou, H.: Fuzzy support vector machine with relative density information for classifying imbalanced data. IEEE Trans. Fuzzy Syst. **27**(12), 2353–2367 (2019)

19. Tao, X., et al.: Affinity and class probability-based fuzzy support vector machine for imbalanced data sets. Neural Netw. **122**, 289–307 (2020)

20. Wang, S., Yao, X.: Diversity analysis on imbalanced data sets by using ensemble models. In: IEEE Symposium on Computational Intelligence and Data Mining, pp. 324–331. IEEE (2009)

21. Chawla, N.V., Lazarevic, A., Hall, L.O., Bowyer, K.W.: SMOTEBoost: improving prediction of the minority class in boosting. In: Lavrač, N., Gamberger, D., Todorovski, L., Blockeel, H. (eds.) PKDD 2003. LNCS (LNAI), vol. 2838, pp. 107–119. Springer, Heidelberg (2003). https://doi.org/10.1007/978-3-540-39804-2_12

22. Krizhevsky, A., Sutskever, I., Hinton, G.E.: Imagenet classification with deep convolutional neural networks. Adv. Neural. Inf. Process. Syst. **25**, 1097–1105 (2012)

23. He, K., Zhang, X., Ren, S., Sun, J.: Deep residual learning for image recognition. In: IEEE Conference on Computer Vision and Pattern Recognition, pp. 770–778 (2016)

24. Ng, W.W., Zeng, G., Zhang, J., Yeung, D.S., Pedrycz, W.: Dual autoencoders features for imbalance classification problem. Pattern Recogn. **60**, 875–889 (2016)

Community Detection Based on Surrogate Network

Chao Lyu[1,2] ⓘ, Yuhui Shi[2(✉)] ⓘ, and Lijun Sun[2,3] ⓘ

[1] Harbin Institute of Technology, Harbin 150001, China
11849557@mail.sustech.edu.cn
[2] Southern University of Science and Technology, Shenzhen 518055, China
shiyh@sustech.edu.cn
[3] University of Technology Sydney, Sydney, Australia
11860004@mail.sustech.edu.cn

Abstract. This paper presents a novel methodology to detect communities in complex networks based on evolutionary computation. In the proposed method, a surrogate network with a more detectable community structure than the original network is firstly constructed based on the eigenmatrix of the adjacent matrix. Then the community partition can be found by successively optimizing the modularity of the surrogate network and the original network with an evolutionary algorithm. The proposed method is tested on both synthetic and real-world networks and compared with some existing algorithms. Experimental results show that employing the constructed surrogate networks can effectively improve the community detection efficiency.

Keywords: Community detection · Complex network · Evolutionary computation

1 Introduction

Community detection is an important research topic of network science. In general, a community in a complex network is defined as a group of nodes with tight connections while nodes which belong to different communities have relative sparse connections [6]. And the aim of community detection is to divide all nodes in a network into different communities, which plays an important role in investigating network topology and has many applications in engineering problems [10]. Therefore, community detection has attracted increasing attention from researchers and many detection algorithms have been proposed in past few decades [12]. Among them, the evolutionary computation (EC) based method

This work is partially supported by the Shenzhen Fundamental Research Program under grant No. JCYJ20200109141235597, National Science Foundation of China under grant No. 61761136008, Shenzhen Peacock Plan under grant No. KQTD2016112514355531, and Program for Guangdong Introducing Innovative and Entrepreneurial Teams under grant No. 2017ZT07X386.

L. Pan et al. (Eds.): BIC-TA 2021, CCIS 1566, pp. 45–53, 2022.
https://doi.org/10.1007/978-981-19-1253-5_4

[17] is an important approach which transfers the community detection into a modularity optimization problem and solves it with evolutionary algorithms (EA) [9]. In this class of methods, the total number of communities in a network does not need to be predefined, which has a higher flexibility than traditional clustering-based methods (e.g., spectral clustering [14]). On the other hand, EA has a more powerful global search ability and a higher robustness than classical optimization methods. Consequently, some EA-based community detection algorithms have been proposed in recent years [2,7,8,19].

However, due to the black box optimization scheme and the complexity of the fitness landscapes, individuals of an EA can be easily trapped into local optima, which can decrease the solution quality. To solve this problem, in addition to improving EAs' optimization performances, utilizing surrogate models [1] which are constructed from optimization problems to assist and accelerate evolutionary search is an effective approach. Compared with original problems, surrogate models have highly similar but much simpler fitness landscapes where global optima can be found more easily.

Based on this motivation, in this paper, we try to improve the community detection efficiency of EAs by constructing surrogate networks which have more significant community structures than the original networks based on the spectral clustering (SC). That is, the unweighted original network is firstly transformed into a weighted surrogate network by resetting the edge weights according to its eigenmatrix where the similarity between two nodes can be measured. Compared with the original network, the surrogate network has a highly similar but more detectable community structure. Then the approximated community division can be easily found by an EA through optimizing the modularity of the surrogate network. Finally, based on this result, the EA-based modularity optimization is performed back on the original network whose accurate community structure can be finally detected.

The rest of this paper is organized as follows: Section 2 introduces the backgrounds and related preliminaries about this research. The proposed method is described in detail in Sect. 3. In Sect. 4, the proposed algorithm is tested on benchmark networks and compared with existing community detection methods. Section 5 summarizes this paper and suggests the future works.

2   Preliminaries

2.1   Spectral Clustering

Spectral clustering (SC) [14] is a widely used clustering method to solve node classification problems. In SC, all nodes of a graph are represented by n-D vectors which can be clustered by traditional clustering methods (e.g., k-means). A classical Ncut SC can be described in Algorithm 1, where D is the degree matrix of W, k_1 is a hyper-parameter.

Algorithm 1: Ncut spectral clustering (NSC)

---

1 **Input:** Adjacent matrix W, number of clusters k_2
2 **Output:** Clustering result C
3 Calculate Laplacian matrix: $L = D - W$.
4 Normalize Laplacian matrix: $L = D^{-1/2}LD^{-1/2}$.
5 Calculate eigenvectors $f_1, f_2, \ldots, f_{k_1}$ of the k_1 minimum eigenvalues of matrix L.
6 Construct eigenmatrix $F = \text{normalize}\left(\text{f}_1^{\text{k}_1}\right)$.
7 $C(c_1, c_2, \ldots, c_{k_2}) = \text{clustering }(F, k_2)$.

2.2   EA-Based Community Detection

In this study, the community detection is formulated as an optimization problem [5]. That is, given a network G, we should find the best community division $\mathcal{D}^*$ that satisfies:

$$\mathcal{D}^* = \arg max \ \mathcal{F}(\mathcal{D}),$$
$$\text{subject to } \mathcal{D} \in \Omega \tag{1}$$

where Ω is the set of all the feasible community divisions of G, and $\mathcal{F} : \mathcal{D} \to \mathbb{R}$ determines the quality of the solution $\mathcal{D}$. In EA-based community detection methods, a solution $\mathcal{D}$ is represented by an individual under a coding scheme and the modularity Q [13] is usually adopted as the fitness function to evaluate the quality of a community division. Q can be calculated as follows:

$$Q = \sum_{i=1}^{q}[\frac{e_i}{S} - (\frac{d_i}{2S})^2] \tag{2}$$

where i is the community index, q is the total number of communities in the network, S is the sum weight of all edges in the network, e_i is the sum weight of the edges within community i, and d_i is the sum of degrees of all nodes in community i.

Particularly, in this paper, the brain storm optimization (BSO) [18], which is a classical evolutionary algorithm with a powerful global search ability, is employed to solve the above problem. BSO can be described in Algorithm 2, where $rand$ is a randomly generated number between 0 and 1, and new individuals are generated by genetic operators of crossover, mutation, and local search.

3   Proposed Method

In the proposed community detection method, we firstly improve the community detectability of a complex network by calculating its eigenmatrix F and modifying the edge weights based on the information provided by F. To be specific,

---

Algorithm 2: Brain storm optimization (BSO)

---

1 **Input:** Parameters N, g, m, P_1, P_2, and P_3
2 **Output:** Best individual of the population
3 Initialize a population with N individuals.
4 **for** $t = 1 : g$ **do**
5   Randomly divide all individuals into m clusters.
6   **while** N *individuals have not been generated* **do**
7   **if** *rand* $< P_1$ **then**
8   Randomly select a cluster c_i.
9   **if** *rand* $< P_2$ **then**
10   Select the best individual of c_i.
11   **else**
12   Randomly select an individual from c_i.
13   Generate an individual based on the selected individual.
14   **else**
15   Randomly select two clusters c_i and c_j.
16   **if** *rand* $< P_3$ **then**
17   Select the best individual of c_i and c_j, respectively.
18   **else**
19   Randomly select an individual from c_i and c_j, respectively.
20   Generate two individuals based on the two selected individuals.
21   Evaluate individuals and update population.

---

for each edge e_{ij} in network G, where i and j are two nodes connected by e_{ij}, we propose the following equation to modify its weights w_{ij} into w^*_{ij}:

$$w^*_{ij} = \frac{r}{1 + \|F_{i.} - F_{j.}\|_2} \tag{3}$$

where $F_{i.}$ and $F_{j.}$ are the ith and jth rows of matrix F, respectively, and $r > 1$ is a predefined parameter. According to the spectral clustering theory, if node i and node j belong to the same community, the value of $\|F_{i.} - F_{j.}\|_2$ tends to be small, otherwise, it tends to be a large number. In this way, the weights of edges within each community can be higher than those of edges which connect different communities so that the community structure of G can be intensified. After calculating w^*_{ij} for each edge in G, we can construct a weighted surrogate network G^* with adjacent matrix W^* whose elements are w^*_{ij}. Compared with the unweighted network G, G^* has a more significant community structure which can be detected more easily.

We firstly maximize the modularity of G^* by initializing and evolving a population of BSO for g_1 generations. Then we return to maximize the modularity of G by changing the fitness function of BSO and continuing evolving the current population for g_2 generations. Finally, the community structure represented by the best individual of the population can be output. The proposed algorithm is called surrogate network assisted community detection (SNACD) which is described in detail in Algorithm 3. Particularly, in the proposed algorithm, individuals are codded by the locus-based representation [15]. Based on this coding scheme, SNACD employs the genetic operators proposed in reference [16] to perform the crossover, mutation, population initialization, and local search operations.

Algorithm 3: Surrogate network assisted community detection (SNACD)

---

1 **Input:** Network G
2 **Output:** Community division $\mathcal{D}$
3 Calculate eigenmatrix F of G by Ncut spectral clustering (see lines 3-6 of Algorithm 1).
4 **for** *each edge e_{ij} in G* **do**
5   ⌊ Compute weight w^*_{ij} according to equation (3).
6 Construct surrogate network G^* with w^*_{ij}.
7 Maximize modularity (equation (2)) of G^* by running BSO for g_1 generations (see Algorithm 2).
8 Save current population and change fitness function.
9 Maximize modularity of G by continuing evolving the population for g_2 generations (see lines 4-21 of Algorithm 2).

---

4 Experiments

4.1 Experimental Setup

In this section, we test the proposed SNACD on benchmark networks and compare its performance with the basic BSO algorithm, the k-means [20] based spectral clustering (KSC) algorithm, and the CoCoMi algorithm [8]. The adopted benchmark consists of three synthetic GN networks [6] with ground-truth community structures and three real-world networks. The parameters for generating these GN networks are summarized in Table 1, where K indicates the total number of communities in the network, N indicates the number of nodes in each community, Z_{in} and Z_{out} indicate the number of internal and external half-edges connected to each node, respectively, and $Diag = 0$ means there is no self-loops in the network. The basic information of all the benchmark networks is summarized in Table 2. It should be pointed out that the tt-tw-yt is a multiplex network, and here we only extract its first layer.

In this experiment, two metrics are adopted to evaluate the performances of algorithms. Modularity Q is used to evaluate the detected community partitions of all networks. Particularly, for synthetic networks, the normalized mutual information (NMI) [3] is used as the metric to measure the similarity between the ground-truth community partition and the detected result. The higher the values of the above two metrics are, the higher the quality of the detected community division is.

Table 1. Parameter setup for generating GN networks

Network	N	K	Z_{in}	Z_{out}	$Diag$
GN1	64	16	20	10	0
GN2	64	16	20	15	0
GN3	16	64	6	4	0

Table 2. Basic information of all benchmark networks

Network	#node	#edge	Type
GN1	1024	15417	Synthetic
GN2	1024	17917	Synthetic
GN3	1024	5098	Synthetic
Football [6]	115	613	Real-world
Books [11]	105	441	Real-world
ff-tw-yt [4]	6401	42320	Real-world

The parameters of the proposed SNACD algorithm are set as follows: $k_1 = 5$, $r = 2$, $N = 50$, $g_1 = 25$, $g_2 = 5$, $m = 5$, $P_1 = 0.8$, $P_2 = 0.8$, $P_3 = 0.7$, the mutation probability is 0.02, and the probability of performing the local search operation for each new generated individual is 0.02.

4.2 Experimental Results and Discussions

For each network, we independently employ the algorithms to detect its community structure for 30 times and the mean values of the performance metrics are summarized in Table 3, where the best results are emphasized in bold.

Table 3. Comparison of the community detection results of different algorithms on benchmark networks

Network	Metric	SNACD	BSO	KSC	CoCoMi
GN1	Q	**0.6039**	0.5555	0.5671	0.5342
	NMI	**1.0000**	0.8790	0.9521	0.8076
GN2	Q	**0.5068**	0.4491	0.4703	0.4011
	NMI	**0.9989**	0.8351	0.9205	0.6882
GN3	Q	**0.5865**	0.5347	0.4454	0.5807
	NMI	**0.9582**	0.7603	0.7552	0.9037
Football	Q	**0.6035**	0.5837	0.5678	0.5886
Books	Q	**0.5265**	0.5251	0.5162	**0.5265**
ff-tw-yt	Q	**0.5190**	0.5115	0.1980	0.4953

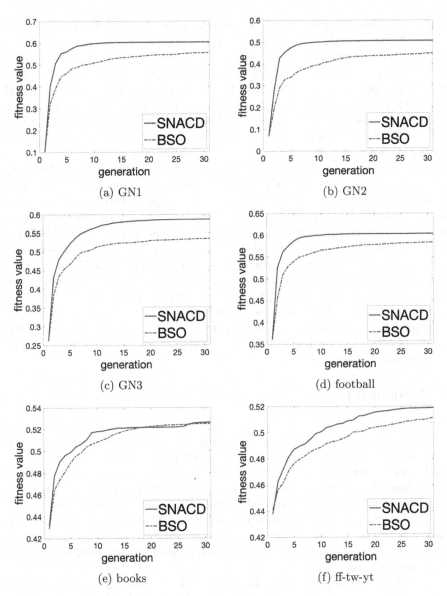

Fig. 1. Comparison of the mean optimization curves of SNACD and BSO on benchmark networks

From Table 3, it can be seen that the proposed SNACD outperforms the other three algorithms on all benchmark networks in terms of both modularity and NMI values. For real-world networks, the community structures output by SNACD have higher qualities than those detected by the other algorithms; For synthetic networks, the community structures output by SNACD have higher similarities with the ground-truth results than those detected by the other algorithms. It can be concluded that SNACD has a superior community detection performance among these algorithms.

Furthermore, to illustrate the effect of the surrogate networks on accelerating modularity optimization, we compare the mean optimization curves of SNACD and BSO on all networks in Fig. 1, where the x-coordinates indicate the generation number, and the y-coordinates indicate the mean fitness value of the best individual evaluated on the original network among the corresponding generation's population over the 30 runs.

From Fig. 1, it can be seen that the proposed SNACD has a higher optimization efficiency than the BSO-based community detection algorithm on most benchmark networks. Even if both algorithms employ BSO as the optimizer to maximize modularity, SNACD firstly constructs surrogate networks which have more significant community structures than the original networks. Benefitting from the highly similar and more optimizable modularity landscapes of the surrogate networks, during the early g_1 generations, SNACD has a higher convergence speed and can find better solutions than BSO which is performed on the original network. Finally, SNACD can output higher-quality community partitions in terms of the metrics of both Q and NMI. Therefore, it can be concluded from the above experimental results that utilizing the constructed surrogate networks can significantly improve the community detection efficiency of evolutionary algorithms.

5 Conclusions

In this paper, a novel community detection algorithm called surrogate network assisted community detection (SNACD) has been presented. In the proposed method, a surrogate network with a more detectable community structure is firstly constructed based on the original network. Then the community division can be found by successively optimizing the modularity of the surrogate network and the original network with BSO algorithm. Community detection experiments on benchmark networks have shown the proposed SNACD has a superior performance among the test algorithms, while utilizing the constructed surrogate networks can significantly accelerate EAs' optimization in solving community detection problems.

To further improve the performance of SNACD, some algorithms with low computational complexity (e.g., network embedding) can be employed to replace the SC-based method to construct surrogate networks. Moreover, the BSO optimizer can be replaced with more advanced EAs to improve its global search ability.

References

1. Audet, C., Denni, J., Moore, D., Booker, A., Frank, P.: A surrogate-model-based method for constrained optimization. In: 8th Symposium on Multidisciplinary Analysis and Optimization, p. 4891 (2000)

2. Cai, Q., Gong, M., Shen, B., Ma, L., Jiao, L.: Discrete particle swarm optimization for identifying community structures in signed social networks. Neural Netw. **58**, 4–13 (2014)
3. Danon, L., Diaz-Guilera, A., Duch, J., Arenas, A.: Comparing community structure identification. J. Stat. Mech. Theory Exp. **2005**(09), P09008 (2005)
4. Dickison, M.E., Magnani, M., Rossi, L.: Multilayer Social Networks. Cambridge University Press, Cambridge (2016)
5. Ferligoj, A., Batagelj, V.: Direct multicriteria clustering algorithms. J. Classif. **9**(1), 43–61 (1992)
6. Girvan, M., Newman, M.E.: Community structure in social and biological networks. Proc. Natl. Acad. Sci. **99**(12), 7821–7826 (2002)
7. Hassan, E.A., Hafez, A.I., Hassanien, A.E., Fahmy, A.A.: A discrete bat algorithm for the community detection problem. In: Onieva, E., Santos, I., Osaba, E., Quintián, H., Corchado, E. (eds.) HAIS 2015. LNCS (LNAI), vol. 9121, pp. 188–199. Springer, Cham (2015). https://doi.org/10.1007/978-3-319-19644-2_16
8. He, S., et al.: Cooperative co-evolutionary module identification with application to cancer disease module discovery. IEEE Trans. Evol. Comput. **20**(6), 874–891 (2016)
9. Holland, J.H., et al.: Adaptation in Natural and Artificial Systems: An Introductory Analysis with Applications to Biology, Control, and Artificial Intelligence. MIT Press, Cambridge (1992)
10. Karataş, A., Şahin, S.: Application areas of community detection: a review. In: 2018 International Congress on Big Data, Deep Learning and Fighting Cyber Terrorism (IBIGDELFT), pp. 65–70. IEEE (2018)
11. Krebs, V.: Political books network. http://www.orgnet.com
12. Lancichinetti, A., Fortunato, S.: Community detection algorithms: a comparative analysis. Phys. Rev. E **80**(5), 056117 (2009)
13. Newman, M.E.: Fast algorithm for detecting community structure in networks. Phys. Rev. E **69**(6), 066133 (2004)
14. Ng, A.Y., Jordan, M.I., Weiss, Y.: On spectral clustering: analysis and an algorithm. In: Advances in Neural Information Processing Systems, pp. 849–856 (2002)
15. Park, Y., Song, M., et al.: A genetic algorithm for clustering problems. In: Proceedings of the Third Annual Conference on Genetic Programming, vol. 1998, pp. 568–575 (1998)
16. Pizzuti, C.: GA-Net: a genetic algorithm for community detection in social networks. In: Rudolph, G., Jansen, T., Beume, N., Lucas, S., Poloni, C. (eds.) PPSN 2008. LNCS, vol. 5199, pp. 1081–1090. Springer, Heidelberg (2008). https://doi.org/10.1007/978-3-540-87700-4_107
17. Pizzuti, C.: Evolutionary computation for community detection in networks: a review. IEEE Trans. Evol. Comput. **22**(3), 464–483 (2017)
18. Shi, Y.: Brain storm optimization algorithm. In: Tan, Y., Shi, Y., Chai, Y., Wang, G. (eds.) ICSI 2011. LNCS, vol. 6728, pp. 303–309. Springer, Heidelberg (2011). https://doi.org/10.1007/978-3-642-21515-5_36
19. Tasgin, M., Herdagdelen, A., Bingol, H.: Community detection in complex networks using genetic algorithms. Computer **2**(1), 3 (2007)
20. Yadav, J., Sharma, M.: A review of k-mean algorithm. Int. J. Eng. Trends Technol. **4**(7), 2972–2976 (2013)

Fault-Tolerant Scheme of Cloud Task Allocation Based on Deep Reinforcement Learning

Hengliang Tang[1], Zifang Tang[1], Tingting Dong[2(✉)], Qiuru Hai[1], and Fei Xue[1]

[1] School of Information, Beijing Wuzi University, Beijing 101149, China
[2] Faculty of Information Technology, Beijing University of Technology, Beijing 100124, China
dongtingting2019@163.com

Abstract. Due to the fact that the resource is prone to be wrong during tasks execution in cloud, which leads to failed tasks, in view of the recent research, the Primary-Backup model (PB model) is mostly used to deal with fault-tolerant tasks, but the selection of passive scheme and active scheme is assumed in advance, and the advantages between the two schemes are not fully utilized. Based on the deep reinforcement learning, this paper proposes an adaptive PB model selection algorithm, Active-Passive Scheme DQN (APSDQN). The process of faulty task tolerance is regarded as a Markov decision process, taking the passive scheme and active scheme as the action spaces, the shortest completion time of the task and the highest resource utilization as the reward feedback, combine with the real environment state information, select the most suitable fault-tolerant scheme for faulty tasks to save resources and improve the robustness of cloud system. The experimental results show that APSDQN has certain advantages in the total task finish time of task allocation, and significantly improves the resource utilization and the task success rate in the cloud.

Keywords: Primary-backup model · Fault-tolerant · Deep reinforcement learning · Passive scheme · Active scheme

1 Introduction

The main role of cloud computing is to calculate through the Internet, share data and resources of software and hardware, and provide other equipment resources on demand [1]. The computing resources of cloud system are flexible and elastic, giving users the illusion of unlimited resources. More and more users choose cloud computing to perform tasks, such as data storage and scientific computing [2]. Although the cloud system has strong computing power in task scheduling, due to the increase of scale and complexity, the cloud system has high dynamic uncertainty and resource failure, which has an adverse impact on resource management and scheduling [3]. Faulty resources in cloud computing may have a devastating impact on tasks execution [4], especially for tasks with deadlines. Because the execution units of cloud fail, the tasks executed on them cannot be completed within the deadline, and the quality of service (QoS) beyond the deadline cannot meet the customer's requirements. Therefore, it is very necessary to provide an effective dynamic fault-tolerant scheme for task sets with deadlines to minimize the total task completion time and system resource consumption.

Fault-tolerant scheme refers to how to assign failed tasks to appropriate processing units and ensuring that the tasks can be completed before the deadline. The existing PB model scheduling strategies are mainly divided into two categories: active scheme and passive scheme [5]. Active scheme means that the primary and the backup are executed at the same time. If the primary fails, the backup can complete the task on time, but this scheme runs multiple copies at the same time, resulting in lots of resource waste and low system resource utilization. Passive scheme means that the primary runs first before the backup, the backup runs after the primary fails. Although this scheme can save resources, the backup may be unsuccessful before the deadline. In the existing studies, many scholars tend to choose the active scheme [6], however, few scholars combine the two schemes to select adaptive fault-tolerant strategies according to the real faulty environment information, so as to balance the time and resource consumption.

Deep reinforcement learning (DRL) has attracted more and more attention in the field of artificial intelligence for its lifelong learning characteristics. Thanks to the success of Atari [7], AlphaGo [8] and AlphaStar [9], scholars quickly realized the power of DRL in optimization and scheduling. Mnih [10] combined convolutional neural network with traditional Q-learning algorithm and proposed Deep Q Network (DQN), which is a typical DRL algorithm. Multi-task scheduling and fault-tolerant processing on cloud platform is a NP-hard problem [11]. This paper proposes a self-adaption Action-Passive Scheme-DQN (APSDQN) algorithm combined with DRL. Firstly, the execution units in the cloud are regarded as virtual machines. Secondly, the fault-tolerant process of fault tasks on the virtual machine is transformed into a Markov decision process (MDP), and then select the corresponding the active or passive scheme according to the real environment information within the deadline to minimize the task completion time and maximize the utilization of system resources. The main contributions of this paper are as follows:

(1) According to the First Come First Serve, this paper designs an allocation algorithm of virtual machine and task.
(2) For faulty tasks, this paper proposes an adaptive PB model selection algorithm (APSDQN) based on deep reinforcement learning. The process of task fault processing is regarded as MDP. Taking the passive scheme and active scheme as the action space, combined with the real environmental state information, the most suitable fault-tolerant scheme is selected for the faulty task.
(3) Based on CloudSim platform, to verify the effectiveness of APSDQN, the simulation comparison experiment with active only scheme and only passive scheme is carried out, the total task finish time, the utilization rate of system resources and the success rate are reference indexes.

2 Related Works

Due to the large scale and high complexity of cloud computing, it faces many challenges, such as system reliability, execution cost and resource utilization, and system reliability is an important challenge. In the existing studies, many fault-tolerant algorithms based on replication strategy have been proposed to improve the reliability of cloud system [12]. In the replication strategy, each task has a primary and backup copy. If the primary of a task cannot be completed normally due to the failure of its execution unit, its backup can continue to be executed and ensure the successful completion of the task on time. There are two types of existing replication strategies: active scheme and passive scheme.

Liu [5] proposed DBSA algorithm based on active scheme to study how to maximize the number of copies of tasks in the system under the given deadline, so as to test the fault tolerance of the system. In order to reduce the execution cost and shorten the resource scheduling time, based on the active scheme and on premise of meeting the system reliability, Xie et al. [13] proposed the quantitative fault-tolerant scheduling algorithms QFEC and QFEC + with the lowest execution cost, and QFSL and QFSL + with the shortest task completion time, but this algorithm didn't consider the task's deadline. Jing et al. [14] designed a fault-tolerant scheduling algorithm CCRH based on passive scheme in cloud system, but didn't consider the on-demand resource supply of cloud system. Wang et al. [15] extended the primary backup model, firstly proposed the elastic resource allocation mechanism in fault-tolerant environment, and designed a new fault-tolerant elastic scheduling algorithm FESTAL for real-time tasks in the cloud to achieve fault tolerance and high resource utilization. Ding et al. [16] considered the characteristics of virtualization and elasticity in cloud system, an offline fault-tolerant elastic scheduling algorithm FTESW is proposed to realize the dynamic resource adjustment of primary and backup. Yan et al. [4] took the uncertainty of task runtime into account in the model, and proposed a dynamic fault-tolerant elastic scheduling mechanism DEFT, which used overlapping mechanism to improve the utilization of cloud resources. Although scholars continue to reduce time consumption and improve resource utilization, fault tolerance based on replication strategy is still a research hotspot.

Now, there is seldom research on using deep reinforcement learning algorithm to realize fault-tolerant processing of cloud resources. Combined with the DQN algorithm and the fault environment of cloud resources, this paper designs a self-adaptive PB model selection algorithm——Action Passive Scheme-DQN (APSDQN). The process of task fault process is regarded as MDP, the passive scheme and active scheme are taken as the action space, combined with the real environmental state information, select the most suitable fault-tolerant processing scheme for fault tasks, so as to shorten the task completion time and improve the utilization of system resources.

3 Cloud System and Fault Model

This part mainly introduces the cloud task allocation system and fault model. Suppose the client uploads the computing task to the cloud, the scheduler allocates the execution unit to the task according to the First Come First Service, and allocates the corresponding fault-tolerant scheme for the task according to the APSDQN algorithm.

The resource monitor is responsible for recording and feeding back the consumption of virtual machines in the system (Fig. 1).

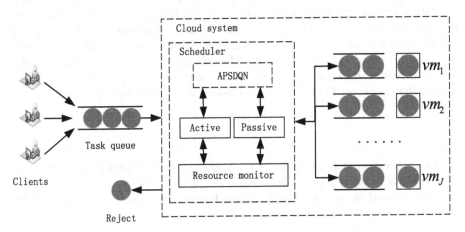

Fig. 1. A figure of the system model.

3.1 Task Model

Clients submit task sets to the cloud $T = \{T_1, T_2, ..., T_K\}$, T_k consists of subtasks: $T_k = \{t_1, t_2, ..., t_I\}$, subtasks t_i are independent of each other and have no priority relationship. K represents the total number of tasks, and I represents the total number of subtasks of each task. $t_i = (a_i, d_i, s_i)$, a_i indicates the arrival time of t_i, d_i indicates the deadline of the subtask; s_i represents the size of the subtask. The deadline of T_k is D_k. Through virtualization technology, the computing host in the cloud can be regarded as a group of virtual machines (VMS), so VM is the smallest processing unit. The cloud system in this paper consists of J VMS, $VM = \{vm_1, vm_2, vm_3, \cdots, vm_J\}$, the computing power of each vm_j is p_j, and its activation time is at_j, vm_{ij} indicates that the subtask t_i is assigned to vm_j. Execution time of subtask t_i on virtual machine vm_j:

$$et_{ij} = \frac{s_i}{p_j} \tag{1}$$

In PB model, each t_i has a primary t_i^P and a backup t_i^B. For tasks with active scheme, the primary and backup will be executed synchronously, for tasks with passive scheme, the backup will be executed after the primary fails. The primary and backup are scheduled on different VMS to avoid that the backup fails for the failure of the execution unit the master is located. vm_{ij}^P indicates that vm_j executes t_i^P, and vm_{ij}^B indicates vm_j executes t_i^B. The predicted finished time of t_i:

$$pft_i = est_i + et_i \tag{2}$$

Where, est_i is the earliest start time of t_i, when vm_{ij} is free: $est_i = \max\{a_i, at_j\}$,when vm_{ij} is busy: $est_i = pft_j^{t-1}$, pft_j^{t-1} is the predicted finished time of vm_j at the last time $t - 1$.

3.2 Fault Model

The existing failure problems in cloud are mainly divided into two types: transient failure and permanent failure [17]. Compared with temporary faults, permanent faults are more troublesome to deal with. Therefore, the faults of the execution unit in this paper are considered as permanent and unrecoverable faults. An error in one execution unit will not affect the other VMS, and only one VM fails in a time step, so as to ensure the smooth execution of the backup, because the primary and backup run on two different VMS at the same time. The failure interval follows the Poisson distribution with failure rate μ:

$$f(t) = e^{-\mu t} \tag{3}$$

This paper designs a fault detection mechanism to find the faulty process unit, such as fault signal or acceptance test [18]. When an error occurs in the process unit where the task is located, the task will fail. This paper focuses on the permanent failure of VM.

3.3 APSDQN MDP Model

This part transforms the fault-tolerant process of faulty tasks into Markov Decision Process (MDP).

State Representation. In most scheduling methods based on reinforcement learning, the state feature representation of the current system is defined as the state indicators, such as the number of tasks, the remaining processing time of unfinished tasks, the load of the current system, the execution of the current task, etc. [19], but in practical applications, the number of tasks in the system is huge, if these indicators directly represent the state characteristics of the task, the input of DQN algorithm will be very complex, and the training results will not be satisfactory. To solve this problem, the state characteristics in this paper are represented by a 4-element array, which correspond to the 4 state components in the system and are recorded as $s_t = (num_k(t), ATFR(t), AFT(t), ARU(t))$. Where, $num_k(t)$ represents the number of subtasks completed in the current time step t, $ATFR(t)$ is the average task finish rate in the current time step t:

$$ATFR(t) = \frac{\sum_{k=1}^{K} tfr_k}{K} \tag{4}$$

Where, fr_k indicates the task T_k finish rate:

$$fr_k = \frac{num_k(t)}{I} \tag{5}$$

$AFT(t)$ indicates the average finish time of the tasks in the current time step t:

$$AFT(t) = \frac{\sum_{i=1}^{num_k(t)} pft_i}{num_k(t)} \times K \tag{6}$$

$ARU(t)$ is the average resource utilization of the current time step t:

$$ARU(t) = \frac{\sum_{k=1}^{K} \sum_{j=1}^{J} \sum_{i=1}^{I} (et_{ij}^P \times x_{ij}^P + et_{ij}^B \times x_{ij}^B)}{\sum_{k=1}^{K} \sum_{j=1}^{J} \sum_{i=1}^{I} (et_{ij}^P \times x_{ij}^P + et_{ij}^B \times x_{ij}^B) + \sum_{j=1}^{J} at_j} \qquad (7)$$

Where, et_{ij}^P indicates the execution time of t_i^P on vm_j, et_{ij}^B indicates the execution time of t_i^B on vm_j, x_{ij}^P indicates t_i^P is assigned to vm_j, and x_{ij}^B indicates that t_i^B is assigned to vm_j.

$$x_{ij}^P = \begin{cases} 0, & t_i^P \text{ not be executed on } rt_j \\ 1, & t_i^P \text{ be executed on } rt_j \end{cases} \qquad (8)$$

Action Representation. Active scheme and passive scheme are two replication policies in PB model. It can be seen from the above that the two schemes have their own advantages and disadvantages. Therefore, at each time step, the best fault-tolerant scheme will be provided for the task according to the real situation of the system. In this paper, the action space is defined as active scheme and passive scheme, that is, action space A = {active, passive}. Agent will combine Q value and $\varepsilon - greedy$ algorithm to select and execute the most appropriate fault-tolerant scheme, and then enter the next state, so as to adapt to the dynamic change of system state information.

Reward Function. The traditional reward settings give positively or negatively discrete rewards when the system reaches a certain state, and do not give rewards when it does not reach the idea state [20]. This design can't immediately offer an exact feedback about agent's selection. Considering the goal of fault-tolerant process in this paper is to minimize the completion time of the task and maximize the resource utilization of the system, the average completion time of the task and the resource utilization in the system are involved in the reward function.

$$r_t = m(1 - \frac{AFT(t)}{d_i}) + nARU(t) \qquad (9)$$

where m and n are the weight coefficients within the range of (0,1). Through repeated experiments, m equals 0.65 and n equals 0.45.

4   APSDQN Implementation

This part further embodies the above designed system in the algorithm implementation. The existing DRL methods are divided into value-function methods and policy-function methods [21]. Compared with the policy-function methods, the methods based on value-function are more intuitive and can directly reflect the advantages and disadvantages of different actions. This paper adopts a classical deep Q network (DQN) algorithm with a dual network structure based on value-function. The target network is used to update network parameters by the experience reply pool D and the predict network is used to make intelligent decision.

The deep neural network structure of APSDQN algorithm is composed of six full connection layers [22]: an input layer, an output layer and four hidden layers. The number of nodes in the input layer equals the number of the state feature components, and the number of nodes in the output layer equals the number of actions. Each hidden layer has 30 nodes. "tansig" is the activation function of input layer and hidden layer, and "softmax" is the activation function of output layer. The Fig. 2 shows the fault-tolerant process framework of APSDQN.

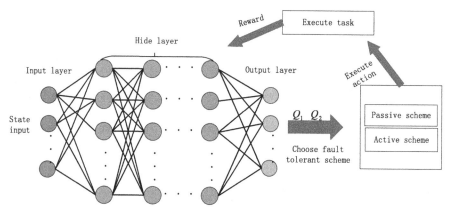

Fig. 2. A figure of the fault-tolerant process framework of APSDQN.

APSDQN algorithm aims to allocate the best fault-tolerant scheme for each ready task to maximize resource utilization and minimize task completion time. In this paper, the pending tasks submitted by customers are divided into K tasks, and each task has I subtasks. Firstly, when a new task T_k arrives, if the maximum completion time *makespan* of T_k isn't within the deadline, the task cannot be completed within QoS, the system will reject T_k. If T_k is accepted, the system calculates the *pft* of each t_i, and select the first two VMs with the shortest *pft* to assign to the primary and backup of each t_i. The *makespan* of T_k is:

$$makespan(T_k) = \max_{i=1,2,..,I} \{pft(t_i)\} \qquad (10)$$

Algorithm 1: APSDQN fault tolerant algorithm

Input: task sets $T = \{T_1, T_2, T_3, ,, T_K\}$, $T_k = \{t_1, t_2, t_3, ,,, t_I\}$, Deadline D_k for T_k, maximum iteration(G=1000); iteration index(t); the learning rate(α); the discount factor(γ)

Output: the fault tolerant scheme; the corresponding optimal VM allocation for each task t_i

01. Initialize replay memory D to capacity O

02. Initialize predict network with weights θ, target network with weights θ^-

03. **While** each new task T_k arrives do

04.   Calculate the $makespan(T_k)$ for task set T_k

05.   **If** $makespan(T_k) > D_k$ then

06.   Reject T_k

07.   **Else**

08.   **For** each arrived task t_i do

09.   Calculate pft_{ij} for each vm_j and order the VMs by the increasing pft_{ij}

10.   Select the first two VMs for the primary t_i^P and backup t_i^B of the task t_i

11.   **For** t = 1 to G do

12.   Observe the current state $s_t = (num_k(t), ATFR(t), AFT(t), ARU(t))$

13. $a_t = \max_a Q^*(s_t, a_t, \theta_t)$, and select a_t with $\varepsilon - greedy$

14.   **If** a_t = resubmission then

15.   Release t_i^B and vm_j

16.   **End if**

17.   Execute action a_t, calculate reward r_t, get the next state s_{t+1}

18.   Store experience sample (s_t, a_t, r_t, s_{t+1}) in D

19.   Sample random minibatch of samples from D

20.
$$y_t = \begin{cases} r_t, & \text{if episode terminates at step t+1} \\ r_t + \gamma \hat{Q}(s_{t+1}, \arg\max_{a_{t+1}} Q(s_{t+1}, a_{t+1}, \theta^-), \theta), & \text{otherwise} \end{cases}$$

21.   Perform a gradient descent on $(y_t - Q(s_t, a_t; \theta))^2$ with parameters θ

22.   Return a_t and allocation scheme

23.   Every C steps reset $\hat{Q} = Q$

24.   **End for**

25.   **End for**

26.   **End if**

27. **End while**

Secondly, APSDQN algorithm uses the convolution neural network (CNN) to preselect fault-tolerant scheme for each t_i. Taking the state information of the system as the input of the CNN, the corresponding Q values of the two fault-tolerant schemes are simulated and calculated through the CNN, and the corresponding fault-tolerant scheme is selected according to $\varepsilon - greedy$. t_i^P and t_i^B with the active scheme are synchronously executed, otherwise, t_i^B will be executed after t_i^P fails. If t_i^P succeeds, t_i^B will be released automatically. Then, after t_i is completed, the reward r_t provide feedback on agent decisions. See algorithm 1 for specific APSDQN.

5   Simulation Experiment

In order to verify the advantage of APSDQN, this paper compares it with only active scheme (OAS) and only passive scheme (OPS) on CloudSim. OAS always runs the primary and backup at the same time. OPS always executes the backup after the primary fails. This paper verifies the performance of APSDQN from the following three indicators: total task completion time (TTFT) [23], system resource utilization (SRU) and success rate (SR) [24]:

(1)   TTFT refers to the total completion time of the task sets in this paper, which reflects the efficiency of cloud system in processing tasks
(2)   SRU refers to the ratio of the total task execution time to the total active time of the execution unit after all tasks are completed, reflecting the resource utilization of VM in the system.
(3)   SR refers to the ratio of the number of tasks completed within the deadline to the total number of tasks when all tasks are completed, reflecting the task success rate in the fault environment.

5.1   Experimental Setup

This paper uses the Google Tracelogs data as the dataset. About 25 million tasks data in 29 days were recorded by Tracelogs. According to [25], the 18th day is a symbol day. Therefore, 1050 tasks were selected on day 18 as samples to test all algorithms in our experiment. Assuming that the length of each task s_i follows the uniform distribution of U (50, 100), and the process capacity p_j of vm_j follows the uniform distribution of U (500, 1000), the deadline d_i of each subtask is:

$$d_i = \frac{(1 + \beta)}{J} \sum_{j=1}^{J} et_{ij} \tag{11}$$

where, β is a random number between (0, 0.5).

In this paper, 10 MVs are set, $J = 10$, the startup time of VM is 15 s, and the arrival time of each task and the failure interval of the virtual machine obey Poisson distribution. The data samples are divided into 6 groups, $K = 6$. The number of subtasks in each group are $I_1 = 50, I_2 = 100, I_3 = 150, I_4 = 200, I_5 = 250, I_6 = 300$. Six groups of experiments are carried out on the above three algorithms to verify the effectiveness of APSDQN compared with the other two algorithms.

5.2   Experimental Results and Analysis

Table 1 shows the results of the three algorithms after performing six groups of tasks. It is obvious that APSDQN and OAS are dominant in the TTFT and SR, and APSDQN

Table 1. The result of three algorithms.

Index	APSDQN	OAS	OPS
TTFT	80.6	79.3	120.5
SRU	0.97	0.82	0.94
SR	0.95	0.94	0.83

and OPS are more prominent in SRU. This is because APSDQN continuously learns the optimal decision according to the system state information and reward feedback when selecting fault-tolerant scheme, besides, APSDQN only receives tasks that are expected to be completed before the deadline; The backup of each task in OAS runs, which wastes a lot of resources, but ensures the smooth completion of the faulty task. OPS does not judge and prepare for the fault task in advance, and doesn't start to execute the backup until the primary fails, which wastes a lot of time. Therefore, in contrast, APSDQN has smaller TTFT and SR, and has obvious advantages in SRU.

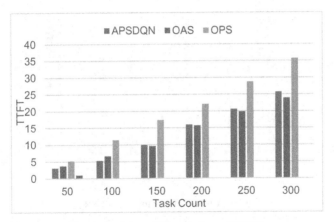

Fig. 3. A figure of Comparison of TTFT.

It can be seen from Fig. 3 that when the number of tasks is small, the TTFT of APSDQN is short, and when the number of tasks becomes large, the TTFT of OAS is short. It can be seen from Figs. 4 and 5 that APSDQN has outstanding advantages in SRU and SR. This is because OAS runs the primary and backup at the same time, which consumes double resources to shorten the finish time of the task, however, APSDQN learns and predicts the possible fault-tolerant schemes of tasks. APSDQN assigns passive schemes to tasks with sufficient deadline, and assigns an active scheme to tasks with tight deadlines, which minimizes the total completion time of tasks and reduces the consumption of cloud resources on the basis of ensuring the tasks are completed within the deadline. Therefore, generally, the APSDQN proposed in this paper is much better in cloud fault-tolerant process.

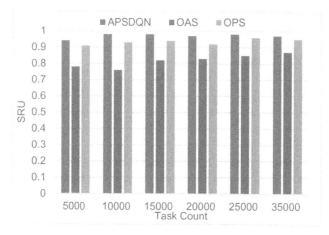

Fig. 4. A figure of Comparison of SRU.

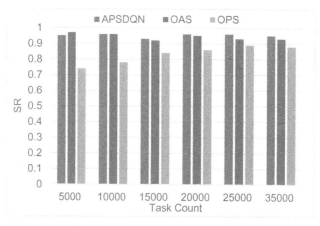

Fig. 5. A figure of Comparison of SR.

6 Conclusion

Based on the background that cloud computing resources are prone to failure, aiming at the problem of excessive resource consumption and long time-consuming in the current fault-tolerant research of PB model, combined with the advantages of DRL, this paper intelligently pre-allocates active scheme or passive scheme to tasks as fault-tolerant scheme according to the real system state information and reward feedback to improve cloud preprocess capability for failed tasks. The experimental results show that APSDQN has certain advantages in the total task finish time for the intelligent decision-making of active scheme and passive scheme, and significantly improves the resource utilization and the task success rate in the cloud. At the same time, it can be seen that APSDQN still has a lot of space for shortening the task completion time. The future research can further focus on reducing TTFT.

References

1. Dähling, S., Razik, L., Monti, A.: Enabling scalable and fault-tolerant multi-agent systems by utilizing cloud-native computing. Auton. Agent. Multi-Agent Syst. **35**(1), 1–27 (2021)
2. Ahmad, Z., Nazir, B., Umer, A.: A fault-tolerant workflow management system with quality-of-service-aware scheduling for scientific workflows in cloud computing. Int. J. Commun. Syst. **34**(1), 66–78 (2021)
3. Yao, G., Ding, Y., Ren, L., et al.: An immune system-inspired rescheduling algorithm for workflow in Cloud systems. Knowl. Based Syst. **99**, 39–50 (2016)
4. Yan, H., Zhu, X., Chen, H., et al.: DEFT: dynamic fault-tolerant elastic scheduling for tasks with uncertain runtime in cloud. Inf. Sci. **477**, 30–46 (2019)
5. Liu, J., Wei, M., Hu, W., et al.: Task scheduling with fault-tolerance in real-time heterogeneous systems. J. Syst. Archit. **90**, 23–33 (2018)
6. Ansari, M., Salehi, M., Safari, S., et al.: Peak-power-aware primary-backup technique for efficient fault-tolerance in multicore embedded systems. IEEE Access **8**, 142843–142857 (2020)
7. Cuccu, G., Togelius, J., Cudré-Mauroux, P.: Playing Atari with few neurons. Auton. Agent. Multi-Agent Syst. **35**(2), 1–23 (2021)
8. Li, Z., Zhu, C., Gao, Y., et al.: AlphaGo policy network: a DCNN accelerator on FPGA. IEEE Access **8**, 203039–203047 (2020)
9. Arulkumaran, K., Cully, A., Togelius, Y.: AlphaStar: an evolutionary computation perspective. GECCO (Companion) 314–315 (2019)
10. Mnih, V., Kavukcuoglu, K., Silver, D., et al.: Playing Atari with deep reinforcement learning (2013). https://arxiv.org/abs/1312.5602
11. Husamelddin, A.M.B., Sheng, C., Jing, W.: Reliability-aware: task scheduling in cloud computing using multi-agent reinforcement learning algorithm and neural fitted Q. Int. Arab J. Inf. Technol. **18**(1), 36–47 (2021)
12. Setlur, A., Nirmala, S., Singh, H., et al.: An efficient fault tolerant workflow scheduling approach using replication heuristics and checkpointing in the cloud. J. Parallel Distrib. Comput. **136**, 14–28 (2020)
13. Xie, G., Zeng, G., Li, R., et al.: Quantitative fault-tolerance for reliable workflows on heterogeneous IaaS clouds. IEEE Trans. Cloud Comput. **8**(4), 1223–1236 (2020)
14. Jing, W., Liu, Y.: Multiple DAGs reliability model and fault-tolerant scheduling algorithm in cloud computing system. Comput. Model. New Techol. **18**(8), 22–30 (2014)
15. Wang, J., Bao, W., Zhu, X., et al.: FESTAL: fault-tolerant elastic scheduling algorithm for real-time tasks in virtualized clouds. IEEE Trans. Comput. **64**(9), 2545–2558 (2015)
16. Ding, Y., Yao, G., Hao, K.: Fault-tolerant elastic scheduling algorithm for workflow in cloud systems. Inf. Sci. **393**, 47–65 (2017)
17. Zhou, J., Cong, P., Sun, J., et al.: Throughput maximization for multicore energy-harvesting systems suffering both transient and permanent faults. IEEE Access **7**, 98462–98473 (2019)
18. Manimaran, G., Murthy, C.S.R.: A fault-tolerant dynamic scheduling algorithm for multiprocessor real-time systems and its analysis. IEEE Trans. Parallel Distrib. Syst. **9**(11), 1137–1152 (1998)
19. Moon, J., Jeong, J.: Smart manufacturing scheduling system: DQN based on cooperative edge computing. IMCOM 1–8 (2021)
20. Wu, Y., Dinh, T., Fu, Y., et al.: A hybrid DQN and optimization approach for strategy and resource allocation in MEC networks. IEEE Trans. Wirel. Commun. **20**(7), 4282–4295 (2021)
21. Lu, H.: Edge QoE: computation offloading with deep reinforcement learning for internet of things. IEEE Internet Things J. **7**(10), 9255–9265 (2020)

22. Shashank, S., Elhadi, M.S., Ansar, Y.: Task scheduling in cloud using deep reinforcement learning. Proc. Comput. Sci. **184**, 42–51 (2021)
23. Wei, C., Rafael, F., Ewa, D., et al.: Dynamic and fault-tolerant clustering for scientific workflows. IEEE Trans. Cloud Comput. **4**(1), 49–62 (2016)
24. Soniya, J., Sujana, J., Revathi, T.: Dynamic fault tolerant scheduling mechanism for real time tasks in cloud computing. ICEEOT 124–129 (2016)
25. Ismael, S., Garraghan, P., Townend, P., et al.: An approach for characterizing workloads in google cloud to derive realistic resource utilization models. SOSE 49–60 (2013)

Attention-Guided Memory Model for Video Object Segmentation

Yunjian Lin[(✉)] and Yihua Tan[(✉)]

National Key Laboratory of Science and Technology on Multi-spectral Information Processing, School of Artificial Intelligence and Automation, Huazhong University of Science and Technology, Wuhan 430074, China
{yjlin0223,yhtan}@hust.edu.cn

Abstract. Semi-supervised video object segmentation (S-VOS) is defined as pixel-wise separating the object of interest specified to initial mask during inference period. For small object, the exploitable information contained in single frame is limited, making S-VOS task more challenging. Existing methods cannot reach a balance between accuracy and speed on small object sequences. To resolve the problem, we develop an Attention-Guided Memory model (AGM) for video object segmentation by introducing two novel modules, namely Joint Attention Guider (JAG) and spatial-temporal feature fusion (STFF). For accuracy, JAG employs multi-dimension attention mechanism to generate salient feature map, which highlights the object area through visual guide, spatial guide and channel guide. Further, STFF integrates more complete spatial-temporal information by fusing previous memory feature, current high-level salient feature and low-level features, which provides an effective representation of small object. For speed, the STFF employs several light-weight RNNs whose embedded computation architecture is more efficient than the explicit query approach used in the state-of-the-art models. We conduct extensive experiments on DAVIS and YouTube-VOS datasets. For small object on DAVIS 2017, AGM obtains 63.5% $\mathcal{J}\&\mathcal{F}$ mean with 28.0 fps for 480p, which achieves similar accuracy with about 5x faster speed compared with the state-of-the-art method.

Keywords: Semi-supervised video object segmentation · Attention mechanism · Feature fusion

1 Introduction

Semi-supervised Video Object Segmentation (S-VOS) [27,28] is defined as pixel-wise separating the object of interest from the background where the annotated ground truth in the first frame provides the prior knowledge of the object during inference period. This technology has amount of applications, such as interactive video editing, automatic surveillance, and advertising recommendation. It is a challenging task as the object may be relatively small or undergoes different difficult situations like large changes in appearance, occluded and drastic motion.

© Springer Nature Singapore Pte Ltd. 2022
L. Pan et al. (Eds.): BIC-TA 2021, CCIS 1566, pp. 67–85, 2022.
https://doi.org/10.1007/978-981-19-1253-5_6

(a)   (b)   (c)

Fig. 1. Visualization of part feature maps. The two rows denote the original image and corresponding feature map. Sub-graph (a), (b) corresponding to large object and small object feature map in the same conv-layer, in which the feature of the large object is rich while that of the small object is hard to be discriminated from the background. Sub-graph (c) represents attention score map of the man in the soapbox car, which can be used to highlight the difference between the object and the background.

Early works [2,5,21,22,34] tackle S-VOS task through an intuitive fine-tuning approach. This kind of methods first uses large-scale static datasets to train a general segmentation network, and then fine-tunes this network with initial annotated mask during inference period. Despite achieving high accuracy, the fine-tuning process seriously slows down the running speed (the speed of most fine-tuning methods does not exceed 0.22 fps), which makes these methods impractical for real-time applications.

Overcoming this shortcoming requires avoiding the inefficient parameter updating process of fine-tuning methods. In essence, fine-tuning methods use the updated parameters to model the differences between the object of interest and background. Therefore, designing more efficient approaches to model the discriminable information of object can alleviate the inefficiency of the fine-tuning process. Applying memory module to segmentation network [1,19,20,25,29] is one of the mainstream approaches, which are normally implemented as the additional memory module or embedding RNN module. The additional memory module [19,20,25] stores the feature maps of historical frames to model the differences between the object and background, and then guide the segmentation of current object with a feature query process. However, the query process leads to limited running speed. For example, the STM [25] model can only achieve about 6 fps even though the down-sampling strategy has been used to reduce the number of the queries. FRTM [29] simplifies the query process but its accuracy significantly decrease. By implementing the memory module as the embedding RNN module, S2S [40] and S2S++ [1] are faster because they model historical information as the network response in the last time step rather than the features of multiple frames. Although the above methods [1,29,40] improve the running speed, they get a significant performance degradation for small object. For example, considering the accuracy for all objects and only the small objects on DAVIS-2017 dataset, $\mathcal{J}\&\mathcal{F}$ mean of FRTM [29] decreases from 76.4% to 58.6%.

Intuitively, making better use of historical information is crucial to improve the segmentation accuracy for small object. For small object, the exploitable feature in single frame are limited compared with that of large object (shown in Fig. 1 (a)&(b)), which are not enough to achieve stable performance. Therefore, historical information is an important supplement to distinguish small object reliably. The additional memory module and embedding RNN module leverage historical information in different ways, leading to different segmentation accuracy of small object. The query process of additional memory module explicitly uses multiple frames feature maps (storing one frame every 5 frames for STM [25]), making it easier to make full use of historical information. However, the embedding RNN module generally use the feature in the last time step to represent historical information that is integrated with the current frame information. This simple architecture needs more effective feature extraction and integration processes to achieve good segmentation accuracy, while the existing methods can hardly meet this requirement. Therefore, improving the feature extraction and integration method is an effective way to benefit the segmentation accuracy of small object.

To improve feature extraction, an effective method is to introduce attention mechanism. For example, as a specific implementation of attention mechanism, spatial attention (shown in Fig. 1 (c)) could highlight the characteristics of the object and its surroundings. Compared with the existing additional memory modules, this kind of attention mechanism has lower computation consumption, and therefore can maintain the efficiency when is combine with the S-VOS model. In this paper, we propose a novel Joint Attention Guider (JAG) module which employs multi-dimensional attention mechanism. Through three guide processes, namely visual guide, spatial guide and channel guide, JAG generates salient feature map to guide network to focus on the object of interest and suppress the background.

As for feature integration between the last and current frames, we design a spatial-temporal feature fusion (STFF) module. STFF employs two embedding RNN modules to integrate the object features both in spatial and temporal dimension at different levels. One RNN is used to record high-level salient feature and provide coarse target areas, while the other is utilized to represent low-level details. In another aspect, the RNN architecture achieves the feature fusion process with an efficient embedded computation process, while maintains the efficiency of the model with speed of 28.0 fps for 480p.

Finally, we integrate the above two modules into a S-VOS network called Attention-Guided Memory model.

In summary, the contributions of this work are as follows:

(1) Taking account of segmentation accuracy for small objects and running speed, we develop an Attention-Guided Memory model, which achieves SOTA performance for small object on DAVIS benchmark and about 5x faster running speed compared with the existing SOTA model.
(2) We propose a novel Joint Attention Guider module based on multi-dimension attention mechanism, which improves the feature saliency of the object of interest.
(3) We design a spatial-temporal feature fusion module, which integrates more complete spatial-temporal information by fusing memory feature of previous moment, current high-level salient feature and different low-level features.

2   Related work

With the release of several large-scale datasets [27,28,40], a large number of models have been emerging, which can be divided into two types according to whether online fine-tuning is required.

Online Learning Based Methods: Fine-tuning methods could achieve satisfactory performance easier with the benefit of fine-tuning, but are also computationally expensive for practical applications. OSVOS [5] adjusts the pre-trained object segmentation network via the annotated frame during inference period. OSVOS-S [22] introduces instance information to distinguish each object, and OnAVOS [34] extends OSVOS by developing an online adaption mechanism to fit large changes in object appearance. Masktrack [26] combines the current frame with previous predict result as input. On the basis of Masktrack, LucidTracker [17] utilizes a series of data augmentation skills to adapt model to diverse scenes. MHP-VOS [41] adapts a multiply hypotheses tracking method for S-VOS task. Furthermore, to achieve satisfactory performance, many methods [2,18,21] integrate fine-tuning with some techniques, such as optical flow [11], re-identification [38] and Markov Random Field [37], while both of them also increase computation burden partly.

Offline Learning Based Methods: Offline learning based methods tackle S-VOS task without updating parameter weights and could achieve faster segmentation speed, which seem more suitable for practical applications. Some of them learn cues from the first frame or the previous frame, which is called matching-based method and propagation-based method respectively. Matching-based models [9,15,35] use scores between current frame and first frame as reference, but cannot deal with objects with large changes in appearance well. Propagation-based models [10,24,42] rely on temporal coherence between sequential adjacent frames while suffering drift problems due to occlusions or fast motions. RGMP [24] imports target frame and reference frame to Siamese encoder for similarity feature matching. OSNM [42] employs meta-learning mechanism to adjust the generic segmentation network to arbitrary object instances.

Hybrid methods [8,16,25,29,33,40,43] use both the first frame and history frame as reference and could avoid the above problems to a certain extent, which becomes the current mainstream method. Hybrid methods gets help from techniques from other fields, such as memory module[31], object tracking [3] and metric learning [12]. SAT [8] fuses object tracking and segmentation into an unified pipeline. Applying memory module [1,19,20,25,29] to segmentation architecture is one of the the mainstream approaches of hybrid methods, which are implemented by introducing additional memory module or embedding RNN module. The additional memory [19,20,25] indirectly stores feature maps of previous frames as source and utilizes current feature as query for feature matching, which leads to limited speed for segmentation. STM [25] uses spatial-temporal attention algorithm to address historical relevant memory. To the contrary, applying embedding memory module could get faster speed while leads performance degradation, as the historical information is updated from time to time. FRTM [29] employs a light-weight appearance model to predict a coarse and robust segmentation. In this work, we employ attention mechanism as main reference to obtain and locate object of interest, and construct a spatial-temporal feature fusion module, which based on embedding memory module, to achieve efficient fusion between current and historical features.

3 Methodology

3.1 Network Overview

To leverage the historical information effectively while maintain fast running speed, we develop an Attention-Guided Memory model (AGM) for S-VOS task, as shown in Fig. 2. AGM is constructed based on an encoder-decoder architecture, in which the encoder performs feature extraction and the decoder generates segmentation results. The improvements of AGM are introducing two modules: Joint Attention Guider based on multi-dimension mechanism and Spatial-temporal feature fusion integrating different levels of temporal features. The inference of the two modules can be described as three parts: feature convert – feature guide – feature fusion. First, *Convert* is used to introduce the historical information into the forward process of the current frame. The input of *Convert* is the response of *Feature Refinement* in the last time step, and the outputs are termed as guidance features. Second, *Joint Attention Guider* takes the guidance features and the current feature extracted by encoder as input, and uses attention mechanism to extract salient feature that highlights the target instance and suppresses the background. Third, *Spatial-temporal Feature Fusion* integrates the salient feature into the historical response, and then fuses it with the high-level and low-level features extracted by the *Backbone*. The fused feature will be considered as the historical information to be used as the input of *Converter* in the next time step.

Integrate the above three steps into the Encoder-Decoder architecture, the inference procedure can be formulated as Eq. 1. At time step t, frame I_t is first processed by *Encoder* to extract feature map x_t. x_t' represents a selected layer of

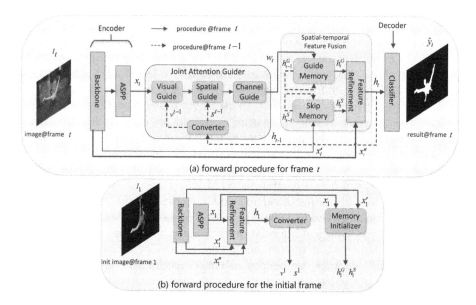

Fig. 2. Subgraph (a), (b) denotes the forward procedure of our Attention-Guided Memory model (AGM) for frame t and the initial frame. For forward procedure for frame t, Joint Attention Guider module guides feature to locate the target object through multiple attention mechanism. To model historical information, Spatial-temporal Feature Fusion integrates high-level guided feature and low-level features of current frame and historical frames. Afterward, the fused feature is fed to Classifier for result prediction and Converter for guidance features updating respectively. For forward procedure for the initial frame, the initial frame without background is fed into Encoder for feature extraction, and then it is feed to Memory Initializer, Feature Refinement and Converter to init two memory module and the Joint Attention Guider module respectively.

high-level feature map. And x_t'' represents the low-level feature map. Then the three steps related to our improvement are performed: (1) *Converter* takes the fused feature map h_{t-1} of previous time step and generates two types of guidance maps: v^{t-1}, s^{t-1}. (2) x_t and v^{t-1}, s^{t-1} are sent as inputs of *Joint Attention Guider* to get salient guided feature map w_t. (3) w_t is sent to *Guide Memory* for guided memory updating, where h_{t-1}^G is the states of *Guide Memory* at time step $t-1$. Correspondingly, h_{t-1}^S is the states of *Skip Memory* at time step $t-1$. The above two memory states h_t^G, h_t^S and skip-connection feature map x_t'' are then sent as inputs of *Feature Refinement* for feature fusion. Finally, the fused feature map h_t is passed into *Classifier* to get final predict segmentation results $\hat{y}_t$.

$$\begin{cases} x_t = Encoder\,(I_t) \\ x'_t, x''_t = Backbone(x_t) \\ v^{t-1}, s^{t-1} = Converter\,(h_{t-1}) \\ w_t = JointAttentionGuider\,\bigl(x_t, v^{t-1}, s^{t-1}\bigr) \\ h^G_t = GuideMemory(w_t, h^G_{t-1}) \\ h^S_t = SkipMemory(x'_t, h^S_{t-1}) \\ h_t = FeatureRefinement(h^G_t, h^S_t, x''_t) \\ \hat{y}_t = Classifier\,(h_t) \end{cases} \tag{1}$$

Among the forward procedure, the *Joint Attention Guider* , *Guide Memory* and *Skip Memory* rely on v^{t-1}, s^{t-1}, h^G_t, h^S_t of the previous time step. While for the forward procedure of the initial frame, these variables do not have the value of the previous time, so these variables need to be initialized. The initial states of v^{t-1}, s^{t-1}, h^G_t, h^S_t can be computed by Eq. 2. The *Encoder* takes the initial frame I_1 as input to obtain the semantic feature map. Note we first set the pixel value of the background in I_1 as zeros according to the annotated mask. The purpose is to make the initial feature focus on the information of the object. The two memory states h^G_1, h^S_1 are produced by *Memory Initializer*, which is designed separately to better initialize the state of two memory modules. In the computation of Feature Refinement, we use x_1, x'_1 rather than h^G_1, h^S_1 as the input, which makes the training more stable. The reason is that the values of h^G_1, h^S_1 are not stable before the Initializer is optimized well. Thus, we replace h^G_1, h^S_1 with x_1, x'_1, passed by *Feature Refinement* and *Converter* to get initial guidance features v^1, s^1.

$$\begin{cases} x_1 = Encoder(I_1) \\ x'_1, x''_1 = Backbone(x_1) \\ h^G_1, h^S_1 = MemoryInitializer(x_1, x'_1) \\ h_1 = FeatureRefinement(x_1, x'_1, x''_1) \\ v^1, s^1 = Converter(h_1) \end{cases} \tag{2}$$

3.2   Joint Attention Guider

The aim of the Joint Attention Guider is to improve the discriminability of the foreground and background and guiding feature of current frame to locate target object and suppress the others. Therefore, we first map the feature in the last time step to the visual and spatial guidance features with the Convert module, and then extract the attention-based features from three different dimensions: the Visual Guide guides current feature map to focus on similar target pixels by matching between previous visual guide feature and current feature; the Spatial Guide use the historical position and shape information of object to highlight the feature representing the nearby position and similar shape; the Channel Guide the weights to different channels of feature to emphasize the channels that are more suitable for the object of interest. Specifically, The inputs of Joint Attention Guider is the guidance features v^{t-1}, s^{t-1} of the previous frame and the semantic feature x_t of the current frame, which are provide by the Converter

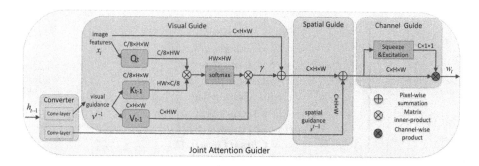

Fig. 3. Detailed implementation of the Joint Attention Guider module.

and Encoder respectively. The implementation of Joint Attention Guider can be depicted as Fig. 3.

Converter: One basic idea of Convert is to introduce the historical information into the forward process of the current frame. Intuitively, the feature h_{t-1} should contain effective visual and spatial information of the object, with which h_{t-1} can be used to classify the object and background while maintaining the clear contour of the object. Therefore, h_{t-1} can be used as the basic information to guide the feature extraction of the current frame.

Taking h_{t-1} as the input, Converter uses two 1×1 convolution layers to further obtain the new features v^{t-1} and s^{t-1} respectively. v^{t-1} and s^{t-1} are fed into the Visual Guide and Spatial Guide module respectively, and then the end-to-end optimization makes v^{t-1} focus on the visual guidance information and s^{t-1} extract the spatial guidance information. Specifically, the similarity between v^{t-1} and the visual feature of the frame t will be computed and considered as the attention weight in the Visual Guide module, which drives v^{t-1} to extract the visual feature. On the other hand, s^{t-1} will be added to the output of the Visual Guide module like the process in the Residual Network. Therefore, s^{t-1} can be considered to learn the residual information of the Visual Guide module, which should mainly contain the spatial information in the last time step, such as the historical position and shape of the object.

Overall, Converter maps the historical feature h_{t-1} to the complementary visual and spatial guidance features v^{t-1}, s^{t-1}, which are used to guide the feature extraction in the Visual Guide and Spatial Guide modules.

Visual Guide: This part is inspired by temporal coherence between adjacent frames. In other words, for the current frame, we should give priority to the features similar to the object of the previous frame. This part is implemented with scaled dot-product attention follows [32]. At first, Visual Guide transfers visual guidance feature v^{t-1} and current semantic feature x_t to Value maps $V_{t-1} \in R^{C \times H \times W}$, Key maps $K_{t-1} \in R^{C/8 \times H \times W}$ and Query maps $Q_t \in R^{C/8 \times H \times W}$ by three 1×1 convolution layers, where C is feature dimension of the encoder output feature map, H and W denotes the height and width respectively. Specifically, the dimension of Key maps and Query maps is compressed to $1/8$ of the originals to reduce the channel size. Then, soft weights are computed by measuring the similarity between Key maps K_{t-1} and Query maps Q_t, which highlights the local region similar to the target instance. Afterward, the guided visual attention map is processed by matrix inner-product between normalized soft weights and corresponding Value maps V_{t-1}. To retain the image feature properly, we set up a hyper-parameter γ to adjust the weight of visual attention map. The output of Visual Guide is processed by the pixel-wise summation of the weighted visual attention maps and current feature x_t and a convolution layer for feature merging. The above procedures can be summarized as:

$$VGF = \gamma softmax\left(\frac{Q_t K_{t-1}^T}{\sqrt{n}}\right) V_{t-1} + x_t \tag{3}$$

where T denotes tensor transposition and n is a scaling factor to prevent excessive results.

Spatial Guide: This part accumulates the visual guided feature map VGF and spatial feature s^{t-1}, then merges the summation features to spatial guided feature map SGF by a 1×1 conv-layer, the procedure can be expressed as Eq. 4. This formulation is inspired by the residual information learning proposed in Residual Network [13]. s^{t-1} will be driven to learn the residual information of the Visual Guide module, which normally mainly contains the spatial information of the last time step.

$$SGF = VGF + s^{t-1} \tag{4}$$

Channel Guide: The above two guides are based on pixel-level operation, which is not robust to deal with objects with large movement. This part uses Squeeze and Excitation block (SEblock) follows [14] which employs a self-attention mechanism for cross-channel interaction. To some extent, Channel Guide can emphasize the channels that are suitable for the object of interest. The output of Channel Guide can be depicted as:

$$CGF_c = SGF_c * v_c \tag{5}$$

where v_c refers to the weight of c-th channel.

3.3 Spatial-Temporal Feature Fusion

Guide Memory: As discussed in Sect. 1, the main idea of this paper is to introduce the embedding RNN to efficiently model the historical information. To achieve that, we employ a ConvLSTM [39] as Guide Memory module at the bottleneck of the encoder-decoder architecture follows [40], which takes the salient feature map extracted by Joint Attention Guider as input. Through capturing object feature of interest with temporal coherence, Guide Memory module could align history features to current guided feature and predict target states of the current time step.

Skip Memory: With only one ConvLSTM served as memory module in the encoder-decoder architecture, we notice that small object often gets lost in early sequence, and its segmentation prediction is also worse than other kinds of object. In other words, guided feature fed into Guide Memory cannot provide much efficient information about small object because the low-resolution guided feature is relatively coarse. Thus, the feature fusion module may need low-level features to provide as much as object details to relieve the above problem. For image segmentation methods like U-Net [30,44], skip connections between encoder and decoder can directly introduce low-level features with fine details to bottleneck. Different from simply passing low-level features to the decoder, we also apply ConvLSTM in the skip connection as Skip Memory, which could restore more low-level historical features about object details. Note it will lead to heavy computation consumption if we directly utilizing all feature maps with higher resolution in the backbone. Therefore, we only use the feature with lowest resolution as the input of Skip Memory module.

In summary, the feature fusion module keeps track of high-level and low-level spatial-temporal features via two ConvLSTMs, Guide Memory module added at the bottleneck of the encoder-decoder network and Skip Memory module added at skip-connection between backbone and decoder.

Feature Refinement: The Feature Refinement module integrates the low-level features extracted by the backbone for the current frame and the output features of Guide Memory and Skip Memory. The outputting feature is fed into the classifier and obtain the segmentation mask for the current frame. Following RGMP [24], we employ three refinement blocks as the building block of our Feature Refinement module. For every stage, the refinement block takes the output of the previous refinement block and low-level feature map of corresponding scale in the Backbone through skip connection. In particular, the first refinement block takes output of Guide Memory, the concatenation feature map between output of Skip Memory and the feature map with the same scale.

3.4   Implementation of Other Modules

Encoder-Decoder: Following Deeplabs [6,7], we utilize a two-stage encoder which consists of a backbone network and an Atrous Spatial Pyramid Pooling (ASPP) [7] module. The backbone of encoder is a shrinked version of ResNet-101 [13]. We remove the last Res-Block and fully-connected layer of ResNet-101 and take the outputs of stage 2, 3, 4 as low-level features for skip connection. Specifically, x_t'' denotes the set of three stage feature maps and x_t' denotes the last stage feature maps for the time step t. After the above three stages, we employ an ASPP module to further get larger receptive fields and merge features of different scales. The decoder consists of a spatial-temporal feature fusion module and a classifier module. The spatial-temporal feature fusion employs three feature refinement blocks as building blocks corresponding to the same scale of Res-blocks in the backbone network. And the classifier module takes fused feature and generates the binary segmentation prediction mask through the final 1×1 convolution layer followed by a softmax operation.

Memory Initializer: The Guide Memory module employs a kernel size of 3×3, and the Skip Memory module employs a larger kernel size of 5×5, which could capture larger displacement of low-level feature. For initialization of two memory module, the Memory Initializer takes the lowest resolution feature map x'_t of backbone and the output feature map x_t of encoder as inputs, generates the initial states of two memory module through two additional 1×1 convolution layer respectively.

3.5 Network Training

During training, we firstly down-sample all the video sequence to half resolution of 480p (864×480). We adapt Adam with an initial learning rate of 10^{-4} to optimize a binary cross-entropy loss. In addition, we apply flipping, shifting, rotating, and scaling as data augmentations. The flipping and shifting possibility is 0.5, the rotate degree is from -3 to $3°$, the scaling range is from 0.97 to 1.03 times with random center positions. To avoid over-fitting, we set a dropout probability with 15% of discarding intermediate templates when the training close to being stable. Besides, we also apply In-Place Activated BatchNorm layer [4] and Mixed Precision strategy [23] during training to reduce GPU consumption.

For making training samples, we set a random probability for the following two methods to sample video sequences: one sampling 5–12 temporally ordered frames from a training video, another randomly skip sampling the same number of frames as the former. The later can help relieve the problem of large changes in appearance for a long-time sequence. For Youtube-VOS experiments, the training process takes about 1 day with a batch size of 2 using a single RTX 2080Ti GPU following the above settings. For DAVIS experiments, we change the learning rate to 10^{-5} for further precision promotion and mix the DAVIS and Youtube-VOS video sequences in a ratio of 2:1 to avoid over-fitting.

4 Experiments

We evaluate our model on DAVIS [27,28] and YouTube-VOS [40] benchmarks: 1) DAVIS-2016 validation set for single object segmentation, 2) DAVIS-2017 and YouTube-VOS 2018 validation set for multi-object segmentation. For the DAVIS datasets, we measure the region similarity $\mathcal{J}$, the contour accuracy $\mathcal{F}$ and overall score $\mathcal{J}\&\mathcal{F}$ using the provided benchmark code [27]. For YouTube-VOS, we upload our results to the online validation server [40] to get $\mathcal{J}$ and $\mathcal{F}$ scores for classes used in the training set (seen) and other ones not be used (unseen). In addition, we compare the running speed of the methods in terms of frames per second (FPS), measured for the time of every forward pass on a single RTX 2080Ti GPU.

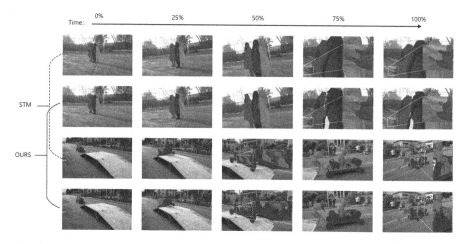

Fig. 4. Qualitative comparison between our AGM and STM for small object on DAVIS-2017 validation. In the first video, STM absolutely loses tiny object (cellphone on hand), while AGM could still predict their mask. In the second video, STM confuses the person in yellow and the car in red. In contrast, AGM successfully generates accurate boundaries between the car and two persons. (Color figure online)

4.1   Comparision to State-of-the-Art

Performance on Small Object: We compare performance for small object on DAVIS-2017 validation between our AGM with current several SOTA methods: STM[25], FRTM [29], and RANet [36], as shown in Table 1. From the last line, we compute overall performance for sequences with the object whose area is smaller than 1% of the input image, and our AGM (63.5%) achieves equal performance of the current Rank-1 methods STM (63.1%) while getting more than 4x speed. Besides, STM and FRTM lose track with tiny objects (such as lab-coat_1&2) easily, while our AGM could still predict their masks stably. From the results, we can conclude that AGM could achieve a robust and accurate segmentation for small object at a favourable. The qualitative comparison between AGM and STM for small objects is reported in Fig. 4. For YouTube-VOS 2018 validation, the online validation server only provides the overall results, thus we do not provide the corresponding comparison on small object.

Overall, the proposed AGM achieves state-of-the-art (SOTA) accuracy for small object, and its speed is more than 4x faster compared with the SOTA STM model.

DAVIS-2017: The validation set for DAVIS-2017 contains 30 sequences, and the results is reported in Table 2. PreMVOS [21], MHPVOS [41] and CINM [2], OnAVOS [34], OSVOS [5] employ extensive fine-tuning process on the initial annotated frame during inference period, resulting in impractical running speed. Besides, FRTM [29] also updates weight parameters of convolution layers of target module during inference period while getting faster running speed. PreMVOS [21], STM [25], AGAME [16], RGMP [24], RANet [36] and OSNM

Table 1. Comparision for small object on DAVIS-2017 validation between ours AGM, STM, FRTM, and RANet. Px-Nums denotes number of initial object pixels.

Sequences	Px-Nums	Ours $\mathcal{J}\&\mathcal{F}$	STM [25] $\mathcal{J}\&\mathcal{F}$	FRTM [29] $\mathcal{J}\&\mathcal{F}$	RANet [36] $\mathcal{J}\&\mathcal{F}$
dogs-jump_1	3548	**91.8**	91.6	66.9	10.8
drift-chicane_1	2370	93.2	**94.4**	79.1	84.6
horsejump-high_2	4168	**90.6**	89.4	78.1	83.6
kite-surf_1	3350	36.9	**56.6**	49.8	39.3
kite-surf_2	340	11.3	31.8	31.0	**44.9**
lab-coat_1	18	**4.8**	0	0	0
lab-coat_2	14	**44.2**	0	6.8	0
mbike-trick_1	2451	80.3	**84.5**	79.1	72.2
mbike-trick_2	2670	73.1	**81.7**	71.8	70.8
paragliding-launch_3	80	16.0	15.3	**36.9**	18.7
scooter-black_1	1335	87.4	**88.2**	58.7	57.4
soapbox_2	1275	78.3	**80.3**	74.3	73.5
soapbox_3	1276	**81.4**	72.4	71.9	70.0
Total	–	**63.5**	63.1	57.8	51.1
Speed(fps)	–	28.0	6.25	14.6	**30.0**

[42] all employ static image augmentation to get more video sequences during pretrain stage, which can largely improve overall segmentation performance but also make training procedure elaborate. The method SAT [8], Siammask [35] and FAVOS [10] seriously rely on object tracking to eliminate redundant computation consumption.

Without using any whistles, like fine-tuning during inference period [2,5, 21,34,41] or pre-training in large augmented simulated data [16,24,25,36], our AGM can still get a reasonable balance between overall performance and speed. For overall $\mathcal{J}\&\mathcal{F}$ average, the proposed AGM achieves competitive accuracy and is only inferior to STM [25] and FRTM[29]. Considering AGM is significantly faster than STM [25] and FRTM[29], it is suitable for the scenes requiring real-time processes. For segmentation speed, our AGM exceeds all of the methods with online fine-tuning and could get competitive performance without relying on object tracking [8,10,35]. Besides, AGM gets a good performance for $\mathcal{F}_D$ decay, which means our AGM is robust for a longer sequence.

YouTube-VOS: YouTube-VOS 2018 validation dataset has 474 sequences with objects from 91 categories and the corresponding report of results is shown in Table 3. AGM is proceeded only by STM and FRTM, while our method can get a nearly equal performance to STM without data augmentation during pretraining.

To further analyze the characteristics of AGM, we show the qualitative result of AGM on DAVIS-2017 and YouTube-VOS benchmarks in Fig. 5. For the normal situations shown in the first and second row, AGM can segment the complete objects and obtain accurate contours. So AGM achieves the competitive performance on the entire DAVIS-2017 and YouTube-VOS 2018 datasets. However, for the objects moving fast (in the third row) and multiple objects with similar

Table 2. Quantitative results on DAVIS-2017 and DAVIS-2016 validation. OL denotes online fine-tuning. Data synth denotes whether additional synthetic data has been used during training. FPS denotes frame per second. The best two results among offline methods are marked in red and blue respectively.

Method	OL	Data synth	DAVIS-2017 $\mathcal{J}_{\mathcal{M}\uparrow}$	$\mathcal{F}_{\mathcal{D}\downarrow}$	$\mathcal{J}\&\mathcal{F}$	DAVIS-2016 $\mathcal{J}\&\mathcal{F}$	FPS
PreMVOS [21]	√	√	73.9	19.5	77.8	86.8	0.01
MHPVOS [41]	√	–	73.4	19.1	76.1	88.6	–
CINM [2]	√	–	67.2	26.2	70.6	84.2	0.01
OSVOS-S [22]	√	–	64.7	18.5	68.0	86.6	0.22
OnAVOS [34]	√	–	61.6	26.6	65.4	85.5	0.08
OSVOS [5]	√	–	56.6	27.0	60.3	80.2	0.22
STM [25]	–	√	79.2	10.5	81.7	89.4	6.25
FRTM [29]	–	–	–	–	76.4	83.5	14.6
SAT [8]	–	–	68.6	–	72.3	83.1	39
FEELVOS [33]	–	–	69.1	20.1	71.5	81.7	2.2
AGAME [16]	–	√	67.0	15.8	70.0	81.9	14.3
RGMP [24]	–	√	64.8	19.6	66.7	81.8	7.7
RANet [36]	–	√	63.2	19.7	65.7	87.1	30
FAVOS [10]	–	–	54.6	18.0	58.2	81.0	0.56
Siammask [35]	–	–	54.3	21.0	56.4	69.8	35
OSNM [42]	–	√	52.5	24.3	54.8	73.5	7.14
Ours(AGM)	–	–	69.7	11.2	73.2	83.9	28.0

Table 3. Quantitative results on YouTube-VOS 2018 validation. OL denotes online fine-tuning. Data synth denotes whether additional synthetic data has been used during training. FPS denotes frame per second. *: denotes without synthetic data during training period. The best two results among offline methods are marked in red and blue respectively.

Method	OL	Data synth	$\mathcal{G}$ overall	$\mathcal{J}_{\mathcal{M}\uparrow}$ seen	unseen	$\mathcal{F}_{\mathcal{M}\uparrow}$ seen	unseen
PreMVOS [21]	√	√	66.9	71.4	56.5	75.9	63.7
OSVOS [5]	√	–	58.8	59.8	54.2	60.5	60.7
OnAVOS [34]	√	–	55.2	60.1	46.1	75.9	63.7
*STM [25]	–	–	68.2	–	–	–	–
STM [25]	–	√	79.4	79.7	84.2	72.8	80.9
FRTM [29]	–	–	71.3	72.2	64.5	76.1	72.7
AGAME [16]	–	√	66.1	67.8	60.8	69.5	66.2
S2S [40]	–	–	64.4	71.0	55.5	70.0	61.2
SAT [8]	–	–	63.6	67.1	55.3	70.2	61.7
RGMP [24]	–	√	53.8	59.5	49.2	–	–
Siammask [35]	–	–	55.8	60.2	45.1	58.2	47.7
OSNM [42]	–	√	51.2	60.0	40.6	60.1	44.0
Ours(AGM)	–	–	68.3	69.1	61.7	73.2	68.9

appearance (in the fourth row), our AGM cannot deal with them well. The reason may be that the representation ability of the used embedding memory module is not enough to handle the objects with fast motion or confused appearance.

Overall, the proposed AGM can obtain good performance in normal situations and achieve superiority for small objects. The accuracy of AGM needs to be further improved on some other challenging situations such as those containing objects moving fast and multiple objects with a similar appearance.

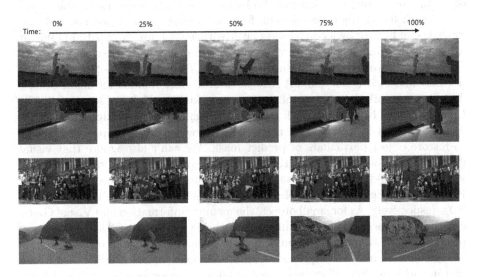

Fig. 5. Qualitative results of AGM

4.2   Ablation Study

We upgrade our model step by step from naive baseline to full-version AGM to analyze the contributions of the key components, and all following ablations are trained on settings in Sect. 3.5 and performed on DAVIS-2017 validation dataset.

Ablation of Spatial-Temporal Feature Fusion: We construct a baseline network called no Guide Memory and no Skip Memory, to analyze the impact of the spatial-temporal feature fusion module. This is performed by removing two memory modules while keeping the remaining unchanged. We train this model with the same methodology as for our proposed network. On the foundation of the baseline network, we further combine one of the Guide Memory and Skip Memory module with the remaining segmentation network: with Skip Memory only, with Guide Memory only, and our AGM (with both GM and SM). As Sect. 3.3 mentioned, we set the memory module for two purposes: first, to remember the object of interest and mask out the rest of the scene, and second, to align the features from the history frames to the current frame. Specifically, the Guide Memory module captures the temporal connection between current guided feature and previous states; the skip Memory module retrains the information of small object and fine details of the object instance.

Ablation of Joint Attention Guider: To analyze the impact of the Joint Attention Guider module, we remove or replace one of the three feature processes. As Sect. 3.2 mentioned, the Visual Guide tackles feature to highlight the local region of similar object, the Spatial Guide leads feature to locate object and eliminate interference, and Channel Guide emphasize the suitable channels of feature for the object of interest. No Visual Guide denotes replacing the Visual Guide with fusing the concatenation features between current feature and previous visual feature by a convolution layer with 1×1 filter. No Spatial Guide or no Channel Guide denotes removing corresponding feature processing directly.

In Table 4, we present the results in terms of $\mathcal{J}\&\mathcal{F}$ on DAVIS-2017 validation dataset, in which $\mathcal{J}\&\mathcal{F}$ (small) denotes overall performance for small object. The base network, without employ memory module, achieves a score of 64.5%. Compared with baseline network, using guide memory only or skip memory only brings 3.3% and 4.9% improvement respectively, which proves skip memory helps to restore object particulars of predict mask. We can't also ignore that visual guide is essential to locate discriminative and similar feature preliminarily for joint feature guider, which leads to a major improvement absolute gain of 9.7%. Further, spatial guide or channel merge improves the overall results by 5.1% and 2.0% respectively. As for small object, the memory information and Visual Guide contribute the accuracy significantly, which bring 12.5% and 8.9% improvement respectively. Without memory information means that once an error occurs, it is difficult to correct later, which is more obvious for small object. Between two memory module, Skip memory or Guide Memory brings 9.1% and 5.0% improvement respectively, which also proves Skip memory could introduce more low-level details about the object. Therefore, constructing temporal coherence is essential for dealing with small object.

Table 4. Ablative study on DAVIS-2017 validation set. We analyze different benefits of memory module of our AGM. GM and SM denote Guide Memory and Skip Memory respectively. Further, we also analyze the role of different feature guides in the Joint feature Guider, no Visual Guide denotes replacing Visual Guide mechanism with simple concatenation, and no Spatial Guide or no Channel Guide denotes removing corresponding processing of feature extraction.

Version	GM	SM	$\mathcal{J}\&\mathcal{F}$	$\mathcal{J}\&\mathcal{F}$ (small)
No Guide Memory and Skip Memory			64.5(−8.7)	54.2(−12.5)
No Skip Memory	√		67.8(−5.4)	57.6(−9.1)
No Guide Memory		√	69.4(−3.8)	61.7(−5.0)
Ours(AGM)	√	√	73.2	66.7
No Visual Guide	√	√	63.5(−9.7)	57.8(−8.9)
No Spatial Guide	√	√	68.1(−5.1)	62.1(−4.6)
No Channel Guide	√	√	71.2(−2.0)	64.9(−1.8)

5 Conclusion

In this paper, taking account of the balance between the segmentation accuracy for small object and running speed, we develop a novel S-VOS pipeline called Attention-Guided Memory model (AGM). AGM employs multi-dimension attention mechanism to guide model to generate salient feature map of the object of interest. For modeling the historical information efficiently, AGM fuses spatial-temporal information at multi-scale to enrich the representation of object. The proposed AGM achieves state-of-the-art (SOTA) accuracy for small objects on DAVIS-2017 dataset while obtaining more than 4x faster speed compared with the existing SOTA model. AGM also while achieves competitive performance on the entire DAVIS-2017 and YouTube-VOS datasets.

References

1. Azimi, F., Bischke, B., Palacio, S., Raue, F., Hees, J., Dengel, A.: Revisiting sequence-to-sequence video object segmentation with multi-task loss and skip-memory. In: 2020 25th International Conference on Pattern Recognition (ICPR), pp. 5376–5383. IEEE (2021)
2. Bao, L., Wu, B., Liu, W.: CNN in MRF: video object segmentation via inference in a CNN-based higher-order spatio-temporal MRF. In: Proceedings of the IEEE Conference on Computer Vision and Pattern Recognition, pp. 5977–5986 (2018)
3. Bertinetto, L., Valmadre, J., Henriques, J.F., Vedaldi, A., Torr, P.H.S.: Fully-convolutional siamese networks for object tracking. In: Hua, G., Jégou, H. (eds.) ECCV 2016. LNCS, vol. 9914, pp. 850–865. Springer, Cham (2016). https://doi.org/10.1007/978-3-319-48881-3_56
4. Bulo, S.R., Porzi, L., Kontschieder, P.: In-place activated batchnorm for memory-optimized training of DNNs. In: Proceedings of the IEEE Conference on Computer Vision and Pattern Recognition, pp. 5639–5647 (2018)
5. Caelles, S., Maninis, K.K., Pont-Tuset, J., Leal-Taixe, L., Gool, L.V.: One-shot video object segmentation. In: 2017 IEEE Conference on Computer Vision and Pattern Recognition (CVPR) (2017)
6. Chen, L.C., Papandreou, G., Kokkinos, I., Murphy, K., Yuille, A.L.: DeepLab: semantic image segmentation with deep convolutional nets, atrous convolution, and fully connected CRFs. IEEE Trans. Pattern Anal. Mach. Intell. 40(4), 834–848 (2017)
7. Chen, L.C., Zhu, Y., Papandreou, G., Schroff, F., Adam, H.: Encoder-decoder with atrous separable convolution for semantic image segmentation. In: Proceedings of the European Conference on Computer Vision (ECCV), pp. 801–818 (2018)
8. Chen, X., Li, Z., Yuan, Y., Yu, G., Shen, J., Qi, D.: State-aware tracker for real-time video object segmentation. arXiv preprint arXiv:2003.00482 (2020)
9. Chen, Y., Pont-Tuset, J., Montes, A., Van Gool, L.: Blazingly fast video object segmentation with pixel-wise metric learning. In: Proceedings of the IEEE Conference on Computer Vision and Pattern Recognition, pp. 1189–1198 (2018)
10. Cheng, J., Tsai, Y.H., Hung, W.C., Wang, S., Yang, M.H.: Fast and accurate online video object segmentation via tracking parts. In: Proceedings of the IEEE Conference on Computer Vision and Pattern Recognition, pp. 7415–7424 (2018)

11. Dosovitskiy, A., et al.: Flownet: learning optical flow with convolutional networks. In: Proceedings of the IEEE International Conference on Computer Vision, pp. 2758–2766 (2015)

12. Fathi, A., et al.: Semantic instance segmentation via deep metric learning. arXiv preprint arXiv:1703.10277 (2017)

13. He, K., Zhang, X., Ren, S., Sun, J.: Deep residual learning for image recognition. In: Proceedings of the IEEE Conference on Computer Vision and Pattern Recognition, pp. 770–778 (2016)

14. Hu, J., Shen, L., Sun, G.: Squeeze-and-excitation networks. In: Proceedings of the IEEE Conference on Computer Vision and Pattern Recognition, pp. 7132–7141 (2018)

15. Hu, Y.T., Huang, J.B., Schwing, A.G.: Videomatch: matching based video object segmentation. In: Proceedings of the European Conference on Computer Vision (ECCV), pp. 54–70 (2018)

16. Johnander, J., Danelljan, M., Brissman, E., Khan, F.S., Felsberg, M.: A generative appearance model for end-to-end video object segmentation. In: Proceedings of the IEEE Conference on Computer Vision and Pattern Recognition, pp. 8953–8962 (2019)

17. Khoreva, A., Benenson, R., Ilg, E., Brox, T., Schiele, B.: Lucid data dreaming for video object segmentation. Int. J. Comput. Vision **127**(9), 1175–1197 (2019)

18. Li, X., Change Loy, C.: Video object segmentation with joint re-identification and attention-aware mask propagation. In: Proceedings of the European Conference on Computer Vision (ECCV), pp. 90–105 (2018)

19. Liu, D., Xu, S., Liu, X.Y., Xu, Z., Wei, W., Zhou, P.: Spatiotemporal graph neural network based mask reconstruction for video object segmentation. arXiv preprint arXiv:2012.05499 (2020)

20. Lu, X., Wang, W., Danelljan, M., Zhou, T., Shen, J., Van Gool, L.: Video object segmentation with episodic graph memory networks. arXiv preprint arXiv:2007.07020 (2020)

21. Luiten, J., Voigtlaender, P., Leibe, B.: PReMVOS: proposal-generation, refinement and merging for video object segmentation. In: Jawahar, C.V., Li, H., Mori, G., Schindler, K. (eds.) ACCV 2018. LNCS, vol. 11364, pp. 565–580. Springer, Cham (2019). https://doi.org/10.1007/978-3-030-20870-7_35

22. Maninis, K.K., et al.: Video object segmentation without temporal information. IEEE Trans. Pattern Anal. Mach. Intell. **41**(6), 1515–1530 (2018)

23. Micikevicius, P., et al.: Mixed precision training. arXiv preprint arXiv:1710.03740 (2017)

24. Oh, S.W., Lee, J.Y., Sunkavalli, K., Kim, S.J.: Fast video object segmentation by reference-guided mask propagation. In: Proceedings of the IEEE Conference on Computer Vision and Pattern Recognition, pp. 7376–7385 (2018)

25. Oh, S.W., Lee, J.Y., Xu, N., Kim, S.J.: Video object segmentation using space-time memory networks. In: Proceedings of the IEEE International Conference on Computer Vision, pp. 9226–9235 (2019)

26. Perazzi, F., Khoreva, A., Benenson, R., Schiele, B., Sorkine-Hornung, A.: Learning video object segmentation from static images. In: Proceedings of the IEEE Conference on Computer Vision and Pattern Recognition, pp. 2663–2672 (2017)

27. Perazzi, F., Pont-Tuset, J., McWilliams, B., Van Gool, L., Gross, M., Sorkine-Hornung, A.: A benchmark dataset and evaluation methodology for video object segmentation. In: Proceedings of the IEEE Conference on Computer Vision and Pattern Recognition, pp. 724–732 (2016)

28. Pont-Tuset, J., Perazzi, F., Caelles, S., Arbeláez, P., Sorkine-Hornung, A., Van Gool, L.: The 2017 davis challenge on video object segmentation. arXiv preprint arXiv:1704.00675 (2017)

29. Robinson, A., Lawin, F.J., Danelljan, M., Khan, F.S., Felsberg, M.: Learning fast and robust target models for video object segmentation. arXiv preprint arXiv:2003.00908 (2020)

30. Ronneberger, O., Fischer, P., Brox, T.: U-Net: convolutional networks for biomedical image segmentation. In: Navab, N., Hornegger, J., Wells, W.M., Frangi, A.F. (eds.) MICCAI 2015. LNCS, vol. 9351, pp. 234–241. Springer, Cham (2015). https://doi.org/10.1007/978-3-319-24574-4_28

31. Sukhbaatar, S., Szlam, A., Weston, J., Fergus, R.: End-to-end memory networks. arXiv preprint arXiv:1503.08895 (2015)

32. Vaswani, A., et al.: Attention is all you need. In: Advances in Neural Information Processing Systems, pp. 5998–6008 (2017)

33. Voigtlaender, P., Chai, Y., Schroff, F., Adam, H., Leibe, B., Chen, L.C.: FEELVOS: fast end-to-end embedding learning for video object segmentation. In: Proceedings of the IEEE/CVF Conference on Computer Vision and Pattern Recognition, pp. 9481–9490 (2019)

34. Voigtlaender, P., Leibe, B.: Online adaptation of convolutional neural networks for the 2017 davis challenge on video object segmentation. In: The 2017 DAVIS Challenge on Video Object Segmentation-CVPR Workshops, vol. 5 (2017)

35. Wang, Q., Zhang, L., Bertinetto, L., Hu, W., Torr, P.H.: Fast online object tracking and segmentation: a unifying approach. In: Proceedings of the IEEE Conference on Computer Vision and Pattern Recognition, pp. 1328–1338 (2019)

36. Wang, Z., Xu, J., Liu, L., Zhu, F., Shao, L.: RANet: ranking attention network for fast video object segmentation. In: Proceedings of the IEEE International Conference on Computer Vision, pp. 3978–3987 (2019)

37. Wu, B., Hu, B.G., Ji, Q.: A coupled hidden Markov random field model for simultaneous face clustering and tracking in videos. Pattern Recogn. **64**, 361–373 (2017)

38. Xiao, T., Li, S., Wang, B., Lin, L., Wang, X.: Joint detection and identification feature learning for person search. In: Proceedings of the IEEE Conference on Computer Vision and Pattern Recognition, pp. 3415–3424 (2017)

39. Xingjian, S., Chen, Z., Wang, H., Yeung, D.Y., Wong, W.K., Woo, W.C.: Convolutional LSTM network: a machine learning approach for precipitation nowcasting. In: Advances in Neural Information Processing Systems, pp. 802–810 (2015)

40. Xu, N., et al.: YouTube-VOS: sequence-to-sequence video object segmentation. In: Proceedings of the European Conference on Computer Vision (ECCV), pp. 585–601 (2018)

41. Xu, S., Liu, D., Bao, L., Liu, W., Zhou, P.: MHP-VOS: multiple hypotheses propagation for video object segmentation. In: Proceedings of the IEEE Conference on Computer Vision and Pattern Recognition, pp. 314–323 (2019)

42. Yang, L., Wang, Y., Xiong, X., Yang, J., Katsaggelos, A.K.: Efficient video object segmentation via network modulation. In: Proceedings of the IEEE Conference on Computer Vision and Pattern Recognition, pp. 6499–6507 (2018)

43. Zeng, X., Liao, R., Gu, L., Xiong, Y., Fidler, S., Urtasun, R.: DMM-Net: differentiable mask-matching network for video object segmentation. In: Proceedings of the IEEE International Conference on Computer Vision, pp. 3929–3938 (2019)

44. Zhou, Z., Siddiquee, M.M.R., Tajbakhsh, N., Liang, J.: UNet++: redesigning skip connections to exploit multiscale features in image segmentation. IEEE Trans. Med. Imaging **39**(6), 1856–1867 (2019)

Multi-workflow Scheduling Based on Implicit Information Transmission in Cloud Computing Environment

Liangqian Ji[1], Tingting Dong[2], Yang Lan[1], and Xingjuan Cai[1(✉)]

[1] School of Computer Science and Technology, Taiyuan University of Science and Technology, Taiyuan 030024, China
xingjuancai@163.com

[2] Faculty of Information Technology, Beijing University of Technology, Beijing 100124, China

Abstract. In the current cloud computing environment, task scheduling and resource allocation are the key and difficult points in the performance improvement. However, there are numerous problems of workflow, such as Montage, Inspiral, Cybershake etc. They have similar workflow structures, which affect the efficiency of task scheduling and resource distribution. In addition, the result obtained by the traditional evolutionary algorithm is the allocation sequence of the virtual machine in the cloud computing environment only for single task, which is a great waste of resources. Aiming at these problems, the multiple workflow tasks are processed in this paper by using implicit information transfer at the same time, that is, to reasonably use the allocation sequence of each task to exchange information so as to share a better virtual machine allocation. Meanwhile, using the potential relationship and differences between different tasks are better able to make population has better convergence and diversity. We proposed a multifactorial evolutionary algorithm based on combinatorial population (CP-MFEA) for multitasking workflows. This paper constructs nine sets of multi-task combination problems, and compares the method with the traditional single-task evolutionary algorithm, the purpose is to describe the superiority of this method clearly. Through the experimental results, we can notice that CP-MFEA's ability is much more obvious than single-task evolutionary algorithms.

Keywords: Cloud computing · Task scheduling · Multifactorial evolutionary algorithm · Multi-workflow scheduling

1 Introduction

Cloud computing is a burgeoning type of resource processing mode. Users can employ the internet to conveniently access the shared resource pools of cloud computing, including dispositivo di elaborazione, memory devices, and applications, anytime and anywhere as needed. And the application of cloud computing is becoming more and more widespread of recent years [1]. There are three types of cloud computing services: Infrastructure as a Service (IaaS), Platform as a Service (PaaS), and Software as a Service

© Springer Nature Singapore Pte Ltd. 2022
L. Pan et al. (Eds.): BIC-TA 2021, CCIS 1566, pp. 86–103, 2022.
https://doi.org/10.1007/978-981-19-1253-5_7

(SaaS). At present, the major cloud computing providers include Microsoft, Amazon, and IBM, etc. However, the number of computing tasks of cloud computing is very large, especially workflow tasks, which makes task scheduling and resource distribution are important for promoting the efficiency of cloud computing, and scheduling issue has been proved to be an NP-hard problem.

Directed Acyclic Graph (DAG) has been widely used in workflow scheduling modeling. In the graph researchers get each node as a subtask, the directed line segments among nodes in graph represents the dependency between each subtask. Currently, the most widely used workflows include Montage, Inspiral, Cybershake, Sipht and other structures. In reality, there are two common optimizing workflow algorithm. One is heuristic algorithm, and the other is a list scheduling algorithm.

Over the years, some heuristic algorithms are put into use in task scheduling resoundingly. Evolutionary algorithm (EA) [2, 3] simulates the evolution of living things in nature, which has been widely used to solve some practical problems, including scheduling problems [4–9], intelligent control [10–14], feature selection [15–21], recommendation system [22, 23] etc. And the populations thinking of EA is very similar to the evolution of human populations [24]. Therefore, Xu et al. [25] proposed a task scheduling blue print for heterogeneous distribute systems on account of genetic algorithms. This scheme assigns priority to each subtask according to the algorithm. And the algorithm takes makespan as the optimization objective. And Yu et al. [26] came up with an adjustment that based on service quality of clients, it can solve scientific workflow scheduling problems by using genetic algorithms. The service quality includes budget constraints and cost constraints. Meanwhile, Kumar et al. [27] merged Min min and Max Min into genetic algorithm to solve the task scheduling problem. In addition, Zhao et al. [28] proposed to regard the maximum completion time and the cost of running the entire task as problems to be optimized, and the above problems were solved through a multi objective evolutionary optimization algorithm. The most basic and most widely applied is the Heterogeneous Earliest Finish Time (HEFT) proposed by H. and others [29]. HEFT arranges all subtasks to be executed on the virtual machine that can make it completed rapidly. Jia, YH et al. [30] proposed an adaptive ant colony optimization algorithm to solve four types of scientific workflow scheduling problems to meet service quality and coordination tasks. Gu, Y et al. [31] proposed an Energy Aware, Time, and Throughput Optimization heuristic (EATTO) based on the bat algorithm. They use this algorithm to minimize the energy consumption and execution time of computationally intensive workflows, while maximizing throughput without causing any significant loss of quality of service (QoS) guarantees. K Sellami et al. [32] proposed a combined chaotic Particle Swarm Optimization (PSO) to solve task resource allocation based on the proposed model.

Above mentioned scientific workflow scheduling problem for single objective or multi-objective is that only one workflow can be solved at a time, and only one task sequence of workflow can be given. Besides, the defects of evolutionary algorithms, such as the slow search speed of the algorithm, it takes a long time to obtain a more accurate solution each time. These greatly limit the work efficiency of cloud computing.

Therefore, inspired by the influence of cultural factors in human evolution, Gupta and other people [33] proposed a multifactorial evolutionary algorithm (MFEA) by the study of multi-objective optimization problems. As a new evolutionary paradigm, MFEA can solve multiple tasks simultaneously, which has been proved to have good optimization ability in both continuous and discrete problems. The performance structure and target model among workflows is basically the same, so using MFEA to process the scheduling of multiple workflows at the same time can significantly save resources.

Subsequently, the ideology of multi-task scheduling has the widespread application in various areas. Iqbal et al. [34] applied multi task optimization to the cross domain reuse of knowledge extraction, and took advantage of the knowledge reuse and information block technology of multi task optimization algorithms to solve complex image classification problems. And Zhou et al. [35] employed the multi task optimization algorithm to solve the vehicle path planning problem, and proposed an improved algorithm based on a unified random key and distributed decoding operator, which is used to analyze the fault tolerance of the multi task vehicle routing problem. To address the low convergence rating issue of MFEA when dealing with complex problems, Gong and others [36] put forward a modified algorithm on account of particle swarm optimization. The improved algorithm is applied to processed complex multi-task problems. Compared with multi-task optimization problems with different dimensions, the performance has been greatly improved.

With the emergence and development of MFEA, and the representation of scientific workflow is also constantly improving and gradually standardized. Bharathi [37] and Juve [38] el al. provided the characterization of workflows, they changed some of the processes in practical applications to direct acyclic graphs, and pointed out that the structure of the workflow is similar when the process is transformed into directed acyclic graphs. In addition, the different workflows have different entrances, and the quantity of jobs is not consistent. But if these workflows are all executed in the same cloud environment, the virtual machines assigned to each workflow may be the same, which makes the allocation sequence of the workflow can be shared with other workflows. And after being assigned to the virtual machines, the virtual machines treat the jobs through same method. Therefore, which task is assigned to a virtual machine multiple times that indicates better performance for the virtual machine. In addition, due to the dependencies between workflow subtasks, different types of workflows can use the same representation, but the corresponding workflow solution cannot be generated at the same time. At the same time, MFEA needs a unified representation of different tasks when solving problems, so there are some defects when solving workflow tasks.

Therefore, based on above reasons, we proposed a multifactorial evolutionary algorithm based on combinatorial population (CP-MFEA) for multitasking workflows. Employing the similarity of the workflow structure, through the evolution operation, the virtual machine allocation sequence results of multiple workflows on cloud computing are exchanged and shared, so as to deliver a better allocation sequence. The contributions made in this paper are as follows:

(1) Because the scientific workflow uses DAG to represent its structure, and there are dependencies between subtasks, in order to better represent the dependencies between subtasks, the distribution sequence can be obtained by topological sorting. Use topological sorting to generate corresponding subpopulations for different types of workflows and merge the subpopulations into one population.

(2) The dependencies of different types of workflows are also different, so the sub-populations generated are different. But because it is processing multi-task, that is, multiple tasks are optimized simultaneously. This paper uses the method of assigning skill factors to distinguish multiple tasks, in the specific form of assigning different skill factors to different types of tasks.

(3) Different crossover and compilation operations are performed depending on whether the two parents are part of the same task. For the same type of workflow, directly carry out crossover and mutation operations to evolve, and different types of workflows transmit information by sharing virtual machine sequences of different workflows.

The remaining organizational structure in the paper described below. The second section introduces the expressive method of workflow and the matter to be solved in this article for multiple workflows. In the third section, we introduced how to solve the information transmission method of multiple workflows and the specific implementation process. The detailed parameter design and result analysis of the experiment are reflected in the fourth section. Finally, in the fifth section, the full text is summarized and the next research direction is proposed.

2 Workflow Schedule Model

2.1 Workflow Model

At present, there have been many successful cases of research on the scheduling of scientific workflow tasks, among them, the well-known scientific workflow structure uses a directed acyclic graph (DAG). This article also employs the aforementioned representation method, using of DAG to represent the dependencies between workflow tasks, and eatablish the scheduling model. Scientific workflow can be represented by a four tuple, $G = \{T, E, D, F\}$, where

- $T = \{t_1, t_2, ..., t_n\}$ denotes the set of n tasks;
- $E = \{(t_i, t_j)|t_i, t_j \in T, i \neq j\}$ is the set of directed edges, using directed edges to represent data transmission and dependencies between subtasks, (t_a, t_b) indicates that task node a has a dependency relationship with task node b and node a is the parent node of node b, child nodes must be processed after all parent nodes are completed;
- $D = \{data_i|t_i \in T\}$ is the set of file sizes that all subtasks need to process;
- $F = \{Transfer_{ij}|i \neq j\}$ is the set of data transmission, $Transfer_{ij}$ indicates that there is a dependency among T_i and T_j, the data transmission size is described as $Transfer_{ij}$.

Figure 1 shows a simple scientific workflow structure. Each node represents a subtask. Each one-way arrow represents the dependency between subtasks and indicates that there is data transfer between them. The numbers on the directed arrows represent the amount of data transferred between subtasks. A subtask that don't have a parent node task is called a start node. A task that don't have a child task is called an end node. For example, in Fig. 1, there are ten subtasks in this workflow, node 1 is a start task, and node 10 is an end task.

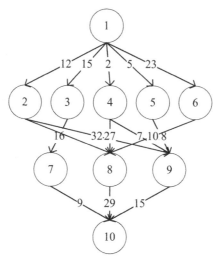

Fig. 1. A simple scientific workflow structure

2.2 Problem Expression

The problem in workflow scheduling to figure out in this manuscript is to assign each task T_i to the most suitable service resource V_i, so that all tasks can be completed according to their dependencies and the final completion time is the shortest. Before establishing the mathematical model, the following constraints need to be considered first.

(1) The priority of each task is equal;
(2) A service resource can handle different kinds of subtasks but it can only serve one subtask each time;
(3) A task node can only be executed on one service resource;
(4) Different service resources have different service quality.

$V = \{v_1, v_2, ..., v_n\}$ is a set of service resources, v_i represents the service quality of the i-th service resource.

The completion time of the workflow is composed of two kinds of time, namely the processing time of the task and the data transmission time. The execution time of the subtask on the virtual machine is represented by processing time (PT). The transmission time (TT) represents the data transmission time between dependent subtasks. Therefore, the start time (ST) of each subtask can be expressed as:

$$ST_j = \begin{cases} pre\_end\_time_i + TT_{ij}, & \text{if } i \text{ and } j \text{ have a dependency} \\ pre\_end\_time_i, & \text{otherwise} \end{cases} \quad (1)$$

where TT_{ij} represents the data transmission time from T_i to T_j, $pre\_end\_time_i$ represents the end time of the i-th subtask and

$$TT_{ij} = \frac{Transfer_{ij}}{v} \quad (2)$$

Thus, the service time of each service resources ($VM\_Finish\_Time_k$) can be expressed as

$$VM\_Finish\_Time_k = \sum_i^j ST_i + PT_i^k \tag{3}$$

where PT_i^k represents the processing time of the T_i on the service resource v_k,

$$PT_i^k = \frac{data_i}{v_k} \tag{4}$$

The final completion time can be expressed as:

$$FT = \max(VM\_Finish\_Time_i), i = 1, 2, ..., n \tag{5}$$

where $VM\_Finish\_Time_i$ refers to the completion of the service resource v_i.

3   Multifactorial Evolutionary Algorithm for DAG Schedule

3.1   MFEA Based on Combinatorial Population (CP-MFEA)

First, we review the basic flow of the MFEA. The structure of the MFEA can be summarized as:

(1) Use uniform representation to generate an initial population with NP individuals. For different tasks, a unified representation must also be defined, and MFEA will perform the following operations on the individuals it encodes.

(2) Evaluate each individual and calculate their *factorial cost, factorial rank, scalar fitness* and *skill factor.*

(3) Use *assortative mating* to perform genetic operations on the current population to generate offspring populations.

(4) Use *vertical cultural transmission* to evaluate individual offspring.

(5) Update the *scalar fitness* and *skill factor* of each individual in the parent population and offspring population.

(6) Select NP individuals from the parent population and the child population to perform the next generation operation.

(7) If the number of iterations is not satisfied, repeat (3) to (6).

In this chapter we will describe in detail the steps to solve the multi-task DAG scheduling. The following is the details of CP-MFEA. In the first, we reviewed the CP-MFEA in algorithm 1, and its flow chart can be represented as Fig. 2.

Algorithm 1 MFEA based on Combinatorial Population(CP-MFEA)

1: Use topological sorting to generate corresponding subpopulations (2/P) for different types of tasks, and combine all subpopulations into one population (P)

2: Evaluate every individual for different task

3: **While** (end demands are not met) **do**

Use Assortative mating to produce offspring (Q)

Evaluate offspring using vertical cultural transmission

Combine initial population (P) and offspring (Q) as a new population

Update the skill factor for every individual in the new population

The best individual is selected as the next generation population based on the fitness value

4: End while

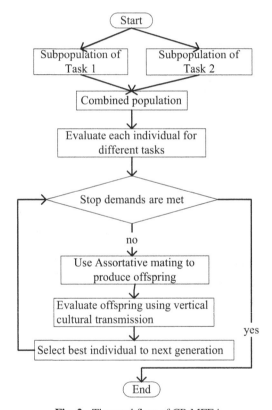

Fig. 2. The workflow of CP-MFEA

3.2   Generation of Population

Because of the dependencies between tasks in scientific workflows, different tasks have their specific individual representations. Therefore, it is necessary to set individual skill factors in advance when the population is initialized.

The individual coding in this paper consists of two parts, one is the topological sorting of all subtasks, and the other is the service resource number assigned to it. Since there are dependencies among all subtasks, the order of execution of the subtasks is extremely important. Topological sorting is a method of arranging subtasks according to their order. Through topological sorting, we can get the execution order of a workflow. The next thing we need to solve is to allocate a suitable service resource for each subtask.

As shown in Fig. 1, it is a simple workflow. It is assumed that there are four service resources whose serial numbers are {1,2,3,4}. A topological sort of subtask is {1,5,4,3,6,7,2,8,9,10}, so the encode of an individual can be expressed as Table 1:

Table 1. The encode individual

TaskID	1	5	4	3	6	7	2	8	9	10
ResourceID	4	2	3	4	2	1	2	4	2	3

The first line is the topological sorting of a workflow, and the second line is the service resources allocated to it. When the entire workflow is completed, it is executed in order. From the perspective of service resources, the individual can be expressed as Fig. 3(a), the completion of all subtasks can be expressed on the timeline as Fig. 3(b).

$$\begin{cases} V_1 : T_7 \\ V_2 : T_5 - T_6 - T_2 - T_9 \\ V_3 : T_4 - T_{10} \\ V_4 : T_1 - T_3 - T_8 \end{cases}$$

(a) Virtual machine perspective

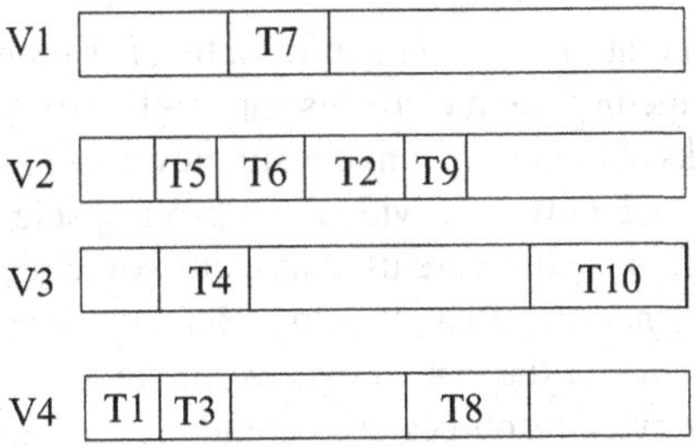

(b) Timeline of task completion

Fig. 3. Individual coding explanation

The basic process of CP-MFEA is shown in Fig. 3. After generating the initial population, evaluate every individual in the population and assign skill factors to the individuals. Then, the population evolution operation is described. The evolution operation in CP-MFEA is described by vertical cultural propagation. After generating offspring, re-evaluate offspring, and finally select the best offspring based on performance.

3.3 Generation of Offspring

There are two methods to produce offspring in CP-MFEA: crossover and mutation. However, the crossover between individuals is not random, which need certain conditions. In reality, individuals are more inclined to cross between the same types. For different types, it can be regraded as a cultural factor to impact on their evolution. The same is true in workflow scheduling. The same type, that is, the same skill factor (τ), will have more opportunities for crossover. For different types of tasks, the crossover operation can be performed only when random mating probability (*rmp*) is satisfied. When the condition is not satisfied, the individual performs mutation operation. The specific operation of creating offspring is described in Algorithm 2.

Algorithm 2: Assortative mating

1: Pick two parents at random p_a & p_b

2: Generate a random number a

3: **If** (skill factors are equal) or ($a<rmp$) **then**

  p_a and p_b cross to produce offspring c_a and c_b

  Else

  p_a mutates into offspring c_a

  p_b mutates into offspring c_b

4: **End if**

3.3.1 Crossover

The main goal of cross operation is to share information between individuals to produce offspring. The crossover method adopted in this paper is that exchange part of the service resources of the child tasks of the two parents. A simple crossover example will be shown as Fig. 4. First, randomly select two individuals as parents, select any position to cross, and the four bits behind this position are used as a crossover segment to exchange with another individual, then generating two offspring. Here, those with the same skill factor and different skill factors adopt the same crossover method, though the order of tasks cannot be changed, the service resources used could are exchanged with each other. If the order of subtasks is crossed, the original dependency relationship of the entire task will be destroyed.

Crossover Position

parent 1

TaskID	1	5	4	3	6	7	2	8	9	10
ResourceID	4	2	3	4	2	1	2	4	2	3

parent 2

TaskID	1	5	2	3	7	6	4	8	9	10
ResourceID	3	2	1	4	2	3	1	2	3	2

⬇

parent 1

TaskID	1	5	4	3	6	7	2	8	9	10
ResourceID	4	2	1	4	2	3	2	4	2	3

parent 2

TaskID	1	5	2	3	7	6	4	8	9	10
ResourceID	3	2	3	4	2	1	1	2	3	2

Fig. 4. An example of crossover

3.3.2 Mutate

The mutation operation is that randomly selects a subtask and then directly changes its service resources. A simple mutation example will be shown in Fig. 5. First, randomly choose a mutation location, and then change its service resource from v_3 to v_2, which represents the change of its service resource.

Mutate position

parent 1

TaskID	1	5	4	3	6	7	2	8	9	10
ResourceID	4	2	3	4	2	1	2	4	2	3

⬇

offsping 1

TaskID	1	5	4	3	6	7	2	8	9	10
ResourceID	4	2	2	4	2	1	2	4	2	3

Fig. 5. An example of mutation

3.4 Evaluate Offspring

The offspring are evaluated by using vertical culture propagation and the skill factor is assessed for every individual. The detailed introduction as shown in Algorithm 3.

Algorithm 3: Vertical cultural transmission

1: offspring q has two parents(crossover) p_a & p_b or one parent(mutation) p

2: **If** (q has two parents) **then**
Randomly generate a number r between 0 and 1
If ($r < 0.5$) **then**
    q inherits p_a, q inherits all the properties of p_a
    Else
    q inherits p_b, q inherits all the properties of p_b
End if
    Else
q inherits p, q inherits all the properties of p
3: **End if**

---

4 Experiment and Discuss

4.1 Basic Workflow Structure

Shishir Bharathi and Gideon Juve et al. [37, 38] provided a characterization of work-flows, which comes from five different scientific applications. And they described the composition of the workflow, data and computing requirements. The five workflow data sets in different scientific fields are Montage, CyberShake, Epigenomics, Inspiral and Sipht.

Montage: NASA/IPAC Infrared Science Archive proposed the Montage application [39]. A simple example of Montage workflow is shown in Fig. 6(a).

CyberShake: CyberShake was proposed by the Southern California Earthquake Center to describe an actual earthquake hazard. The visualization of the simplest task structure of CyberShake scientific workflow is shown in Fig. 6(b).

Epigenomics: the USC Epigenome Center and the Pegasus team proposed the epigenome workflow. This workflow is spent on various operations that automate genome sequence processing. The visualization of the simplest task structure of Epigenomics scientific workflow is shown in Fig. 6(c).

Inspiral: The Inspiral workflow is generated by summarizing the data collected when the compact binary system merges. The visualization of the simplest task structure of Inspiral scientific workflow is shown in Fig. 6(d).

Sipht: The Sipht workflow was developed by Harvard University's Bioinformatics Project. This workflow is spent on automatically find for RNA that don't be translated from bacterial replicators in the NCBI database. A simple example of Sipht workflow is shown in Fig. 6(e).

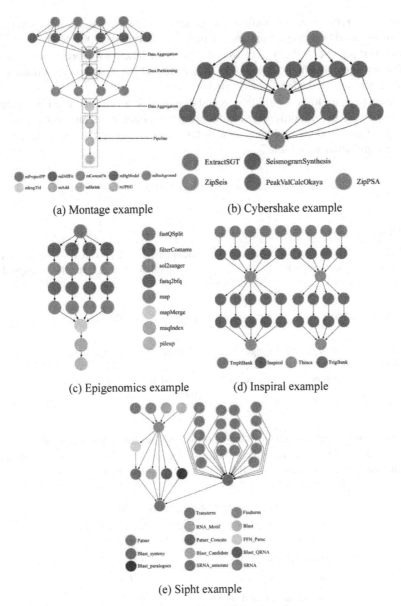

(a) Montage example   (b) Cybershake example

(c) Epigenomics example   (d) Inspiral example

(e) Sipht example

Fig. 6. Five types of workflow examples

4.2 Experimental Setup

For the multi-task experimental setup in the cloud computing environment, we adopt some the real world workflows that Pegasus has previously released. These workflows include many types, just as those workflows mentioned in the previous Sect. 4.1. Our commonly used scientific workflow also contains some attributes, such as the number of subtasks, the number of directed edges, the runtime of every subtask, the data transfer size, etc. Different types of workflows are generally expressed as a combination of the name of the workflow and a number, for instance, 'Montage_100', 'Cybershake_50'. The first part represents the type of workflow, and the latter part represents the number of subtasks owned by the workflow. The dimensions of the workflow are different, and the number of directed edges it has is also different.

Therefore, a multi-task workflow scheduling problem is constructed by matching workflow instances with different workflow attributes but has the uniform subtask. The 9 groups of multitasking problems used in this paper to verify the performance of the algorithm are detailed in Table 2.

Table 2. Instances of multitasking workflow for investigating

Multi-tasking problems	P1	P2	P3	P4	P5
Workflow instances	CyberShake 30 + Inspiral 30	Montage 50 + CyberShake 50	Montage 50 + Inspiral 50	CyberShake 50 + Inspiral 50	Montage 100 + Inspiral 100
Multi-tasking problems	P6	P7	P8	P9	
Workflow instances	Montage 100 + Epigenomics 100	Epigenomics 100 + Inspiral 100	Montage 100 + CyberShake 100	CyberShake 100 + Epigenomics 100	

Next, in the research of this article, the traditional single-task evolutionary algorithm is used for comparison. For the sake of fairness, the single-task evolution algorithm uses the same evolution parameters as MFEA. The detailed parameters are as Table 3.

Table 3. Experimental parameter setup

Attributes	Values
Population Size	N = 300
Generation Size	gen = 1000
Independent Run Times	time = 20
Random Mating Probability	rmp = 0.8 [40, 41]
The Number of Virtual Machine	num = 4

4.3 Results and Analysis

In the subsequent operation of generating offspring, the individual in the original unified space cannot represent the information of different tasks, so this article deals with workflow tasks of the same dimension. Because of the dependence between the sub-tasks of each task, every individual has a corresponding task, so the skill factors of the individual are allocated when they are initialized. The comparison results of the single-task evolutionary algorithm is established in Table 4. And the multifactorial evolutionary algorithm. Each result was run 20 times. It should be noted that the processing method of single-task evolutionary algorithm is to run 20 times for each workflow, while CP-MFEA is to process and run two tasks together 20 times. In the table, B.finish_time represents the best minimum completion time for the workflow in 20 runs, Ave.finish_time represents the minimum completion time of the evaluation, and Std.finish_time represents the variance of the results of the 20 runs. After comparison, the better performance is shown in bold in Table 4.

Table 4. CP-MFEA & Single comparative results

Multi-tasking problems	Workflow	CP-MFEA			Single Solver		
		B.finish_time	Ave.finish_time	Std.finish_time	B.finish_time	Ave.finish_time	Std.finish_time
P1	CyberShake 30	**18.9775**	33.3687	12.8338	25.4708	**25.4708**	31.9976
	Inspiral 30	**134.2750**	**142.5863**	4.8549	197.4092	208.3391	13.3670
P2	Montage 50	**10.4755**	**455.1545**	393.2457	25.4319	742.8012	242.1589
	CyberShake 50	**31.4513**	**40.9741**	22.3152	41.8857	87.6131	37.6759
P3	Montage 50	818.5323	842.3183	17.2094	**25.4319**	**742.8012**	11.5377
	Inspiral 50	**253.9945**	**248.7472**	15.0657	284.5383	300.2587	11.8458
P4	CyberShake 50	**30.7145**	**51.2976**	20.2091	41.8857	87.6131	37.6759
	Inspiral 50	**236.0365**	**244.3737**	6.3752	284.5383	300.2588	15.8458
P5	Montage 100	842.5150	1045.3674	340.0573	**828.2413**	**906.5372**	210.5172
	Inspiral 100	**437.2634**	**456.8720**	12.1120	439.1689	458.2343	27.1828
P6	Montage 100	839.3809	975.3207	289.6624	**828.2413**	**906.5372**	210.5172
	Epigenomics 100	**8705.9608**	**9160.5553**	293.6800	8958.3632	9303.0728	515.3847
P7	Epigenomics 100	**8767.9897**	9499.2797	294.4247	8958.3632	**9303.0728**	515.3847
	Inspiral 100	446.1519	470.7739	14.7826	**439.1689**	**458.2343**	27.1828
P8	Montage 100	**44.8498**	1125.6559	1554.0101	828.2413	**906.5372**	210.5172
	CyberShake 100	74.4345	**30733.2401**	19048.8920	**73.7803**	33796.6432	16906.0324
P9	CyberShake 100	**65.8927**	**29888.7325**	14411.7174	73.7803	33796.6432	16906.0324
	Epigenomics 100	**8201.0600**	**8424.7696**	149.7236	8958.3632	9303.0728	515.3847

In Table 4, we can see that there is a total of 9 sets of multi-task combination problems, of which 3 sets of minimum finish time and average finish time are completely better than single-task processing methods, and multi-task evolutionary algorithms show better problem-solving ability. The three sets of combined workflow tasks are P2, P4 and P9 respectively. In the remaining six groups, there are a total of 24 results. Among them, CP-MFEA is better than the single-task evolutionary algorithm with 12 results.

From the perspective of dimensionality, CP-MFEA is basically better than single-task evolutionary algorithm in a total of 4 sets of multi-task workflows of 30-dimensional and 50-dimensional. In the remaining 5 groups of experiments, they are all 100-dimensional combined workflow tasks. CP-MFEA is also better than single-task evolutionary algorithms in the two aspects of B.finish_time and Ave.finish_time.

After observing the data, it can be seen that there is a workflow of Montage 50 in both P2 and P3, but the value of B.finish_time is quite different. In problem P2, Montage 50 is the same as CyberShake 50 Combine them into a multi-workflow problem. In problem P3, Montage 50 is combined with Inspiral 50 to form a multi-workflow problem, while in P2, the value of B.finish_time of Montage 50 It is 10.475 5. In P3, the value of B.finish_time of Montage 50 is 818.532 3. In the single-task evolutionary algorithm, the value of B.finish_time of Montage 50 is 25.431 9, which is still not as good as the result obtained by CP-MFEA. Therefore, it can be explained that CP-MFEA can better obtain the better solution about the problem, and transmit information through different types of workflows, which can make the solution escape from the local optimum.

Figure 7 shows the situation where the convergent is finally reached for the simultaneous processing of 2 tasks in the 9 groups of problems. The x-axis in the Fig. 7 means the algebra in the evolution process, and the y-axis in the Fig. 7 means the sum of the objective values of the two tasks solved at the same time. Through the convergence graph, we can notice that whether it is 30-dimensional, 50-dimensional or 100-dimensional, the final convergence speed of the two tasks is relatively good. For 30-dimensional combined multitasking, the overall convergence was achieved in the 449 generation, and for the 50-dimensional combined multitasking, the overall convergence was basically reached around the 680 generation. In addition, from the Fig. 7 we can also observe that P1, P2, P3, P4, and P5 rush to a place very close to the x-axis at the beginning of algebra. This is due to the random allocation of virtual machines when the population is initialized. The amount of data exchange between dependent subtasks is too large. Therefore, through the mutual influence and optimization between different tasks, the subtasks with dependent relationships and large data transmission volume are assigned to the same virtual machine, which can greatly reduce the overall Complete time.

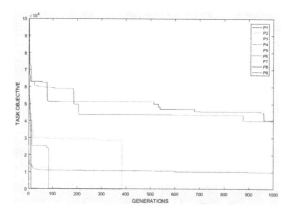

Fig. 7. Convergence rate indication

From the perspective of Montage_50, both P2 and P3 have this task, and when Montage_50 is processed together with Cybershake_50, a better target value can be obtained, indicating that the combination of multitasking is effective. The same is true for Epigenomics_100 in the 100-dimensional combination task P9. When combined with Cybershake_100, it gets a better target value than P6 and P7.

The time complexity is the number of operations an algorithm performs to complete its task. The algorithm that performs the task in the smallest number of operations is considered the most efficient one in terms of the time complexity. The algorithm used in this article and the algorithm compared are all evolutionary algorithms. The biggest factor affecting time complexity in evolutionary algorithms is the number of iterations. Therefore, the algorithm used in this article and the algorithm for comparison are both O(N) in time complexity.

5   Conclusion

Due to the diversity of user needs in the cloud computing environment, this paper uses CP-MFEA to obtain the solution of multi-workflow scheduling and allocation problem of the same-dimensional multi-task scientific workflow. First, when the population is initialized, corresponding subpopulations are generated for different types of workflows, and a skill factor is assigned to it, and then the populations are merged. In the evolution operation, the evolution operation is directly performed for the same type of individuals, and the different types of individuals perform the evolution operation by sharing information, and this method completes the implicit information transmission of different types of workflows. The experimental results indicate that the performance of multi-task processing through this implicit information transfer method is better than single-task processing.

Since this article only deals with different types of workflow problems in the same dimension, the next step will continue to deal with workflow tasks in different dimensions, while also taking into account other optimization goals in the workflow.

Acknowledgment. This work is supported by the National Key Research and Development Program of China under Grant No.2018YFC1604000, the National Natural Science Foundation of China under Grant No.61806138, No. U1636220, No.61961160707 and No.61976212, Key R&D program of Shanxi Province (International Cooperation) under Grant No.201903D421048. Australian Research Council (ARC) projects DP190101893, DP170100136, and LP180100758.

References

1. Chen, T.G., Peng, L.J., Yin, X.H., Rong, J.T., Yang, J.J., Cong, G.D.: Analysis of user satisfaction with online education platforms in china during the COVID-19 pandemic. Healthcare **8**(3), 200 (2020)
2. Coello Coello, C.A.: Evolutionary multi-objective optimization: a historical view of the field. IEEE Comput. Intell. Magaz. **1**(1), 28–36 (2006)
3. Back, T., Hammel, U., Schwefel, H.P.: Evolutionary computation: comments on the history and current state. IEEE Trans. Evolution. Comput. **1**(1), 3–17 (1997)

4. Li, N., Wang, S., Li, Y.: A hybrid approach of GA and ACO for VRP. J. Comput. Inf. Syst. **7**(13) (2011)
5. Rabbouch, B., Saâdaoui, F., Mraihi, R.: Efficient implementation of the genetic algorithm to solve rich vehicle routing problems. Oper. Res. **21**(3), 1763–1791 (2019)
6. Yusuf, I., Baba, M.S., Iksan, N.: Applied genetic algorithm for solving rich VRP. Appl. Artif. Intell. **28**(10), 957–991 (2014)
7. Andrew, O.: A genetic algorithm model for vehicle routing problem (VRP) (2015)
8. Xu, J., Zhang, Z., Hu, Z., et al.: A many-objective optimized task allocation scheduling model in cloud computing. Appl. Intell. 1–18
9. Cai, X., Geng, S., Wu, D., Cai, J., Chen, J.: A multi-cloud model based many-objective intelligent algorithm for efficient task scheduling in internet of things. IEEE Internet Things J. (2020). https://doi.org/10.1109/JIOT.2020.3040019
10. Ming-Si, S.: Intelligent control method of ship course based on genetic learning algorithm. Ship Sci. Technol. (2019)
11. Yan, L.: Intelligent control technology of ultra-high voltage grid. J. Adv. Comput. Intell. Intell. Inf. (2019)
12. Wang, G., Xiao, S., Chen, X., et al.: Application of genetic algorithm in automatic train operation. Wirel. Person. Commun. (2018)
13. Sun, J., Wang, R., Yu, K., Miao, K., Deng, H.: Application of genetic algorithm and neural network in ship's heading PID tracking control. In: Qiao, F., Patnaik, S., Wang, J. (eds.) ICMIR 2017. AISC, vol. 691, pp. 436–442. Springer, Cham (2018). https://doi.org/10.1007/978-3-319-70990-1_64
14. Cui, Z.H., et al.: A hybrid blockchain-based identity authentication scheme for Multi-WSN. IEEE Trans. Serv. Comput. **13**(2), 241–251 (2020)
15. Yusof, R., Khairuddin, U., Khalid, M.: A new mutation operation for faster convergence in genetic algorithm feature selection. Int. J. Innov. Comput. Inf. Control **8**(10B), 7363–7378 (2012)
16. Wong, W.K., Chekima, A., Ahmad, I.O.B., et al.: Genetic algorithm feature selection and classifier optimization using moment invariants and shape features. Int. Conf. Artif. Intell. IEEE Comput. Soc. (2013)
17. Devaraj, N.: Feature Selection using Genetic Algorithm to Improve SVM Classifier (2019)
18. Yildiz, O., Dogru, I.A.: Permission-based android malware detection system using feature selection with genetic algorithm. Int. J. Softw. Eng. Knowl. Eng. **29**(2), 245–262 (2019)
19. Zhang, Z., Xie, L.: A many objective integrated evolutionary algorithm for feature selection in anomaly detection. Concurr. Comput. Pract. Exp. **32**(22) (2020)
20. Zhang, Z., Wen, J., Zhang, J., Cai, X., Xie, L.: A many objective-based feature selection model for anomaly detection in cloud environment. IEEE Access **8**, 60218–60231 (2020)
21. Chen, T.G., Wang, Y.L., Yang, J.J., Cong, G.D.: Modeling public opinion reversal process with the considerations of external intervention information and individual internal characteristics. Healthcare **8**(2), 160 (2020)
22. Cui, Z.H., et al.: Personalized recommendation system based on collaborative filtering for IoT scenarios. IEEE Trans. Serv. Comput. **13**(4), 685–695 (2020)
23. Cai, X., Hu, Z., Zhao, P., et al.: A hybrid recommendation system with many-objective evolutionary algorithm. Exp. Syst. Appl. **159**, 113648 (2020)
24. Chen, T.G., Shi, J.W., Yang, J.J., Cong, G.D., Li, G.F.: Modeling public opinion polarization in group behavior by integrating SIRS-based information diffusion process. Complexity **2020**, 4791527 (2020)
25. Xu, Y., Li, K., Hu, J., et al.: A genetic algorithm for task scheduling on heterogeneous computing systems using multiple priority queues. Inf. Sci. **270**, 255–287 (2014)
26. Jia, Y., Buyya, R.: Scheduling scientific workflow applications with deadline and budget constraints using genetic algorithms. Sci. Program. **14**(3–4), 217–230 (2006)

27. Kumar, P., Verma, A.: Independent task-scheduling in cloud computing by improved genetic algorithm. Int. J. Adv. Res. Comput. Sci. Softw. Eng. (2012). https://doi.org/10.1145/234 5396.2345420

28. Zhu, Z., Zhang, G., Li, M., et al.: Evolutionary multi-objective workflow scheduling in cloud. IEEE Trans. Parallel Distrib. Syst. 27(5), 1344–1357 (2016)

29. Topcuoglu, H., Hariri, S., Min-You, W.: Performance-effective and low-complexity task scheduling for heterogeneous computing. IEEE Trans. Parall. Distrib. Syst. 13(3), 260–274 (2002)

30. Jia, Y.H., Chen, W.N., Yuan, H., et al.: An intelligent cloud workflow scheduling system with time estimation and adaptive ant colony optimization. IEEE Trans. Syst. Man Cybern. Syst. 1–16 (2018)

31. Yi, G., Budati, C.: Energy-aware workflow scheduling and optimization in clouds using bat algorithm. Future Gen. Comput. Syst. 113, 106–112 (2020)

32. Sellami, K., Tiako, P.F., Sellami, L., et al.: Energy efficient workflow scheduling of cloud services using chaotic particle swarm optimization. In: 2020 IEEE Green Technologies Conference (GreenTech). IEEE (2020)

33. Gupta, A., Ong, Y.-S., Feng, L.: Multifactorial evolution: towards evolutionary multitasking. In: IEEE Transactions on Evolutionary Computation (99), 1 (2015)

34. Iqbal, M., Xue, B., Al-Sahaf, H., et al.: Cross-domain reuse of extracted knowledge in genetic programming for image classification. IEEE Trans. Evol. Comput. 21(4), 569–587 (2017)

35. Zhou, L., Feng, L., Zhong, J., et al.: Evolutionary multitasking in combinatorial search spaces: a case study in capacitated vehicle routing problem. In: Computational Intelligence. IEEE (2017)

36. Xie, T., Gong, M., Tang, Z., et al.: Enhancing evolutionary multifactorial optimization based on particle swarm optimization. In: IEEE Congress on Evolutionary Computation (CEC). IEEE (2016)

37. Bharathi, S., Chervenak, A., Deelman, E., et al.: Characterization of scientific workflows. In: Workshop on Workflows in Support of Large-scale Science. IEEE (2008)

38. Juve, G., Chervenak, A., Deelman, E., et al.: Characterizing and profiling scientific workflows. Futur. Gener. Comput. Syst. 29(3), 682–692 (2013)

39. Berriman, G.B., Good, J.C., Laity, A.C., et al.: Montage: a grid-enabled engine for delivering custom science-grade mosaics on demand. Proc. SPIE Int. Soc. Opt. Eng. 2004, 5493 (2004)

40. Oliver, I.M.: A study of permutation crossover operations on the traveling salesman problem. Proceedings of the International Conference on GA Lawrence Erlbaum Associates Hillsdale, NJ (1987)

41. Potvin, J.-Y., Duhamel, C., Guertin, F.: A genetic algorithm for vehicle routing with backhauling. Appl. Intell. 6(4), 345–355 (1996)

Pose Estimation Based on Snake Model and Inverse Perspective Transform for Elliptical Ring Monocular Vision

Cong Qian[1]($\boxtimes$), Guohua Wang[1], Jiajian Zhang[1], Renjie Wang[1], and Pengshuai Li[2]

[1] Maintenance Branch of State Grid Jiangsu Electric Power Co., Ltd., Nanjing, China
1381521995@163.com
[2] School of Mechanical Science and Engineering, Huazhong University of Science and Technology, Wuhan 430074, Hubei, China

Abstract. In the pose estimation of the elliptical ring contour in monocular vision, it is difficult to achieve high precision midline contour extraction and pose estimation, because of the close distance between the inner and outer contours. To ensure measurement accuracy, a high-precision contour separation scheme is proposed in this paper based on Zernike moment detection and the Snake model. Specifically, the sub-pixel edge detection method based on Zernike moment is designed to achieve the rough extraction of internal and external contour, in which the adaptive binarization method is used to obtain the coordinates of the internal and external contours as maskers. Then, combined with mask operation to obtain the coordinates of the separated contours, an iterative contour finding algorithm based on the Snake model is designed to obtain the high-precision inner and outer contour. In addition, an ellipse correction method based on inverse perspective transformation is proposed to solve the problem of difficult matching of ellipse feature points when identifying pixel coordinates of feature points. Finally, the proposed method is applied to the static contact hole oval pose estimation of switchgear on a high voltage power system. The results show that depth measurement error is ±0.5 mm, to moderate repeated measurement precision of ±0.3 mm, indicating that this algorithm can achieve higher accuracy of elliptical ring pose estimation.

Keywords: Snake model · Inverse perspective transformation · Ellipse correction · Pose estimation · Fault diagnosis of the circuit breaker

1 Introduction

Visual measurement has been widely used in industrial system detection due to its good stability and accuracy [1,2,9]. Configure extraction and feature point matching are two key steps that can determine the accuracy of pose estimation. The key problem of contour extraction is to filter a large number of non-target

© Springer Nature Singapore Pte Ltd. 2022
L. Pan et al. (Eds.): BIC-TA 2021, CCIS 1566, pp. 104–117, 2022.
https://doi.org/10.1007/978-981-19-1253-5_8

contours to obtain high precision target contours. The main purpose of feature point matching is to find corners and templates on the target contour to achieve pose estimation.

Common contour extraction methods include edge-based pixel-level detection operators (e.g., Prewitt operator and canny operator [6]) and threshold-based methods (e.g., adaptive binarization [4]). These traditional contour extraction methods are generally pixel-level precision, high efficiency but poor accuracy. Some scholars propose contour extraction based on the moment method [8]. This method is insensitive to noise and can achieve detection accuracy at the sub-pixel level. For example, the rotation invariance of Zernike orthogonal moment can be used to achieve a high precision edge detection, but it generally requires square images with high image quality [3]. For the above methods, one of the common features is that using the classical hierarchical processing technology, i.e., extracting the contour information through the step-by-step process of point-surface-body. This processing method reduces the difficulty of contour extraction but results in insufficient accuracy since the low error is transmitted to the high level. Kass [5] et al. proposed an iterative algorithm of the Snake model. Through the target contour curve energy function with high-low level information, it achieves a higher precision contour location. However, it requires the initial contour with a certain precision as the initial iterative solution.

Many scholars have studied feature point matching of ellipse contour. Song Limei [10] proposed an affine LOG polar coordinate transformation that transforms local concentric ellipses into parallel lines. The obtained image features are used for decoding, which could realize the classification of different ellipse contours, but could not realize the pose estimation. The monocular vision vehicle distance measurement can be realized by the inverse perspective transformation relation of road vanishing points, but it needs to combine the constraint of polygon corner points of the road itself [7].

Inspired by the above analysis, this paper proposes an elliptic ring pose estimation method based on the Snake model and the inverse perspective transformation. Based on the Zernike model, an adaptive threshold binarization is designed to obtain the elliptic ring contour with sub-pixel accuracy. And the precision of the target elliptic contour is enhanced through the Snake model iterative algorithm. To correct the ellipse contour, an inverse perspective transform algorithm based on installation position calibration is proposed to obtain a more accurate estimation of the ellipse contour pose. Experimental results on the dynamic and static contacts of switch cabinet circuit breakers show that the proposed algorithm can achieve a more accurate estimation of the elliptical ring pose because it has less depth error and higher accuracy for moderate repeated measurement.

Notation: Px represents the X-axis coordinates of the center of the ellipse, Py represents the Y-axis coordinates of the center of the ellipse, Ls represents the length of the short axis, Ll represents the length of the long axis, and R represents the rotation angle.

2 Ellipse Ring Contour Extraction Based on Snake Model

In this paper, we extract the initial positions of two ellipse contours by the contour extraction method based on the moment and obtain the coordinates of two mask regions at the same time. Firstly, the original rectangular image is cut into squares required by the Zernike moment detection. The inner and outer ellipse contours are separated by mask operation. The internal and external elliptical contour obtained by Zernike moment detection is used as the initial contour of the Snake model to iteratively search for a more accurate elliptical contour. The final pose estimation contour is obtained by thinning algorithm. The algorithm flow is shown in Fig. 1.

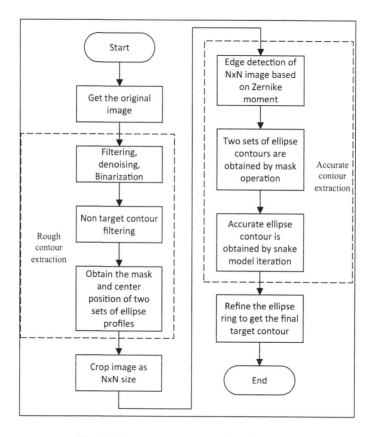

Fig. 1. Ring contour extraction algorithm

2.1 Rough Contour Extraction

In the rough contour extraction stage, the prediction operation is performed to remove the noise of the original image and the information irrelevant to the contour, which includes the steps of filtering, denoising, and adaptive binarization.

Taking the original image of circuit breaker contact (1600 × 1200) as an example, the results are shown in Fig. 2. From the analysis of the local image of the target contour, it can be found that the target elliptic ring can be completely preserved.

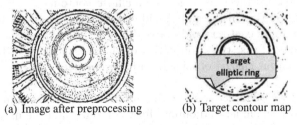

(a) Image after preprocessing   (b) Target contour map

Fig. 2. Image preprocessing

Then the filtering schemes such as area filtering, roundness filtering, and center filtering are successively employed to filter the non-target contour.

During the engagement of the circuit breaker's dynamic and static contacts, the area threshold is set as 90000 of the inner contour of the ellipse when the meshing depth is 0 because the area of the elliptical ring is constantly changing. The area threshold is set as 220,000 of the outer contour when the meshing depth is fully engaged. Filtering parameters are shown in Table 1.

Table 1. Filter parameters table

Area threshold/pixels	Roundness evaluation	Center position/pixels
90000 ∼ 220000	5 > 4	$600 < x < 1000, 400 < y < 800$

The existence of the non-target ellipse contour makes the target contour easy to be misidentified. Therefore, a non-circular contour filtering method based on roundness evaluation parameters is proposed in this paper. The roundness calculation formula is shown in (1).

$$roundness = 4\pi/c^2 \tag{1}$$

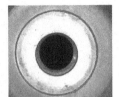

(a) Filtered profile   (b) The position of contour in the original image

Fig. 3. Non-target contour filtering

where s is the area of the ellipse contour, and c is half of the length of the long axis of the ellipse contour. After contour filtering, the image is shown in Fig. 3. It can be found that the hierarchical filtering scheme has a better effect.

A refinement algorithm-based contour boundary extraction scheme is designed to separate the inner and outer ellipse contours. Through obtaining the filtered elliptic ring inside and outside the contour line, the combination of internal and external contours and line width is set inside and outside boundary elliptical contour. Thus, the coordinates of the mask region of the inner and outer ellipse contour can be obtained, and the inner and outer contour can be separated.

According to Table 2, there is a difference of about 10 pixels in the length of the axes between the inner and outer ellipse contours, and the meshing depth is 0. With the increase of the meshing depth of the dynamic and static contacts, the difference in the length of the two ellipses will be bigger and bigger. Therefore, as long as the depth is 0, the elliptical ring can be separated by thinning the contour boundary, to realize the separation of the elliptical ring in the whole meshing process.

Table 2. Feature extraction after ellipse fitting of object contour

Px/Pixels	Py/Pixels	Ls/Pixels	Ll/Pixels	R/Degree
873.79	557.38	383.55	385.72	163.34
872.80	556.80	372.20	372.66	21.25

The elliptical ring in Table 2 is refined to obtain a single-pixel elliptical contour, as shown in Fig. 4. It can be seen from the refined renderings that the dividing line obtained by the refinement can better separate the two target contours.

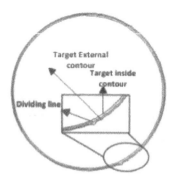

Fig. 4. The dividing line of inner and outer contour after thinning

In Table 2, the long and short axis of the outer ellipse contour increase or decrease the width of the boundary line and the inner and outer contour boundary, respectively. They serve as internal and external boundaries. Since the width of the inner and outer boundary is about 10 pixels, the major and minor axis of the outer ellipse contour are increased by 5 pixels as the outer boundary, and the inner contour is reduced by 5 pixels as the inner boundary, as shown in Table 3. After the contour coordinates of the inner and outer boundaries are obtained, the area between the outer boundary and the contour boundary is used as the mask of the outer ellipse contour. The area between the contour boundary and the inner boundary is used as the mask of the internal ellipse contour.

Table 3. The characteristics of ellipse outline with the inner and outer boundary

Px/Pixels	Py/Pixels	Ls/Pixels	Ll/Pixels	R/Degree
873.79	557.38	388.55S	390.72	163.34
872.80	556.80	367.20	367.66	21.25

2.2   Refined Contour Extraction

In this subsection, contour extraction is refined to sub-pixel accuracy based on Zernike moment detection and the Snake model.

According to the edge coordinates of the ellipse contour in Table 2, the center of the circle is located near (873,557). The original image is clipped to 1200×1200 for Zernike detection. The calculation formula of Zernike detection edge point coordinates is shown as follows:

$$\begin{bmatrix} x_m \\ y_m \end{bmatrix} = \begin{bmatrix} x_e \\ y_e \end{bmatrix} + \frac{Nd}{2} \begin{bmatrix} \cos \alpha \\ \sin \alpha \end{bmatrix} \tag{2}$$

where $\begin{bmatrix} x_e \\ y_e \end{bmatrix}$ is the origin coordinate and N is the size of the template.

A 7×7 template size is used to construct two corresponding templates M1,1, M2,0. As shown in the detection results in Fig. 5, it can accurately extract the contour of the countersunk hole and effectively filter out the noise edge.

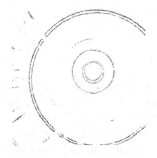

Fig. 5. Zernike moment subpixel detection result graph

The Zernike moment detection results are cut back according to the original cutting method and then restores to the original size. Mask the image with mask contour, and obtain two independent ellipse profiles, as shown in Fig. 6.

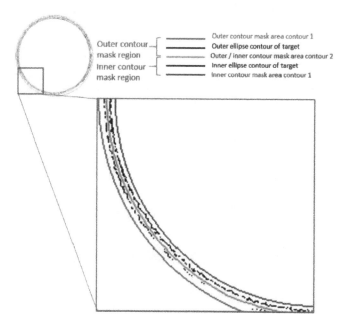

Fig. 6. Schematic diagram of the relationship between mask contour and target profile position

It can be found that the outer and inner contour masks can achieve a more accurate separation of the target ellipse ring contour. The two ellipse contour features obtained by ellipse fitting are shown in Table 4.

Table 4. Recognition of ellipse features after contour fitting by Zernike moment

Px/Pixels	Py/Pixels	Ls/Pixels	Ll/Pixels	R/Degree
873.34	556.73	381.99	382.84	58.29
872.61	556.91	370.53	370.87	76.96

For the inner hole of the static contact, the contour of its elliptical ring is concentric in theory. Given this context, the identification accuracy can be judged according to the difference of the center and angle of the two identified contours. As can be seen from Table 4, the coordinate of the center point of the ellipse contour obtained by Zernike moment detection and fitting has a large difference on the X-axis and a small difference on the Y-axis. The rotation angle has a small difference compared with the direct adaptive threshold segmentation method, which is closer to the actual circular contour.

To obtain a more accurate ellipse contour, an ellipse contour searching method is designed based on the Snake model. It iterates through an initial contour to find a more accurate target contour nearby. The cost function is the energy function defined by the snake model. $I(X, Y)$, $C(q) = C(x(q), y(q))$ is the evolution curve of an image. The energy of the evolution curve is defined as:

$$E(c) = E_{int} + E_{ext} \tag{3}$$

where E_{int} is the internal energy function and E_{ext} is the external energy function. The smallest $E(c)$ satisfies

$$\inf_{c \in C} J(c) = \alpha \int_a^b \left(|c'(q)|^2 \, dq \right) + \beta \int_a^b \left(|c''(q)|^2 \, dq \right) + \int_a^b (E_{ext}(c(q)) \, dq) \tag{4}$$

Combining the Euler-Lagrange formula of curve $C(q)$ with the Euler-Lagrange formula of (2) can obtain:

$$- ac''(q) + \beta c^{(4)}(q) + \nabla E_{ext} = 0 \tag{5}$$

By combining (4) and (5), the iterative evolution mode of the curve is shown in

$$\begin{cases} \frac{\partial c(q,t)}{\partial t} = F_{int} + F_{ext} \\ c(q, 0) = c_0(q) \\ c(a, t) = c(b, t) \end{cases} \tag{6}$$

The initial evolution curve of Snake is set as the ellipse contour detected by Zernike moment. The target contour is obtained through the iterative evolution based on the Snake algorithm, and the final elliptical contour is shown in Table 5.

Table 5. Snake model to extract ellipse feature of contour fitting

Px/Pixels	Py/Pixels	Ls/Pixels	Ll/Pixels	R/Degree
872.82	556.40	385.14	385.30	50.64
872.26	556.56	370.60	370.83	55.68

It can be seen from Table 5 that the center point of the ellipse obtained by fitting the two groups of contour data is almost the same. The rotation angle is also slightly different. Compared with the Zernike moment detection method, this method has higher detection accuracy.

After obtaining two sets of ellipse contours, the thinning algorithm is used to extract the middle contour. The refined contour is fitted to get the final target ellipse contour, as shown in Table 6.

Table 6. Feature extraction of target ellipse after thinning

Px/Pixels	Py/Pixels	Ls/Pixels	Ll/Pixels	R/Degree
872.69	556.40	378.65	379.02	30.62

3   Ellipse Correction Based on Inverse Perspective Transformation

Generally speaking, the initial circular contour will undergo perspective transformation to become an elliptical contour since the camera and the initial circular contour are not parallel. This leads to the problem that there is no feature point for pose estimation. In this section, an ellipse correction method is proposed based on inverse perspective transformation. Firstly, the pose transformation matrix of the camera installation position and the ideal position is obtained through the calibration of the camera installation position. The ideal position is parallel to the camera plane and the object plane. Then the inverse perspective transformation matrix is obtained. Then the approximate circular contour is obtained by inverse transformation of the ellipse contour. The center and endpoints of the circular contour are selected as feature points to realize pose estimation.

3.1   Solving Inverse Perspective Transformation Matrix

In this paper, the installation position calibration is designed, and the correction perspective transformation matrix of the camera installation position and ideal position is solved. To obtain the relationship between the ellipse contour before and after the perspective transformation, the rotation matrix of the calibration matrix is set as the unit matrix, and the perspective transformation matrix is obtained after correction. Through the perspective transformation matrix before and after correction, four groups of points are selected to obtain the coordinates. Thus, the image coordinate relations before and after perspective transformation can be solved to realize ellipse correction.

Through camera position calibration, the rotation matrix R_C and translation matrix T_C are obtained.

$$R_c = \begin{bmatrix} 0.9999 & 2.8575e-06 & 1.8126e-03 \\ 3.7777e-06 & 0.9999 & -3.6606e-03 \\ -1.812e-03 & 3.6606e-03 & 0.9999 \end{bmatrix}$$

$$T_C = \begin{bmatrix} 2.2863 \\ -4.7803 \\ 67.2903 \end{bmatrix}$$

The general perspective transformation is shown as follows

$$\begin{bmatrix} x \\ y \\ z \end{bmatrix} = \begin{bmatrix} a_{11} & a_{12} & a_{13} \\ a_{21} & a_{22} & a_{23} \\ a_{31} & a_{32} & a_{33} \end{bmatrix} \begin{bmatrix} u \\ v \\ 1 \end{bmatrix} \tag{7}$$

where u and v are the pixel coordinates of the original image, respectively, x, y, and z are the three-dimensional coordinates after the perspective transformation, $x/z, y/z$ are the two-dimensional coordinates after the perspective transformation, $\begin{bmatrix} a_{11} & a_{12} & a_{13} \\ a_{21} & a_{22} & a_{23} \\ a_{31} & a_{32} & a_{33} \end{bmatrix}$ is the perspective transformation matrix, $\begin{bmatrix} a_{11} & a_{12} \\ a_{21} & a_{22} \end{bmatrix}$ represents the image linear transformation matrix, $\begin{bmatrix} a_{31} & a_{32} \end{bmatrix}$ is the image translation matrix.

Table 7. World coordinate system point coordinates

Point number	1	2	3	4
X coordinate	17.5	0	−17.5	0
Y coordinate	0	17.5	0	−17.5

Four groups of points in the world coordinate system are selected as shown in Table 7. Before and after ellipse correction, there is a set of pose transformation matrices respectively. In the corrected rotation matrix and pose transformation matrix, the difference lies in the identity matrix. The unit matrix means that no rotation occurs and it is parallel. Before the correction, M is the pose transformation matrix obtained by calibration, i.e.,

$$M = \begin{bmatrix} 0.9999 & 2.85e-06 & 1.81e-03 & 2.276 \\ 3.7e-06 & 9.99e-01 & -3.6e-03 & -4.789 \\ -1.8e-03 & 3.66e-03 & 9.9e-01 & 67.29 \end{bmatrix} \tag{8}$$

The corrected matrix is shown in (9).

$$M_C = \begin{bmatrix} 1 & 0 & 0 & 2.27619614 \\ 0 & 1 & 0 & -4.78912334 \\ 0 & 1 & 1 & 67.29001199 \end{bmatrix} \tag{9}$$

The coordinates of the midpoint in Table 7 are multiplied by M_b and M_a to obtain the pixel coordinates before and after correction. The inverse perspective transformation matrix M is obtained by four groups of pixel coordinates before and after correction, i.e.,

$$M = \begin{bmatrix} 9.988e-01 & 3.407e-03 & -4.216e-01 \\ -1.203e-03 & 1.00e+00 & -3.012e-01 \\ -1.989e-06 & 4.014e-06 & 1.000e+00 \end{bmatrix} \tag{10}$$

3.2 Ellipse Correction and Pose Estimation

To realize ellipse pose estimation, it is necessary to find the feature points of the actual 3D model and those corresponding to the 2D image. By transforming the original image, the approximate circular contour is obtained through the inverse perspective transformation matrix. At this time, the center point of the circular contour corresponds to the center point of the 3D model. The ellipse pose estimation is realized through the coordinates of the center point and the endpoint.

The single-pixel ellipse contour obtained in Table 6 is corrected by inverse perspective transformation. The ellipse features obtained by fitting are shown in Table 8.

Table 8. Recognition of ellipse features after contour fitting by Zernike moment

Trans	Px/Pixels	Py/Pixels	Ls/Pixels	Ll/Pixels	R/Degree
Before	873.34	556.73	381.99	382.84	58.29
After	872.61	556.91	370.53	370.87	76.96

The PnP algorithm [11] is used to realize pose estimation. The endpoints of the horizontal and vertical axes and the center of the circle of the circular contour are selected as feature points for pose estimation.

The center coordinates of the circular contour are $[821.25, 620.02]$ and the radius is 378.64. The coordinates of the pixels to be matched are $[821.25, 620.02]$, $[821.25, 241.38]$, $[821.25, 998.66]$, $[1199.89, 620.02]$, $[442.61, 620.02]$. The actual coordinates of the 3D object are $[[0, 0, 0], [0, -17.5, 0], [0, 17.5, 0], [17.5, 0, 0], [-17.5, 0, 0]]$.

The transformation matrix T between the camera and the static contact is calculated by the solvent method

$$T = \begin{bmatrix} X_{Phase-staticcontact} \\ Y_{Phase-staticcontact} \\ Z_{Phase-staticcontact} \end{bmatrix} = \begin{bmatrix} 2.27619614 \\ -4.63912334 \\ 84.18001199 \end{bmatrix}$$

The rotation vector R is as follows:

$$R = \begin{bmatrix} 5.97577166e - 03 \\ -3.56256301e - 03 \\ 1.98851307e - 05 \end{bmatrix}$$

By combining the geometric dimensions of the moving and static contacts of the circuit breaker, the deviations in X, Y, and Z directions are obtained, as shown in Table 9.

It can be found from Table 9 that the errors in X, Y, and Z directions are less than 0.2 mm, which conforms to the theoretical state at the beginning of meshing.

Table 9. Recognition of ellipse features after contour fitting by Zernike moment

Classification of dynamic and static contact deviation	Results (mm)
X direction	−0.01
Y direction	0.14
Z direction	0.11

4 Experimental Results and Analysis

A switchgear experimental platform is built to verify the accuracy of meshing state detection, as shown in Fig. 7. The actual depth is obtained through scratch measurement. The resin is smeared on the static contact, and the measured scratches are taken out as the actual depth after meshing. Since there is no accurate verification method for moderate deviation, the method of measuring repeated positioning accuracy is adopted to verify the moderate deviation. By constantly pushing the moving contact handcart, the moderate deviation positioning accuracy is measured by changing state, since moderate deviation does not change with the increase of meshing depth in general.

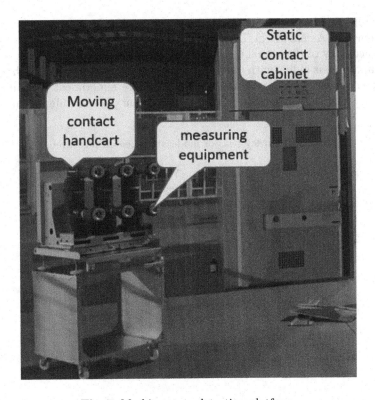

Fig. 7. Meshing state detection platform

The experimental results are shown in Table 10. From the analysis of the experimental results, it can be seen that the error range between the actual meshing depth and the measuring engagement is within ±0.5 mm which is in line with the required accuracy of ±2.5 mm.

Table 10. Comparative test of meshing depth

Serial number	Ad(mm)	Md(mm)	Error(mm)	Speed(times/s)
1	14.7	15.2	0.5	1.2
2	14.8	15.2	0.4	1.0
3	16.0	15.8	−0.2	0.9
4	17.3	17.0	−0.3	1.0
5	18.0	17.5	−0.5	1.1
6	18.1	18.4	0.3	1.3
7	20.7	20.3	−0.4	0.9

Where A_d is the actual meshing depth, and M_d is the Measuring engagement depth.

The repeated positioning accuracy is used to verify the accuracy of moderate measurements. As shown in Table 11, it can be found that the repeated positioning accuracy of the actual measurement of moderate measurements is about ±0.3 mm, which is in line with the experimental environment of actual changes in the measurement of moderate measurements. These experimental results prove the effectiveness of this method for the measurement of center alignment degree.

Table 11. Accuracy test for moderate repeated measurement

Serial number	Measurement alignment $X/Y(mm)$	Measuring engagement depth(mm)	Error(mm)
1	3.2/3.5	15.2	0.0/0.0
2	3.0/3.8	15.2	−0.2/0.3
3	3.1/3.5	15.8	−0.1/0.0
4	2.9/3.2	17.0	−0.3/−0.3
5	3.5/3.5	17.5	0.3/0.0
6	3.2/3.5	18.4	0.0/0.0
7	3.2/3.8	20.3	0.0/0.3

5   Conclusion

To solve the problem of target contour extraction and feature point matching for elliptical ring pose estimation, a contour extraction method based on Snake, and an ellipse correction method based on inverse perspective transform are proposed in this paper. Compared with the traditional binary contour extraction methods, the contour extracted by this method is close to the contour features of the elliptical ring. The ellipse correction based on inverse perspective transform is used to estimate the ellipse contour with high accuracy. At the same time, the validity and application prospect of the method is verified by the dynamic and static contacts of switchgear as the experimental object.

References

1. Chen, H., Sun, Y., Gong, Y., Huang, L.: Visual measurement and data analysis of pool boiling on silicon surfaces. J. Chem. Ind. Eng. **90**, 1309–1317 (2019)
2. Chen, P., Huangfu, D., Luo, Z., Li, D.: Visualization analysis of learning attention based on single-image PnP head posture estimation. J. Commun. **39**, 141–150 (2018)
3. Ghosal, S., Mehrotra, R.: Orthogonal moment operators for subpixel edge detection. Pattern Recogn. **26**(2), 295–306 (1993)
4. Hsia, C.H., Lin, T.Y., Chiang, J.S.: An adaptive binarization method for cost-efficient document image system in wavelet domain. J. Imaging Sci. Technol. **64**(3), 30401-1–30401-14 (2020)
5. Kass, M., Witkin, A., Terzopoulos, D.: Snakes: active contour models. Int. J. Comput. Vision **1**(4), 321–331 (1988)
6. Lee, D.H., Chen, P.Y., Yang, F.J., Weng, W.T.: High-efficient low-cost VLSI implementation for canny edge detection. J. Inf. Sci. Eng. **36**(3), 535–546 (2020)
7. Liu, J., Hou, S., Zhang, K., Yan, X., et al.: Vehicle distance measurement with implementation of vehicle attitude angle estimation and inverse perspective mapping based on monocular vision. Trans. Chin. Soc. Agric. Eng. **34**(13), 70–76 (2018)
8. Lyvers, E.P., Mitchell, O.R., Akey, M.L., Reeves, A.P.: Subpixel measurements using a moment-based edge operator. IEEE Trans. Pattern Anal. Mach. Intell. **11**(12), 1293–1309 (1989)
9. Shi, J., Chen, G., Shen, X.: Visual measurement system for three dimensional rotation attitudes of the air float turntable. Optik **222**, 165229 (2020)
10. Song, L., Chen, C., Chen, Z., Tan, M., Li, D.: Detection and recognition of ring coded markers. Opt. Precis. Eng. **21**(012), 3239–3247 (2013)
11. Tsai, C.Y., Hsu, K.J., Nisar, H.: Efficient model-based object pose estimation based on multi-template tracking and PnP algorithms. Algorithms **11**(8), 122 (2018)

Enhancing Aspect-Based Sentiment Classification with Local Semantic Information

Hengliang Tang, Qizheng Yin$^{(\boxtimes)}$, Liangliang Chang, Huilin Qin, and Fei Xue

School of Information, Beijing Wuzi University, Beijing 101149, China
dazhengyin@outlook.com

Abstract. The research goal of aspect-level sentiment analysis is to analyze the sentiment polarity expressed by a given sentence according to its specific aspect. The Graph Convolutional Network (GCN) model based on attention mechanism performs better among the existing solutions. This kind of method uses syntactic dependency information and semantic information to adjust and optimize attention. Still, the experimental results show that this kind of model does not perform well in complex sentences. We consider that attention mechanism is good at capturing global feature information, while Convolutional Neural Networks can effectively utilize local features. In this work, we study how to use attention mechanism and Convolutional Neural Networks to extract sentiment features better and propose a Graph Convolutional Network Model (DWGCN) of Depthwise separable convolution. Moreover, the basic design idea is to obtain syntactic dependency information utilizing graph convolution network learning and use the corresponding attention mechanisms to interact syntactic features with contextual information about word order to get semantic information. Then, we extract the emotional statement about the given Aspect-term from the semantic information. Therefore, we design a Feature extraction module based on a Depthwise separable convolution network and GLU (FMDG). To verify the effectiveness of the model, we test it on five benchmark datasets. The experimental results show that the proposed model outperforms the current relevant work in classification accuracy and generalization ability.

Keywords: Aspect-level sentiment analysis · Graph Convolutional Network · Depthwise separable convolution network

1 Introduction

Compared with general sentiment classification, aspect-level sentiment classification can provide more detailed sentiment polarity information because it aims to distinguish the sentiment polarity of one or more specific aspect words in a sentence [10,22,23]. The aspect-level sentiment analysis problem studied in this paper is to analyze the sentiment polarity of A in the semantics of sentence S,

L. Pan et al. (Eds.): BIC-TA 2021, CCIS 1566, pp. 118–131, 2022.
https://doi.org/10.1007/978-981-19-1253-5_9

given a specific aspect A of the object O described by sentence S. As shown in Fig. 1, the sentence is taken from the SemEval2014 Restaurant data set. The sentiment polarity of "CPU" and "software compatibility" mentioned in the sentence is positive and negative. Since aspect-level sentiment classification needs to match aspect words and their corresponding parts, it is more complicated than ordinary sentence-level sentiment analysis. Aspect-level sentiment classification is widely used in many fields, such as public opinion analysis, e-commerce..., and extensive attention in natural language processing (NLP).

With the development of neural networks, early aspect-level sentiment classification problems mainly use recurrent neural networks or convolutional neural network methods [5]. Such models are greatly affected by syntax analysis errors. Tang et al. discovered the effectiveness of modeling the semantic connection between context words and aspects words through research [16]. Inspired by this, they combined attention mechanisms with RNNs to model extensive attempts [6,10,11,17,22].

Although attention-based models have made significant progress in aspect-level sentiment classification tasks, because such models lack a mechanism to capture syntactic dependencies, it may cause the attention mechanism to misassign the weights of the essential relationships of words. For example, "The pizza, though server with poor service, is delicious". For the aspect word "pizza" in the absence of syntactic dependency, the attention mechanism is likely to assign a greater weight to "poor". This will cause significant interference to the classification task. In response to the above problems, Zhang et al.innovatively proposed an aspect-based GCN method (Aspect-based GCN method), which is the first to introduce syntactic dependency information in aspect-level sentiment classification tasks [24]. Figure 1 provides a syntactic dependency tree of a sentence. The dependency relationship between aspect words and related emotional semantic information can be easily obtained on the syntactic dependency tree. After syntactic dependency information was proved to be effective, it was widely used by attention mechanism, graph convolutional network, Transformer, and achieved excellent results [9,25,26].

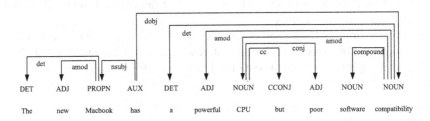

Fig. 1. An example of a syntactic dependency tree.

However, the above methods all number on the dependency information and global features between words, the above methods all focus on the dependent information between words and global features, after our experimental research, some local features of the sentence contain essential information, and Xue and Li [21] also confirmed that specific key phrases in a sentence rather than a word often determine the emotional polarity of the aspect word. When the current method applies syntactic dependency information, due to the current imperfect dependency information analysis mechanism (ignoring the relationship type of word dependency information), it is inevitable to lose some local critical information. Therefore, the improved method in this paper hopes to fully and effectively utilize the local features and global syntactic dependency features of sentences to enhance the accuracy of aspect-level sentiment classification.

In order to solve the above limitations, this paper proposes a graph convolutional network model (DWGCN) with deep separable convolution enhancement for aspect-level sentiment classification. As far as we know, this is the first method that combines the application of global syntactic dependency features with local text features and uses them efficiently. Then we further used the multi-head attention mechanism to obtain profound text semantic information through syntactic dependency features and word order context features. Finally, we cleverly designed a Feature extraction module based on a Gated linear units (GLU) and Depthwise separable convolution network (FMDG) from the profound text. Semantic information extracts local semantic information and combines the obtained local semantic features with syntactic dependent features as the final feature representation for sentiment classification.

According to the results of experiments on five benchmark test sets, DWGCN effectively solves the limitations of the current aspect-level sentiment classification method we mentioned above. The main contributions of this paper are as follows:

1. We improve the method of acquiring deep semantic features of the text. In this model, we use a multi-head attention(MHAM) mechanism to combine syntax-dependent features and word order text features to obtain deep semantic features of a text.
2. We accurately designed a local feature extraction module based on a gated linear unit (GLU) and deep separable convolutional network (FMDG). FMDG can efficiently mine local semantic features that determine emotional polarity from deep semantic features.
3. Many experiments have proved the value of the local semantic features used in this article in aspect-level sentiment classification and proved the efficiency of capturing and using local semantic features of the FMDG proposed in this paper.

2   Related Work

Recently, traditional neural networks are widely used in aspect-level sentiment classification, such as RNNs and CNN, and have achieved good results in some sentiment classification tasks [1,14,16,23]. With the in-depth study of the attention mechanism, it is found that the introduction of the attention mechanism can capture the detailed emotional characteristics related to the aspect words from the complex sentences. Some researchers use a method that combines the attention mechanism with CNN and RNNs for sequence classification tasks. [22,23] Tai et al. proposed a MemNet model based on the attention mechanism, which performs attention learning based on the external memory formed by the word vector of the input sentence [15]. Chen et al. proposed a RAM model based on the attention mechanism on the basis of movement [2]. In order to reduce the complexity of the model and consider the decisive role of local features in sentiment classification, Xue et al. proposed a model based on CNN and gate mechanism. GCN is a neural network used to process non-European data [21]. It has strong advantages for graph structure data processing in the field of natural language processing. On the other hand, the introduction of the Syntactic dependency tree also brings new ideas to researchers. Zhang et al. proposed an Aspect-specific Graph Convolutional Networks, which uses a multi-layer GCN to extract syntactic dependent features to perform sentiment classification [24]. Tang et al. used Bi-GCN to obtain the syntactic information of the dependency tree and the iterative interaction mode of the text plane representation obtained by the Transformer and proposed a Dependency Graph Enhanced Dual-transformer Structure for aspect-level sentiment classification [18].

3   Preliminaries

Since the attention mechanism [19], Deep Convolutional Neural Networks [4] and GCN [7,20] are the three key modules in DWGCN, and we will briefly introduce them here.

Attention Mechanism. Suppose there are three matrix inputs, key $K \in \mathbb{R}^{n \times d_k}$, query $K \in \mathbb{R}^{m \times d_k}$ and value $V \in \mathbb{R}^{m \times d_v}$ where n and m represent the length of these two inputs, d_k and d_v Represents the dimension size of the key and value. The attention mechanism is also equipped with multiple heads, and each head can pay attention to different position information and can also learn different features. It calculates the key and value dot product, then normalizes it through SoftMax, and finally uses the value projection (V) into the output to calculate the weighted sum:

$$Attention(Q, K, V) = softmax(\frac{QK^T}{\sqrt{d_k}})V \qquad (1)$$

Depthwise Convolutions. The deep Convolutional Neural Networks operation is similar to the conventional CNN operation and can be used to extract features efficiently, but compared with the conventional convolution operation, its parameter amount and computational cost are lower. One convolution kernel of deep convolution is responsible for one channel, and one channel is convolved by only one convolution kernel. In this way, the number of parameters can be reduced from d^2k of conventional convolution to dk, where d is the width of the convolution kernel.

$$O_{i,c} = Depthwise \quad convolutions(X, W_c, :, i, c) \tag{2}$$

$$Depthwise \quad convolutions(X, W_c, :, i, c) = \sum_{j=1}^{k} W_{c,j} \cdot X_{(i+j-\lfloor \frac{k+1}{2} \rfloor),c} \tag{3}$$

The output of the deep convolution is $O_{i,c} \in \mathbb{R}^{d \times k}$, i represents the element i, the output dimension is c, and the weight $W \in \mathbb{R}^{d \times k}$

Graph Convolutional NetworkGCN. Graph Convolutional Network is a feature extractor used to process unstructured data, and it has strong advantages for graph structure data processing in the field of natural language processing. Suppose a graph containing K nodes is given, and the adjacency matrix $A \in \mathbb{R}^{k \times k}$, h_i^l of the graph is obtained. Here, the output of node i in the i-th layer of GCN is expressed as h_i^l, h_i^l represents the initial state of node i when the first layer of GCN is input. For an l-layer GCN,$l \in [1, 2, \ldots, L]$, the final state of node i can be expressed as h_i^l. The following formula is the calculation process of graph convolution on node i.

$$h_i^l = \sigma(\sum_{j=1}^{k} A_{ij} W^l h_i^{l-1} + b^l) \tag{4}$$

Among them, W^l is the weight of the linear transformation, b^l is the deviation term, and σ represents the activation function. Commonly used activation functions such as ReLU and so on.

4   Methodology

Through in-depth research on the existing Aspect-level sentiment analysis methods based on neural networks, in this paper, we propose DWGCN, and Fig. 2 gives an overview of our proposed DWGCN network structure. The entire process of DWGCN can be divided into the steps of extracting text word order features, learning semantic features based on syntactic dependence, constructing and extracting text features based on syntactic dependence, training neural networks, and obtaining final prediction results. The first input text uses GloVe to obtain the word embedding representation. Then, Bi-LSTM is used to obtain the text word order feature H^c. In order to obtain the dependency information between sentence words, the output of Bi-LSTM and the adjacency matrix A of the syntax dependency tree is used as the input of L-layer GCN. The syntactic dependency feature H^g is obtained after tuning the self-attention mechanism. Subsequently, the MHAM is used to perform attention coding on the syntactic dependence features and the text word order features to obtain deeper text featuresH^m, and then obtain the final semantic features through DCGM. Finally,H^g and H^m are spliced to obtain the final feature representation H^f.

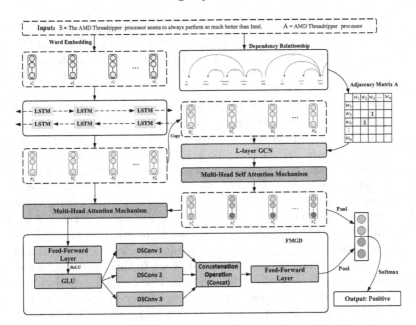

Fig. 2. An overall demonstration of DWGCN.

4.1 Embedding and Bidirectional LSTM

Given a sentence C of n words, expressed as $C = \{w_1, w_2, \ldots, w_{t+1}, \ldots, w_{t+m-1}, \ldots, w_n\}$, which contains m aspect words, t is the mark of the beginning of the aspect word. The subsequent word embedding operation maps the words in the sentence to the high dimensional vector space. In this paper, we use the pre-trained embedding matrix GloVe to obtain the word embedding vector of the word. The embedding vector of the input sentence is expressed as $E \in \mathbb{R}^{N \times d_{emb}}$, N represents the number of words, and d_emb represents the dimension of the word embedding vector. Then input the word vector of the sentence into a Bi-LSTM (bidirectional LSTM) to construct a hidden state vector matrix containing the word order feature of the text $H^c = \{h_1^c, h_2^c, \ldots, h_{t+1}^c, \ldots, h_{t+m-1}^c, \ldots, h_n^c\}$, where the hidden state vector at time step t is expressed as $h_t^c \in \mathbb{R}^{2d_h}$, d_h is the dimension of the hidden state vector output by the one-way LSTM.

4.2 Obtaining Semantic Information

In this paper, we plan to capture the local semantic features that determine the emotional polarity of the terms in the deep semantic features that combine syntactically dependent information. Therefore, in this part, we obtain deep semantic features by applying an L-Layer GCN and MHAM. First, the output of Bi-LSTM and the adjacency matrix A of the syntax-dependent tree is used as the input of L-layer GCN, and the syntax-dependent feature H^g is obtained after tuning by the self-attention mechanism. Subsequently, the MHAM is used to perform attention coding on the syntactic dependence features and the text word order features to obtain deeper text features H^m, and then obtain the final semantic features through DCGM. Finally, H^g and H^m are spliced to obtain the final feature representation H^f.

As mentioned above, in order to obtain the deep semantic features combined with syntactic dependence information, we apply an L-Layer GCN on the syntactic dependence tree. It is worth noting that the method of applying GCN to the syntactic dependency tree is proposed by Zhang et al. Specifically, given a sentence and constructs a syntactic dependency tree of the sentence, and we can easily get the adjacency matrix $A \in \mathbb{R}^{n \times n}$ for each word in the sentence according to the syntactic dependency tree, n represents the number of words in the sentence. In addition, according to the self-circulation thought of Kipf and Welling (2017), each word is manually set to be adjacent to itself, that is, the diagonal value of A is 1. Since graph convolution encodes the information of each node's neighbor nodes, the L-Layer GCN set in this paper can make each node be affected by L times of neighbor nodes. This method convolves the syntactic dependency tree, adds the syntactic dependency information to the text features of the word order, and realizes the collection of the syntactic dependency features. We have improved a method of combining GCN and multi-head self-attention applied to the syntactic dependency tree to obtain grammatical information.

First, input H^o into L-Layer GCN, that is $H^o = H^c$. The purpose of this step is to make the node aware of the context. Then use the normalization factor to perform the graph convolution operation, as follows:

$$\widetilde{h}_i^l = \sum_{j=1}^{n} A_{ij} W^l x_j^{l-1} \tag{5}$$

$$h_i^l = ReLU(\frac{\widetilde{h}_i^l}{d_i + 1} + b^l) \tag{6}$$

Where $x_j^{l-1} \in \mathbb{R}^{2d_n}$ represents the representation of the j-th token's evolved from the previous GCN layer, and $h_i^l \in \mathbb{R}^{2d_n}$ represents the current GCN The calculation result of the layer. $d_i = \sum_{j=1}^{n} A_{ij}$ is the degree of the i-th token in the syntactic dependency tree. The weight W^l and the bias b^l are trainable parameters.

It is worth noting that, considering the importance of context words similar to aspect words, we perform position-aware transformation before sending h_i^l to the next layer each time, as follows:

$$x_j^l = F(h_i^l) \tag{7}$$

Among them, $F(\cdot)$ is a function for assigning position weights to context words, and the purpose is to reduce the noise and deviation that naturally occur in the process of relying on parsing. The specific form of the position weight function $F(\cdot)$ is as follows:

$$q_i = \begin{cases} 1 - \frac{\tau+1-i}{n} & 1 \leq i \leq \tau+1 \\ 0 & \tau+1 \leq i \leq \tau+m \\ 1 - \frac{i-\tau-m}{n} & \tau+m \leq i \leq n \end{cases} \tag{8}$$

$$F(h_i^l) = q_i h_i^l \tag{9}$$

Among them, $q_i \in \mathbb{R}$ is the position weight of the i-th tag. The final result of L-layer GCN is $H^L = \{h_1^l, h_2^l, \ldots, h_{t+1}^l, \ldots, h_{t+m-1}^l, \ldots, h_n^l\}$ Then input H^L to the multi-head self-attention mechanism (MHSA)layer for attention coding to obtain the syntax-dependent coding H^{L_a}. The MHSA is a situation where the key and the value are equal, which is specifically defined as the following formula.

$$H^{L_a} = MHSA(H^L, H^L) = (head_1 \oplus head_2 \oplus \ldots \oplus head_n) \cdot W_m \tag{10}$$

$$head_i = Attention(H^L, H^L) \tag{11}$$

$$Attention(H^L, H^L) = softmax(\frac{H^L H^{L^T}}{\sqrt{d_K}})H^L \tag{12}$$

Where $head_i$ represents the definition of the i-th head in MHSA, $i \in [1, 2, \cdots, n]$, The self-attention codes obtained by each head are grouped together by means of vector splicing, and $\oplus$ represents vector splicing. W_m is a matrix of trainable parameters.

Get syntax dependent coding $H^{L_a} = \{h_1^{l_a}, h_2^{l_a}, \ldots, h_{t+1}^{l_a}, \ldots, h_{t+m-1}^{l_a}, \ldots, h_n^{l_a}\}$, where $h_i^{l_a} \in \mathbb{R}^{2d_h}$. At last, we use the syntax-dependent coding H^{L_a} obtained above and the semantic feature H^c of the text containing the word order through Multi-Head Interactive Attention (MHSA) coding to obtain the deep semantic features that merge the syntax dependency H^d. Multi-Head Interactive Attention is an attention mechanism with $K \neq Q$. Its definition is similar to MHSA. Finally, we get the deep semantic features $H^d = \{h_1^d, h_2^d, \ldots, h_{t+1}^d, \ldots, h_{t+m-1}^d, \ldots, h_n^d\}$,where $h_i^d \in \mathbb{R}^{2d_h}$.

4.3   FMDG: Obtaining Local Semantic Information

In this part, we designed a Feature extraction module based on a Gated linear units (GLU) and Depthwise separable convolution network. As shown in Fig. 2, first, we apply a feedforward network from dimension d to dimension 2d in this module, and then apply a gated linear unit (GLU). GLU uses CNN and gating mechanism to keep the information strictly according to the time sequence position when processing time-series data, thereby improving performance and can use parallel computing to increase the calculation speed. Then we applied three deep separable convolutional networks with three convolution kernel widths of 3, 5, and 7, each of these three deep separable convolutional networks has 6 layers, each of which is used after the deep convolutional network A layer of the point-by-point convolutional network. We hope that the deep convolutional network using three different convolution kernels can capture local semantic information of different sizes. Next, the outputs of the three depth separable convolutional networks are combined by splicing, and finally, the dimension is converted to dimension d through another feedforward network.

First input H^d into the feedforward network, and convert the dimension d to dimension 2d.

$$H^{d_l} = linear(H^d) = W_{l1}H^{d^T} + b_{l1} \tag{13}$$

Followed by a linear gating unit, the following is the calculation process of this layer, where W_G and V_G are two convolution kernel parameters, and b_G and c_G are bias parameters.

$$H^G = GLU(H^{d_l}) \tag{14}$$

$$GLU(H^{d_l}) = (H^{d_l} + b_G) \otimes \sigma(H^{d_l}V_G + C_G)) \tag{15}$$

The specific meaning is that H^{d_l} is processed by the convolution of the parameters W_G and b_G, and then the final output H^G is controlled by the convolution processed and activated outputs of V_G and c_G.

Then input H^G into three depth separable convolutional networks, and their convolution kernel widths are 3, 5, and 7, respectively. The specific definition of deep convolutional network is as follows:

$$h^{N_d} = Depthwise \quad convolutions(h^G, W_C, :, i, c) \tag{16}$$

$$Depthwise \quad convolutions(H^{(G)}, W_c, :, i, c) = \sum_{j=1}^{k} W_{c,j} \cdot h^G_{(i+j-\lceil \frac{k+1}{2} \rceil),c} \tag{17}$$

Where i represents the elementi, the output dimension is c, and W is the weight matrix.

After each layer of deep convolutional network, there is a layer of point-by-point convolution, and the size of the convolution kernel of point-by-point convolution is 1. Specifically defined as:

$$h_i^{N_p} = PWC(h_i^{N_d}) = \sigma(h_i^{N_d} \times w_{pwc} + b_{bwc}) \tag{18}$$

Then stitch the outputs of the three deep separable networks:

$$H^N = [H_1^{N_P} \oplus H_2^{N_P} \oplus H_3^{N_P}] \tag{19}$$

The output of the depth convolution obtained by splicing $H^N = \{h_1^N, h_2^N, \ldots, h_{t+1}^N, \ldots, h_{t+m-1}^N, \ldots, h_n^N\}$, $h_i^N \in \mathbb{R}^{6d_h}$. Finally, a feedforward network maps H^N from dimension $6d_h$ to $2d_h$ to obtain the final local semantic coding $H^N = \left\{h_1^f, h_2^f, \ldots, h_{t+1}^f, \ldots, h_{t+m-1}^f, \ldots, h_n^f\right\}$, $h_i^f \in \mathbb{R}^{6d_h}$.

4.4 Information Fusion

First, the local semantic feature H^f and the syntax dependent feature H^{L_a} are averagely pooled:

$$H_{avg}^f = \sum_{i=1}^{n} H_i^f / n \tag{20}$$

$$H_{avg}^{L_a} = \sum_{i=1}^{n} H_i^{L_a} / n \tag{21}$$

Then they are spliced to get the final representation r:

$$r = [H_{avg}^f \bigoplus H_{avg}^{L_a}] \tag{22}$$

4.5 Sentiment Classification

The final feature representation H^f is fed to the fully connected layer, followed by the SoftMax normalization layer, and finally the emotional polarity decision space of the probability distribution $P \in \mathbb{R}^{d_p}$ s generated.

$$P = softmax(W_p r + b_p) \tag{23}$$

Among them, d_p has the same dimension as the emotion label, the learning weight is expressed as $W_p \in \mathbb{R}^{d_p \times 2d_h}$, and the bias is expressed as $b_p \in \mathbb{R}d_p$.

4.6 Training

The DWGCN proposed in this paper is trained using the standard gradient descent algorithm of cross-entropy loss and L2 regularization.

$$Loss = -\sum_{(c,p)} \log P_{\widetilde{p}} + \lambda \|\theta\|_2 \tag{24}$$

5 Experiments

5.1 Dataset and Experiment Setup

The experiments in this paper are conducted on five data sets, including a Twitter data set [5], and Semeval2014 task4 [8], Semeval2015 task12 [13], and Four data sets (rest14, lap14, rest15, rest16) obtained in semeval2016 task5 [12], these four data sets are people's evaluation of laptops and restaurants. In our experiment, a 300-dimensional pre-trained GloVe vector () is used for initial word embedding. The model weight initialization is uniformly distributed. The hidden state vector is set to 300 dimensions. The model uses the Adam optimizer with a learning rate of 0.001. The coefficient of L2-regularization is 105, and the batch size is set to 32. The number of GCN layers is set to 2, which is the best performance after the study (Zhang et al.). In addition, we train the model to 30 epochs, and take the average of the results of three experiments, and each experiment uses random initialization. The evaluation indicators of the experimental results are the accuracy rate and the macro-average F1 value (Table 1).

Table 1. Dataset statistics

Dataset	Category	Pos	Neu	Neg
Twitter	Train	1561	3127	1560
	Test	173	346	173
Rest14	Train	994	464	870
	Test	341	169	128
Lap14	Train	2164	637	807
	Test	728	196	196
Rest15	Train	912	36	439
	Test	326	34	182
Rest16	Train	1240	69	439
	Test	469	30	117

5.2 Models for Comparison

In order to comprehensively evaluate and analyze our proposed model, we compare DWGCN with a series of benchmark models and the latest models (state-of-the-art models). Including LSTM, MemNet [17], AOA [6], IAN [11], CAPSNet [3], Transfer-CAPS [3], AS-CNN [24], AS-GCN [24]In order to study the role played by the key modules in the model, we set up a variant of DWGCN: DWGCN (-FMDG) means that only the multi-head attention layer is retained and FMDG is deleted.

5.3 Overall Result

As shown in Table 2, our proposed DWGCN is better than all the compared models on the five data sets, especially on the three test sets of Twitter, Lap14 and Rest14, which has achieved a great improvement. By comparing DWGCN (Attention) and DWGCN, we found that when deep semantic features are directly combined with syntactic dependent features for sentiment classification, the effect does not achieve further performance compared with AS-GCN. So we

Table 2. Comparison of the accuracy and F1 value of the model on the five data sets with the benchmark model

Model	Twitter		Lap14		Rest14		Rest15		Rest16	
	Acc	F1	Acc	F1	Acc	F1	Acc	F1	Acc	F1
LSTM	69.6	67.7	69.3	63.1	78.1	67.5	77.4	55.2	86.8	63.9
MemNet	71.5	69.9	70.6	65.2	79.6	69.6	77.3	58.3	85.4	66.0
AOA	72.3	70.2	72.6	67.5	80.0	70.4	78.2	57.0	87.5	66.2
IAN	72.5	70.8	72.1	67.4	79.3	70.1	78.6	52.7	84.7	55.2
AS-CNN	73.0	71.4	74.6	70.1	80.4	71.0	78.5	59.5	87.4	64.6
CAPSNet	–	–	72.7	68.8	78.8	69.7	–	–	–	–
Transfer-CAPS	–	–	73.9	70.2	79.3	70.9	–	–	–	–
AS-GCN	72.2	70.4	75.6	71.1	80.8	72.0	79.9	61.9	89.0	67.5
DWGCN(-FMGD)	72.03	69.87	75.24	70.21	80.59	71.69	79.05	60.08	88.64	70.76
DWGCN	**73.12**	**71.81**	**76.80**	**72.43**	**82.86**	**74.43**	**80.01**	**62.94**	**89.32**	**71.61**

can conclude: The local semantic features captured and used in this paper are of great value for improving aspect-level sentiment classification, and the local feature extraction module FMDG designed by us is efficient in extracting local semantic features.

5.4 Ablation Study

Table 2 compares the experimental effects of DWGCN (-FMDG) and DWGCN, showing the ability of FMGD to efficiently capture local semantic features. In this part, we will explore the degree of influence of each component of FMGD on performance in detail. As shown in Table 3, we use the experimental results of DWGCN (-FMDG) as the baseline and the experimental results of the ablation study as a comparison. We use -GLU to represent the deletion of GLU in FMDG; Set DWP*0, DWP*1 and DWP*2 respectively to set 0 to 2 depth separable convolutional networks.

Table 3. Ablation study results

Model	Twitter		Lap14		Rest14		Rest15		Rest16	
	Acc	F1	Acc	F1	Acc	F1	Acc	F1	Acc	F1
DWGCN	73.12	71.81	76.80	72.43	82.86	74.43	80.01	62.94	89.32	71.61
DWGCN(-FMGD)	72.03	69.87	75.24	70.21	80.59	71.69	79.05	60.08	88.64	70.76
-GLU	69.6	67.7	69.3	63.1	78.1	67.5	77.4	55.2	86.8	63.9
DWP*0	72.79	70.61	75.46	71.74	80.94	72.50	78.61	61.27	89.21	71.43
DWP*1	72.36	71.04	75.69	72.03	81.62	72.83	78.24	60.54	89.42	71.92
DWP*2	72.87	70.92	76.21	72.20	82.06	72.77	79.94	62.46	89.07	71.26

The results of ablation experiments confirmed the rationality of the various components of FMGD and the excellent performance of the module in capturing local features.

6   Conclusion

Through the research of Aspect-level sentiment classification models in recent years, we found that the information in local semantic information has excellent value for emotion classification. Therefore, we tried a new network to capture and use deep local semantic information. We have conducted good experiments on five data sets. The experimental results prove that the FMDG we designed can efficiently capture and utilize local semantic information and improve the overall performance.

In future work, we will improve our method from the following two aspects. First, we consider reducing the trainable parameters of FMDG to reduce computational complexity while improving performance. Then, we hope to study how to use tag information of syntactic dependency.

References

1. Castellucci, G., Filice, S., Croce, D., Basili, R.: UNITOR: aspect based sentiment analysis with structured learning. In: Proceedings of the 8th International Workshop on Semantic Evaluation (SemEval 2014), pp. 761–767 (2014)
2. Chen, P., Sun, Z., Bing, L., Yang, W.: Recurrent attention network on memory for aspect sentiment analysis. In: Proceedings of the 2017 Conference on Empirical Methods in Natural Language Processing, pp. 452–461 (2017)
3. Chen, Z., Qian, T.: Transfer capsule network for aspect level sentiment classification. In: Proceedings of the 57th Annual Meeting of the Association for Computational Linguistics, pp. 547–556 (2019)
4. Chollet, F.: Xception: deep learning with depthwise separable convolutions. In: Proceedings of the IEEE Conference on Computer Vision and Pattern Recognition, pp. 1251–1258 (2017)
5. Dong, L., Wei, F., Tan, C., Tang, D., Zhou, M., Xu, K.: Adaptive recursive neural network for target-dependent twitter sentiment classification. In: Proceedings of the 52nd Annual Meeting of the Association for Computational Linguistics (Volume 2: Short Papers), pp. 49–54 (2014)
6. Huang, B., Ou, Y., Carley, K.M.: Aspect level sentiment classification with attention-over-attention neural networks. In: Thomson, R., Dancy, C., Hyder, A., Bisgin, H. (eds.) SBP-BRiMS 2018. LNCS, vol. 10899, pp. 197–206. Springer, Cham (2018). https://doi.org/10.1007/978-3-319-93372-6_22
7. Kipf, T.N., Welling, M.: Semi-supervised classification with graph convolutional networks. arXiv preprint arXiv:1609.02907 (2016)
8. Kirange, D., Deshmukh, R.R., Kirange, M.: Aspect based sentiment analysis SemEval-2014 task 4. Asian J. Comput. Sci. Inf. Technol. (AJCSIT) **4**, 72–75 (2014)

9. Li, R., Chen, H., Feng, F., Ma, Z., Wang, X., Hovy, E.: Dual graph convolutional networks for aspect-based sentiment analysis. In: Proceedings of the 59th Annual Meeting of the Association for Computational Linguistics and the 11th International Joint Conference on Natural Language Processing (Volume 1: Long Papers), pp. 6319–6329 (2021)

10. Liu, J., Zhang, Y.: Attention modeling for targeted sentiment. In: Proceedings of the 15th Conference of the European Chapter of the Association for Computational Linguistics: Volume 2, Short Papers, pp. 572–577 (2017)

11. Ma, D., Li, S., Zhang, X., Wang, H.: Interactive attention networks for aspect-level sentiment classification. arXiv preprint arXiv:1709.00893 (2017)

12. Pontiki, M., et al.: SemEval-2016 task 5: aspect based sentiment analysis. In: International Workshop on Semantic Evaluation, pp. 19–30 (2016)

13. Pontiki, M., Galanis, D., Papageorgiou, H., Manandhar, S., Androutsopoulos, I.: SemEval-2015 task 12: aspect based sentiment analysis. In: Proceedings of the 9th International Workshop on Semantic Evaluation (SemEval 2015), pp. 486–495 (2015)

14. Rakhlin, A.: Convolutional neural networks for sentence classification. GitHub (2016)

15. Tai, K.S., Socher, R., Manning, C.D.: Improved semantic representations from tree-structured long short-term memory networks. arXiv preprint arXiv:1503.00075 (2015)

16. Tang, D., Qin, B., Feng, X., Liu, T.: Effective LSTMs for target-dependent sentiment classification. arXiv preprint arXiv:1512.01100 (2015)

17. Tang, D., Qin, B., Liu, T.: Aspect level sentiment classification with deep memory network. arXiv preprint arXiv:1605.08900 (2016)

18. Tang, H., Ji, D., Li, C., Zhou, Q.: Dependency graph enhanced dual-transformer structure for aspect-based sentiment classification. In: Proceedings of the 58th Annual Meeting of the Association for Computational Linguistics, pp. 6578–6588 (2020)

19. Vaswani, A., et al.: Attention is all you need. arXiv preprint arXiv:1706.03762 (2017)

20. Wang, X., et al.: Heterogeneous graph attention network. In: The World Wide Web Conference, pp. 2022–2032 (2019)

21. Xue, W., Li, T.: Aspect based sentiment analysis with gated convolutional networks. arXiv preprint arXiv:1805.07043 (2018)

22. Yang, M., Tu, W., Wang, J., Xu, F., Chen, X.: Attention based LSTM for target dependent sentiment classification. In: Proceedings of the AAAI Conference on Artificial Intelligence, vol. 31 (2017)

23. Zeng, J., Ma, X., Zhou, K.: Enhancing attention-based LSTM with position context for aspect-level sentiment classification. IEEE Access **7**, 20462–20471 (2019)

24. Zhang, C., Li, Q., Song, D.: Aspect-based sentiment classification with aspect-specific graph convolutional networks. arXiv preprint arXiv:1909.03477 (2019)

25. Zhao, W., Zhao, Y., Lu, X., Qin, B.: An aspect-centralized graph convolutional network for aspect-based sentiment classification. In: Wang, L., Feng, Y., Hong, Yu., He, R. (eds.) NLPCC 2021. LNCS (LNAI), vol. 13029, pp. 260–271. Springer, Cham (2021). https://doi.org/10.1007/978-3-030-88483-3_20

26. Zhu, X., Zhu, L., Guo, J., Liang, S., Dietze, S.: GL-GCN: global and local dependency guided graph convolutional networks for aspect-based sentiment classification. Expert Syst. Appl. **186**, 115712 (2021)

A Chinese Dataset Building Method Based on Data Hierarchy and Balance Analysis in Knowledge Graph Completion

Yunwei Shi, Kuangrong Hao$^{(\boxtimes)}$, Xuesong Tang, and Tong Wang

Donghua University, Shanghai, China
krhao@dhu.edu.cn

Abstract. This paper mainly studies the problem of knowledge graph completion. After analyzing the characteristics of the English dataset of knowledge graph, it is pointed out that many triples are meaningless. At the same time, it is found that there is no good construction method for the Chinese dataset. Then, based on two metrics, the method to create a Chinese dataset is proposed, and two Chinese data subsets are then created, which can well represent the special relations and the overall hierarchy of the dataset. Then, by selecting the existing model, it is concluded that the effect of the created Chinese datasets is better than the effect of the existing English datasets. At the same time, it is found that the uneven amount of data in the dataset may affect the accuracy of the model. Experiments results can conclude that when the amount of data is more uneven, the accuracy of the model will be worse.

Keywords: Knowledge graph completion · Chinese dataset building · ATTH

1 Introduction

Semantic web is made up of a lot of semantic data [1]. It provides semantic understanding of what people look up on the Internet and returns information they want to know, and knowledge graph is a technology to help semantic web understand. The concept of knowledge graph was proposed by Google Company. It is a structured semantic knowledge base that describes concepts and their interrelations through semantic information [2]. The basic unit of knowledge graph is the triple (head entity, relation entity, tail entity), and the entities are connected with each other through relations to form a networked knowledge structure. Through knowledge graph, web links can be transformed from web pages to conceptual links, so that users can accurately locate and acquire knowledge without browsing a lot of web pages.

Since the number of entities and relations in the knowledge graph is limited, there may be some entities and relations not in the knowledge base, which leads to the completion task of the knowledge graph. The main goal of the knowledge graph completion task is to predict the missing part of the triple and make the knowledge graph more complete. According to the specific prediction objects in the triple, the knowledge graph completion

© Springer Nature Singapore Pte Ltd. 2022
L. Pan et al. (Eds.): BIC-TA 2021, CCIS 1566, pp. 132–141, 2022.
https://doi.org/10.1007/978-981-19-1253-5_10

task can be divided into three sub-tasks: head entity prediction, tail entity prediction and relation prediction. For the head entity prediction, the tail entities and their relations of the triples should be given. For tail entity prediction, we need to give the head entity and the relation of the triple, and then predict the entities that can form the correct triple. For relation prediction, it is given the header and tail entities, and then predicts the possible relation between the two entities.

In recent years, through the research of many scholars, the effect of knowledge graph completion has been continuously improved and developed. On the traditional model, [3] proposes a model to deal with multiple relation data. Based on the distributed vector representation of entities and relations, the TransE model ensures that the addition of the header and the relation vector is as equal as possible to the tail entity vector. [4] believes that different relations should focus on different attributes of entities and have different semantic spaces. [5] presents an idea to solve the heterogeneity and imbalance of entities and relations in knowledge graph by using sparse matrix instead of dense matrix in the original model. [6] thinks to use Gaussian distribution to represent entities and relations to deal with the uncertainty inherent in the semantics of relations and entities in the knowledge graph. [7] puts forward a new linear model to learn the knowledge graph representation, using the core tensor scale to measure the interaction level between the elements of the triple by using the mathematical Tucker decomposition. [8] adopts the method of mapping triples to complex vector space. On the neural network model, a new graph convolution network is proposed, which defines a different weight for different relations, and transforms a multi-graph into several single graphs with different strength relations [9, 10]. In [11], a new embedded model is proposed, which is used to model triple relations by capsule network. [12] uses the method of LSTM memory gate to relearn the relation between triples.

However, although the above scholars have made great contributions to the task of knowledge graph completion, they all focus on model improvement and innovation on the basis of the existing knowledge graph dataset, without paying much attention to the possible problems in the dataset itself. Although some articles believe that the existing English datasets have unreasonable problems in the data, such as FB15k [13] and WN18 [14], but none of them analyze Chinese datasets. Moreover, it is worth affirming that both English and Chinese datasets have the problem of meaningless data and unbalanced data quantity, and they all present a tree structure. In terms of semantic richness, Chinese datasets are more polysemy hierarchical than English datasets. Therefore, a more effective method to analyze and build Chinese datasets is urgently needed. In order to solve the above problems, this paper gives a method to optimize the Chinese dataset and builds two Chinese datasets. This method is more hierarchical than other methods to build English datasets, and can better reflect the special structure of different entities and relations, which is more convenient for the subsequent processing of model completion tasks. Then, this paper uses related model to test the effect of the established Chinese datasets and the existing English datasets.

This paper consists of the following parts. Section 2 analyzes some unreasonable problems in the existing English datasets and the methods given in related articles. Section 3 introduces the method of optimizing the Chinese dataset and how to construct a Chinese dataset in detail, and then introduces related model and reason. Section 4 shows the effects of different models on the constructed Chinese dataset, and analyzes the reasons for the good and bad effects and related verification. Section 5 summarizes the main conclusions and some work that can be carried out in the future.

2 Problem Analysis

Nowadays, there are many open-source English datasets for knowledge graph completion tasks, such as FB15k and WN18, they are extracted from the huge knowledge base Freebase and WordNet through related methods, respectively. They can represent a certain knowledge graph structural, and it is widely used. But this kind of dataset is not perfect and has two problems of meaningless triples and unbalanced data volume.

2.1 Existence of Meaningless Triples

Obviously, there are a large number of reverse triples and repeated triples in the open-source English dataset. The meaning of reverse triples is that there are two triples, and the semantics expressed by their relation are opposite. [15] finds that in the FB15k test set and WN18 test set, about 70% of the reverse triples of the triples exist in the training set. However, for these triples, when one of them appears in the test set, the other There is no need for triples to appear in the test set anymore, because their reverse relation can already be determined, so the existence of such a large number of reverse triples will cause the test set and the training set to have a high similarity. It will improve the accuracy of the model in disguise.

At the same time, there is a Cartesian product relation in the dataset. For a Cartesian product relation, the head entity-tail entity pairs in the involved triples constitute the corresponding Cartesian product. For example, if there are city entity a and month entity b widely in the dataset, then for the triples (a, *climate*, b), each possible city a and month b are valid triples, because for each *climate*, different cities can be established in different months, then *climate* is a Cartesian product relation.

For such a Cartesian product relation, the problem of complementing the knowledge map becomes predicting whether a city has its climate in a certain month. The existence of these relations will improve the accuracy of the model in disguise, and such prediction tasks are of little significance. Cartesian product relations and reverse relations are both artificially constructed and widely exist in the FB15k dataset and WN18 dataset. Therefore, it is necessary to artificially delete the head and tail entity pairs that exist in these relations. This problem will cause the existing performance indicators of the embedded model to be inconsistent with reality.

2.2 Unbalanced Data Volume

In addition to the widespread existence of meaningless triples, these datasets also have the problem of uneven data volume. [15] also finds through experiments that among the 37 relations in the YAGO3-10 dataset, there are two relations, *isAffiliatedto* and *playsFor*, whose triples account for 35% and 30% of all triples, respectively, which shows that the amount of triple data contained in the other 35 relations is very different from them.

At the same time, these two relations can be regarded as the same semantic relation in semantics, and there are also problems described before.

However, the work of [15] is aimed at open-source English datasets. Currently, there is no open-source Chinese dataset. There are only some general knowledge bases similar to WordNet, such as CN-DBpedia and zhishi.me. Similarly, there is no open-source Chinese dataset after the meaningless and unreasonable relation has been eliminated. Therefore, it is necessary to propose a method that can construct a certain rigorous Chinese dataset.

3 Methods

To build a Chinese dataset, we need to structure the dataset itself, and then refer to the method of constructing the English open-source dataset for analysis and summary.

3.1 Use Indicators to Measure Dataset Structure

We use two mathematical indicators to measure the overall and local structure of the knowledge graph dataset. The indicator that can reflect the overall structure of the dataset is ξ_G, and the formula is:

$$\xi_G = \frac{d(a,m)^2 + \frac{d(b,c)^2}{4} - \frac{d(a,b)^2 + d(a,c)^2}{2}}{2d(a,m)} \tag{1}$$

where a, b, c represent the three vertices of the triangle, m represents the midpoint of the shortest distance between the two vertices b and c of the triangle. $d(\cdot)$ indicates the shortest distance between two points.

The specific principle of this formula is to use the mathematical Toponogov theorem, which can show that the smaller the negative value, the better it reflects the structure of the tree. This theorem is the parallelogram law in Euclidean space, and the value is negative in spaces with negative curvature, such as hyperbolic space.

We define a parameter to represent the weight of different triples under the same relation, this parameter is:

$$k = \frac{e^{n_i}}{\sum\limits_{i=1}^{q} e^{n_i}} \tag{2}$$

where q represents the number of all connected triples in the knowledge graph dataset, and n_i represents the number of nodes in the triple. We sample 2000 k triangles from these triples that contain this relation in the dataset. By calculating ξ_G of these 2000 k triangles, we use the average value $\overline{\xi_G}$ to represent the overall structure of the dataset under this relation.

$$\overline{\xi_G} = \frac{\sum \xi_G}{2000k} \tag{3}$$

For the entire knowledge graph dataset, we use a weighted average method to obtain the index value of the entire dataset. The weight is:

$$w = \frac{k_r}{\sum\limits_{r=1}^{p} k_r} \tag{4}$$

where p represents the number of relations in the whole dataset.

Another indicator Khs_G is used to measure whether there is a reverse relation between entities and entities within the dataset. The formula is:

$$Khs_G = \frac{\sum R_{i,j}(1 - R_{j,i})}{\sum R_{i,j}} \tag{5}$$

where i, j represent the interconnected entities. For each relation, if there is only one edge from entity i to entity j, then

$$R_{i,j} = 1 \tag{6}$$

else

$$R_{i,j} = 0 \tag{7}$$

It can be found that if there is a set of reverse relations between every two entities, then $R_{i,j} = 0$, if every two entities are connected in a one-way relation, then $R_{i,j} = 1$.

3.2 Method of Constructing Chinese Dataset

With the above indicators as the criterion, we summarize several steps to build Chinese dataset.

Table 1. Five relations.

Coupling between triple relations	Examples
Symmetric	Marriage relation
Anti-symmetric	Dependency relation
Reversed	Inclusion relation
Combined	Family relation
Independent	Ubiquitous

Firstly, we make it clear that most of the relations in the dataset are coupled. This means that they follow some kind of logical connection. The coupling relations can be divided into four categories: symmetric, anti-symmetric, reversed and combined. These four types of relations need to be focused on and obtained from the dataset for subsequent model analysis. For ease of representation, we add a class to represent relations without any coupling. These relations and corresponding examples are shown in Table 1. Then, we give the specific implementation steps. The overall step flow chart is shown in Fig. 1.

1) Find that the data library basically presents a tree structure by using $\overline{\xi_G}$,
2) Screen out entities with higher frequency,
3) Sort the results obtained by calculating the relation between the selected entities in ascending order by using $\overline{\xi_G}$ and Khs_G,
4) Extract the first 100 –200 relations and all entities corresponding to these relations,
5) Extract most symmetric, anti-symmetric, reversed or combined relations and all related head and tail entities from these relations as the final data subset.

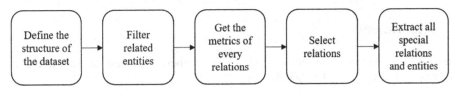

Fig. 1. Flow chart of dataset establishment steps.

3.3 Knowledge Graph Completion Model Selection

After establishing the basic steps of Chinese dataset construction, we need to use the model to verify whether the experimental effect of Chinese dataset constructed by us is better than that of English dataset.

We take the ATTH model proposed by [16] as our selected model into the task of knowledge graph completion. The ATTH model maps entities and relations in triples to hyperbolic-tangent space, and uses $Rot(\cdot)$ and $Ref(\cdot)$ to learn the coupling between different relations in triples. These two parameters were originally used to deal with the hyperbolic space to express the tangent formula, by constructing the diagonal matrix of sine and cosine, and then using the parameter matrix to map the tangent points, complete the mapping of space. $Rot(\cdot)$ can deal with anti-symmetric and combined relations, $Ref(\cdot)$ can deal with symmetric and reversed relations.

The formula related to the ATTH model is as follows.

$$q_{Rot} = Rot(\cdot)x \tag{8}$$

$$q_{Ref} = Ref(\cdot)x \tag{9}$$

where x represents the header and tail entities in triples.

$$Att(q_{Rot}, q_{Ref}, a) = \exp^c(\alpha_1 q_{Rot} + \alpha_2 q_{Ref}) \tag{10}$$

where a represents an attention vector, α_1 is the result of softmax between a and q_{Rot}, and α_2 in the same way. $\exp^c()$ represents the mathematical formula for the transformation from hyperbolic space to tangent space.

$$Q = Att(q_{Rot}, q_{Ref}, a) \oplus r \tag{11}$$

where r represents the relations in triples, $\oplus$ represents the Mobius addition. Finally, Q is put into the distance function and trained.

The reason why we choose ATTH model is that ATTH model is very sensitive to data with hierarchical structure, and it can well separate the coupling of different relations in knowledge graph dataset. Any other model is far less effective than it. The Chinese dataset we build is the dataset with this hierarchical structure, so we can observe the construction effect of Chinese dataset with this model.

4   Experiments

In this section, we need to use the model to verify whether the Chinese dataset we created is more efficient than the English dataset.

First of all, according to the method of creating Chinese dataset proposed previously, we select two general knowledge bases, one is CN-DBpedia [17], and the other is zhishi.me [18]. Then, we screen 30000 entities with high occurrence frequency, and then measure these triples according to the relation with $\overline{\xi_G}$ and Khs_G. And then we pick 200 of those relations in ascending order, then we find that in CN-DBpedia dataset, most of the 200 relations are coupled with each other, but in zhishi.me dataset, 130 of the 200 relations are uncoupled, we manually remove 54 uncoupled relations and retain 146 relations.

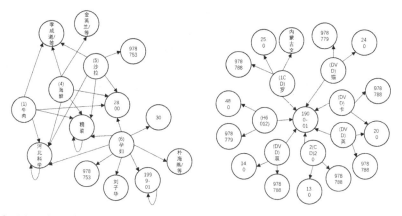

Fig. 2. The schematic diagram of the complexity of the internal relation of the Chinese dataset.

Finally, we constructed Chinese datasets CNDBp-200 and zhishi-146, the related information of the created Chinese datasets is shown in Table 2. The English datasets

Table 2. Details of datasets.

Dataset	#entities	#relations	#triples
CNDBp-200 (Chinese)	13k	200	103k
zhishi-146 (Chinese)	9k	146	85k
FB15k-237 (English)	15k	237	310k
WN18RR (English)	41k	11	93k

we selected are also shown in Table 2. The schematic diagram of CNDBp-200 dataset is shown in Fig. 2.

For the measurement index of model accuracy, we choose H@10 and MRR. H@10 checks whether the correct result of each triple in the test set is in the top ten of the sequence, and then calculate the probability that the correct result of all triples is in the top ten. MRR is an international general mechanism to evaluate search algorithms. When the rank of each result is obtained, the reciprocal of each result is calculated first and the average is calculated. The ATTH model test results are shown in Table 3.

Table 3. Test results of ATTH model on different datasets.

Dataset	MRR	H@10
CNDBp-200	0.291	0.483
zhishi-146	**0.325**	**0.494**
FB15k-237	0.307	0.49
WN18RR	0.266	0.447

From the results, we find that the ATTH model is the best on the zhishi-146 Chinese dataset and the worst on the WN18RR English dataset in H@10 index and MRR.

We notice that the effect of WN18RR is much worse than that of other datasets, which may be caused by the large difference in the amount of data between different relations in the dataset.

We also analyzed the proportion of the two relations with the largest difference in the number of relations in each dataset. The results are shown in Table 4.

Then we find that the proportion of the two groups with the largest difference in the number of relations in the WN18RR English dataset is very different from other datasets. Therefore, in order to prove that too much difference in the amount of data leads to poor model effect, we delete some triples with less relation data from our CNDBp-200 dataset to enlarge the difference, and finally maintain it at about 15:1.

Table 4. Comparison of the difference of relation data volume among different datasets.

Dataset	The proportion of the two relations with the biggest difference in quantity
CNDBp-200	3:1
FB15k-237	6:1
WN18RR	12:1

Then we use ATTH model to test again on the modified dataset, and the results are shown in Table 5.

Table 5. Comparison between the modified Chinese dataset and the original one.

Dataset	MRR	H@10
CNDBp-200	**0.291**	**0.483**
CNDBp-200(modified)	0.280	0.467

It can be apparently seen from the results that the problem of unbalanced data quantity will affect the accuracy of the model and make the accuracy worse.

5 Conclusions

This paper focuses on the completion of the knowledge graph. It first analyzes the characteristics of the English dataset of the knowledge graph, and then points out that the English dataset is unreasonable in terms of data. Many triples in the English dataset are meaningless. At the same time, it also found that although some of the problems in the English dataset have been improved by others, there is still no good way to improve the Chinese dataset. Then, on the basis of avoiding these existing problems, a method to create a Chinese dataset was given, and two Chinese data subsets were created. Then choose the ATTH model, and conclude that the effect of the Chinese dataset obtained by this method is better than that of the existing English dataset. This means that these Chinese datasets can have a better effect on the completion model. At the same time, it is found that the uneven amount of data in the dataset may affect the accuracy of the model. Through experiments it is concluded that when the amount of data is more uneven, the accuracy of the model will be worse.

The main tasks in the future are as follows. The method of dataset analysis and creation studied in this paper is relatively static, this means that adding some newly emerging entities, such as new network terms, to the existing knowledge graph dataset may have a significant impact on the completion task performance. If this method can be further improved in the future, the position and hierarchy of these newly introduced entities can be well reflected in the whole knowledge graph, and they can perform better in some intelligent scene dialogues and question answering systems. These are the contents that can continue to be studied in the future.

Acknowledgement. This work was supported in part by the Fundamental Research Funds for the Central Universities (2232021A-10, 2232021D-37), National Natural Science Foundation of China (61806051), and Natural Science Foundation of Shanghai (20ZR1400400, 21ZR1401700).

References

1. Hitzler, P.: A review of the semantic web field. Commun. ACM **64**(2), 76–83 (2021)
2. Paulheim, H.: Knowledge graph refinement: a survey of approaches and evaluation methods. Semant. Web **8**(3), 489–508 (2017)
3. Bordes, A., Usunier, N., Garcia-Duran, A., et al.: Translating embeddings for modeling multi-relational data. In: Advances in Neural Information Processing Systems, pp. 2787–2795 (2013)
4. Lin, Y., Liu, Z., Sun, M., Liu, Y., Zhu, X.: Learning entity and relation embeddings for knowledge graph completion. In: Proceedings of the AAAI Conference on Artificial Intelligence, vol. 29, no. 1, February 2015
5. Ji, G., Liu, K., He, S., Zhao, J.: Knowledge graph completion with adaptive sparse transfer matrix. In: Proceedings of the Thirtieth AAAI Conference on Artificial Intelligence (AAAI 2016), pp. 985–991. AAAI Press (2016)
6. He, S., Liu, K., Ji, G., et al.: Learning to represent knowledge graphs with Gaussian embedding. In: Proceedings of the CIKM, pp. 623–632. ACM, New York (2015)
7. Balazevic, I., Allen, C., Hospedales, T.M.: TuckER: tensor factorization for knowledge graph completion. arXiv:1901.09590 (2019). n. pag
8. Sun, Z., Deng, Z., Nie, J., Tang, J.: RotatE: knowledge graph embedding by relational rotation in complex space. arXiv:1902.10197 (2019)
9. Shang, C., Tang, Y., Huang, J., Bi, J., He X., Zhou, B.: End-to-end structure-aware convolutional networks for knowledge base completion. arXiv:1811.04441 (2019). n. pag
10. Nguyen, D.Q., Nguyen, T.D., Nguyen, D.Q., Phung, D.: A novel embedding model for knowledge base completion based on convolutional neural network. arXiv preprint arXiv:1712.02121 (2017)
11. Nguyen, D.Q., Vu, T., Dinh Nguyen, T., Phung, D.: A capsule network-based embedding model for search personalization. arXiv e-prints, arXiv-1804 (2018)
12. Santoro, A., et al.: Relational recurrent neural networks. arXiv:1806.01822 (2018)
13. Cai, H., Zheng, V.W., Chang, K.C.C.: A comprehensive survey of graph embedding: problems, techniques, and applications. IEEE Trans. Knowl. Data Eng. **30**(9), 1616–1637 (2018)
14. Chen, D., Fisch, A., Weston, J., Bordes, A.: Reading wikipedia to answer open-domain questions. arXiv preprint arXiv:1704.00051 (2017)
15. Akrami, F., Saeef, M.S., Zhang, Q., Hu, W., Li, C.: Realistic re-evaluation of knowledge graph completion methods: an experimental study. In: Proceedings of the 2020 ACM SIGMOD International Conference on Management of Data, pp. 1995–2010, June 2020
16. Chami, I., Wolf, A., Juan, D.C., Sala, F., Ravi, S., Ré, C:. Low-dimensional hyperbolic knowledge graph embeddings. arXiv preprint arXiv:2005.00545 (2020)
17. Xu, B., et al.: CN-DBpedia: a never-ending chinese knowledge extraction system. In: Benferhat, S., Tabia, K., Ali, M. (eds.) IEA/AIE 2017. LNCS, vol. 10351, pp. 428–438. Springer, Cham (2017). https://doi.org/10.1007/978-3-319-60045-1_44
18. Wu, T., Qi, G., Li, C., Wang, M.: A survey of techniques for constructing Chinese knowledge graphs and their applications. Sustainability **10**(9), 3245 (2018)

A Method for Formation Control of Autonomous Underwater Vehicle Formation Navigation Based on Consistency

Rui Wu, Xuan Guo, Hao Zhou$^{(\boxtimes)}$, Dongming Zhao, and Yunsheng Mao

School of Automation, Wuhan University of Technology, Wuhan 430000,
People's Republic of China
{233980,zhzmq,dmzhao}@whut.edu.cn

Abstract. In the process of underwater unmanned submarine operations, an important issue is formation control. In this paper, a method for formation control of AUV formation navigation based on consistency is designed, second-order kinematics model is used to describe the system, and the related knowledge of graph theory is used to express the communication network structure. The leader-follower control structure and the consistency control theory are combined, on the basis of model predictive control, a collaborative control which does not require that every unmanned submarine can receive the leader status information is proposed, so they can change the direction of travel without changing the formation during the formation navigation process. At the same time, this control algorithm also has convergence when the scale of AUV formation is large. Finally, the effectiveness of the control algorithm is verified by simulation.

Keywords: Autonomous Underwater Vehicle · Consistency control · Formation control · Model predictive control

1 Introduction

AUV is an unmanned underwater submarine that relies on its own sensors and other task modules to perform ocean reconnaissance, ocean survey, anti-submarine, mine clearance and so on. It can perform autonomous navigation and autonomous control by its own energy, navigation equipment and thrusters [1–5].

In order to solve complex marine missions, on the one hand, AUVs with stronger capabilities and more functions can be developed [6]; On the other hand, a distributed AUV group can be built through coordination and cooperation among multiple AUVs. since the 1990s, distributed AUV systems have been receiving a lot of attention. for distributed AUV formations, the core idea is to make multiple AUVs form an organic whole, and complete a given formation task through a certain collaborative strategy [7,8]. In order to solve distributed formation control problem, there are several methods: follower-navigator method [9],

© Springer Nature Singapore Pte Ltd. 2022
L. Pan et al. (Eds.): BIC-TA 2021, CCIS 1566, pp. 142–157, 2022.
https://doi.org/10.1007/978-981-19-1253-5_11

virtual structure method [10], artificial potential function [11], and analysis based on graph theory [12] to analyze and design the method of consensus agreement. Among the above control methods, the distributed consistency control of AUV formation based on graph theory has developed rapidly in recent years.

Many scholars had done a lot of research on the issue of AUV formation consistency control. A decentralized leader-follower formation structure was used in [13] to design a robust multivariable controller, which completed the horizontal formation control of the submarine formation, the effectiveness of this method was verified by experiment. A decentralized coordinated control architecture based on the concept of space-time decoupling was proposed in [14], in this method, the space path tracking task was decomposed into two parts: space path tracking and time formation coordination control. A distributed control strategy for submarine formations based on the theory of passivity and consistency theory was designed in [15, 16], the coordinated path tracking of the underwater submarine formation was realized. A method of non-linear formation keeping and parking control for submarines was proposed in [17], etc. However, the scale of AUV formation is too small in the scope of application of above methods, once the scale becomes larger, the control effect will decrease.

In this paper, the formation control problem of group AUV formation sailing is designed. Combining the consistency control theory with the leader-follower method, a consistency cooperative control algorithm is proposed, with the combination of the algorithm mentioned above and the model predictive control algorithm [18], the consistent coordinated variables are converted into the more commonly used speed, heading angle and trim angle, which improves the applicability of the consistent algorithm. The formation control algorithm proposed in this paper, compared with traditional methods, can maintain the formation during the formation sailing process, and can also change the navigation direction accordingly in the case that some AUVs cannot receive leader status information [19].

The remainder of this paper is organized into four main sections. In Sect. 2, a description of AUV formation system is presented. In Sect. 3, a formation control algorithm is designed. Section 4 contains a detailed description of the USV formation control test, the results will presented here, and the performance of the suggested method will be compared with the performance of other methods. In Sect. 5, the main conclusions is presented.

2   AUV Formation System Description

2.1   Graph Theory

Graph theory is a powerful tool to deal with consistency of multi-agent systems. If regard each AUV as a node in algebraic graph, the information connection between AUVs is an edge on the way, and the multi-AUV system is a graph. So the graph can be used to describe the information transfer relationship between AUVs.

$G = (V(G), E(G))$ is often used to define a graph, where $V(G) = \{1, ..., n\}$ represents a set of non-empty vertex nodes, $E(G) \subseteq V(G) \times V(G)$ represents a set of edges composed of pairs of nodes.

In order to describe the relationship between nodes and edges, and to characterize the information interaction topology of the multi-agent system, the adjacency matrix $A(G)$ is introduced. The values of the elements in $A(G)$ are as follows:

$$a_{kn} = \begin{cases} 1 & (v_n, v_k) \in E(G) \\ 0 & (others) \end{cases} \tag{1}$$

When G is an undirected graph, $A(G)$ is a symmetric matrix with all zeros on the main diagonal.

Generally, the weighted adjacency matrix $A_w(G)$ is defined as:

$$A_w(G) = [a_{kn}] = \begin{cases} w_{kn} & (v_n, v_k) \in E(G) \\ 0 & (others) \end{cases} \tag{2}$$

Laplacian matrix $L(G)$ is another matrix that describes the relationship between nodes and edges. Its elements have the following values:

$$l_{kn} = -a_{kn}, k \neq n, l_{kk} = \sum_{n=1}^{N} a_{kn}, k = n \tag{3}$$

The point-edge incidence matrix $I(G)$ is also a matrix similar to the Laplacian matrix $L(G)$, which is defined as follows:

$$I(G) = [i_{ke}] = \begin{cases} 1 & \text{Node } k \text{ is the end point of edge } e \\ -1 & \text{Node } k \text{ is not the end point of edge } e \\ 0 & \text{others} \end{cases} \tag{4}$$

Then another way to obtain the Laplacian matrix can be expressed: $L(G) = I(G)I^T(G)$, by weighting it, it can be obtained the weighted Laplacian matrix: $L_w(G) = I(G)WI^T(G)$, where $W = [w_{kn}]$.

2.2   Kinematic Model

The research of AUV movement includes two aspects: static and dynamic. Static refers to the stability of the equipment in a stable or uniform motion state, while dynamic is related to accelerated motion. Generally, research on dynamics is divided into two parts: the study of kinematics about geometric metric of motion and the analysis of dynamics which generate motion force [20]. Figure 1 shows an example of dynamic variables of the AUV in a fixed coordinate system and its position relative to inertial coordinate system. Table 1 is AUV motion based on the different model variables, which defined by the Society of Naval Engineers (SNAME).

The six-degree-of-freedom motion model (6DOF) [21] of AUV can be expressed as:

$$\begin{cases} \dot{\eta} = J(\eta)\nu \\ M\dot{\nu} + C(\nu)\nu + D(\nu)\nu + g(\eta) = \tau + \omega \end{cases} \tag{5}$$

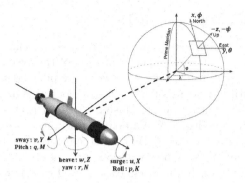

Fig. 1. Model diagram of underactuated AUV in inertial and fixed coordinates

Table 1. Symbolic representation of model

Degree of freedom	Position and Euler Angle	Linear velocity and angular velocity	Force and moment
Surging	x	u	X
Swaying	y	v	Y
Heaving	z	w	Z
Rolling	ϕ	p	K
Pitching	θ	q	M
Yawing	ψ	r	N

where $\eta \in \mathbb{R}^6$ is spatial position and posture of AUV in the fixed coordinate system. $\nu \in \mathbb{R}^6$ is linear velocity and angular velocity of the AUV in motion coordinate system. $J(\eta)$ is rotation transformation matrix from the motion coordinate system to fixed coordinate system. And M is inertia matrix of system (Including additional mass), $C(\nu)$ is Coriolis force matrix (including additional mass), $D(\nu)$ is damping matrix, $g(\eta)$ is gravity/buoyancy and moment vector, τ is thrust and moment vector, ω is external disturbance and internal disturbance.

The six-degree-of-freedom motion equation of AUV can be expressed as:

$$
\begin{aligned}
X &= m\left[\dot{u} - vr + wq - x_G\left(q^2 + r^2\right) + y_G(pq + \dot{r}) + z_G(pr + \dot{q})\right], \\
Y &= m\left[\dot{v} - wp + ur + x_G(pq + \dot{r}) - y_G\left(r^2 + p^2\right) + z_G(qr + \dot{p})\right], \\
Z &= m\left[\dot{w} - uq + vp + x_G(rp + \dot{q}) + y_G(rq + \dot{p}) - z_G\left(p^2 + q^2\right)\right], \\
K &= I_{xx}\dot{p} + \left(I_{zz} - I_{yy}\right)qr + m\left[y_G(\dot{w} - uq + vp) - z_G(\dot{v} - wp + ur)\right], \\
M &= I_{yy}\dot{q} + \left(I_{xx} - I_{zz}\right)rp + m\left[z_G(\dot{u} - vr + wq) - x_G(\dot{w} - uq + vp)\right], \\
N &= I_{zz}\dot{r} + \left(I_{yy} - I_{zz}\right)pq + m\left[x_G(\dot{v} - wp + ur) - y_G(\dot{u} - vr + wp)\right].
\end{aligned}
\tag{6}
$$

2.3   Information Interaction Model

From the existing research results, it can be seen that usually only one pilot is defined in a system, and the consistency process of the system is controlled by controlling the information interaction between the pilot boat and other AUVs. In this paper, multiple leaders-followers in topological structure are adopted, AUV group is divided into multiple clusters to form a cluster network, each cluster which includes multiple AUVs defines a leader. Moreover, it is defined that there is one and only one AUV in first cluster as virtual target, which is named virtual pilot boat. A personal computer is used on the pilot boat to simulate a virtual AUV with a mathematical model similar to the actual AUV. The dynamics and kinematics characteristics of the leader and the formation AUV are the same, and the desired speed and desired position of the follower are given as control inputs. In other words, a mixed-mode topology is designed to jointly solve the consistency problem of the AUV group system. The schematic diagram of the topology is shown in Fig. 2.

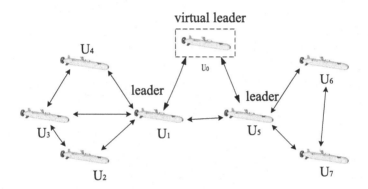

Fig. 2. Communication topology

3   Formation Control Algorithm Design

Two parts are included in AUV group collaborative control: consensus protocol control and coordinated navigation control. Coordinated navigation control is the inner loop, which is used to control the navigation attitude of the AUV. Consensus protocol control is the outer loop, which is used to control the navigation trajectory, the output of outer loop is used as the input of the inner loop. The consensus protocol control calculates the corresponding pitch angle, yaw angle, speed and other track commands, which based on predetermined navigation information and navigation information of adjacent AUVs in topology network, and then transmits them to coordinated navigation control. Algorithmically, trajectory command is introduced into information consistency as a reference state. After receiving the command, the navigation control will track the consistency control command by solving the control rudder angle and thruster.

The cooperative control structure is shown in the Fig. 3. In this work, consistency protocol is a second-order consistency control protocol, and cooperative navigation controller uses a model predictive controller.

3.1   Definition of Covariate

The control of co-variables is core content of the consistency theory, huge advantages in practical application would be obtained by choosing appropriate co-variables. Coordinated variables will all reach asymptotic consistency and stability with information consistency. Using information consistency to complete coordinated navigation, appropriate coordinated variables must be defined and selected firstly. The goal of collaboration will be achieved with controlling 6 basic state variables of AUV, its specific expression are $\xi_i = (r_i, V_i)^T, r_i = (x_i, y_i, z_i), V_i = (u_i, v_i, w_i)$. The speed of each AUV can be directly used as a coordinated variable, but the position can not, because the center of mass of each AUV cannot be overlapped when the coordinated navigation is stable. Therefore, the distance between boats requires for safe navigation and formation maintenance, which determine each position of the boat cannot be directly used as a coordinated variable. It is necessary to define a reference point to make the state of each AUV consistent.

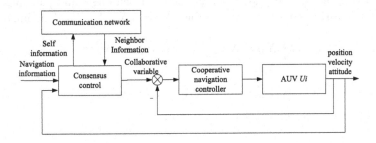

Fig. 3. Cooperative control structure

Define the location coordination variable $r_{iF} = (x_{ciF}, y_{ciF}, z_{ciF})^T$. It is calculated and generated by each AUV, the initial time is different, and the steady state has same value. The relationship between the actual position and the reference position is as follows:

$$\begin{cases} x_{ci} = x_{ciF} - \left\| r_{iF}^d \right\| \cos \bar{\theta}_{iF} \cos \bar{\psi}_{iF} \\ y_{ci} = y_{ciF} - \left\| r_{iF}^d \right\| \sin \bar{\theta}_{iF} \\ z_{ci} = z_{ciF} - \left\| r_{iF}^d \right\| \cos \bar{\theta}_{iF} \sin \bar{\psi}_{iF} \end{cases} \tag{7}$$

where $r_{iF}^d = (x_{iF}^d, y_{iF}^d, z_{iF}^d)^T$ represents the set distance between U_i and formation reference point F_r, reflecting the geometric constraints of the formation.

By transforming Eq. 7, and removing the influence of the distance between the boats from position quantity of the AUV, it can be obtained:

$$\tilde{r}^d_{iF} = \left(\tilde{x}^d_{iF}, \tilde{y}^d_{iF}, \tilde{z}^d_{iF}\right)$$
$$= \left[\left\|r^d_{iF}\right\| \cos \bar{\theta}_{iF} \cos \bar{\psi}_{iF}, \left\|r^d_{iF}\right\| \sin \bar{\theta}_{iF}, \left\|r^d_{iF}\right\| \cos \bar{\theta}_{iF} \sin \bar{\psi}_{iF}\right] \tag{8}$$

The coordinate position equation is written in following vector form:

$$r_{iF} = r_i + \tilde{r}^d_{iF} \tag{9}$$

When all coordination variables are consistent, the stability of the formation position and the synchronization of the attitude are realized, and the stable maintenance of the formation is realized.

The above description is the definition of coordination variables in a single formation. According to communication topology, it is also necessary to complete information synchronization between formations. The topology structure between formation pilot boats can be regarded as a pilot-follow structure, where the virtual pilot boat l_0 is pilot boat of the structure, and pilot boat l_i in other formations is the follower in structure. In this topology, followers use the reference point $R_i = (X_{ci}, Y_{ci}, Z_{ci})^T$ in their formations as the coordinated variable that needs to be synchronized. $R_0 = (X_0, Y_0, Z_0)^T$ represents the x, y, and z coordinate of the virtual pilot boat. $\bar{\vartheta}_0, \bar{\psi}_0$ are pitch angle and yaw angle, and the global position coordination variable $R_{iF} = (X_{0i}, Y_{0i}, Z_{0i})^T$ is introduced, namely:

$$\begin{cases} X_{0i} = X_{ci} + \left\|R^d_{iF}\right\| \cos \bar{\theta}_{iF} \cos \bar{\psi}_{iF} \\ Y_{0i} = Y_{ci} + \left\|R^d_{iF}\right\| \sin \bar{\theta}_{iF} \\ Z_{0i} = Z_{ci} + \left\|R^d_{iF}\right\| \cos \bar{\theta}_{iF} \sin \bar{\psi}_{iF} \end{cases} \tag{10}$$

Define a new predetermined distance vector:

$$\begin{cases} \tilde{R}^d_{iF} = \left(\tilde{X}^d_{iF}, \tilde{Y}^d_{iF}, \tilde{Z}^d_{iF}\right) \\ = \left[\left\|R^d_{iF}\right\| \cos \bar{\theta}_{iF} \cos \bar{\psi}_{iF}, \left\|R^d_{iF}\right\| \sin \bar{\theta}_{iF}, \left\|R^d_{iF}\right\| \cos \bar{\theta}_{iF} \sin \bar{\psi}_{iF}\right] \end{cases} \tag{11}$$

Finally, the coordinated position formula that combines global and local information is obtained in following vector form:

$$r_{iF} = r_i + \tilde{r}^d_{iF} + \tilde{R}^d_{iF} \tag{12}$$

When the formation does not reach a stable state, the position coordination variables generated by each AUV are different. The purpose of coordinated control is to make position coordination variables overlap, and finally achieve the asymptotic consistency and stability of global position in formation.

3.2   Second-Order Consistency Control Algorithm

The second-order consensus protocol is used to design the cooperative control law, and three positions and speed channel are designed separately:

$$
\begin{cases}
\dot{V}_{xi}^g = - \sum_{j \in N_i} a_{ij} \left[e^{S(t-t_{k_i}^i)} x_i(t_{k_i}^i) - e^{S(t-t_{k_j}^j)} x_j(t_{k_j}^j) \right] \\
\dot{V}_{zi}^g = - \sum_{j \in N_i} a_{ij} \left[e^{S(t-t_{k_i}^i)} z_i(t_{k_i}^i) - e^{S(t-t_{k_j}^j)} z_j(t_{k_j}^j) \right] \\
\dot{V}_{yi}^g = - \sum_{j \in N_i} a_{ij} \left[e^{S(t-t_{k_i}^i)} y_i(t_{k_i}^i) - e^{S(t-t_{k_j}^j)} y_j(t_{k_j}^j) \right]
\end{cases}
\tag{13}
$$

where $\dot{V}_{xi}^g$, $\dot{V}_{yi}^g$ and $\dot{V}_{zi}^g$ respectively represent the control quantity in the east, north and longitudinal direction. $e^{S(t-t_{k_i}^i)}$ and $e^{S(t-t_{k_j}^j)}$ are the control gain. The velocity of AUV U_j relative to U_i is:

$$
\begin{cases}
\dot{x}_{ij} = V_{xi} - V_{xj} \\
\dot{z}_{ij} = V_{zi} - V_{zj} \\
\dot{y}_{ij} = V_{yi} - V_{yj}
\end{cases}
\tag{14}
$$

Define acceleration command:

$$
\dot{V}_i^g = \left[\dot{V}_{xi}^g, \dot{V}_{zi}^g, \dot{V}_{yi}^g \right]^{\mathrm{T}}
\tag{15}
$$

where $\dot{V}_i^g$ is a second-order consensus algorithm, which contains both position information and speed information. In order to control more clearly, the control of yaw angle and pitch angle is added below, and $\dot{V}_i^g$ is converted into the more commonly used navigation command $\left[\dot{u}_i^g, \dot{v}_i^g, \dot{w}_i^g, \dot{\theta}_i^g, \dot{\psi}_i^g \right]$. According to the relationship between pitch angle, yaw angle and velocity component:

$$
\theta_i = \arctan \left(\frac{V_{zi}}{V_{xi}} \right)
$$

$$
\psi_i = \arctan \left(\frac{V_{yi}}{V_{xi}} \right)
\tag{16}
$$

Take the derivative of the Eq. 16, Eq. 17, 18 are obtained:

$$
\dot{\theta}_i^g = \left[\arctan \left(\frac{V_{yi}^g}{V_{xi}^g} \right) \right]' = \frac{\dot{V}_{yi}^g \int_0^t \dot{V}_{xi}^g dt - \dot{V}_{xi}^g \int_0^t \dot{V}_{yi}^g dt}{\left(\int_0^t \dot{V}_{xi}^g dt \right)^2 + \left(\int_0^t \dot{V}_{yi}^g dt \right)^2}
\tag{17}
$$

$$
\dot{\psi}_i^g = \left[\arctan \left(\frac{V_{zi}^g}{V_{xi}^g} \right) \right]' = \frac{\dot{V}_{zi}^g \int_0^t \dot{V}_{xi}^g dt - \dot{V}_{xi}^g \int_0^t \dot{V}_{zi}^g dt}{\left(\int_0^t \dot{V}_{xi}^g dt \right)^2 + \left(\int_0^t \dot{V}_{zi}^g dt \right)^2}
\tag{18}
$$

Using the control command of Eq. 17, 18, and giving an appropriate sailing controller, the formation can be maintained. The coordinated control instruction u_i for each AUV can be defined as:

$$
u_i = \left[\dot{u}_i^g, \dot{v}_i^g, \dot{w}_i^g, \dot{\theta}_i^g, \dot{\psi}_i^g \right]
\tag{19}
$$

3.3 Model Predictive Control Rate Design

Based on idea of model predictive control of MPC, its basic structure can be represented by Fig. 4. A function of the prediction error is usually used as cost function in predictive control. In most cases, the change of the control signal is also included in cost function. By minimizing this function, the prediction error and the change of the control signal are optimized. Cost function may be single-step or multi-step, so the prediction error and the change of the control signal may only be considered in the cost function at a certain point in the future, or their sum may be included in the cost function at several points in the future.

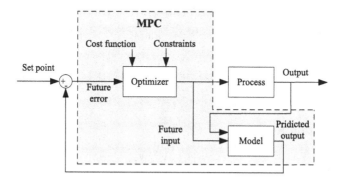

Fig. 4. Model predictive controller

Although the AUV moving in the real world is a continuous physical system, the position and posture information collected by the sensor is discrete. The control signal sent by the controller also controls the ship in the form of discrete time, so the controller should be designed for discrete systems. The Eq. 20 is discretized with the step size h to obtain the low-frequency discrete-time state space model of AUV:

$$\begin{cases} \mathbf{x}_m(k+1) = \mathbf{A_d}\mathbf{x}_m(k) + \mathbf{B}_d\mathbf{u}(k) \\ \mathbf{y}(k) = \mathbf{C}_d\mathbf{x}_m(k) \end{cases} \tag{20}$$

where $\mathbf{x}_m(k)$ is state of the system at time k, $\mathbf{u}(k)$ is input of the system, $\mathbf{y}(k)$ is output of the system at time k, and $\mathbf{A}_d, \mathbf{B}_d, \mathbf{C}_d$ are coefficients of the discrete constant matrix. Generally, $\mathbf{u}$ is modified to a discrete integral $\Delta\mathbf{u}$ to obtain the augmented state space model to eliminate interference and reduce errors. Equation 20 is rewritten into a discrete form:

$$\begin{aligned} x_m(k+1) - x_m(k) &= \Delta x_m(k+1) \\ &= A_d(x_m(k) - x_m(k-1)) + B_d(u(k) - u(k-1)), \\ y(k+1) - y(k) &= C_d(x_m(k+1) - x_m(k)) \\ &= C_d A_d \Delta x(k) + C_d B_d \Delta u(k) \end{aligned} \tag{21}$$

The state space equation can be written as:

$$\begin{bmatrix} \Delta x(k+1) \\ y(k+1) \end{bmatrix} = \begin{bmatrix} A_d & 0_{12\times6} \\ C_d A_d & I_{6\times6} \end{bmatrix} \begin{bmatrix} \Delta x(k) \\ y(k) \end{bmatrix} + \begin{bmatrix} B_d \\ C_d B_d \end{bmatrix} \Delta u(k) \qquad (22)$$

$$y(k) = \begin{bmatrix} 0_{6\times12} & I_{6\times6} \end{bmatrix} \begin{bmatrix} \Delta x(k) \\ y(k) \end{bmatrix} \qquad (23)$$

where I is a 6×6-dimensional identity matrix, and 0 is a 6×12-dimensional 0 matrix. In order to obtain predictive model of the controlled system, the following two vectors are defined:

$$\Delta U = \begin{bmatrix} \Delta u(k)^T & \Delta u(k+1)^T & \cdots & \Delta u(k+N_c-1)^T \end{bmatrix}^T$$

$$Y = \begin{bmatrix} y(k+1|k)^T & y(k+2|k)^T & \cdots & y(k+N_p|k)^T \end{bmatrix}^T \qquad (24)$$

$y(k+1|k)$ represents the output at time $k+1$ based on state at time k, N_c and N_p represent the length of control and prediction respectively. Based on new state space model, the output vector can be written in the following matrix form:

$$Y = Fx(k) + H\Delta U$$

$$F = \begin{bmatrix} C_d A_d \\ C_d A_d{}^2 \\ \vdots \\ C_d A_d{}^{N_P} \end{bmatrix} \qquad (25)$$

$$H = \begin{bmatrix} C_d B_d & 0_{6\times6} & \cdots & 0_{6\times6} \\ C_d A_d B_d & C_d B_d & \cdots & 0_{6\times6} \\ \vdots & C_d A_d B_d & \ddots & \vdots \\ C_d A_d{}^{N_p-1} B & C_d A_d{}^{N_p-2} B_d & \cdots & C_d A_d{}^{N_p-N_c} B_d \end{bmatrix}$$

A quadratic performance indicator function is constructed as follows:

$$J = E^T Q E + \Delta U^T R \Delta U,$$
$$E = W - Y = W - (Fx(k) + H\Delta U) \qquad (26)$$

where Y is predicted output value of the system at a certain time in the future, W is the size of reference signal at future time, and ΔU is the control signal value at future time obtained after optimizing the cost function. Finding the partial derivative from performance index function and make the derivative zero, the optimal control semaphore can be obtained:

$$\Delta U_{optimal} = (H^T Q H + RI)^{-1} H^T Q(W - Fx(k)) \qquad (27)$$

The optimal response is a sequence of input signals, only the first element of this sequence is applied as the optimized control input, and the calculation is repeated again in the next interval to obtain a new control input.

Due to the influence of the mechanical properties of the equipment, the thrust and rudder angle generated by AUVs are limited, which are divided into static constraints and dynamic constraints.

The former means that the maximum thrust generated by the propeller and the maximum rudder angle generated by the steering gear are constrained, another expression, the input is saturated:

$$T_{\min} \leq T \leq T_{\max}$$
$$\delta_{r,s,\min} \leq \delta_{r,s} \leq \delta_{r,s,\max} \tag{28}$$

The constraint for all predictive control inputs u is:

$$u_{\min} \leq u \leq u_{\max} \tag{29}$$

The latter is the process of the thrust and rudder angle generated by the propeller and the steering gear, in a unit time, the increase in the change of the thrust and the rudder angle is limited, another expression, the input change rate is saturated:

$$\dot{T}_{\min} \leq \dot{T} \leq \dot{T}_{\max}$$
$$\dot{\delta}_{r,s,\min} \leq \dot{\delta}_{r,s} \leq \dot{\delta}_{r,s,\max} \tag{30}$$

At the same time, for the safety of AUV navigation, it is necessary to limit its motion trajectory, put another way, to restrict the output:

$$y_{\min} \leq y \leq y_{\max} \tag{31}$$

Considering that the cost function is based on the change of the control signal Δu, the constraints and restrictions must be transformed into constraints and restrictions of Δu. And because of $\Delta \mathbf{u}(k) = \mathbf{u}(k) - \mathbf{u}(k-1)$, it can be obtained:

$$\mathbf{u}_{\min} \leq \mathbf{u}(k) = \mathbf{u}(k-1) + \Delta \mathbf{u}(k) \leq \mathbf{u}_{\max} \tag{32}$$

According to the Eq. 32:

$$U_{\min} \leq T\Delta U + u(t-1) \times I_{N_c \times 1} \leq U_{\max} \tag{33}$$

$$\Delta u_{\min} I_{N_c \times 1} \leq \Delta U \leq \Delta u_{\max} I_{N_c \times 1} \tag{34}$$

where $U_{\min}$ and $U_{\max}$ represent the set of the minimum and maximum values of the control quantity in control time domain, and T is an upper triangular matrix which non-zero element is one. Two constraints of output and output equation are Combined:

$$y_{\min} I_{N_p \times 1} \leq Fx(k) + H\Delta U \leq y_{\max} I_{N_p \times 1} \tag{35}$$

Therefore, the equation of the final constrained optimization problem is as follows:

$$\begin{aligned}
\min \ & J = [\omega - Fx(k) - H\Delta U]^T Q[\omega - Fx(k) - H\Delta U] + \Delta U^T R\Delta U, \\
s.t. \ & U_{\min} \leq T\Delta U + u(t-1) \times I_{N_c \times 1} \leq U_{\max}, \\
& y_{\min} I_{N_p \times 1} \leq Fx(k) + H\Delta U \leq y_{\max} I_{N_p \times 1}, \\
& \Delta u_{\min} I_{N_c \times 1} \leq \Delta U \leq \Delta u_{\max} I_{N_c \times 1}
\end{aligned} \tag{36}$$

4   Simulation Research

4.1   Simulation Setup

In this section, simulation examples are used to verify the tracking ability of multiple AUV formations. The reference path is a space spiral curve, and the specific form is as follows:

$$x(t) = 100\cos(0.05\pi t) - 100$$
$$y(t) = 100\sin(0.05\pi t)$$
$$z(t) = -0.1t$$

The topological structure of the formation is shown in Fig. 5, including three heterogeneous AUV formations. Formation 1 is a triangular formation, formation 2 is a vertical formation and formation 3 is a parallel formation. Node 0 is a virtual node, 1th, 4th and 7th node are pilot boat nodes of each formation. The initial yaw angle is a random number between 0 to 359, and the initial trim angle is 0. The position simulation parameters are shown in Table 2.

All AUVs use MPC based on model decoupling, the specific control parameters are horizontal plane: $N_p = 40, N_c = 4, \alpha = 0.95$; vertical plane: $N_p = 60, N_c = 4, \alpha = 0.85$. The consistency protocol control parameters are $\gamma_x = \gamma_y = 2.6, \gamma_z = 1.2$. And the simulation duration is set to 500 s.

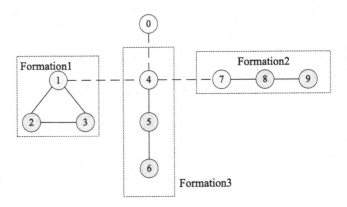

Fig. 5. Formation topology

Table 2. Position simulation parameter

AUV	Initial position(m)	AUV	Initial position(m)
U_0	(0, 0, 0)	U_5	(10, −40, 0)
U_1	(−60, 0, 0)	U_6	(0, −60, 0)
U_2	(−50, −20, 0)	U_7	(10, 20, 0)
U_3	(−40, 10, 0)	U_8	(50, 40, 0)
U_4	(0, −30, 0)	U_9	(60, 0, 0)

4.2   Simulation Results and Analysis

Simulation results of heterogeneous AUV formation are shown in Figs. 6, 7, 8, 9. It can be seen from simulation results that three groups of AUV formation can converge stably and track the preset path in initial state. In about 100 s, the speed, attitude and position of the formation reached consistency of the formation. Since the simulation path is a spiral path, the speed of each AUV is different on navigation path in order to maintain the formation, due to better maneuverability, the light formation has the fastest convergence speed and smaller overshoot.

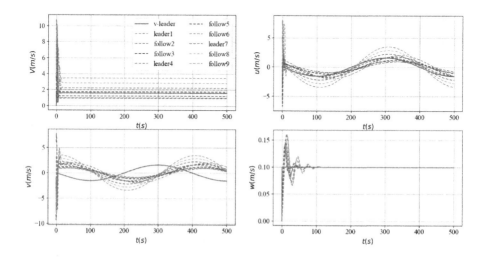

Fig. 6. Collaborative track control speed response

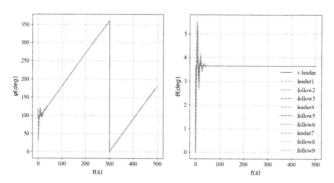

Fig. 7. Collaborative track control of heading Angle and trim Angle response

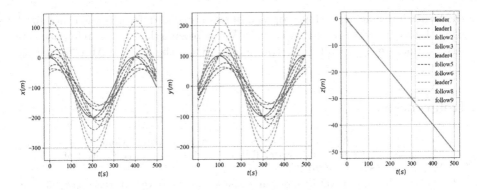

Fig. 8. Collaborative track control position response

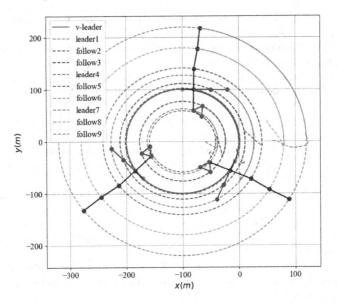

Fig. 9. Collaborative track control of two dimensional position

5   Conclusion

In this paper, the second-order kinematics model is used to describe the AUV formation system, based on the knowledge of graph theory, the communication network structure of this system can be expressed. On the basis of setting consistent coordination variables, an AUV formation control algorithm is proposed by the combination of leader-follower control structure, consistency control theory and MPC control. When the leader changes the direction of travel, it can correspondingly change the direction of movement of remaining AUVs and maintain the formation. The algorithm proposed in this paper is different from centralized control, it does not require that each AUV can receive the leader's reference status information, and it also has convergence when the scale of AUV formation is large.

References

1. Antonelli, G.: Underwater Robots: Motion and Force Control of Vehicle-Manipulator Systems. Underwater Robots: Motion and Force Control of Vehicle-Manipulator Systems (2010)
2. Wynn, R.B., et al.: Autonomous underwater vehicles (AUVs): their past, present and future contributions to the advancement of marine geoscience. Mar. Geol. **352**, 451–468 (2014)
3. Aman, B., Ciobanu, G.: Travelling salesman problem in tissue p systems with costs. J. Membr. Comput. **3**(2), 97–104 (2021)
4. Blidberg, D.R.: The development of autonomous underwater vehicles (AUV); a brief summary. In: IEEE ICRA (2001)
5. Licht, S., Polidoro, V., Flores, M., Hover, F.S., Triantafyllou, M.S.: Design and projected performance of a flapping foil AUV. IEEE J. Ocean. Eng. **29**(3), 786–794 (2004)
6. Buiu, C., Florea, A.G.: Membrane computing models and robot controller design, current results and challenges (2019)
7. Wu, D., Yan, Z., Chen, T.: Cooperative current estimation based multi-AUVs localization for deep ocean applications. Ocean Eng. **188**(Sep. 15), 106148.1–106148.9 (2019)
8. Juayong, R., Adorna, H.N.: A survey of results on evolution-communication p systems with energy. J. Membr. Comput. **2**(2) (2020)
9. Wei, Q., Wang, X., Zhong, X., Wu, N.: Consensus control of leader-following multi-agent systems in directed topology with heterogeneous disturbances. IEEE/CAA J. Autom. Sin. **8**(2), 423–431 (2021)
10. Yan, X., Jiang, D., Miao, R., Li, Y.: Formation control and obstacle avoidance algorithm of a multi-USV system based on virtual structure and artificial potential field. J. Mar. Sci. Eng. **9**(2), 161 (2021)
11. Harder, S.A., Lauderbaugh, L.K.: Formation specification for control of active agents using artificial potential fields (2019)
12. Wang, S., Zhan, X., Zhai, Y., Shen, J., Wang, H.: Performance estimation for Kalman filter based multi-agent cooperative navigation by employing graph theory. Aerosp. Sci. Technol. **112**, 106628 (2021)
13. Bian, X., Mou, C., Yan, Z., Wang, H.: Formation coordinated control for multi-AUV based on spatial curve path tracking. In: OCEANS 2011 (2011)
14. Wang, Y., Yan, W., Li, J.: Passivity-based formation control of autonomous underwater vehicles. IET Control Theory Appl. **6**(4), 518–525 (2012)
15. Wang, Y.T., Yan, W.S.: Consensus formation tracking control of multiple autonomous underwater vehicle systems. Control Theory Appl. **30**(3), 379–384 (2013)
16. Yang, E., Gu, D.: Nonlinear formation-keeping and mooring control of multiple autonomous underwater vehicles. IEEE/ASME Trans. Mechatron. **12**, 164–178 (2007)

17. Cui, R.X., Yan, W.S., Demin, X.U.: Synchronization of multiple autonomous underwater vehicles without velocity measurements. Sci. China Inf. Sci. **55**(007), 1693–1703 (2012)
18. Budiyono, A.: Model predictive control for autonomous underwater vehicle. Indian J. Geo-Marine Sci. **40**(2), 191–199 (2011)
19. Paull, L., Saeedi, S., Seto, M., Li, H.: AUV navigation and localization: a review. IEEE J. Ocean. Eng. **39**(1), 131–149 (2014)
20. Fjellstad, O.-E., Fossen, T.I.: Position and attitude tracking of AUV'S: a quaternion feedback approach. IEEE J. Ocean. Eng. **19**(4), 512–518 (1994)
21. Borlaug, I., Pettersen, K.Y., Gravdahl, J.T.: Trajectory tracking for an articulated intervention AUV using a super-twisting algorithm in 6 DOF. IFAC-PapersOnLine **51**(29), 311–316 (2018)

A Formation Control Method of AUV Group Combining Consensus Theory and Leader-Follower Method Under Communication Delay

Xuan Guo, Yuepeng Chen$^{(\boxtimes)}$, Guangyu Luo, and Guangwu Liu

School of Automation, Wuhan University of Technology, Wuhan 430070, China
{233980,luoguangyu,gliu}@whut.edu.cn, chenyuepengneu@163.com

Abstract. A consistency control algorithm for AUV(Autonomous Underwater Vehicle) group combining with the leader-follower approach under communication delay is proposed. Firstly, the graph theory is used to describe the communication topology of AUV group. Specially, a hybrid communication topology is introduced to adapt to large formation control. Secondly, the distributed control law is constructed by combining consensus theory with leader-following method. Two consistency control algorithms for AUV group based on leader-follower approach with and without communication delay are proposed. Stability criteria are established to guarantee the consensus based on Gershgorin disk theorem and Nyquist law, respectively. Finally, the simulation experiment is carried out to show the effectiveness of the proposed algorithms.

Keywords: AUV group · Formation control · Consensus theory · Leader-follower · Communication delay

1 Introduction

AUV is a device that can perform a variety of tasks underwater instead of a human [1]. In general, complex underwater operations are usually accomplished by multi-AUV group. Compared to a single AUV, multi-AUVs own powerful and comprehensive capabilities to accomplish difficult tasks [2–4]. At the same time, the formation control problem is of great interest in the study of multi-AUV group. Various formation control approaches have been reported in the literature, such as path following approach [5,6], leader-follower approach [7–11], behavioral approach [12,13], virtual structure approach [14], consensus theory [15–17]. The leader-follower method is widely used because of its simple structure and easy implementation in engineering, but it relies too much on the leader. If the leader fails, the entire formation system will collapse. Consensus theory usually assumes that AUVs only interact with information from their neighboring AUVs, which can be suitable for large scale formation control. However, it is difficult to find appropriate quantization information and topology to ensure

© Springer Nature Singapore Pte Ltd. 2022
L. Pan et al. (Eds.): BIC-TA 2021, CCIS 1566, pp. 158–173, 2022.
https://doi.org/10.1007/978-981-19-1253-5_12

that the consistency algorithm converges in a limited time. Meanwhile, there are time delays in the hydro acoustic communication among AUVs in underwater environment. In this paper, the consistency algorithm is combined with the leader-follower approach under communication delay in order to be applied to large formation control of AUV group.

The problem of multi-AUVs formation control has received increasing attention from both marine technology and control engineering communities. In [18], a classification framework with three dimensions, including AUV performance, formation control, and communication capability was proposed, which provides a comprehensive classification method for AUV formation research in this paper. In [19], a distributed leader-following control method combining consensus theory and artificial potential field method (CMM-AUV) for the multi AUV system with a leader was designed. In this method, communication delay was not taken into account. In [20], a new path planning method for AUV group moved in the leader-followers mode was proposed, which can not be used in large formation because of huge amount of information interaction. In [21], a dual closed-loop fast integral terminal sliding mode control method of AUV group was proposed, which overcomes the problem that the formation tracking errors of the traditional method may not converge to zero in finite time. In this method, communication topology was redundant and prone to message blocking. In [22], a new concept of formation learning control was introduced to the field of formation control of AUV group without considering more realistic underwater control circumstances, including imperfect inter-AUV communication with time delays.

Although a lot of literatures was proposed in the AUV formation control field, there still exist critical issues that have not been adequately addressed to date. In particular, formation control issues of large AUV group need to be addressed. Specifically, realistic underwater control circumstances about communication delays need to be considered. The contributions of this paper can be understood as follows. A formation control method of AUV group combining consensus theory and leader-follower method under communication delay is proposed. At the same time, a virtual leader is used in order to overcome the problem of over-reliance on leader. The method distinguishes itself from many existing formation control techniques in the following aspects.

- It establishes a hybrid communication topology that can be applied to formation control of large AUV group.
- It achieves distributed control by combining consistency algorithm with leader-following method.
- It realizes consistent control of AUV groups while taking into account communication delay conditions.

The rest of this paper is organized as follows. Some preliminary reviews and modelling are given in Sect. 2. The consistency control method for AUV group based on leader-follower approach with and without communication delay is addressed in Sect. 3. Simulation results are provided in Sect. 4. The conclusions are drawn in Sect. 5.

2   Preliminaries and Modelling

2.1   Graph Theory

Graph theory is a powerful tool to deal with the consensus problem of multi-agent systems. It is very effective to use graphs to represent the communication topology of information exchange between AUVs. Assume that each AUV is a node in the graph, and the information connection between AUVs is the edge in the graph, then the multi-AUV system can be referred as a graph. The basic theory of graph can be found in [23], which is omitted for simplicity.

In order to describe the relationship between nodes and edges and to characterize the information interaction topology of AUV group, the adjacency matrix $A(G)$ is introduced. The values of the elements in $A(G)$ are as follows:

$$a_{kn} = \begin{cases} 1 & (v_n, v_k) \in E(G) \\ 0, others \end{cases} \tag{1}$$

When G is an undirected graph, $A(G)$ is a symmetric matrix with all zeros on the main diagonal. Generally, the weighted adjacency matrix $A_w(G)$ is defined as:

$$A_w(G) = [a_{kn}] = \begin{cases} w_{kn} & (v_n, v_k) \in E(G) \\ 0, others \end{cases} \tag{2}$$

Laplacian matrix $L(G)$ is another matrix that describes the relationship between nodes and edges in graph. Its elements have the following values:

$$l_{kn} = -a_{kn}, k \neq n, l_{kk} = \sum_{n=1}^{N} a_{kn}, k = n \tag{3}$$

The adjacency matrix and Laplacian matrix have some following remarkable properties:

Lemma 1. *Given a directed graph G and its adjacence matrix $A(G)$, If $A(G)$ is irreducible, then G is a strongly connected graph.*

Lemma 2. *The rank of a strongly connected directed graph G with N nodes is $rank(L(G)) = N - 1$.*

Lemma 3. *A symmetric graph G is connected if and only if $rank(L(G)) = N - 1$.*

Lemma 4. *1. $L(G)$ is positive semi-definite.*
2. If zero is the eigenvalue of $L(G)$, the graph is connected. $1_N \in R^N$ is its corresponding eigenvector, where $1_N = [1 \ldots 1]^T$.
3. The eigenvalues of the Laplacian matrix are always non-negative. Moreover, they can always be ordered as follows:

$$0 = \lambda_1(L(G)) < \lambda_2(L(G)) < \cdots < \lambda_n(L(G))$$

2.2   AUV Model

The study of AUV motion includes the static and dynamic aspects. Statics is the stability of the device in steady or moving at constant velocity states and the dynamics is related to the accelerated motion. Usually, dynamic studies are divided into two parts: kinematics that only examines the geometric dimension of motion and kinetics that analyzes the forces that generate motion. Figure 1 presents an example of AUV and its dynamic variables in the body-fixed coordinate frame and its position relative to the inertial coordinate frame. Table 1 indicates different model variables defined as AUV's motion behaviors in accordance with the Society of Naval Architects and Marine Engineers (SNAME).

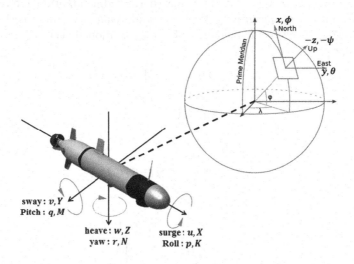

Fig. 1. Model diagram of underdriven AUV in inertial and fixed coordinate systems

Table 1. Symbolic representation of model

Degree of freedom	Position and Euler angle	Linear velocity and angular velocity	Force and moment
Surging	x	u	X
Swaying	y	v	Y
Heaving	z	w	Z
Rolling	ϕ	p	K
Pitching	θ	q	M
Yawing	ψ	r	N

The relationship between velocity and acceleration is mainly considered by AUV dynamic equation. AUV is a rigid body with uniform mass distribution, and its shape is symmetrical from left to right and approximately symmetrical from top to bottom. The six degree of freedom motion model of AUV can be expressed as:

$$\begin{cases} \dot{\eta} = J(\eta)\nu \\ M\dot{\nu} + C(\nu)\nu + D(\nu)\nu + g(\eta) = \tau \end{cases} \tag{4}$$

where $\eta \in \mathbb{R}^6$ is spatial position and posture of AUV in the fixed coordinate system. $\nu \in \mathbb{R}^6$ is linear velocity and angular velocity of the AUV in motion coordinate system. $J(\eta)$ is rotation transformation matrix from the motion coordinate system to fixed coordinate system. And M is inertia matrix of system (Including additional mass), $C(\nu)$ is Coriolis force matrix (including additional mass), $D(\nu)$ is damping matrix, $g(\eta)$ is gravity/buoyancy and moment vector, τ is thrust and moment vector. The specific meanings of above-mentioned vectors and matrices are as follows:

$$\eta = [\eta_1, \eta_2]^T$$
$$\eta_1 = [x, y, z] \tag{5}$$
$$\eta_2 = [\varphi, \theta, \psi]$$

$$\nu = [\nu_1, \nu_2]^T \tag{6}$$
$$\nu_1 = [u, v, w], \quad \nu_2 = [p, q, r]$$

$$\tau = [\tau_1, \tau_2]^T \tag{7}$$
$$\tau_1 = [X, Y, Z], \tau_2 = [K, M, N]$$

$$\begin{bmatrix} \dot{\eta}_1 \\ \dot{\eta}_2 \end{bmatrix} = \begin{bmatrix} J_1(\eta_2) & 0 \\ 0 & J_2(\eta_2) \end{bmatrix} \begin{bmatrix} \nu_1 \\ \nu_2 \end{bmatrix} \tag{8}$$

$$J_1 = \begin{bmatrix} \cos\psi\cos\theta & \cos\psi\sin\theta\sin\varphi - \sin\psi\cos\varphi & \cos\psi\sin\theta\cos\varphi + \sin\psi\cos\varphi \\ \sin\psi\cos\theta & \sin\psi\sin\theta\sin\varphi + \cos\psi\cos\varphi & \sin\psi\sin\theta\cos\varphi - \cos\psi\sin\varphi \\ -\sin\theta & \cos\theta\sin\varphi & \cos\theta\cos\varphi \end{bmatrix}$$
$$J_2 = \begin{bmatrix} 1 & \sin\varphi t\theta & \cos\varphi\tan\theta \\ 0 & \cos\varphi & -\sin\varphi \\ 0 & \frac{\sin\varphi}{\cos\theta} & \frac{\cos\varphi}{\cos\theta} \end{bmatrix}, \theta \neq \pm\frac{\pi}{2} \tag{9}$$

The six-degree-of-freedom motion equation of AUV can be expressed as:

$$X = m\left[\dot{u} - vr + wq - x_G\left(q^2 + r^2\right) + y_G(pq + \dot{r}) + z_G(pr + \dot{q})\right],$$
$$Y = m\left[\dot{v} - wp + ur + x_G(pq + \dot{r}) - y_G\left(r^2 + p^2\right) + z_G(qr + \dot{p})\right],$$
$$Z = m\left[\dot{w} - uq + vp + x_G(rp + \dot{q}) + y_G(rq + \dot{p}) - z_G\left(p^2 + q^2\right)\right], \tag{10}$$
$$K = I_{xx}\dot{p} + (I_{zz} - I_{yy})qr + m\left[y_G(\dot{w} - uq + vp) - z_G(\dot{v} - wp + ur)\right],$$
$$M = I_{yy}\dot{q} + (I_{xx} - I_{zz})rp + m\left[z_G(\dot{u} - vr + wq) - x_G(\dot{w} - uq + vp)\right],$$
$$N = I_{zz}\dot{r} + (I_{yy} - I_{zz})pq + m\left[x_G(\dot{v} - wp + ur) - y_G(\dot{u} - vr + wp)\right].$$

2.3   Communication Modelling

At present, only one leader is defined in a group in most cases. The consistency process of the system is controlled by controlling the information interaction between leader and other AUVs. In this paper, multiple leaders-followers in topological structure is adopted. AUV group is divided into multiple small groups to form a swarm network. Each group that includes multiple AUVs has its own leader AUV. Moreover, there is one and only one AUV in first group as virtual AUV, which is named virtual leader. The dynamics and kinematics characteristics of the virtual leader and the real AUV are the same. The desired speed and desired position of the follower are given as control inputs of virtual leader. In other words, a mixed-mode topology to jointly is designed to solve the consistency problem of the AUV swarm system. The schematic diagram of the topology is shown in Fig. 2.

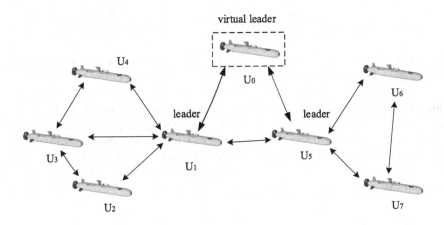

Fig. 2. Hybrid communication topology

3   Consistency Control Algorithm Based on Leader-Following Method for AUV Group

In this section, the motion controller of AUV group is designed based on consistency theory and leader-follower method, so that all the followers can follow the leader for motion. Further, a distributed controller is designed for each AUV with communication time delay to enable them to move according to a given queue.

3.1   Consistency Control Algorithm Without Communication Delay

In this section, a motion controller of AUV group is designed based on consistency theory and leader-follower model. Furthermore, a distributed controller is designed for each AUV with communication delay. The model of AUV is shown in Eq. (4). The control algorithm is given as Eq. (11).

$$u_i(t) = -\sum_{j=1}^{m} a_{ij}(t)[(\eta_i - \eta_j) + \gamma(t)(v_i - v_j)], \ i = 1, 2, \ldots, m \qquad (11)$$

where $u_i(t)$ denotes control input, $a_{ij}(t)$ denotes the elements in directed graph G_m adjacency matrix, η_i and η_j denote the position of different AUVs, v_i and v_j denote the velocity. $\gamma(t)$ denotes control gain.

Lemma 5. *When G_m is a directed spanning tree, suppose $\mu_i(i = 1, 2, ..., m)$ denotes the eigenvalue of $-L_m$ of AUVi. If Eq. (11) arrives at consistency, then $\gamma > \bar{\gamma}$ needs to be satisfied, where all $m - 1$ non-zero eigenvalues of $-L_m$ are negative, $\bar{\gamma} \overset{\Delta}{=} 0$. Otherwise, Eq. (12) is met.*

$$\bar{\gamma} = \max_{\forall Re(\mu_i) < 0 \ and \ Im(\mu_i) > 0} \sqrt{\frac{2}{|\mu_i| \cos\left[\tan^{-1} \frac{Im(\mu_i)}{-Re(\mu_i)}\right]}} \qquad (12)$$

Since communication topology among AUVs is a directed graph, Eq. (4) achieves consistency for all $i = 1, 2, \ldots, m$, $\eta_i(0)$ and $v_i(0)$, when $\|\eta_i(t) - \eta_j(t)\| \to 0$, $\|v_i(t) - v_j(t)\| \to 0$ and $t \to 0$, the control gain γ satisfies Eq. (12). Only horizontal plane motion is taken into account. The position of AUVi is $\eta_i = (x_i, y_i, z_i)$, and the velocity is v_i. Suppose AUV group keep the horizontal plane speed as v_0, the rotary motion angular speed as r_0, and the vertical speed as v_{z_0}. Suppose (x_{f_i}, y_{f_i}) denotes the position of point f_i on AUVi with distance d_i from the center of gravity (x_i, y_i). The simplified control algorithm is expressed as Eq. (13).

$$\begin{aligned}
\dot{x}_{f_i} &= v_{x_i} \\
\dot{y}_{f_i} &= v_{y_i} \\
\dot{z}_i &= v_{z_i} \\
\dot{v}_{x_i} &= u_{x_i} \\
\dot{v}_{y_i} &= u_{y_i} \\
\dot{v}_{z_i} &= u_{z_i}
\end{aligned} \qquad (13)$$

The motion model of the virtual leader AUV can be represented as

$$\begin{aligned}
\dot{x}_l &= v_{x_l} \\
\dot{y}_l &= v_{y_l} \\
\dot{z}_l &= 0 \\
\dot{v}_{x_l} &= f(t, x_l) \\
\dot{v}_{y_l} &= f(t, y_l)
\end{aligned} \qquad (14)$$

Therefore, consistency of AUV group can be achieved by designing control inputs $u_{x_i}, u_{y_i}, u_{z_i}$. Suppose that each AUV has a unique number and all AUVs update their state parameters at the same moment based on a time-triggered. When all followers can maintain traffic with the leader AUV without communication delay, the control algorithm is shown as Eq. (15), (16), and (17).

$$u_{x_i} = f(t, x_l) - \sum_{j=1}^{m} a_{ij}[(x_{f_i} - x_{f_j}) - (\delta_i^x - \delta_j^x) + \gamma_x(v_{x_i} - v_{x_j})]$$
$$- a_{i(m+1)}[(x_{f_i} - x_l + \delta_i^x) + \gamma_x(v_{x_i} - v_{x_l})] \tag{15}$$

$$u_{y_i} = f(t, y_l) - \sum_{j=1}^{m} a_{ij}[(y_{f_i} - y_{f_j}) - (\delta_i^y - \delta_j^y) + \gamma_y(v_{y_i} - v_{y_j})]$$
$$- a_{i(m+1)}[(y_{f_i} - y_l + \delta_i^x) + \gamma_y(v_{y_i} - v_{y_l})] \tag{16}$$

$$u_{z_i} = -v_{z_i} - \sum_{j=1}^{m} a_{ij}[(z_i - z_j) + \gamma_z(v_{z_i} - v_{z_j})]$$
$$- a_{i(m+1)}[(z_i - z_l) + \gamma_z v_{z_i}] \tag{17}$$

where control gain γ_x, γ_y, γ_z are greater than 0. $a_{ij}(i, j = 1, 2, ..., m)$ denotes the i, j element of the adjacency matrix X of the directed graph G_m. When there is information interaction between the leader AUV and the follower AUV, $a_{i(m+1)} > 0, i = 1, 2, ..., m$. Otherwise, $a_{i(m+1)} = 0$. Suppose adjacency matrix $X_{m+1} = [a_{ij}] \in {}^{(m+1) \times (m+1)}$, where a_{ij} and $a_{i(m+1)}$ denote the elements in the adjacency matrix X_m. $a_{k(m+1)} = 0, \forall k \in (1, 2, ..., m + 1)$ is satisfied. X_{m+1} denotes the adjacency matrix of the directed graph G_{m+1}. L_{m+1} denotes the laplacian matrix of the directed graph G_{m+1}.

Theorem 1. *When the model of virtual leader in the AUV group is Eq. (4), the follower AUV control inputs are Eq. (15), Eq. (16), and Eq. (17), respectively. When all follower AUVs can maintain normal communication with the leader AUV, the AUV group can maintain a fixed formation forward at a fixed depth when and only when the communication network topology between the follower AUVs contains a spanning tree. The control gains satisfies equation Eq. (12).*

Proof. When the communication network topology among followers contains a spanning tree and all follower AUVs are able to communicate with the leader AUV normally, the graph G_{m+1} contains a spanning tree. Suppose $z_l = z_{m+1}$, u_{z_i} can be written as

$$u_{z_i} = -v_{z_i} - \sum_{j=1}^{m+1} a_{ij}[(z_i - z_j) + \gamma_z(v_{z_i} - v_{z_j})] \tag{18}$$

According to Lemma 5, when the graph G_{m+1} contains a spanning tree and the control gain γ_z satisfies Eq. (12) and Eq. (19) can be satisfied.

$$\begin{cases} z_i \to z_j \to z_l \\ v_{z_i} \to v_{z_j} \to 0 \end{cases} \tag{19}$$

Suppose $\tilde{x}_{f_i} = x_{f_i} - x_l - \delta_i^x$ and $\tilde{v}_{x_i} = v_{x_i} - v_{x_l}$, u_{x_i} can be written as

$$
\begin{cases}
\dot{\tilde{x}}_{f_i} = \tilde{v}_{x_i} \\
\dot{\tilde{v}}_{x_i} = -\sum_{j=1}^{n} a_{ij} \left[(\tilde{x}_{f_i} - \tilde{x}_{f_j}) + \gamma_x(\tilde{v}_{x_i} - \tilde{v}_{x_j}) \right] - a_{i(m+1)}(\tilde{x}_{f_i} + \gamma_x \tilde{v}_{x_i})
\end{cases}
\tag{20}
$$

$$
\begin{bmatrix} \dot{x}_f \\ \dot{v}_x \end{bmatrix} = \begin{bmatrix} 0 & I_n \\ -(L + diag(a_{i(m+1)})) & -\gamma_x(L + diag(a_{i(m+1)})) \end{bmatrix} \begin{bmatrix} x_f \\ v_x \end{bmatrix}
\tag{21}
$$

According to Gershgorin disk theorem, the eigenvalues of the matrix $-(L + diag(a_{i(m+1)}))$ all have non-negative real parts. When γ_x satisfies Eq. (12), $\tilde{x}_{f_i} \rightarrow \tilde{x}_{f_j} \rightarrow 0$ and $\tilde{v}_{x_i} \rightarrow \tilde{v}_{x_j} \rightarrow 0$. At the same time, when γ_y satisfies Eq. (12), $y_{f_i} \rightarrow y_l + \delta_i^y$ and $v_{y_i} \rightarrow v_{y_l}$. Consequently, the AUV group reaches stability.

3.2   Consistency Control Algorithm with Communication Delay

Since there is a hydroacoustic communication delay among AUVs in the underwater environment, the consistency control algorithm for the AUV under the time delay condition is considered below. Similarly, assuming that the AUV group maintains a fixed depth motion when there is a time delay in the inter-AUV communication, the controller is designed as follows.

$$
\begin{aligned}
u_{x_i} = \dot{f}^x(t) &- \gamma \left(v_{x_i}(t - \tau_{ij}(t)) - f^x(t - \tau_{ij}(t)) \right. \\
&- \sum_{j=1}^{m} a_{ij} \left[(x_{f_i}(t) - x_{f_j}(t - \tau_{ij}(t)) - (\delta_i^x - \delta_j^x) \right] \\
&- \sum_{j=1}^{m} a_{ij} \left[\gamma \left(v_{x_i}(t - \tau_{ij}(t)) - v_{x_j}(t - \tau_{ij}(t)) \right) \right]
\end{aligned}
\tag{22}
$$

$$
\begin{aligned}
u_{y_i} = \dot{f}^y(t) &- \gamma \left(v_{y_i}(t - \tau_{ij}(t)) - f^y(t - \tau_{ij}(t)) \right. \\
&- \sum_{j=1}^{m} a_{ij} \left[y_{f_i}(t) - y_{f_j}(t - \tau_{ij}(t)) - (\delta_i^y - \delta_j^y) \right] \\
&- \sum_{j=1}^{m} a_{ij} \left[\gamma \left(v_{y_i}(t - \tau_{ij}(t)) - v_{y_j}(t - \tau_{ij}(t)) \right) \right]
\end{aligned}
\tag{23}
$$

where control gain $\gamma > 0$, $\tau_{ij}(t)$ denotes communication time delay between AUVi and AUVj. $f^x(t)$ and $f^y(t)$ are continuous differentiable functions that denote the velocity characteristics of the AUV motion. δ_i^x, δ_i^y denote the desired position. When the upper limit of time delay is τ_0, $0 < \tau_{ij}(t) < \tau_0$. Eq. (24) is satisfied.

$$
0 \leq \tau_{ij}(t) \leq \frac{1}{\omega_0} \arctan \frac{(1 + \lambda_i)\omega_0 \gamma}{\lambda_i}
\tag{24}
$$

where

$$\omega_0 = \sqrt{\frac{(1+\lambda_i)^2\gamma^2 \pm \sqrt{(1+\lambda_i)^4\gamma^4 + 4\lambda_i^2}}{2}}$$

where λ_i is the characteristic root of the Laplacian matrix L of the graph G.

Theorem 2. *When Eq. (12) and Eq. (24) are satisfied, AUV group can maintain a stable formation.*

Proof. For control input u_{x_i}, suppose

$$\begin{cases} \tilde{x}_{f_i} = x_{f_i} - \int_0^1 f^x(s)dt - \delta_i^x \\ \tilde{v}_{x_i} = v_{x_i} - f^x(t) \end{cases} \tag{25}$$

According to Eq. (22)

$$\begin{cases} \dot{\tilde{x}}_{f_i}(t) = \tilde{v}_{x_i}(t) \\ \dot{\tilde{v}}_{x_i}(t) = -\gamma\tilde{v}_{x_i}(t - \tau_{ij}(t)) \\ \quad - \sum\limits_{j=1}^{m} a_{ij}\left[\tilde{x}_{f_i}(t) - \tilde{x}_{f_j}(t - \tau_{ij}(t))\right] \\ \quad - \sum\limits_{j=1}^{m} a_{ij}\left[\gamma\left(\tilde{v}_{x_i}(t - \tau_{ij}(t)) - \tilde{v}_{x_j}(t - \tau_{ij}(t))\right)\right] \end{cases} \tag{26}$$

Assume that all AUVs in homogeneous AUV swarm have the same upper limit of delay τ_0, suppose $x(t) = [\tilde{x}_f(t), \tilde{v}_x(t)]^T$

$$\dot{x}(t) = \begin{bmatrix} 0 & I_n \\ 0 & 0 \end{bmatrix} x(t) + \begin{bmatrix} 0 & 0 \\ -L & -\gamma(I_m + L) \end{bmatrix} x(t - \tau_0) \tag{27}$$

A Laplace variation of Eq. (27) is

$$sx(s) = \begin{bmatrix} 0 & I_m \\ 0 & 0 \end{bmatrix} x(s) + \begin{bmatrix} 0 & 0 \\ -L & -\gamma(I_m + L) \end{bmatrix} e^{-\tau_0 s} x(s) \tag{28}$$

The characteristic equation satisfies Eq. (29)

$$\det(s^2 I_m + e^{-\tau_0 s}\gamma(I_m + L)s + e^{-\tau_0 s}L) = 0 \tag{29}$$

It follows from the Theorem 2 that for an undirected connected graph G, the rank of L is $rank(L) = m - 1$, the eigenvalue of L is $0 = \lambda_1 < \lambda_2 \leq \ldots \leq \lambda_m = \lambda_{\max}$, then

$$s\prod_{i=2}^{m}\left[s^2 + e^{-\tau_0 s}(\gamma(1 + \lambda_i)s + \lambda_i)\right] = 0 \tag{30}$$

When $i = 2, \ldots, m$, Eq. (17) can be organized as

$$1 + e^{-\tau_0 s}[\frac{1}{s}\gamma(1 + \lambda_i) + \frac{1}{s^2}\lambda_i] = 0 \tag{31}$$

Suppose $G_i(s) = e^{-\tau_0 s}[\frac{1}{s}\gamma(1 + \lambda_i) + \frac{1}{s^2}\lambda_i]$, the number of unstable poles $P = 0$ is consistent with the minimum phase system characteristics. Based on Nyquist stability criterion, the roots of Eq. (31) are in the left half-open plane of the s-plane when the Nyquist curve $G_i(s)$ does not enclose the critical point $(-1, j0)$. Then the system reaches asymptotic consistency. Consequently, when Eq. (24) is satisfied, the roots of Eq. (31) are in the left half-open plane of the s-plane, and the system can reach agreement. At this time, $x_{f_i} - x_{f_j} \to \delta_i^x - \delta_i^x$, $v_{x_i} \to v_{x_j} \to f^x(t)$. Similarly, when control inputs u_{y_i} satisfies Eq. (24), $y_{f_i} - y_{f_j} \to \delta_i^y - \delta_i^y$, $v_{y_i} \to v_{y_j} \to f^y(t)$.

4   Simulation Results

4.1   Simulation of Consistency Control Algorithm Without Communication Delay

In this subsection, a simulation experiment is conducted for the consistency control algorithm without communication delay proposed in Sect. 3.1. One leader and four followers are set to form a AUV group. The initial position of the leader is randomly distributed between $[-4, 4]$, the initial position of each follower is randomly distributed in the interval $[-8, 8]$, the initial combined speed is 5 m/s, and the initial values of other state variables are set to 0. The communication topology diagram is defined as an undirected connectivity diagram, as shown in Fig. 3. The system weighted adjacency matrix is shown as follows.

$$A = \begin{bmatrix} 0 & 1 & 1 & 0 & 0 \\ 1 & 0 & 0 & 1 & 1 \\ 1 & 0 & 0 & 0 & 1 \\ 0 & 1 & 0 & 0 & 0 \\ 0 & 1 & 1 & 0 & 0 \end{bmatrix} D = \begin{bmatrix} 2 & 0 & 0 & 0 & 0 \\ 0 & 3 & 0 & 0 & 0 \\ 0 & 0 & 2 & 0 & 0 \\ 0 & 0 & 0 & 1 & 0 \\ 0 & 0 & 0 & 0 & 2 \end{bmatrix}$$

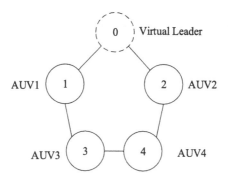

Fig. 3. Communication topology diagram

A parallel formation is designed with the leader as the center and four followers evenly distributed around it. Control gain factor $\gamma_x = \gamma_y = 2$, $\gamma_z = 1$. The simulation results are shown from Fig. 4, 5, 6, 7, 8 and Fig. 9. In Fig. 4 and Fig. 5, it can be seen that the AUV group maintains a stable parallel formation, and the followers in the multi-AUV group formation pair can keep the desired relative distance from the leader to leader. From Fig. 6, 7, 8 and Fig. 9, it can be seen that the position of each follower in the formation in three directions and the velocity can converge to the value of the leader after about 30s, and the value of acceleration gradually converges to zero. Therefore, the effectiveness of the control algorithm without communication delay is proved.

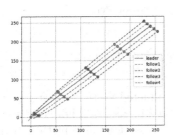

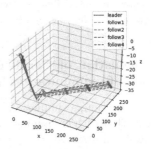

Fig. 4. Formation formation process without communication delay (2-D)

Fig. 5. Formation formation process without communication delay (3-D)

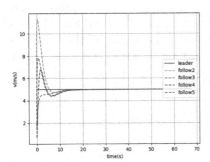

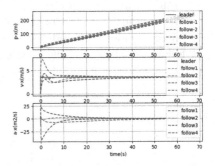

Fig. 6. The combined velocity in the x and y directions without communication delay

Fig. 7. Position, velocity, and acceleration states in the x-direction without communication delay

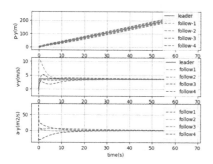

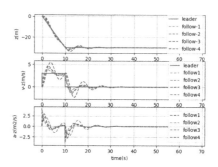

Fig. 8. Position, velocity, and acceleration states in the y-direction without communication delay

Fig. 9. Position, velocity, and acceleration states in the z-direction without communication delay

4.2 Simulation of Consistency Control Algorithm with Communication Delay

In this subsection, a simulation experiment is conducted for the consistency control algorithm with communication delay proposed in Sect. 3.2. For comparison, the initial conditions of the simulations in this subsection are kept the same as in Sect. 4.1. The difference is that the communication time lag is set to $\tau = 0.5$. The simulation results are shown as follows.

In Fig.10 and Fig. 11, it can be seen that the AUV group has a lag in the state of the follower in the condition of the presence of communication delay. The followers can not keep a horizontal line with the leader, which means that the parallel formation can not be maintained. However, the AUV group can still maintain a steady state moving forward. From Fig. 12, 13, 14 and Fig. 15, it can be seen that under the condition of communication time delay, the velocity of each follower AUV in x, y, and z directions is jittered and then converges rapidly. Simultaneously, the acceleration of each follower finally converges to zero.

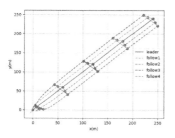

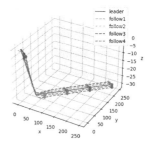

Fig. 10. Formation process with communication delay (2-D)

Fig. 11. Formation process with communication delay (3-D)

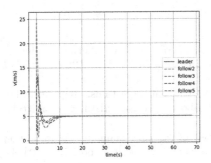

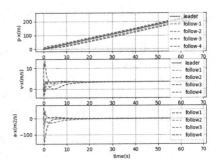

Fig. 12. The combined velocity in the x and y directions with communication delay

Fig. 13. Position, velocity, and acceleration states in the x-direction with communication delay

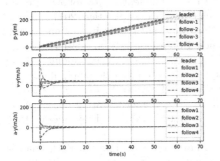

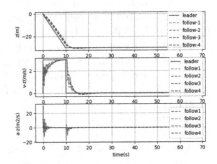

Fig. 14. Position, velocity, and acceleration states in the y-direction with communication delay

Fig. 15. Position, velocity, and acceleration states in the z-direction with communication delay

5   Conclusion

In this paper, a formation control method of AUV group combining consensus theory and leader-follower method under communication delay is proposed. A hybrid communication topology that can be applied to formation control of large AUV group is established. At the same time, a virtual leader is used in order to overcome the over-reliance on leader. The simulation results show that the consistency control algorithm designed in this paper can make all follower AUVs able to follow the leader for stable motion under both communication delay and no communication delay conditions. The difference is that with the consideration of communication delay, the transient performance of the system will be reduced and the steady-state error will be increased, which is reflected in Sect. 4.2. In the future, a compensator will be designed to overcome the interference in complex ocean environment.

References

1. Sánchez, P.J.B., Papaelias, M., Márquez, F.P.G.: Autonomous underwater vehicles: instrumentation and measurements. IEEE Instrum. Meas. Mag. **23**(2), 105–114 (2020)
2. Connor, J., Champion, B., Joordens, M.A.: Current algorithms, communication methods and designs for underwater swarm robotics: a review. IEEE Sens. J. **21**(1), 153–169 (2020)
3. Hadi, B., Khosravi, A., Sarhadi, P.: A review of the path planning and formation control for multiple autonomous underwater vehicles. J. Intell. Robot. Syst. **101**(4), 1–26 (2021)
4. Park, D., Li, J.H., Ki, H., Kang, H., Kim, M.G., Suh, J.H.: Selective AUV guidance scheme for structured environment navigation. In: OCEANS 2019-Marseille, pp. 1–5. IEEE (2019)
5. Yu, C., Xiang, X., Zuo, M., Xu, G.: Robust variable-depth path following of an under-actuated autonomous underwater vehicle with uncertainties (2017)
6. Xinjing, H., Yibo, L., Fei, D., Shijiu, J.: Horizontal path following for underactuated AUV based on dynamic circle guidance. Robotica **35**(4), 876–891 (2017)
7. Heshmati-Alamdari, S., Bechlioulis, C.P., Karras, G.C., Kyriakopoulos, K.J.: Cooperative impedance control for multiple underwater vehicle manipulator systems under lean communication. IEEE J. Oceanic Eng. **46**(2), 447–465 (2020)
8. Zhang, W., Zeng, J., Yan, Z., Wei, S., Tian, W.: Leader-following consensus of discrete-time multi-AUV recovery system with time-varying delay. Ocean Eng. **219**, 108258 (2021)
9. Wang, J., Wang, C., Wei, Y., Zhang, C.: Neuroadaptive sliding mode formation control of autonomous underwater vehicles with uncertain dynamics. IEEE Syst. J. **14**(3), 3325–3333 (2019)
10. Renjie, F., Xin, W., Zhenlong, X., Rongfu, L., Xiaodi, L., Xiaotian, C.: Underwater robot formation control based on leader-follower model. In: 2020 16th International Conference on Control, Automation, Robotics and Vision (ICARCV), pp. 98–103. IEEE (2020)
11. Bechlioulis, C.P., Giagkas, F., Karras, G.C., Kyriakopoulos, K.J.: Robust formation control for multiple underwater vehicles. Front. Robot. AI **6**, 90 (2019)
12. Chen, G., Shen, Y., Qu, N., He, B.: Path planning of AUV during diving process based on behavioral decision-making. Ocean Eng. **234**, 109073 (2021)
13. He, B., Ren, H., Kan, W.: Design and simulation of behavior-based reactive decision-making control system for autonomous underwater vehicle. In: 2010 2nd International Conference on Advanced Computer Control, vol. 5, pp. 647–651. IEEE (2010)
14. Zhang, L.C., Wang, J., Wang, T., Liu, M., Gao, J.: Optimal formation of multiple AUVs cooperative localization based on virtual structure. In: OCEANS 2016 MTS/IEEE Monterey, pp. 1–6. IEEE (2016)
15. Xia, G., Zhang, Y., Zhang, W., Chen, X., Yang, H.: Multi-time-scale 3-D coordinated formation control for multi-underactuated AUV with uncertainties: design and stability analysis using singular perturbation methods. Ocean Eng. **230**, 109053 (2021)
16. Qin, H., Chen, H., Sun, Y.: Distributed finite-time fault-tolerant containment control for multiple ocean bottom flying nodes. J. Franklin Inst. **357**(16), 11242–11264 (2020)

17. Zhang, W., Zeng, J., Yan, Z., Wei, S., Zhang, J., Yang, Z.: Consensus control of multiple AUVs recovery system under switching topologies and time delays. IEEE Access **7**, 119965–119980 (2019)
18. Yang, Y., Xiao, Y., Li, T.: A survey of autonomous underwater vehicle formation: performance, formation control, and communication capability. IEEE Commun. Surv. Tutor. **23**(2), 815–841 (2021)
19. Xia, G., Zhang, Y., Yang, Y.: Control method of multi-AUV circular formation combining consensus theory and artificial potential field method. In: 2020 Chinese Control and Decision Conference (CCDC), pp. 3055–3061. IEEE (2020)
20. Filaretov, V., Yukhimets, D.: The method of path planning for AUV-group moving in desired formation in unknown environment with obstacles. IFAC-PapersOnLine **53**(2), 14650–14655 (2020)
21. Xia, G., Zhang, Y., Zhang, W., Chen, X., Yang, H.: Dual closed-loop robust adaptive fast integral terminal sliding mode formation finite-time control for multi-underactuated AUV system in three dimensional space. Ocean Eng. **233**, 108903 (2021)
22. Yuan, C., Licht, S., He, H.: Formation learning control of multiple autonomous underwater vehicles with heterogeneous nonlinear uncertain dynamics. IEEE Trans. Cybern. **48**(10), 2920–2934 (2017)
23. Liu, Y., Nicolescu, R., Sun, J.: An efficient labelled nested multiset unification algorithm. J. Membr. Comput. **3**(3), 194–204 (2021). https://doi.org/10.1007/s41965-021-00076-0

stigLD: Stigmergic Coordination of Linked Data Agents

René Schubotz[✉], Torsten Spieldenner, and Melvin Chelli

German Research Center for Artificial Intelligence,
Saarland Informatics Campus D 3 2, Saarbrücken, Germany
rene.schubotz@dfki.de

Abstract. While current Semantic Web technologies are well-suited for data publication and integration, the design and deployment of dynamic, autonomous and long-lived multi-agent systems (MAS) on the Web is still in its infancy. Following the vision of hypermedia MAS and Linked Systems, we propose to use a value-passing fragment of Milner's Calculus to formally specify the generic hypermedia-driven behaviour of Linked Data agents and the Web as their embedding environment. We are specifically interested in agent coordination mechanisms based on stigmergic principles. When considering transient marker-based stigmergy, we identify the necessity of generating server-side effects during the handling of safe and idempotent agent-initiated resource requests. This design choice is oftentimes contested with an imprecise interpretation of HTTP semantics, or with rejecting environments as first-class abstractions in MAS. Based on our observations, we present a domain model and a SPARQL function library facilitating the design and implementation of stigmergic coordination between Linked Data agents on the Web. We demonstrate the efficacy our modeling approach in a Make-to-Order fulfilment scenario involving transient stigmergy and negative feedback.

Keywords: Linked Data · Semantic Web · Multi-agent systems · Stigmergy · Nature inspired algorithm · RDF · SPARQL

1 Introduction

Hypermedia multi-agent systems [4, 6], sometimes also referred to as Linked Systems [20], are receiving increasing research attention. The hypothesis is that the Web provides a scalable and distributed hypermedia environment that embedded agents can use to uniformly discover and interact with other agents and artifacts. Following a set of design principles very much aligned with REST and Linked Data best practices [2], the design and deployment of world-wide and long-lived hypermedia MASs with enhanced scalability and evolvability is aspired. In this context, we are specifically interested in stigmergic coordination principles for hypermedia MASs. The concept of stigmergy [22] provides an indirect and mediated feedback mechanism between agents, and enables complex,

© Springer Nature Singapore Pte Ltd. 2022
L. Pan et al. (Eds.): BIC-TA 2021, CCIS 1566, pp. 174–190, 2022.
https://doi.org/10.1007/978-981-19-1253-5_13

coordinated activity without any need for planning and control, direct communication, simultaneous presence or mutual awareness. A crucial part of a stigmergic system is its stigmergic environment [35] given that "it is its mediating function that underlies the power of stigmergy" [23]. Accounting for the importance of distributed hypermedia environments as first-class abstractions in hypermedia MASs and the environment's pivotal role in stigmergic systems, we examine the use of hypermedia-enabled Linked Data as a general stigmergic environment.

We briefly present core concepts and variations of stigmergic systems and summarise existing literature relevant to our work in Sect. 2. Next in Sect. 3, we propose to use a value-passing fragment of Milner's Calculus to formally specify generic, hypermedia-driven Linked Data agents and the Web as their embedding environment. We composed Linked Data agents and their environment into a Linked System (or equivalently a hypermedia MAS). Based on this formalism, we consider transient marker-based stigmergy as coordination mechanism between Linked Data agents in Sect. 4. We identify the necessity of generating server-side effects during the handling of safe and idempotent agent-initiated requests, and present a domain model and a SPARQL function library facilitating the design and implementation of stigmergic environments on the Web. Section 5 illustrates and evaluates our approach in a Make-to-Order fulfilment scenario involving transient stigmergy and negative feedback. We conclude and point out future work in Sect. 6.

2 Varieties of Stigmergy and Related Work

In collective stigmergic systems, groups of *agents* perform work by executing *actions* within their environment [23]. An action is considered a causal process that produces a change in the environment. Agents choose actions based on condition-action rules, and perform an action as soon as its condition is found to be met. Conditions are typically based on environmental states as *perceived* by the agent. Examples from nature are the presence of specific (food) resources, semiochemical traces, progress in

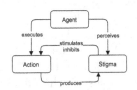

Fig. 1. Stigmergic feedback loop

building nest structures, etc. Which actions an agent can perform, how the agent will perform them, and which condition-action rules an agent will follow, is considered the agent's *competence* [25]. The part of the environment that undergoes changes as a result of executing an action, and the state of which is perceived to incite further actions, is called the *medium*. Each action produces, either as byproduct of an action, or the deliberate goal of the action itself, a *stigma* in the medium. Consequently, the behaviour of agents in a collective stigmergic system can be understood as a cycle of executing actions based on existing stigmata, and as result, leaving stigmata that stimulate or inhibit future actions (see Fig. 1). In essence, stigmata work as indirect communication mechanism between agents [37], potentially leading to coordination between agents, and, ideally, a self-organising behaviour of the entire system [22–24]. Based on these core concepts, i.e. *action*, *medium* and *stigma*, stigmergic systems can be further classified [23]. In *sematectonic* stigmergy, a stigma is a perceivable modification of the environment as result of work that was carried out by the agent, e.g. giving some new shape to a working material, or re-arranging order of objects in the world. In *marker-based* stigmergy, stigmata are markers, e.g. semiochemicals, that are specifically added to the environment as means for indirect communication between agents. When perceiving stigmata, agents may choose their actions based on the mere existence of a stigma in the medium (*qualitative stigmergy*), or also take into account quantities, like semiochemcial concentration levels, number of stigmata left, etc. (*quantitative stigmergy*). Moreover, stigmata present in the medium may stay until actively being removed by an agent (*persistent stigmata*) or until dissipated over time due to agent-less processes (*transient stigmata*).

Since the concept of stigmergy was coined as inherent underlying principle of coordination found in nature, it has faced a history of thorough research [36]. There is a profound understanding of the many variations of stigmergic systems, and how these are suited to model and implement efficient, flexible, and scalable algorithms for AI-based coordination and optimization [7,23,24].

Stigmergy is recognized as suitable underlying principle for multi-agent systems [17,18,37,38] and is applied in a variety of practical domains, e.g. digital manufacturing [39], robotics [27,30] or public transport [1,29].

Stigmergic systems can be considered a variation of *situated agent systems*, in which the interaction of agents with their environment is reduced to direct reaction based on perception, rather than complex knowledge processing and inference [41–43]. Principles in these systems were also developed around an indirect, influence-based interaction mechanism between agents and their environment as chosen for our proposed stigmergic system [13].

Web technologies have been found a suitable basis for implementation of multi agent systems [5,6,26,28]. Meanwhile, it came to attention that stigmergic principles are the underlying concept of many applications in the World Wide Web [8] including coordination in Web-based IoT systems [33].

Self-organizing multi agent systems and agent systems that rely on stigmergy as coordination mechanism have been exhaustively reviewed in [3]. This review concludes that a common understanding of such systems is widely lacking, and suggests a generic domain model to describe self-organizing system. From the review, we conclude additionally that the interaction between agents and environment is often described only vaguely, and is generally underspecified. As a solution, we provide in this paper a formal and generic specification of hypermedia driven agents and the respective agent-server interaction for stigmergic systems.

3 Process Algebra, Agents and Linked Systems

In what follows, we recap the syntax and semantics of a value-passing fragment of Milner's Calculus of Communicating Systems (CCS) [31,32]. This process algebra allows us to (i) specify the notion of Linked Data servers, (ii) formally model the *generic* hypermedia-driven behaviour of *Linked Data agents*, and (iii) compose a collection of Linked Data agent and server processes into a concurrent system that is denoted as a *Linked System* [20] or a hypermedia MAS [6].

3.1 Theoretical Setting: CCS with Value-Passing

Let $\mathcal{A}$ be a set of channel names; $\bar{\mathcal{A}} = \{\bar{a} \mid a \in \mathcal{A}\}$ be the set of co-names; $Act = \mathcal{A} \cup \bar{\mathcal{A}} \cup \{\tau\}$ be the set of actions where τ is the silent action; and $\mathcal{K}$ be a set of process identifiers.

The set $\mathcal{P}$ of all *process expressions* is the set of all terms generated by the right-hand side abstract syntax. Here, $\mathbf{0}$ is the atomic inactive process; $K \in \mathcal{K}$ is a process identifier; $\alpha \in Act$; $\vec{x} = (x_1, \ldots, x_n)$ is a n-dimensional vector of variables; $P_{1 \leq i \leq 2} \in \mathcal{P}$ are process expressions; and e is a Boolean expression.

$$
\begin{array}{llr}
P & := \quad \mathbf{0} & \text{(inaction)} \\
 & \mid \quad K & \text{(process labelling)} \\
 & \mid \quad \alpha.P & \text{(prefixing)} \\
 & \mid \quad \alpha(\vec{x}).P & \text{(value passing)} \\
 & \mid \quad P_1 + P_2 & \text{(choice)} \\
 & \mid \quad P_1 \parallel P_2 & \text{(parallel composition)} \\
 & \mid \quad \text{if } e \text{ then } P_1 \text{ else } P_2 & \text{(conditional)}
\end{array}
$$

A *process definition* is an equation system of the form $(K_{1 \leq i \leq k} = P_{1 \leq i \leq k})$ where $P_{1 \leq i \leq k} \subset \mathcal{P}$ is a set of process expression with process identifiers from $K_{1 \leq i \leq k} \subset \mathcal{K}$. Each process definition determines an Act-labelled transition system whose transitions can be inferred from the following Structural Operational Semantics rules

$$
\frac{}{\alpha.P \xrightarrow{\alpha} P} \qquad \frac{P \xrightarrow{\alpha} P' \quad (K = P)}{K \xrightarrow{\alpha} P'} \qquad \frac{P \xrightarrow{\alpha} P'}{(P + Q) \xrightarrow{\alpha} P'} \qquad \frac{Q \xrightarrow{\alpha} Q'}{(P + Q) \xrightarrow{\alpha} Q'}
$$

$$
\frac{P \xrightarrow{\alpha} P'}{(P \parallel Q) \xrightarrow{\alpha} (P' \parallel Q)} \qquad \frac{Q \xrightarrow{\alpha} Q'}{(P \parallel Q) \xrightarrow{\alpha} (P \parallel Q')} \qquad \frac{P \xrightarrow{a} P' \quad Q \xrightarrow{\bar{a}} Q'}{(P \parallel Q) \xrightarrow{\tau} (P' \parallel Q')}
$$

$$
\frac{}{\bar{a}(\vec{x}).P \xrightarrow{\bar{a}(\vec{v})} P} \qquad \frac{}{a(\vec{x}).P \xrightarrow{a(\vec{v})} P[v_1/x_1, \ldots, v_n/x_n]} \qquad \frac{P \xrightarrow{\bar{a}(\vec{v})} P' \quad Q \xrightarrow{a(\vec{v})} Q'}{(P \parallel Q) \xrightarrow{\tau} (P' \parallel Q')}
$$

$$
\frac{P \xrightarrow{\alpha} P'}{\text{if } true \text{ then } P \text{ else } Q \xrightarrow{\alpha} P'} \qquad \frac{Q \xrightarrow{\alpha} Q'}{\text{if } false \text{ then } P \text{ else } Q \xrightarrow{\alpha} Q'}
$$

where $P, P', Q, Q' \in \mathcal{P}$ are process expressions; $K \in \mathcal{K}$ is a process identifier; $\alpha \in Act$; $\vec{x} = (x_1, \ldots, x_n)$; $a, \bar{a} \in \mathcal{A} \cup \bar{\mathcal{A}}$; $P[v/x]$ is the process expression obtained from P by substituting a data value v for all occurrences of x.

3.2 Linked Data Servers, Agents and Linked Systems

Let $\mathbf{I}$, $\mathbf{L}$ and $\mathbf{B}$ be pairwise disjoint sets of resource identifiers, literals and blank nodes, respectively. The set of all *RDF triples* is $\mathcal{T} = (\mathbf{I} \cup \mathbf{B}) \times \mathbf{I} \times (\mathbf{I} \cup \mathbf{B} \cup \mathbf{L})$; a *RDF graph* $G \subset \mathcal{T}$ is a finite set of RDF triples. Given a formal RDF query language Q, we define the *query answering* functions $\mathrm{ans} : Q \times 2^{\mathcal{T}} \to 2^{\mathcal{T}}$, $\mathrm{ask} : Q \times 2^{\mathcal{T}} \to \mathbb{B}$, $\mathrm{sel} : Q \times 2^{\mathcal{T}} \to 2^{\mathbf{I}}$ and $\mathrm{descr} : \mathbf{I} \times 2^{\mathcal{T}} \to 2^{\mathcal{T}}$.

A *resource structure* is a tuple $(\mathbf{I}, R, \eta, \mathrm{OPS}, \mathrm{RET})$ where $\mathbf{I}$ is given as above; $R \subset \mathbf{I}$ is a finite set of root identifiers; $\eta : \mathbf{I} \to \mathbb{N}$ is a function that maps resource identifier i to its origin server $\mathrm{SERVER}_{\eta(i)}$; $\mathrm{OPS} = \{\mathrm{GET}, \mathrm{PUT}, \mathrm{POST}, \mathrm{DEL}\}$ is a set of method names; and $\mathrm{RET} = \{\mathrm{OK}, \mathrm{ERR}\}$ is a set of return codes.

We now fix a set of channel names as $\mathcal{A} = \{req_i, res_i \mid i \in \mathbb{N}\}$, and give CCS-style process specifications of *Linked Data servers* as well as *Linked Data agents* defined over the given resource structure $(\mathbf{I}, R, \eta, \mathrm{OPS}, \mathrm{RET})$.

Linked Data Servers. We conceive a Linked Data server SERVER_k as a reactive component that maintains an RDF graph G. It receives requests to perform a CRUD operation $op \in \mathrm{OPS}$ on a resource i via channel req_k

$$\mathrm{SERVER}_k(G) = req_k(op, i, G').\mathrm{PROC}_k(op, i, G', G)$$

where $G' \subset \mathcal{T}$ is a (potentially empty) request body. The server employs a constrained set of operations to process client-initiated requests for access and manipulation of the server-maintained RDF graph G

$$\mathrm{PROC}_k(\mathrm{GET}, i, G', G) = \mathrm{RESP}_k(\mathrm{OK}, (\emptyset, \mathrm{descr}(i, G)), G) + \mathrm{RESP}_k(\mathrm{ERR}, (\emptyset, \emptyset), G)$$
$$\mathrm{PROC}_k(\mathrm{PUT}, i, G', G) = \mathrm{RESP}_k(\mathrm{OK}, (\emptyset, \emptyset), (G \setminus \mathrm{descr}(i, G)) \cup G') + \mathrm{RESP}_k(\mathrm{ERR}, (\emptyset, \emptyset), G)$$
$$\mathrm{PROC}_k(\mathrm{POST}, i, G', G) = \mathrm{RESP}_k(\mathrm{OK}, (\{i'\}, \emptyset), G \cup G') + \mathrm{RESP}_k(\mathrm{ERR}, (\emptyset, \emptyset), G)$$
$$\mathrm{PROC}_k(\mathrm{DEL}, i, G', G) = \mathrm{RESP}_k(\mathrm{OK}, (\{i\}, \emptyset), G \setminus \mathrm{descr}(i, G)) + \mathrm{RESP}_k(\mathrm{ERR}, (\emptyset, \emptyset), G)$$

where $i' \in \mathbf{I}$ is a "fresh" IRI with $\eta(i') = k$. The server responds to requests via channel $\overline{res}_k$

$$\mathrm{RESP}_k(rc, rval, G) = \overline{res}_k(rc, rval).\mathrm{SERVER}_k(G)$$

with return code $rc \in \mathrm{RET}$ and with a linkset and response graph in $rval \in (2^{\mathbf{I}} \times 2^{\mathcal{T}})$.

Tropistic Linked Data Agents. We specify a *tropistic* [16, section 13.1] Linked Data agent AGENT_k as an active component

$$\mathrm{AGENT}_k = \mathrm{PERC}_k(i \in R, G = \emptyset, L = \{i\})$$

being initially situated at a resource $i \in R$ without a-priori agent knowledge $(G = \emptyset)$ and a linkset $L = \{i\}$ restricted to i. Our specification of AGENT_k puts emphasis on a direct response to its perceptions and favours to employ *situated perceptions* [34] of the environment as the basis for deciding which action to perform next. We model situated perception in CCS-style as

$$\text{PERC}_k(i, G, L) = \overline{req}_{\eta(j)}(\text{GET}, j, \emptyset).res_{\eta(j)}(rc, (L', G')).$$

$$\left(\text{PERC}_k(i, G'', L'') + \text{REACT}_k(i, G'', L'') \right) \tag{1}$$

where AGENT_k - while being situated at i - will at first issue a GET request for a resource j in its current linkset L via channel $\overline{req}_{\eta(j)}$ and then awaits the server's response via channel $res_{\eta(j)}$ with return code $rc \in \text{RET}$, response linkset $L' \subset \mathbf{I}$ and response graph in $G' \in \mathcal{T}$. Subsequently, the agent executes (i) a *perceptional query* q_{PERC_k} over G' in order to update its situational knowledge to

$$G'' = G \cup \text{ans}(q_{\text{PERC}_k}, G')$$

as well as (ii) a *navigational query* q_{NAV_k} over its updated knowledge graph in order to update its linkset to

$$L'' = L \cup L' \cup \text{sel}(q_{\text{NAV}_k}, G''))$$

On the basis of G'' and L'', AGENT_k chooses to either recurse into its situated perception process $\text{PERC}_k(i, G'', L'')$ or to enter the process $\text{REACT}_k(i, G'', L'')$ in order to select an action on the basis of a local, short-time view of its environment. An action selected only on the basis of a situated perception is called a *reaction*.

We model the process of selecting reactions in the following way

$$\text{REACT}_k(i, G, L) = \text{PERC}_k(j \in L, \emptyset, \{j\}) +$$

$$\sum_{m \in \text{OPS} \setminus \{\text{GET}\}} \left(\text{if } \text{ask}(\widehat{q}_{m_k}, G, L) \text{ then } m_k(i, G, L) \text{ else } \text{REACT}_k(i, G, L) \right) \tag{2}$$

In essence, an agent may choose to either

(i) re-situate and perform situated perception of resource $j \in L, j \neq i$ with the implication that its situational knowledge and linkset will be reset; hence it does neither maintain a long-term internal model of its environment nor pursues explicit goals;

(ii) request the execution of operation $m \in \text{OPS} \setminus \{\text{GET}\}$ against resource i given that the *conditional query* $\widehat{q}_{m_k}$ over its knowledge graph G holds; possible instantiations of $m_k(i, , L)$ are given by

$$\text{PUT}_k(i, G, L) = \overline{req}_{\eta(i)}(\text{PUT}, i, \text{ans}(q_{\text{PUT}_k}, G)).res_{\eta(i)}(rc, (\emptyset, \emptyset)).\text{REACT}_k(i, G, L)$$
$$\text{POST}_k(i, G, L) = \overline{req}_{\eta(i)}(\text{POST}, i, \text{ans}(q_{\text{POST}_k}, G)).res_{\eta(i)}(rc, (L', \emptyset)).\text{REACT}_k(i, G, L \cup L')$$
$$\text{DEL}_k(i, G, L) = \overline{req}_{\eta(i)}(\text{DEL}, i, \emptyset).res_{\eta(i)}(rc, (L', \emptyset)).\text{REACT}_k(j \in L \setminus L', G, L \setminus L')$$

where $\text{ans}(q_{m_k}, G)$ is the result graph of executing an *effectual query* q_{m_k} over the agent's knowledge graph G with $m \in \{\text{PUT}, \text{POST}\}$.

Given the formal notation of Linked Data servers and agents, we can now focus on composing a collection of Linked Data agent and server processes into a concurrent system that is denoted as a hypermedia MAS [6] or a *Linked System* [20].

Linked Systems. A *Linked System* [20] is the parallel composition

$$\texttt{LINKED-SYSTEM} = (\texttt{AGENTS} \parallel \texttt{ENVIRONMENT})$$

with $\texttt{AGENTS} = (\texttt{AGENT}_1 \parallel \cdots \parallel \texttt{AGENT}_m)$ and $\texttt{ENVIRONMENT} = (\texttt{SERVER}_1 \parallel \cdots \parallel \texttt{SERVER}_n)$ for a collection of Linked Data agents $\texttt{AGENT}_{1 \leq k \leq m}$ and Linked Data servers $\texttt{SERVER}_{1 \leq k \leq n}$ respectively. All direct interaction within $\texttt{LINKED-SYSTEM}$ is between agent and server processes.

The *state space* of $\texttt{LINKED-SYSTEM}$ is given by the nodes of an *Act*-labelled transition system whose transitions can be inferred from the Structural Operational Semantics rules given in Sect. 3.1.

A *computation* is an alternating sequence of global states and actions, where an *action* is either a communication between an agent and a server, or an internal process transition. A computation of a Linked System induces an *interaction sequence* given by the sequence of actions along that computation.

3.3   Synthesis

With the notions of Linked Data servers, tropistic Linked Data agents, and finally Linked Systems as defined above, the resulting value-passing CCS fragment enables us to formally specify the generic hypermedia-driven behaviour of tropistic Linked Data agents. We would like to emphasise the fact that the general behaviors as described by the CCS fragment are generic and independent of the scenarios in which they are applied. Domain- or application-specific behaviors of agents and systems are entirely encoded in terms of the queries that are evaluated as part of the different processes. For these, we identified four different type of queries:

(i) *Perceptional queries* specify the subsets of the environment representation relevant to the agent.

(ii) *Navigational queries* constrain the agent navigation with respect to such relevant subsets of the environment.

(iii) *Conditional queries* guard the selection of particular reactions.

(iv) *Effectual queries* describe how the agent intends to manipulate a given resource.

The per se generic framework can be applied to different scenarios by supplying respective specific queries. In the following section, we will extend Linked Systems to support stigmergy by an additional class of queries: *evolutional queries* that drive the dynamics of the underlying $\texttt{ENVIRONMENT}$.

4   Stigmergy in Linked Systems

A $\texttt{LINKED-SYSTEM}$ as specified previously provides an indirect, mediated mechanism of coordination between $\texttt{AGENTS}$. It therefore enables the realisation of sematectonic and *persistent* marker-based stigmergy. However, when considering some of the prime examples of stigmergy, e.g. ant colony optimization [9–12] and termite colony optimisation methods [21], it becomes apparent that a purely reactive ENVIRONMENT is insufficient for the implementation of *transient marker-based stigmergic* mechanisms.

In fact, a stigmergic environment typically demonstrates some immanent dynamics that may modify the environment's state independent of any agent's actions [23, p. 24]. These endogenous dynamics, e.g. diffusion, evaporation, dissipation, atrophy or erosion of stigmata, constitute a crucial component of transient marker-based stigmergic systems ([40], cf. Fig. 2), and more importantly, they are *not* subjected to agent-driven processes. 5 We call the part of a stigmergic environment that, in addition

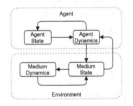

Fig. 2. Stigmergic system components

to being malleable and perceivable by all agents under coordination, *actively* drives the evolution of such agent-less dynamic processes a *stigmergic medium*.

Taking into account the notion of a stigmergic medium, we define a *stigmergic Linked System* as the parallel composition

$$\text{STIGMERGIC-LINKED-SYSTEM} = (\text{AGENTS} \parallel (\text{MEDIUM} \parallel \text{ENVIRONMENT}))$$

where the stigmergic $\text{MEDIUM} = \text{MEDIUM}_1 \parallel \cdots \parallel \text{MEDIUM}_l$ relates to the parallel composition of a collection of *extended* LD server components.

A MEDIUM_k component is a Linked Data server that offers a constrained set of operations to access and manipulate server-provided resource states, but *in addition*, generates server-side side-effects[1]

$$\text{MEDIUM}_k(G) = req(op, i, G').\text{PROC}_k(op, i, G', G))$$
$$\text{RESP}_k(rc, rval, G) = \overline{res}(rc, rval).\text{MEDIUM}_k(G)$$
$$\text{PROC}_k(\text{GET}, i, G', G) = \text{EVOLVE}_k(i, G)$$

as evolution $\text{EVOLVE}_k(i, G)$ of the environment during the handling of safe and idempotent agent-initiated resource request. The generation of such side-effects is subjected to an *internal* process

$$\text{EVOLVE}_k(i, G) = \text{RESP}(\text{OK}, (\emptyset, \text{descr}(i, G')), G'') + \text{RESP}_k(\text{ERR}, (\emptyset, \emptyset), G) \qquad (3)$$

where the result of executing an *evolutional query* q_{EVO_k} over a given RDF graph G is given by $G' = \text{ans}(q_{\text{EVO}_k}, G)$ and the server state after an evolutional state update is $G'' = G \setminus \text{descr}(i, G) \cup \text{descr}(i, G')$. Executing an evolutional query drives the endogenous dynamics of MEDIUM_k over time, e.g. diffusion and evaporation of semiochemicals, irrespectively of *agent-initiated requests for* resource state *change*.

Next, we address the definition of evolutional queries; towards this end, we introduce the **stigLD** domain model and the **stigFN** SPARQL function library.

---

[1] We emphasise that this conception is not in violation with HTTP semantics [14, sections 4.2.1,4.2.2] [15].

4.1   stigLD: A Domain Model for Stigmergic Linked Systems

Our domain model (cf. Fig. 3) defines four basic concepts: stig:Medium, stig:Law, stig:Topos and stig:Stigma.

A stig:Medium instance is a resource that allows for interaction between different actions, and therefore, it enables the stigmergic coordination between agents performing such actions. In order to fulfil its "mediating function that underlies the true power of stigmergy" [23], a stig:Medium must be similarly perceivable and malleable by all agents under stigmergic coordination. A stig:Medium is considered a part of a larger environment, and it undergoes changes only through agents' actions or through a set of stig:Law governing its endogenous dynamics.

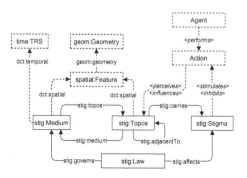

Fig. 3. stigLD domain model

A stig:Medium may optionally detail on its spatio-temporal characteristics[2], however, it must introduce a structure of interconnected stig:Topos instances in which an agent navigates, experiences situated perception and exerts situated behaviour.

A stig:Topos resource is the fundamental structural element of a stig:Medium and carries a potentially empty set of stig:Stigma instances. It has a potentially empty set of directed connections to other stig:Topos instances within the same stig:Medium instance. Furthermore, a stig:Topos may be identified with any domain- or application-specific resource using an owl:sameAs link and optionally detail on its spatial characteristics. An agent situated in a specific stig:Topos partially perceives the medium state and may try to influence the medium as a result of its action.

A stig:Stigma is a perceivable change made in a stig:Medium by an agent's action. The perception of a stig:Stigma may stimulate (or inhibit) the performance of a subsequent action, i.e. the presence of a stig:Stigma makes the performance of this action more (or less) likely. Hence, actions stimulate (or inhibit) their own continued execution via the intermediary of stig:Stigma (cf. Fig. 1).

A stig:Law describes the spatio-temporal evolution of stigmata within the medium. For this, a stig:Law describes itself in terms of its specific effect, e.g. linear decay, to a set of affected stig:Stigma sub classes. A stig:Law may link to an *evolutional query* which may be used to calculate the evolution of the medium's endogenous dynamics.

---

[2] For example via dct:spatial and dct:temporal links.

4.2 stigFN: SPARQL Functions for Stigmergic Linked Systems

In order to facilitate the implementation of transient marker-based stigmergic Linked Systems, we supplement our domain model with the stigFN SPARQL function library. It provides the fundamental operations required for implementing the endogenous dynamics of a stigmergic medium:

1. *Decay functions.* Transient marker-based stigmergy may require certain stigmata to be subjected to dissipation processes. With stigFN:linear_decay and stigFN:exponential_decay, we provide two standard decay models.
2. *Diffusion functions.* In diffusion processes, the intensity of a stigma does not decay over time but rather spreads over a spatial dimension from the point of its deposition. With stigFN:diffuse_1D, the 1D diffusion equation is made available.
3. *Handling temporal and spatial values.* Decay and diffusion functions require arithmetic operations on temporal data, e.g. xsd:duration, xsd:dateTime or xsd:time. Due to lack of built-in support in SPARQL and XPATH, we provide stigFN:duration_secs and stigFN:duration_msecs for conversions from a xsd:duration value to (milli)seconds. Additionally, stigFN:dist_manhattan is provided as a means to find the Manhattan distance between topoi when the medium is discretised into grids.

We implemented stigFN using SPARQL user-defined functions[3] in Apache Jena[4]. https://github.com/BMBF-MOSAIK/StigLD-DemoDocumentation and source code[5] is publicly available; we intend to extend stigFN with additional decay and diffusion models as well as auxiliary functions.

5 Use Case: Make-to-Order Fulfilment

We apply the previously established concepts to a Make-to-Order (MTO) fulfilment process from the production domain. MTO is a production approach in which manufacturing starts only after a customer's order is received.

Let us consider a shop floor area that is represented by a discrete grid; in each grid cell is a shop floor location and can accommodate a single production resource. We distinguish between three types of production resources: machines, output slots assigned to individual machines and transporters.

Machines produce a product of not further specified kind in response to a confirmed order received for it from a final customer. Whenever a machine finishes production of a product, the product is placed into an output slot awaiting pickup by a transporter unit. *Output slots* have limited capacity. If any of the output slots are full, the associated machine cannot produce any new products until the output slot is emptied by the transporters. *Transporters* are initially situated in idle locations spread throughout the grid; they can move to any

---

[3] https://jena.apache.org/documentation/query/writing_functions.html.
[4] https://jena.apache.org/.
[5] https://github.com/BMBF-MOSAIK/StigLD-Demo.

unoccupied location within their respective Manhattan distance neighbourhood. Their task is to pick up finished products from the output slots of machines, so that production can go on without significant interruptions.

The shop floor will continuously receive new customer orders; we aim to coordinate the MTO fulfilment process such that customer orders should be assigned to machines in such a way that the overall machine work load is balanced, and make-shift times of individual products – the time from start of production to delivery of the finished product – should be minimized. More specifically, we are interested in improving the following metrics

(i) average number of steps moved by the transporters
(ii) average maximum and minimum machine loads
(iii) deviation in maximum load experienced by machines
(iv) average time between start of production of a product until pickup by a transport unit (mean time to deliver)

All material needed to set up and run the example are provided https://github. com/BMBF-MOSAIK/StigLD-Demoonline along with an http://mosaik.dfki. deinteractive demo instance[6].

5.1   Shop Floor Representation in StigLD

In our example, the `stig:Medium` represents the overall shop floor area as a 10×10 grid of `stig:Topos` instances. Neighborhood relations depend on the type of agent that is exploring the medium (see also Sect. 5.2): For transporter agents that navigate the shopfloor, each `st:Topos` links via `stig:adjacentTo` predicates to the `stig:Topos` instances in its Manhattan distance neighborhood. Order assignment agents ignore spatial information, and consider all topoi that carry a machine unit as mutually connected. Production resources are assigned to their individual `stig:Topos` instances using `stig:locatedAt` link predicates; the Transporters' idle locations – the grid cells to which they return after having finished a pickup – are given by `ex:idlePosition` link predicates.

5.2   Agent Models

We employ *marker-based stigmergy* with *transient* semio-chemical marker models to achieve the desired coordination. For this, we employ two types of agents: one type assigns open orders to available machines on the shop floor, the other controls transport units.

Order Assignment Agents: Transient Stigmergy Based on Linear Decay. For an open order, an order assignment agent $\mathtt{OAA} = \mathrm{PERC}(i, G = \emptyset, L = \emptyset)$ is placed on a randomly chosen topos i that is accommodating a machine; the agent performs situated perception as specified in Eq. 1 with

---

[6] http://mosaik.dfki.de.

$$(G'' = \text{ans}(q_{\text{PERC}}, G')) \equiv (\forall t \in G' \Rightarrow t \in G'')$$

$$(L'' = \text{sel}(q_{\text{NAV}}, G'')) \equiv (L'' = \{j \mid \underset{j}{\text{argmin}} \begin{pmatrix} \text{<j> stig:carries [} & \text{stig:level ?val;} \\ & \text{a ex:NFMarker];} \\ \hat{} \ \text{(stig:locatedAt) [a ex:Machine].} \end{pmatrix} \})$$

When selecting its reaction (cf. Eq. 2)

$$\text{REACT}(i, G, L) = \text{if } i \notin L \text{ then } \text{PERC}(j \in L, \emptyset, \emptyset) \text{ else } \text{MARK}(i, G, L)$$

the agent OAA will either (i) re-situate to a topos with lower concentration of negative feedback or (ii) leave a *negative feedback marker*[7] on its current topos:

$$\text{MARK}(i, G, L) = \overline{req}_{\eta(i)}(\text{PUT}, i, \text{ans}(q_{\text{PUT}}, G)).res_{\eta(i)}(rc, (\emptyset, \emptyset)).\mathbf{0}$$

$$\text{ans}(q_{\text{PUT}}, G) \equiv \text{descr}(i, G) \cup \{\text{<i> stig:carries [a ex:NFMarker; stig:level 1.0].}\}$$

Negative feedback markers will decay linearly over time; the system's endogenous dynamics with respect to negative feedback markers is given by Eq. 3 with

$$\text{ans}(q_{\text{EVO}}, G) \equiv \begin{pmatrix} \text{?i stig:carries [a ex:NFMarker; stig:level ?c; stig:decayRate ?d].} \\ \Downarrow \\ \text{?i stig:carries [stig:level stigFN:linear\_decay}(\Delta t, \text{?d, ?c)].} \end{pmatrix}$$

Leaving a negative feedback marker *inhibits* future selection of a machine, and increases the likelihood of balancing machine workloads during the MTO process.

Transporter Agents: Transient Stigmergy Based on Diffusion. Whenever a new finished product is put into a machine's output slot, *transportation markers* (ex:TMarker) are added to the topos containing the respective slot. These markers do not decay linearly in-place, but diffuse and spread over the entire shop floor.

A transporter agent $\text{TA} = \text{PERC}(s, G = \emptyset, L = \emptyset)$ is initially situated in its idle location s; the agent performs situated perception as specified in Eq. 1 with

$$(G'' = \text{ans}(q_{\text{PERC}}, G')) \equiv (\forall t \in G' \Rightarrow t \in G'')$$

$$(L'' = \text{sel}(q_{\text{NAV}}, G'')) \equiv (L'' = \{l \mid \underset{l}{\text{argmax}} \begin{pmatrix} \text{<l> stig:carries [stig:level ?val;} \\ \text{a ex:TMarker].} \end{pmatrix} \})$$

When selecting its reaction (cf. Eq. 2)

$$\text{REACT}(i, G, L) = \text{if } i \notin L \text{ then } \text{PERC}(j \in L, \emptyset, \emptyset) \text{ else } \text{PICKUP}(i, G, L)$$

$$\text{PICKUP}(i, G, L) = \text{if } \exists p : (\text{<p> a ex:Product; stig:locatedAt <i>}) \in G$$
$$\text{then } \text{DEL}(p, \emptyset, \emptyset).\text{MOVE}(s, p).\text{PERC}(s, \emptyset, \emptyset)$$
$$\text{else } \text{PERC}(j \in L, \emptyset, \emptyset)$$

the agent TA will either (i) re-situate to a neighboring topos with higher concentration of ex:TMarker and hence climb the diffusion gradient, or (ii) attempt to pickup and move a product from its current location to its idle location.

---

[7] – as well as a production task into the respective machine's task queue –.

As described in Sect. 4, any `GET` request as part of a `TA` agent's situated perception (cf. Eq. 1) will trigger a diffusion update

$$
\mathrm{ans}(q_{\mathrm{EVO}, G}) \equiv
\begin{pmatrix}
\texttt{?i stig:carries [a ex:TMarker; stig:level ?c;].} \\
\Downarrow \\
\texttt{?j stig:carries [a ex:TMarker;} \\
\qquad\qquad\qquad\texttt{stig:level stigFN:diffuse1D(} \\
\qquad\qquad\qquad\texttt{?i, stigFN:dist\_manhattan(?i, ?j), ?c, } \Delta\texttt{t} \\
\qquad\qquad\qquad\texttt{)].}
\end{pmatrix}
$$

and drive the evolution of the system's transportation markers.

Table 1. Results of simulations

	Random walk	Stigmergic coordination
Avg. number of updates	85	58
Avg. transporter steps	262	132
Mean time to deliver	112 s	67 s
Avg. max machine load	13	12
Avg. min machine load	6	8

5.3   Evaluation

We evaluated above scenario with fifty orders for products to be produced and picked up by the transporters from output slots. The shop floor contains five production machines and four transporter artifacts. For the sake of uniformity while running these simulations, all machines have output slots with a capacity of holding five finished products.

We employ the agent models as described in the previous section and benchmark against a simplified transporter agent model that only scans for finished products in its surroundings to initiate pick up, but otherwise move around randomly, i.e. not following any marker trace.

We compare the total number of updates required in each instance to complete producing fifty orders, as well as emptying them from the output slots. In addition, we compare the average number of steps moved by the transporters, the deviation in maximum load experienced by machines in each simulation and the average time that a finished product spends in an output slot before being picked up by transporters. These results can be seen in Table 1. The stigmergic coordination based shop floor simulation requires around 30% less updates in order to complete the simulation run of producing fifty orders and transporting them away from the output slots of machines. Also, it takes half as many movements by transporters compared to randomly moving transporters. Moreover, the average time it takes from a product from beginning of production to pickup by a transporter (mean time to deliver) is reduced by 40% in the stigmergy based simulation.

Average maximum and minimum machine loads are comparable in both cases, but slightly worse in the random walk simulations. Ideally, given that we have five machines and fifty orders, the average number of orders at each machine should be ten. But, since the randomly moving transporters often take longer to empty some output slots, the corresponding machines are loaded less relative to the other machines. Each update query (which includes the implicit diffusion and linear decay of stigmergic markers) takes an average of 500 milliseconds to complete.

6 Conclusions and Future Work

We propose to use a value-passing fragment of Milner's Calculus to formally specify the *generic* hypermedia-driven behaviour of Linked Data agents and the Web as their embedding environment. Based on this formalism, agents and their environment can be composed into a concurrent Linked System with declarative queries serving as extension mechanism for specifying the *domain-specific* hypermedia-driven behaviour of Linked Data agents.

Next, we took first steps into investigating stigmergic coordination principles within such Linked Systems. When considering transient marker-based stigmergy, we have identified the necessity of generating server-side effects during the handling of safe and idempotent agent-initiated resource requests. This is due to the fact that stigmergic environments may exhibit agent-less, endogenous dynamic evolution.

Based on this observation, we developed the stigLD domain model and the stigFN function library facilitating the design and declarative implementation of stigmergic principles within the agent as well as server components of a Linked System.

We demonstrate the genericity and effectiveness of our modeling approach by implementing a make-to-order (MTO) scenario from the production domain using two transient semio-chemical marker models. Our implementation displays emergence of self-organized coordination from simple agent behaviour and compares favourably against a random walk baseline strategy.

We intend to expand the stigFN function library with additional decay and diffusion models as well as auxiliary functions; scalability experiments and application to additional domains are subject to future work. Translating given CCS specifications of (stigmergic) Linked Systems into executable labelled-transition systems [19] is an issue for future research.

Acknowledgements. This work has been supported by the German Federal Ministry for Education and Research (BMBF) as part of the MOSAIK project (grant no. 01IS18070-C).

References

1. Alfeo, A.L., Cimino, M.G., Egidi, S., Lepri, B., Vaglini, G.: A Stigmergy-based analysis of city hotspots to discover trends and anomalies in urban transportation usage. IEEE Trans. Intell. Transp. Syst. **19**(7), 2258–2267 (2018). https://doi.org/10.1109/TITS.2018.2817558
2. Bizer, C., Heath, T., Idehen, K., Berners-Lee, T.: Linked data on the web (LDOW2008). In: Proceedings of the 17th International Conference on World Wide Web, pp. 1265–1266 (2008)
3. Charpenay, V., et al.: MOSAIK: a formal model for self-organizing manufacturing systems. IEEE Pervasive Comput. **20**, 9–18 (2020)
4. Ciortea, A., Boissier, O., Ricci, A.: Engineering world-wide multi-agent systems with hypermedia. In: Weyns, D., Mascardi, V., Ricci, A. (eds.) EMAS 2018. LNCS (LNAI), vol. 11375, pp. 285–301. Springer, Cham (2019). https://doi.org/10.1007/978-3-030-25693-7_15
5. Ciortea, A., Mayer, S., Boissier, O., Gandon, F.: Exploiting interaction affordances: on engineering autonomous systems for the web of things. In: Second W3C workshop on the Web of Things: The Open Web to Challenge IoT Fragmentation, Munich, Germany (2019)
6. Ciortea, A., Mayer, S., Gandon, F., Boissier, O., Ricci, A., Zimmermann, A.: A decade in hindsight: the missing bridge between multi-agent systems and the World Wide Web. In: Proceedings of the International Joint Conference on Autonomous Agents and Multiagent Systems, AAMAS, vol. 3, pp. 1659–1663 (2019). https://www.alexandria.unisg.ch/256718/
7. Dipple, A., Raymond, K., Docherty, M.: General theory of Stigmergy: modelling stigma semantics. Elsevier (2014). https://doi.org/10.1016/j.cogsys.2014.02.002
8. Dipple, A.C.: Standing on the shoulders of ants: Stigmergy in the web. In: Proceedings of the 20th International Conference Companion on World Wide Web, pp. 355–360 (2011)
9. Dorigo, M., Bonabeau, E., Theraulaz, G.: Ant algorithms and Stigmergy. Future Generation Comput. Syst. **16**(8), 851–871, June 2000. https://doi.org/10.1016/S0167-739X(00)00042-X
10. Dorigo, M., Di Caro, G.: Ant colony optimization: a new meta-heuristic. In: Proceedings of the 1999 Congress on Evolutionary Computation, CEC 1999, vol. 2, pp. 1470–1477. IEEE Computer Society (1999). https://doi.org/10.1109/CEC.1999.782657
11. Dorigo, M., Maniezzo, V., Colorni, A.: Ant system: optimization by a colony of cooperating agents. IEEE Trans. Syst. Man Cybern. B Cybern. **26**(1), 29–41 (1996). https://doi.org/10.1109/3477.484436
12. Dorigo, M., Stützle, T.: Ant colony optimization: overview and recent advances. In: Gendreau, M., Potvin, J.-Y. (eds.) Handbook of Metaheuristics. ISORMS, vol. 272, pp. 311–351. Springer, Cham (2019). https://doi.org/10.1007/978-3-319-91086-4_10
13. Ferber, J., Müller, J.P.: Influences and reaction: a model of situated multiagent systems. In: 2nd International Conference on Multi-Agent Systems (ICMAS-96), pp. 72–79 (1996)
14. Fielding, R.: hypertext transfer protocol (http/1.1): semantics and content. Technical report
15. Fielding, R.: Re: draft findings on unsafe methods (whenToUseGet-7) (2002). https://lists.w3.org/Archives/Public/www-tag/2002Apr/0207.html. Accessed Apr 2021

16. Genesereth, M.R., Nilsson, N.J.: Logical Foundations of Artificial Intelligence. Morgan Kaufmann (2012)

17. Hadeli, K., Valckenaers, P., Kollingbaum, M., Van Brussel, H.: Multi-agent coordination and control using Stigmergy. Comput. Ind. **53**(1), 75–96 (2004). https://doi.org/10.1016/S0166-3615(03)00123-4

18. Hadeli, K., et al.: Self-organising in multi-agent coordination and control using Stigmergy. In: Di Marzo Serugendo, G., Karageorgos, A., Rana, O.F., Zambonelli, F. (eds.) ESOA 2003. LNCS (LNAI), vol. 2977, pp. 105–123. Springer, Heidelberg (2004). https://doi.org/10.1007/978-3-540-24701-2_8

19. Harth, A., Käfer, T.: Towards specification and execution of linked systems. In: GvD (2016)

20. Harth, A., Käfer, T.: Towards specification and execution of linked systems. In: CEUR Workshop Proceedings, vol. 1594, pp. 62–67 (2016)

21. Hedayatzadeh, R., Akhavan Salmassi, F., Keshtgari, M., Akbari, R., Ziarati, K.: Termite colony optimization: a novel approach for optimizing continuous problems. In: 2010 18th Iranian Conference on Electrical Engineering, pp. 553–558 (2010). https://doi.org/10.1109/IRANIANCEE.2010.5507009

22. Heylighen, F.: Stigmergy as a generic mechanism for coordination: definition, varieties and aspects. Cognition, pp. 1–23 (2011)

23. Heylighen, F.: Stigmergy as a universal coordination mechanism I: definition and components. Cogn. Syst. Res. **38**, 4–13 (2016). https://doi.org/10.1016/j.cogsys.2015.12.002

24. Heylighen, F.: Stigmergy as a universal coordination mechanism II: varieties and evolution. Cogn. Syst. Res. **38**, 50–59 (2016). https://doi.org/10.1016/j.cogsys.2015.12.007

25. Heylighen, F., Vidal, C.: Getting things done: the science behind stress-free productivity. Long Range Plan. **41**(6), 585–605 (2008)

26. Hunt, E.R., Jones, S., Hauert, S.: Testing the limits of pheromone Stigmergy in high-density robot swarms. Roy. Soc. Open Sci. **6**(11) (2019). https://doi.org/10.1098/rsos.190225

27. Jevtić, A., Gutierrez, Á., Andina, D., Jamshidi, M.: Distributed bees algorithm for task allocation in swarm of robots. IEEE Syst. J. **6**(2), 296–304 (2012). https://doi.org/10.1109/JSYST.2011.2167820

28. Jochum, B., Nürnberg, L., Aßfalg, N., Käfer, T.: Data-driven workflows for specifying and executing agents in an environment of reasoning and RESTful systems. In: Di Francescomarino, C., Dijkman, R., Zdun, U. (eds.) BPM 2019. LNBIP, vol. 362, pp. 93–105. Springer, Cham (2019). https://doi.org/10.1007/978-3-030-37453-2_9

29. Kanamori, R., Takahashi, J., Ito, T.: Evaluation of traffic management strategies with anticipatory stigmergy. J. Inf. Process. **22**(2), 228–234 (2014). https://doi.org/10.2197/ipsjjip.22.228

30. Krieger, M.J., Billeter, J.B., Keller, L.: Ant-like task allocation and recruitment in cooperative robots. Nature **406**(6799), 992–995 (2000). https://doi.org/10.1038/35023164

31. Milner, R. (ed.): A Calculus of Communicating Systems. LNCS, vol. 92. Springer, Heidelberg (1980). https://doi.org/10.1007/3-540-10235-3

32. Milner, R.: Communication and concurrency. PHI Series in Computer Science. Prentice Hall (1989)

33. Privat, G.: Phenotropic and stigmergic webs: the new reach of networks. Univ. Access Inf. Soc. **11**(3), 323–335 (2012). https://doi.org/10.1007/s10209-011-0240-1

34. Smith, G.J., Gero, J.S.: What does an artificial design agent mean by being 'situated'? Des. Stud. **26**, 535–561 (2005). https://doi.org/10.1016/j.destud.2005.01.001

35. Spieldenner., T., Chelli., M.: Linked data as stigmergic medium for decentralized coordination. In: Proceedings of the 16th International Conference on Software Technologies - ICSOFT, pp. 347–357. INSTICC. SciTePress (2021). https://doi.org/10.5220/0010518003470357

36. Theraulaz, G., Bonabeau, E.: A brief history of stigmergy. Artif. Life **5**(2), 97–116 (1999)

37. Tummolini, L., Castelfranchi, C.: Trace signals: the meanings of stigmergy. In: Weyns, D., Parunak, H.V.D., Michel, F. (eds.) E4MAS 2006. LNCS (LNAI), vol. 4389, pp. 141–156. Springer, Heidelberg (2007). https://doi.org/10.1007/978-3-540-71103-2_8

38. Valckenaers, P., Kollingbaum, M., Van Brussel, H., et al.: Multi-agent coordination and control using stigmergy. Comput. Ind. **53**(1), 75–96 (2004)

39. Valckenaers, P., Van Brussel, H., Kollingbaum, M., Bochmann, O.: Multi-agent coordination and control using stigmergy applied to manufacturing control. In: Luck, M., Mařík, V., Štěpánková, O., Trappl, R. (eds.) ACAI 2001. LNCS (LNAI), vol. 2086, pp. 317–334. Springer, Heidelberg (2001). https://doi.org/10.1007/3-540-47745-4_15

40. Dyke Parunak, H.: A survey of environments and mechanisms for human-human stigmergy. In: Weyns, D., Van Dyke Parunak, H., Michel, F. (eds.) E4MAS 2005. LNCS (LNAI), vol. 3830, pp. 163–186. Springer, Heidelberg (2006). https://doi.org/10.1007/11678809_10

41. Weyns, D., Agentwise, T.H.: A formal model for situated multi-agent systems. Technical report (2004)

42. Weyns, D., Holvoet, T.: Model for simultaneous actions in situated multi-agent systems. In: Schillo, M., Klusch, M., Müller, J., Tianfield, H. (eds.) MATES 2003. LNCS (LNAI), vol. 2831, pp. 105–118. Springer, Heidelberg (2003). https://doi.org/10.1007/978-3-540-39869-1_10

43. Weyns, D., Omicini, A., Odell, J., Weyns, D., Omicini, A., Odell, J.: Environment as a first class abstraction in multiagent systems model of the environment. Auton. Agent Multi-Agent Syst. **14**(1), 5–30 (2007). https://doi.org/10.1007/s10458-006-0012-0

An Approach for Optimal Coverage of Heterogeneous AUV Swarm Based on Consistency Theory

Yongzhou Lu[1], Guangyu Luo[2(✉)], Xuan Guo[2], and Yuepeng Chen[2]

[1] Naval Research Institute, Wuhan 430000, People's Republic of China
[2] School of Automation, Wuhan University of Technology,
Wuhan 430000, People's Republic of China
{luoguangyu,233980}@whut.edu.cn

Abstract. Target search mission in given 3-D underwater environments is a challenge in heterogeneous AUV swarms exploration. In this paper, an effective and low consumption strategy is focused for the challenge. With consistency theory, two problems are proposed: optimal partition of regions and cooperative search of targets. First, the original computational geometry of spatial structures is exploited using centroidal Voronoi tessellation. Then, the optimal distribution of the regions under weighted condition of the target probability is obtained by using the mission load dynamic model. Next, a distributed cooperative protocol based on consensus strategy is proposed to solve the cooperative search problem. Finally, theoretical results are validated through simulations on heterogeneous AUV swarms.

Keywords: Consensus theory · Optimal partition of regions · Bioinspired model · Cooperative target search · Optimal coverage control

1 Introduction

Autonomous underwater vehicle (AUV) is a submarine robot that can cruise underwater freely without the restriction of umbilical cable. With a variety of sensors, it is capable of performing various underwater tasks, such as marine resource exploitation, underwater scientific research and hydrological environmental exploration [1–4]. However, with the increasing complexity and dangerous of underwater tasks, a single AUV or a homogeneous AUV swarm is difficult to complete the tasks. In order to improve efficiency of such situation, AUVs with different characteristics and abilities are grouped to perform tasks collaboratively, which is called heterogeneous AUV swarm. The fundamental research of heterogeneous AUV swarm is how to search targets, and how to reach a sensing consensus of targets in the given underwater region [5–7].

© Springer Nature Singapore Pte Ltd. 2022
L. Pan et al. (Eds.): BIC-TA 2021, CCIS 1566, pp. 191–205, 2022.
https://doi.org/10.1007/978-981-19-1253-5_14

This problem had received a consistent attention in the research community over the past decade. In [8], an internal wave detection experiment conducted by the Massachusetts Institute of Technology (MIT) Laboratory of Autonomous Ocean Sensing System (LAMSS) was summarized in August 2010. The goal was to allow AUV swarm to collaborate autonomously through on-board autonomous software and real-time hydroacoustic communication, but no relevant research of search locational optimization has been conducted. A distributed cooperative search strategy for multiple AUVs based on initial target information was introduced in [9]. The process of target searching was decomposed into two stage, in the first stage, the possible range of the target was predicted based on its speed and elapsed time, in the second stage, AUV entered the prediction range, and then updated the target existence probability in real time according to the sensor detection results, and used predictive control to make optimal decisions based on the target existence probability. This method can detect the existence of targets quickly, however, it can cause waste of resources and unnecessary time consumption, and the search region was not divided optimally, because it did not consider the functional differences between the individual AUV of the swarm. A cooperative combat strategy based on simultaneous survey was presented in [10], which can solve the problem of AUV task region partition, however, this method required AUV to meet and exchange information with its neighbors periodically, which increased the difficulty of formation control and the load of the information network. There were also methods such as the multi-AUV target allocation strategy based on improved communication network which was proposed in [11].

In this work, the collaborative search task of heterogeneous AUV swarm was decomposed into two sub-problems: optimal partition of regions and cooperative search of targets.

Different types of AUVs in a heterogeneous AUV swarm usually carry devices and sensors with different performance. Therefore, when dealing with the problem of optimal partition of regions, we address a control protocol involving the voronoi partition with consensus approach, which makes the best of heterogeneous AUV swarm, and then makes all the sub-detection regions of the AUV reach an even distribution.

After the sub-detection region is determined, each AUV reaches its respective search area to perform target search task. A distributed collaborative search method is designed to solve the problem of cooperative search of targets. Through the information exchange between the AUV swarm, each AUV can determine for themselves whether there is duplication of targets, then recounts and sorts the targets until the target information of all AUVs reach consensus.

2   Problem Formulation and Preliminaries

2.1   Voronoi Partition

According to the optimal partition strategy of target region, the region is divided by Voronoi partition principle [12–16]. Compared with other regional partition strategies, Voronoi partition has the characteristics of strong pertinence and high computational efficiency.

Consider a target region S with i AUVs, and the collection of position of AUVs is given by $\eta = \{\eta_1, \eta_2, ..., \eta_n\}$. The density function of the target region is $\phi(\xi)$, ξ is defined as a function to describe the measurement cost of i-th AUV to any point in the target region. The i-th Voronoi cell is thus defined as:

$$V_i = \{\xi \in S | f(\eta_i, \xi) \leq f(\eta_j, \xi), \forall i \neq j, \forall i, j \in n\} \tag{1}$$

Lemma 1. *n AUVs are randomly distributed in target region S, the collection of position of AUVs is given by η. According to the current location information, the optimal region partition principle for heterogeneous AUV swarm is Voronoi partition principle.*

According to Lemma 1, within the target region, the optimal coverage region of each AUV is Voronoi region, which size and shape are not only related to the location information of the AUV and its neighbors, but also related to the measurement cost function of each AUV. Therefore, the measurement cost function of each AUV needs to be predefined. Suppose $f(\eta_i, \xi) = \|\eta_i - \xi\|$ denotes the distance between any AUV and the target point. At present, $f(\eta_i, \xi)$ is used as the cost function by most studies. It is easy to understand and calculate the distance as the measuring cost function of the vehicle.

2.2 Bioinspired Model

On biological cell membranes, there are a series of contents such as voltage, current, signal input and output, and conclusions based on their mutual interaction can solve many problems [17,18].

The bioinspired model was first proposed by British scientist Hodgeto while studying the action potential of squid neurons. The mathematical model of this kind of neuron potential is also called H-H model, The dynamic characteristic equation of the cell membrane voltage V_m in this model is as follows:

$$C_m \frac{dV_m}{dt} = -(E_p + V_m) \cdot g_p + (E_{Na} - V_m) \cdot g_{Na} - (E_K + V_m) \cdot g_K \tag{2}$$

where V_m represents the membrane voltage of the cell membrane, C_m represents the membrane capacitance of the cell membrane; E_p, E_{Na} and E_K represent the energy of the negative current, sodium ion and potassium ion in the cell membrane respectively. g_p, g_{Na}, and g_K are the conductivities corresponding to negative current, sodium ion, and potassium respectively.

H-H model coefficients are simplified by further improving. Suppose $C_m = 1$, $\partial = E_p + V_m$, $A = g_p$, $B = E_p + E_{Na}$, $D = E_K - E_p$, $f(e_i) = \max(e_i, 0)$, $g(e_i) = \max(-e_i, 0)$, the bioinspired models can be obtained:

$$\frac{d\partial}{dt} = -A\partial_i + (B - \partial_i)f(e_i) - (D + \partial_i)g(e_i) \tag{3}$$

where $f(e_i)$ is the excitatory input and $g(e_i)$ is the inhibitory input. The membrane voltage of neuron ∂_i is the output of the system, and any excitation and inhibition signal can be controlled within the range of [-D,B] to make the output signal ∂_i smooth. The bioinspired model can be used in AUV swarm to solve the problems of speed jump in formation and cooperative operation [19,20].

2.3   Region Partition Model

In this work, a position-probability model is proposed to describe the probability of the target appear in the search region. The larger the probability is, the wider the search area of the AUV swarm is, which means the larger the task payload of this AUV swarm. For any position r in a task region, assuming that there are m suspicious positions in the region. Target occurrence probability utilized by gaussian probability function can be expressed as:

$$target(r) = \sum_{i=1}^{m} \frac{1}{2\pi} \exp[-\frac{1}{2}(r - r_i)^T K_i (r - r_i)] \tag{4}$$

r_i represents the location where the target is most likely to appear, which is mainly judged according to environmental features and prior knowledge, random value is used in this work. K_i is a diagonal matrix, represents the probability weight of occurrence of r_i. According to the Eq. 4, the probability of occurrence of the target is a continuous function. Assuming that the position information of the ith AUV is η_i, the search mission payload of the ith AUV can be expressed as the sum of the probability of occurrence of all targets in its task partition V_i:

$$task(i) = \int_{r \in V_i} target(r)dr \tag{5}$$

Consider a convex polygon with N vertices as task region, V_i is also convex polygon. Suppose $\{v_1, v_2, ..., v_N\}$ denotes the vertices, the task region can be divided into N triangles whose vertices are respectively represented as (η_i, v_j, v_{j+1}), where $j \in \{1, 2, ..., N-1\}$. The mission payload of the ith AUV can be expressed by double integral:

$$task(i) = \sum_{j=1}^{N} \int_{s_j} \sum_{i=1}^{m} \frac{1}{2\pi} \exp[-\frac{1}{2}(r - r_i)^T K_i (r - r_i)]dr \tag{6}$$

The optimal partition problem of target region can be described as the consistency of all AUV groups to the mission payload:

$$task(1) = task(2) = ... = task(n) \tag{7}$$

3   Optimal Region Partition with Consensus Protocol

3.1   Control Strategy Design

In order to realize the reasonable partition of target search region, the dynamic process of search task of heterogeneous AUV swarm is simulated based on the biological competition mechanism in the bioinspired model. Consider the dynamic characteristics, sensor performance, computing power and other factors of the AUV swarm, control force is used to indicate the search ability of each AUV, the main system variables in the model are mapped to the partition problem, the territory is used to represent the search region for each AUV swarm, total resources indicates the task payload of the AUV swarm.

According to the biological competition mechanism model, the greater the control power, the more its total resources. The utilization resource ratio represents the resources occupied by the unit's control power, which is the ratio of total resources to control power. Based on the bioinspired model, combined with the Voronoi partition and the optimal partition problem model for target region search, the task allocation model for the AUV swarm is established.

Assuming that the heterogeneous AUV swarm is randomly distributed in the search region S, and the position is represented as $\eta = \{\eta_1, \eta_2, ...\eta_n\}$, $\eta_i \in \mathbb{R}^2$ (2 D plane), with the partitioning method defined:

$$V_i = \{\xi \in S \,|\, f(\eta_i, \xi) \leq f(\eta_j, \xi), \forall i \neq j, \forall i, j \in n\} \tag{8}$$

The initial detection partition $\{V_1, V_2, ..., V_n\}$ of all AUVs can be obtained, and the mission payload of each AUV can be calculated by combining the target occurrence probability $target(r)$, the sum of target occurrence probability $task(i)$ and mission payload $task(i)$, which is represented as $\{T_{auv1}, T_{auv2}, ..., T_{auvi}\}$. Set a constant for the search capability of each AUV, the ratio of task and capability $R_{auvi} = {T_{auvi}}/{E_{auvi}}$ of each AUV can be calculated. Therefore, the consistency formula of the mission payload can be represented as below:

$$R_{auv1} = R_{auv2} = ... = R_{auvn} \tag{9}$$

AUV_i will move toward AUV_j, When $R_{auvi} < R_{auvj}$ and $i \neq j$. Since the search task assignment is based on the Voronoi partitioning principle, the search task region of AUV_j will be reassigned to AUV_i. The dynamics of the ith AUV is modelled as an integrator: $\dot{\eta}_i = u_i$, the control input u_i of the system can be defined based on consistency theory and biological invasion mechanism:

$$u_i = -\gamma_i \sum_{j=1}^{n} \vec{n}_{ij} a_{ij} (R_{auvi} - R_{auvj}) \tag{10}$$

where γ_i is the feedback control gain coefficient greater than zero. $\vec{n}_{ij} = \frac{\eta_i - \eta_j}{\|\eta_i - \eta_j\|}$ is the direction vector. a_{ij} represents the degree of coupling between AUV_i and

AUV_j in the search task region. According to the occurrence probability of the target, it can be obtained:

$$a_{ij} = \int_{r \in V_i \cap V_j} \text{target}(r) dr \tag{11}$$

3.2 Consistency Analysis

In order to prove whether the uniform distribution of the search region can be achieved based on the above theory, it is necessary to analyze its consistency.

Lemma 2. *For n variables $\{\delta_1, \delta_2, ..., \delta_n\}$, satisfy $\sum_{i=1}^{n} \delta_i = \Delta$, where Δ is a constant value. Then for a set of positive real numbers $\{\beta_1, \beta_2, ..., \beta_n\}$, there exists:*

$$\min(\sum_{i=1}^{n} \frac{\delta_i^2}{\beta_i}) = \frac{\Delta^2}{\sum_{i=1}^{n} \beta_i}$$

And for any variable $\{\delta_1, \delta_2, ..., \delta_n\}$, it satisfies:

$$\frac{\delta_i}{\beta_i} = \frac{\Delta}{\sum_{i=1}^{n} \beta_i}$$

According to the Lemma 2, if the minimum value of the objective function can be obtained, the consistency of the variables can be achieved. If the mission payload T_{auvi} of AUV_i is taken as δ_i in the lemma, and the search capability E_{auvi} is taken as β_i, when the search region does not change:

$$T_{auv1} + T_{auv2} + ... + T_{auvn} = T_S \tag{12}$$

where T_S is a constant and represents the sum of the probability of occurrence of targets in the search region. Consider a Lyapunov function candidate:

$$V = V_1 + V_2 + ... + V_n$$
$$= \frac{T_{auv1}^2}{E_{auv1}} + \frac{T_{auv2}^2}{E_{auv2}} + ... + \frac{T_{auvn}^2}{E_{auvn}} \tag{13}$$

Lemma 3. *For a first-order integral system $\dot{\eta}_i = u_i$:*

with $u_i = -\gamma_i \sum_{j=1}^{n} \vec{n}_{ij} a_{ij} (R_{auvi} - R_{auvj})$ as the system input. If and only if lyapunov function achieves minimum value, the task-capability ratio of each AUV in the heterogeneous AUV swarm is consistent. That is the search region is evenly distributed according to the load.

Taking the derivative of Eq. 13:

$$\frac{\partial V}{\partial t} = \frac{\partial V_1}{\partial t} + \frac{\partial V_2}{\partial t} + ... + \frac{\partial V_n}{\partial t}$$
$$= (\frac{\partial V_1}{\partial \xi} + \frac{\partial V_2}{\partial \xi} + ... + \frac{\partial V_n}{\partial \xi}) \frac{\partial \xi}{\partial t} \tag{14}$$
$$= \sum_{i=1}^{n} \frac{\partial V}{\partial \eta_i} \frac{\partial \eta_i}{\partial t}$$

where $\frac{\partial \eta_i}{\partial t} = u_i$, For $j \neq i$, and N_i denote the set of neighbors of the ith AUV:

$$\frac{\partial T_{auvi}}{\partial \eta_j} = 0 \tag{15}$$

Then

$$\frac{\partial V}{\partial \eta_i} = \frac{2T_{auvi}}{E_{auvi}} \frac{\partial T_{auvi}}{\partial \eta_i} + \sum_{j \in N_i} \frac{2T_{auvj}}{E_{auvj}} \frac{\partial T_{auvj}}{\partial \eta_j} \tag{16}$$

T_{auvi} can be represented as:

$$\frac{\partial T_{auvi}}{\partial \eta_k} = \frac{\partial}{\partial \eta_k} \int\limits_{r \in V_i} \text{target}(r) dr$$

$$= \int\limits_{r \in V_i} \frac{\partial}{\partial \eta_k} \text{target}(r) dr + \int\limits_{\partial V_i} \text{target}(\mu) n^T(\mu) \frac{\partial \mu}{\partial \eta_k} d\mu \tag{17}$$

where ∂V_i represents the boundary of V_i, μ is the parameterized expression of the boundary. $n^T(\mu)$ is the outgoing normal line at the boundary, which is the unit vector. Since the probability distribution function $\text{target}(r)$ of the occurrence of the target does not depend on the position of η_k, $\int\limits_{r \in V_i} \frac{\partial}{\partial \eta_k} \text{target}(r) dr$ is always zero. So we have the following Eq. 18:

$$\frac{\partial T_{auvi}}{\partial \eta_k} = \int\limits_{\partial V_i} \text{target}(\mu) n^T(\mu) \frac{\partial \mu}{\partial \eta_k} d\mu \tag{18}$$

With $\partial V_i = \sum_{j \in N_i} V_i \cap V_j$, the Eq. 18 can be expressed as:

$$\frac{\partial T_{auvi}}{\partial \eta_k} = \sum_{j \in N_i} \int\limits_{V_i \cap V_j} \text{target}(\mu_{ij}) n^T(\mu_{ij}) \frac{\partial \mu_{ij}}{\partial \eta_k} d\mu_{ij} \tag{19}$$

To summarize:

$$\frac{\partial V}{\partial \eta_i} = \frac{2T_{auvi}}{E_{auvi}} \sum_{j \in N_i} n^T(\mu_{ij}) \int\limits_{V_i \cap V_j} \text{target}(\mu_{ij}) \frac{\partial \mu_{ij}}{\partial \eta_i} d\mu_{ij}$$
$$+ \sum_{j \in N_i} \frac{2T_{auvj}}{E_{auvj}} n^T(\mu_{ij}) \int\limits_{V_i \cap V_j} \text{target}(\mu_{ji}) \frac{\partial \mu_{ji}}{\partial \eta_i} d\mu_{ji} \tag{20}$$

For any two adjacent i and j, μ_{ij} can be expressed as:

$$\mu_{ij} : \frac{\eta_i + \eta_j}{2} + \begin{bmatrix} 0 & -1 \\ 1 & 0 \end{bmatrix} \frac{\eta_i - \eta_j}{\|\eta_i - \eta_j\|} \lambda_{ij}, \lambda_{ij} \in [-a_{ij}, b_{ij}]$$

It can be seen that μ_{ij} is the midperpendicular line of η_i and η_j, λ_{ij} represents the boundary length. Since μ_{ij} and $n(\mu_{ij})$ are orthogonal, it can be concluded that:

$$n^T(\mu_{ij}) \frac{\partial \mu_{ij}}{\partial \eta_i} = n^T(\mu_{ij}) \frac{\partial \mu_{ij}}{\partial \eta_j} = \frac{1}{2} n^T(\mu_{ij}) \tag{21}$$

Substituted into the Eq. 21:

$$\frac{\partial V}{\partial \eta_i} = \frac{T_{auvi}}{E_{auvi}} \sum_{j \in N_i} n^T(\mu_{ij}) \int_{V_i \cap V_j} \text{target}(\mu_{ij})d\mu_{ij}$$
$$+ \sum_{j \in N_i} \frac{T_{auvi}}{E_{auvi}} n^T(\mu_{ij}) \int_{V_i \cap V_j} \text{target}(\mu_{ji})d\mu_{ji} \qquad (22)$$
$$+ \sum_{j \in N_i} \frac{2T_{auvj}}{E_{auvj}} n^T(\mu_{ij}) \int_{V_i \cap V_j} \text{target}(\mu_{ji})\frac{\partial \mu_{ji}}{\partial \eta_i}d\mu_{ji}$$

$n^T(\mu_{ij}) = -n^T(\mu_{ji})$, simplify Eq. 22:

$$\frac{\partial V}{\partial \eta_i} = \sum_{j \in N_i} (R_{auvi} - R_{auvj})n^T(\mu_{ij}) \int_{V_i \cap V_j} \text{target}(\mu_{ji})d\mu_{ji} \qquad (23)$$

Then

$$\frac{\partial P}{\partial t} = -\sum_{i=1}^{n} k_i \left\| \sum_{j \in N_i} (R_{auvi} - R_{auvj})n(\mu_{ij})a_{ij} \right\|^2 \qquad (24)$$

Since V is continuously differentiable and $\dot{V} \leq 0$, according to the LaSalle invariance principle, if $\dot{V} = 0$, the system state values will converge to the maximum invariant set of the system. According to the Eq. 24, when $\dot{V} = 0$:

$$\sum_{j \in N_i} (R_{auvi} - R_{auvj})n(\mu_{ij})a_{ij} = 0_{2 \times 1} \qquad (25)$$

The matrix form of the Eq. 25 is expressed as:

$$\begin{pmatrix} l_{11} & \cdots & l_{1n} \\ \vdots & \ddots & \vdots \\ l_{m1} & \cdots & l_{mn} \end{pmatrix} \begin{pmatrix} R_{auv1} \\ \vdots \\ R_{auvn} \end{pmatrix} = \begin{pmatrix} 0_{2 \times 1} \\ \vdots \\ 0_{2 \times 1} \end{pmatrix} \qquad (26)$$

where $l_{ij} \in \mathbb{R}^2$, then:

$$l_{ij} = \begin{cases} \sum_{k \in N_i} n(\mu_{ik})a_{ik}, j = i \\ -n(\mu_{ij})a_{ij}, j \in N_i \end{cases} \qquad (27)$$

Suppose $L_\alpha = L_\alpha^U \otimes \begin{bmatrix} 1 \\ 0 \end{bmatrix} + L_\alpha^D \otimes \begin{bmatrix} 0 \\ 1 \end{bmatrix}$, where L_α^U, L_α^D represent the weighted Laplacian matrix of the system:

$$\begin{cases} L_\alpha^U R_{auv} = 0 \\ L_\alpha^U R_{auv} = 0 \end{cases} \qquad (28)$$

where $R_{auv} = \begin{bmatrix} R_{auv1} & \cdots & R_{auvn} \end{bmatrix}^T$, and R_{auv} is a column vector with the same elements, which is $R_{auv1} = R_{auv2} = \cdots = R_{auvn}$, then the theorem is proved.

4 Collaborative Target Search Based on Consensus Protocol

4.1 Collaborative Target Search Problem Modeling

Assuming that n AUVs of different types have arrived in their respective subregion and started to perform target search tasks, the search range of the ith AUV is centered on itself with radius of D_{auvi}, the target state information detected by each AUV includes the following types:

(1) Position information: $O_{ij}(t) = (x_{ij}(t), y_{ij}(t), z_{ij}(t))$ represents the spatial coordinate of T_j detected by AUV_i in the geodetic coordinate system.
(2) Velocity information: $v_{ij}(t)$ represents the velocity of T_j detected by AUV_i.
(3) Target type: K_{ij} represents the type of T_j detected by AUV_i.
(4) Time information: s_{ij} represents the time stamp of T_j detected by AUV_i.
(5) Number of targets: m_i represents the number of targets detected by AUV_i. Including the number of targets detected by itself and the number of targets obtained from the neighboring AUV.
(6) Target label: n_{ij} represents the label of T_j detected by AUV_i, which does not exceed the value of m_i.

When m_i targets are detected, the status information of AUV_i is established as follows:

$$S_i(t) = (S_{i1}^T(t), S_{i2}^T(t), ..., S_{im_i}^T(t)) \tag{29}$$

where $S_{ij}^T(t) = \{O_{ij}(t), v_{ij}(t), K_{ij}, s_{ij}, m_i, n_{ij}\}$ denotes the set of the status information of target T_j detected by AUV_i. If and only if $\|S_i(t) - S_k(t)\| \to 0$, the system is consistent, which means the AUV swarm completes the cooperative search task. The consistency model of heterogeneous AUV swarms can be expressed as:

$$\begin{cases} |x_{ij}(t) - x_{kj}(t)| < \varepsilon_x \\ |y_{ij}(t) - y_{kj}(t)| < \varepsilon_y \\ |z_{ij}(t) - z_{kj}(t)| < \varepsilon_z \\ |v_{ij}(t) - v_{kj}(t)| < \varepsilon_v \\ K_{ij} - K_{kj} = 0 \\ s_{ij} - s_{ik} = 0 \\ m_i - m_k = 0 \\ n_{ij} - n_{ik} = 0 \end{cases} \tag{30}$$

where ε_x, ε_y, ε_z, ε_v are respectively denote the allowable errors of position information and velocity information of the same target detected by different AUVs.

4.2 Consistency Condition

Consider a heterogeneous AUV swarm composed of n AUVs, which communication network topology is $G = (V, E)$. While $V = \{1, 2, ..., n\}$ is a set of non-empty nodes, and each node represents an AUV. $E \subseteq V \times V$ is a set of connecting edges, represents the communication relationship between AUVs. $G(t) = [g_{ik}(t)]$ is the adjacency relation of the topology, where $g_{ik}(t) = 1$ means that the communication between AUV_i and AUV_k is connected at time t, and $g_{ik}(t) = 0$ means that the communication is interrupted. The Laplace matrix $L = [l_{ik}]$ is:

$$l_{ik} = \begin{cases} \sum_k a_{ik}, i = k \\ -a_{ik}, i \neq k \end{cases} \tag{31}$$

Suppose that AUV_i sends the detected target information T_j to its neighbor AUV_k, and AUV_k compares the received target information T_j with the target information T_q detected by itself, if the following conditions are met:

$$\begin{cases} |x_{ij}(t) - x_{kq}(t)| < \varepsilon_x \\ |y_{ij}(t) - y_{kq}(t)| < \varepsilon_y \\ |z_{ij}(t) - z_{kq}(t)| < \varepsilon_z \\ |v_{ij}(t) - v_{kq}(t)| < \varepsilon_v \\ K_{ij} - K_{kq} = 0 \end{cases} \tag{32}$$

Target T_j and target T_q can be determined as the same target, otherwise, they are marked as different targets. Then, the target is renumbered and updated with n_{kq}.

If T_j and T_k are the same target, compare the timestamp:

(1) If $s_{ij} < s_{kq}$, let $s_{kq} = s_{ij}$.
(2) If $s_{kq} = s_{ij}$, AUV_k reorder the targets according to the detected timestamp.

If T_j and T_q are not the same target, add T_j to the probe list of AUV_k:

$$\begin{cases} m_k = m_k + 1 \\ O_{kq}(t) = O_{ij}(t) \\ v_{kq}(t) = v_{ij}(t) \\ s_{kq} = s_{ij} \end{cases} \tag{33}$$

The target is reordered according to the time stamp, and the sorted result is taken as the new number of the target. If and only if the target information states of all AUVs are identical and tend to be consistent, which means $\|S_i(t) - S_k(t)\| \to 0$. The heterogeneous AUV swarms complete the cooperative search task.

5   Simulation Experiment and Analysis

5.1   Simulation of Optimal Region Partition

The task range is set to 1000×1000. Consider seven AUV swarms, each AUV swarm is represented by the leader AUV within the swarm. The initial position and mission payload are shown in Table 1.

Table 1. Initial position and mission payload

Heterogeneous AUV swarm	The initial position	The mission payload
Swarm 1	[860, 552]	80.1498165
Swarm 2	[428, 527]	32.72320087
Swarm 3	[547, 1]	72.49389006
Swarm 4	[718, 97]	80.03960203
Swarm 5	[368, 687]	33.54609727
Swarm 6	[522, 91]	92.11312154
Swarm 7	[411, 837]	62.61293414

According to the information in Table 1, we calculate the probability of occurrence of the target at each position:

$$\text{target}(x, y) = \sum_{i=1}^{7} \text{target}_i \exp(-10^{-3}((x_i - x)^2 + (y_i - y)^2)) \qquad (34)$$

After the initial Voronoi diagram is produced, the state information is updated according to the bioinspired model in this paper until the task loads of all AUV swarms are consistent. The task region generation process is illustrated in Fig. 1.

As can be seen from the final distribution diagram, the gray value of each region is the same, achieving uniform distribution. The final consistency state is shown in Fig. 2.

In Fig. 2, the algorithm adopted in this paper can effectively realize the average distribution of the task load of different AUV swarms in the specified search region. The final task load ratio R tends to be consistent, and the velocity of each AUV group in the x and y directions also tends to be consistent. The area value of the assigned area eventually tends to be stable.

5.2 Simulation of Cooperative Target Search

Consider that there are 3 AUVs in a swarm, and each AUV carries out target search in a distributed manner. The target information detected by the AUV is shown in Table 2.

Suppose $\varepsilon_x = \varepsilon_y = \varepsilon_z = 0.02$ and $\varepsilon_v = 1$. The simulation was carried out according to the distributed collaborative algorithm proposed in this paper, the simulation results were shown in Table 3.

As shown in Table 3, three AUVs in the group detect six targets. Target 1 and 2 detected by AUV1 were the same as target 4 and 5 detected by AUV2, and target 1, 2 and 3 detected by AUV2 were the same as target 5, 6 and 3 detected by AUV3. The results show that the algorithm can eliminate the repeated target information among each AUV, and it can effectively realize distributed collaborative detection in AUV swarm.

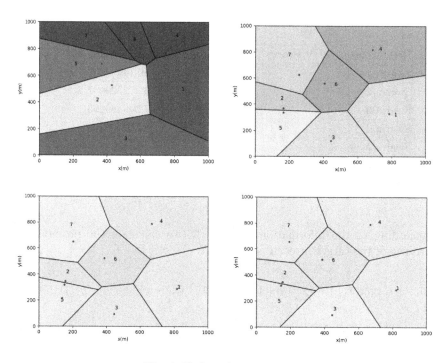

Fig. 1. Task region generation

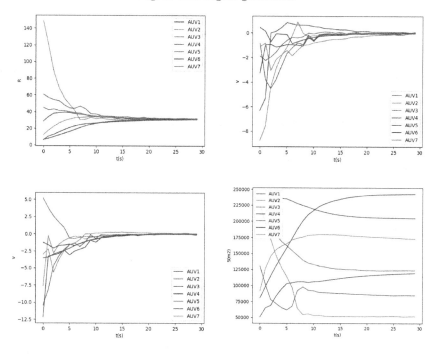

Fig. 2. Consistent state

Table 2. Detecting target information 1

	Target number n_{ij}	Target coordinate $O_{ij}(t)$	The target speed $v_{ij}(t)$	Time information s_{ij}
AUV1	1	[6.32, 2.56, 4.11]	5	08:55:53
AUV1	2	[11.32, 19, 21, 9.31]	5	08:56:28
AUV2	1	[17, 33, 16.21, 3.85]	6	08:55:56
AUV2	2	[5.21, 12.49, 18, 75]	10	08:58:35
AUV2	3	[10.21, 15.45, 9.08]	8	08:58:41
AUV3	1	[1.35, 16.76, 9.75]	5	08:56:00
AUV3	2	[2.49, 6.55, 10.69]	8	08:57:19
AUV3	3	[10.21, 1.33, 16.76]	10	09:05:03
AUV3	4	[8.37, 13.75, 17.44]	8	09:09:53

Table 3. Detecting target information 2

	Target number n_{ij}	Target coordinate $O_{ij}(t)$	The target speed $v_{ij}(t)$	Time information s_{ij}
AUV1	1	[6.32, 2.56, 4.11]	5	08:55:53
AUV1	2	[11.32, 19, 21, 9.31]	5	08:56:28
AUV1	3	[1.35, 16.76, 9.75]	5	08:56:00
AUV1	4	[5.21, 12.49, 18, 75]	10	08:58:35
AUV1	5	[10.21, 15.45, 9.08]	8	08:58:41
AUV1	6	[2.49, 6.55, 10.69]	8	08:57:19
AUV2	1	[17, 33, 16.21, 3.85]	6	08:55:56
AUV2	2	[5.21, 12.49, 18, 75]	10	08:58:35
AUV2	3	[10.21, 15.45, 9.08]	8	08:58:41
AUV2	4	[6.32, 2.56, 4.11]	5	08:55:53
AUV2	5	[11.32, 19, 21, 9.31]	5	08:56:28
AUV2	6	[1.35, 16.76, 9.75]	5	08:56:00
AUV3	1	[1.35, 16.76, 9.75]	5	08:56:00
AUV3	2	[2.49, 6.55, 10.69]	8	08:57:19
AUV3	3	[10.21, 1.33, 16.76]	10	09:05:03
AUV3	4	[8.37, 13.75, 17.44]	8	09:09:53
AUV3	5	[17.33, 16.21, 3.85]	6	08:55:56
AUV3	6	[5.21, 12.49, 18, 75]	10	08:58:35

6   Conclusion

In this paper, the problems of search region partition and collaborative target detection faced by heterogeneous AUV swarms in implementing collaborative search tasks are studied. According to different stages of detection, two different types of tasks are divided: region partition and target detection. Firstly, the target occurrence probability model is established for the region partition task, and the initial detection region partition is carried out by using Voronoi partitioning principle. By analyzing the detection capability of each AUV and transforming it into the detection mission load index, a dynamic model of AUV mission load based on bioinspired model is proposed and established. The consistency theory is used to prove that this model can realize the uniform distribution of regional detection tasks under the probability weighted condition of target presence. Secondly, A distributed collaborative detection method based on the principle of consistency is proposed, which realizes the detection of repeated targets in the target detection process. By judging the target information status of all AUVs is all the same and tends to be consistent, the heterogeneous AUV swarms completes the collaborative detection task. Finally, the effectiveness and convergence of the proposed method have been validated by the performance presented in numerical experiments on heterogeneous AUV swarms.

References

1. Gafurov, S.A., Klochkov, E.V.: Autonomous unmanned underwater vehicles development tendencies. Procedia Eng. **106**, 141–148 (2015)
2. Yuh, J.: Design and control of autonomous underwater robots. Auton. Rob. **8**, 7–24 (2000)
3. Fiorelli, E., Leonard, N.E., Bhatta, P., Paley, D.A., Fratantoni, D.M.: Multi-AUV control and adaptive sampling in monterey bay. IEEE J. Oceanic Eng. **31**, 935–948 (2007)
4. Blidberg, D.R.: The development of autonomous underwater vehicles (AUV); a brief summary. In: IEEE ICRA (2001)
5. Aman, B., Ciobanu, G.: Travelling salesman problem in tissue p systems with costs. J. Membr. Comput. **3**(2), 97–104 (2021)
6. Juayong, R., Adorna, H.N.: A survey of results on evolution-communication p systems with energy. J. Membr. Comput. **2**(2) (2020)
7. Hert, S., Tiwari, S., Lumelsky, V.: A terrain-covering algorithm for an AUV. In: Yuh, J., Ura, T., Bekey, G.A. (eds.) Underwater Robots, pp. 17–45. Springer, Boston (1996). https://doi.org/10.1007/978-1-4613-1419-6_2
8. Petillo, S., Schmidt, H.: Exploiting adaptive and collaborative AUV autonomy for detection and characterization of internal waves. IEEE J. Oceanic Eng. **39**(1), 150–164 (2014)
9. Jia, Q., Xu, H., Feng, X., Gu, H., Gao, L.: Research on cooperative area search of multiple underwater robots based on the prediction of initial target information. Ocean Eng. **172**, 660–670 (2019)
10. Yoon, S., Qiao, C.: Cooperative search and survey using autonomous underwater vehicles (AUVs). IEEE Trans. Parallel Distrib. Syst. **22**(3), 364–379 (2011)
11. Li, J., Zhang, K., Xia, G.: [IEEE 2017 IEEE International Conference on Mechatronics and Automation (ICMA) - Takamatsu, Japan (2017.8.6–2017.8.9)] 2017 IEEE International Conference on Mechatronics and Automation (ICMA) - Multi-AUV Cooperative Task Allocation Based on Improved Contra, pp. 608–613 (2017)
12. Kim, D.S., Chung, Y.C., Seo, S., Kim, S.P., Kim, C.M.: Crystal structure extraction in materials using Euclidean Voronoi diagram and angular distributions among atoms (2005)
13. Yan, C., Guo, T., Sun, W., Bai, J.: Voronoi diagrams' eccentricity measurement and application. In: International Conference on Geoinformatics (2010)
14. Senechal, M.: Spatial tessellations: concepts and applications of Voronoi diagrams. In: Spatial Tessellations: Concepts and Applications of Voronoi Diagrams (2000)
15. Okabe, A., Boots, B.N., Sugihara, K., Chiu, N.: Spatial Tesselations: Concepts and Applications of Voronoi Diagrams, Wiley, New York (2000)
16. Fortune, S.: Voronoi Diagrams and Delaunay Triangulations (2004)
17. Wu, T., Jiang, S.: Spiking neural p systems with a flat maximally parallel use of rules. J. Membr. Comput., 1–11 (2021)

18. Ren, T., Cabarle, F., Macababayao, I., Adorna, H.N., Zeng, X.: Homogeneous spiking neural P systems with structural plasticity. J. Membr. Comput., 1–12 (2021)
19. Rout, R., Subudhi, B.: A backstepping approach for the formation control of multiple autonomous underwater vehicles using a leader-follower strategy. J. Mar. Eng. Technol. **15**(1), 38–46 (2016)
20. Wang, J., Wang, C., Wei, Y., Zhang, C.: Sliding mode based neural adaptive formation control of underactuated AUVs with leader-follower strategy. Appl. Ocean Res. **94**, 101971 (2020)

An Improved Event-Triggered Control Method Based on Consistency Algorithm in Heterogeneous AUV Swarm Under Communication Delay

Ke Chen[1], Guangyu Luo[2(✉)], Hao Zhou[2], and Dongming Zhao[2]

[1] Naval Research Institute, Beijing 100094, China
[2] School of Automation, Wuhan University of Technology, Wuhan 430070, China
{luoguangyu,zhzmq,dmzhao}@whut.edu.cn

Abstract. The method for continuous time sampling suffers from communication interruptions in AUV (Autonomous Underwater Vehicle) swarm for underwater communication. In this paper, an improved event triggering mechanism is introduced to control the communication among heterogeneous AUV swarm. Each AUV only updates control input at its own event triggering time, without considering the triggering time of neighboring AUVs. In this method, the frequency of control signal updates has been reduced. Meanwhile, two consistency control algorithms for heterogeneous AUV swarm are studied with time delay and without time delay, respectively. The simulation results show that when time delay is reduced, the transient performance of the system will be increased and the steady-state error will be reduced. The heterogeneous AUV swarm under event-triggered control can significantly reduce the number of communications and the Zeno phenomenon will not occur. Consequently, the stability of the system has been improved.

Keywords: Heterogeneous AUV swarm · Event trigger control · Consistency control · Communication delay

1 Introduction

AUV is a cable-free, self-propelled underwater vehicle [1,2]. Due to small size and flexibility of AUV, an increasingly important position in future military activities will be occupied [3]. Because it is difficult for a single AUV to perform complex tasks, multiple AUVs are usually utilized to form a swarm to coordinate tasks [4]. Generally speaking, each AUV usually comes from different manufacturers, so types and platforms of AUVs are different. The formation of a swarm often reflects a heterogeneous type, so there are difficulties in information interaction [5,6]. While the amount of information interaction can be reduced by consistency algorithm [7]. In underwater environment, hydroacoustic communication is widely used among AUVs. Compared with time-sampled communication method, resource consumption can be reduced by event-triggered method

© Springer Nature Singapore Pte Ltd. 2022
L. Pan et al. (Eds.): BIC-TA 2021, CCIS 1566, pp. 206–221, 2022.
https://doi.org/10.1007/978-981-19-1253-5_15

[8]. Therefore, a formation control method based on event-triggered mechanism for heterogeneous AUV swarm is proposed.

In [9], the event-triggered tracking control problem of fully driven AUVs in the vertical plane was studied. Meanwhile, a reinforcement learning method was introduced to optimize the long-term tracking performance. In [10], a fixed-time leader-following formation control method for a set of AUVs with event-triggered acoustic communications was investigated. In [11], a distributed event-driven adaptive formation control strategy was proposed to achieve three-dimensional formation tracking of AUV swarm. In [12], asynchronous and synchronous communication strategies were proposed. Moreover, the consistency of the algorithm with limited information exchange and distributed communication delays was proved. In [13], the event-triggered consensus problem of multiagent systems with input time delay is investigated, which could be applied to AUV swarm. In [14], the problem of fixed-time event-triggered formation control for multi-AUV systems with external uncertainty was investigated. A distributed control strategy was considered, which can realize the control of arbitrary initial states of multi-AUVs. While the time delay was not taken into account. In [15], an event-triggered integral sliding-mode fixed-time control method was proposed to solve the trajectory tracking problem of AUVs with interference without considering communication delay. In [16], the problem of event-triggered distributed adaptive bipartite consensus control for multi-AUV systems with a fixed topology was studied. Although the competition among AUVs was considered, the heterogeneity of swarm was not taken into account.

In this paper, a distributed event-triggered control algorithm is proposed for heterogeneous AUV swarm under communication delay. In this algorithm, each AUV updates control input at its own trigger moment without considering neighboring AUVs. Consumption of communication resources and the update frequency of control signals is reduced through the algorithm. The consistency stability of the algorithm is proved by Lyapunov theory. Meanwhile, Zeno phenomenon will not occur. Finally, the correctness and the effectiveness of the algorithm are demonstrated by numerical simulations.

2 Problem Description

2.1 Multi-AUV Swarm

The model of AUV is studied in a right-angle coordinate system [16]. Suppose that AUVi can detect its own position and angle from neighboring AUVj. E is defined as the fixed coordinate system while B is defined as the motion coordinate system. Ignoring sea surface interference, mathematical model of AUV can be expressed as Eq. (1).

$$\begin{cases} \dot{\eta}_i = R_i(\psi_i)v_i \\ M_i\dot{v}_i + C_i(v_i)v_i + D_iv_i = \tau_i \end{cases} \tag{1}$$

where $\eta_i = [x_i, y_i, \psi_i]^T$ denotes the position of AUVi, $v_i = [u_i, v_i, r_i]^T$ denotes the velocity of AUVi, $\tau_i = [\tau_{1i}, \tau_{2i}, \tau_{3i}]^T$ denotes the motion thrust, M_i denotes inertia matrix, C_i denotes koch force matrix, D_i denotes damping matrix. $R_i(\psi_i)$ denotes coefficient matrix.

$$R_i(\psi_i) = \begin{bmatrix} \cos(\psi_i) & -\sin(\psi_i) & 0 \\ \sin(\psi_i) & \cos(\psi_i) & 0 \\ 0 & 0 & 1 \end{bmatrix} \tag{2}$$

In this section, a distributed controller is designed under a fixed undirected topology graph, which make all AUVs maintain the same position, attitude, and velocity asymptotically.

$$\begin{aligned} \lim_{t\to\infty} \eta_i - \eta_j = 0 \\ \lim_{t\to\infty} v_i - v_j = 0 \end{aligned} \tag{3}$$

Suppose $R_i(\psi_i)v_i = \gamma_i$. Due to $R_i^{-1}(\psi_i) = R_i^T(\psi_i)$, $(R_i^{-1})^T(\psi_i) = R_i^{-T}(\psi_i)$, $v_i = R_i^{-1}(\psi_i)\gamma_i$, Eq. (1) can be written as

$$\begin{cases} \dot{\eta}_i = \gamma_i \\ M_i R_i^{-1}(\psi_i)(\dot{\gamma}_i - \dot{R}_i(\psi_i)R_i^{-1}(\psi_i)\gamma_i) \\ = -C_i(R_i^{-1}(\psi_i)\gamma_i)R_i^{-1}(\psi_i)\gamma_i - D_i R_i^{-1}(\psi_i)\gamma_i + \tau_i \end{cases} \tag{4}$$

Suppose

$$Q_i = R_i^{-T}(\psi_i)M_i R_i^{-1}(\psi_i)$$

$$G_i = R_i^{-T}(\psi_i)[C_i(R_i^{-1}(\psi_i)\dot{\eta}_i) - M_i R_i^{-1}(\psi_i)\dot{R}_i(\psi_i) - D_i]R_i^{-1}(\psi_i)$$

$$p_{ij} = \eta_i - \eta_j$$

Equation (4) can be written as

$$\begin{cases} \dot{p}_{ij} = \gamma_i - \gamma_j \\ \dot{\gamma}_i = -Q_i^{-1}(G\gamma_i - \tau_{qi}) \end{cases} \tag{5}$$

where $\tau_{qi} = R_i^{-T}(\psi_i)\tau_i$ denotes control input.

An event-triggered consistent controller is designed for multi-AUV swarm in Eq. (6).

$$\tau_{qi}(t) = -\sum_{j\in N_i} a_{ij}(\eta_i(t_k^i) - \eta_j(t_k^j)) - \omega\gamma_i(t_k^i), t \in [t_k, t_{k+1}] \tag{6}$$

where $\eta_i(t_k^i)$, $\gamma_i(t_k^i)$ denotes the state information sampled by AUVi at the moment of t_k^i. t_k^i denotes the k trigger moment of AUVi, $k \in \{0, 1, 2, ...\}$. $\eta_j(t_k^j)$ denotes the sampled value of latest trigger moment of AUVj. Position error and velocity error are expressed as Eq. (7).

$$
\begin{aligned}
e_{\eta i}(t) &= \eta_i(t_k^i) - \eta_i(t) \\
e_{\gamma i}(t) &= \gamma_i(t_k^i) - \gamma_i(t)
\end{aligned}
\tag{7}
$$

Furthermore, Eq. (5) can be written as

$$
\begin{cases}
\dot{p}_{ij} = \gamma_i - \gamma_j \\
\dot{\gamma}_i = -Q_i^{-1}(G\gamma_i + \sum_{j \in N_i} a_{ij}(\eta_i(t_k^i) - \eta_j(t_k^j)) + \omega\gamma_i(t_k^i) \\
\quad + \sum_{j \in N_i} a_{ij}((e_{\eta i}(t) - e_{\gamma i}(t)) + \omega e_{\gamma i}(t))
\end{cases}
\tag{8}
$$

Event triggering function is designed as Eq. (9).

$$
f_i(t) = \|e_i(t)\| - \zeta_i \|\gamma_i(t)\| - \delta_i(t)
\tag{9}
$$

where $e_i(t) = [e_{\eta i}^T, e_{\gamma i}^T]^T$ denotes state error, $\zeta_i = \sqrt{\frac{c\alpha_i\beta_i}{2\theta_i}}$, where $0 < \alpha_i < 1$, $\beta_i = \frac{\omega(2-c)}{2} - c|N_i| > 0$, $\theta_i = \max(|N_i|, \frac{\omega}{2}) > 0$. $\delta_i(t) = \kappa_i e^{-\varepsilon(t-t_0)}$ denotes compensation function, where $\kappa_i > 0$, $0 < \varepsilon < 1$. The sequence of trigger moment is shown as Eq. (10).

$$
t_{k+1}^i = \inf\{t : t > t_k^i, f_i(t) > 0\}
\tag{10}
$$

when $f_i(t) > 0$, the control protocol $\tau_{qi}(t)$ of AUVi updates once. Meanwhile, the position state $\eta_i(t_k^i)$ is passed to AUVj. At the same time, the state value updates once: $\eta_i(t_k^i) = \eta_i(t)$, $\gamma_i(t_k^i) = \gamma_i(t)$. The error $e_i(t)$ is set to zero. After AUVj is triggered in $t \in [t_k, t_{k+1}]$, the corresponding sampling information is received by AUVi. The control protocol of AUVi updates. Therefore, the measurement error of AUVi should be known while the state information of AUVj is not necessary. communication burden and bandwidth resource are reduced. by the improved event-trigger method. The system stability is demonstrated below.

Suppose a Lyapunov function:

$$
V = \frac{1}{2} \sum_{i=1}^{n} \sum_{j=1}^{n} a_{ij} p_{ij}^T p_{ij} + \frac{1}{2} \sum_{i=1}^{n} \gamma_i^T Q_i \gamma_i
\tag{11}
$$

where Q_i is a symmetric and positive definite matrix. $V > 0$ when p_{ij} and γ_i are not simultaneously 0. The derivative of V is

$$
\begin{aligned}
\dot{V} &= \sum_{i=1}^{n}\sum_{j=1}^{n} a_{ij} p_{ij}^{T}(\gamma_i - \gamma_j) + \sum_{i=1}^{n}\gamma_i^{T} Q_i \dot{\gamma}_i + \frac{1}{2}\gamma_i^{T}\dot{Q}_i\gamma_i \\
&= \sum_{i=1}^{n}\sum_{j=1}^{n} a_{ij} p_{ij}^{T}(\gamma_i - \gamma_j) - \sum_{i=1}^{n}\gamma_i^{T}\left(G_i\gamma_i + \sum_{j\in N_i} a_{ij}\left(\eta_i(t) - \eta_j(t)\right)\right) \\
&\quad - \sum_{i=1}^{n}\gamma_i^{T}\left(\omega\gamma_i(t) + \sum_{j\in N_i} a_{ij}\left(\left(e_{\eta i}(t) - e_{\gamma i}(t)\right) + \omega e_{\gamma i}(t)\right)\right) \\
&\quad + \frac{1}{2}\sum_{i=1}^{n}\gamma_i^{T}\dot{Q}_i\gamma_i \\
&\leq \sum_{i=1}^{n}\sum_{j=1}^{n} a_{ij} p_{ij}^{T}(\gamma_i - \gamma_j) - \sum_{i=1}^{n}\gamma_i^{T}\left(G_i\gamma_i + \sum_{j\in N_i} a_{ij}(\eta_i(t) - \eta_j(t))\right) \\
&\quad - \sum_{i=1}^{n}\gamma_i^{T}\left(\omega\gamma_i(t) + \sum_{j\in N_i} a_{ij}\left(\left(e_{\eta i}(t) - e_{\gamma i}(t)\right) + \omega e_{\gamma i}(t)\right)\right) \\
&\leq \sum_{i=1}^{n}\gamma_i \sum_{j=1}^{n} a_{ij} p_{ij}^{T} - \sum_{i=1}^{n}\gamma_i^{T}\sum_{j=1}^{n} a_{ij}(\eta_i(t) - \eta_j(t)) \\
&\quad - \sum_{i=1}^{n}\omega\gamma_i^{T}\gamma_i - \sum_{i=1}^{n}\gamma_i^{T}\sum_{j=1}^{n} a_{ij}\left(\left(e_{\eta i}(t) - e_{\gamma i}(t)\right)\right) - \sum_{i=1}^{n}\omega\gamma_i^{T} e_{\gamma i}(t) \\
&\leq -\sum_{i=1}^{n}\omega\gamma_i^{T}\gamma_i - \sum_{i=1}^{n}\gamma_i^{T}\sum_{j=1}^{n} a_{ij} e_{\eta i}(t) \\
&\quad + \sum_{i=1}^{n}\gamma_i^{T}\sum_{j=1}^{n} a_{ij} e_{\eta j}(t) - \sum_{i=1}^{n}\omega\gamma_i^{T} e_{\gamma i}(t)
\end{aligned}
$$
(12)

Due to

$$
\sum_{i=1}^{n}\sum_{j=1}^{n} a_{ij}\left\|e_{\eta i}(t)\right\| = \sum_{i=1}^{n}\sum_{j=1}^{n} a_{ij}\left\|e_{\eta j}(t)\right\|
$$
(13)

where $a_{ij} = 1$ when AUVi maintains communication with AUVj , $a_{ij} = 0$ when AUVi disconnect from AUVj. According to $xy \leq \frac{c}{2}x^2 + \frac{1}{2c}y^2$ and $0 < c <$

$\frac{2\omega}{(2|N_i|+\omega)}$, the upper bound of $\dot{V}$ is obtained as Eq. (14).

$$
\begin{aligned}
\dot{V} &\leq -\sum_{i=1}^{n}\omega\gamma_i^{T}\gamma_i + 2\sum_{i=1}^{n}\|\gamma_i^{T}\|\sum_{j=1}^{n}a_{ij}\|e_{\eta i}(t)\| - \sum_{i=1}^{n}\omega\gamma_i^{T}e_{\gamma i}(t) \\
&\leq -\sum_{i=1}^{n}\omega\gamma_i^{T}\gamma_i + \sum_{i=1}^{n}|N_i|\left(c\gamma_i^{T}\gamma + \frac{1}{c}e_{\eta i}^{T}(t)e_{\eta i}(t)\right) \\
&\quad + \sum_{i=1}^{n}\omega\left(\frac{c}{2}\gamma_i^{T}\gamma_i + \frac{1}{2c}e_{\gamma i}^{T}(t)e_{\gamma i}(t)\right) \\
&\leq \sum_{i=1}^{n}\left(-\omega + c\left(|N_i| + \frac{\omega}{2}\right)\right)\gamma_i^{T}\gamma_i \\
&\quad + \sum_{i=1}^{n}\frac{|N_i|}{c}e_{\eta i}^{T}(t)e_{\eta i}(t) + \sum_{i=1}^{n}\frac{\omega}{2c}e_{\gamma i}^{T}(t)e_{\gamma i}(t)
\end{aligned}
\tag{14}
$$

When $f_i(t) \leq 0$,

$$
\|e_i(t)\|^2 \leq 2\zeta_i^{2}\|\gamma_i(t)\|^2 + 2\delta_i^{2}(t)
\tag{15}
$$

Consequently, Eq. (13) can be written as

$$
\begin{aligned}
\dot{V} &\leq -\sum_{i=1}^{n}\beta_i\|\gamma_i\|^2 + \sum_{i=1}^{n}\frac{|N_i|}{c}\|e_{\eta i}\|^2 + \sum_{i=1}^{n}\frac{\omega}{2c}\|e_{\gamma i}\|^2 \\
&\leq -\sum_{i=1}^{n}\beta_i\|\gamma_i\|^2 + \sum_{i=1}^{n}\frac{\theta_i}{c}\|e\|^2 \\
&\leq -\sum_{i=1}^{n}(1-\alpha_i)\beta_i\|\gamma_i\|^2 + \sum_{i=1}^{n}\frac{2\theta_i}{c}\kappa_i^{2}e^{-2\varepsilon(t-t_0)}
\end{aligned}
\tag{16}
$$

Integrating over Eq. (16):

$$
\sum_{i=1}^{n}(1-\alpha_i)\beta_i\int_0^t\|\gamma_i(\partial)\|^2d\partial \leq V(0) + \sum_{i=1}^{n}\frac{\theta_i\kappa_i^{2}}{c\varepsilon_i}
\tag{17}
$$

In Eq. (17), V and $\int_0^t\|\gamma_i(\partial)\|^2d\partial$ is bounded. Equation (11) shows that both position error p_{ij} and velocity γ_i are bounded, then $\|p_{ij}\| \leq p_{\max}$ and $\|\gamma_i(t)\| \leq \gamma_{\max}$. According to $\dot{\gamma}_i = -Q_i^{-1}(G\gamma_i + \sum_{j\in N_i}a_{ij}(\eta_i(t_k^i) - \eta_j(t_k^j)) + \omega\gamma_i(t_k^i))$, $\|\dot{\gamma}_i\| \leq \|Q_i^{-1}\|\,(((\|G_i\|+1)\gamma_{\max} + \sum_{j\in N_i}a_{ij}p_{\max}$. Due to Q_i and G_i are bounded, $\dot{\gamma}_i$ is bounded. Therefore, $\lim_{t\to\infty}\gamma_i = 0$, $\dot{\gamma}_i \to 0$, $\eta_i(t_k^i) - \eta_j(t_k^j) \to 0$ when $t \to \infty$. Consequently, multi-AUV swarm can remain consistent and stable.

Lemma 1 is given to show that Zeno phenomenon does not exist in multi-AUV swarm based on event-triggered mechanisms.

Lemma 1. *In a directionless communication topology, when trigger function satisfies $f_i(t) \leq 0$ and $0 < c < \frac{2\omega}{(2|N_i|+\omega)}$, the neighboring trigger moment time interval satisfies $\Delta t_k^i > 0$ [2].*

2.2 Heterogeneous AUV Swarm

A formation control problem for a heterogeneous AUV swarm is studied in this section. When The swarm consists of N AUVs, the dynamic equation of AUVi is given by [17], which is shown as Eq. (18).

$$\dot{x}_i(t) = Ax_i(t) + Bu_{x,i}(t) + \theta_i^*, i = 1, 2, ..., N \tag{18}$$

where $x_i(t) \in R^n$ denotes state variables, $u_{x,i}(t) \in R^n$ denotes control inputs, $\theta_i^* \in R^n$ denotes bounded vectors of AUVi. $A \in R^{n \times n}$ and $B \in R^{n \times n}$ are system parameters. Each disparate $\theta_i^* \in R^n$ is characteristic of the heterogeneous AUV swarm.

$$rank([\theta_i^*, B]) = rank(B), i = 1, 2, ..., N \tag{19}$$

$$B\theta_i = \theta_i^*, i = 1, 2, ..., N \tag{20}$$

Then Eq. (18) can be written as

$$\dot{x}_i(t) = Ax_i(t) + B(u_{x,i}(t) + \theta_i), i = 1, 2, ..., N \tag{21}$$

Event trigger policy is activated when the system state function or measurement data exceeds a certain threshold value. Event trigger time series is composed of a strictly increasing sequence $\{t_k^i, k \geq 0\}$. The control input $u_{x,i}(t)$ keeps constant at $t \in [t_k^i, t_{k+1}^i)$.

$$u_{x,i}(t) = z_i(t) + K \sum_{j \in N_i} a_{ij}(\hat{x}_j(t) - \hat{x}_i(t)), t \in [t_k^i, t_{k+1}^i) \tag{22}$$

where $K \in R^{n \times n}$ is control gain matrix, $\hat{x}_i(t) = e^{A(t-t_k^i)}x_i(t_k^i)$ is estimated value at t. $E_{x,i}(t) = \hat{x}_i(t) - x_i(t)$ denotes corresponding estimation error. a_{ij} is the i,j element of the adjacency matrix A in communication network topology. $z_i(t)$ is subsequent compensation variable. In order to compensate for the heterogeneity in AUV swarm, variable $z_i(t)$ is introduced. $z_i(t)$ updates when event trigger condition is activated.

$$\dot{z}_i(t) = u_{z,i}(t) = H \sum_{j \in N_i} a_{ij}(\hat{z}_j(t) - \hat{z}_i(t)) \tag{23}$$

where $z_i(t) \in R^n$, $\hat{z}_i(t) = \theta_i + z_i(t_k^i)$. $H \in R^{n \times n}$ is the corresponding control gain matrix. $E_{z,i}(t) = z_i(t_k^i) - z_i(t)$ is the measurement error.

3   Controller Design

3.1   Heterogeneous AUV Swarm Consistency Control Algorithm Based on Event-Triggered

In this section, consistency problem of heterogeneous AUV swarm under fixed topology is studied. A distributed consistency control algorithm based on event-triggered is given as [18].

Suppose event trigger time sequence $\{t_k^i\} = \inf_{k \in +} \{t > t_{k-1}^i : f_i(t) > 0\}$. The corresponding event trigger function is shown as Eq. (24).

$$f_i(t) = \|e_i(t)\| - c_1 \left\| \sum_{j \in N_i} a_{ij}(\hat{x}_j(t) - \hat{x}_i(t)) + \sum_{j \in N_i} a_{ij}(\hat{z}_j(t) - \hat{z}_i(t)) \right\| \tag{24}$$
$$- c_2 e^{-\alpha t}$$

where $e_i(t) = \left[E_{x,i}^T(t), E_{z,i}^T(t)\right]^T$.

When a known constant scalar $\lambda > 0$ and control gains $K = M_1 \bar{P}_1^{-1}$, $H = M_2 \bar{P}_2^{-1}$, there exist positive definite matrices $\bar{P} = diag\{\bar{P}_1, \bar{P}_2\}$ and $\bar{M} = diag\{M_1, M_2\}$. The stability of the system can be achieved when Eq. (25) is satisfied.

$$\begin{cases} 0 < \alpha < \frac{\lambda}{2} \\ 0 < c_1 < \min\left\{ \sqrt{\frac{1}{\lambda_{\max}(\bar{P}^{-1})}}, \frac{1}{N\|L \otimes I_{2n}\|} \right\} \\ 0 < c_2 < \sqrt{\frac{1}{\lambda_{\max}(\bar{P}^{-1})}} \end{cases} \tag{25}$$

Proof. A Lyapunov function is chosen for a fixed topology [19].

$$V(\delta(t)) = \delta(t)^T P \delta(t) \tag{26}$$

where $P = I_N \otimes P$, $P = diag\{P_1, P_2\}$. Taking the derivative of $V(\delta(t))$:

$$\begin{aligned} \dot{V}(\delta(t)) &= 2\delta(t)^T P[\hat{A}\delta(t) + \hat{B}\delta(t) + \hat{B}e(t)] \\ &\leq \tilde{\eta}(t)^T \prod_1 \tilde{\eta}(t) - \lambda \delta(t)^T P \delta(t) + e(t)^T P e(t) \\ &\leq \tilde{\eta}(t)^T \prod_1 \tilde{\eta}(t) - \lambda \delta(t)^T P \delta(t) + \lambda_{\max}(P) e(t)^T e(t) \end{aligned} \tag{27}$$

According to Eq. (28)

$$\begin{aligned} \|e_i(t)\| &\leq c_1 \left\| \sum_{j \in N_i} a_{ij}(\hat{x}_j(t) - \hat{x}_i(t)) + \sum_{j \in N_i} a_{ij}(\hat{z}_j(t) - \hat{z}_i(t)) \right\| + c_2 e^{-\alpha t} \\ &\leq c_1 \|(L \otimes I_{2n})\delta(t) + (L \otimes I_{2n})e(t)\| + c_2 e^{-\alpha t} \end{aligned} \tag{28}$$

After deflating and accumulating, Eq. 28 can be written as

$$\sum_{i=1}^{N} \|e_i(t)\|^2 \le 4Nc_1{}^2\|(L \otimes I_{2n})\delta(t)\|^2$$
$$+ 4Nc_1{}^2\|(L \otimes I_{2n})e(t)\|^2$$
$$+ 2Nc_2{}^2e^{-2\alpha t}$$

(29)

Due to $c_1^2 c_2^2 \in (0, \lambda_{\max}(P))$, Eq. (27) can be written as

$$\dot{V}(\delta(t)) \le \tilde{\eta}(t)^T \prod_2 \tilde{\eta}(t) - \lambda\delta(t)^T P\delta(t) + 2Ne^{-2\alpha t}$$
$$\le -\lambda V(\delta(t)) + 2Ne^{-2\alpha t}$$

(30)

Integrating over Eq. (30):

$$V(\delta(t)) \le V(\delta(t_0))e^{-\lambda(t-t_0)} + 2N \int_{t_0}^{t} e^{-2\alpha t} ds$$
$$= V(\delta(t_0))e^{-\lambda(t-t_0)} + \frac{2N}{\lambda - 2\alpha}e^{-2\alpha t} - \frac{2Ne^{(\lambda-2\alpha)t_0}}{\lambda - 2\alpha}e^{-\lambda t}$$
$$\le V(\delta(t_0))e^{-\lambda(t-t_0)} + \frac{2N}{\lambda - 2\alpha}e^{-2\alpha t}$$

(31)

Suppose $q_1 = \lambda_{\min}(P)$, $q_2 = \lambda_{\max}(P)$

$$q_1\|\delta(t)\|^2 \le V(\delta(t)) \le q_2\|\delta(t)\|^2$$

(32)

$$\|\delta(t)\|^2 < \frac{q_2\|\delta(t)\|^2}{q_1}e^{\lambda(t-t_0)} + \frac{2N}{q_1(\lambda - 2\alpha)}e^{-2\alpha t}$$

(33)

In summary, the heterogeneous AUV swarm can reach agreement with the control gain of $K = M_1\bar{P}_1^{-1}$, $H = M_2\bar{P}_2^{-1}$. According to Lemma 1, Zeno phenomenon will not occur.

In this section, a consistency control algorithm based on event-triggered mechanism is proposed for heterogeneous AUV swarm. Due to the adoption of estimation-based trigger conditions, the designed algorithm can effectively extend the release time and reduce the number of event trigger.

3.2 Heterogeneous AUV Group Consistency Algorithm Based on Event-Triggered Control Under Communication Time Delay

In this section, a distributed event-triggered controller is implemented using a state feedback approach. When communication delay exists, the output of all AUVs is progressively consistent. Meanwhile, Zeno phenomenon will not occur. The system dynamic equation is shown as Eq. (21).

The event trigger controller under communication time delay is shown as Eq. (34).

$$\begin{cases} \dot{\eta}_i(t) = S\eta_i(t) - \sum_{j \in N_i} a_{ij} \left(e^{S(t-t^i_{k_i})}\eta_i(t^i_{k_i}) - e^{S(t-t^j_{k_j})}\eta_j(t^j_{k_j}) \right) \\ u_i(t) = K_i \left(x_i(t - \tau_i(t)) - \prod_i \eta_i(t) \right) + \eta_i(t) - \alpha_i \mathrm{sgn}(x_i - \prod_i \eta_i) \end{cases} \tag{34}$$

where $i, j = 1, \ldots, N$, $\tau_i(t) > 0$ denotes the underwater communication time delay, $t^i_{k_i}$ is the most recent trigger moment of AUVi, $k_i = 1, 2, \ldots, \eta_i(t^i_{k_i})$ is the controller state of the last broadcast of AUVi, α_i is the normal number gain, sgn is the sign function. Define a measurement error based on the controller state:

$$e_i(t) = e^{S(t-t^i_{k_i})}\eta_i(t^i_{k_i}) - \eta_i(t) \tag{35}$$

The trigger function of AUVi is given by Eq. (36).

$$f_i(t, e_i(t)) = \|e_i(t)\| - ce^{-\alpha t} \tag{36}$$

where $c > 0$, α is a normal number to be determined. When $f_i(t, e_i(t)) > 0$, AUVi triggers an event. Simultaneously, AUVi updates its controller. At the same time, the measurement error is set to zero. If the error is less than a given threshold, no communication between intelligences is required until the next event is triggered.

Suppose t^* denotes the most recent trigger moment. The tracking error $\delta_i(t) = x_i(t) - \prod_i \eta_i(t)$ is defined. When $c > 0$, $0 < \alpha < -\max_i \mathrm{Re}(\lambda_i)$, $\alpha_i > \max_i \|f_i\|$, system consistency can be achieved. Moreover, Zeno phenomenon will not occur based on Lemma 1.

4   Simulation and Analysis

4.1   Simulation of Heterogeneous AUV Cluster Consistency Algorithm under Event Trigger Control

In this section, a simulation is conducted for the consistency control algorithm of heterogeneous AUV swarm under event-triggered control proposed in Sect. 3.1. Suppose a heterogeneous AUV swarm consists of a navigator and four followers, where $x_i(t) = [s_i(t), v_i(t), a_i(t)]^T$ denotes state variables of AUVi, $s_i(t)$ denotes distance, $v_i(t)$ denotes velocity, and $a_i(t)$ denotes acceleration. Suppose that the initial position of navigator is randomly distributed between $[-10, 10]$. The initial position of each follower is randomly distributed in the interval $[-20, 20]$. The initial combined velocity is $5\,\mathrm{m/s}$. The initial values of other state variables are set to 0. The expected formation is designed as a parallel formation with the leader as the center and the four followers evenly distributed around it. The heterogeneity of the swarm is ensured by setting the constant vector of each AUV with $\theta^*_1 = [0, -0.0325, 0]^T$, $\theta^*_2 = [0, -0.0319, 0]^T$, $\theta^*_3 = [0, -0.0428, 0]^T$, $\theta^*_4 = [0, -0.0258, 0]^T$, $\theta^*_5 = [0, -0.0637, 0]^T$. The control input of leader AUV is

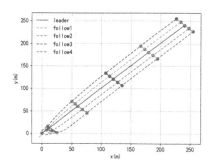

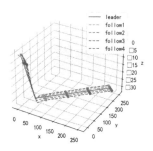

Fig. 1. Heterogeneous AUV group formation (2-D)

Fig. 2. Heterogeneous AUV group formation (3-D)

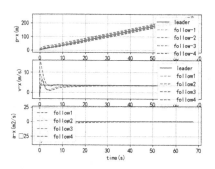

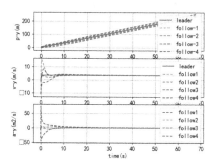

Fig. 3. Position, velocity and acceleration state quantities in x-direction without communication time

Fig. 4. Position, velocity and acceleration state quantities in y-direction without communication time

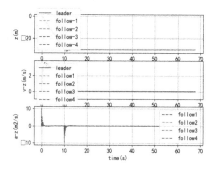

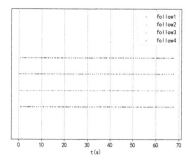

Fig. 5. Position, velocity and acceleration state quantities in z-direction without communication time delay

Fig. 6. Event trigger time without communication time delay

set to $u_0(t) = t \sin t$ and the trigger interval is set to 0.1s. The communication delay is not considered. According to Eq. (22), the simulation results are shown from Fig. 1 to Fig. 6.

The formation process of the heterogeneous AUV swarm can be seen in Fig. 1 and Fig. 2. The position and velocity of the follower can reach the leader, and the acceleration of the follower eventually converges to zero as shown in Fig. 3, Fig. 4, and Fig. 5. The event trigger moments are shown in Fig. 6. It can be seen that the proposed control method can significantly reduce the number of communications. Meanwhile, there is no Zeno behavior.

The simulation results show that the algorithm proposed in Sect. 3.1 updates the control signal of each follower AUVs at its own event-triggered moment, which can effectively reduce a large amount of communication information among AUVs. Moreover, the number of event triggering is reduced and the release time of event triggering is extended by using estimation-based trigger conditions. The speed and position state convergence is better. Consistency can be obtained faster.

4.2 Simulation of Heterogeneous AUV Cluster Consistency Algorithm with Time Delay Under Event Trigger Control

In this section, the simulation is carried out for the algorithm proposed in Sect. 3.2. In order to conduct the comparative analysis, one leader and four followers are also considered to form a heterogeneous AUV group. The rest of the state initial conditions are the same as Sect. 4.1. The following simulation experiments are designed with time delays of 0.1s and 0.5s, respectively. The simulation results for a time delay of 0.5s are shown in Fig. 7, 8, 9, 8, 9, 10, 11 and Fig. 12. The simulation results for a time delay of 0.5s are shown in Fig. 13, 14, 15, 16, 17 and Fig. 18.

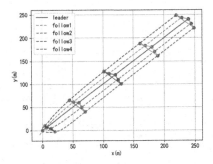

Fig. 7. Heterogeneous AUV group formation (2-D) with communication time delay = 0.5

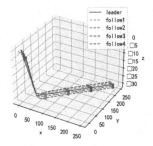

Fig. 8. Heterogeneous AUV group formation (3-D) with communication time delay = 0.5

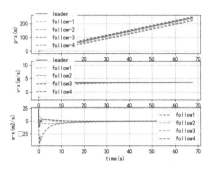

Fig. 9. Position, velocity and acceleration state quantities in x-direction with time delay = 0.5

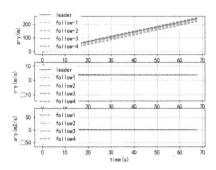

Fig. 10. Position, velocity and acceleration state quantities in y-direction with time delay = 0.5

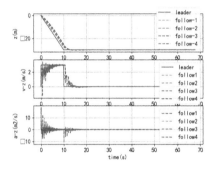

Fig. 11. Position, velocity and acceleration state quantities in z-direction with time delay = 0.5

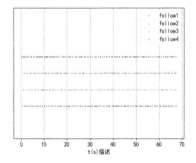

Fig. 12. Event trigger time with time delay = 0.5

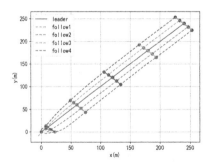

Fig. 13. Heterogeneous AUV group formation (2-D) with communication time delay = 0.1

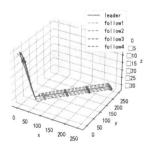

Fig. 14. Heterogeneous AUV group formation (3-D) with communication time delay = 0.1

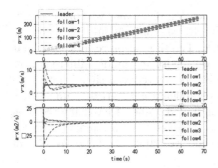

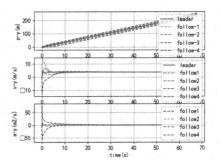

Fig. 15. Position, velocity and acceleration state quantities in x-direction with time delay = 0.1

Fig. 16. Position, velocity and acceleration state quantities in y-direction with time delay = 0.1

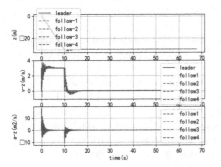

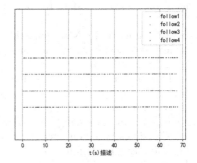

Fig. 17. Position, velocity and acceleration state quantities in z-direction with time delay = 0.1

Fig. 18. Event trigger time with time delay = 0.1

The simulation results show that the heterogeneous AUV swarm based on event-triggered control algorithm can still maintain a stable formation under different time delay conditions. The number of communications can be reduced significantly while there is no Zeno behavior. Comparing the simulation results under different time delay conditions, the transient performance will increase and steady-state error will be reduced when time delay is reduced.

5   Conclusion

In this paper, a distributed consistency control algorithm based on event-triggered mechanism for heterogeneous AUV swarm under communicaton delay is proposed. Firstly, an improved method is proposed by using estimation-based trigger conditions. In this method, the release time of event trigger is extended and the number of event triggers is reduced. Secondly, the consistency stability of the algorithm is proved by Lyapunov theory and Zeno phenomenon will not occur. Thirdly, two algorithms with communication delay and without communication delay are proposed respectively. Finally, simulations are conducted to demonstrate the effectiveness of the algorithm. The simulation results show that a fixed formation can be achieved by the two algorithms under different conditions. Meanwhile, the number of communications is reduced significantly and no Zeno phenomenon is found. In order to establish a comparison, simulations under different time delay conditions are conducted. When time delay reduces, the transient performance increases and the steady-state error reduces. In the future, a better compensator can be set in order to adjust the heterogeneity of AUV swarm.

References

1. Raanan, B.Y., et al.: Automatic fault diagnosis for autonomous underwater vehicles using online topic models. In: OCEANS 2016 MTS/IEEE Monterey, pp. 1–6. IEEE (2016)
2. Su, B., Wang, H., Li, N.: Event-triggered integral sliding mode fixed time control for trajectory tracking of autonomous underwater vehicle. Trans. Inst. Meas. Control, 0142331221994380 (2021)
3. Al Issa, S., Kar, I.: Design and implementation of event-triggered adaptive controller for commercial mobile robots subject to input delays and limited communications. Control. Eng. Pract. **114**, 104865 (2021)
4. Xiang, X., Xu, G., Zhang, Q., Xiao, Z., Huang, X.: Coordinated control for multi-AUV systems based on hybrid automata. In: 2007 IEEE International Conference on Robotics and Biomimetics (ROBIO), pp. 2121–2126. IEEE (2007)
5. Yu, M., Yan, C., Li, C.: Event-triggered tracking control for couple-group multi-agent systems. J. Franklin Inst. **354**(14), 6152–6169 (2017)
6. Yue, D., Tian, E., Han, Q.L.: A delay system method for designing event-triggered controllers of networked control systems. IEEE Trans. Autom. Control **58**(2), 475–481 (2012)
7. Liu, W., Yang, C., Sun, Y., Qin, J.: Observer-based event-triggered control for consensus of multi-agent systems with time delay. In: 2016 Chinese Control and Decision Conference (CCDC), pp. 2515–2522. IEEE (2016)
8. Antunes, D.J., Khashooei, B.A.: Consistent dynamic event-triggered policies for linear quadratic control. IEEE Trans. Control Netw. Syst. **5**(3), 1386–1398 (2017)
9. Deng, Y., Liu, T., Zhao, D.: Event-triggered output-feedback adaptive tracking control of autonomous underwater vehicles using reinforcement learning. Appl. Ocean Res. **113**, 102676 (2021)
10. Gao, Z., Guo, G.: Fixed-time leader-follower formation control of autonomous underwater vehicles with event-triggered intermittent communications. IEEE Access **6**, 27902–27911 (2018)
11. Kim, J.H., Yoo, S.J.: Distributed event-driven adaptive three-dimensional formation tracking of networked autonomous underwater vehicles with unknown nonlinearities. Ocean Eng. **233**, 109069 (2021)
12. Li, L., Ho, D.W.C., Lu, J.: Event-based network consensus with communication delays. Nonlinear Dyn. **87**(3), 1847–1858 (2016). https://doi.org/10.1007/s11071-016-3157-7
13. Mu, N., Wu, Y., Liao, X., Huang, T.: Input time delay margin in event-triggered consensus of multiagent systems. IEEE Trans. Cybern. **49**(5), 1849–1858 (2018)

14. Su, B., Wang, H., Wang, Y., Gao, J.: Fixed-time formation of AUVs with disturbance via event-triggered control. Int. J. Control Autom. Syst. **19**(4), 1505–1518 (2021)
15. Su, H., Wang, Z., Song, Z., Chen, X.: Event-triggered consensus of non-linear multi-agent systems with sampling data and time delay. IET Control Theory Appl. **11**(11), 1715–1725 (2017)
16. Xu, Y., Li, T., Tong, S.: Event-triggered adaptive fuzzy bipartite consensus control of multiple autonomous underwater vehicles. IET Control Theory Appl. **14**(20), 3632–3642 (2020)
17. Li, Y., Zhang, P., Wang, C., Wang, D., Wang, J.: Distributed event-triggered consensus of multi-agent systems with input delay. IFAC-PapersOnLine **53**(2), 2550–2555 (2020)
18. Wang, S., Cao, Y., Huang, T., Chen, Y., Li, P., Wen, S.: Sliding mode control of neural networks via continuous or periodic sampling event-triggering algorithm. Neural Netw. **121**, 140–147 (2020)
19. Wang, Y., Gu, Y., Xie, X., Zhang, H.: Delay-dependent distributed event-triggered tracking control for multi-agent systems with input time delay. Neurocomputing **333**, 200–210 (2019)

Edge Computing Energy-Efficient Resource Scheduling Based on Deep Reinforcement Learning and Imitation Learning

Hengliang Tang[1], Rongxin Jiao[1]([⊠]), Tingting Dong[2], Huilin Qin[1], and Fei Xue[1]

[1] School of Information, Beijing Wuzi University, Beijing 101149, China
`jeorgea@163.com`
[2] Faculty of Information Technology, Beijing University of Technology, Beijing 100124, China

Abstract. Task scheduling is one of the key technologies in edge computing. End devices can significantly improve the quality of service by offloading some latency-sensitive tasks to edge servers, but a large amount of power and compute units are wasted. Therefore, this paper proposes a two-stage task offloading approach to ensure low latency while reducing the energy consumption of edge computing units and cloud computing centers. The mobile edge computing environment contains edge computing nodes as well as cloud computing centers. A two-stage processing mechanism based on deep Q-learning is used to automatically generate optimal long-term scheduling decisions that reduce power consumption while ensuring quality of service. Imitation learning is also used in the reinforcement learning process to reduce the training time of the optimal policy. To evaluate the effectiveness of the model, we use the Shortest job first (SJF) algorithm and the Heterogeneous Earliest Finish Time (HEFT) into as comparison algorithms, comparing the running time and energy consumption as a measure. Our proposed algorithm has 13% more running time but 34% lower average energy consumption compared to other algorithms.

Keywords: Edge computing · Resource scheduling · Deep reinforcement learning · Imitation learning

1 Introduction

In the past few years, with the growth of data volume of terminal devices and the continuous development of artificial intelligence applications, the limited computing power of terminal devices cannot meet the application scenarios such as unmanned driving, smart manufacturing and smart cities. This has led to the proposed edge computing service model. Edge computing is the processing of latency-sensitive partial requests through micro computing units such as base stations in the vicinity of mobile end devices, thus improving the response speed as well as the stability and continuity of services. Requests for non-delay-sensitive types are processed by means of cloud computing, thus reducing the load pressure on the edge computing units. Currently, the edge processing units are underutilized, leading to idle equipment and energy waste. The data shows [1]. For

© Springer Nature Singapore Pte Ltd. 2022
L. Pan et al. (Eds.): BIC-TA 2021, CCIS 1566, pp. 222–231, 2022.
https://doi.org/10.1007/978-981-19-1253-5_16

traditional computing centers, the optimal energy utilization is 70–80%, but the actual service delivery is unpredictable in terms of user requests, so the energy utilization is usually below 50%. We need to simulate user requests and find a reasonable scheduling scheme to ensure the quality of service and energy consumption.

In the MEC (Mobile Edge Computing) scenario, by deploying micro-servers in the communication base stations near the terminal devices, part of the computing resources are sunk to the user side, which shortens the distance on the physical path, reduces the communication overhead, and also relieves the load pressure on the cloud computing center. The whole edge computing service system has two service parties, which are the edge computing nodes and the cloud computing center. The service process of the system starts with the end device sending requests to the edge computing node, and the edge computing node sends part of the non-delay-sensitive requests to the cloud for processing back to the edge server, and then the edge server returns to the end device. For some delay-sensitive requests, the edge computing nodes process and return the results directly to the terminal.

Traditional deep learning resource management schemes have long training time and slow convergence [2]. This is mainly due to the fact that RL is completely ignorant of "expert knowledge", which allows RL to learn the optimal policy from scratch through trial and error, which motivates us to adopt a more efficient training method [3]. The training time can be significantly reduced by imitation learning.

In this project, the system consists of two main parts: workload processor and two-level resource decision system. The workload processor receives user requests and adds them to the task queue of the edge computing nodes and the task queue of the cloud computing center, respectively. The two-level resource decision system allocates the appropriate computing units based on the provided task information. To improve the processing efficiency of compute units, we dynamically update the ready task queues to achieve the parallel operation of the impractical virtual machines (VMS). Our task scheduling optimization goal is to minimize the long-term energy cost by training while ensuring the quality of service. We first implement this system and then verify the effectiveness of our system by benchmarking algorithms. Our main contributions are listed below.

(1) We implemented a two-level scheduling algorithm based on deep Q-learning. The two-level decision can minimize the energy cost while satisfying the service quality.
(2) We built an edge computing service simulation system to simulate the requests of end devices, edge computing service devices, resources and other information.
(3) To speed up model training and convergence, we integrate imitation learning in reinforcement learning to mimic the behavior of some classical heuristics (e.g., minimum average waiting time). These scheduling methods are considered as 'experts' for specific scenarios, thus improving the effectiveness of agent training and substantially reducing the training time.

2   Related Works

In recent years, academic circles have been enthusiastic about research in the field of MEC: at the theoretical level, a number of literature reviews [4] summarized the existing theoretical framework and architecture of MEC and looked forward to the future development of MEC; Mao Y et al. [5] investigated MEC supporting technologies, including technologies such as virtualization and software-defined networking; Zhang K et al. [6] classified MEC scenes, models, and deployment in detail. At the application level, Yang X et al. [7] expounded the application and value of MEC in the field of Internet of Things; Huang X [8] et al.

Computing offloading is a process in which mobile users delegate computing-intensive tasks to cloud computing platforms for execution. It has been fully and widely applied in the field of MCC [9]. In the field of MEC, computing offloading technology is the first of the three design elements of the MEC system (the other two major elements are resource allocation and mobility management), which can not only optimize resource utilization, but also reduce service delay, extend equipment life, and improve user experience, so it is also of great research value [10]. In general, the key to the design of the calculation offloading algorithm is to decide which tasks to uninstall and which devices to offload tasks to execute. Starting from the scope of computational offloading, Yang J et al. [11] divided the computational offloading model into two basic categories: single server model and multi-server model.

Under the single-server computing offloading model, Yuan J et al. [12] used a convex optimization method to achieve the optimal computational offloading decision.

At present, there is little research on edge computing resource allocation using deep reinforcement learning algorithm. On the basis of [1], combined with Deep Reinforcement Learning (DQN) algorithm and edge computing environment model, we propose an edge computing task allocation model for energy efficient utilization, and use imitation learning method to speed up the model training speed and realize the efficient use of energy under the condition of meeting task constraints.

3   Scheduling System

We expect our system to minimize long-term energy consumption. To achieve this goal, we built a platform that simulates the MEC environment model, which calculates energy consumption and costs. We use real user request data and the workload model is handled by the user. After that, we built an environmental model that provides information on resource usage and energy consumption.

3.1   Workload Processor

Our system contains edge computing node processing units as well as cloud computing center virtual machine processing units, where the edge node device set is represented by set E_i and the computing center virtual machine is represented by set VM_i. The set of devices is represented as Eqs. 1 and 2.

$$E = \{E_1, E_2, \cdots, E_n\} \tag{1}$$

$$VM = \{VM_1, VM_2, \cdots, VM_n\} \tag{2}$$

We abstract each user request into a DAG graph, which is represented by a binary G $< V, E >$, where V is the task vertex and E is the edge associated with the vertex. Each vertex represents a task, and the edge represents the relationship between the two tasks. The workload processor is responsible for classifying the tasks in the DAG diagram, and then dynamically adding sub tasks to the edge node task queue Q_e, T in the set of Q_e denotes the set of task queues on edge node e and the cloud environment task queue Q_c, T in the set denotes the set of task queues on the central server. The above two sets are expressed by the following Eqs. 3 and 4.

$$Q_e = \left\{ T_1^E, T_2^E, \cdots, T_n^E \right\} \tag{3}$$

$$Q_c = \left\{ T_1^C, T_2^C, \cdots, T_n^C \right\} \tag{4}$$

Each task is represented by Ti. The workload resolves Ti based on the information provided by the dataset include Ti_{start} (Start execution time), Ti_{ddl} (Task deadline), Ti_{res} (Computing resources required), Ti_s (Whether the task is delay-sensitive is represented by a binary number, where 1 is delay-sensitive) and relevance to other tasks. Relevance refers to the constraint relationship before and after task execution. For example, if task a depends on the results and data of Task B, task a can only be executed after task B is completed. Tasks are added to different queues according to the Tis value, and the process is as in Eq. 5.

$$\begin{cases} Add \ Q_e(T), \ if \ T_{tag} = 1 \\ Add \ Q_c(T), \ if \ T_{tag} = 0 \end{cases} \tag{5}$$

T_i^{time} indicates that the workload processor calculates the running time required for each task at different nodes, where i represents the task number. The runtime on edge nodes and compute center VMs is calculated by the following Eqs. 5 and 6.

$$T_i^{time} = \frac{T_i res}{VM_i^P} \tag{6}$$

$$T_i^{time} = \frac{T_i res}{E_i^P} \tag{7}$$

We use the HEFT algorithm to obtain the priority queue Q to provide to the agent for selecting the appropriate computational unit. The HEFT algorithm is a static scheduling algorithm that calculates the priority of tasks by computing the rank value from the bottom up. It first calculates the earliest completion time of all tasks on each virtual machine according to the dependencies in the DAG before scheduling, then compares the smallest earliest completion time and its corresponding computational unit, matches the task with the virtual machine and corresponds to the corresponding occupied time slot, and then schedules the tasks of the whole workflow to the corresponding virtual machine after all tasks and virtual machines are matched. After all the tasks and virtual machines are matched, the tasks of the entire workflow are scheduled to the corresponding virtual machines for operation.

3.2 Problem Definition

We use deep reinforcement learning methods to generate reasonable task allocation schemes that minimize energy consumption while meeting latency requirements and quality of service. Therefore, we build a 2-level decision system. to handle task queues at the edge nodes as well as at the cloud computing center, respectively. Figure 1 shows the flowchart of task queue processing by the smart body. The task queues are generated by the Workload Processor and used as the input to the neural network. The intelligence automatically generates the best decision based on the reward function.

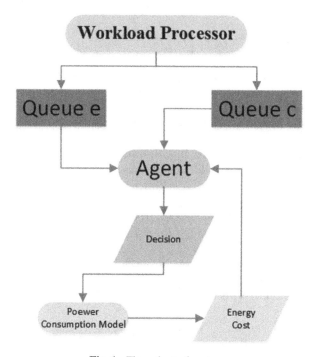

Fig. 1. Flow chart of system.

Power Consumption Model: We calculate the utilization of node i by expressing it in the following equation, where Runtime(m) is the total running time of the node, $\sum_{i=1}^{n} \text{Ti}_{res}^{time}$ is the amount of time being occupied, where Ti_{res}^{time} is the amount of resources required for each task, and i represents the tasks that currently running on this node.

$$U_m = \frac{\sum_{i=1}^{n} T_i^{time}}{Runtime} \tag{8}$$

The power of a computational node consists of two components: static power Pwrs and dynamic power Pwrd. where the static power is fixed while the node is operating, while the dynamic power varies as the utilization increases.

$$Pwr_s = \begin{cases} 0 & U_m = 0 \\ const & U_m > 0 \end{cases} \tag{9}$$

$$Pwr_D = \begin{cases} \alpha * U_m & U_m < \tilde{U}_m \\ \alpha * \tilde{U}_m + (U_m - 0.7)^2 \beta & U_m \geq \tilde{U}_m \end{cases} \tag{10}$$

Um is the utilization rate of server m, $\alpha = 0.5$, $\beta = 10$, $\tilde{U}_m$ is the optimal utilization which is 0.7 [13]. And the total power of server m Pwrm is the sum of static power Pwrs and dynamic power Pwrd.

Each task's runtime takes up a non-infinite amount of computational resources. In reality, it will be automatically released at the end of the process. To simulate this process, we set a random runtime for each task. During this time, some resources of the computational unit will be occupied by that task. In other words, when the agent assigns a task to a computing unit, we can get an end time which represents the expected completion time of the task. When the occupancy time is over, we change the status of the task from "ready" to "finished" and release the corresponding resources. In this way, we can dynamically model the changes of resources in the server system and help the agent to make decisions.

3.3 Environment Model

Figure 2 below shows the workflow of the two-level decision processor [14, 15]. Tasks are added to the edge node compute waiting queue as well as the cloud computing center waiting queue based on latency sensitive markers, respectively. The system keeps track of the resource status, information, records of the current cloud server platform and basic information about the new tasks. The agent makes a decision based on the current task and status information through a reward function. The pseudo code of two-layer deep reinforcement learning is shown in Fig. 3.

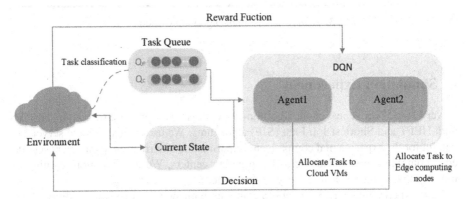

Fig. 2. Two-stage processor based on deep reinforcement learning.

State Space: In the two-stage decision-making process, the current state information and task information are obtained as the input information of the environment. For the agent of stage1, it will get the current resource status information and single task information. For the second stage, the agent will obtain the resource status information of all base stations and the task information of virtual machines in the base station.

Action Space: Just like the state space, the action space defines the operations available to the agent [16]. In the first stage, DQN needs to select a server farm from all the server farms of the current task, and the agent of stage2 will select the appropriate base station from the base station set.

Reward Functions: The following are the reward functions of our two agents [15].

$$R = P[t_n, Pwr_D(t_{n-1}) - Pwr_D(t_n)] \tag{11}$$

t_n is the current time, and $Pwr_f(t)$ represents the total power of servers in the farm on time t, and $Pwr_m(t)$ represents the power of individual server on time t.

DQN Resource Scheduling Algorithm

Input: Ready Tasks

Output: Scheduling Matrix

01. Initialize environment information
02. Initialize workload processor
03. Q_e workloadprocessor() , Q_c workloadprocessor()   //Get Task Queue
04. **For** each Calculation unit do C_i
05.   **For** each task unit do T_i
06.   Unit_Task_ arrays   calculate τ_i^{time} //Calculate the T_i runtime on C_i
07. **For** each task in Qe
08.   Scheduling Matrix   RunAgent1(Unit_Task_ arrays)
09. **For** each task in Qc
10.   Scheduling Matrix   RunAgent2(Unit_Task_ arrays)
11. Return Scheduling Matrix

Fig. 3. Resource scheduling algorithm pseudo code.

4   Simulation Experiment

To verify the effectiveness of our algorithm, we compared the proposed algorithm HEFT* with HEFT and Shortest Job First (SJF) algorithms. We used a real Google server log dataset for the experimental comparison. Experimental environment parameters set 100 edge computing nodes and 3 cloud computing centers, We use imitation learning to improve the convergence efficiency of the model.

The experimental environment is a computer with Windows 10 Home Edition, Intel i7–6700 CPU, 16G memory, and NVIDIA GeForce GTX 1050Ti graphics card with 8G memory.

We use the above parameters and data set and the experimental results are as follows (Figs. 4 and 5).

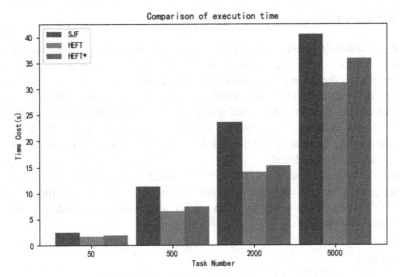

Fig. 4. Scheduling runtime comparison.

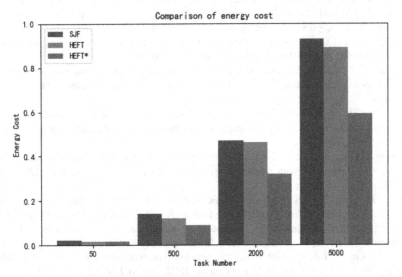

Fig. 5. Energy cost comparison.

This shows that the execution time of our proposed algorithm HEFT* is on average 13% more compared to the HEFT algorithm, but the average energy consumption of scheduling is reduced by 34%. Because the DQN agent learns from the reward function and continuously selects the server group and base station with the largest reward.

5 Conclusion

The task scheduling problem in edge computing environments requires rational algorithms to reduce energy consumption. Although traditional algorithms have shorter scheduling time, their energy consumption is not considered.

The HEFT* algorithm is experimentally tested in an environment with edge computing nodes and cloud computing virtual machines. The time required for task scheduling and the energy consumption are tested. And the convergence time is reduced by using imitation learning method in training the DQN model. Task fault tolerance, network failure, etc. can be considered.

In the future, a combination of fault-tolerant approaches to task fault tolerance in edge computing environments such as those considered in [17–19] and more precise methods for algorithms to determine whether a task is latency-sensitive can be considered to be closer to the real situation.

References

1. Kozyrakis, C.: Resource efficient computing for warehouse-scale datacenters. In: Design, Automation & Test in Europe Conference & Exhibition (DATE), pp. 1351–1356 (2013)
2. Tong, Z., Chen, H., Deng, X., Li, K., Li, K.: A scheduling scheme in the cloud computing environment using deep Q-learning. Inf. Sci. **512**, 1170–1191 (2020)
3. Wen, G., et al.: Cloud resource scheduling with deep reinforcement learning and imitation learning. IEEE Internet Things J. **8**(5), 3576–3586 (2021)
4. Bellavista, P., Chessa, S., Foschini, L., et al.: Human-enabled edge computing: exploiting the crowd as a dynamic extension of mobile edge computing. IEEE Commun. **56**(1), 145–155 (2018)
5. Mao, Y., Zhang, J., Song, S.H., et al.: Stochastic joint radio and computational resource management for multi-user mobile-edge computing systems. IEEE Trans. Wireless Commun. **16**(9), 5994–6009 (2017)
6. Zhang, K., Mao, Y., Leng, S., et al.: Mobile-edge computing for vehicular networks: a promising network paradigm with predictive off-loading. IEEE Veh. Technol. Mag. **12**(2), 36–44 (2017)
7. Yang, X., Chen, Z., Li, K., et al.: Communication-constrained mobile edge computing systems for wireless virtual reality: scheduling and trade-off. IEEE Access **6**, 16665–16677 (2018)
8. Huang, X., Yu, R., Kang, J., et al.: Distributed reputation management for secure and efficient vehicular edge computing and networks. IEEE Access **1**, 99 (2017)
9. Xu, X., Liu, J., Tao, X.: Mobile edge computing enhanced adaptive bitrate video delivery with joint cache and radio resource allocation. IEEE Access **1**, 99 (2017)
10. Morabito, R., Cozzolino, V., Ding, A.Y., et al.: Consolidate IoT edge computing with lightweight virtualization. IEEE Netw. **32**(1), 102–111 (2018)
11. Duan, Y., Sun, X., Che, H., et al.: Modeling data, information and knowledge for security protection of hybrid IoT and edge resources. IEEE Access **7**, 1 (2019)
12. Liu, Z., Choo, K.K.R., Grossschadl, J.: Securing edge devices in the post-quantum Internet of Things using lattice-based cryptography. IEEE Commun. Mag. **56**(2), 158–162 (2018)
13. Yang, J., Zhihui, L., Jie, W.: Smart-toy-edge-computing-oriented data exchange based on blockchain. J. Syst. Archit. **87**, 36–48 (2018). https://doi.org/10.1016/j.sysarc.2018.05.001
14. Gao, Y., et al.: An energy and deadline aware resource provisioning, scheduling and optimization framework for cloud systems. In: Hardware/Software Co-Design and System Synthesis. IEEE, pp. 1–10 (2013)

15. Mao, H., Alizadeh, M., Menache, I., Kandula, S.: Resource management with deep reinforcement learning. In: Proceedings of the 15th ACM Workshop on Hot Topics In Networks - HotNets 2016 (2016). https://doi.org/10.1145/3005745.3005750
16. Mnih, V., et al.: Human-level control through deep reinforcement learning. Nature, **518**(7540), 529–533 (2015). https://doi.org/10.1038/nature14236
17. Xie, G., Zeng, G., Li, R., et al.: Quantitative fault-tolerance for reliable workflows on heterogeneous IaaS clouds. IEEE Trans. Cloud Comput. **8**(4), 1223–1236 (2020)
18. Moon, J., Jeong, J.: Smart manufacturing scheduling system: DQN based on cooperative edge computing. IMCOM, 1–8 (2021)
19. Wu, Y., Dinh, T., Fu, Y., et al.: A hybrid DQN and optimization approach for strategy and resource allocation in MEC networks. IEEE Trans. Wirel. Commun. **20**(7), 4282–4295 (2021)

Metric Learning with Distillation for Overcoming Catastrophic Forgetting

Piaoyao Yu[1,2], Juanjuan He[1,2(✉)], Qilang Min[1,2], and Qi Zhu[1,2]

[1] College of Computer Science and Technology, Wuhan University of Science and Technology, Wuhan, China
{yupiaoyao,juanjuanhe,zhuqi}@wust.edu.cn
[2] Hubei Province Key Laboratory of Intelligent Information Processing and Real-Time Industrial System, Wuhan, China

Abstract. In incremental learning, reducing catastrophic forgetting always adds additional weights to the classification layer when a new task comes. Moreover, it focuses on prediction accuracy, ignores mislabeling differences, and causes the learned features to be scattered. This paper removes the softmax and integrates depth metric learning to compute image embeddings, which doesn't need to add extra weights or additional space for new classes. The distances of the data mapped in the old and new task spaces are calculated separately. Then, the distillation of depth metric learning is used to make the two distances as similar as possible to improve the performance of the old knowledge. The experimental results on Cifar10 and Tiny-ImageNet show that the proposed method can effectively alleviate catastrophic forgetting and enhance the effectiveness of incremental learning.

Keywords: Class incremental learning · Metric learning · Knowledge distillation · Deep learning

1 Introduction

When samples are acquired incrementally, catastrophic forgetting occurs. This is because a model continuously receives knowledge from non-stationary data distributions. The new knowledge can interfere with or even overwrite the old knowledge, significantly degrading the model's performance in recognizing the old knowledge. Incremental learning aims to solve this problem. It continuously acquires knowledge from a stream of data while retaining the old knowledge learned previously.

Incremental learning has three cases [1]: task-incremental learning (TIL), class-incremental learning (CIL), and domain-incremental learning (DIL). TIL provides a task ID for each task to select the associated classifier. It is mainly applicable to network structures with "multi-head" output layers. There is no

The work was supported by National Natural Science Foundation of China under Grants 61702383.

task ID in DIL, and there is no need to infer which task the input data belongs to. DIL is usually used in cases with the same task structure and different input distributions. However, in some practical cases, it is necessary to infer which task the input data belongs to without a task ID., and CIL is usually used in such cases. Therefore, CIL is the most complex among these three cases. Since CIL does not know the task ID, inferring old tasks' input data is challenging. This paper focuses on overcoming catastrophic forgetting in CIL. In recent years, some scholars have also proposed many improvements. For example, tao used NG networks and enhanced topology stability to solve the CIL catastrophic forgetting problem [3]. Yu proposed to apply embedded networks in class incremental learning [2]. Rebuffi combined replay and distillation loss and applied to class incremental learning [14]. However, these networks introduce new neurons as classes increase [37].

Metric learning is used to measure the similarity between images, which makes the similarity between images of different categories smaller and the similarity between images of the same category larger [4]. It was first proposed by Xing at NIPS 2002 [5]. In this work, the input images are classified into the category with high similarity. Deep metric learning is a method of metric learning. It uses triple loss to learn the mapping from the original features to a low-dimensional dense vector space (called embedding space). The mapping distance of the images on the embedding space is changed by using deep metric learning. Images in the same class are closer, while images of different classes are further apart. Deep metric learning has achieved many successful applications [26], such as face recognition, face verification, image retrieval, signature verification, and pedestrian re-identification.

This paper proposes an incremental class learning framework based on metric learning with distillation (MLDCIL). MLDCIL applies a triple loss function to incremental class learning by constraining the sample metric distance through metric learning. Moreover, MDDCIL utilizes distillation loss functions to preserve the relationships between samples and resist catastrophic forgetting. The main contributions of this framework are as follows:

1) Use deep metric learning to compute image embeddings. It can avoid adding extra weights to the network.
2) The softmax function is replaced by a triple loss. It makes the distance between the same classes smaller, while the distance between different classes larger.
3) Apply the distillation loss function from metric learning to incremental learning. Make the embedding distances of images on the old and new models as similar as possible to resist the occurrence of catastrophic forgetting.

Experiments are conducted on two public datasets, Cifar10 and Tiny-ImageNet, and compared with oEWC [35], SI [7], FDR [8], LWF [19], HAL [9], and SDC [2] for a total of six methods. The experiments show that our method effectively prevents catastrophic forgetting, and the average forgetting rate is about 20% lower than the other methods.

2   Related Work

2.1   Incremental Learning

With the popularity of neural networks, incremental learning and catastrophic forgetting have received increasing attention in the last decades. For two consecutive tasks, there are several experiments [10] that have investigated the effect of different activation functions on forgetting. There are also some works [11] that have studied theoretical perspectives. To reduce forgetting, the mainstream methods are generally classified into three categories. 1) Replay methods. 2) Regularization-based methods. 3) Parameter isolation methods [12].

1) Replay methods are used by storing some of the original samples or using a generative model to generate pseudo-samples. These initial samples or pseudo-samples are re-entered when learning a new task to reduce forgetting. This method [13] readjusts the subset of samples stored in training. For example, in incremental learning, ICARL [14] stores a subset of examples for each class and selects the best approximate class mean. However, this method may overfit the stored sample subsets. If previous samples are not available, a pseudo-training method can be used. First, the pseudo-training method inputs new samples to the previous model. Then the output data is added to the training as previous samples [15]. In recent years, some generative models have been able to output very similar images [16] They are well used in incremental learning [17].

2) Regularization-based methods avoid storing the original input data and reduce memory. This method reduces catastrophic forgetting by constraints on the optimization direction of the model on the new task. Constraints include adding distillation losses using the old model, constraining essential parameters of the model, projecting the gradient direction of the parameters, etc.

   2.1) Use knowledge to distill. Silver and Mercer [18] first proposed to use the output of the previous task model. LWF uses the previous output model as the soft label of the previous task to reduce forgetting. Rannen et al. [20] improved and mapped the features to the low-dimensional learning space.

   2.2) Parameter constraints estimate the distribution of parameters and are used prior when learning new data. EWC [21] first uses this method. It assesses the importance of the network parameters and restricts the variety of important parameters during the after-task training. Zenke et al. [22] the importance of online estimation of weights. The significance of unsupervised estimation [23] was proposed by Aljundi et al. However, for long sequence tasks [24], the limitation of regularization may be insufficient, and it leads to more forgetting of old tasks.

2.2   Metric Learning

Metric learning is also called similarity learning. Chopra et al. [25] first proposed Siamese contrast loss and applied it to deep metric learning. Later, Schroff et al.

proposed triplet loss [26] based on Euclidean embedding and used to face recognition. Making face verification only requires thresholding the distance between the two embeddings.

2.3 Knowledge Distillation

Knowledge distillation is mainly used for specific visual computing tasks. First, it [27] uses large-scale data to train an extensive complex network. Then the pseudo-data generated by the large-scale network is predicted to obtain pseudo-labels. Finally, a small-scale network is trained with this pseudo-labeled pseudo-data and the original training data. This makes the small network similar to the large network. The work of [28] uses the concept of temperature T in the Boltzmann distribution. It applies a fixed $T = 1$ to knowledge distillation. However, the distillation does not work well. This inspired [29] to propose knowledge distillation in neural networks, which uses different T and increases the small probability impact. Mirzadeh S-I et al. [30] found that knowledge distillation is ineffective when the model sizes of two networks differ too much, leading to a degradation in the performance of smaller networks. Therefore, they proposed a multi-step distillation method. By using the teaching assistant network, the teacher network and the teaching assistant network are distilled. Then knowledge distillation is performed in the teaching assistant network and the student network. The purpose of [31] is the same as Mirzadeh S-I et al. However, they argue that the multi-step distillation method is ineffective. It is proposed that the training of the teacher network should be stopped early. LWF uses the knowledge distillation method for incremental learning for the first time. Due to the use of the softmax function, the parameters change as the model learns new data. To make the parameters remember the original data, LWF treats the old model as a teacher network and the new model to be trained as a student network. First, the old model is used to label some of the new data. Then during the training process, this part of the training data labeled with "pseudo-label" can be regarded as the original data and put into training with the remaining new data.

3 Proposed Method

We apply deep metric learning and knowledge distillation to incremental class learning and design a class incremental learning framework(MDLCIL). Suppose the training dataset for the t-th task is $D^{(t)}$ and the class set is $C^{(t)}$. We can only access $D^{(t)}$ and train the model. The training dataset is a new class for each task and there is no overlap between classes for different tasks: $C^{(i)} \cap C^{(j)} = \emptyset$. This section briefly describes our method, and the flowchart of the method is shown in Fig. 1.

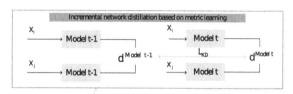

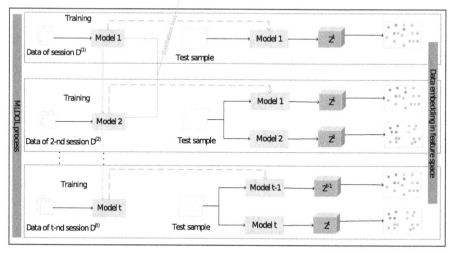

Fig. 1. Description of the flowchart. When $t = 1$, the model is trained on task 1. When $t > 1$, a copy of the model t is read and frozen. The data of the t-th task is fed to the model t and the frozen model for training, respectively. Then the model is updated by knowledge distillation. The final model t is obtained. The orange dashed line is a diagram of knowledge distillation loss. The L_{KD} aims to make the embedding distances of the same two images in both models as similar as possible.

3.1 Network Structure and its Losses

We apply deep metric learning (embedding network) in the resnet network. The network is structurally identical to a normal resnet. However, it removes the softmax layer and adds the embedding layer at the network's last layer. This lets the output be mapped into a low-dimensional space. Then, using the Euclidean distance, a distance metric is applied to the two samples in turn. This is to compare the similarity between the samples. Triple loss is the metric loss function of the embedding network. It will close the distance between the anchor and the positive, while distancing the anchor and the negative (the positive belongs to the same class as the anchor, and the negative does not belong to the same class as the anchor.) The structure of the Triple loss is as follows:

$$L_{ML} = max(0, d_+ - d_- + \alpha) \tag{1}$$

The formula of d_+ and d_- is:

$$d_+ = ||f(x_i^a) - f(x_i^p)||_2^2 \tag{2}$$

$$d_- = ||f(x_i^a) - f(x_i^n)||_2^2 \tag{3}$$

d_+ and d_- are the Euclidean distances between $f(x_i^a)$ and $f(x_i^p$ and $f(x_i^n)$ respectively. $f(x_i^\varphi)$ is the embedding of the i sample x_i^φ in space. $x_i^\varphi = \{x_i^a, x_i^p, x_i^n\}$. a, p, n stand for anchor, positive, and negative respectively. The smaller the $d_+ - d_-$, the closer the distance between the a and the p. When the a is close enough to p and far enough away from n, L_{ML} will be 0. This metric is determined by the margin α.

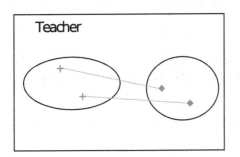 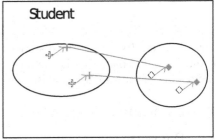

Fig. 2. Example. The same points in the embedding space indicate the same class. The dotted line in the Student embedding space indicates the position of this sample in the Teacher embedding. (Color figure online)

3.2 Knowledge Distillation Embedded in the Network

The traditional knowledge distillation method mainly uses the softmax function. Later [6] proposed relative teachers, which extended the knowledge distillation method to metric learning. As long as the data in the embedding space are similar in distance, it forces the student network to learn all embeddings. In this paper, the old model is considered the teacher network, and the new model under training is regarded as the student network. Distillation loss functions constrain the feature distances of teachers and students. For the same two images, let the feature distances of the student network and the teacher network resemble each other as much as possible. This will avoid the relationship between the data being affected. As shown in Fig. 2. The figure (above) pointed to by the orange dashed line in Fig. 1 is the diagram of L_{KD} in the network, and its distillation loss is as follows:

$$L_{KD} = ||d^S - d^T|| \tag{4}$$

Where $||.||$ refers to the Frobinius norm. d^S and d^T are the distances of sample x_i, x_j in the student and teacher embedding space:

$$d^S = ||f^S x_i - f^S x_j|| \tag{5}$$

$$d^T = ||f^T x_i - f^T x_j|| \tag{6}$$

When d^S and d^T are as similar as possible, L_{KD} is closer to 0.

We use both metric L_{ML} (1) and L_{KD} (4) to train the network to prevent forgetting during continuous training of embeddings:

$$L = L_{ML} + \lambda L_{KD} \tag{7}$$

Where λ is a trade-off between L_{ML} and L_{KD}.

3.3 Classifier

Due to the introduction of the metric network, we use the nearest class mean (NCM) classifier [2] for joint training, which is defined as:

$$\hat{y}_j = \underset{C \in U_i C^{(i)}}{argmin}\, dist(f(x_j), U_C) \tag{8}$$

Among them, $dist(.,.)$ is the distance metric, and $f(x_j)$ is the embedding of the j sample x_j in space. U_C is the mean value of the features extracted from the embedding of all samples in class C.

4   Experiment

4.1   Datasets

We used the following two benchmark data sets to evaluate our framework:

Cifar10 [32] contains 60,000 RGB images, and all images are divided into 10 classes. 50,000 of these images are divided into the training set, and the remaining 10,000 are the test set.

Tiny-ImageNet [33] is an image classification dataset provided by Stanford University. It has 120,000 images and is divided into 200 classes. Each class has 500 training images, 50 validation images, and 50 test images.

4.2   Implementation Details

This section uses Pytorch1.4 and python3.7 to compile all models. All the experiments were trained on GTX2070 GPU, Intel Core i5-9400F CPU, and 8G RAM. We use the Resnet18 [34] model (without pre-training) as the backbone network, add a linear 512-dimensional embedding layer after the average pooling layer, and use the triple loss for training. Using Adam optimizer, for Cifar10 and Tiny-ImageNet, the training images are randomly flipped horizontally, and the images are 32×32 and 28×28, respectively. Our Batch size is 64, epoch is 50, and the λ in Eq. 7 is 1. Then, for the experiments, we randomly input classes for class incremental training.

4.3   Ablation Experiment

The results of the ablation experiments are shown in Fig. 3. The Cifar10 and Tiny-ImageNet datasets are evaluated in 2 and 5 increments, respectively. FT learns the regular Resnet18 classification network. Its loss function is softmax, and no measures are taken to prevent catastrophic forgetting. M-FT adds metric learning to Resnet18 classification, and its loss function is triple loss. The results in Fig. 3 show that triple loss outperforms softmax for different class increment

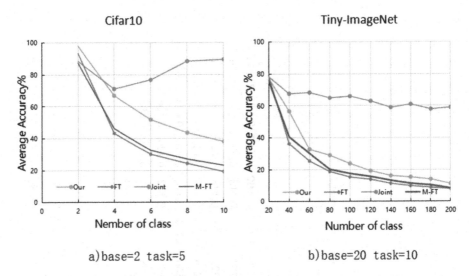

Fig. 3. Results of ablation experiments performed on Cifar10 and Tiny-ImageNet. base: The number of classes for the initial training, and the number of tasks. M-FT: Add metric learning to the Resnet network. FT: lower-pound. Join: upper-pound. Our: Our method.

conditions, with FT always obtaining the worst results. This proves that catastrophic forgetting is indeed the main problem of class incremental learning. Our method prevents catastrophic forgetting by using distillation loss during learning after each task.

4.4   Comparison Methods

In this section, our methods are compared with some advanced incremental learning methods, as shown in Table 1 (the best results for each learning session have been bolded). These incremental learning methods include LWF, oEWC, HAL, SI, and FDR, as well as SDC, which also uses an embedding layer. The test accuracies of the above methods on 2 datasets are reported separately. Ten trials were performed to avoid idiosyncrasies and chance in the results. Their average classification accuracies are calculated and analyzed.

It can be seen from Table 1 and Fig. 4 that oEWC, SI and LWF perform the same as FT in class incremental learning, with no delayed catastrophic forgetting at all, and they all have an average forgetting rate of 100%. HAL and SDC have higher accuracy rates. However, they have very high forgetting rates, which are basically above 50%. Our method is 4% more accurate on average, while the forgetting rate is less than 30%, which shows that we are significantly effective in resisting catastrophic forgetting.

Table 1. Class incremental learning results on the Cifar10 (accuracy percentage).

Method	Cifar10					Tiny-ImageNet learning sessions									
	Learning sessions					Learning sessions									
	1	2	3	4	5	1	2	3	4	5	6	7	8	9	10
Our	0.980	**0.668**	**0.514**	**0.436**	**0.427**	0.735	**0.566**	**0.326**	**0.289**	**0.237**	**0.192**	**0.162**	**0.157**	**0.139**	**0.112**
oEWC	**0.989**	0.463	0.317	0.246	0.195	0.781	0.363	0.253	0.187	0.153	0.138	0.113	0.098	0.087	0.076
SDC	0.954	0.654	0.499	0.428	0.380	0.713	**0.556**	0.322	0.275	0.225	0.178	0.138	0.122	0.101	0.084
HAL	0.987	0.658	0.479	0.418	0.364	0.794	0.573	0.325	0.271	0.226	0.170	0.149	0.122	0.110	0.081
SI	0.988	0.458	0.319	0.247	0.195	0.790	0.364	0.251	0.183	0.156	0.136	0.110	0.916	0.082	0.066
FDR	0.988	0.487	0.429	**0.439**	0.271	**0.791**	0.413	0.296	0.263	0.209	0.160	0.142	0.126	0.106	0.088
LWF	0.981	0.468	0.315	0.247	0.195	0.786	0.436	0.302	0.259	0.188	0.153	0.140	0.121	0.098	0.085

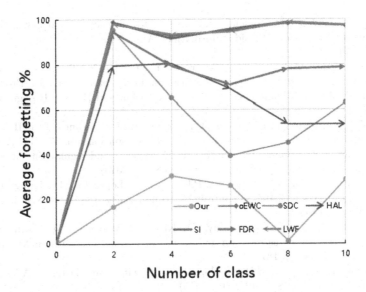

Fig. 4. On the Cifar10 dataset, the average forgetting [36] is compared with the other six methods. The results for LWF and these data agree, making the presentation of the data overlap.

5 Conclusions

The incremental class learning framework based on metric learning and distillation is proposed in this paper. In MDLCIL, distillation by metric learning allows the network to remember the distance between samples. This alleviates the problem of catastrophic forgetting. Compared with other incremental class methods, the accuracy of the MDLCIL method is improved by 4%, and it has a forgetting rate of less than 30%. It shows that we have a significant effect in resisting catastrophic forgetting. The experimental results show that the proposed method outperforms other class incremental methods and substantially impacts fighting forgetting.

References

1. Van de Ven, G.M., Tolias, A.S.: Three scenarios for continual learning. arXiv preprint arXiv:1904.07734 (2019)
2. Yu, L., et al.: Semantic drift compensation for class-incremental learning. In: Proceedings of the IEEE/CVF Conference on Computer Vision and Pattern Recognition, pp. 6982–6991 (2020)
3. Tao, X., Hong, X., Chang, X., Dong, S., Wei, X., Gong, Y.: Few-shot class-incremental learning. In: Proceedings of the IEEE/CVF Conference on Computer Vision and Pattern Recognition, pp. 12183–12192 (2020)
4. Hu, J., Lu, J., Tan, Y.P.: Discriminative deep metric learning for face verification in the wild. In: Proceedings of the IEEE Conference on Computer Vision and Pattern Recognition, pp. 1875–1882 (2014)

5. Xing, E., Jordan, M., Russell, S.J., Ng, A.: Distance metric learning with application to clustering with side-information. Adv. Neural. Inf. Process. Syst. **15**, 521–528 (2002)

6. Yu, L., Yazici, V.O., Liu, X., Weijer, J.V.D., Cheng, Y., Ramisa, A.: Learning metrics from teachers: compact networks for image embedding. In: Proceedings of the IEEE/CVF Conference on Computer Vision and Pattern Recognition, pp. 2907–2916 (2019)

7. Wu, Y., et al.: Large scale incremental learning. In: Proceedings of the IEEE/CVF Conference on Computer Vision and Pattern Recognition, pp. 374–382 (2019)

8. Benjamin, A.S., Rolnick, D., Kording, K.: Measuring and regularizing networks in function space. arXiv preprint arXiv:1805.08289 (2018)

9. Chaudhry, A., Gordo, A., Dokania, P.K., Torr, P., Lopez-Paz, D.: Using hindsight to anchor past knowledge in continual learning. arXiv preprint arXiv:2002.08165, vol. 2, no. 7 (2020)

10. Hsu, Y.C., Liu, Y.C., Ramasamy, A., Kira, Z.: Re-evaluating continual learning scenarios: a categorization and case for strong baselines. arXiv preprint arXiv:1810.12488 (2018)

11. Pentina, A., Lampert, C.H.: Lifelong learning with non-IID tasks. Adv. Neural. Inf. Process. Syst. **28**, 1540–1548 (2015)

12. De Lange, M., et al.: Continual learning: a comparative study on how to defy forgetting in classification tasks. arXiv preprint arXiv:1909.08383, vol. 2, no. 6 (2019)

13. Isele, D., Cosgun, A.: Selective experience replay for lifelong learning. In: Proceedings of the AAAI Conference on Artificial Intelligence, vol. 32 (2018)

14. Rebuffi, S.A., Kolesnikov, A., Sperl, G., Lampert, C.H.: ICARL: incremental classifier and representation learning. In: Proceedings of the IEEE Conference on Computer Vision and Pattern Recognition, pp. 2001–2010 (2017)

15. Robins, A.: Catastrophic forgetting, rehearsal and pseudorehearsal. Connect. Sci. **7**(2), 123–146 (1995)

16. Bengio, Y., LeCun, Y. (eds.): 2nd International Conference on Learning Representations, ICLR 2014, Banff, AB, Canada, 14–16 April 2014, Conference Track Proceedings (2014). https://openreview.net/group?id=ICLR.cc/2014

17. Shin, H., Lee, J.K., Kim, J., Kim, J.: Continual learning with deep generative replay. arXiv preprint arXiv:1705.08690 (2017)

18. Silver, D.L., Mercer, R.E.: The task rehearsal method of life-long learning: overcoming impoverished data. In: Cohen, R., Spencer, B. (eds.) AI 2002. LNCS (LNAI), vol. 2338, pp. 90–101. Springer, Heidelberg (2002). https://doi.org/10.1007/3-540-47922-8_8

19. Li, Z., Hoiem, D.: Learning without forgetting. IEEE Trans. Pattern Anal. Mach. Intell. **40**(12), 2935–2947 (2017)

20. Rannen, A., Aljundi, R., Blaschko, M.B., Tuytelaars, T.: Encoder based lifelong learning. In: Proceedings of the IEEE International Conference on Computer Vision, pp. 1320–1328 (2017)

21. Kirkpatrick, J., et al.: Overcoming catastrophic forgetting in neural networks. Proc. Natl. Acad. Sci. **114**(13), 3521–3526 (2017)

22. Zenke, F., Poole, B., Ganguli, S.: Improved multitask learning through synaptic intelligence

23. Aljundi, R., Babiloni, F., Elhoseiny, M., Rohrbach, M., Tuytelaars, T.: Memory aware synapses: learning what (not) to forget. In: Proceedings of the European Conference on Computer Vision (ECCV), pp. 139–154 (2018)

24. Farquhar, S., Gal, Y.: Towards robust evaluations of continual learning. arXiv preprint arXiv:1805.09733 (2018)

25. Chopra, S., Hadsell, R., LeCun, Y.: Learning a similarity metric discriminatively, with application to face verification. In: 2005 IEEE Computer Society Conference on Computer Vision and Pattern Recognition (CVPR 2005), vol. 1, pp. 539–546. IEEE (2005)

26. Schroff, F., Kalenichenko, D., Philbin, J.: Facenet: a unified embedding for face recognition and clustering. In: Proceedings of the IEEE Conference on Computer Vision and Pattern Recognition, pp. 815–823 (2015)

27. DaWaK'10: Proceedings of the 12th International Conference on Data Warehousing and Knowledge Discovery. Springer, Heidelberg (2010)

28. Li, J., Zhao, R., Huang, J.T., Gong, Y.: Learning small-size DNN with output-distribution-based criteria. In: Fifteenth Annual Conference of the International Speech Communication Association (2014)

29. Hinton, G., Vinyals, O., Dean, J.: Distilling the knowledge in a neural network. arXiv preprint arXiv:1503.02531 (2015)

30. Mirzadeh, S.I., Farajtabar, M., Li, A., Levine, N., Matsukawa, A., Ghasemzadeh, H.: Improved knowledge distillation via teacher assistant. In: Proceedings of the AAAI Conference on Artificial Intelligence, vol. 34, pp. 5191–5198 (2020)

31. Cho, J.H., Hariharan, B.: On the efficacy of knowledge distillation. In: Proceedings of the IEEE/CVF International Conference on Computer Vision, pp. 4794–4802 (2019)

32. Krizhevsky, A., Hinton, G., et al.: Learning multiple layers of features from tiny images (2009)

33. Le, Y., Yang, X.: Tiny imagenet visual recognition challenge. CS 231N **7**(7), 3 (2015)

34. He, K., Zhang, X., Ren, S., Sun, J.: Deep residual learning for image recognition. In: Proceedings of the IEEE Conference on Computer Vision and Pattern Recognition, pp. 770–778 (2016)

35. Schwarz, J., et al.: Progress & compress: a scalable framework for continual learning. In: International Conference on Machine Learning, pp. 4528–4537. PMLR (2018)

36. Chaudhry, A., Dokania, P.K., Ajanthan, T., Torr, P.H.: Riemannian walk for incremental learning: understanding forgetting and intransigence. In: Proceedings of the Proceedings of the European Conference on Computer Vision (ECCV), pp. 532–547 (2018)

37. Masana, M., Ruiz, I., Serrat, J., van de Weijer, J., Lopez, A.M.: Metric Learning for Novelty and Anomaly Detection. arXiv preprint arXiv:1808.05492 (2018)

Feature Enhanced and Context Inference Network for Pancreas Segmentation

Zheng-hao Lou[1], Jian-cong Fan[1,3(✉)], Yan-de Ren[2], and Lei-yu Tang[1]

[1] College of Computer Science and Engineering, Shandong University of Science and Technology, Qingdao, China
fanjiancong@sdust.edu.cn
[2] The Affiliated Hospital of Qingdao University, Qingdao, China
[3] Provincial Key Lab for Information Technology of Wisdom Mining of Shandong Province, Shandong University of Science and Technology, Qingdao, China

Abstract. Segmenting pancreas from CT images is of great significance for clinical diagnosis and research. Traditional encoder-decoder networks, which are widely used in medical image segmentation, may fail to address low tissue contrast and large variability of pancreas shape and size due to underutilization of multi-level features and context information. To address these problems, this paper proposes a novel feature enhanced and context inference network (FECI-Net) for pancreas segmentation. Specifically, features are enhanced by imposing saliency region constraints to mine complementary regions and details between multi-level features; Gated Recurrent Unit convolution (ConvGRU) is introduced in the decoder to fully contact the context aimed to capture task-relevant fine features. By comparing experimental evaluations on the NIH-TCIA dataset, our method improves IOU and Dice by 5.5% and 4.1% respectively compared to the baseline, which outperforms current state-of-the-art medical image segmentation methods.

Keywords: Deep learning · Pancreas segmentation · Multi-level feature fusion · Context inference

1 Introduction

Medical image segmentation is a complex and critical step in medical image processing and analysis. It aims to segment the parts with certain special meanings of medical images and extract the relevant features [1] to assist doctors in making the more accurate diagnosis [2]. Automatic pancreas segmentation from CT images is deemed to be a challenging task. First, the boundary between pancreas and other neighboring tissues is usually blurred due to the gray-scale proximity [3] and partial volume effect [4], which makes the segmentation more difficult. Second, owing to individual difference, pancreas have different shapes, sizes, and locations, which also limit the accurate segmentation of targets.

With the rise of deep learning [5], Convolutional Neural Networks (CNNs) have shown a great potential in medical image segmentation in decade years. As many segmentation methods [6–8] have proved, different feature maps extract different information.

© Springer Nature Singapore Pte Ltd. 2022
L. Pan et al. (Eds.): BIC-TA 2021, CCIS 1566, pp. 244–257, 2022.
https://doi.org/10.1007/978-981-19-1253-5_18

Feature maps at low level have more spatial information to help refine the target edges; while feature maps at high level have richer semantic information to help locate where the targets are. Multi-level features fusion strategy have introduced in many deep learning methods. Fully convolutional neural networks (FCNs) have semantic segmentation capabilities at the pixel level, which gradually fuse multi-level features in element-wise addition manner during decoder phase. PSP-Net [7] fused multi-level features by applying pyramid pooling to aggregate context information from different regions. Feature Pyramid Network (FPN) [9] used top-down pathway and lateral connections to merge multi-level features to deal with multi-scale variations in object detection. U-Net [10] has achieved good segmentation performance by gradually fusing feature maps at different levels in a bottom-up manner, which has a profound impact on medical image segmentation. Inspired by this, U-Net++, U-Net3+ [11, 12] have been successively applied to medical image segmentation tasks by fusing multi-level features through different kinds of skip connections. But these methods directly fuse multi-level features without imposing any constraints, which may not be able to fuse features efficiently due to information redundancy and insufficient use of context information.

To solve the above problems, this paper proposes a novel end-to-end network, called Feature Enhanced and Contextual Inference Network (FECI-Net). During the encoding phase, we enhance the feature representation at each level by imposing saliency region constraints on the multi-level features to fully exploit and utilize the complementary regions and details. During the decoding phase, we introduce Gated Recurrent Convolution (ConvGRU) to control the information flow, which enhances the prediction of different layers by selective accumulation of information at the pixel level. In short, we have the following contributions:

1. For better feature extraction, a semantic supervision strategy is applied during the encoder to generate more discriminative feature representations.
2. To fully and efficiently utilize the feature representations at different levels, we propose a feature enhancement approach with spatial constraints. Features are enhanced by imposing saliency region constraints on features at different levels before fusion, which preserves the original feature representation through mining and utilizing complementary regions and details from other levels.
3. ConvGRU is introduced during the decoding phase to link contextual information, which uses different gating mechanisms to control the input and output information across layers. It implement a selective fusion of enhanced features from different layers and to continuously capture task-relevant fine structures to produce accurate segmentation results.

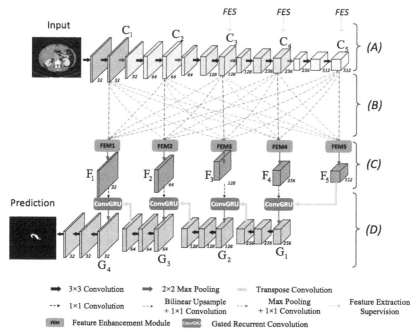

Fig. 1. Proposed feature enhanced and context inference network (FECI-Net) architecture for medical image segmentation.

2 Related Work

2.1 Deep Learning Methods

Long et al. [13] first proposed a fully convolutional neural network (FCN) for the semantic segmentation tasks. U-Net [11] was proposed by Ronneberger et al., which sequentially fuse multi-level features by stacking the convolution channel to generate more accurate segmentation results. Kaku et al. [14] proposed Dense-U-Net to segment brain tumors by introducing dense skip connections to make full use of multi-level feature maps. Zhou et al. [12] proposed U-Net++ with nested and dense skip connections to reduce the semantic gap between the encoder and decoder. Huang et al. [13] proposed U-Net3+, which captures fine-grained details from full levels through remodifying the inter-connection during the encoder connected to the decoder phase. While the intra-connection in the decoders are redesigned to obtain the coarse-grained semantic information. Crosslink-Net [15] proposed by Yu et al., which design a new network with double-branch encoder to get more detailed feature information. Gu et al. [16] proposed CE-Net, which design a new dense connections and residual pooling block with multi-kernel to extract context information.

2.2 Attention Mechanism

Attention mechanisms are widely used in natural image analysis, knowledge graphs, and natural language processing for image captioning [17], machine translation [18], and classification [19] tasks. Sanghyun et al. [20] proposed a generalized attention module that generates attention in the spatial and channel domains by compressing the space and channel generate attention in the channel and spatial domains, respectively. Oktay et al. [21] proposed Attention U-Net introduced attention during the decoder phase before skip connections to achieve selective fusion of features. Sinha et al. [22] integrated all level feature maps by different levels of feature maps by applying global spatial attention and channel attention to fuse multi-level prediction maps. Fan et al. [23] proposed Pra-Net to introduce reverse attention to capture fine details during the decoder process.

3   Methods

The proposed FECI-Net consists of four major parts: the feature encoder part, the full-level feature mapping part, the feature enhancement part, and the feature selection and decoder part, as shown in Fig. 1. The feature encoder part extracts feature maps at different levels through a backbone network and the feature extraction supervision strategy; the full-level feature mapping part consists of dense skip connections to map features at all levels to the uniform feature space; the feature enhancement part is to enhance features by mining complementary regions and details of features among different levels through the feature enhancement module; ConvGRU is introduced in the feature selection and decoder part, which capture the fine structure relevant to the segmentation task in a bottom-up manner from enhanced features.

3.1   Feature Encoder

Encoder. The backbone network for the feature encoder includes five steps, as shown in Fig. 1(A), each of which consists of two convolutional layers and a maximum pooling layer, where the convolutional layers are composed of 3×3 convolution, batch normalization, and ReLU function sequences. The stacking of the convolutional and max-pooling layers is used to generate feature maps at different levels. As shown in Fig. 1, features at five different levels $\{E_i | i = 1, 2, 3, 4, 5\}$ extracted by the backbone network are represented, corresponding to the feature space $\left\{ E_i \in R^{w/2^{i-1} \times h/2^{i-1} \times c/2^{1-i}} | i = 1, 2, 3, 4, 5 \right\}$, where w, h, and c represent the width, height, and the number of channels of the feature map.

Feature Extraction Supervision. To exact more discriminative features, we use a multi-level feature extraction supervision strategy, as shown in Fig. 1(A). Applying supervision to shallow layers may lead to information loss [24], so we generate the initial prediction maps with 2 dimensions by applying 1×1 convolution to the feature maps $\{E_i | i = 3, 4, 5\}$, and then up-sample all the generated prediction maps to the same scale as the input image through bilinear interpolation sampling. During the training process, more discriminative feature maps are generated by learning the differences from the true value. Formally we describe this process as follows.

$$cpm_i = \varphi(\theta_i, E_i)   i = 3, 4, 5 \tag{1}$$

$$Loss_f = Loss(cpm_i, label) \quad i = 3, 4, 5 \tag{2}$$

Where $\varphi(\cdot)$ denotes different 1*1 convolution operations, θ_i indicates the learning parameter of the convolution operation, cpm_i defines the prediction maps generated by features maps at different levels, $label$ is the true value, $Loss$ represents the Tversky loss, $Loss_f$ defines the feature extraction loss, and the implementation details and parameter settings will be expressed in detail in the Sect. 4.1.

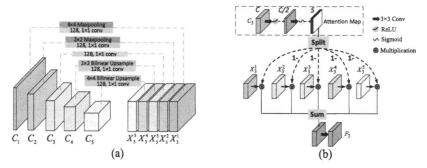

Fig. 2. (a). Illustration of how to get the mapped feature maps for FEM3 (b). Illustration of feature enhancement module (FEM)

3.2 Feature Space Mapping

Since the saliency regions of feature maps at different levels are varied, and the saliency regions at the same level are also distributed on different channels of the features, we map all the feature maps at all levels to the same feature space.

The feature space mapping process is shown in Fig. 1(B), where we first sample (including bilinear up-sampling operation, maximum pooling, and down-sampling operation) all the features to the same scale, and then perform channel mapping to unify the feature dimensions to obtain the feature maps at different levels. Formally, we formulate the feature space mapping as follows.

$$X_i^j = \begin{cases} \varphi(\theta_1; X_i) & i = j \\ \varphi(\theta_2; \mu(X_i)) & i > j \\ \varphi(\theta_3; \upsilon(X_i)) & i < j \end{cases} \tag{3}$$

Where $\varphi(\cdot)$ denotes 1×1 convolution, batch normalization, and ReLU activation operations, θ_* is the learnable parameters, $\mu(\cdot)$, $\upsilon(\cdot)$ indicate up- and down-sampling operation respectively, X_i represents feature maps of i-th layer extracted by the encoder, X_i^j represents feature map X_i mapped to j-th enhancement module.

Figure 2(a) illustrates how to get the mapped feature maps for the third feature enhancement module. The feature maps C_3 are directly received, while the low-level detailed information from the feature maps with the larger scale C_1, C_2 and the high-level semantic information from the feature maps with the smaller scale C_4, C_5 are delivered through a set of skip connections by applying max pooling and bilinear interpolation operation respectively. We further unify the number of channels of the five feature maps by the same filters of size 1×1 convolution, batch normalization, and ReLU function.

3.3 Feature Enhancement

The direct fusion of multi-level feature maps may lead to suboptimal results due to information redundancy and saliency differences. The proposed feature enhancement modules apply different spatial constraints to feature maps at different levels, which retains the original feature representation and taps the complementary regions and details of feature maps at other levels. The constrained feature maps are fused aiming to enhance the non-significant regions. The feature enhancement process is simply shown in Fig. 1(C). As an example, the workflow of the third feature enhancement module is shown in Fig. 2(b). A 5-dimensional saliency region map is generated from the feature maps C_3 through the attention head, which represents the saliency score of the features at each spatial location. One of them is used to retain the saliency regions of the feature maps X_3^3, and the other is used to extract the complementary regions and details of other feature maps after the inverse operation, and finally fuse and recode all the constrained feature maps to prevent feature degradation.

The red dashed box shows the process of generating the saliency region map, where we first compress the dimension of the feature maps to half by 3×3 convolution, and then go through the ReLU function, and finally generate the saliency region maps by 3×3 convolution and Sigmoid function. Formally we describe it as:

$$\alpha = \delta_2(q_{att}(\delta_1(f(E; \theta_1)); \theta_{att})) \tag{4}$$

Where α defines the generated saliency maps, E is the input feature maps, $f(\cdot)$ represents the 3×3 convolution operation, $q_{att}(\cdot)$ represents the convolution operation for generating saliency maps, θ_* is the learnable parameter of the convolution operation, δ_1, δ_2 indicate ReLU function and Sigmoid function respectively.

To get the enhanced feature maps F_3, the 5-dimensional saliency region map is been splitting, one of which is multiplied with the feature maps X_3^3, while other saliency region maps are subtracted by 1 to erase the existing saliency regions, and then multiplied with other mapped feature maps, and finally the five parts after multiplication operation are added together and then recoded to generate the enhanced feature maps. The five different colored blocks in the middle part represent the different feature maps mapped to the same feature space, and the block in the lower right corner represents the enhanced feature maps after feature re-encoding. We describe this process as follows.

$$\alpha_1, \alpha_2, \alpha_3, \alpha_4, \alpha_5 = \phi(\alpha) \tag{5}$$

$$F_{out} = \eta \left(\alpha_3 X_3^3 + \sum_{i=1,2,4,5} (1 - \alpha_i X_3^i; \theta) \right) \tag{6}$$

Where F_{out} defines the output feature maps after the enhancement module, $\phi(\cdot)$ represents the spilt operation, $\{\alpha_i | i = 1, 2, 3, 4, 5\}$ indicates saliency region maps, $\eta(\cdot)$ represents the 3×3 convolution, batch normalization, and ReLU function.

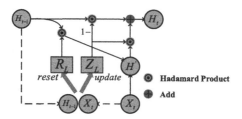

Fig. 3. Illustration of gated recurrent convolution (ConvGRU).

3.4 Decoder

Gated Recurrent Convolution (ConvGRU). We first review gated recurrent convolution [25], which controls the flow of information in the sequence through the gate mechanism as shown in Fig. 3. The reset gate determines how to combine the input information memorized in the previous step, and the update gate determines the amount of information saved from the previous state to the current state. The reset gate and the update gate are generated by combining the feature maps after decoding in the previous step with the input feature maps at current state. The reset feature maps are obtained by multiplying the reset gate with the input feature maps. Combining the reset features with the current input, we generate a feature representation of the current state, and then selectively fuse the feature maps of the previous state after the reset with the features of the current state through the update gating. We describe this process as follows:

$$G_r = \sigma\left(g\left(\left[X_t, H_{t-1}\right]; \theta_r\right)\right) \tag{7}$$

$$G_z = \sigma\left(g\left(\left[X_t, H_{t-1}\right]; \theta_z\right)\right) \tag{8}$$

$$H' = \mu\left(h\left(\left[G_r H_{t-1}, X_t\right]; \theta_h\right)\right) \tag{9}$$

$$H_t = (1 - G_z)H_{t-1} + G_z H' \tag{10}$$

Where H_{t-1} represents the feature maps after decoding at the previous step, and X_t represents the input feature maps at the current step, G_r, G_z indicate the reset gate and the update gate respectively, H' defines the feature representation of the current state.

Decoding Process. Figure 1(D) shows the process of the decoder. After feature enhancement, we obtain the features $\{F_i | i = 1, 2, 3, 4, 5\}$, ConvGRU accepts the feature map in the previous step after convolutional layers and transposition convolution and the new input features by the skip connection, resets the features passed in the previous step through the reset gate, preserving the feature representation needed for the task, and then convolves the reset features with the new input features superimposed to generate the features for the current step, and finally by updating them from the previous reset features and the current features The fine structure relevant to the task is selected and passed through two convolutional layers, which we describe as:

$$G_i = g\left(\zeta(F_i, up(G_{i+1})); \theta_i^1, \theta_i^2\right) \quad i = 1, 2, 3, 4 \tag{11}$$

$$Prediction = p(G_4; \theta_p) \tag{12}$$

Where $G_5 = F_5$, $up(\cdot)$ represents the deconvolution operation, $\zeta(\cdot)$ represents ConvGRU, $g(\cdot)$ represents two convolution layers, where each convolution layer is composed of 3×3 convolution, batch normalization and ReLU activation operations, $p(\cdot)$ represents the 1×1 convolution operation, θ_* is the learnable parameter of the operation corresponding to the convolution.

4 Experiment

4.1 Experiment Setup

Data Pre-processing and Partitioning. The dataset NIH-TCIA [26] contains 82 3D CT images. The data preprocessing consists of window adjustment and data slicing. Window adjustment is performed to increase the grayscale difference between tissues. Pancreatic region is identified by the labeled region where is 1, then we determine the window width and window center based on maximum and minimum Hu values of the pancreatic region. Window width is equal to the maximum Hu value minus the minimum value, window center is half of the maximum and minimum Hu values. Finally we adjust and normalize the Hu values of the entire image to between 0 and 1. We describe it as follows:

$$wt = (Hu_{max} + Hu_{min})/2 - \mu * (Hu_{max} - Hu_{min}) \tag{13}$$

$$Hu_{new} = (Hu - wt)/(Hu_{max} - Hu_{min}) \tag{14}$$

$$Hu_{new} = \begin{cases} 0 \ Hu_{new} \leq 0 \\ 1 \ Hu_{new} > 1 \end{cases} \tag{15}$$

Where Hu_{max}, Hu_{min} is the maximum and minimum Hu values of the pancreatic region, wt indicates the window value needed to be adjusted, μ is the adjustment parameter and it is set to 0.5 in this paper, Hu_{new} defines the adjusted Hu values.

After the window adjustment, we randomly divide all 3D CT images into training set, validation set, and testing set in the ratio of 7:1:2. All 3D CT images are $512 \times 512 \times N$ (N is the number of the slices in transverse-section plane). We then slice them in the transverse-section plane into N 2D images and discard slices without pancreas region according to the segmentation label, and finally 4743 2D images in the training set, 610 in the validation set and 1446 in the testing set are obtained.

Environment Settings. To verify the performance of our proposed method, the parameters of the experiments are as follows: the initial learning rate is 3e-4, the learning rate adjustment strategy is to adjust StepLR at equal intervals, the learning rate decays by a factor of 0.5 every 32 rounds, the optimizer is Adam, and the batch size is 4. We trained 100 rounds on an NVIDIA Tesla v100.

Loss Function. Our loss function consists of two components, the feature extraction loss and the final prediction loss. As the number of training rounds increases, we let the feature extraction loss gradually converge to 0, making the overall loss gradually converge to the final prediction loss. The details are described as follows:

$$Loss_{tversky} = \frac{|A \cap B|}{|A \cap B| + \alpha|A - B| + \beta|B - A|} \tag{16}$$

$$Loss_f = \sum_{i=3}^{5} \varepsilon_i Loss_{tversky}(cpm_i, labels) \tag{17}$$

$$Loss_p = Loss_{tversky}(prediction, labels) \tag{18}$$

$$Loss = Loss_p + Loss_f * \left(1 - \frac{ep}{eps}\right) \tag{19}$$

Where A, B indicate the set of points contained in the foreground region of the prediction and true value respectively, $\alpha = 0.7$ and $\beta = 0.3$ are set to balance the dataset, $Loss_f$ represents the feature extraction loss, $\varepsilon = 0.5$ is set uniformly, $Loss_p$ represents the final prediction loss, and ep, eps defines the number of training rounds and the total number of rounds, respectively.

Evaluation Metrics. We evaluate model performance in terms of four metrics: Precision (P), Sensitivity (S), Intersection over Union (IOU) and Dice Similarity Coefficient (DSC).

$$P = TP/TP + FP \tag{20}$$

$$S = TP/TP + FN \tag{21}$$

$$IOU = TP/FP + TP + FN \tag{22}$$

$$DSC = 2TP/2TP + FP + FN \tag{23}$$

Where TP, FP, FN is true positive, false positive, and false negative respectively.

4.2 Comparative Experiments

We compared several popular medical image segmentation algorithms, FCN-8s [13],
We compare PSP-Net [7], Attention U-Net [21], Dense-U-Net [14], U-Net++ [11], and U-Net3+ [12] with our method. Among them, we halve the initial channels of U-Net and add BN layers after each convolutional layer to improve the network performance and accelerate the convergence, and the adjusted U-Net is used as the baseline for the comparison in this paper.

Table 1. Comparison of proposed method with several popular segmentation frameworks

Method	P	S	IOU	DSC
FCN (pretrained vgg16)	0.733	0.750	0.589	0.742
PSP-Net (pretrained resnet50)	0.748	0.741	0.593	0.744
Attention U-Net	0.790	0.766	0.636	0.777
Dense-U-Net	0.785	0.791	0.651	0.788
U-Net++	0.797	0.762	0.645	0.784
U-Net3+	0.797	0.773	0.646	0.785
Baseline(U-Net)	0.787	0.756	0.628	0.771
Ours	**0.803**	**0.820**	**0.683**	**0.812**

4.3 Comparative Experiments

We compared several popular medical image segmentation algorithms, FCN-8s [13], PSP-Net [7], Attention U-Net [21], Dense-U-Net [14], U-Net++ [11], and U-Net3+ [12]. Among them, we halve the initial channels of U-Net and add BN layers after each convolutional layer to improve the network performance and accelerate the convergence, and the adjusted U-Net is used as the baseline for the comparison in this paper.

Quantitative Results. Table 1 shows the quantitative comparison results of our method with other advanced segmentation methods, and we can see that our method is better than the others in all metrics. The precision of our method is improved by 1.6% compared to the baseline, and there is also a improvement of 0.6%–7% compared to other methods, indicating that our method can better distinguish the target from other tissues; in terms of sensitivity, our method has a more obvious advantage, improving by 4.7% compared to the second highest Unet3+, indicating that our method can more effectively identify the pixel points in the target region and reduces the risk of missed detection; in the IOU metric, our method are 5.5% higher than the baseline, with a 3%–9% improvement compared to other advanced methods, which indicates that our method predicts regions with higher regional agreement with the real target regions; Dice score of our method is 4.1% higher compared to the baseline, while compared to the higher scoring U-Net++, U-Net3+ are also higher by 2.6% and 2.7%, respectively, indicating that our predicted results have higher similarity to the real ones, demonstrating the stronger segmentation ability of our method.

Qualitative Results. Some challenging cases are selected to validate the performance of our proposed method. The segmentation results are shown in Fig. 4, where the different colors represent TP (orange), FN (red), and FP (blue), respectively. Criteria for evaluating the performance of segmentation algorithms is more orange region consistent with the labeled region and less blue and red region.

We can see in Fig. 4, the orange region of our method are much closer to the true value than other advanced methods. In (a) we can observe that the predicted result of

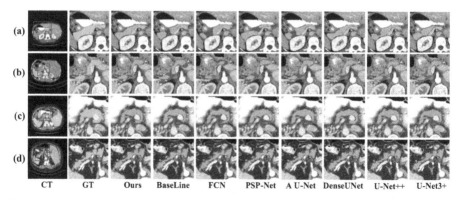

Fig. 4. Comparisons of our methods, Baseline(U-Net), FCN-8s, PSP-Net, Attention-U-Net, Dense-U-Net, U-Net++, U-Net3+ on four different slices. Region in ▪show labeled pancreas region, grayscale region is background. Segments in ▪show false positive, segments in ▪show false negative and segments in ▪show true positive.

our method has less red region, which demonstrates other methods miss a large number of pixels that should belong to the target region while our method misses very few. The results in (b) show that the segments of other methods have more blue region, which indicates they incorrectly identify other tissue regions as the target region, while our method more accurately distinguishes the target from other tissue regions and alleviates the misdetection problem. Furthermore, the segmentation results for targets with more complex edges are shown in (c,d), where our method can identify finer boundary information, which is attributed to the ability of ConvGRU to continuously capture the fine structure and continuously enhance local predictions. All the above segmentation results demonstrate the effectiveness of our method in improving segmentation accuracy.

Table 2. Verify the effects of each component on the baseline. Among them, FES: Feature Extraction Supervision. FEM: Feature Enhancement Module. ConvGRU: Gated recurrent convolution used in decoder.

FES	FEM	ConvGRU	P	S	IOU	DSC
			0.787	0.756	0.628	0.771
✓			0.761	0.791	0.634	0.776
	✓		**0.791**	0.786	0.650	0.788
		✓	0.790	**0.796**	0.657	0.793
✓	✓		**0.818**	0.782	**0.667**	**0.800**
✓	✓	✓	0.803	**0.820**	**0.683**	**0.812**

Ablation Experiments. To examine the contribution of each module to the overall approach, we present the scores of each component on each indicator, as shown in Table

2. We can see that the feature extraction supervision improves DSC by around 0.5%, indicating that improving feature quality by supervision alone does not achieve good performance, possibly due to limited information utilization as a result of not utilizing all the hierarchical features.

The addition of the feature enhancement module improves both accuracy and sensitivity, indicating that the use of complementary regions and details of multilevel features helps to locate organ locations and boundaries, which can alleviate the problems of missed and wrong detections, and its improvement in IOU and Dice scores is more obvious, reaching 2.2% and 1.7%, respectively, while the addition of these two components results in precision, IOU, and DSC. The improvement is even more pronounced at 3.1%, 3.9%, and 2.9%, respectively.

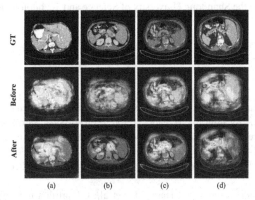

Fig. 5. Activation region of the feature maps before and after the FEM5 on four different slices.

To see the effect of the feature enhancement module more visually, we compared the activation region of the feature maps before and after enhancement. Since the semantics of the deeper layers of the network are obvious, we visualized the saliency map of the features before and after the fifth feature enhancement module, as shown in Fig. 5, where the pink color represents the true value. We can see that in the enhanced features, there are fewer activated background regions and more activated target regions activated, indicating that the feature enhancement module not only suppresses the activation of irrelevant regions and focuses more on target regions, but also enhances the feature representation using regions and details that are complementary to other levels of features.

The addition of ConvGRU improves the sensitivity by 4%, indicating that it can effectively capture fine structure during decoding, accurately detect pixels in the target region, reduce the risk of missing detection, enhance the model's ability to obtain information through context, and improve the accuracy of segmentation.

5   Discussion and Conclusion

In this paper, we propose a feature enhancement module to enhance feature representation by fully exploiting the complementary regions and details between feature maps at different levels, and to improve the performance of medical image segmentation by introducing ConvGRU in the decoder to better link contextual information, capture more task-relevant fine structures, and gradually refine the segmentation results. Full experiments are conducted on the NIH-TCIA dataset, and by evaluating the comparison with several advanced medical image segmentation algorithms, the experimental results show that our method has improved for target localization and edge detection, and in the future, we will try to improve the quality of extracted features by using feature reuse on the encoder to achieve better performance.

Acknowledgments. We would like to thank the anonymous reviewers for their valuable comments and suggestions. This work is supported by Shandong Provincial Natural Science Foundation of China under Grant ZR2018MF009, the State Key Research Development Program of China under Grant 2017YFC0804406, the Taishan Scholars Program of Shandong Province under Grant ts20190936, and the Shandong University of Science and Technology Research Fund under Grant 2015TDJH102.

References

1. Li, Z., Fan, J., Ren, Y., Tang, L.: A novel feature extraction approach based on neighborhood rough set and PCA for migraine rs-fMRI. J. Intell. Fuzzy Syst. **38**(6), 1–11 (2020)
2. Patil, D.D., Deore, S.G.: Medical image segmentation: a review. Int. J. Comput. Sci. Mob. Comput. **2**(1), 22–27 (2013)
3. Liu, Y., Chen, S.: Review of medical image segmentation method. Electr. Sci. Technol. **30**(8), 169–172 (2017)
4. Popilock, R., Sandrasagaren, K., Harris, L., et al.: CT artifact recognition for the nuclear technologist. J. Nucl. Med. Technol. **36**(2), 79–81 (2008)
5. Cui, Z., Xue, F., Cai, X., Cao, Y., Wang, G., Chen, J.: Detection of malicious code variants based on deep learning. IEEE Trans. Industr. Inf. **14**(7), 3187–3196 (2018)
6. Chen, L.-C., Zhu, Y., Papandreou, G., Schroff, F., Adam, H.: Encoder-decoder with atrous separable convolution for semantic image segmentation. In: Ferrari, V., Hebert, M., Sminchisescu, C., Weiss, Y. (eds.) Computer Vision – ECCV 2018: 15th European Conference, Munich, Germany, September 8–14, 2018, Proceedings, Part VII, pp. 833–851. Springer International Publishing, Cham (2018). https://doi.org/10.1007/978-3-030-01234-2_49
7. Zhao, H.S., Shi, J.P., Qi, X.J., Wang, X.G., Jia, J.Y.: Pyramid scene parsing network. In: 2017 IEEE Conference on Computer Vision and Pattern Recognition, pp. 6230–6239. Honolulu, HI, USA (2017)
8. Kumar, N., Hoffmann, N., Oelschlägel, M., Koch, E., Kirsch, M., Gumhold, S.: Structural similarity based anatomical and functional brain imaging fusion. In: Zhu, D., et al. (eds.) MBIA/MFCA -2019. LNCS, vol. 11846, pp. 121–129. Springer, Cham (2019). https://doi.org/10.1007/978-3-030-33226-6_14
9. Vo, X.-T., Tran, T.-D., Nguyen, D.-L., Jo, K.-H.: Stair-step feature pyramid networks for object detection. In: Jeong, H., Sumi, K. (eds.) IW-FCV 2021. CCIS, vol. 1405, pp. 168–175. Springer, Cham (2021). https://doi.org/10.1007/978-3-030-81638-4_13
10. Ronneberger, O., Fischer, P., Brox, T.: U-Net: convolutional networks for biomedical image segmentation. In: Navab, N., Hornegger, J., Wells, W.M., Frangi, A.F. (eds.) MICCAI 2015. LNCS, vol. 9351, pp. 234–241. Springer, Cham (2015). https://doi.org/10.1007/978-3-319-24574-4_28

11. Zhou, Z., Rahman Siddiquee, M.M., Tajbakhsh, N., Liang, J.: UNet++: a nested u-net architecture for medical image segmentation. In: Stoyanov, D., et al. (eds.) DLMIA/ML-CDS -2018. LNCS, vol. 11045, pp. 3–11. Springer, Cham (2018). https://doi.org/10.1007/978-3-030-00889-5_1

12. Huang, H., et al.: UNet 3+: a full-scale connected UNet for medical image segmentation. In: ICASSP 2020 - 2020 IEEE International Conference on Acoustics, Speech and Signal Processing (ICASSP), pp. 1055–1059. Barcelona, Spain (2020)

13. Shelhamer, E., Long, J., Darrell, T.: Fully convolutional networks for semantic segmentation. IEEE Trans. Pattern Anal. Mach. Intell. **39**(4), 640–651 (2017)

14. Kaku, A., Hegde, C.V., Huang, J., et al.: DARTS: DenseUnet-based automatic rapid tool for brain segmentation. arXiv preprint arXiv:1911.05567 (2019)

15. Yu, Q., et al.: Crosslink-Net: double-branch encoder segmentation network via fusing vertical and horizontal convolutions. arXiv preprint arXiv:2107.11517 (2021)

16. Gu, Z., et al.: CE-Net: context encoder network for 2D medical image segmentation. IEEE Trans. Med. Imaging **38**(10), 2281–2292 (2019)

17. Anderson, P., et al.: Bottom-Up and top-down attention for image captioning and visual question answering. In: 2018 IEEE/CVF Conference on Computer Vision and Pattern Recognition, pp. 6077–6086. Salt Lake City, UT, USA (2018)

18. Bahdanau, D., et al.: Neural machine translation by jointly learning to align and translate. CoRR abs/1409.0473 (2015)

19. Liang, L., Cao, J., Li, X., You, J.: Improvement of residual attention network for image classification. In: Cui, Z., Pan, J., Zhang, S., Xiao, L., Yang, J. (eds.) IScIDE 2019. LNCS, vol. 11935, pp. 529–539. Springer, Cham (2019). https://doi.org/10.1007/978-3-030-36189-1_44

20. Woo, S., Park, J., Lee, J.-Y., Kweon, I.S.: CBAM: convolutional block attention module. In: Ferrari, V., Hebert, M., Sminchisescu, C., Weiss, Y. (eds.) ECCV 2018. LNCS, vol. 11211, pp. 3–19. Springer, Cham (2018). https://doi.org/10.1007/978-3-030-01234-2_1

21. Oktay, O., Schlemper, J., Folgoc, L., et al.: Attention U-Net: learning where to look for the pancreas. arXiv preprint arXiv:1804.03999 (2018)

22. Sinha, A., Dolz, J.: Multi-scale self-guided attention for medical image segmentation. IEEE J. Biomed. Health Inform. **25**(1), 121–130 (2021)

23. Fan, D.-P., et al.: PraNet: parallel reverse attention network for polyp segmentation. In: Martel, A.L., et al. (eds.) MICCAI 2020. LNCS, vol. 12266, pp. 263–273. Springer, Cham (2020). https://doi.org/10.1007/978-3-030-59725-2_26

24. Wang, Y., Ni, Z., Song, S., et al.: Revisiting locally supervised learning: an alternative to end-to-end training. In: International Conference on Learning Representations (2021)

25. Ballas, Nicolas, et al.: Delving deeper into convolutional networks for learning video representations. arXiv preprint arXiv:1511.06432 (2015)

26. Roth, H., Farag, A., Turkbey, E.B., Lu, L., Liu, R.M.: Data from pancreas-CT. Cancer Imag. Arch. (2016). https://doi.org/10.7937/K9/TCIA.2016.tNB1kqBU

Object Relations Focused Siamese Network for Remote Sensing Image Change Detection

Jie-pei Wang[1], Lei-yu Tang[2], Jian-cong Fan[1,3(✉)], and Guo-qiang Liu[1]

[1] College of Computer Science and Engineering, Shandong University of Science and Technology, Qingdao, China
fanjiancong@sdust.edu.cn
[2] College of Mathematics and System Science, Shandong University of Science and Technology, Qingdao, China
[3] Provincial Key Lab for Information Technology of Wisdom Mining of Shandong Province, Shandong University of Science and Technology, Qingdao, China

Abstract. In recent years, deep learning methods, especially convolutional neural networks (CNNs), have shown powerful discriminative ability in the field of remote sensing change detection. However, the multi-temporal remote sensing images often have a long time interval, which leads to the geographical objects with the same semantic may have different spectral representations in different spatial and temporal locations, thus affecting the performance of network detection. Exploring the latent connections between different objects helps promote the discrimination of feature maps, so as to suppress the generation of pseudo changes because the geographical objects are not isolated. In this paper, we propose a novel change detection network focused on the object relations (ORFNet), which can capture relevant context by exploring the relations between objects in dual spatio-temporal scenes, so as to enhance the discrimination of original image features. Experiments on CDD data sets show that our method only increases 0.4M parameters compared with the baseline, and improves F1 by 3.6%.

Keywords: Deep learning · Convolutional neural networks · Object relations · Feature enhancement

1 Introduction

Change detection is a branch of remote sensing image processing that aims to mark the pixels of change between remote sensing images of the same region acquired at different times, and it plays an important role in the fields of environmental monitoring, urban change analysis, agricultural surveys, and disaster monitoring [1, 2]. However, variations in factors such as seasons, weather, and lighting, differences in imaging conditions between images [3], and heterogeneity within geographic objects result in objects with the same semantic concept in remote sensing images that may have different spectral representations at different spatial-temporal spaces. Change detection, as a challenging task, requires features with sufficient discriminative power to overcome the interference caused by these pseudo-variations.

© Springer Nature Singapore Pte Ltd. 2022
L. Pan et al. (Eds.): BIC-TA 2021, CCIS 1566, pp. 258–270, 2022.
https://doi.org/10.1007/978-981-19-1253-5_19

Many recent methods improve the discriminative power of the feature by designing multilevel feature fusion structures [4], combining GAN-based optimization [5], and increasing the reception field of the model for better context modeling [6].

Since geographic objects do not exist in isolation, there are often some inter-relationships between different geographic objects. For example, vehicles often travel on roads or in parking lots, so detecting the roads or parking lots can helps us segment the cars. In addition, there may also be some connections between geographic objects in different spatial-temporal spaces, for example, in the process of urban expansion, previously vacant land either does not undergo semantic changes or is more likely to be replaced by buildings. Thus, extracting these feature inter-relations in the same and different spatio-temporal helps us to reduce the search scope of changing pixel types.

Previous methods for acquiring bi-temporal image context usually have large limitations. Change detection networks based on FCN [7], UNet [8] architectures enlarger receptive fields by stacking convolution kernels. Although the use of atrous convolution [9] can establish dependencies between remote pixels faster, some studies [10] have shown that the actual receptive field of such networks is usually much smaller than the theoretical receptive field, making it difficult to establish inter-connections between remote geographic objects or even objects across space and time. Non-local self-attention methods have shown outstanding performance by establishing dense relations between pixels, but their computational efficiency is relatively low. In addition, some new studies [11] show that the reason for the excellent performance achieved by Transformer does not depend entirely on its attention mechanism and that even using a simple fully connected structure still achieves performance close to that of state-of-the-art methods.

FarSeg [12] focuses on the problem of large intra-class variation in remote sensing image segmentation and introduces an additional branch to encode contextual information on top of the FPN architecture to enhance the foreground feature representation by establishing connections between foreground and scene. Inspired by FarSeg, we design a lightweight geographic objects relations module to model the connections between all blocks in dual spatial-temporal space, and then use the feature representation containing global contextual information to enhance the discrimination of the original image features.

2   Related Work

Traditional change detection methods focus mainly on the extraction of spectral values, shape and texture information between images, while ignoring modeling contextual information, and thus the accuracy is often low. [13] used a fuzzy hidden Markov chain algorithm to avoid spurious changes and missed detections caused by threshold segmentation. [14] used a super-position-constrained Boltzmann machine to analyze the differential images between the multi-phase SAR image. In addition, some machine learning methods such as artificial neural networks [15], clustering algorithms [16–18] and SVM [19] are able to handle larger datasets and avoid the dimensional explosion problem well.

With the development of deep learning, deep feature-based methods have achieved great success in the field of change detection. FC-Siam-conc [20] and FC_Siam_diff [20] are two siamese architectures of change detection networks that can receive bi-temporal images and predict the changed region, enabling end-to-end training. IFN [21], SNUNet [22], and FDCNN [23] further develop the siamese architecture and improve the network performance by extracting the difference features more adequately. However these methods using pure convolutions cannot explore and utilize long-range concepts in space-time. The use of atrous convolution [9, 24, 25] enables the establishment of connections between more remote pixels, thus expanding the theoretical field of perception and acquiring richer contextual information. All of the above methods expand the receptive field mainly by stacking convolution kernels and down-sampling consecutively, but some studies [11] show that the actual receptive field of such networks is usually much smaller than the theoretical field.

Some attention-based methods assign larger weights to important channels through pooling and non-linear operations but ignore the inter-relationships between pixels. Self-attention mechanisms [26–28] enlarger receptive fields by establishing dense relationships among all pixels, but lower computational efficiency and high memory overhead limit the application of this technique.

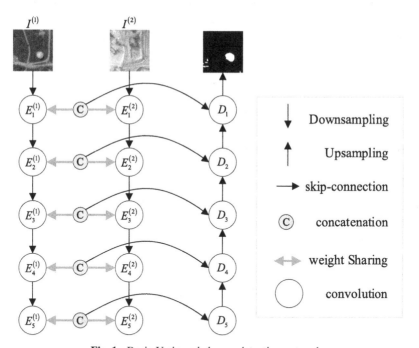

Fig. 1. Basic U-shaped change detection network.

3 Methods

In this paper, we generate a relation map that contains the relevant context by establishing potential connections between all geographic objects in dual spatial-temporal space, and then use the relationship map to enhance the features of the original image.

3.1 Basic Network Architecture

The goal of our network is to receive the bi-temporal images and predict the corresponding changed regions. We combine the siamese architecture with UNet, where the encoder is used to extract more representative features of the original bi-temporal images, while the decoder combines these features to further obtain changed information. As shown in Fig. 1, the UNet single-branch encoder is expanded into a dual-flow structure with shared weights to receive the bi-temporal images simultaneously, while the decoder receives both the feature maps from the encoder after concatenate and the disparity feature maps from the upper level of the decoder.

Specifically, the encoder consists of a total of 5 stages, with the first stage containing two 3×3 convolutions and each subsequent stage consisting of a down-sampling operation and two 3×3 convolutions. The bi-temporal image generates five feature maps at different scales in each of these five stages, and these extracted feature maps are concatenated together and fed to the decoder to extract the disparity information. Denote $\left\{ E_i^{(N)} | i = 1, 2, 3, 4, 5; N = 1, 2 \right\}$ as the set of feature maps of the bi-temporal image extracted by the encoder, i is the layer index, and N denotes the corresponding two flow branches of the encoder, then $E_i^{(N)}$ can be represented as

$$E_i^{(N)} = \begin{cases} C(I^{(N)}), & i = 1 \\ C\left(D\left(E_{i-1}^{(N)}\right)\right), & i = 2, 3, 4, 5 \end{cases} \tag{1}$$

Here, $I^{(N)}$ denotes the original bi-temporal image, $C(\cdot)$ denotes two 3×3 convolution operations (each followed by a batch normalization layer and a ReLU activation function), and $D(\cdot)$ denotes a down-sampling operation (max-pooling), after which doubles the number of channels of the feature map.

To obtain the discrepancy information, we concatenate the feature maps with the same scale in the dual-flow structure. Let E_i denote the feature map after concatenate, then it can be expressed as

$$E_i = \left[E_i^{(1)}, E_i^{(2)} \right] \tag{2}$$

Here, $E_i^{(1)}$ and $E_i^{(2)}$ denote the extracted feature maps of the same scale of the bi-temporal image, respectively, and $[\cdot]$ denote the concatenating operation.

As can be seen from Fig. 1, each layer of the decoder consists of two 3×3 convolutions (each followed by a batch normalization layer and a ReLU activation function) to fit the disparity information of the bi-temporal image and up-sample the feature map by bilinear interpolation to recover the resolution of the semantic feature map. $\{D_i | i = 1, 2, 3, 4, 5\}$ denotes the set of feature maps generated by each layer of the decoder, i is the layer index, then D_i can be expressed as

$$D_i = \begin{cases} C(E_5), & i = 5 \\ C\left([E_i, U(D_{i+1})]\right), & i = 1, 2, 3, 4 \end{cases} \tag{3}$$

Here, E_i denotes the feature map after concatenating generated by encoder, $U(\cdot)$ denotes the up-sampling operation (bilinear interpolation), $[\cdot]$ denotes the concatenation of the feature map, and $C(\cdot)$ denotes the two 3×3 convolution operations (each layer followed by a batch normalization layer and a ReLU activation function).

We recover the deepest decoder feature map D_1 by a plain 1×1 convolution into 2 dimensions (changed or unchanged) for the final change detection task.

3.2 Geo-Objects Relations Module

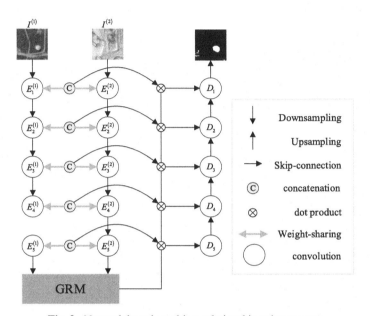

Fig. 2. Network based on object relationship enhancement.

The performance of the change detection task, a challenging task, is extremely dependent on the discrimination of the extracted features. Since our network uses a general encoder-decoder structure, this suffers from two drawbacks: first, the network can only slowly increase the receptive field by stacking convolutional kernels, making it difficult to directly capture the inter-connections between different features in dual spatial-temporal space; second, there is a large semantic gap between the original image features extracted by the encoder and the difference features generated by the decoder. These two shortcomings lead to the change detection network having a low discriminative power for these pseudo-variations when the background is complex or when there are obvious seasonal and lighting differences between the bi-temporal images.

As shown in Fig. 2, we propose the Geo-objects relations module (GRM) to explicitly establish the inter-relationships between all blocks in dual spatial-temporal space to obtain global contextual information, and then use the relation map containing the context to enhance the features of the original image, which not only enhances the semantics of the original features but also obtains the global receptive field.

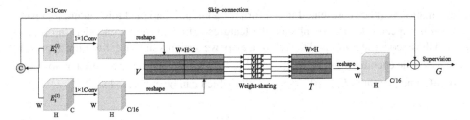

Fig. 3. Geo-objects relations module

Figure 3 illustrates how the Geo-objects relations are constructed. The purpose of our relation module is to receive the deepest feature maps of the dual-flow encoder, and establish valid links between all blocks in the dual spatial-temporal space, and then generate a relation map that contains contextual information.

Here, $E_5^{(1)}, E_5^{(2)} \in R^{C \times H \times W}$, we first reduce the number of channels of both to C/16 by 1×1 convolution to ensure that the model is light-weighting. Each dimension of $E_5^{(1)}$ and $E_5^{(2)}$ is then spread linearly and the two linear vectors are stitched together, and the stitched tensor $V \in R^{C/16 \times (H \times W \times 2)}$. Each dimension of V is passed through a multilayer perceptron (MLP) to capture the Geo-objects relations and to further reduce the computational effort, the multilayer perceptron used by different channels will share weights. It can be seen that using two layers of fully connected for each dimension of the stitched vector, each element of the resulting tensor is inter-connected with all pixels of $E_5^{(1)}, E_5^{(2)}$.

The transformation of the dimensional space is achieved through the multilayer perceptron: $V \in R^{C/16 \times (H \times W \times 2)} \rightarrow T \in R^{C/16 \times (H \times W)}$, as shown in Eq. 4. We revert to the dimensions of the original feature map, $R^{C/16 \times (H \times W)}$, for each dimension of T, which achieves a mapping of all pixels in the bi-temporal image to all pixels in the relational map.

$$T = g_{\theta_1}\left(\delta\left(f_{\theta_2}(V)\right)\right) \tag{4}$$

f and g represent two full connection functions of MLP respectively, θ_1 and θ_2 denotes the learnable parameters of f and g, respectively. δ denotes the ReLU function.

Although the two layers fully connected captures the inter-relationships between all blocks, this also leads to the destruction of the spatial information, so we introduce skip connection with element-by-element summation of the relational map, thus aiding the relational map to recover its spatial resolution.

To establish valid relationships in the relational map, we enhance valid connections in the GRM and suppress invalid connections by deep supervision. It is evident that the feature representation generated by the relation map establishes all valid relations between the bi-temporal images and generates the relevant context.

3.3 Feature Enhancement

The relation map generated by ground-truth supervision contains valid relations between dual spatial-temporal space features that capture the relevant context, and this contextual information will be represented in the form of a feature map, and this feature representation is expected to use to enhance the features extracted by the encoder. In order to align the encoder features and the relation map, we design a simple calibration approach. First, for the encoder input $E_i \in R^{(C \times 2^{i-1}) \times H \times W}$, we use learnable parameters to map it to difference features $E'_i \in R^{(C \times 2^{i-1}) \times H \times W}$, which can be expressed as.

$$E'_i = \psi_{\theta_i}(E_i) \tag{5}$$

θ_i is the learnable parameter of the function $\psi(\cdot)$, $\psi(\cdot)$ consisting of a 1×1 convolution that recodes the encoder features E_i into a difference feature representation.

At the same time, we utilize a set of learnable parameters to map the relational map G to a set of weights, and then enhance the E'_i, the transformation of G can be expressed as

$$G_i = \varphi_{\theta_i}(U(G)) \tag{6}$$

where $U(\cdot)$ denotes the up-sampling operation (bilinear interpolation) and θ_i is the learnable parameter of the function $\varphi(\cdot)$. $\varphi(\cdot)$ implements the mapping of the relational map into a set of weights to enhance the encoder features. For simplicity, $\varphi(\cdot)$ consists of a 1×1 convolution. $U(\cdot)$ and $\varphi(\cdot)$ transform $G \in R^{C/16 \times H \times W}$ to $G \in R^{(C \times 2^{i-1}) \times H \times W}$ together, thus adjusting the dimensionality of the relational map to be consistent with the encoder features.

As shown in Fig. 2, we enhance the encoder-generated feature maps one by one using the relational map. To achieve this, the relation map G is mapped to multiple sets of weights, and the encoder feature map is re-weighted by G. This is different from the general attention mechanism, for the relation map obtains valid relationships between all features in dual spatial-temporal space through deep supervision, enabling a more accurate and fine-grained enhancement of the encoder feature representation. Let S_i denote the enhanced encoder feature map, then the alignment of G_i with E'_i is as follows.

$$S_i = E'_i \otimes G_i \tag{7}$$

$\otimes$ represents the dot product operation, which can directly establish the connection between the relation map G_i and the feature map E'_i, utilize G_i re-weighting the E'_i to achieve feature enhancement.

4 Experiment

To evaluate our methods, we compare other advanced networks in Sect. 4.3 and make ablation experiments for the Geo-objects relations module in Sect. 4.2.

4.1 Experiment Settings

Dataset. We experimented on the CDD [29] dataset, a publicly available large-scale dataset in the field of remote sensing change detection, containing a total of 10,000 pairs of training samples and 3,000 pairs of validation and test samples, each with a spatial resolution of 3–100 cm per pixel and a pixel count of 256 × 256. LEVIR-CD [26] is a public building CD dataset containing 637 pairs of RS images with a size of 1024 × 1024 pixels. To save GPU memory, we splited the images into patches of size 256 × 256 pixels.

Parameter Settings. The baseline network for our model is the expanded UNet, as shown in Fig. 1. We performed flip and rotate operations on the input images for data augment. Use a BCE loss function, an optimizer AdamW, and a learning rate initially set to 1e-3, decaying to 0.5 of the original every 8 epochs. Our model converged after 100 epochs of training on an NVIDIA Tesla V100 graphics card.

Evaluation Metrics. Here, precision rate, recall rate, and F1 score are used to evaluate the algorithm performance comprehensively. These metrics are defined as follows.

$$F1 = 2TP/(2TP + FP + FN) \tag{8}$$

$$precision = TP/(TP + FP) \tag{9}$$

$$recall = TP/(TP + FN) \tag{10}$$

$$IoU = TP/(FP + TP + FN) \tag{11}$$

4.2 Ablation Experiments

To explore the role of the GRM, we perform ablation experiments on the baseline network and the network focused on the object relations (ORFNet) in this section. Our baseline network is shown in Fig. 1, and the ORFNet is shown in Fig. 2. As can be seen from Table 1, our proposed network ORFNet increases the accuracy, recall, and F1 score by 1.1%, 5.8%, and 3.6%, respectively, compared to the baseline network by just adding 0.40M parameters and 0.21GFLOPs. This indicates that the feature relationship module is very lightweight and efficient, and can be easily inserted into change detection networks with an encoder-decoder structure.

Table 1. Comparison of baseline network and ORFNet.

Methods	Params. (M)	GFLOPS	Precision	Recall	IoU	F1
Baseline	13.55	45.18	0.955	0.900	0.862	0.926
ORFNet	13.95	45.39	0.966	0.958	0.927	0.962

To analyze in detail the reasons for the improved performance of the GRM, we visualize in Fig. 4 a sample of the baseline network and a portion of the ORFNet on the

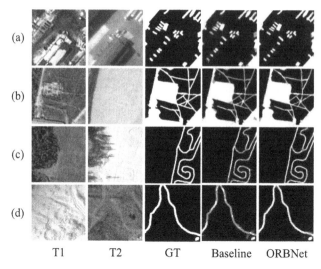

T1	T2	GT	Baseline	ORBNet

Fig. 4. Visualization results of the baseline network and ORFNet on the CDD test set. (Color figure online)

CDD test set. To show the segmentation results more clearly, we use different colors to indicate TP (white), TN (black), FP (red), and FN (green). It can be visually seen that ORFNet's segmentation is significantly better than the baseline network, with few missed and wrong detections.

In Fig. 4(a), some vehicles are parked on the roadside, and because of the strong correlation between roads and vehicles and between vehicles and vehicles, the network can easily exclude changes in other irrelevant features such as buildings or farmland by detecting roads and other vehicles, thus reducing the search range of change categories. It can be easily seen from the prediction results that some missed vehicle changes are clearly segmented in ORFNet.

In Fig. 4(c), there is a clear seasonal variation between the bi-temporal images, and some of the newly constructed roads in T2 are also covered by snow, which leads to a degree of similar spectral representation of objects with different semantic concepts in the same space-time, thus significantly affecting the detection of newly constructed roads. Our network significantly enhances the feature representation of the encoder through the GRM, making the features passed into the decoder highly dis-crimination of these pseudo-variations in snow, and thus the ORFNet can detect road changes more accurately and more clearly.

In the Fig. 4 (d), there are large illumination changes between the bi-temporal images T1 and T2, and the original network has significant missed detection for these changes, while our network significantly improves detection performance by enhancing the discrimination of the feature maps.

4.3 Comparative Experiments

We compare several other state-of-the-art change detection methods. FC-EF [20], FC-Siam-Diff [20], and FC-Siam-Conc [20] are three different architectures of change detection networks, the latter two of which use a siamese encoder architecture for end-to-end training. IFN [21] introduces an attention mechanism on top of the siamese architecture and multi-level deep supervision, prompting the generated feature maps to segment change targets more clearly. DASNet [27] uses a self-attention mechanism to model remote relationships, resulting in more discriminative feature maps. SNUNet [22] combines the siamese architecture with NestedUNet [30] and alleviates the loss of deep feature localization information through tight information transfer.

Table 2. Performance comparison with other advanced change detection networks.

Methods	Params. (M)	GFLOPS (G)	CDD				LEVIR-CD			
			Pre	Rec	IoU	F1	Pre	Rec	IoU	F1
FC-EF	1.35	7.14	0.749	0.494	0.423	0.595	0.754	0.730	0.590	0.742
FC-Siam-Conc	1.55	10.64	0.779	0.622	0.529	0.692	0.852	0.736	0.653	0.790
FC-Siam-Diff	1.35	9.44	0.786	0.588	0.507	0.673	0.861	0.687	0.618	0.764
IFN	35.73	164.58	0.950	0.861	0.823	0.903	0.903	0.876	0.800	0.889
DASNet	16.26	113.09	0.914	0.925	0.850	0.919	0.811	0.788	0.665	0.799
SNUNet-c32	12.03	109.62	0.956	0.949	0.910	0.953	0.889	0.874	0.787	0.881
Ours	13.95	45.39	0.966	0.958	0.927	0.962	0.925	0.890	0.830	0.907

Table 2 shows the overall comparison results of the models on the test set. The quantitative results show that ORFNet consistently outperforms the other methods on the CDD dataset. For example, compared to SNUNet, ORFNet has slightly more parameters but is significantly less computationally intensive, and it outperforms by 1.0%/0.9%/0.9% in terms of precision/recall/F1, respectively. To evaluate the generalization performance of the established network model, we supplemented the experiment on the LEVIR-CD dataset. Table 2 reports the comparison results. The quantitative results show our model still outperforms the other methods on this dataset. For example, compared to SNUNet, ORFNet outperforms by 3.6%/1.6%/2.6% in terms of precision/recall/F1, respectively. This can be attributed to the fact that ORFNet explores the relations between all objects in dual spatial-temporal space and uses these relations to significantly enhance the discrimination of the feature maps.

We visualize the prediction map for a portion of the network on the CDD test set as shown in Fig. 5, which includes FC-EF, FC-Siam-Conc, FC-Siam-Diff, SNUNet, and our ORFNet. It can be visualized from Fig. 5 that the detection performance of our network is significantly better than other networks, since our network explores a larger range of relationships between features and significantly enhances the feature discrimination through such relations.

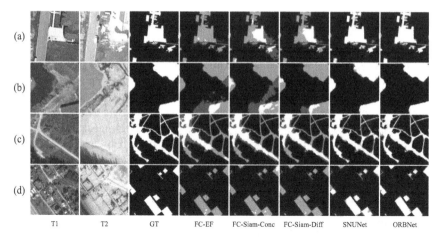

Fig. 5. Visualization results of different methods on the CDD test set.

In Fig. 5(a), Region marked with red circles in the figure, which is a part of buildings, is difficult to determine its type by local pixels alone, so other CD models misdetected this part. Our network establishes the relations between it and other buildings through the GRM, thus narrowing down the search range of pixel types and well avoiding the occurrence of false detections.

In Fig. 5(b-d), there are obvious seasonal variations between the bi-temporal images, and compared to other methods, our network achieves better detection by enhancing the discrimination of the enhanced feature maps, which makes the network more robust to the interference caused by these external factors.

5   Conclusion

In this paper, we designed a lightweight and efficient Geo-objects relations module to explore the effective connections between all objects in dual spatial-temporal space, and enhance the discrimination of the encoder feature map through these connections, which makes the network have high detection performance even in complex backgrounds. The experimental results on the CDD dataset show that our approach provides a good balance between performance and efficiency. In the future, we will try to embed the relationship module into other more advanced models.

Acknowledgments. We would like to thank the anonymous reviewers for their valuable comments and suggestions. This work is supported by Shandong Provincial Natural Science Foundation of China under Grant ZR2018MF009, the State Key Research Development Program of China under Grant 2017YFC0804406, the Taishan Scholars Program of Shandong Province under Grant ts20190936, and the Shandong University of Science and Technology Research Fund under Grant 2015TDJH102.

References

1. Gong, M., Zhang, P., Su, L., Liu, J.: Coupled dictionary learning for change detection from multi-source data. IEEE Trans. Geosci. Remote Sens. **54**(12), 7077–7091 (2016)
2. Jin, S., Yang, L., Danielson, P., Homer, C., Fry, J., Xian, G.: A comprehensive change detection method for updating the national land cover database to circa. Remote Sens. Environ. **132**, 159–175 (2011)
3. Chen, H., Qi, Z., Shi Z.: Efficient Transformer based Method for Remote Sensing Image Change Detection (2021)
4. Liu, Y., Pang, C., Zhan, Z., et al.: Building change detection for remote sensing images using a dual-task constrained deep Siamese convolutional network model. IEEE Geosci. Remote Sens. Lett. **18**, 811–815 (2021)
5. Zhao, W., Mou, L., Chen, J., Bo, Y., Emery, W.J.: Incorporating metric learning and adversarial network for seasonal invariant change detection. IEEE Trans. Geosci. Remote. Sens **58**(4), 2720–2731 (2020)
6. Jiang, H., Hu, X., Li, K., Zhang, J., et al.: Pga-siamnet: pyramid feature-based attention-guided siamese network for remote sensing orthoimagery building change detection. Remote Sens. **12**(3), 484 (2020)
7. Long, J., Shelhamer, E., Darrell, T.: Fully convolutional networks for semantic segmentation. IEEE Trans. Pattern Anal. Mach. Intell. **39**(4), 640–651 (2015)
8. Ronneberger, O., Fischer, P., Brox, T.: U-net: Convolutional networks for biomedical image segmentation. Med. Image Comput. Comput. Assist. Intervent. MICCAI **9351**, 234–241 (2015)
9. Zhang, M., Xu, G., Chen, K., Yan, M., Sun, X.: Tripletbased semantic relation learning for aerial remote sensing image change detection. IEEE Geosci. Remote. Sens. Lett. **16**(2), 266–270 (2019)
10. Zhao, H., Shi, J., Qi, X., Wang, X., Jia, J.: Pyramid scene parsing network. In: 2017 IEEE Conference on Computer Vision and Pattern Recognition (CVPR), pp. 6230–6239 (2017)
11. Tolstikhin, I., Houlsby, N., Kolesnikov, A., Beyer, L., Zhai, X., Unterthiner, T., Yung, J., Keysers, D., Uszkoreit, J., Lucic, M., et al.: MLP-Mixer: An all-MLP Architecture for Vision. arXiv preprint arXiv:2105.01601 (2021)
12. Zheng, Z., Zhong, Y., Wang, J., Ma, A.: Foreground-aware relation network for geospatial object segmentation in high spatial resolution remote sensing imagery. In: 2020 IEEE/CVF Conference on Computer Vision and Pattern Recognition (CVPR), pp. 4095–4104 (2020)
13. Carincotte, C., Derrode, S., Bourennane, S.: Unsupervised change detection on SAR images using fuzzy hidden Markov chains. IEEE Trans. Geosci. Remote Sens. **44**(2), 432–441 (2006). https://doi.org/10.1109/TGRS.2005.861007
14. Liu, J., Gong, M., Zhao, J., Li, H., Jiao, L.: Difference representation learning using stacked restricted Boltzmann machines for change detection in SAR images. Soft. Comput. **20**(12), 4645–4657 (2014). https://doi.org/10.1007/s00500-014-1460-0
15. Kayikcioglu, I., Kose, C., Kayikcioglu T.: ECG ST segment change detection using Born-Jordan time-frequency transform and artificial neural networks. In: Signal Processing and Communications Applications Conference (SIU) (2018)
16. Wang, H., Cui, Z., Sun, H., Rahnamayan, S., Yang, X.-S.: Randomly attracted firefly algorithm with neighborhood search and dynamic parameter adjustment mechanism. Soft. Comput. **21**(18), 5325–5339 (2016). https://doi.org/10.1007/s00500-016-2116-z
17. Fan, J.: OPE-HCA: an optimal probabilistic estimation approach for hierarchical clustering algorithm. Neural Comput. Appl. **31**(7), 2095–2105 (2015). https://doi.org/10.1007/s00521-015-1998-5

18. Tang, L., Wang, C., Wang, S., et al.: A novel fuzzy clustering algorithm based on rough set and inhibitive factor. Concurr. Comput. Pract. Exper. **33**(6), e6078 (2021)
19. Li, W., Lu, M., Chen, X.: Automatic change detection of urban land-cover based on SVM classification. In: Geoscience & Remote Sensing Symposium. IEEE 1686–1689 (2015)
20. Daudt, R.C., Saux, B.L., Boulch, A.: Fully convolutional siamese networks for change detection. In: ICIP (2018)
21. Cz, A., Peng, Y., Dt, E., et al.: A deeply supervised image fusion network for change detection in high resolution bi-temporal remote sensing images. ISPRS J. Photogramm. Remote. Sens. **166**, 183–200 (2020)
22. Fang, S., Li, K., Shao, J., Li, Z.: SNUNet-CD: a densely connected Siamese network for change detection of VHR Images. IEEE Geosci. Remote Sens. Lett. **19**, 1–5 (2022). https://doi.org/10.1109/LGRS.2021.3056416
23. Lopez-Pacheco, M., Morales-Valdez, J., Wen, Y.: Frequency domain CNN and dissipated energy approach for damage detection in building structures. Soft Comput. **24**(20), 15821–15840 (2020). https://doi.org/10.1007/s00500-020-04912-w
24. Chen, L.C., Papandreou, G., et al.: Rethinking atrous convolution for semantic image segmentation. arXiv (2017)
25. Liu, S., Huang, D., Wang, Y.: Receptive field block net for accurate and fast object detection. In: Ferrari, V., Hebert, M., Sminchisescu, C., Weiss, Y. (eds.) ECCV 2018. LNCS, vol. 11215, pp. 404–419. Springer, Cham (2018). https://doi.org/10.1007/978-3-030-01252-6_24
26. Chen, H., Shi, Z.: A spatial-temporal attention-based method and a new dataset for remote sensing image change detection. Remote Sens. **12**(10), 1662 (2020). https://doi.org/10.3390/rs12101662
27. Chen, J., Yuan, Z., Peng, J., Chen, L., Huang, H., Jiawei Zhu, Y., Liu, H.L.: DASNet: dual attentive fully convolutional siamese networks for change detection in high-resolution satellite images. IEEE J. Select. Top. Appl. Earth Observ. Remote Sens. **14**, 1194–1206 (2021). https://doi.org/10.1109/JSTARS.2020.3037893
28. Diakogiannis, F.I., Waldner, F., Caccetta, P.: Looking for change? roll the dice and demand attention. Remote Sens. **13**(18), 3707 (2021). https://doi.org/10.3390/rs13183707
29. Lebedev, M.A., Vizilter, Y.V., Vygolov, O.V., Knyaz, V.A., Rubis, A.Y.: Change detection in remote sensing images using conditional adversarial networks. Int. Arch. Photogramm. Remote Sens. Spat. Inf. Sci. **XLII–2**, 565–571 (2018). https://doi.org/10.5194/isprs-archives-XLII-2-565-2018
30. Zhou, Z., Rahman Siddiquee, M.M., Tajbakhsh, N., Liang, J.: UNet++: A nested U-Net architecture for medical image segmentation. In: Stoyanov, D., et al. (eds.) DLMIA/ML-CDS-2018. LNCS, vol. 11045, pp. 3–11. Springer, Cham (2018). https://doi.org/10.1007/978-3-030-00889-5_1

MLFF: Multiple Low-Level Features Fusion Model for Retinal Vessel Segmentation

Tao Deng[✉], Yi Huang, and Junfeng Zhang

School of Information Science and Technology, Southwest Jiaotong University, Chengdu 611756, China
tdeng@swjtu.edu.cn

Abstract. Imaging is increasingly used for the diagnosis of retinal normality and the monitoring of retinal abnormalities. Many retinal vessel properties, such as small artery aneurysms, narrowing of incisions, etc., are related to systemic diseases. The morphology of retinal blood vessels themselves is related to cardiovascular disease and coronary artery disease in adults. The fundus image can intuitively reflect the retinal vessel lesions, and the computer-based image processing method can be used for auxiliary medical diagnosis. In this paper, a retinal vessel segmentation model, named as MLFF, is proposed to effectively extract and fuse multiple low-level features. Firstly, there are 25 low-level feature maps of fundus retinal vessel images that are analyzed and extracted. Then, the feature maps are fused by an AdaBoost classifier. Finally, the MLFF is trained and evaluated on public fundus images for vessel extraction dataset (DRIVE). The qualitative and quantitative experimental results show that our model can effectively detect the retinal vessels and outperforms other models including deep learning-based models.

Keywords: Vessel segmentation · Low-level features · Feature fusion · AdaBoost

1 Introduction

The fundus retinal vessels are the parts of the human body vessels that can be directly and non-invasively observed. By observing the changes in the retinal vascular network structure or morphology of retinal vessels, like diameter, branch morphology and angle, lots of ophthalmological and cardiovascular diseases can be diagnosed, such as glaucoma, diabetic retinopathy, hypertension, and arteriosclerosis [1]. Fundus retinal images have been commonly used for screening of diabetic patients. Using computer-assisted methods to automatically generate segmented blood vessel images can effectively help clinicians save their time [2].

In order to facilitate the diagnosis and surgery planning of those diseases, the first thing we have to do is to distinguish between the blood vessels and the background in the fundus images. Since it is labor-intensive and time-consuming

© Springer Nature Singapore Pte Ltd. 2022
L. Pan et al. (Eds.): BIC-TA 2021, CCIS 1566, pp. 271–281, 2022.
https://doi.org/10.1007/978-981-19-1253-5_20

to perform the segmentation manually by the clinicians, we want to achieve computer-aided automatic segmentation. Hence, the automatic detection and extraction of retinal vascular structure in color fundus images are of great significance. However, retina vessel segmentation (RVS) has been a challenge for long. In the fundus images, the intricacies of retinal vessel network and the changing brightness of the vessels with the extension of the vessels cause the segmentation challenging [3–5]. Furthermore, because of the lack of retinal vessel datasets, the deep learning-based models, which rely heavily on datasets, could be not effective.

In this paper, there are total of 25 low-level features of fundus retinal image are analyzed and extracted. Then, we design a multiple low-level features fusion model (MLFF) for retinal vessel segmentation. The extracted low-level features are fused by an AdaBoost classifier. By training and testing MLFF on the public digital retinal images for vessel extraction dataset (DRIVE) [6], the experimental results show that our model can effectively detect the retinal vessels and outperforms the SOTA models including deep learning-based methods.

2   Related Works

Researchers have worked on the RVS and made some achievements for many years. There are numerous methods of RVS published, which can be roughly classified into supervised and unsupervised methods.

Supervised methods require annotated standard images for training and thus show better performance. Among these methods, the commonly used techniques include Neural Networks, Gaussian Mixture Models, Conditional Random Fields, AdaBoost and Convolutional Neural Networks, etc. [7–9]. Lupascu et al. [10] buildt a RVS method based on Adaboost classifier, constructing the 41-D feature vector including local information, shape information and structural information of each pixel in the fundus image to train a classifier. Yang et al. [11] designed a multi-scale feature fusion model based on U-Net, which included data augmentation and preprocessing. The inception structure was introduced in the multi-scale feature extraction encoder for different sizes in the retina, showing a better segmentation effect on blood vessels. Recently, Wu et al. [12] constructed a NFN+ model, in which the multi-scale information was extracted and deep feature maps was fully used. A unique cascaded networks structure with network connection was designed to improve segmentation accuracy and solve the problem of under-segmenting of faint blood vessels. The models achieved high accuracy on DRIVE [6], STARE [13] and CHASE [14,15] databases. Shi et al. [16] proposed a multi-scale U-Net for RVS, called MSU-Net. Zhang et al. [17] built a pyramid context-aware network (PCANet) for RVS. Besides, a fast and efficient RVS model was proposed by Boudegga et al. [18].

Unsupervised methods do not need to rely on labeled samples and analyzes similarities or features between images. Such methods include matched filtering, morphological processing, model based approach, thresholding, etc. Image matting was also applied to the retinal vessel segmentation. Zhao et al. [19]

transformed the segmentation problem into a matting task, combining the local matting loss and global pixel loss to discern the ambiguous pixels around small vessels. The method can be either supervised or unsupervised. Ding et al. [20] proposed a new deep neural networks(DNNs) to detect vessels in FA images. Ramos-Soto et al. [21] built an efficient RVS model with optimized top-hat and homomorphic methods. The proposed methodology included previous, main, and post processing stages.

3   Multiple Low-Level Feature Fusion Model

3.1   Multiple Low-Level Feature Extraction

There are various features in the image, but not all of them are useful for improve the performance of different detection or segmentation task. Feature selection improves classification accuracy by identifying the most distinct features. In this work, the multiple low-level features of retinal vessel image, including gray, color, intensity, edge, morphology, texture, and multi-scales linearity, are analyzed and extracted detailedly. There are total of 25 low-level image features are extracted in our work. Specifically, 2 color feature maps on RGB and HSV color space, 1 luminance feature map, 8 edge features by Canny and Scharr operators, 7 morphological feature maps of Dilation, Erosion, Opening, Closing and TopHat operations, 6 texture feature maps by Gabor, Hessian and Frangi filters and 1 multi-scale feature map.

Color. As we know, the color image includes red, green and blue channel features. For retinal vessel image, the color fundus images separated by channels showed the strongest contrast in the images separated by green channels [10]. So, we choose the green gray feature map $\mathcal{F}_{Green}$ as one important low-level feature.

In terms of color feature analysis, HSV color space was selected to extract the colors of black and white. It was found that the whole range of red included the large vessels, while the background and small vessels were orange. We extract the red and orange color feature map $\mathcal{F}_{HSV}$ in the HSV color system. Compared with RGB color space, HSV color space can directly show the type, light and shade of color, and the color distribution of blood vessels and background in the color retinal vessel image is obvious. So, it is convenient and clear to extract the color information by using HSV color space.

Luminance. The luminance value of blood vessels in each area of fundus image is different from that of background. Threshold segmentation can effectively select the blood vessels, so the luminance value is taken as a feature. The brightness of blood vessels and background in different areas is obviously different in the color retinal vessel images. In terms of luminance feature analysis, the luminance value of each pixel is obtained through the calculation method of extracting luminance value. The luminance feature map of retinal vessel image is extracted by follow formula:

$$\mathcal{F}_{Lum} = \lambda_R * R + \lambda_G * G + \lambda_B * B \tag{1}$$

where λ_R, λ_G and λ_B are the weights of red (R), green (G), blue (V) channels of retinal vessel image on the RGB space, respectively. As mentioned above, the green channel includes the strongest contrast feature information. So, we set the weight of G as the biggest one $\lambda_G = 0.587$, and $\lambda_R = 0.299$ and $\lambda_B = 0.114$. The selection of the weights of each RGB channel are based on our experimental experience.

Edge Features. Retinal vessel images have obvious edge features, and the junction between blood vessels and background has obvious changes of gray scale or other characteristic values. The edge features are important for the retinal vessel segmentation. In this case, we extract the edge feature maps $\mathcal{F}_{Edge} = \{\mathcal{F}_{Cany}, \mathcal{F}_{Sobel}, \mathcal{F}_{Scharr}\}$, 2 low-level feature maps are obtained by using Canny operator with 3×3 and 5×5 different cores, and 4 low-level feature maps are obtained by using Scharr operator in X and Y directions with 3×3 and 9×9 different cores. The weighted square of two directions is used to obtain 2 low-level feature maps. The Canny feature map $\mathcal{F}_{Cany}$ can judge whether edge points are edges. In order to extract more edge information of retinal vessel, the Sobel feature map $\mathcal{F}_{Sobel}$ are also considered as another low-level edge feature in this work. However, although the Sobel operation can effectively extract image edges, but cannot extract the unclear edges. Compared with the edge features extracted by Sobel, the edge feature map extracted by Scharr operator $\mathcal{F}_{Scharr}$ can significantly improve the information of small blood vessels.

Morphological Characteristics. The mathematical morphology operation can remove the noise in the image and connect the image area. So, we use the 3×3 structure operator to extract the morphological characteristics by Dilation, Erosion, Opening, Closing and TopHat operations, and obtain the feature maps $\mathcal{F}_{Dila}$, $\mathcal{F}_{Ero}$, $\mathcal{F}_{Opening}$, $\mathcal{F}_{Closing}$ and $\mathcal{F}_{TopHat}$ respectively. Note that, three cores with different structures, i.e. (80,800), (800,80) and (800,800), are selected to perform operation on grayscale images, and 3 TopHat feature vectors are obtained.

Texture. We choose the Gabor, Hessian and Frangi filters to extract the texture features. Gabor feature $\mathcal{F}_{Gabor}$ is extracted with scale equals 1, and Hessian feature map $\mathcal{F}_{Hessian}$ is with stride equals 10, λ equals 10. Furthermore, the sensitivity coefficient of Frangi filter is set to 10, and four scales are selected to filter the retinal images by 0.002, 0.004, 0.008 and 0.01. So, we obtain four Frangi feature maps, $\mathcal{F}_{Frangi_i}$ ($i = 0.002, 0.004, 0.008, 0.01$).

Multi-scale. In the multi-scale linear analysis, a total of 12 linear detectors were established from 0 to 180° according to the gray distribution of blood vessels, and 1 feature was obtained. By analyzing the transverse information, we can find that the gray distribution of retinal vessels conforms to the Gaussian matched filtering function, that is, the shape of Gaussian matched filtering is similar to the characteristics of retinal vessels in the direction of the bottom of the eye. The Gaussian filter is defined as:

$$\mathcal{G}_\theta(x,y) = -\frac{1}{\sqrt{2\pi}\sigma} \exp\left(-\frac{x^2}{2\sigma^2}\right), f \text{ or } |x| \leq t \cdot \sigma, |y| \leq L/2 \qquad (2)$$

where θ is the rotation Angle ($[0°, 180°]$), L and σ represent the length of detectable omental vessels and their cross-sectional stretch, respectively. In this paper, $\sigma = 1.5$, $L = 9$, and 12 directions $[0°, 15°, ...180°]$ were selected to carry out linear retinal vascular Gaussian matched filtering, and operation was carried out on the mask to remove the information outside the mask, and a feature map $\mathcal{F}_M$ was established.

3.2 Multiple Low-Level Feature Fusion

After extracting the low-level features of retinal vessel images, we design a RVS model using the Adaboost learning method (MLFF) in this section. The architecture of MLFF is introduced in Fig. 1. AdaBoost, proposed by Freund and Shapire [22], is an adaptive supervised machine learning technique, which combines a set of low-level classifiers with low discrimination (called weak learners) to construct a powerful classifier. The AdaBoost algorithm is easy to implement and relatively fast, making it popular for computer vision. Furthermore, the AdaBoost can reduce the bias and variance during training phase, which can effectively solve the overfitting problem caused by the small sample learning. The final classifier is a weighted combination of weak classifiers, which is defined as following formula:

$$G(f) = \text{sign}\left(\sum_{t=1}^{T} \alpha_t g_t(f)\right) \qquad (3)$$

where $g_t(\cdot)$ is the weak classifier and $G(\cdot)$ is the strong AdaBoost classifier. α_t is the weight of $g_t(\cdot)$. T is the number of weak classifiers. More details are shown in Algorithm 1 and shown in Fig. 1.

The algorithm has two stages, i.e. Training and Testing. In the training, the low-level feature maps of retinal vessel images are extracted firstly. Then, the feature maps are stacked together as the feature vector for training. Finally, weak classifiers of AdaBoost are combined to a strong classifier. In the testing, the low-level feature maps of test images are extracted as same as the training stage. Then, the features are used to train strong classifier. Finally, the vessel segmentation results are obtained by the post-processing.

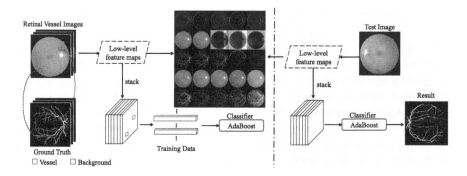

Fig. 1. The architecture of MLFF, including train and test phases.

Algorithm 1: Learning a Multiple Low-level Feature Fusion Using AdaBoost

---

Input: Training dataset with N retinal vessel images and ground truth from expert. Testing images I_{test}.

Output: Retinal vessel segmentation map.

Training stage:

1. Extract the the multiple low-level features of fundus vessel images $\mathcal{F}_i$
2. For N retinal vessel images, sample $x_s(S = 1)^S$ with labels $y_s(S = 1)^S$.
   Compute features $f_s(S = 1)^S = f(x_s)_{(S=1)^S}$.
3. Initialization $w_s = 1/S$.
4. **for** $t = 1, ... T$ **do**

   a. train a weak classifier $g_t : R^d \rightarrow \{-1, 1\}$, by $g_t = \arg\min_{g_n \in \mathcal{G}}$, where

   $$\varepsilon_u = \sum_{s=1}^{S} w_t(s) \, [y_s \neq g_u(\mathbf{f}_s)]$$

   b. set the weight of g_t: $\alpha_t = \frac{1}{2} \log \frac{1-\varepsilon_t}{\varepsilon_t}$
   c. update weights

   $$w_{t+1}(s) = \frac{w_t(s) \exp\left[-\alpha_t \cdot y_s \cdot g_t(\mathbf{f}_s)\right]}{Z_t}$$

   where Z is a normalization factor.
end

5. Final classifier is trained $G(f) = \text{sign}\left(\sum_{t=1}^{T} \alpha_t g_t(f)\right)$

Testing stages:

Extract the feature vector $f(x)$ of each location x in I_{test}, obtain the detected vessel segmentation map by the trained strong classifier $g_t : R^d \rightarrow \{-1, 1\}$.

3.3   Post-processing

While a single classifier is used to segment the vessels of fundus image, there will be noise or other impurities in the segmentation results. Therefore, morphological operator $\mathcal{S}$ is established in this paper to calculate the number of blood vessel pixels contained in the connected region of S. The connected area refers to: from the gray level image, the gray value of one or more of the 8 pixel points around the pixel point or the four pixel points around the pixel point is the same as the gray value of the point, and so forth, until the gray value of no pixel point is the same. In this paper, we select 8 surrounding pixel points, and the structural operator S judged by the classification model as blood vessel is calculated. The connected area with less than 20 pixel points is changed as the background.

4   Experiments

The DRIVE dataset [6] is used often in RVS. It includes 20 training and 20 testing fundus images with 584×565 resolution and JPEG-compressed. We evaluated the performance of MLFF on DRIVE dataset.

4.1   Qualitative Evaluation

Figure 2 presents a visual comparison of our model and other models, such as 2D matched filtering, Random Forest learning method. The results indicate that MLFF can much more accurately detect the retinal vessels than others. Furthermore, the comparison of local segmentation results is showed in the third row of Fig. 2. As expected, our model can detect more vessel information than others.

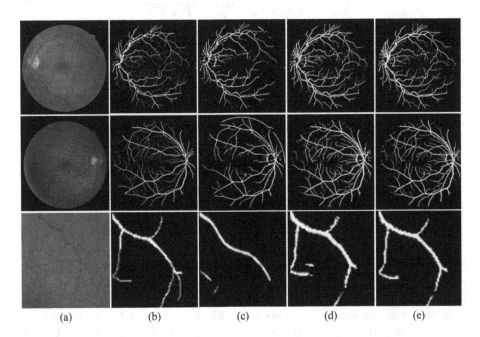

Fig. 2. Qualitative comparison our model with other method. (a) Retinal vessel images. (b) Ground truth. (c) Results of 2D matched filtering. (d) Random Forest. (e) Ours.

Table 1. Comparisons of our model on DRIVE dataset.

	Models	ACC(%)	SP(%)	SE(%)
Classical method	Random Forest	94.70	95.67	84.82
	Azzopardi (2015)	94.42	97.04	76.55
	Orlando (2017)	/	96.84	78.97
	Li (2016)	95.27	98.16	75.69
Deep learning-based	Liskowski (2016)	95.35	98.07	78.11
	Yan (2018)	95.42	98.18	76.53
	Wu (2018)	95.67	**98.19**	78.44
	NFN+ (2020)	95.82	98.13	79.96
Ours (MLFF)		**96.17**	96.77	**87.83**

4.2 Quantitative Evaluation

In this work, we employ the accuracy (ACC), sensitivity (SE) and specificity (SP) [12] to quantitatively compare the performance of our model.

$$ACC = \frac{TP + TN}{TP + TN + FP + FN} \tag{4}$$

$$SP = \frac{TN}{TN + FP}, SE = \frac{TP}{TP + FN} \tag{5}$$

where SP denotes that the manually annotated non-vessel pixels that are correctly classified as non-vessel pixels divided by the total number of non-vessel pixels (TN) in the gold standard. Similarly, the SE is determined by dividing the number of pixels correctly classified as vessel pixels (TP) by the total number of vessel pixels in the ground truth.

In Table 1, the performance of our model is compared with other classical model and deep learning model, such as Random Forest [23], some retinal vessel segmentation model (proposed by Azzopardi [24], Liskowski [25], Li [26], Orlando [27], Yan [28] and Wu [29] et al., respectively) and NFN+ [12] model. The comparison results show that the ACC and SE scores of our model are the highest one. Moreover, our model outperforms some deep learning-based vessel segmentation models, such as Liskowski, Yan, Wu and NFN+.

4.3 Ablation Study

To investigate the effects of the proposed MLFF with and without post-processing, the qualitative and quantitative comparisons are shown in Fig. 3 and Table 2, respectively. As shown in Fig. 3 (b) and (c), we can see that the noise and some irrelevant information of retinal vessel are eliminated after the post-processing. In addition, the segmentation results with post-processing are very close to the ground truth visually (Fig. 3 (d)). Furthermore, the quantitative comparison is discussed in Table 2. As expected, we can find that the

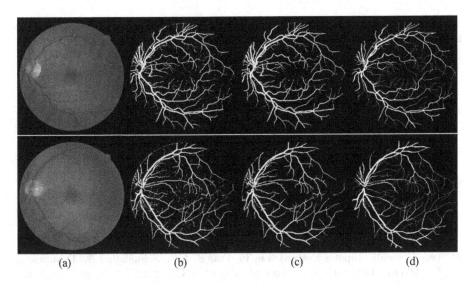

Fig. 3. Qualitative comparison of the proposed MLFF with and without post-processing. (a) Retinal vessel images. (b) Segmentation results without post-processing. (c) Segmentation results with post-processing. (d) Ground truth.

Table 2. Performance of MLFF with and without post-processing.

Models	ACC(%)	SP(%)	SE(%)
MLFF without post-processing	95.12	96.24	83.59
MLFF with post-processing	**96.17**	**96.77**	**87.83**

evaluation scores of MLFF with post-processing are all higher than the without post-processing. Therefore, we can conclude that the post-processing is effective for RVS.

5 Conclusion and Discussion

In this work, we analyze and extract total of 25 low-level features of the fundus retinal images. A multiple low-level features fusion model (MLFF) is proposed for retinal vessel segmentation. The extracted multiple low-level features are fused by an AdaBoost classifier. By training and testing the MLFF on DRIVE dataset, the results show that our model can precisely detect the retinal vessels and outperforms other SOTA models including deep learning-based methods. However, due to the lack of retinal vessel segmentation datasets, the proposed model is only verified on DRIVE. In the future, the proposed model will be trained and tested on more fundus vessel datasets.

Acknowledgments. This work was supported by the National Natural Science Foundation of China (62106208), the Sichuan Science and Technology Program (2020JDRC0031) and the China Postdoctoral Science Foundation (2021TQ0272, 2021M702715).

References

1. Abràmoff, M.D., Garvin, M.K., Sonka, M.: Retinal imaging and image analysis. IEEE Rev. Biomed. Eng. **3**(3), 169–208 (2010)
2. Fraz, M., et al.: Blood vessel segmentation methodologies in retinal images - a survey. Comput. Methods Programs Biomed. **108**(1), 407–433 (2012)
3. Waheed, Z., Usman Akram, M., Waheed, A., Khan, M.A., Shaukat, A., Ishaq, M.: Person identification using vascular and non-vascular retinal features. Comput. Electr. Eng. **53**, 359–371 (2016)
4. Zhao, Y., et al.: Retinal artery and vein classification via dominant sets clustering-based vascular topology estimation. In: Frangi, A.F., Schnabel, J.A., Davatzikos, C., Alberola-López, C., Fichtinger, G. (eds.) MICCAI 2018. LNCS, vol. 11071, pp. 56–64. Springer, Cham (2018). https://doi.org/10.1007/978-3-030-00934-2_7
5. Zheng, H., Chang, L., Wei, T., Qiu, X., Lin, P., Wang, Y.: Registering retinal vessel images from local to global via multiscale and multicycle features. In: IEEE Computer Vision and Pattern Recognition Workshops, pp. 50–57, June 2016
6. Staal, J., Abramoff, M., Niemeijer, M., Viergever, M., van Ginneken, B.: Ridge-based vessel segmentation in color images of the retina. IEEE Trans. Med. Imaging **23**(4), 501–509 (2004)
7. Srinidhi, C.L., Aparna, P., Rajan, J.: Recent advancements in retinal vessel segmentation. J. Med. Syst. **41**(4), 1–22 (2017)
8. Li, T., Bo, W., Hu, C., Kang, H., Liu, H., Wang, K., Fu, H.: Applications of deep learning in fundus images: a review. Med. Image Anal. **69**, 101971 (2021)
9. Alyoubi, W.L., Shalash, W.M., Abulkhair, M.F.: Diabetic retinopathy detection through deep learning techniques: a review. Inform. Med. Unlocked **20**, 100377 (2020)
10. Lupascu, C.A., Tegolo, D., Trucco, E.: FABC: retinal vessel segmentation using adaboost. IEEE Trans. Inf. Technol. Biomed. **14**(5), 1267–1274 (2010)
11. Yang, D., Liu, G., Ren, M., Xu, B., Wang, J.: A multi-scale feature fusion method based on u-net for retinal vessel segmentation. Entropy **22**(8), 811 (2020). https://doi.org/10.3390/e22080811
12. Wu, Y., Xia, Y., Song, Y., Zhang, Y., Cai, W.: NFN+: a novel network followed network for retinal vessel segmentation. Neural Netw. **126**, 153–162 (2020)
13. Hoover, A., Kouznetsova, V., Goldbaum, M.: Locating blood vessels in retinal images by piecewise threshold probing of a matched filter response. IEEE Trans. Med. Imaging **19**(3), 203–210 (2000)
14. Fraz, M.M., et al.: An ensemble classification-based approach applied to retinal blood vessel segmentation. IEEE. Trans. Biomed. Eng. **59**(9), 2538–2548 (2012)
15. Owen, C.G., et al.: Measuring retinal vessel tortuosity in 10-year-old children: validation of the computer-assisted image analysis of the retina (CAIAR) program. Inve. Ophtha. Vis. Sci. **50**(5), 2004–2010 (2009)
16. Shi, Z., Wang, T., Xie, F., Huang, Z., Zheng, X., Zhang, W.: MSU-net: a multi-scale u-net for retinal vessel segmentation. In: International Symposium on Artificial Intelligence in Medical Sciences, pp. 177–181 (2020)

17. Zhang, Y., Chen, Y., Zhang, K.: PCANet: pyramid context-aware network for retinal vessel segmentation. In: International Conference on Pattern Recognition, pp. 2073–2080 (2021)

18. Boudegga, H., Elloumi, Y., Akil, M., Bedoui, M.H., Kachouri, R., Abdallah, A.B.: Fast and efficient retinal blood vessel segmentation method based on deep learning network. Comput. Med. Imaging Graph. **90**, 101902–101902 (2021)

19. Zhao, H., Li, H., Cheng, L.: Improving retinal vessel segmentation with joint local loss by matting. Pattern Recognit. **98**, 107068 (2020)

20. Ding, L., Bawany, M.H., Kuriyan, A.E., Ramchandran, R.S., Wykoff, C.C., Sharma, G.: A novel deep learning pipeline for retinal vessel detection in fluorescein angiography. IEEE Trans. Image Process. **29**, 6561–6573 (2020)

21. Ramos-Soto, O., et al.: An efficient retinal blood vessel segmentation in eye fundus images by using optimized top-hat and homomorphic filtering. Comput. Methods Programs Biomed. **201**, 105949 (2021)

22. Freund, Y., Schapire, R.E.: A short introduction to boosting. J. Jpn. Soc. Artif. Intell. **14**(5), 771–780 (1999)

23. Breiman, L.: Random forests. Mach. Learn. **45**(1), 5–32 (2001)

24. Azzopardi, G., Strisciuglio, N., Vento, M., Petkov, N.: Trainable COSFIRE filters for vessel delineation with application to retinal images. Med. Image Anal. **19**(1), 46–57 (2015)

25. Liskowski, P., Krawiec, K.: Segmenting retinal blood vessels with deep neural networks. IEEE Trans. Med. Imaging **35**(11), 2369–2380 (2016)

26. Li, Q., Feng, B., Xie, L., Liang, P., Zhang, H., Wang, T.: A cross-modality learning approach for vessel segmentation in retinal images. IEEE Trans. Med. Imaging **35**(1), 109–118 (2016)

27. Orlando, J.I., Prokofyeva, E., Blaschko, M.B.: A discriminatively trained fully connected conditional random field model for blood vessel segmentation in fundus images. IEEE. Trans. Biomed. Eng. **64**(1), 16–27 (2017)

28. Yan, Z., Yang, X., Cheng, K.T.: Joint segment-level and pixel-wise losses for deep learning based retinal vessel segmentation. IEEE. Trans. Biomed. Eng. **65**(9), 1912–1923 (2018)

29. Wu, Y., Xia, Y., Song, Y., Zhang, Y., Cai, W.: Multiscale network followed network model for retinal vessel segmentation. In: Frangi, A.F., Schnabel, J.A., Davatzikos, C., Alberola-López, C., Fichtinger, G. (eds.) MICCAI 2018. LNCS, vol. 11071, pp. 119–126. Springer, Cham (2018). https://doi.org/10.1007/978-3-030-00934-2_14

Location Analysis of Urban Electric Vehicle Charging Metro-Stations Based on Clustering and Queuing Theory Model

Chongyu Chen[1], Teng Li[1], Shugui Wang[1], Zhenyao Hua[1,2,3], Zecheng Kang[1,2,3], Dongyang Li[2,3], and Weian Guo[1,2,3](✉)

[1] Sino-German College of Applied Sciences, Tongji University, Shanghai 201804, China
guoweian@tongji.edu.cn
[2] School of Information and Electronics Engineering, Tongji University, Shanghai, China
[3] Shanghai Institute of Intelligent Science and Technology, Tongji University, Shanghai 200092, China

Abstract. The holding capacity of electric vehicles becomes increasingly huge. Limited by the battery capacity and charging speed, the market of the electric charging stations is very large. Moreover, due to the restrict of the urban planning resources, it is important that electric charging stations are reasonably located. In this paper, through the analysis of electric vehicles' trajectory in Chengdu and the application of K-Means clustering algorithm and Queuing Theory, the reasonable charging station locations and the numbers of charging piles are proposed. The model is conducive to reduce the users' queue length for charging.

Keywords: Electric charging station · Queuing theory · Clustering

1 Introduction

With the shortage of fossil energy and environmental pollution, the development of new alternative energy has been drawn attentions world-widely. By reducing carbon dioxide emissions and switching to electricity in the ground transport sector, China will achieve carbon neutral target by 2060 [1]. Therefore, the Chinese government has introduced policy measures and financial incentives to promote the development of electric vehicles [2]. Compared with traditional fuel vehicles, electric vehicles not only have lower noise, but also have stronger start dynamic. In addition, electric vehicles will not emit nitrogen oxides and other polluting gases [3], which play an important role in protecting the environment. With the dual support of national policy measures and market demand, the research and development of electric vehicles in China will become the future traffic industry main trend. More and more papers and related products have laid a solid foundation for the development of electric vehicles [4]. The literature [5] mainly discussed the comparison between the resource consumption of electric vehicles and that of traditional fuel vehicles in China. After analyzing the resource consumption of the production, using and recycling of the two kinds of vehicles, it is concluded that

© Springer Nature Singapore Pte Ltd. 2022
L. Pan et al. (Eds.): BIC-TA 2021, CCIS 1566, pp. 282–292, 2022.
https://doi.org/10.1007/978-981-19-1253-5_21

the resource consumption of an electric vehicle is less than that of a fuel vehicle [6]. In order to encourage the public to use electric vehicles, China has introduced many specific measures. Relevant policy ran in 25 demonstration cities, which also had subsidies and policies [7, 8]. AI is also used in developing cruising strategy of electric taxis [9]. By then, the number of electric vehicles will be further increasing. The following electric vehicle facilities also need to be improved.

Electric charging station is an essential foundation facility for electric vehicles. The location and capacity of charging station play a very crucial role in improving the efficiency of charging service. Up to date, many researchers focused on this topic and conduct many works on this area. Wei [10] used a hybrid model combining Cellular Automata (CA) and Agent-Based-Modeling (ABM) to analyze the location of electric vehicle charging stations. In order to minimize the total cost, Xiao [11] established a charging queuing model considering the limited queue length and different location constraints, and determined the optimal location and capacity of electric vehicle charging facilities. Huang [12] proposed a robust deep K-Means model to exploit the hierarchical semantics of data in a layer wise way. Zhang and Yang [13] optimized the application of Simultaneous Heat Transfer Search (SHTS) in K-Means.

These literatures only carried out theoretical analysis without combination with the actual travel behavior of users and the city's street layout to make specific suggestions on the charging station location. At present, there are few literatures about the location of charging stations, though there are many benefits of large charging stations, such as safety, efficiency, manageability and high capacity. Due to large investments, the location of the large charging station is particularly important. Through reasonable location and unified management, large charging stations can not only satisfy and promote the popularization of electric vehicles, but also bring huge economic benefits to the society. To address these problems, in this paper we propose a reasonable charging station location proposal based on a specific operating vehicle trajectory in our research. In order to obtain the proposed location, this paper uses K-Means clustering algorithm to analyze urban driving trajectory data set of electric operating vehicles. Then, in order to optimize the charging piles' number of each station, this paper analyze the average queuing time of users using the queuing theory M/M/C model.

The rest of this paper is organized as follows. In Sect. 2, we come up with assumptions and describe a model. In Sect. 3, we briefly introduce a clustering algorithm and queuing theory. In Sect. 4, we take Chengdu City, China as an example to implement the algorithms and provide analysis on it. With the implementation, we find that the charging efficiency is improved and the queue length is reduced. Finally, we end this paper in Sect. 5 with conclusions and future works.

2 Model Establishment

In order to count the electric vehicle order data within a specific range, the origin of the order is taken as the geographic information data point, and the data point information includes the longitude and latitude of the point. The format of driving trajectory data set is shown in formula (1).

$$(X, Y) = \{(x_i, y_i) | i = 1, 2, \ldots, t, \ldots, n\} \tag{1}$$

To obtain the coordinate points of the charging station, it is necessary to first determine the number of the charging stations K in a limited area. The location of the charging station is expressed in formula (2).

$$(X', Y') = \left\{ \left(x'_k, y'_k \right) | k = 1, 2, \ldots, K \right\} \tag{2}$$

For each charging station, in order to meet the charging need of the majority of electric vehicles, it is also necessary to set the value of charging piles in each charging station as formula (3).

$$C = \{C_1, C_2, \ldots, C_K\} \tag{3}$$

All the processes of the model can be concluded in Table 1.

Table 1. Process of model

Input	The urban driving trajectory data set (X, Y)
Output	①The proposed number of charging stations K
	②The proposed locations of charging stations (X', Y')
	③The proposed values of charging piles in each charging station C

In this paper, the M/M/C queuing theory model is used to model the charging pile design problem based on order distribution.

In the arrival process, there are C charging piles in the charging service system. Customers arrive at the system according to Poisson flow and queue up to receive service on the first come first served basis.

In the service process, the charging time of each vehicle is also different, but the overall service time follows a negative exponential distribution. Each charging pile can only charge one car at the same time, which does not interfere with each other.

We hope to optimize the cost of the model results and satisfy the queuing requirements in the same time. We come up with an evaluation variable in the form of formula (4).

$$U = min\{aK_iC_i + b(L_s)\} \tag{4}$$

Where U is the evaluation variable, a and b are two positive coefficients. In formula (4), the first term is the cost and the second term is queuing requirement. $[KC]$ and $[L_s]$ are dimensionless constants that have been processed separately. The queue length should be as short as possible. Therefore, we introduce some constraints (5) and (6) to our model.

$$\text{For each } K_i, C_i = \lim_{L_s \to \infty} [C] + 1 \tag{5}$$

Where $[C]$ is defined as the integer part of C, and they are all integers.

$$C \geq C_i, \quad C, C_i \in N^* \tag{6}$$

3   Brief of Methods and Algorithms

3.1   The Method of K-means Clustering Analysis

Clustering analysis is a method of data mining, which is often used to analyze a large number of sample data. Clustering analysis basing on a certain feature between various sample points (usually the distance between sample points) divided each sample point into different clusters, in order to simplify the sample data and find the same features of the data. There are many clustering algorithms that are widely used. The algorithm used in this paper is K-Means clustering algorithm based on Euclidean distance, namely K-Means clustering algorithm. The Advantage of K-Means clustering algorithm is that the closer the distance of the sample points is, the higher the similarity of the points is.

In K-Means clustering algorithm, the clustering results of a certain sample data set can be obtained through continuous iteration as long as the number of clusters K is given. Therefore, whether an appropriate K value is selected determines the quality of clustering results. In order to select an optimal K value, the sum of the squares of the distance from each sample point after iteration to the center of the cluster (the Sum of the Squares of the Errors, SSE) is often used as the evaluation index. The calculation formula is as (7).

$$SSE = \sum_{k=1}^{K} \sum_{p \in C_k} \left[dis(p, m_k) \right]^2 \tag{7}$$

Among the formula (7): C_k is the k-th cluster, p is the data point of C_k, m_k is the cluster center of C_k, $dis(p, m_k)$ is the distance between p and m_k.

The smaller the SSE is, the more convergent the cluster is, and the better the clustering result is. Obviously, smaller SSE does not mean better. This is because SSE is zero when K value is taken as the number of the sample points. On this occasion it certainly cannot achieve the purpose of clustering. In order to find the balance between smaller SSE and more reasonable K value, the elbow method is often used to determine the optimal K value. This method is outlined below.

As the value of K is gradually increased to a large enough value, calculate the SSE corresponding to every K value, then draw the broken line graph of SSE changing with K value. Obviously, it should be a line which keeps falling. The K value corresponding to the obvious inflection point can be selected as the optimal number of clusters.

The pseudo-codes of these processes above are given as follows.

Procedure: K-Means clustering algorithm and the elbow method
Input: One coordinate data set $(X, Y) = \{(x_i, y_i) | i = 1, 2, \dots, t, \dots, n\}$
Output: The count of clusters K, the coordinates of final cluster centers (X', Y')
1: Initialize the coordinates of cluster centers
$\quad (X', Y') = \{(x'_k, y'_k) | k = 1, 2, \dots, K\} = \{(x'_1, y'_1), (x'_2, y'_2), \dots, (x'_K, y'_K)\}$
2: K is the count of clusters
3: *for K in range (1, t) do*
4:   *while* the elements in (X', Y') do not change any more
5:     *for i in range (1, n) do*
6:       Assign the point (x_i, y_i) to the nearest cluster center (x'_k, y'_k)
7:     *end for*
8:     *for* each (x'_k, y'_k) *in* (X', Y') *do*
9:       Take the average coordinate of all data points that belongs to this cluster
          center (x'_k, y'_k) as the new cluster center point coordinate (x'_k, y'_k)
10:    *end for*
11: *end while*
12: Calculate the *SSE*
13: *end for*
14: Draw the broken line graph of SSE changing with K value
15: Select the K value corresponding to the obvious inflection point as output

3.2 The Method of M/M/C Queuing Theory

Queuing theory, a branch of operational research, also known as stochastic service system theory, is a mathematical theory and method to study the phenomenon of random aggregation and dispersion of systems and the working process of stochastic service systems. In this paper, we use queuing theory to get the quantity index of service objects, so as to determine and optimize the parameters of related systems, and so as to make the target service system play the best benefits.

The mathematical model of queuing theory established in this paper is M/M/C type. The definition of this kind of model is that the customer flow obeys Poisson distribution of the parameter λ. The service time obeys the exponential distribution of the parameter μ. The number of service desks is constant C. And the services of each service desk are independent of each other.

Without considering other relevant constraints, the operation indexes can be obtained from the existing data to facilitate the evaluation of the system. When the expectation of a certain operation index has been obtained, the reasonable range of several important parameters can also be deduced.

After the clustering points are obtained, a mathematical model related to queuing theory can be applied to analyze the number C of charging piles. In the absence of constraints such as cost or achievability, we hope that the number of charging piles of each charging station corresponding to each clustering point can exactly meet the customers' needs, which means that the system service intensity $\rho = \frac{\lambda}{C\mu} \leq 1$. From this formula we'll get a constrain about C, which is $C \geq \frac{\lambda}{\mu}$.

From the mean value of the Poisson distribution $E[N(t)] = \lambda t$, it can be seen that the number of cars arriving per hour is the value of the Poisson index in actual situations. Therefore, we multiply the total number of orders with a proportional coefficient f to get the K we need. In this article, we take f as 1/25.

As mentioned earlier, the average charging time μ is determined to be 1 h as an inherent attribute of the entire service system.

The formula (8) is the specific formula used to calculate the queue length index.

$$L_s = \frac{1}{C!} \frac{(C\rho)^C \rho}{(1-\rho)^2} P_0 + \frac{\lambda}{\mu} \tag{8}$$

where P_0 is calculated as formula (9).

$$P_0 = \left[\left(\sum_{k=0}^{C-1} \frac{1}{k!} \left(\frac{\lambda}{\mu}\right)^k \right) + \frac{1}{C!} \frac{1}{(1-\rho)} \left(\frac{\lambda}{\mu}\right)^C \right]^{-1} \tag{9}$$

3.3 The Application Processes

The main procedures of the practical application in a specific city are as follows.

Firstly, cutting the longitude and latitude of the city into x segments respectively, or rather, dividing the urban area of the city into a set number of small grids.

Secondly, counting the numbers of electric vehicles' start points in each grid as the outdegree of this grid. The result can be expressed by a x-order matrix.

Thirdly, replacing all electric vehicles' starting points in every grid with the central coordinates of this grid.

Fourthly, selecting the top $y\%$ outdegree of grids as the aforementioned urban driving trajectory data set (X, Y).

Fifthly, using K-Means clustering algorithm and the elbow method to determine the proposed locations of charging stations (X', Y') and the proposed number of charging stations K.

Sixthly, using the M/M/C queuing theory to determine the proposed values of charging piles in each charging station C.

In these procedures, x and y are undermined constants.

4   Practical Application and Results Analysis

It is the city of Chengdu, China that was chosen as the research object in this paper. The number of the longitude and latitude segments x is taken as 100, which means the urban area of Chengdu is divided into 10,000 small grids. The percentage of the top outdegree of grids $y\%$ is taken as 5%.

The data all comes from Didi company, which published in GAIYA plan (https://out reach.didichuxing.com/research/opendata/). In the data source, it concludes more than 6,000,000 electric operating vehicle orders in 30 days in November 2016. The northeast corner of the vehicle operation area is Qilong Temple with geographic coordinates of

Table 2. Data format

Timestamp of departure	Arrival timestamp	Longitude of beginning	Latitude of beginning	Longitude of ending	Latitude of ending
1478091677	1478092890	104.00816	30.70622	104.064147	30.685848
......	......	......	......	......	......

$30.734868°N$, $104.180312°E$, while the southwest is the Joy Park with coordinates of $30.60068°N$, $103.983974°E$. The Table 2 describes the data format.

In the actual experiment, we researched the urban driving trajectory data of 30 days in November 2016. In this paper the result on November 2nd is taken as an example. It concludes about 200,000 orders.

The coordinates of the top 5% outdegree of those grids are selected as the urban driving trajectory data set (X, Y).

In the fifth step, the SSE-K image obtained by elbow method is shown in the Fig. 1.

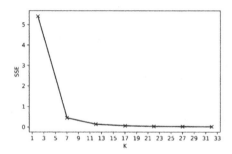

Fig. 1. The elbow method

It can be clearly seen from the figure that $K = 7$ is the obvious inflection point, so according to the elbow method mentioned earlier the proper cluster number K should be approximately equal to 7.

Here we list the results of clustering with K of 7, 9, 11, 13 in Fig. 2.

In the calculation, we calculate the total number of orders contained in a certain cluster center corresponding to each K value for different cluster K values. Since the data and coordinate position corresponding to this point are relatively stable, there is an obvious trend of change, which is convenient for analysis. In the subsequent processing, the data at this point shall prevail. When this analysis method is applied to the processing of other points, it needs to be modified (such as adding a correction coefficient) to meet the actual situation.

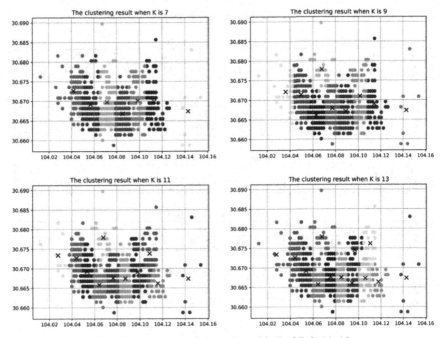

Fig. 2. The results of clustering with K of 7, 9, 11, 13

First, we need to compare the value of the queue length L_s corresponding to each K value when the number of charging piles is different. According to the value of the total number of orders and the principle that the overall average service intensity ρ is as close as possible to 1, we take the value of C from 35 to 51. Because some data cannot correctly reflect the status of the queuing system, we deleted the redundant data and put the data that can visually express the length of the queue in the Table 3.

There are negative numbers in Table 3. The reason is that the function of the queue length is a hyperbolic function, which is close to negative infinity on the left side of the asymptote. If a negative number appears in the table, we can consider that the queue length is close to infinity here. The C value corresponding to the number marked in gray is the value of C_i in formula (5), (6). This value is a limit, which means that when C is smaller than this value, the queue length is closed to infinity.

Use KC as the independent variable and L_s as the dependent variable to draw the picture. The result is shown in Fig. 3.

Table 3. Calculation result

Table 3.1 (K=7, λ=36.5)

C	35	37	39	41	43	45	47	49	51
L_s	4.07	102.51	45.10	39.47	37.72	37.02	36.72	36.59	36.54

Table 3.2 (K=9, λ=30.3)

C	29	31	33	35	37	39	41	43	45
L_s	-0.31	67.37	36.26	32.31	31.08	30.61	30.42	30.35	30.32

Table 3.3 (K=11, λ=24.6)

C	23	25	27	29	31	33	35	37	39
L_s	2.43	80.41	30.12	26.27	25.19	24.82	24.68	24.63	24.61

Table 3.4 (K=13, λ=23.9)

C	23	25	27	29	31	33	35	37	39
L_s	-8.96	40.37	27.26	25.00	24.29	24.04	23.95	23.92	23.90

Table 3.5 (K=15, λ=18.6)

C	17	19	21	23	25	27	29	31	33
L_s	0.99	60.21	22.40	19.64	18.93	18.70	18.63	18.61	18.60

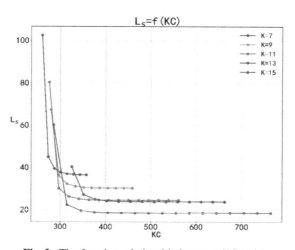

Fig. 3. The function relationship between KC and L_s

In the previous analysis, we got the mathematical relationship between KC and L_s, that is, cost and queue length. On this basis, we hope to construct an evaluation variable that can contain the function of KC and L_s at the same time, and use the function value and the current curve to optimize the whole method. In the formula (4), we take $a = 0.1$ and $b = 0.8$ as examples and draw the image of U in Fig. 4 for optimization analysis.

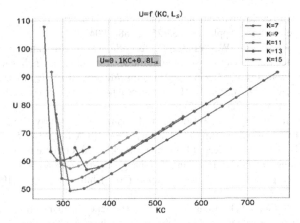

Fig. 4. The function relationship between U and KC, L_S

5   Conclusions

In this paper, we mainly use M/M/C queuing theory and K-Means algorithm to calculate the number of the electric vehicle charging stations and to complete the positioning of electric vehicle charging station. We take the actual social environment as background, and believe that these results can provide some help for the actual construction of charging stations. We use the selected hot points data to simulate the operation of the charging stations. All in all, the contributions of this paper are summarized as follows:

1. To establish stations, we employ K-Means algorithm by real data to analyze customers features of driving behavior/tracing. In this way, we cluster a large number of scattered points into hot spots for analysis.
2. In the modeling, we consider the queue length for each vehicle by queuing theory, so that we can obtain a reasonable number of charging piles to optimize the customer queuing time.

References

1. Zhang, R., Hanaoka, T.: Deployment of electric vehicles in China to meet the carbon neutral target by 2060: provincial disparities in energy systems, CO_2 emissions, and cost effectiveness. Resour. Conser. Recycl. **170**, 105622 (2021). https://doi.org/10.1016/j.resconrec.2021.105622
2. Yang Andrew, W.: A review of evolutionary policy incentives for sustainable development of electric vehicles in China: Strategic implications. Energy Policy **148**, 111983 (2021). https://doi.org/10.1016/j.enpol.2020.111983
3. Schnell, J.L., Peters, D.R., Wong, D.C., Lu, X., Guo, H., Zhang, H., Kinney, P.L., Horton, D.E.: Potential for electric vehicle adoption to mitigate extreme air quality events in China. Earth's Future **9**(2), e2020EF001788 (2021). https://doi.org/10.1029/2020EF001788
4. Hsieh, Y.L., Pan, M.S., Green, W.H.: Transition to electric vehicles in China: Implications for private motorization rate and battery market. Energy Policy, **144** (2020)

5. Zhao, L.: The life cycle environmental rebound effect of battery electric vehicles in China. A provincial level analysis. Appl. Econ. **53**(25), 2888–2904 (2021)
6. Li, J., Liang, M., Cheng, W., Wang, S.: Life cycle cost of conventional, battery electric, and fuel cell electric vehicles considering traffic and environmental policies in China. Int. J. Hydrog. Energy **46**(14), 9553–9566 (2021). https://doi.org/10.1016/j.ijhydene.2020.12.100
7. Graham, J.D., Belton, K.B., Xia, S.: How china beat the US in electric vehicle manufacturing. Iss. Sci. Technol. **37**(2), 72–79 (2021)
8. Zhou, M.: Characterizing the motivational mechanism behind taxi driver's adoption of electric vehicles for living: Insights from China. Transp. Res. Part A **144**, 134–152 (2021)
9. Hua, Z., Li, D., Guo, W.: A deep q-learning network based reinforcement strategy for smart city taxi cruising. In: Zhang, H., Yang, Z., Zhang, Z., Wu, Z., Hao, T. (eds.) NCAA 2021. CCIS, vol. 1449, pp. 59–70. Springer, Singapore (2021). https://doi.org/10.1007/978-981-16-5188-5_5
10. Wei, G., Lin, R., Jianping, L., Jiang, W., Wei, C.: The generalized dice similarity measures for probabilistic uncertain linguistic MAGDM and its application to location planning of electric vehicle charging stations. Int. J. Fuzzy Syst. **54**, 1–16 (2021). https://doi.org/10.1007/s40815-021-01084-z
11. Xiao, D., An, S., Cai, H., Wang, J., Cai, H.: An optimization model for electric vehicle charging infrastructure planning considering queuing behavior with finite queue length. J. Energy Stor. **29**, 101317 (2020). https://doi.org/10.1016/j.est.2020.101317
12. Huang, S., Kang, Z., Zenglin, X., Liu, Q.: Robust deep k-means: an effective and simple method for data clustering. Patt. Recog. **117**, 107996 (2021). https://doi.org/10.1016/j.patcog.2021.107996
13. Zhang, X., Yang, F.: Information guiding and sharing enhanced simultaneous heat transfer search and its application to k-means optimization. Appl. Soft Comput. **109**, 107476 (2021). https://doi.org/10.1016/j.asoc.2021.107476

Multi-feature Fusion Based Deep Forest for Hyperspectral Image Classification

Xiaobo Liu[1,2,3(✉)], Mostofa Zaman Mohammad[1,2,3], Chaochao Zhang[1,2,3], Xin Gong[1,2,3], and Zhihua Cai[4]

[1] School of Automation, China University of Geosciences, Wuhan 430074, China
xbliu@cug.edu.cn

[2] Hubei Key Laboratory of Advanced Control and Intelligent Automation for Complex Systems, Wuhan 430074, China

[3] Engineering Research Center of Intelligent Technology for Geo-Exploration, Ministry of Education, Wuhan 430074, China

[4] School of Computer Science, China University of Geosciences, Wuhan 430074, China

Abstract. Multi-feature fusion is a useful way to improve the classification of hyperspectral image (HSI). But the multi-feature fusion is usually at the decision level of classifier, which causes less link between features or poor extensibility of feature. In this paper, we propose a multi-feature fusion based deep forest method for HSI classification, named mfdForest. In mfdForest, the morphological features, saliency features, and edge features are extracted, then the three deep multi-grained scanning branches in dgcForest (one of improved deep forest) are used to extract and fuse the extracted features deeply, and the fused features are sent into cascade forest in dgcForest for classification. Experimental results indicate that the proposed framework consumes less training time and has better performance on two HSI data sets.

Keywords: Deep forest · Hyperspectral image classification · Multi-feature fusion

1 Introduction

Hyperspectral images (HSI) are widely used in many fields, such as agriculture, military, medicine, due to the rich information it contains [1–4]. The increase in spatial resolution and spectral resolution makes HSI contain more fine-grained feature information. As the amount of information increases, stronger feature extraction capabilities are needed, multi-feature extraction and fusion are proven to be an effective way to improve feature extraction [5–7].

To make full use of information contained in hyperspectral data, multi-feature based strategy has been widely applied to current popular method. He et al. [8] proposed a multi-scale 3D deep convolutional neural network to jointly learn both 2D multi-scale spatial feature and 1D spectral feature from HSI data in an end-to-end approach, achieved better results with large-scale data set. However, Deep Neural Network (DNN) is hard

© Springer Nature Singapore Pte Ltd. 2022
L. Pan et al. (Eds.): BIC-TA 2021, CCIS 1566, pp. 293–302, 2022.
https://doi.org/10.1007/978-981-19-1253-5_22

to fuse multi-feature obtained by different methods limited by the structure of neural network. Some methods use traditional extractor to extract multiple shallow features to improve utilization of HSI information by enhancing the diversity of features, such as Extended Morphological Profile (EMP), Gabor, Local Binary Patterns (LBP), Scale-invariant Feature Transform (SIFT), etc. [9–12]. Li et al. [13] used linear divergence analysis (LDA) to extract spectral features, and adaptive weighted filters (AWFs) to extract spatial information. After multiple iterations, they were fused with LBP features. The experimental results proved that the method can extract feature information further effectively. Zhang et al. [14] used Principal Component Analysis (PCA), Extended morphological profile (EMP), Differential Morphological Profiles (DMP), and Gabor filters to extract different features, and used Support Vector Machine (SVM) and Gabor filters for fusion and classification, achieved good performance. The aforementioned methods combine traditional feature extractor and extracted features have no ability to present well. Liu et al. [15] firstly extracted EMP features from HSI that was reduced by PCA, and then extracted Boolean Map based Saliency (BMS) visual features and fused them. While data redundancy is reduced, feature extraction is improved. However, BMS can not extract edge information well due to the less focus on edge of object. The above methods do not fully extract the spatial features.

After multi-feature extraction provides guarantee for HSI classification, the use of high-performance classifiers is also crucial in HSI classification. Deep forest is a new deep model of the alternative DNN proposed by Zhou et al. [11]. The deep forest used non-differentiable modules to build deep model, and the modules can be decision trees, random forest, et al. As the deep forest inherits the advantages of decision-tree ensemble approach, with fewer hyper-parameters than deep neural networks, and its model complexity can be automatically determined in a data-dependent way. The deep forest includes multi-grained scanning and cascade forest, the multi-grained scanning further enhanced the representational learning ability, potentially enabling deep forest to be contextually or structurally aware; the cascade levels can be automatically determined such that the model complexity can be determined in a data-dependent way. Yin et al. [12] applied deep forest to HSI classification, making it possible for deep forest to be used for HSI classification. Liu et al. [13] proposed a deep multi-grained scanning cascade forest (dgcForest), and improved the deep forest to make it more suitable for HSI classification by deep multi-grained scanning. But the dgcForest extracts features just using different sizes of sliding windows, not making full use of spatial information on HSI.

Extended morphological profile (EMP) is a simple and commonly used feature map method that can denoise images [19]. Saliency detection can highlight the spatial scene features [20]. However, saliency detection will weaken the boundary information of each area in HSI. Edge detection can detect the edge feature of feature map, which makes up for the deficiency of saliency detection. Thus, the combination of three features has a certain rationality.

In this paper, we proposed a multi-feature fusion based deep forest method for HSI classification. The main contributions of this paper are summarized as follows.

1) Three deep multi-grained scanning branches in dgcForest were used to deeply extract EMP features, saliency features and edge features, which can supplement each other, to make full use of spatial information of HSI.

2) In order to enhance features, voting fusion method was used to fuse three deeply extracted features, which can make the link between features closer than decision-level fusion method.

2 Proposed Method

Reasonable multi-feature selection, efficient multi-feature extraction and fusion are essential for promoting HSI classification. In this part, a novel framework is proposed to extract multiple complementary features in depth and fuse them effectively to improve the classification of HSI. The framework is shown in Fig. 1. Firstly, in order to decrease the redundancy of HSI in the spectral channel, PCA is introduced. Secondly, following the role played by EMP and Visual Saliency Detection (VSD) in previous studies, EMP operation is used on the global PCA image to remove the noise and smooth the image. And then VSD is used on EMP image to extract the more salient information, thereby reducing the impact of irrelevant background on HSI classification. However, VSD is difficult to detect the edge of ground objects, which will cut down the classification of pixels in the edge area. Therefore, edge detection (ED) is introduced to compensate for the loss of edge information caused by VSD, which is used to determine the edge by detecting the dramatic changes in the gray value around the pixel and calculating the reciprocal of the gray value change, and locate the edge by detecting the dramatic changes in the gray value around the pixel, that is, calculating the reciprocal of the gray value change. In the process of extracting edge information from EMP images, first, the EMP feature map is denoised by Gaussian blur. Second, a discrete differential operator called the Sobel operator is used to calculate the approximate gradient of the image, and Non-Maximum Suppression (NMS) is used to obtain the point with the largest gradient. Finally, the edge point is obtained by setting the threshold, and the edge maps are obtained by calculating all the edge points. The calculation process is shown in Eq. 1.

$$\begin{cases} C(E) = DUAL\_THRESHOLD\big(NMS\big(G_f\big)\big) \\ G_f = \big(arctan\big(\frac{G_x}{G_y}\big), \sqrt{G_x^2 + G_y^2} \\ G_x, G_y = \frac{\partial f}{\partial x}, \frac{\partial f}{\partial y} \end{cases} \tag{1}$$

In the Eq. 1, $C(E)$ represents the operation of edge detection on the EMP feature map, DUAL_THRESHOLD indicates dual threshold filtering in CED, NMS is non-maximum suppression, G_f is the gradient of the pixel (x, y), including the horizontal gradient G_f and the vertical gradient G_f.

Although VSD and ED can extract semantic features, which is high-level feature compared to texture features. But in the face of HSI, traditional methods are difficult to extract enough useful information. To extract multi-feature effectively, our proposed method uses the efficient feature extractor of dgcForest, deep multi-grain scanning, to extract these three features separately. Firstly, each pixel of HSI is set as the center pixel and the sub-block is obtained by choosing a neighbor region of this pixel with size of $(2 * w - 1)*(2 * w - 1)$, where w and l is the size and step length of multi-grained scanning window of dgcForest, which ensures that each neighbor region obtained by deep multi-grained scanning contains the central pixel uniquely. Next, these sub-pixels blocks containing global spatial and local spatial information are input in deep multi-grained scanning, and three multi-grained scanning will output three class probability vectors in parallel (random forest, the core component of deep multi-grain scanning, can output a probability vector of class that this sample belongs to). Then, the three feature vectors are simply added to obtain the final deep feature vector containing global and local information. Finally, the fused vector was sent into cascade forest to obtain final prediction.

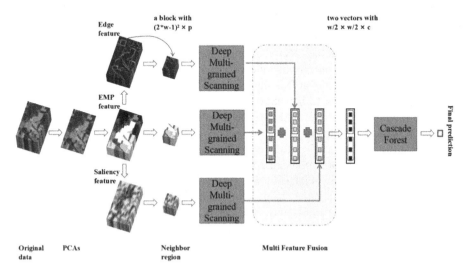

Fig. 1. The flowchart of our proposed method: mfdForest.

3   Experimental Results

This section presents the classification accuracy of several states-of-the-art methods and three cases that our method used different types of features. The performance of our proposed algorithm will be demonstrated through extensive experiments on two well-known HSI datasets, using three evaluative metrics including average accuracy (AA), overall accuracy (OA) and Kappa coefficient (Kappa). 10% of each category is selected as the training set on the two datasets, and the rest data as testing data, which are described in Table 1. The effects of several contributions of the proposed approach also be summarized in this section. All experiments were implemented on ubuntu16.04, with the CPU of Xeon E5-1603 and GPU of GeForce RTX1080Ti.

Table 1. The detail of two data sets.

Data set	Class	Pixel	Band	Resolution	Sample
Indian Pine	16	145*145	200	20 m	10249
Salinas	16	512*217	200	3.7 m	43980

To ensure the validity of the experiment, the parameters involved in our methods are consistent with comparative methods: ACGAN [18], ResNet [19], dgcForest [14]. The parameters involved are number of PCA, the number of morphological opening and closing operations on EMP, the size of neighbor region in dgcForest, the number of decision tree in random forest and completely random forest, the number of random forest and completely random forest in deep multi-grained scanning and cascade forest. In order to ensure the consistency of the experiment, the above parameters are set to the same. It's just that the layer of cascading forest is increased to 2. Table 2 shows the parameters setting. The number of features selected through the first layer of the cascading forest will be different according to the datasets. Except for the experiment about selecting the different number of features, other experiments uniformly use the optimal number corresponding to the datasets.

Table 2. Parameters setting of proposed method.

	PCA	3
Multi-feature extraction branches	Number of morphological opening and closing operations	4
	Neighbor region size	7
	Number of Random Forest	1
	Number of Completely Random Forest	1
	Number of Decision Tree	40
	Number of k-Fold Cross-Validation	5
Cascade Forest	Number of Levels	1
	Number of Random Forest	4
	Number of Completely Random Forest	4
	Number of Decision Tree	80

In order to evaluate the contribution of edge detection, two sets of experiments are prepared. It can be seen from in Fig. 2, Fig. 3, Table 3, Table 4, that the addition of feature extraction branches improves OA, AA, and KAPPA on three datasets. The EMP, EMP + Saliency, mfdForest means that our algorithm uses different type of feature extraction branch, the EMP just uses extended morphological profile feature for mfdForest, the EMP + Saliency uses extended morphological profile and Boolean Map Saliency Detection features for mfdForest, mfdForest uses extended morphological profile, Boolean Map Saliency Detection, and edge detection features together.

In Fig. 2 and Fig. 3, our algorithm has a better performance than other methods in OA in two data sets. Although our method has a lower accuracy than ResNet when using less than three branches in Indian Pines data set, but three branches can still have a best performance. What's more, in the case of our method using different number of extraction branches, the accuracy was increased with more branches. As can be seen from Table 3 and Table 4, with the addition of the morphological features, saliency features, and edge features extracted, the classification accuracy increases. It shows that each feature we chosen and feature fusion method we used has played a significant role. In Table 3 and Table 4, our method also has superiority in OA, AA and Kappa comparing to other methods, and AA has a subtle change in the case of using two extraction branches in Indian Pines data set. It shows that saliency detection hasn't improve classification in some classes, which is the point we need to solve later.

In terms of running time in Table 3 and Table 4, which is the total time of training and testing, although our improved algorithm is slower than dgcForest, the reduction in speed has not been presented as multiple, the accuracy of both is higher than the dgcForest, indicating that the three extracted features can improve the classification accuracy and complement each other.

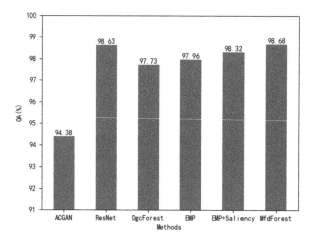

Fig. 2. OA of different methods in Indian Pines

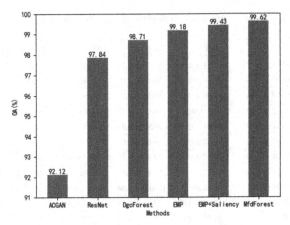

Fig. 3. OA of different methods in Salinas.

Table 3. Accuracy comparison of different algorithms in Indian Pines datasets.

Method	ACGAN	ResNet	DgcForest	EMP	EMP + Saliency	mfdForest
OA	94.38 ± 1.88	98.63 ± 0.25	97.73 ± 0.23	97.96 ± 0.3	98.32 ± 0.14	**98.68 ± 0.15**
AA	76.29 ± 3.28	90.33 ± 0.29	95.92 ± 0.51	94.62 ± 2.62	94.59 ± 2.02	**96.8 ± 1.54**
K*100	93.58 ± 2.15	98.44 ± 0.28	97.41 ± 0.18	96.23 ± 0.77	97.37 ± 1.01	**98.55 ± 0.71**
1	57.14 ± 46.78	**100.00 ± 0.00**	89.63 ± 2.30	96.97 ± 2.93	96.10 ± 1.95	97.56 ± 1.95
2	90.41 ± 4.26	**98.81 ± 00.46**	96.58 ± 0.66	96.45 ± 0.91	97.70 ± 0.92	98.44 ± 0.69
3	**99.41 ± 0.40**	98.35 ± 1.33	96.32 ± 0.90	96.78 ± 2.05	98.39 ± 1.14	97.72 ± 1.75
4	91.97 ± 1.58	98.64 ± 1.92	**99.06 ± 0.39**	95.21 ± 1.44	97.84 ± 0.97	98.6 ± 1.25
5	97.11 ± 1.46	98.06 ± 1.81	94.08 ± 0.51	96.14 ± 2.30	96.05 ± 1.88	**98.39 ± 2.13**
6	98.32 ± 0.60	98.59 ± 1.29	**99.32 ± 0.25**	98.6 ± 1.07	98.00 ± 1.32	99.09 ± 0.86
7	20.00 ± 40.00	66.67 ± 27.14	84.00 ± 1.73	67.2 ± 19.82	64.8 ± 14.4	**90.00 ± 13.24**
8	94.82 ± 2.94	99.39 ± 00.54	**99.88 ± 0.10**	99.81 ± 0.17	99.67 ± 0.35	99.07 ± 0.35
9	0.00 ± 0.00	0.00 ± 0.00	94.44 ± 0.00	85.56 ± 20.96	81.11 ± 19.12	**99.53 ± 0.16**
10	93.88 ± 2.50	97.34 ± 2.31	96.46 ± 0.09	97.17 ± 1.00	97.44 ± 1.17	**97.49 ± 0.06**
11	98.94 ± 0.97	98.87 ± 0.28	98.89 ± 0.24	99.24 ± 0.88	99.15 ± 0.61	**99.82 ± 0.17**
12	82.54 ± 29.04	**99.56 ± 0.09**	96.86 ± 0.07	97.45 ± 1.14	98.84 ± 0.89	98.13 ± 0.32
13	97.61 ± 2.96	97.78 ± 2.14	98.38 ± 0.00	98.6 ± 1.21	98.27 ± 0.99	**98.92 ± 1.00**
14	98.64 ± 0.41	99.24 ± 0.22	99.60 ± 0.16	**99.82 ± 0.12**	99.75 ± 0.23	99.74 ± 0.13
15	**99.78 ± 0.20**	98.19 ± 1.11	99.50 ± 0.36	99.77 ± 0.16	99.42 ± 0.73	97.7 ± 0.90
16	0.00 ± 0.00	95.86 ± 2.96	91.67 ± 0.00	90.00 ± 11.82	90.95 ± 8.54	**98.96 ± 0.96**
Running time(s)	836.15	923.48	**94.6**	114.37	139.93	152.11

Table 4. Accuracy comparison of different algorithms in Salinas datasets.

Method	ACGAN	ResNet	DgcForest	EMP	EMP + Saliency	mfdForest
OA	92.12 ± 1.42	97.84 ± 0.12	98.71 ± 0.11	99.18 ± 0.22	99.43 ± 0.28	**99.62 ± 0.21**
AA	86.59 ± 2.96	98.63 ± 0.27	98.63 ± 0.09	99.18 ± 0.28	99.43 ± 0.49	**99.62 ± 0.32**
K*100	86.59 ± 2.96	97.59 ± 0.13	98.68 ± 0.12	99.09 ± 0.33	99.36 ± 0.24	**99.57 ± 0.15**
1	91.18 ± 1.59	100.0 ± 0.00	98.96 ± 0.12	99.8 ± 0.12	98.53 ± 0.15	**100.00 ± 0.00**
2	44.71 ± 37.94	99.94 ± 0.05	**99.99 ± 0.03**	99.78 ± 0.6	99.38 ± 0.31	99.87 ± 0.13
3	96.00 ± 4.38	99.22 ± 0.01	98.60 ± 0.61	99.3 ± 1.39	98.8 ± 1.01	**100.00 ± 0.00**
4	95.02 ± 2.70	99.22 ± 0.01	97.86 ± 0.14	99.25 ± 0.19	98.57 ± 0.17	**99.28 ± 0.53**
5	32.29 ± 39.59	99.17 ± 0.22	**99.87 ± 0.09**	97.9 ± 1.96	99.44 ± 0.26	99.48 ± 0.49
6	94.38 ± 1.62	99.78 ± 0.07	**100.00 ± 0.00**	99.32 ± 0.25	99.42 ± 0.4	99.87 ± 0.12
7	95.15 ± 3.89	**99.98 ± 0.03**	95.98 ± 0.03	99.83 ± 0.11	99.83 ± 0.14	99.89 ± 0.01
8	97.58 ± 2.02	**99.77 ± 0.27**	98.55 ± 0.15	98.92 ± 0.12	99.52 ± 0.1	99.36 ± 0.19
9	97.16 ± 1.68	96.63 ± 0.21	97.99 ± 0.03	99.51 ± 0.29	**99.87 ± 0.22**	99.65 ± 0.27
10	98.06 ± 1.25	99.73 ± 0.05	98.88 ± 0.13	98.57 ± 1.08	99.69 ± 0.13	**100.00 ± 0.00**
11	98.61 ± 0.96	99.15 ± 0.27	97.77 ± 0.35	99.62 ± 0.2	99.25 ± 0.44	**100.00 ± 0.00**
12	94.33 ± 6.11	96.24 ± 2.09	97.74 ± 0.34	99.69 ± 0.27	**100.00 ± 0.00**	99.84 ± 0.13
13	99.22 ± 0.70	98.84 ± 1.13	98.71 ± 0.29	**100.00 ± 0.0**	**100.00 ± 0.00**	98.68 ± 0.21
14	90.50 ± 4.79	**99.16 ± 0.91**	98.50 ± 0.71	97.59 ± 3.28	98.33 ± 1.37	98.61 ± 0.05
15	73.42 ± 36.72	91.72 ± 0.42	99.07 ± 0.63	99.04 ± 0.35	99.12 ± 0.28	**99.56 ± 0.23**
16	94.21 ± 5.26	**100.0 ± 0.00**	97.92 ± 0.12	99.28 ± 0.16	99.61 ± 0.31	99.34 ± 0.32
Running time(s)	1020.11	1861.4	368.9	437.21	472.98	531.29

4 Conclusion

In this paper, we introduce a multi-feature fusion based deep forest to extract and fuse three feature maps of the HSI for improving classification accuracy. For a certain pixel, even the classification improved by certain feature map is not good, but one of the other two features may have a better effect, so it can work together for each pixel to get the best results. Although we use three branches to increase the size of the model, which result in the running time longer than dgcForest. This problem can be solved by parallel computing, and we will set three branches of mfdForest in parallel in the future work.

Acknowledgement. This work was supported by National Nature Science Foundation of China (Grant Nos. 61973285, 62076226, 61873249).

References

1. Tang, Y., et al.: Apple bruise grading using piecewise nonlinear curve fitting for hyperspectral imaging data. IEEE Access **8**, 147494–147506 (2020)
2. Shimoni, M., Haelterman, R., Perneel, C.: Hypersectral imaging for military and security applications: combining myriad processing and sensing techniques. IEEE Geosci. Remote Sens. Mag. **7**(2), 101–117 (2019)

3. Pike, R., Lu, G., Wang, D., Chen, Z.G., Fei, B.: A Minimum spanning forest-based method for noninvasive cancer detection with hyperspectral imaging. IEEE Trans. Biomed. Eng. **63**(3), 653–663 (2016)
4. Zhang, L., Zhang, L., Du, B.: Deep learning for remote sensing data: a technical tutorial on the state of the art. IEEE Geosci. Remote Sens. **4**(2), 22–40 (2016)
5. Yang, C., Li, Y., Peng, B., Cheng Y., Tong, L.: Road material information extraction based on multi-feature fusion of remote sensing image. In: 2019 IEEE International Geoscience and Remote Sensing Symposium (IGARSS). pp. 3943–3946, IEEE (2019)
6. Lu, J., Ma, C., Zhou, Y., Luo, M., Zhang, K.: Multi-feature fusion for enhancing image similarity learning. IEEE Access **7**, 167547–167556 (2019)
7. Zhao, S., Nie, W., Zhang, B.: Multi-feature fusion using collaborative residual for hyperspectral palmprint recognition. In: 2018 IEEE 4th International Conference on Computer and Communications (ICCC), Chengdu, China, pp. 1402–1406, IEEE (2018)
8. He, M., Li, B., Chen, H.: Multi-scale 3D deep convolutional neural network for hyperspectral image classification. In: 2017 IEEE International Conference on Image Processing (ICIP). pp. 3904–3908. IEEE (2018)
9. Gu, Y., Liu, T., Jia, X., et al.: Nonlinear multiple kernel learning with multiple-structure-element extended morphological profiles for hyperspectral image classification. IEEE Trans. Geosci. Remote Sens. **54**(6), 3235–3247 (2016)
10. Jia, S., Lin, Z., Deng, B., et al.: Cascade superpixel regularized gabor feature fusion for hyperspectral image classification. IEEE Trans. Neural Netw. Learn. Syst. **31**(5), 1638–1652 (2019)
11. Jia, S., Deng, B., Zhu, J., et al.: Local binary pattern-based hyperspectral image classification with superpixel guidance. IEEE Trans. Geosci. Remote Sens. **56**(2), 749–759 (2017)
12. He, Z., Li, J., Liu, K., et al.: Kernel low-rank multitask learning in variational mode decomposition domain for multi-hyperspectral classification. IEEE Trans. Geosci. Remote Sens. **56**(7), 4193–4208 (2018)
13. Li, F., Wang, J., Lan, R., et al.: Hyperspectral image classification using multi-feature fusion. Opt. Laser Technol. **110**, 176–183 (2019)
14. Zhang, C., Han, M., Xu, M.: Multi-feature classification of hyperspectral image via probabilistic SVM and guided filter. In: 2018 International Joint Conference on Neural Networks (IJCNN). pp. 1–7. IEEE (2018)
15. Liu, X., Yin, X., Cai, Y., et al.: Visual saliency-based extended morphological profiles for unsupervised feature learning of hyperspectral images. IEEE Geosci. Remote Sens. Lett. **17**(11), 1963–1967 (2019)
16. Zhou, Z., Feng, J.: Deep forest: towards an alternative to deep neural networks. In: 2017 International Joint Conference on Artificial Intelligence Organization (IGCAI). pp. 3553–3559
17. Yin, X., Wang, R. et al.: Deep forest-based classification of hyperspectral images. In: Chinese Control Conference, pp. 10367–10372, IEEE (2018)
18. Liu, X., Wang, R., Cai, Z., et al.: Deep multigrained cascade forest for hyperspectral image classification. IEEE Trans. Geosci. Remote Sens. **57**(10), 8169–8183 (2019). https://doi.org/10.1109/TGRS.2019.2918587
19. Luo, H., Tang, Y.Y., Yang, X., et al.: Autoencoder with extended morphological profile for hyperspectral image classification. In: 2017 IEEE International Conference on Cybernetics (CYBCONF). pp. 293–296. IEEE (2017)
20. Zhang, J., Sclaroff, S.: Saliency detection: a Boolean map approach. In: 2013 IEEE International Conference on Computer Vision (ICCV). pp. 153–160. IEEE (2013)
21. Guo, G., Neagu, D., Huang, X., Bi, Y.: An effective combination of multiple classifiers for toxicity prediction. In: Wang, L., Jiao, L., Shi, G., Li, X., Liu, J. (eds.) Fuzzy Systems and

Knowledge Discovery, pp. 481–490. Springer Berlin Heidelberg, Berlin, Heidelberg (2006). https://doi.org/10.1007/11881599_56

22. Zhu, L., Chen, Y., Ghamisi, P., Benediktsson, J.A.: Generative adversarial networks for hyperspectral image classification. IEEE Trans. Geosci. Remote Sens. **56**(9), 5046–5063 (2018)

23. Zhong, Z., Li, J., Luo, Z., Chapman, M.: Spectral-spatial residual network for hyperspectral image classification: A 3-D deep learning framework. IEEE Trans. Geosci. Remote Sens. **56**(2), 847–858 (2018)

Pulse Wave Recognition of Pregnancy at Three Stages Based on 1D CNN and GRU

Nan Li[1], Jiarui Yu[1], Xiaobo Mao[1(✉)], Pengyuan Zheng[3], Liguo Li[3], and Luqi Huang[1,2(✉)]

[1] School of Electrical Engineering, Zhengzhou University, Zhengzhou 450001, China
810920179@qq.com, 670993930@qq.com
[2] China Academy of Chinese Medical Sciences, Beijing 100020, China
[3] The Fifth Affiliated Hospital of Zhengzhou University, Zhengzhou 450001, China

Abstract. The aim of the present study is to achieve the discrimination of pulse at each stage of pregnancy by 1D convolutional neural network (1D CNN) and gated recurrent unit(GRU) classifier. Firstly, the pulse signals of Chi acquisition position were collected from 160 healthy pregnancy women. Secondly, a new deep learning classifier was proposed by combining 1D CNN and GRU technologies for pulse classification that learns the representation directly from the wave signal. Finally, the classifier proposed is used to classify the pregnancy pulse at three stages of pregnancy. The classifier proposed combines the advantages of CNN and GRU, which greatly improve the accuracy of pregnancy pulse identification. The classification accuracy of three stages of pregnancy pulse achieved satisfactory accuracy of 85%, 88% and 86%, respectively. Furthermore, the average sensitivity, precision and F1-score can reach 88.18%, 86.25% and 87.42%, respectively. The experiment results demonstrated that the method has a good recognition effect and promoted the objective development of TCM.

Keywords: TCM · Pregnancy pulse · 1D CNN · GRU

1 Introduction

Pulse diagnosis is an important part of Traditional Chinese medicine(TCM) method and has a history of thousands of years [1–3]. TCM doctors take the patient's wrist with their index finger, middle finger and ring finger. Based on the touch of fingertips, doctors can judge the patient's physiological condition [4]. As one of the four diagnostic methods in TCM, pulse diagnosis, does take on special significance, which reflect the functional and physiological activities of the visceral and cardiovascular, including relationships among organ groupings [5,6].

Supported by national key R&D program of China (2020YFC2006100) and key project at central government level: the ability establishment of sustainable use for valuable Chinese medicine resources (2060302-2101-16).

TCM has used pulse feeling to diagnose pregnancy for thousands of years and accumulated rich clinical experience [7,8]. Pregnancy is usually divided into three stages, namely early stage(E), middle stage(M) and late stage(L) three stages according to gestational age (9–14 weeks; 20–28 weeks; 32–37 weeks). Usually, pregnant women have profound physiological changes in the cardiovascular system during pregnancy. It starts in E stage of pregnancy, reaches its peak in the M stage of pregnancy, and peaking again around full term [9–11]. In particular, these changes will affect different organs of pregnant women, including cardiovascular, blood, metabolism, kidney and respiratory system, and have different effects on pregnancy pulse with different gestational periods.

From the perspective of TCM, the pulse shape during pregnancy, including rhythm, wave amplitude and arterial pulse speed etc., which can be used to reflect the physiological and pathological changes of pregnant women [12,13]. In the three stages of pregnancy, there will be obvious differences in the wrist pulse of pregnant women due to the changes of organ system. Therefore, the pulse of study in each pregnancy period will help us to identify abnormal pregnancy changes. Experienced and famous traditional Chinese medicine can even determine the sex, development and health status of the fetus through the pregnancy pulse, and give rational treatment [14,15]. However, it takes a long time to master pulse diagnosis and is considered to be a problem of subjective experience by western medicine. Thus, how to recognize and judge different pregnancy pulse with a more objective and accurate method has been a long time challenge.

With the rapid development of artificial intelligence (AI), the combination of TCM and AI to realize intelligent diagnosis of TCM has become a hot spot in the reform of TCM. Especially combined with AI technology, such as deep learning [16], decision tree [17] and convolutional neural network [18], etc., it has become a new diagnostic method of TCM. Fortunately, the method of intelligent diagnosis of TCM has been widely used, and many useful achievements have been made during this period. Chen et al. extracted the time-domain and energy characteristics of pulse wave by using time-frequency analysis method, and constructed BP neural network to distinguish different pulse conditions, and achieved good results [19]. Huang et al. explored the correlation between PPW and pregnancy through deep learning technology, and the calculation method showed that the accuracy of PPW in detecting pregnancy was 84%, and the area under the curve (AUC) was 91% [20]. Mao proposed a one-dimensional convolutional neural network (1D CNN) model with transmission block. The network structure can be used to distinguish pregnant pulse from normal pulse, and the classification accuracy is 97% [21]. Zhang et al. studied the changes of radial artery pulse and photoelectric volume pulse (PPG) pulse waveform with gestational age in normal pregnant women. They measured pulse waveforms in each trimester of pregnancy and extracted and calculated three pulse features [22]. Li studied the correlation and difference of pulse acquisition location and found that the difference of the three parts is mainly reflected in the time-frequency domain and power spectrum [23]. Liu et al. proposed a new and effective classification method of wrist pulse blood flow signals, which combined multiple features with multi-core learning (MKL) algorithm for classification [24]. Lu et al. used four algorithms of machine learning to analyze digital pulse wave form signal for recognition of pregnancy [25]. Shi et al. systematically reviewed the development of TCM intelligence, summarized the bottlenecks and shortcomings of TCM development, and put forward the future development direction [26]. Due to the rapid development of computer technology and deep learning, the reform of TCM has been accelerated, which contribute to the inheritance and development of TCM [27,28].

However, most studies focused on the characteristics and morphology of pulse in the past, few works have focused on the analysis of pulse distinguish in different stages of pregnancy. As a matter of fact, there is a strong relationship and difference among the three trimesters. To identify the three trimesters of pregnancy pulse effectively can help us better understand the working state and external connection of pregnancy. To the best of our knowledge, the research on pulse of pregnancy identification problem is still open and remains challenging.

Motivated by the previous works, the discrimination of pulse at each stage of pregnancy was studied by the combination of CNN and gated recurrent unit(GRU) classifier. Firstly, the pulse signals of Chi position were collected from 160 healthy pregnancy women, which the number of women in the three stages are 50, 60, 50, respectively. Secondly, a new deep learning classifier by combining the technical advantages of GRU and CNN for pulse classification that learns the representation directly from the wave signal. Finally, the proposed classifier is used to classify the pulse in three stages of pregnancy.

The remainder of the paper is organized as follows. In Sect. 2, some introductions about pulse data collection and processing work are given. In Sect. 3, the methods designed and the network model are described in detail. In Sect. 4, the obtained results and analysis are given. Finally, we briefly outline the conclusions drawn from this study, which in turn serve as the basis for future work in Sect. 5.

2   Subjects and Methods

2.1   Volunteer Recruitment and Data Acquisition

For this study, pulse waveform recordings were available from 160 volunteers at the Affiliated Obstetrics and Gynecology Hospital of Fudan University, who were divided into three trimesters of pregnancy. The demographics of the group are provided in Table 1. During the examination, the volunteers were instructed to follow the standard. The research received the ethics approval from the Affiliated Obstetrics and Gynecology Hospital of Fudan University.

The wrist pulse measurements were performed in a quiet clinical measurement room at the Affiliated Obstetrics and Gynecology Hospital of Fudan University, Shanghai, China. In order to ensure the data quality, all pregnant women were required to rest quietly for 5 min and collect pulse after reaching a stable heart rate. The pressure sensor of TZ-2 data acquisition instrument was fixed

Table 1. Subjects index

Variable	Statistic
Amount(n)	160 (E = 50, M = 60, L = 50)
Age (year)	28.4 ± 3.5
Height (cm)	166.2 ± 6.4
Weight (kg)	64.3 ± 8.7
BMI (kg/m^2)	22.4 ± 3.8

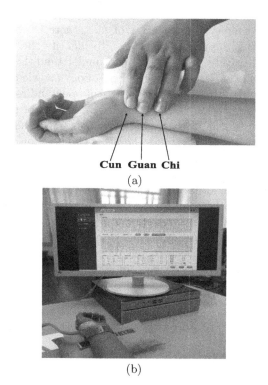

Cun Guan Chi
(a)

(b)

Fig. 1. The pulse acquisition.

to Chi position of the left wrist, and the radial pulse was recorded for 3 min by applying continuous pressure. The waveform acquisition is shown in Fig. 1.

2.2 Pulse Data Pre-processing

In order to optimize the performance of the proposed model, it is necessary to preprocess the original data. Data pre-processing mainly includes the following two aspects.

(a) Wavelet denoise and Baseline removed

The pulse signal will inevitably be polluted by the subjects' breathing, artifact movement and other factors in the process of pulse acquisition. Therefore, preprocessing is the key to reduce noise and eliminate baseline drift of pulse waveform before further analysis. In this paper, a robust signal preprocessing framework and a cascade adaptive filter based on wavelet were used to denoise and remove baseline drift, respectively. The original pulse wave and pulse wave preprocessed are shown in Fig. 2.

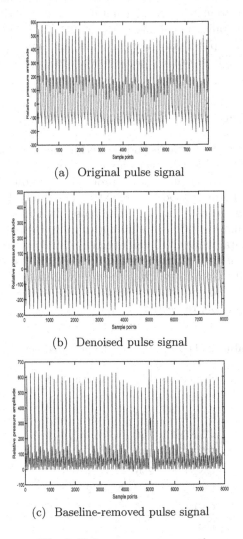

(a) Original pulse signal

(b) Denoised pulse signal

(c) Baseline-removed pulse signal

Fig. 2. Pulse wave preprocessed.

(b) Normalization

Data normalization processing is a basic work of data mining. After the original data is normalization, all indicators are in the same order of magnitude, which is suitable for comprehensive comparison and evaluation.

2.3 Data Augmentation

Data amplification is the process of not actually adding to the original data, but simply making changes to the original data to create more data. The purpose of data amplification is to increase the amount of data, enrich the diversity of data and improve the generalization ability of the model. By augmenting the original data, 7650 pregnancy pulse data were included in the early, middle and late stages, respectively. These original pulse waves are used as analysis sequences for pulse analysis.

3   The Architecture of Proposed Model

This section describes the methods and the techniques used in the present work in detail. Because the pulse signal is a one-dimensional time series, the proposed network model needs to be suitable for processing one-dimensional data. The model should not only have good feature extraction ability, but also reconstruct the pulse waveform, so as to analyze the pulse data as accurately as possible. Generally speaking, CNN can automatically extract features and process high-dimensional data, while GRU can effectively analyze time series data. The network structures of the proposed model are shown in Table 2. CNN(ith/jth) represent the ith/jth CNN network, respectively. Among these eight convolutional structures, the number of convolutional kernels at 8 layers is 32, 32, 64, 64, 128, 128, 256 and 256, respectively.

Table 2. The structure of the proposed network.

Structures	Filters	Length	Stride
Input		748 * 1	1
CNN1/2	32	9 * 1	1
CNN3/4	64	3 * 1	1
CNN5/6	128	3 * 1	1
CNN7/8	256	3 * 1	1
Pool		2 * 2	1
GRU		1 * 748	1
Dense		96	1
Softmax		5	1

3.1   Description of the CNN Module

Considering that pulse signals are all time series, the 1D CNN structure can effectively extract the features of the original pulse signals. Therefore, the 1D CNN model is used to carry out convolution layer and filter layer functions, features extraction, as is shown in Fig. 3.

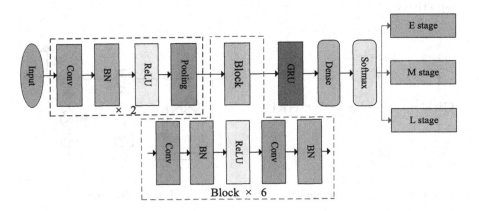

Fig. 3. The architecture of proposed model.

The forward extraction model, which consists of convolution layer, normalization (BN) operation layer, a rectified linear unit (ReLU) and pooling layer, are used for feature extraction of pulse data. By trying different number of feature extraction blocks, it is found that too many or too few feature modules will lead to feature redundancy or lack of feature, which directly affects the classification effect. In order to improve the classification accuracy, six feature extraction modules were superimposed to form the backbone of the model, and the extracted features were further processed to achieve the best classification effect. Furthermore, each block was mixed ReLU and BN in the operation process. The pulse characteristics of the backbone module are sent to the GRU module for processing, and finally classified by Dense and Softmax layer. The 1D CNN layer can be described by the following equation,

$$x_k^l = f(\sum_{i \in M_k} x_i^{l-1} \omega_{ik} + b_k) \tag{1}$$

where M_k is defined as the effective range of the convolution kernel, x_k^l and b_k represent input and bias of the kth neuron at layer l, respectively. ω_{ik} is the kernel from the ith neurons at layer l to the kth neurons at layer $l-1$, $f(*)$ is the ReLU activation function. The structure of the proposed CNN module is shown in Table 2.

3.2   Description of the GRU Module

GRU is a variant of LSTM, which is a model that maintains the LSTM effect, has simpler structure, fewer parameters and better convergence. Compared with LSTM, GRU has only two gates: update gate(z_t) and reset gate(r_t). GRU can save a lot of time in the case of large training data, and avoids the disappearance of the gradient. Figure 4 and Fig. 5 are GRU network model and unit, respectively.

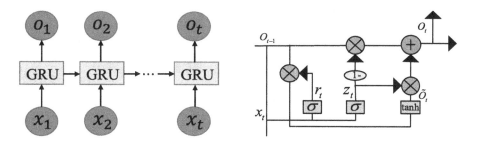

Fig. 4. GRU network model.   **Fig. 5.** GRU unit.

$$r_t = \delta(W_{xr}^T x_t + W_{or}^T o_{t-1} + b_r) \tag{2}$$

$$z_t = \delta(W_{xz}^T x_t + W_{oz}^T o_{t-1} + b_z) \tag{3}$$

$$\widetilde{o}_t = tanh(W_x^T x_{\widetilde{o}} + W_{o\widetilde{o}}^T(r_t \otimes o_{t-1}) + b_{\widetilde{o}}) \tag{4}$$

$$o_t = z_t \otimes o_{t-1} + (1 - z_t) \otimes \widetilde{o}_t \tag{5}$$

where $W_{xr}, W_{xz}, W_{x\widetilde{o}}$ are the weight matrix of the corresponding vector, $W_{or}, W_{oz}, W_{o\widetilde{o}}$ are the weight matrix of the $t-1$ moment, and $b_r, b_r, b_{\widetilde{o}}$ represent the deviation, respectively. GRU network are connected behind the Block unit composed of CNN network, which realize the characteristic processing of the output data of Block unit, as show in Fig. 3.

3.3   Loss Function

The loss function a function that maps the value of a random event or its related random variables to a non negative real number to represent the risk or loss of the random event. In application, the loss function is usually associated with the optimization problem as a learning criterion, that is, the model is solved and evaluated by minimizing the loss function. The cross entropy loss function is a smooth function. Its essence is the application of cross entropy in information theory in classification problems. In this work, the cross-entropy function is selected as the cost function. The formula is as follows,

$$L = -\frac{1}{N}[y_n log(\hat{y}) + (1 - y)log(1 - \hat{y})] \tag{6}$$

where L represents the total cost, N is the number of training data, y_n is the expected output and $\hat{y}$ is the actual output generated by the network.

4   Results

In our experiment, we adopt CNN and GRU to classify the three stages of pregnancy pulse.

4.1   Set Up

The data set was randomly split into a ratio of 8:2, i i.e., 80% for training, and 20% for testing. This experimental scheme is implemented through Python coding, and the framework used is Keras framework. The experiment environment was set up on an Intel i9-10900 3.10 GHz CPU, the GPU was NVIDIA GeForce GTX1050 and 32G.

4.2   Evaluation

In this paper, pulse data were used for both training and performance evaluation. The four commonly used performance indicators: F1 score, accuracy, precision and recall, which are adopted to evaluate the diagnostic performance by 4-fold cross validation. The four indicators are defined as Eqs.

$$Accuracy, ACC = \frac{TP + TN}{(TP + TN) + (FP + FN)} \times 100\% \tag{7}$$

$$Recall\ or\ Sensitivity, SEN = \frac{TP}{TP + FN} \times 100\% \tag{8}$$

$$Precision, PRE = \frac{TP}{TP + FP} \times 100\% \tag{9}$$

$$F1 - score = \frac{2Precision \cdot Recall}{Precision + Recall} \tag{10}$$

where, TP is the number of positive training data are evaluated as positive, TN is the number of activities correctly predicted to be negative, FP is the classification result where negative training data are evaluated as positive, and FN Is the classification result that evaluates positive training data as negative. $F1$-score is the harmonic mean of accuracy and recall, with a maximum of 1 and a minimum of 0. Obviously, the higher the recall and precision results, the greater the F1 score.

4.3   Experiment

In this section, the 1D CNN and GRU structure proposed will be comprehensively evaluated efficiency and performance when performing pregnancy pulse classification tasks, using a balanced data set containing data amplification strategies. In order to find the most suitable classification model, 5 kinds of 1D CNN structures were used for evaluation. The 5 kinds of 1D CNN layer are 4, 5, 6, 7, and 8 respectively. The Table 3 shows the classification accuracy of each structure. As can be seen from Table 3, when the number of 1D CNN layers increases, the accuracy of classification also increases. When the number of 1D CNN layers is 6, the classification accuracy is maximum. After that, with the increase of the number of 1D CNN layers, the accuracy of classification decreased. This phenomenon indicated that the classification results will be affected by the number of 1D CNN layer. Actually, when the 1D CNN layer deepens to a certain threshold, the performance of classifier is no longer strong and the training time will become longer. Therefore, six CNN layers were selected as the main structure of this experiment for pulse classification and discrimination.

Based on the results of the experiment, we found that the capability of the entire network model was significantly improved to recognize pregnancy pulse signals by applying the combined model of CNN and GRU. The confusion matrices and evaluation metrics for pulse discrimination with training and test data are presented in Fig. 6, Fig. 7 and Fig. 8, respectively. The confusion matrices mainly used to compare the classification results with the actual measured values, and the accuracy of the classification results can be displayed in a confusion matrix. It can be observed from Fig. 6 that, for the test data, the 1D CNN model can achieve 85% for E stage, 88% for M stage and 86% for L stage.

Table 3. Basic physiological data of the participants

CNN layers	4	5	6	7	8
Numbers	85.7%	85.9%	86.3%	85.5%	84.6%

For pregnancy pulse, we can observe the stable accuracy and loss values after 1500 iterations in Fig. 7 and Fig. 8, respectively. The accuracy and loss are obtained through different iterations. With the increase of iteration times, the accuracy is improved and the loss is reduced. The accuracy increases as

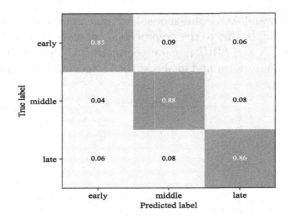

Fig. 6. Confusion matrix of the proposed model.

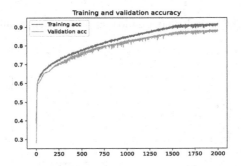

Fig. 7. Training and validation accuracy curve for each training epoch.

the number of iteration increases, and the loss decreases at the same time in a certain range. Figure 9 shows the receiver operating characteristic (ROC) curve of the model in this paper. It is a comprehensive index reflecting the continuous variables of sensitivity and specificity, and calculates a series of sensitivity and specificity. A curve was drawn with sensitivity as ordinate and specificity as abscissa. The larger the area under the curve(AUC), the higher the diagnostic accuracy. From the Fig. 9, we find that the AUC achieve 97% for E stage, 95% for M stage and 97% for L stage, respectively. In addition, $F1$-score was calculated and found that the pulse classification accuracy of the network structure in pulse can reach 90.61%, the average sensitivity, precision and F1-score are 88.18%, 86.25% and 87.42%, respectively.

4.4 Compared

Table 4 shows the comparison between the proposed method and the existing pulse classification methods in accuracy and ROC. Compared with the Chen et al.'s [20] and Lu et al.'s [25] proposed network whose performance are 84.7% and

83.9% in accuracy and AUC, ours model have much more in accuracy and AUC, respectively. It may be due to the preprocessing of waveform, and the combined network of 1DCNN and GRU is more conducive to the extraction of effective characteristics of waveform and analysis, thus achieving a better results.

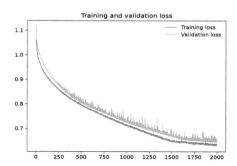

Fig. 8. Training and validation loss curve for each training epoch.

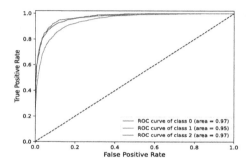

Fig. 9. ROC curve

Table 4. Basic physiological data of the participants

Work	Accuracy (%)	AUC (%)
Chen et al. [20]	84.7%	91%
Lu et al. [25]	83.9%	94%
Proposed model	**86.3%**	**96%**

5 Conclusion and Recommendations

This paper proposed a new classification method that introduces the advantage of 1D CNN and GRU into learning approach for pregnancy pulse. Conclusions are summarized as follows. Firstly, the pulse signals of Chi acquisition position were collected from healthy pregnancy. Secondly, the proposed 1D CNN model has been applied to classify the pregnancy pulse that learns the representation directly from the wave signal. Finally, the classification results show that the proposed network model has better ability of learning and feature extraction and shows significant advantages in the accuracy, the precision, and the recall etc. In the future, the improvement of the proposed model will be studied and further explore the scope of application.

Acknowledgments. We acknowledge the support of the Affiliated Obstetrics and Gynecology Hospital of Fudan University for the facilities and all volunteers for their collaboration. This work was supported by National Key R&D Program of China (2020YFC2006100) and Key Project at Central Government Level: The ability establishment of sustainable use for valuable Chinese medicine resources (2060302-2101-16).

Conflict of Interest. The authors declare that they have no conflicts of interest.

References

1. Wei, M., Chen, Z., Chen, G., et al.: A portable three-channel data collector for Chinese medicine pulses. Sens. Actuators A Phys. **323**(1), 112669 (2021)
2. Wu, H.K., Ko, Y.S., Lin, Y.S., Wu, H.T., Tsai, T.H., Chang, H.H.: The Correlation between pulse diagnosis and constitution identification in traditional Chinese medicine. Complement. Ther. Med. **30**, 107–112 (2017)
3. Velik, R.: An objective review of the technological developments for radial pulse diagnosis in traditional Chinese medicine. Eur. J. Integr. Med. **7**(4), 321–331 (2015)
4. Nie, J., Ji, M., Chu, Y., et al.: Human pulses reveal health conditions by a piezo-electret sensor via the approximate entropy analysis. Nano Energy **58**, 528–535 (2019)
5. Qiao, L., Qi, Z., Tu, L., et al.: The association of radial artery pulse wave variables with the pulse wave velocity and echocardiographic parameters in hypertension. Evid. Based Complement. Alter. Med. **2018**, 1–12 (2018)
6. Moura, N.G.R., Ferreira, A.S.: Pulse waveform analysis of Chinese pulse images and its association with disability in hypertension. J. Acupunct. Meridian Stud. **9**(2), 93–98 (2016)
7. Chen, H.Q., Zou, S.H., Yang, J.B., et al.: A survey and analysis of using traditional Chinese medicine during pregnancy. Inter. J. Clin. Exper. Med. **8**(10), 19496 (2015)
8. Tsai, Y.N., Huang, Y.C., Lin, S.J.S., et al.: Different harmonic characteristics were found at each location on TCM radial pulse diagnosis by spectrum analysis. Evid. Based Complement. Altern. Med. **2018**, 1–11 (2018)
9. Jakes, A., Wade, J., Vowles, Z., et al.: Validation of the BPro radial pulse waveform acquisition device in pregnancy and gestational hypertensive disorders. Blood Press. Monit. **26**(5), 380–384 (2021)
10. Varshavsky, J.R., Robinson, J.F., Zhou, Y., et al.: Association of polybrominated diphenyl ether (PBDE) levels with biomarkers of placental development and disease during mid-gestation. Environ. Health **19**, 1–16 (2020)
11. Su, F., Li, Z., Sun, X., et al.: The pulse wave analysis of normal pregnancy: investigating the gestational effects on photoplethysmographic signals. Bio-med. Mater. Eng. **24**(1), 209–219 (2014)

12. Stirrat, L.I., Walker, J.J., Stryjakowska, K., et al.: Pulsatility of glucocorticoid hormones in pregnancy: changes with gestation and obesity. Clin. Endocrinol. **88**(4), 592–600 (2018)
13. Fernandez, L.A., Sousa, A.K.S., Doi, L.M., et al.: Analysis of ocular pulse amplitude values in different pregnancy stages as measured by dynamic contour tonometry. CLEVER Clin. Exper. Vis. Eye Res. **1**(1), 14–18 (2018)
14. Zhang, L., Meng, X., Wang, Y., et al.: Mode energy ratio analysis using pulse signals for diagnosis of pregnancy conditions. In: 2nd World Conference on Mechanical Engineering and Intelligent Manufacturing, pp. 479–482 (2019)
15. Tang, A.C.Y., Chung, J.W.Y., Wong, T.K.S.: Validation of a novel traditional Chinese medicine pulse diagnostic model using an artificial neural network. Evid. Based Complement. Altern. Med. **2012**, 1–7 (2012)
16. Zhang, Q., Bai, C., Chen, Z., et al.: Smart Chinese medicine for hypertension treatment with a deep learning model. J. Netw. Comput. Appl. **129**, 1–8 (2019)
17. Guo, R., Wang, Y., Yan, H., et al.: Analysis and recognition of traditional Chinese medicine pulse based on the Hilbert-Huang transform and random forest in patients with coronary heart disease. Evid. Based Complement. Altern. Med. **2015**, 1–8 (2015)
18. Hu, Q., Yu, T., Li, J., et al.: End-to-end syndrome differentiation of Yin deficiency and Yang deficiency in traditional Chinese medicine. Comput. Meth. Prog. Biomed. **174**, 9–15 (2019)
19. Chen, Z., Huang, A., Qiang, X.: Improved neural networks based on genetic algorithm for pulse recognition. Comput. Biol. Chem. **88**, 107315 (2020)
20. Chen, J., Huang, H., Hao, W., et al.: A machine learning method correlating pulse pressure wave data with pregnancy. Inter. J. Num. Meth. Biomed. Eng. **36**(1), e3272 (2020)
21. Li, N., Jiao, Y., Mao, X., Zhao, Y., Yao, G., Huang, L.: Analysis of pregnancy pulse discrimination based on wrist pulse by 1D CNN. In: Pan, L., Pang, S., Song, T., Gong, F. (eds.) BIC-TA 2020. CCIS, vol. 1363, pp. 336–346. Springer, Singapore (2021). https://doi.org/10.1007/978-981-16-1354-8_23
22. Li, K., Zhang, S., Chi, Z., et al.: Arterial pulse waveform characteristics difference between the three trimesters of healthy pregnant women. In: 40th Annual International Conference of the IEEE Engineering in Medicine and Biology Society (EMBC), pp. 5317–5320 (2018)
23. Li, N., Yu, J., Hu, H., et al.: The correlation study of Cun, Guan and Chi position based on wrist pulse characteristics. IEEE Access **9**, 28917–28929 (2021)
24. Liu, L., Zuo, W., Zhang, D., et al.: Combination of heterogeneous features for wrist pulse blood flow signal diagnosis via multiple kernel learning. IEEE Trans. Inf. Technol. Biomed. **16**(4), 598–606 (2012)
25. Lu, X., Wu, Y., Yan, R., et al.: Pulse waveform analysis for pregnancy diagnosis based on machine learning. In: IEEE 3rd Advanced Information Technology, Electronic and Automation Control Conference (IAEAC), pp. 1075–1079 (2018)
26. Wang, Y., Shi, X., Li, L., et al.: The impact of artificial intelligence on traditional Chinese medicine. Am. J. Chin. Med. **49**, 1297–1314 (2021)
27. Feng, C., Shao, Y., Wang, B., et al.: Development and application of artificial intelligence in auxiliary TCM diagnosis. Evid. Based Complement. Altern. Med., 1–8 (2021). ID 6656053
28. Chen, Z., Zhang, X.Y., Qiu, R.J.: Application of artificial intelligence in tongue diagnosis of traditional Chinese medicine: a review. TMR Mod. Herb. Med. **4**(2), 14–30 (2021)

Prognostic Staging System for Esophageal Cancer Using Lasso, Cox and CS-SVM

Qing Liu[1,2], Wenhao Zhang[1,2], Junwei Sun[1,2](✉), and Yanfeng Wang[1,2]

[1] Henan Key Lab of Information-Based Electrical Appliances,
Zhengzhou University of Light Industry, Zhengzhou 450002, China
junweisun@yeah.net
[2] School of Electrical and Information Engineering,
Zhengzhou University of Light Industry, Zhengzhou 450002, China

Abstract. Esophageal cancer is a heterogeneous malignant tumor with high mortality. Design constructing an effective prognostic staging system would help to improve the prognosis of patients. In this paper, blood indexes and TNM stages of patients with esophageal cancer are analyzed using the Lasso algorithm and Cox Proportional Hazards analysis. Two indicators significantly correlated with postoperative survival time and status of esophageal cancer patients are screened out. PI prognostic index is established by Cox Proportional Hazards Models. PI prognostic system can effectively predict the survival status of patients, which has been verified by ROC curve. PI prognostic staging system was established by ROC curve results. PI prognostic staging system was validated using kaplan-Meier curves, $P < 0.0001$. Cuckoo search algorithm-support vector machine can accurately predict PI prognostic staging system, and the accuracy of 10-fold cross-validation is 97.6721%. Therefore, the constructed PI prognostic staging system has the value of predicting the risk level of esophageal cancer patients.

Keywords: ESCC · Lasso algorithm · Cox Proportional Hazards analysis · CS-SVM · Prognostic staging system

1 Introduction

Esophageal cancer is a multi-process heterogeneous disease. In recent years, the morbidity and mortality rates of the disease continue to rise. According to a

This work was supported in part by the Joint Funds of the National Natural Science Foundation of China under Grant U1804262, in part by the Foundation of Young Key Teachers from University of Henan Province under Grant 2018GGJS092, in part by the Youth Talent Lifting Project of Henan Province under Grant 2018HYTP016, in part by the Henan Province University Science and Technology Innovation Talent Support Plan under Grant 20HASTIT027, in part by the Zhongyuan Thousand Talents Program under Grant 204200510003, and in part by the Open Fund of State Key Laboratory of Esophageal Cancer Prevention and Treatment under Grant K2020-0010 and Grant K2020-0011.

© Springer Nature Singapore Pte Ltd. 2022
L. Pan et al. (Eds.): BIC-TA 2021, CCIS 1566, pp. 317–329, 2022.
https://doi.org/10.1007/978-981-19-1253-5_24

report by the WHO's International Agency for Research on Cancer, there were 570,000 new cases of esophageal cancer worldwide in 2018, the death toll was 508,000 cases, and more than 60% of the patients came from Asia [1]. Because the early onset of esophageal cancer is insidious, diagnosis is often in the middle and late stage, which leads to more difficult treatment. In the current environment of the high incidence of esophageal cancer, the treatment of esophageal cancer still lacks clear management guidelines, and the 5-year survival rate of esophageal cancer patients is poor [2]. Moreover, there was significant survival heterogeneity among patients. Clinical data provide evidence that similar treatment for patients with similar physical conditions and the same TNM stages has different outcomes. It suggests that TNM stages may not be sufficient to determine the risk level of patients [3].

With the development of research on disease markers, prediction models have been widely concerned based on disease markers. Several studies [4] have revealed that the blood parameters of cancerous patients are significantly different from those of normal people. Especially cancerous patients after surgery, the abnormal changes in tumor markers and blood indicators often mean metastasis or recurrence of cancer cells. PT was considered by Alhenc Gelas Marion et al. [5] as the strongest independent prognostic indicator for tumor patients. Some blood indicators have been found to correlate with the prognostic effects of cancer patients, which guides clinicians to make diagnosis and treatment decisions. Lasso algorithm is often used to select variables. Two predictors of COVID-19 infection were screened by Liu Jingyuan et al. [6] using Lasso algorithm, and neutrophil/lymphocyte ratio was considered as a risk factor for survival of esophageal cancer. The features of the progression-free survival (PFS) chart were selected by Zhang Bin et al. [7] through Lasso algorithm. Nomogram discrimination and calibration were evaluated. This paper aims to develop a new prognostic staging system based on blood indexes and TNM stages through Lasso algorithm and Cox Proportional Hazards analysis, so as to improve the prognostic effect of esophageal cancer patients. This prognostic staging system has certain advantages in predicting the risk of esophageal cancer. This will help experts make decisions and contribute to improving clinical diagnosis and treatment outcomes. With the continuous improvement of intelligent medical treatment, many machine learning methods combined with group optimization algorithms have been used to study cancer prognosis and diagnosis, which has an important contribution to improving patient survival rates [8–10]. Machine learning techniques are considered by Kourou K. et al. [11] to improve the accuracy of tumor susceptibility, recurrence, and survival prediction. Kanghee Park et al. [12] developed a prediction model to evaluate the survival of cancer patients. The best performance of support vector machine (SVM), artificial neural network (ANN), and semi-supervised learning (SSL) classification models are compared. They proposed a method to optimize the SVM classifier using swarm intelligence algorithm, which achieved better performance of the model. Zhu X et al. [13] compared the optimization performance of particle swarm optimization algorithm-support vector machine (PSO-SVM), genetic algorithm-support vector machine (GA-SVM) and artificial bee colony algorithm-support vector machine(ABC-SVM). The convergence speed and accuracy of the three swarm intelligence algorithms are found to be different. Zhou Jian et al. [14] compared the prediction accuracy of grey Wolf optimization algorithm-support vector machine (GWA-SVM), Whale optimization algorithm-support vector machine (WOA-SVM), and Moth Flame optimization algorithm-support vector machine (MFO-SVM). They proved that the swarm intelligence algorithm hybrid SVM could improve the prediction accuracy of the model. M. Prabukumar et al. [15] extracted features of CT scan images of lung cancer and used CS-SVM to accurately and effectively classify lung cancer.

In this paper, the blood indexes and TNM stages of esophageal cancer patients are selected by Lasso algorithm and Cox proportional risk analysis. TNM stage and prothrombin time (PT) are identified as independent factors, it is affecting the prognosis of esophageal cancer. PI prognostic index is constructed by cox proportional risk model. ROC curve verified that $AUC = 0.623$, $P < 0.001$. PI has a significant relationship with survival status. PI is divided into high-risk and low-risk categories by ROC curve, PI prognostic staging system is obtained. Kaplan-Meier survival curve reveals that the survival rate of the low-risk levels is significantly higher than that of the high-risk levels. Finally, seven algorithms are used in the prediction accuracy of the PI prognostic staging system, which is gravity search algorithm-support vector machine (GSA-SVM), cuckoo search algorithm-support vector machine (CS-SVM), particle swarm optimization-support vector machine (PSO-SVM), simulated annealing-support vector machine (SA-SVM), artificial swarm algorithm-support vector machine (ABC-SVM), firefly algorithm-support vector machine (FA-SVM), gray Wolf optimization algorithm-support vector machine (GWO-SVM). The cuckoo search algorithm-support vector machine (CS-SVM) verify the validity of the PI prognosis staging system. The accuracy of the 10-fold cross-validation is 97.6721%. Moreover, CS-SVM is superior to GSA-SVM, PSO-SVM, SA-SVM, ABC-SVM, FA-SVM, and GWO-SVM in predicting accuracy of PI prognosis staging system.

The purpose of this paper is to develop a prognostic staging system for esophageal cancer using blood indicators and TNM staging. Based on Lasso algorithm, Cox Proportional Hazards analysis, and Cuckoo search algorithm-support vector machine, a method to construct staging system for esophageal cancer is proposed. The main contributions of this paper are summarized as follows.

(1) Two blood indicators prominently correlated with survival time and status of patients with esophageal cancer are found using Lasso algorithm and Cox Proportional Hazards analysis.
(2) A prognostic staging system with predictive value for the survival time and status of patients with esophageal cancer is established.
(3) Cuckoo search algorithm-support vector machine is proposed to effectively predict the established prognostic staging system.

2   Dataset Analysis

2.1   Data Introduction

The dataset for this paper included 383 samples. Each sample contains seventeen blood indicators, TNM stage, survival time and survival status. Seventeen blood indexes include: lymphocyte count (LY), white blood cell count (WBC), neutrophil count (NEUT), monocyte count (MONO), BASO, eosinophil count (EOS), hemoglobin (HB), red blood cell count (RBC), totalProtein (TP), platelet count (PLT), globulin (GLB), albumin (ALB), international standardized ratio (INR), prothrombin time (PT), fibrinogen (FIB), thrombin time (TT), activated partial thrombin time (APTT). TNM stages and survival time information of dataset are shown in Table 1. Information of seventeen blood indicators are shown in Table 2.

Table 1. TNM stages and survival time information of dataset

Project	Category	Number of population	Percentage of population
TNM stages	I	41	11%
	II	165	43%
	III	157	41%
	IV	2	5%
Survival time	>3	224	58%
	≤ 3	159	42%
	>5	148	39%
	≤ 5	235	61%

3   Construct for Prognostic Staging System

3.1   Lasso Algorithm Analysis

In this paper, 383 cases of data contain eighteen indicators, and each variable has its unique characteristics. In the case of multivariable features, the training model can always fit the training data well. At this time, the loss function is very close to zero, but the model can not be extended to new data samples. This phenomenon is called over-fitting. To solve the over-fitting problem, Tibshirani [16] proposed the least absolute shrinkage and selection operator (lasso) algorithm in 1996. The Lasso algorithm constructs a penalty function to earn a more elaborate model, which compresses some coefficients and sets some coefficients to zero [17]. The shortcomings of traditional methods in model selection are compensated by Lasso algorithm, which has the advantage of subset shrinkage. It influences on variable selection is pass beyond stepwise regression, principal component regression, ridge regression and partial least squares [7]. The penalty function is constructed by adding L_1 regularization after the loss function, as shown in Eq. (1).

Table 2. Information on seventeen blood indicators

Variable	Mean	Median (Range)	Variance
LY	1.7622	1.8(0–4)	0.3652
WBC	6.5366	6.2(2.5–13.6)	3.6958
NEUT	4.0011	3.7(0–9.8)	2.8097
MONO	0.3899	0.4(0–1.4)	0.06661
BASO	0.04163	0(0–5)	0.005549
EOS	0.1238	0.1(0–0.9)	0.0198
HB	137.4347	138(64–169)	223.7577
RBC	4.43	4.48(2.73–5.75)	0.2289
TP	71.0377	71(50–92)	54.4092
PLT	236.8518	231(100–448)	52.606
GLB	29.1533	29(16–45)	28.8656
ALB	42.0201	42(26–59)	25.1281
INR	0.7837	0.78(0.45–1.56)	0.02919
PT	10.2271	10.2(7–16.6)	2.4610
FIB	387.3433	378.3960(167.613–774.433)	985.7021
TT	15.3420	15.5(10.9–21.3)	2.9607
APTT	35.9095	35.1(15.4–62.2)	52.9934

$$J(\theta) = \frac{1}{2m} \left[\sum_{i=1}^{m} \left(h_\theta(x^{(i)}) - y^{(i)} \right)^2 + \lambda \sum_{j=1}^{k} |\omega_j| \right] \tag{1}$$

Where, θ is the parameter of the solution. m is the number of samples. h_θ is the hypothesis function. $x^{(i)}$ is the input to the sample. $y^{(i)}$ is the output to the sample. $h_\theta(x^{(i)}) - y^{(i)})^2$ is the square error of single sample. λ is the regularization parameter. k is the number of parameters. ω_j is k-th weight. $\lambda \sum_{j=1}^{k} |\omega_j|$ is the L_1 regularization parameter.

L_1 regularization reduces the order of magnitude characteristic variables in exchange for preserving all characteristic variables. Insignificant variable coefficients are compressed tend to zero, the significant variables are screened out. Therefore, L_1 regularization plays a role in preventing the over-fitting phenomenon and keeping the parameter value small. The complexity of Lasso is commanded by λ. As *lambda* increases, the penalty increases, thus serving to reduce the variables in the linear model.

In this paper, seventeen blood indicators and TNM stages are inputs. The survival time is output. The Lasso algorithm is used to analyze the correlation between inputs and output. This process runs in MATLAB. Six blood indicators and TNM stages are found by Lasso algorithm. The six blood indicators are LY, NEUT, Hb, ALB, GLB, PT.

3.2   Cox Proportional Hazards Model

Common survival analysis models include Kaplan-Meier survival estimate and Cox proportional hazards analysis. Kaplan-Meier survival estimate belongs to univariate analysis, which could only describe the relationship between this variable and survival. It only applies to categorical variables, but the impact of continuous variables on survival cannot be analyzed. Therefore, Kaplan-Meier survival estimate cannot be used for further analysis of the seven indicators in this paper.

Cox proportional hazards model is a semi-parametric regression model [18]. The model explores the effect of multiple characteristic variables on mortality at some point. Cox proportional hazards model is a significant model in survival analysis. At present, Cox proportional hazards model has become the main method of multivariate analysis. The definition of the Cox proportional hazards model is shown in Eq. (2).

$$h(t, X_i) = h_0(t) \times \exp(X_i \beta) \tag{2}$$

where, t is time. X_i is the eigenvector of data i. $h_0(t)$ is any non-negative equation for time t, namely the benchmark risk equation. β is the parameter vector obtained by maximizing cox partial likelihood. β is an important factor to judge the patient's cancer risk. If β is greater than zero, the higher X, the higher the patient's death risk. If β is less than zero, the higher X, the smaller the patient's death risk. If β is equal to zero, and X is independent of survival. The parameters in Cox proportional hazards model could predict the prognosis of an individual. The higher the prognostic index, the higher the risk, and the worse the prognosis.

In this study, seven indicators are inputs, the survival time and survival state are outputs, a Cox proportional hazards model is established to further screen the seven indicators. Overall model fit results for two indicators are shown in Table 3. Coefficient and standard error for two indicators are shown in Table 4. Survival curves for two indicators is shown in Fig. 1. The results suggest that PT and TNM stages are associated with the survival risk of patients. PT and TNM stages are the strongest independent prognostic factors. PI prognostic index is established as follows:

$$PI = 0.904 * PT + 1.6319 * TNM stages \tag{3}$$

The Receiver Operating Characteristic (ROC) curve is a common statistical analysis method. It is widely used to judge classification and test results. The area under curve (AUC) is surrounded by the coordinate axes under the ROC curve. Model performance is closely related to the value of AUC. When the value of AUC is greater than 0.5, the model has statistical significance. When the value of AUC is closer to 1, the model has more authenticity. Higher authenticity means better classification performance of the model. In this paper, the accuracy and classification prediction of PI are analyzed by the ROC curve. ROC curve of PI is illustrated in Fig. 2, ROC curve results of PI are indicated in Table 5.

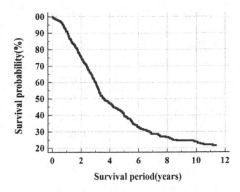

Fig. 1. Survival curves for two indicators

Table 3. Overall model fit results for two indicators

Project	Parameter
No model -2 logarithmic probability	3033.624
Full model -2 logarithmic probability	2990.137
Chi-square	43.486
DF	2
Significance level	$P < 0.0001$

From Table 5, $AUC = 0.623$, $P < 0.0001$, The survival status of esophageal cancer patients can be accurately estimated by PI. Based on the relevant criteria of 4.1678, PI is divided into different risk group. High-risk levels and low-risk levels for PI are represented in Table 6. Next, two risk levels of PI are inputs, and survival time and survival state are outputs. The Kaplan-Meier survival curve is used to determine whether PI risk levels could reflect the survival time and survival rate of patients. Kaplan-Meier survival curve for PI is demonstrated in Fig. 3. Figure 3 clearly shows that low-risk patients have the highest prognostic effect, while high-risk patients have a poor survival rate. PI classification is proven to be effective using Kaplan-Meier survival curve.

Table 4. Coefficient and standard error for two indicators

Project	PT	TNM stages
B	-0.1009	0.4898
SE	0.03915	0.08551
Wald	6.6473	32.8044
P	0.0099	<0.0001
$Exp(\beta)$	0.9040	1.6319
95%CI for $Exp(\beta)$	0.8372–0.9761	1.3801–1.9297

Table 5. ROC curves results for PI

Project	Parameter
AUC	0.623
Standard error	0.0322
95% confidence interval	0.560–0.686
Z statistics	3.811
P-value	0.0001
Youden index	0.1974
Relevant standard	≤ 4.1678
Sensitivity	51.42
Specificity	68.32

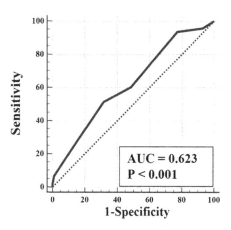

Fig. 2. Roc curve for PI.

4   Prognostic Staging System Prediction

4.1   Cuckoo Search Algorithm-Support Vector Machine

Support vector machine (SVM) [19] is a binary classification model based on structural risk minimization. SVM can calculate empirical risk through hinge loss function, and regularization items are added into the solving system to optimize structural risk [20]. It is suitable for small and medium-sized data samples.

Table 6. High-risk levels and low-risk levels for PI

Project	Proportion	Scope
High-risk levels	46%	0.4898
Low-risk levels	54%	0.08551

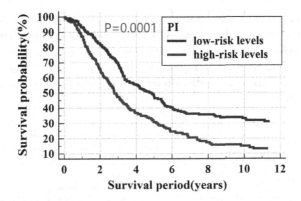

Fig. 3. Kaplan-Meier survival curve for PI

And it solves nonlinear and high-dimensional classification problems. SVM is a sparse and robust classifier. When the data is not linearly separable, SVM introduces the mapping function to map the original feature space into a higher-dimensional space, and non-fractional data is converted into linearly separable space in the higher dimensional space. The introduction of kernel function solves the problem of sample distance in higher dimensional space after mapping, so that k-dimensional space can be mapped into infinite-dimensional space. The kernel function is shown in Eq. (4),

$$K(x^{(i)}, y^{(i)}) = \exp(-g\left\|x^{(i)} - y^{(i)}\right\|^2), g > 0 \tag{4}$$

Where, $x^{(i)}$ is the eigenvalue of the $i-th$ sample, and $y^{(i)}$ is the category label of $x^{(i)}$. The parameter coefficient of kernel function g is closely related to the performance of SVM. If the parameter g is smaller, the classification is finer and the model will be overfitted. If the parameter g is larger, the classification will be coarser and the data cannot be separated.

The objective function and constraints of support vector machine optimization are as follows:

$$\begin{cases} min\frac{1}{2}\|\omega\|^2 + C\sum_{i=1}^{n}\xi(i) \\ s.t. y^{(i)}(\omega^T\Phi(x^{(i)} + b)) \geq 1 - \xi(i), i = 1, 2...n \end{cases} \tag{5}$$

Where, ω is a normal vector, it determines the direction of the hyperplane. C is the penalty factor. $\xi(i)$ is the relaxation factor. $\Phi(x)$ is the mapping function. b is the displacement, it determines the distance between the hyperplane and the origin. The value of penalty factor C balances empirical risk and structural risk. If C is larger, the empirical risk is smaller and the structural risk is larger, and overfitting is easy to occur. If C is smaller, the model complexity is lower, and underfitting is easy to occur.

Its performance is closely related to the penalty parameter C and parameter coefficient g of the kernel function. At present, parameter optimization of SVM has become a research hotspot in the machine learning. Therefore, in this paper, the parameter coefficients g and penalty parameter C are optimized by Cuckoo Search(CS) algorithm. The prediction model has high precision in a certain solution space is ensured.

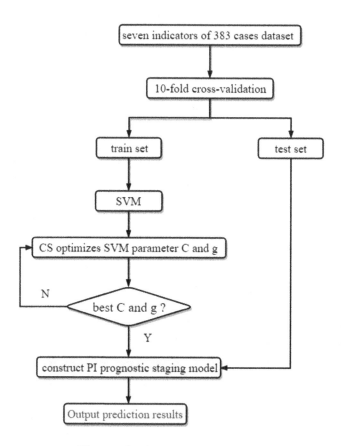

Fig. 4. The flow chart of CS-SVM

CS algorithm [21] is a swarm intelligent search algorithm developed in 2009. It simulated the nest-seeking parasitic characteristics of cuckoos to obtain the local optimal solution and searched for an optimal host nest globally to hatch its eggs through Levy flight. The cuckoo is a parasitic bird. Usually cuckoos lay eggs in another nest, and the young cuckoos are hatched and raised by the host bird. If the eggs are found by the host, the host may discard them or build a new nest. The optimization process of cuckoo algorithm is the process of cuckoo searching for parasitic eggs that are not easy to be found by the host. To avoid host discovery of parasitic eggs, cuckoos use Levy flights to constantly search for new nest sites. They compare the detection probability of old and new nests, which determines whether to keep or change their location. Until it find the best place to nest. The above process is cuckoo algorithm optimization process. The above process is cuckoo algorithm optimization process. CS-SVM is to find the best penalty parameter C and the parameter coefficients g through the CS algorithm. The flow chart of CS-SVM is represented in Fig. 4.

4.2 Prognostic Staging System Prediction of Esophageal Cancer

In the existing data set, PI prognostic staging system is significantly associated with survival in esophageal cancer patients. To evaluate the accuracy of the PI prognostic staging system, seven indexes significantly correlated with survival time are taken as inputs. PI prognostic staging system is taken as output. CS-SVM algorithm is used to predict the PI prognostic staging system. The parameter part of CS-SVM is designed as follows.

The data set is divided into test set and train set for 10-fold cross-validation. Set the number of host nests to 20, the maximum iteration times to 100, the search range is $[0.01, 100]$, and the P_a value is 0.25. When the feature dataset is introduced into CS-SVM model, the prediction accuracy of 10-fold cross-validation reached 97.6721%. CS-SVM could effectively predict the PI prognostic staging system.

Time complexity is a function, and the running time of CS-SVM algorithm is qualitatively described by time complexity. O is usually used to measure the complexity of an algorithm. In this paper, the time complexity of CS-SVM was evaluated by O. The computational efficiency of SVM parameters C and g reflects the time complexity of CS-SVM algorithm. The time complexity of CS-SVM can be expressed as:

$$T_n = O(2n + f(n)) = O(n) \tag{6}$$

Where, $f(n)$ is the calculation rate of parameters C and g. n is the number of variables.

With the deepening of research, swarm intelligence algorithm mixing SVM to optimize and improve the performance of SVM, this method has been recognized. In this paper, CS-SVM is implemented to predict high-risk levels and low-risk levels. GSA-SVM, PSO-SVM, SA-SVM, ABC-SVM, FA-SVM and GWO-SVM are respectively used to predict high-risk levels and low-risk levels. The prediction results of the seven algorithms are shown in Table 7. The 10-fold cross-validation accuracy rates of the seven algorithms are 94.2645%, 93.2119%, 95.5803%, 95.3171%, 95.027%, 95.027%, 91.8961%, respectively. CS-SVM algorithm has the best prediction effect, while the GWO-SVM algorithm has the weakest prediction effect. It shows that the CS-SVM algorithm has high accuracy in the prediction of esophageal cancer. Moreover, these algorithms have achieved good accuracy, the PI prognostic staging system could reflect the survival rate of esophageal cancer patients.

Table 7. Prediction results of seven algorithms.

Project	Accuracy rate (%)	Running times (s)
GSA-SVM	94.2645	11.6
CS-SVM	97.6721	28.36
PSO-SVM	93.2119	4.85
SA-SVM	95.5803	17.26
ABC-SVM	95.3171	23.18
FA-SVM	95.027	11.66
GWO-SVM	91.8961%	16.2

5   Conclusion

A new prognostic index PI and prognostic staging system are proposed. First, the two indicators are significantly correlated with the survival time and status of patients with esophageal cancer using the Lasso algorithm and Cox proportional hazards analysis. PT and TNM stages are found to have independent predictive values. The prognostic index PI of esophageal cancer is established by Cox proportional hazards model. Secondly, PI is divided into different risk levels by the ROC curve. Patients in the low-risk level had the highest survival rate, while patients in the high-risk level had the lowest survival rate. The difference in survival between the two groups was verified by kaplan-Meier survival curve. The PI staging system can effectively reflect the survival status of different patients. Finally, the cuckoo search algorithm-support vector machine (CS-SVM) is proposed to predict PI prognosis staging system effectively. Moreover, CS-SVM is superior to GSA-SVM, PSO-SVM, SA-SVM, ABC-SVM, FA-SVM, and GWO-SVM in predicting accuracy of PI prognosis staging system.

References

1. Arnold, M., et al.: Global burden of 5 major types of gastrointestinal cancer. Gastroenterology **159**(1), 335–349 (2020)
2. Zhang, Z., et al.: Development of a prognostic signature for esophageal cancer based on nine immune related genes. BMC Cancer **21**(1), 1–16 (2021)
3. Huang, Q., et al.: A nomogram-based immune-serum scoring system predicts overall survival in patients with lung adenocarcinoma. Cancer Biol. Med. **18**(2), 517 (2021)
4. Petrella, F., et al.: Prognostic value of the hemoglobin/red cell distribution width ratio in resected lung adenocarcinoma. Cancers **13**(4), 710 (2021)
5. Alhenc-Gelas, M., et al.: Characteristics and outcome of breast cancer-related microangiopathic Haemolytic anaemia: a multicentre study. Breast Cancer Res. **23**(1), 1–10 (2021)
6. Liu, J., et al.: Neutrophil-to-lymphocyte ratio predicts critical illness patients with 2019 coronavirus disease in the early stage. J. Transl. Med. **18**, 1–12 (2020)

7. Zhang, B., et al.: Radiomics features of multiparametric MRI as novel prognostic factors in advanced nasopharyngeal carcinoma. Clin. Cancer Res. **23**(15), 4259–4269 (2017)
8. Wang, H., Zheng, B., Yoon, S.W., Ko, H.S.: A support vector machine-based ensemble algorithm for breast cancer diagnosis. Eur. J. Oper. Res. **267**(2), 687–699 (2018)
9. Wang, M., Chen, H.: Chaotic multi-swarm whale optimizer boosted support vector machine for medical diagnosis. Appl. Soft Comput. **88**, 105946 (2020)
10. Tao, Z., Huiling, L., Wenwen, W., Xia, Y.: GA-SVM based feature selection and parameter optimization in hospitalization expense modeling. Appl. Soft Comput. **75**, 323–332 (2019)
11. Kourou, K., Exarchos, T.P., Exarchos, K.P., Karamouzis, M.V., Fotiadis, D.I.: Machine learning applications in cancer prognosis and prediction. Comput. Struct. Biotechnol. J. **13**, 8–17 (2015)
12. Park, K., Ali, A., Kim, D., An, Y., Kim, M., Shin, H.: Robust predictive model for evaluating breast cancer survivability. Eng. Appl. Artif. Intell. **26**(9), 2194–2205 (2013)
13. Zhu, X., Li, N., Pan, Y.: Optimization performance comparison of three different group intelligence algorithms on a SVM for hyperspectral imagery classification. Remote Sens. **11**(6), 734 (2019)
14. Zhou, J., et al.: Optimization of support vector machine through the use of meta-heuristic algorithms in forecasting TBM advance rate. Eng. Appl. Artif. Intell. **97**, 104015 (2021)
15. Prabukumar, M., Agilandeeswari, L., Ganesan, K.: An intelligent lung cancer diagnosis system using cuckoo search optimization and support vector machine classifier. J. Ambient Intell. Humanized Comput. **10**(1), 267–293 (2017). https://doi.org/10.1007/s12652-017-0655-5
16. Tibshirani, R.: Regression shrinkage and selection via the lasso: a retrospective. J. R. Stat. Soc. Ser. B (Stat. Methodol.) **73**(3), 273–282 (2011)
17. Li, J., et al.: Feature selection: a data perspective. ACM Comput. Surv. (CSUR) **50**(6), 1–45 (2017)
18. Wang, Y., Liang, E., Zhao, X., Song, X., Wang, L., Sun, J.: Prediction of survival time of patients with esophageal squamous cell carcinoma based on univariate analysis and ASSA-BP neural network. IEEE Access **8**, 181127–181136 (2020)
19. Sun, J., Yang, Y., Wang, Y., Wang, L., Song, X., Zhao, X.: Survival risk prediction of esophageal cancer based on self-organizing maps clustering and support vector machine ensembles. IEEE Access **8**, 131449–131460 (2020)
20. Wang, Y., Yang, Y., Sun, J., Wang, L., Song, X., Zhao, X.: Development and validation of the predictive model for esophageal squamous cell carcinoma differentiation degree. Front. Genet. **11**, 595638 (2020)
21. Sharma, P., Dinkar, S.K., Gupta, D.: A novel hybrid deep learning method with cuckoo search algorithm for classification of arrhythmia disease using ECG signals. Neural Comput. Appl. **33**, 1–21 (2021)

Federated Neural Architecture Search Evolution and Open Problems: An Overview

Detian Liu and Yang Cao$^{(\boxtimes)}$

School of Information, Beijing Wuzi University, Beijing 101149, China
caoyangcwz@126.com

Abstract. As an effective optimization technique that automatically tunes the architecture and hyperparameters of deep neural network models, neural architecture search (NAS) has made significant progress in deep learning model design and automated machine learning (AutoML). However, with the widespread attention to privacy issues, privacy-preserving machine learning approaches have received much attention. Federated learning (FL) is a machine learning paradigm that addresses data privacy issues, mainly facing heterogeneous and distributed scenarios. Therefore, combining FL with NAS can effectively address the privacy issues faced in NAS. Several studies have proposed federated neural architecture search methods, which provide a feasible solution for the joint construction of deep learning models with optimal performance for multiple parties without data sharing. Federated neural architecture search focuses on solving the design challenges of deep neural network models for distributed data and making the models more suitable for heterogeneous scenarios. In this paper, a summary of research related to neural architecture search and FL. We give a review of current work in federated neural architecture search and summarize open issues of existing research. The objective is to offer an overview of a survey on combining FL with NAS, balancing the privacy protection issues of deep neural network models with efficient design. Privacy protection is the primary goal of federated neural architecture search while ensuring model performance.

Keywords: Federated learning · Neural architecture search · Federated NAS · Security and privacy

1 Introduction

Due to the speedy advancement of information technology, breakthroughs in artificial intelligence continue to be made. Machine learning, deep learning, and other technologies are widely used to achieve good results in natural language processing, image recognition, automatic control, and other fields. Following the development of deep neural network models, as AlexNet [17], VGG [38], ResNet

© Springer Nature Singapore Pte Ltd. 2022
L. Pan et al. (Eds.): BIC-TA 2021, CCIS 1566, pp. 330–345, 2022.
https://doi.org/10.1007/978-981-19-1253-5_25

[45], etc., the performance of these models is sufficiently advanced. Still, their network architectures have all become very complex, efficient design of deep learning models requires much effort and cost. Therefore, neural architecture search (NAS) [8] becomes very important and has high application in deep learning model design to automatically search for good neural network architectures. Recently, NAS has been widely researched and applied to automatically tune the neural network model's architecture and hyperparameters.

Development in deep learning relies on massive data support, and traditional deep learning models work with data in a centralized manner. However, with the concern of privacy protection and the continuous improvement of laws and regulations, it is impractical to process data centrally. Federated learning [21] is a novel paradigm for machine learning that addresses privacy protection issues, and a distributed approach that does not require centralized processing of data. The participants do not need to upload data to the cloud or central server in a federated setting. Still, they train locally using the generated data and the device's computing power and only upload the parameters of the trained model, which can effectively protect the private user data. Federated learning (FL) provides a new practical and effective way to protect user privacy in machine learning techniques and has been heavily researched and applied.

Federated learning (FL) protects privacy by avoiding sharing data between parties and instead uses the transmission of model parameters to build globally feasible machine learning models, which improves the level of privacy protection but still faces some problems. Communication resources and computational efficiency are two critical issues in FL [19]. In addition, the local training of FL still needs to be trained based on machine learning models such as NNs, and distributed setting brings more significant difficulties to the design of the model structure of FL. Moreover, FL mostly faces heterogeneous scenarios, and the data are primarily non-independent identical distribution (Non-IID), which makes FL's model performance mostly non-optimal, which further increases the difficulty of designing the neural network architecture.

In traditional machine learning, model design requires data analysis to gain the necessary insight into the architecture to be employed. Although neural architecture search(NAS) extends some new ways for automatic machine learning and neural network model structure design, NAS still faces many open problems when performed in a distributed environment. In FL, the data is not shared, and one party can only analyze that party's data and not the data of other parties. Once there is no global data analysis, it is impossible to directly use the traditional NAS approach for the automatic search of model architectures in the FL setting. Therefore, it is essential to combine NAS techniques with FL effectively, and research on the combination of FL and NAS has a broad prospect.

In Sect. 2, we summarize and provide an overview of related research on NAS, discussing research on reinforcement learning-based, evolutionary algorithm-based, and gradient-based NAS. In Sect. 3, the detailed process and classical algorithms of FL are outlined, and novel research directions of FL are summarized. Section 4 focuses on the summary of research combining FL with NAS and provides an overview of currently existing research on federated neural architecture search. Section 5 discusses the open challenges and significant research problems, such as NAS and federated neural architecture search, exploring feasible future solutions based on existing research. Finally, the full text is summarized, and future research directions and work are proposed.

2   Neural Architecture Search

It has been shown that the quality of Deep Neural Networks (DNNs) models has become very dependent on their architecture, and better architectures mean better performance. Therefore, with many applications of DNNs in AI, optimization of DNNs architectures already got a lot of attention. NAS is a research direction derived precisely from the growing need for DNNs architecture design. It is closely related to automatic machine learning (AutoML) and DNNs architecture design. The primary process of neural architecture search is shown in Fig. 1. Many excellent results have been achieved in the research of NAS, mainly for RL-based, EA-based, and gradient-based neural architecture search methods, and most of the existing NAS schemes are most of these three types. [35] presents a detailed description and summary of the research related to neural architecture search and presents some challenges and solutions. The difficulties in implementing neural architecture search in a distributed scenario of FL are significant and face many open challenges.

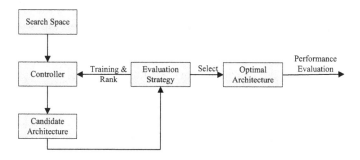

Fig. 1. The overall process of NAS

2.1   NAS Based on Reinforcement Learning

The search strategy of NAS aims to find well-performing neural network architectures in the dataset as a way to speed up the application of deep learning models and reduce the significant overhead of neural network model design. Most of the early NAS research was conducted using reinforcement learning methods [62,63], where the design task of the network model was taken as an action of an agent, it can represent the network structure of a sub-model, network is trained with results obtained by validation on the dataset can be returned as a reward. The reinforcement learning-based NAS approach mainly uses training to get reward values to determine the optimal network, which requires a lot of training and may incur a significant overhead. In addition, as research on reinforcement learning continues to evolve, Q-learning [49] has become a mainstream technology, and applying Q-learning to NAS is an effective way to do so. The MetaQNN model was proposed in [2], the method depends on Q-learning for selecting network layers and their parameters sequentially in a limited space. It begins by defining each state of the learning agent as a layer containing all relevant parameters. For fast convergence, constraints can be set to assimilate the agent operation space to the suitable layers to which the agent could move. [58] used the Q-learning paradigm to design block network generation methods that repeatedly stack the best blocks to build the entire network and can speed up the search process using distributed asynchronous strategies and early stop methods. The NAS based on reinforcement learning effectively combines the automatic learning idea of reinforcement learning by making good use of it. [18] gave an overall overview of the study and progress in the automation of reinforcement learning for extensive use in CNN model design and details the challenges that still need further consideration for reinforcement learning methods in NAS. As the research on neural networks continued to grow, Graph Neural Networks (GNNs) are already widely applied to analyze non-Euclidean data. They have been successfully applied, but GNNs still needs much manual work and lots of knowledge for its design. For the NAS method of GNNs, [10] proposed a reinforcement learning-based graph NAS method that can automatically search for the best of graph neural architecture. NAS methods based on reinforcement learning still have a broad development prospect. As deep reinforcement learning research continues to expand, there are still multiple solutions to the neural architecture search problem that can be explored.

2.2 NAS Based on Evolutionary Algorithm

Methods in evolutionary algorithm (EA)-based approaches are commonly utilized to handle multi-objective optimization in NAS. NAS based on EA only optimizes the model structure of itself, with conventional gradient descent methods to train the model parameters [32,43]. This is significantly different from neuroevolutionary techniques [1,54], which the objective is to optimize the weights and architecture of NNs, where evolutionary NAS starts with randomly generated populations of parent models with different architectures that are trained in parallel. Adaptation values were computed by the evaluation of the models in proof datasets after all models had learned for some predefined periods. Then, genetic operations like crossover and mutations were performed for both parents to generate a population of progeny formed by the new model. In next step, a selection operation is performed to choose the better offspring model as the parent for the next period, which is commonly referred to a survival of the fittest.

By repeating such selection and reproduction of processes over several generations, until some conditions are fulfilled. Traditional evolutionary NAS requires evaluating a set of NNs at any generation. All new neural network models generated were trained from the beginning, which is unsuitable for optimization tasks online. A genetic CNN approach was presented in [51], which was among the initial researches of optimizing CNN with EA. The genetic CNN approach searched the whole architecture space and used a fixed-length binary string for representing connections among many ordered nodes (e.g., evolutionary operations). The method has some limitations, but the generated network structure has good results. There are numerous studies on evolutionary algorithm-based NAS, the mainstream approach in early NAS research. Still, most of the studies have limitations, and excessive training overhead is the main problem of EA-based NAS.

2.3 NAS Based on Gradient

Gradient-based neural architecture search studies are gradually becoming popular. The main reason is that the GD-based methods have much better search speed than other methods, resulting in a good improvement in inefficiency. [29] proposed DARTS algorithm, a gradient-based NAS method that optimizes both model weights and architectures. And the application of gradient descent with the help of relaxation techniques allows the direct training of weights. Recently, the GD-based NAS approach has been formulated as a two-layer optimization problem. However, He et al. [15] observed that the two-layer optimization of the present approaches were designed based on heuristic solutions. They show this approximation has overlapping effects, mostly as it is based on a one-step approximation of the network weights. Therefore, the gradient error might prevent the algorithm converge to the (local) optimal solution. Experimental results show a higher classification accuracy of MiLeNAS over original two-layer optimization method. Most gradient-based NAS methods can optimize the weights and architecture directly. It is feasible to combine gradient-based methods with FL to form federated neural architecture search. [24] observed in one gradient optimization-based NAS method, relaxing the problem to continuous optimization on architectures and shared weights, a geometric-aware framework with fast convergence guarantees is proposed based on minimizing the single-level empirical risk. A principled approach for co-designing the optimizer and continuously relaxing the discrete NAS search space is demonstrated using experiments. The literature [36] provided an overview and summary of the application of gradient descent to different neural architecture searches. It also explored the effect of gradient descent for NAS and investigated how the candidate architectures were generated during the search process.

3   Federated Learning

The federated averaging algorithm presented by McMahan [30], could reduce the number of communication rounds and improve the communication efficiency by reduce the local training mini-batchsize or increase the number of local training rounds. Due to the increasing attention to data privacy and security, FL has been widely studied, and the heterogeneity problem, model accuracy, and communication efficiency of FL have received a lot of attention. [37] proposed a clustered federated learning approach to classify different clients based on their similarity to each other, allowing different clients to use more data for training, improving model accuracy and reducing the impact of data heterogeneity. [27] used gradient compression to reduce the size of uploaded and downloaded model parameters, which in turn enables communication efficiency and accelerates training efficiency. [25] is improved based on the federated average algorithm by adding an approximation term so that the final obtained model can be more suitable for different clients, which in turn improves the overall performance of the federated learning model. However, most of the current federated optimization [21] approaches are dedicated to optimizing one objective alone, which makes it possible to optimize one objective always with different degrees of other aspects.

FL is considered as a distributed machine learning method that can efficiently utilize computing power among different devices. Training is performed without data leaving the device to build a local model, and with a limited amount of local training, server to aggregate local models to achieve a global model with better performance. After the model aggregation completed, global model was assigned to each participant and iterations were executed till the model converged and stopped updating. The whole architecture of Federated Learning is shown in Fig. 2. A typical FL approach to training consists of three main steps:

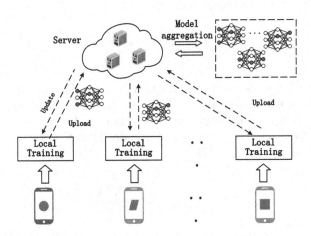

Fig. 2. Federated learning architecture

1. Each clients utilize local data to train independently and in parallel to get a local model.

2. Upload the local model parameters to server, while the server receives all the model parameters to aggregate them for a global model.
3. The server broadcasts the aggregated global model to each clients, and all clients update model after receiving it, and iteratively updates multiple rounds until the model converges to obtain the final global model.

3.1 Federated Learning Optimization Objective and FedAvg Algorithm

In FL, aim to find the best parameter $omega_*$ minimizing the global objective function:

$$\omega^* = \arg\min_{\omega} f(\omega), where \ f(\omega) = \sum_{k=1}^{N} \frac{p_k}{P} F_k(\omega) \tag{1}$$

where N denotes the number of participating client, P_k the contribution of client k in the federation, $P = \sum p_k$ the normalization factor, $\sum_k^N \frac{p_k}{P} = 1$, and $F_k(w)$ the local objective function of client k. We refer to the model computed using Eq. (1) as the global model w_c. Every client computes its local objective by minimizing the empirical risk over its local training set D_K^T as $F_k(\omega) = \mathbb{E}_{x_k \sim D_K^T}[l_k(\omega; x_k)]$, while l_k being the loss function. Thus, for each clients k in a training round, the update process is as formula:

$$\omega_{t+1}^k = w_t^k - \eta_t \nabla f(\omega) \tag{2}$$

Besides, let $g(\omega_t)$ denote the aggregated value of local model update gradient in the round t, the formulation as flowing:

$$g(\omega_t) = \sum_{k}^{N} \frac{p_k}{P} \nabla f(\omega) \tag{3}$$

In a typical FL system, where a fraction of clients are chosen for training at each iteration, it is assumed that K clients are chosen in one round. In addition, stochastic gradient descent algorithm used in training. In our research, we assume a total of I rounds of local training and update. Therefore, the update rules for the model parameters are as follows:

$$\omega_{t+1} = \omega_t - \eta_t \sum_{k=1}^{K} \frac{p_k}{P} \sum_{i=0}^{I} \nabla f(\omega) \tag{4}$$

In addition, the pseudo-code of the federated averaging algorithm(FedAvg), which we give in Algorithm 1, will randomly select a portion of clients for each round of local training, and each clients will also perform a certain number of rounds of training locally, and then upload the model parameters for aggregation and updating after the local training is completed.

Algorithm 1: Federated Average Algorithm

Input: FL Server Initialize global model ω_0; $f(\omega)$: objective function;
Output: *results*: update parameters of $f(\omega)$;

1 **for** *each communication round $t = 1, 2, \ldots, T$* **do**
2 | Randomly select K clients from N clients
3 **end**
4 $C_t \leftarrow$ Sever broadcasts ω_t to the selected clients.
5 **for** *each clients $c_i \in C_t$ parallelly* **do**
6 | $\omega_{t+1}^i \leftarrow Update(i, \omega_t)$
7 **end**
8 $\omega_{t+1} \leftarrow \omega_t + \sum_{c_i \in C_t} \frac{p_k}{P} \omega_{t+1}^i$
9 **Return**(ω_{t+1});

3.2 Distributed Optimization for FL

With the Federated Average algorithm as the typical algorithm for FL, it was also the first algorithm to be applied. As the research on FL continues to expand, much research has been done on improving the *FedAvg* algorithm. In this section, we summarize the distributed optimization algorithms for FL. [33] combined adaptive optimization methods, widely used in non-federated settings, with federated learning to form a federated version of the adaptive optimizer. [47] proposed the *FedMA* algorithm to construct a shared global model hierarchically by matching and averaging features with similar characteristics and extracting the hidden states of the invisible elements of the features. [42] proposed a federated multi-task learning approach that solves the challenges of statistical and system heterogeneity in a multi-task format and proposed the system-aware optimization method *MOCHA*, which is robust to real-world problems. A variational federated multi-task learning method was proposed in [5] as a federated multi-task learning algorithm for nonconvex models, which uses approximate variational inference to perform learning on the network with better performance. [31] proposed a fast federated optimization algorithm framework for solving distributionally convex minimization problems with additive structures based on an algorithm for operator splitting processes. [20] proposed the stochastic controlled averaging algorithm for FL, named *SCAFFOLD*, which uses control variables to correct the "client-side drift" problem in local updates. [48] proposed a common framework for analyzing the convergence of heterogeneous federated optimization algorithms. And *FedNova* normalized averaging method is proposed to eliminate factual inconsistencies while maintaining fast convergence. [26] proposed the *FedDANE* method, a federated Newton-type method, improved from the classical distributed optimization algorithm *DANE* [34,39], *FedDANE* can be used for dealing with the practical limitations of FL and can give a guarantee of convergence when learning convex and non-convex functions.

3.3   Non-IID and Model Personalization for FL

FL is mainly performed in heterogeneous environments, so it especially faces scenarios with large amount of Non-IID data distribution and faces specific performance loss and efficiency degradation. The personalized federated learning model is an effective solution proposed to address Non-IID data distribution and heterogeneous devices. This section summarizes the Non-IID and personalization problems of federated learning. [16] provided a general overview of the non-IID data problem for decentralized machine learning, investigated the data skew distribution using experiments, and analytically derived the significant effect of data skew on the loss of model accuracy. [60] provided a sound introduction and summary of federated learning of Non-IID data, reviewing current research efforts dealing with Non-IID data. A lot of research on Non-IID data in FL has been conducted by [3,40,46,57]. Semi-Federated learning [4] is proposed to be applied to solve the Non-IID data problem by clustering local clients and performing intra-cluster training so that neighboring clients can share their models. $FedCD$ [23] is proposed as a method that can improve the performance of FL under Non-IID data by dynamically grouping devices with similar data, achieving higher accuracy and convergence. [22] proposed the $FedFMC$ method, which dynamically updates the device crossover into different global models and then merges the separate models into a single model. It can effectively improve the Non-IID problem without increasing the communication cost. A Meta-Learning approach is proposed in [9] that investigates a resonant variable of $FedAvg$ and evaluates the performance based on the gradient parametrization of a non-convex loss function. The $pFedMe$ method is proposed in [6] to use Moreau envelope as a regularized loss function for clients, it helps to decouple personalized model optimization and global model learning in personalized FL.

3.4   Hierarchical and Clustered FL

The efficiency of federated learning is still a vital issue and practical federated learning algorithms need to be explored, with hierarchical and clustered federated learning being feasible approaches. In this section, a summary of the existing hierarchical and clustered federated learning will be presented. A cluster federated learning framework in [37] is proposed, which uses the geometric characteristics of federated learning loss to perform clustering after federated learning training converges to a stable point and divides users into different clusters. The model trained after clustering can be more suitable for users, thus reducing heterogeneity's impact. An efficient federated learning framework [12] is proposed to alternately estimate user clustering identities and optimize model parameters based on gradient descent. This method can effectively speed up the convergence of the model but may require a lot of communication. $FedGroup$ [7] is a clustering federated learning framework that groups clients based on the similarity of client optimization directions and constructs a data-driven distance metric to improve clustering efficiency. A semi-decentralized federated edge learning is proposed [44], which allows model aggregation between different edge clusters, reduces training delay, and improves model convergence speed. A low-overhead federated learning semi-asynchronous protocol [50] is proposed to reduce the impact of client dropout, crash, and model obsolescence. $CSAFL$ [56] combining the advantages of the synchronous communication strategy and asynchronous communication strategy of federated learning, a clustering semi-asynchronous architecture is proposed, and experiments have verified that the model's accuracy can be improved.

4   Federated Neural Architecture Search

Research on federated NAS is still in its infancy. There is still no general paradigm for federated NAS, and more in-depth research is still needed.

Zhu et al. in [61] gives a specific overview of both FL and federated neural architecture search. They summarize the classification of federated learning, the training process, and the current research progress and organize a large amount of research on NAS. Our classification approach for NAS is based on the classification approach they proposed. Their work proposed that the neural architecture for search optimization in the FL framework is particularly demanding and faces many open challenges, and the federated neural architecture search was classified as online and offline implementations, single-objective and multi-objective search methods. It is crucial for studying federated neural architecture search and will be helpful for future research.

Furthermore, Zhu et al. [59] also proposed a real-time federated evolutionary search algorithm, which is mainly designed to address the communication and computational resource challenges. The algorithm introduces a double sampling technique in the search process. Sub-models for random sampling of the master model are delivered to multiple randomly sampled clients, trained on each one, reducing the initialization process and effectively reducing optimization costs.

There are still some other studies on federated neural architecture search, and we will summarize all of them. Singh et al. [41] proposed differential privacy for federated neural architecture search to solve the privacy problem by applying differential privacy techniques to federated neural architecture search. This study proposes the FNAS method, where fewer parties jointly search for microscopic architectures by swapping the gradients of architecture variants with no data sharing. And further adds differential privacy to the FNAS algorithm to propose the DP-FNAS algorithm, which uses the differential privacy mechanism to add random noise to achieve gradient fuzzing of architecture parameters, which can improve the search performance while protecting privacy.

Grag et al. [11] proposed direct federated NAS, hoping to automatically search global and personalized models of non-iid data, thus avoiding the non-optimal performance problem of FL of predefined models. This study points out that most NAS methods have high computational costs and require post-search adjustments, complicating overall process. The proposed direct federated neural architecture search method, a one-stage search method with hardware diagnostics and computational lightweight, can improve computational efficiency.

Xu et al. [52] proposed an automatic neural architecture search to decentralize training in a way that makes it applicable to design neural network architectures in heterogeneous environments and proposed the DecNAS method, which is an efficient federated NAS method. DecNAS takes full advantage of the insufficient model candidate retraining during architecture search and further optimizes it to improve model performance and effectively reduce clients' costs.

Zhang et al. [55] investigate data privacy and model diversity issues in AutoML, mainly by integrating federated learning with NAS and proposing the FDNAS framework that allows clients to obtain hardware-aware NAS from Non-IID data. This research proposes to combine meta-learning with FDNAS to form a clustered federated direct neural architecture search (CFDNAS) framework to implement a client-aware NAS where each client can learn a customized deep learning model that matches the data distribution.

He et al. [13] proposed to implement the FedNAS method for federated neural architecture search using the FedNAS method, mainly for Non-IID and invisible data cases. And in the proposed FedML [14] platform, a FedNAS-based system is constructed, and experiments on the Nn-IID dataset are used to show that the model structure is obtained by FedNAS search outperforms the manually predefined architecture.

Liang et al. [28] proposed a Cross-silo federated neural architecture search and utilized a sub-supervised learning approach, mainly applied in a VFL environment. The SS-VFNAS method is proposed to automate the FL of the participating parties holding partitioned feature data. It is a self-supervised vertical federated NAS. Each party executes the NAS by using a self-supervised approach for finding the locally best architecture with their data. This approach offers better performance, more efficient communication and privacy protection than normal Federated NAS, generating high-performance and highly transferable heterogeneous architectures.

In addition, [53] presented a RL-based method to federated model search using ideas from reinforcement learning, and the framework samples and distributes participants' submodels and updates their model selection strategies by reward maximization.

5   Open Problems of NAS and Federated NAS

NAS as a technique to design neural networks automatically. That can use the various algorithms described above to automatically create high-performance network architectures based on sample sets that exhibit excellent model performance on specific tasks and effectively reduce the cost of using and implementing neural networks. As the research on neural architecture search continues to grow and evolve in its applications, it faces new challenges. In addition, the study of combining FL techniques with NAS is still in its infancy, and many problems have not been effectively solved. The research on both neural architecture search and federated neural architecture search faces numerous open challenges that require more study and feasible solutions. This section provides an overview of the critical issues and available challenges of neural architecture search and federated neural architecture search.

5.1   Open Problems of NAS

Theoretical Flaws of NAS. NAS research has covered a variety of approaches and content, but compared to the pace of development in areas such as artificial intelligence, NAS is not yet complete. Current NAS research focuses on image classification recognition tasks, aiming to automatically search for neural network architectures with optimal performance, improve image classification accuracy, and reduce the cost and time required to train neural network models. The primary use of the current NAS research is mostly based on the supernet search strategy. However, there are still some shortcomings in the theoretical background. Lacking perfect academic support and perfect research background is of great significance for NAS.

NAS Performance and Cost Trade-Offs. Early research on neural network architecture search focused on using large-scale evolutionary algorithms as a search strategy to find the optimal network architecture as little intervention from humans as possible. Evolutionary algorithms allow the algorithm to determine the neural network's evolutionary direction autonomously. Still, the computational overhead of evolutionary algorithms is too large, the efficiency of evolutionary search is low, and it isn't easy to obtain a neural network architecture with excellent performance. As NAS research expands, gradient-based methods are gradually becoming mainstream and expanding the NAS progressively into a modular process. Global search is transformed into modular search, improving search efficiency. Therefore, the search efficiency of NAS and the tradeoff between performance and search cost for the acquired model remains a critical issue, and balancing performance and cost overhead is essential.

NAS Performance Measurement Strategy. The objective of the NAS search strategy for finding a neural network architecture to maximize certain performance metrics. To provide guidance for a search process, it is necessary for NAS to estimate the performance for a given NNs architecture, which requires an evaluation strategy for performance. Search strategies for the neural network architecture searched need to be evaluated on training sets and tested for accuracy on verification sets. Therefore, adopting effective measures to reduce performance evaluation cost is also a vital issue for NAS. A reasonable performance evaluation strategy can effectively reduce the cost overhead of NAS. Designing and selecting an efficient performance evaluation strategy is also of great importance for NAS-related research.

5.2   Open Problems of Federated NAS

Non-IID Data for Federated NAS. Some problems related to federated neural architecture search mainly originate from federated learning, which is primarily studied for heterogeneous environments with mostly Non-IID data. Therefore, the primary concern of federated neural architecture search is closely related to data distribution. It is a crucial challenge to address the impact of unbalanced data distribution in federated neural architecture search. There is no general method to effectively address training issues caused by Non-IID in FL. Further research is still needed to deal with the search efficiency and model performance issues caused by the unbalanced data distribution in federated neural architecture search.

Resource Limitation Issues with Federated NAS. Federated neural architecture search is designed to obtain superior performance neural network models in a distributed environment without centralized data processing. However, since the local resources of each participant device of federated learning in a distributed environment are different, the overall efficiency of federated neural architecture search may be affected due to the limitation of the devices' communication capacity and computational resources. Once the search space occupies too many resources in a resource-limited environment, it can lead to the possibility of not being able to proceed or a system crash.

Privacy Protection for Federated NAS. Federated neural architecture search is a good application of the privacy-preserving property of FL without sharing data, which an excellent solution to the problem of data privacy leakage, but there are still many shortcomings. Since simply not sharing data does not achieve a high level of privacy protection and is not perfect enough, applying security techniques such as encryption algorithms and differential privacy is a complete solution. To effectively combine cryptographic techniques such as cryptographic algorithms with federated neural architecture search still needs to be studied in depth. The application of encryption algorithms causes different degrees of performance loss, making the search less efficient, making the neural architecture search more complex and therefore requires an effective solution.

6   Conclusion

Our article provides a brief overview of the research on FL and NAS. After summarizing some researches on NAS, we explore practical ways to combine federated learning with NAS and summarize the existing research on federated neural architecture search. The overview of current research shows us that introducing FL into NAS is a practical approach to address the privacy issues arising from NAS, which can automatically search the neural network architecture and obtain models with better performance without centralized data processing. Most of the existing research on neural architecture search does not apply to the federated setting, so it is crucial for a more effective and feasible solution of FL with NAS. Federated NAS is at the beginning stage of research, which is of great practical importance, but it still faces many problems and needs to be studied more thoroughly.

Acknowledgements. This work is supported by the General Program of Science and Technology Development Project of Beijing Municipal Education Commission of China (No. KM202110037002), the Youth Fund Project of Beijing Wuzi University (No. 2020XJQN02).

References

1. Angeline, P.J., Saunders, G.M., Pollack, J.B.: An evolutionary algorithm that constructs recurrent neural networks. IEEE Trans. Neural Netw. **5**(1), 54–65 (1994)
2. Baker, B., Gupta, O., Naik, N., Raskar, R.: Designing neural network architectures using reinforcement learning. arXiv preprint arXiv:1611.02167 (2016)
3. Briggs, C., Fan, Z., Andras, P.: Federated learning with hierarchical clustering of local updates to improve training on non-IID data. In: 2020 International Joint Conference on Neural Networks (IJCNN), pp. 1–9. IEEE (2020)
4. Chen, Z., Li, D., Zhao, M., Zhang, S., Zhu, J.: Semi-federated learning. In: 2020 IEEE Wireless Communications and Networking Conference (WCNC), pp. 1–6. IEEE (2020)
5. Corinzia, L., Beuret, A., Buhmann, J.M.: Variational federated multi-task learning. arXiv preprint arXiv:1906.06268 (2019)
6. Dinh, C.T., Tran, N.H., Nguyen, T.D.: Personalized federated learning with Moreau envelopes. arXiv preprint arXiv:2006.08848 (2020)
7. Duan, M., et al.: FedGroup: efficient clustered federated learning via decomposed data-driven measure (2020)
8. Elsken, T., Metzen, J.H., Hutter, F.: Neural architecture search: a survey. J. Mach. Learn. Res. **20**(1), 1997–2017 (2019)
9. Fallah, A., Mokhtari, A., Ozdaglar, A.: Personalized federated learning: a meta-learning approach. arXiv preprint arXiv:2002.07948 (2020)
10. Gao, Y., Yang, H., Zhang, P., Zhou, C., Hu, Y.: GraphNAS: graph neural architecture search with reinforcement learning. arXiv preprint arXiv:1904.09981 (2019)
11. Garg, A., Saha, A.K., Dutta, D.: Direct federated neural architecture search. arXiv preprint arXiv:2010.06223 (2020)
12. Ghosh, A., Chung, J., Yin, D., Ramchandran, K.: An efficient framework for clustered federated learning. arXiv preprint arXiv:2006.04088 (2020)
13. He, C., Annavaram, M., Avestimehr, S.: Towards non-IID and invisible data with FedNAS: federated deep learning via neural architecture search. arXiv preprint arXiv:2004.08546 (2020)
14. He, C., et al.: FedML: a research library and benchmark for federated machine learning. arXiv preprint arXiv:2007.13518 (2020)
15. He, C., Ye, H., Shen, L., Zhang, T.: MiLeNAS: efficient neural architecture search via mixed-level reformulation. In: Proceedings of the IEEE/CVF Conference on Computer Vision and Pattern Recognition, pp. 11993–12002 (2020)
16. Hsieh, K., Phanishayee, A., Mutlu, O., Gibbons, P.: The non-IID data quagmire of decentralized machine learning. In: International Conference on Machine Learning, pp. 4387–4398. PMLR (2020)
17. Iandola, F.N., Han, S., Moskewicz, M.W., Ashraf, K., Dally, W.J., Keutzer, K.: SqueezeNet: AlexNet-level accuracy with 50x fewer parameters and <0.5 mb model size. arXiv preprint arXiv:1602.07360 (2016)
18. Jaafra, Y., Laurent, J.L., Deruyver, A., Naceur, M.S.: Reinforcement learning for neural architecture search: a review. Image Vis. Comput. **89**, 57–66 (2019)
19. Kairouz, P., et al.: Advances and open problems in federated learning. arXiv preprint arXiv:1912.04977 (2019)
20. Karimireddy, S.P., Kale, S., Mohri, M., Reddi, S., Stich, S., Suresh, A.T.: SCAFFOLD: stochastic controlled averaging for federated learning. In: International Conference on Machine Learning, pp. 5132–5143. PMLR (2020)

21. Konečnỳ, J., McMahan, H.B., Yu, F.X., Richtárik, P., Suresh, A.T., Bacon, D.: Federated learning: strategies for improving communication efficiency. arXiv preprint arXiv:1610.05492 (2016)
22. Kopparapu, K., Lin, E.: FedfMC: sequential efficient federated learning on non-IID data. arXiv preprint arXiv:2006.10937 (2020)
23. Kopparapu, K., Lin, E., Zhao, J.: FedCD: improving performance in non-IID federated learning. arXiv preprint arXiv:2006.09637 (2020)
24. Li, L., Khodak, M., Balcan, M.F., Talwalkar, A.: Geometry-aware gradient algorithms for neural architecture search. arXiv preprint arXiv:2004.07802 (2020)
25. Li, T., Sahu, A.K., Zaheer, M., Sanjabi, M., Talwalkar, A., Smith, V.: Federated optimization in heterogeneous networks. arXiv preprint arXiv:1812.06127 (2018)
26. Li, T., Sahu, A.K., Zaheer, M., Sanjabi, M., Talwalkar, A., Smithy, V.: FedDANE: a federated Newton-type method. In: 2019 53rd Asilomar Conference on Signals, Systems, and Computers, pp. 1227–1231. IEEE (2019)
27. Li, Z., Kovalev, D., Qian, X., Richtárik, P.: Acceleration for compressed gradient descent in distributed and federated optimization. arXiv preprint arXiv:2002.11364 (2020)
28. Liang, X., Liu, Y., Luo, J., He, Y., Chen, T., Yang, Q.: Self-supervised cross-silo federated neural architecture search. arXiv preprint arXiv:2101.11896 (2021)
29. Liu, H., Simonyan, K., Yang, Y.: DARTS: differentiable architecture search. arXiv preprint arXiv:1806.09055 (2018)
30. McMahan, B., Moore, E., Ramage, D., Hampson, S., Arcas, B.A.: Communication-efficient learning of deep networks from decentralized data. In: Artificial Intelligence and Statistics, pp. 1273–1282. PMLR (2017)
31. Pathak, R., Wainwright, M.J.: FedSplit: an algorithmic framework for fast federated optimization. arXiv preprint arXiv:2005.05238 (2020)
32. Real, E., et al.: Large-scale evolution of image classifiers. In: International Conference on Machine Learning, pp. 2902–2911. PMLR (2017)
33. Reddi, S., et al.: Adaptive federated optimization. arXiv preprint arXiv:2003.00295 (2020)
34. Reddi, S.J., Konečnỳ, J., Richtárik, P., Póczós, B., Smola, A.: AIDE: fast and communication efficient distributed optimization. arXiv preprint arXiv:1608.06879 (2016)
35. Ren, P., et al.: A comprehensive survey of neural architecture search: challenges and solutions. ACM Comput. Surv. (CSUR) 54(4), 1–34 (2021)
36. Santra, S., Hsieh, J.W., Lin, C.F.: Gradient descent effects on differential neural architecture search: a survey. IEEE Access 9, 89602–89618 (2021)
37. Sattler, F., Müller, K.R., Samek, W.: Clustered federated learning: model-agnostic distributed multitask optimization under privacy constraints. IEEE Trans. Neural Netw. Learn. Syst. 32, 3710–3722 (2020)
38. Sengupta, A., Ye, Y., Wang, R., Liu, C., Roy, K.: Going deeper in spiking neural networks: VGG and residual architectures. Front. Neurosci. 13, 95 (2019)
39. Shamir, O., Srebro, N., Zhang, T.: Communication-efficient distributed optimization using an approximate Newton-type method. In: International Conference on Machine Learning, pp. 1000–1008. PMLR (2014)
40. Shoham, N., et al.: Overcoming forgetting in federated learning on non-IID data. arXiv preprint arXiv:1910.07796 (2019)
41. Singh, I., Zhou, H., Yang, K., Ding, M., Lin, B., Xie, P.: Differentially-private federated neural architecture search. arXiv preprint arXiv:2006.10559 (2020)
42. Smith, V., Chiang, C.K., Sanjabi, M., Talwalkar, A.: Federated multi-task learning. arXiv preprint arXiv:1705.10467 (2017)

43. Suganuma, M., Shirakawa, S., Nagao, T.: A genetic programming approach to designing convolutional neural network architectures. In: Proceedings of the Genetic and Evolutionary Computation Conference, pp. 497–504 (2017)

44. Sun, Y., Shao, J., Mao, Y., Zhang, J.: Semi-decentralized federated edge learning for fast convergence on non-IID data. arXiv preprint arXiv:2104.12678 (2021)

45. Szegedy, C., Ioffe, S., Vanhoucke, V., Alemi, A.A.: Inception-v4, inception-ResNet and the impact of residual connections on learning. In: Thirty-First AAAI Conference on Artificial Intelligence (2017)

46. Wang, H., Kaplan, Z., Niu, D., Li, B.: Optimizing federated learning on non-IID data with reinforcement learning. In: IEEE INFOCOM 2020-IEEE Conference on Computer Communications, pp. 1698–1707. IEEE (2020)

47. Wang, H., Yurochkin, M., Sun, Y., Papailiopoulos, D., Khazaeni, Y.: Federated learning with matched averaging. arXiv preprint arXiv:2002.06440 (2020)

48. Wang, J., Liu, Q., Liang, H., Joshi, G., Poor, H.V.: Tackling the objective inconsistency problem in heterogeneous federated optimization. arXiv preprint arXiv:2007.07481 (2020)

49. Watkins, C.J.C.H.: Learning from delayed rewards (1989)

50. Wu, W., He, L., Lin, W., Mao, R., Maple, C., Jarvis, S.A.: SAFA: a semi-asynchronous protocol for fast federated learning with low overhead. IEEE Trans. Comput. **70**, 655–668 (2020)

51. Xie, L., Yuille, A.: Genetic CNN. In: Proceedings of the IEEE International Conference on Computer Vision, pp. 1379–1388 (2017)

52. Xu, M., Zhao, Y., Bian, K., Huang, G., Mei, Q., Liu, X.: Federated neural architecture search. arXiv preprint arXiv:2002.06352 (2020)

53. Yao, D., et al.: Federated model search via reinforcement learning (2021)

54. Yao, X.: Evolving artificial neural networks. Proc. IEEE **87**(9), 1423–1447 (1999)

55. Zhang, C., Liang, Y., Yuan, X., Cheng, L.: FDNAS: improving data privacy and model diversity in AutoML. arXiv preprint arXiv:2011.03372 (2020)

56. Zhang, Y., et al.: CSAFL: a clustered semi-asynchronous federated learning framework. arXiv preprint arXiv:2104.08184 (2021)

57. Zhao, Y., Li, M., Lai, L., Suda, N., Civin, D., Chandra, V.: Federated learning with non-IID data. arXiv preprint arXiv:1806.00582 (2018)

58. Zhong, Z., et al.: BlockQNN: efficient block-wise neural network architecture generation. IEEE Trans. Pattern Anal. Mach. Intell. **43**(7), 2314–2328 (2020)

59. Zhu, H., Jin, Y.: Real-time federated evolutionary neural architecture search. IEEE Trans. Evol. Comput. (2021). https://doi.org/10.1109/TEVC.2021.3099448

60. Zhu, H., Xu, J., Liu, S., Jin, Y.: Federated learning on non-IID data: a survey. arXiv preprint arXiv:2106.06843 (2021)

61. Zhu, H., Zhang, H., Jin, Y.: From federated learning to federated neural architecture search: a survey. Complex Intell. Syst. **7**(2), 639–657 (2021). https://doi.org/10.1007/s40747-020-00247-z

62. Zoph, B., Le, Q.V.: Neural architecture search with reinforcement learning. arXiv preprint arXiv:1611.01578 (2016)

63. Zoph, B., Vasudevan, V., Shlens, J., Le, Q.V.: Learning transferable architectures for scalable image recognition. In: Proceedings of the IEEE Conference on Computer Vision and Pattern Recognition, pp. 8697–8710 (2018)

Face Detection on Thermal Infrared Images Combined with Visible Images

Yujia Chen[1], Liqing Wang[2], and Guangda Xu[3]($\boxtimes$)

[1] School of Mathematics and Statistics, Xi'an Jiaotong University, Xi'an, China
`jerryniu520126@foxmail.com`
[2] Infrared Division, Wuhan Huazhong Numerical Control Co., Ltd., Wuhan, China
[3] National Numerical Control System Engineering Research Center, Huazhong University of Science and Technology, Wuhan, China
`xu_guangda@hust.edu.cn`

Abstract. Due to COVID-19, intelligent thermal imagers are widely used all over the world. Since intelligent thermal imagers usually require real-time temperature measurement, it is significant to find a method to quickly and accurately detect human faces in thermal infrared images. This paper mainly proposes two different methods. One is to use image processing methods and face detected from visible images to determine the position of the face in the infrared image, while the other is to use target detection algorithms on infrared images, including YOLOv3 and Faster R-CNN. This paper uses the two methods on a self-collected dataset containing 944 pairs of visible and infrared images and observes the robustness of methods by adding random noise to images. Experiments show that the first one has much lower latency and the latter one has higher accuracy in both cases.

Keywords: Face detection · Thermal infrared image · YOLOv3 · Faster R-CNN · Intelligent thermal imagers

1 Introduction

Visible images refer to images formed by visible light (light with a wavelength between 390 nm–780 nm). The photos taken by ordinary cameras are visible images. In recent years, target detection, especially face detection for visible images, is developing rapidly and many effective algorithms can be used. For example, it is a good choice to use R-CNN (Region-based Convolutional Neural Networks) [5] and its derivative algorithms, including Fast R-CNN [4], Faster R-CNN [14], Mask R-CNN [6] and R-FCN [3]. Different versions of YOLO (You only look once) are also effective, including YOLOv1 [11], YOLOv2 [12], YOLOv3 [13], YOLOv3 [1] and PP-YOLO [10].

Because of COVID-19, intelligent thermal imagers are widely used all over the world. To prevent interference caused by the ambient temperature, the intelligent thermal imager needs to narrow down the temperature measurement area.

© Springer Nature Singapore Pte Ltd. 2022
L. Pan et al. (Eds.): BIC-TA 2021, CCIS 1566, pp. 346–357, 2022.
https://doi.org/10.1007/978-981-19-1253-5_26

Given that the skin of the human face is exposed to the air, the human face is considered a suitable temperature measurement area. Therefore, an intelligent thermal imager usually needs to find the position of the human face in the infrared image as the temperature measurement area [16]. Face detection in thermal infrared images becomes an important issue.

In recent years, there are some papers on face detection in thermal infrared images [7–9,15]. Most previous papers used high-resolution single-person thermal infrared images with little noise in the environment. However, in actual application scenarios of intelligent thermal imagers, thermal infrared images may have low resolution, many people, or much environmental noise. The facial features in the thermal infrared image are probably not visible due to low resolution, which means they may perform badly in a real situation.

In addition, since intelligent thermal imagers usually require real-time temperature measurement, they usually do not use target detection algorithms directly on infrared images because their processing speed is not fast enough. Instead, many intelligent thermal imagers copy the faces detected in visible images to the corresponding infrared images [16]. However, the results of this method are not very accurate. For example, Fig. 1 is a screenshot of HY-2005B intelligent thermal imager, produced by Wuhan Huazhong Numerical Control Co., Ltd. [17].

Fig. 1. A screenshot of an intelligent thermal imager

Figure 1 shows that faces detected in visible images are quite precise, while faces detected in infrared images have noticeable offsets. The main reason is that these two different types of images are captured by two different cameras and there is a small distance between them (shown as Fig. 2), which leads to different optical axes of the two cameras. This means that even the same pixel in the infrared image and the visible image corresponds to a different position.

In conclusion, it is significant to find a method to quickly and accurately detect human faces in thermal infrared images with corresponding visible images.

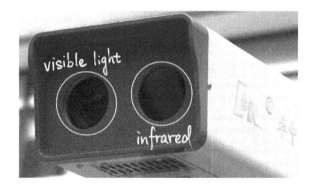

Fig. 2. The infrared camera and the visible light camera

2 Principle of Image Calibration

Given that the distance between the two cameras is small, it can be assumed that the mapping between infrared images and visible images is a rigid transformation. In other words, the pixel (x, y) in the visible image and the pixel (x', y') in the infrared image satisfy the following relationship (shown as Eq. (1)).

$$\begin{cases} x' = a_{11}x + a_{12}y + a_{13} \\ y' = a_{21}x + a_{22}y + a_{23} \end{cases} \tag{1}$$

where $a_{ij}(i = 1, 2; j = 1, 2, 3)$ are all constants.

The matrixed equation is as follows

$$\begin{bmatrix} x' \\ y' \end{bmatrix} = \begin{bmatrix} a_{11} & a_{12} & a_{13} \\ a_{21} & a_{22} & a_{23} \end{bmatrix} \cdot \begin{bmatrix} x \\ y \\ 1 \end{bmatrix} = \mathbf{A} \cdot \begin{bmatrix} x \\ y \\ 1 \end{bmatrix} \tag{2}$$

If the coordinates of the three corresponding point pairs are known and they are $(x_k, y_k)(x'_k, y'_k)(k = 1, 2, 3)$, then the parameters $a_{ij}(i = 1, 2; j = 1, 2, 3)$ can be determined by the following equation:

$$\begin{cases} x'_k = a_{11}x_k + a_{12}y_k + a_{13} & (k = 1, 2, 3) \\ y'_k = a_{21}x_k + a_{22}y_k + a_{23} & (k = 1, 2, 3) \end{cases} \tag{3}$$

This method is simple and easy to implement. By using this method, people can determine the position of human faces in the infrared image through the face box in the corresponding visible image.

However, it should be noticed that this method ignores the distance between the object and the camera, which will affect the calibration. For example, if all the calibration point pairs are obtained at a distance of 5 m from the camera, the calibration of the object at 2 m will have an offset. This paper will analyze the causes of offset in detail and propose ways to reduce it.

3   Optical Analysis for Calibration Offset

This section tries to explain the reasons why the calibration offset occurs by performing an optical analysis.

3.1   Optical Model Derivation

The optical model of the intelligent thermal imager is shown in Fig. 3. $\overline{BG}$ represents the optical axis of the visible camera, while $\overline{CT}$ represents the optical axis of the infrared camera. $\overline{FG}$ and $\overline{ST}$ are the light screens of the visible camera and infrared camera respectively. Note that the light screens are on the same plane. The point P represents the object being photographed.

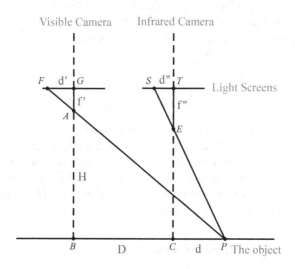

Fig. 3. The optical representation of an intelligent thermal imager

The geometric similarity tells that

$$\frac{FG}{BP} = \frac{AG}{AB}$$

$$\frac{ST}{CP} = \frac{ET}{CE}$$

Namely,

$$\frac{d'}{D+d} = \frac{f'}{H} \tag{4}$$

$$\frac{d''}{d} = \frac{f''}{H + f' - f''} \tag{5}$$

Since $H \gg f', f''$ and $f' \approx f''$, $H \gg f' - f''$. Thus, the Eq. (5) can be simplified as

$$\frac{d''}{d} = \frac{f''}{H} \qquad (6)$$

By combining the Eqs. (4) and (6), the following relationship can be obtained

$$d'' = d' \cdot \frac{f''}{f'} - \frac{Df''}{H} \qquad (7)$$

Let $k = \frac{f''}{f'}$ and $C = \frac{Df''}{H}$. Then the Eq. (7) becomes

$$d'' = d' \cdot k - C \qquad (8)$$

Suppose that at a fixed distance H_0, take any two calibration points. The distances between these two points and point C are d_1 and d_2 respectively. d'_1 and d''_1 correspond to d_1, while d'_2 and d''_2 correspond to d_2. Then, the following linear equations can be obtained

$$\begin{cases} d''_1 = d'_1 \cdot k - C \\ d''_2 = d'_2 \cdot k - C \end{cases} \qquad (9)$$

By solving the Eq. (9), k and C can be determined.

The calibration method introduced in Sect. 2 regards the distance between the object and the two cameras H as a constant H_0. In other words, This calibration method only uses constants k and C for calibration, regardless of the distance between the object and the camera. However, H is changing, which causes C is also changing. That is the reason why the calibration has an offset.

3.2 Analysis for Calibration Offset

Assume that the calibration is performed at H_0. Then, the calibration offset is $\frac{Df''}{H} - \frac{Df''}{H_0}$. When $H > H_0$ (that is, when the actual object is farther from the camera), $\frac{Df''}{H} - \frac{Df''}{H_0} < 0$ because D and f'' keep unchanged. This means that d'' will be smaller than it should be, if we still use k and C obtained by H_0 for calibration in this case. Similarly, when $H < H_0$ (that is, the actual object is closer to the camera), d'' will be larger than it should be.

However, it should be noticed that $\frac{1}{H}$ is an inverse function. Hence, the calibration offset at $H < H_0$ is much larger than the calibration offset at $H > H_0$. For example, suppose $H_0 = 5$ meters. On the one hand, when $H = 1$ meter, the calibration offset is

$$\frac{Df''}{H} - \frac{Df''}{H_0} = \frac{4}{5}Df''$$

On the other hand, when $H = 9$ meters, the calibration offset is

$$\frac{Df''}{H} - \frac{Df''}{H_0} = -\frac{4}{45}Df''$$

In this case, $\frac{4}{5}Df'' > \frac{4}{45}Df''$.

3.3   Methods to Reduce Calibration Offset

The first two methods try to reduce the calibration offset on the physical level, while the latter two methods try to rectify the calibration results from the perspective of image processing.

Method 1: Using the Exact H Instead of H_0. This method can even eliminate the calibration offset. However, it should be noted that this method requires real-time measurement of the distance between each object and the camera, which needs very professional equipment and incurs huge costs. Therefore, this method is theoretically usable but not practically affordable.

Method 2: Decreasing the Distance Between the Two Cameras. Since the calibration offset $\frac{Df''}{H} - \frac{Df''}{H_0}$ is linear to the distance between the two cameras D, decreasing it is another choice. However, it should be noticed that the ideal situation $D = 0$ cannot be implemented physically because the visible camera and the infrared camera are two different cameras.

Method 3: Looking for the Largest Connected White Area. This method mainly has 4 steps (shown in Fig. 4). The largest connected white area is the precise face box as required.

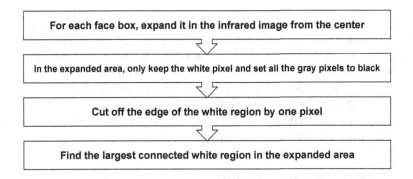

Fig. 4. A flowchart of the procedure of Method 3

Take Fig. 5 as an example. The red rectangle in Fig. 5 shows the face box obtained by using the calibration method above.

First, expand the red rectangle by half of its side length to obtain the green rectangle in Fig. 5.

Fig. 5. An example for Method 3 (Color figure online)

Second, set all the pixels with a gray-scale value between 221 and 255 to 1 (i.e. white) and setting the other pixels to 0 (i.e. black).

Next, traverse all the white pixels and determine whether the four pixels up, down, left, and right are all 1 (i.e. white). Save the positions of the pixels that do not meet this condition and set them to 0 (i.e. black).

Finally, use the seed-filling algorithm or the two-pass algorithm to find all the connected white regions, which are both traditional and classical algorithms to do that. Then compute the area of all connected regions and find the largest one, which is the blue rectangle in Fig. 5.

Method 4: Using Target Detection Algorithms. Method 3 uses classic image processing methods to detect faces. Thus, combining some more advanced algorithms seems to be a good option, especially some mature and effective target detection algorithms, such as Faster-RCNN [14] or YOLOv3 [13].

The first step of Method 4 is the same as the one of Method 3, which is expanding each face box from the center. However, Method 4 directly uses target detection algorithms to detect a human face in the expanded area, while Method 3 uses 3 more steps to process the infrared image.

4   Experiments and Results

4.1   Experimental Setup

Data Collection. Since there are few pairs of infrared and visible images in the public data set containing clear human faces, this paper uses a self-collected data set containing 944 pairs of infrared and visible images. Some pairs of images are shown in Fig. 6. All the infrared images are grayscale images consisting of 256 * 320 pixels, while all the visible images are RGB images consisting of 1024

* 1280 pixels. The faces in each image are labeled with rectangular boxes as ground truths. Labels are stored in XML files.

Fig. 6. A few examples of the data set

For data augmentation, this paper performs a horizontal flip for all image pairs. Besides, this paper standardizes all the images before training, evaluation, and final testing.

This paper shuffles all preprocessed image pairs and extracts 70% of them as the training set, 15% as the validation set, and the remaining 15% as the test set.

Performance Measurement. This paper mainly uses two parameters to measure the performance of methods: average precision (AP) when the threshold is intersection over union (IoU) = 0.5 and frames per second (FPS) in the following experimental environment

> GPU: Tesla V100. Video Mem: 16 GB
> CPU: 4 Cores. RAM: 32 GB. Disk: 100 GB

For each method, the AP and FPS of the optimal model on the test set will be collected as its final performance.

Optimization and Evaluation. This paper uses a trained PP-YOLO model to detect faces in visible images, whose FPS is about 50 in the above environment [10].

For Method 4, this paper uses two algorithms, YOLOv3 [13] and Faster R-CNN [14], to detect faces in infrared images. The optimization and evaluation strategy is shown in Table 1, where LR is the abbreviation of learning rate.

This paper mainly compares the performance of the following five methods.

Table 1. Optimization and evaluation strategy

Algorithms	Backbone	LR	Epochs	LR decay epochs	Optimizer
YOLOv3	DarkNet53	0.000125	50	[30, 40]	Momentum
Faster R-CNN	ResNet50	0.0025	12	[10, 11]	Momentum

---

1. PP-YOLO + Image Processing (Method 3)

2. PP-YOLO + YOLOv3 (Method 4)

3. YOLOv3 only

4. PP-YOLO + Faster R-CNN (Method 4)

5. Faster R-CNN only

The optimization and evaluation strategy of PP-YOLO + YOLOv3 is the same as YOLOv3 only. Similarly, the optimization and evaluation strategy of PP-YOLO + Faster R-CNN is the same as Faster R-CNN only.

Random Noise. In order to compare the robustness of methods, this paper conducts experiments in two situations: with random noise and without random noise.

The random noise is added by randomly scaling the brightness and contrast of images. The probability of whether randomly scaling contrast or brightness is 0.5. When scaling is required according to the random result, take a random value from $[0.5, 1.5]$ as the scaling factor s_b, s_c and distort the image according to the following formulas.

$$\text{Brightness}: \textbf{Image}(i, j) \Longrightarrow s_b \cdot \textbf{Image}(i, j)$$

$$\text{Contrast}: \textbf{Image}(i, j) \Longrightarrow s_c \cdot \textbf{Image}(i, j) + (1 - s_c) \cdot \overline{\textbf{Image}}$$

where $\textbf{Image}(i, j)$ refers to each pixel and $\overline{\textbf{Image}}$ is the mean of the image. Namely,

$$\overline{\textbf{Image}} = \frac{1}{M \cdot N} \sum_{i=1}^{M} \sum_{j=1}^{N} \textbf{Image}(i, j)$$

4.2 Results

The experimental results are shown in Table 2.

Experiments show that Method 3 has a much higher FPS than the other methods, which means that Method 3 can quickly find the positions of human faces in infrared images. However, the AP of Method 3 is much worse than Method 4's AP. That is mainly because Method 3 has weaker robustness than that of Method 4. For example, if a person wears a mask, Method 3 tends to

Table 2. The experimental results

Algorithms	Without noise		With noise	
	AP (%)	FPS (Hz)	AP (%)	FPS (Hz)
PP-YOLO + Image Processing	58.13	42	49.64	36
PP-YOLO + YOLOv3	91.03	11	91.05	10
YOLOv3 only	90.33	16	90.27	14
PP-YOLO + Faster R-CNN	91.60	10	91.62	9
Faster R-CNN only	90.80	13	90.83	13

output the part without the mask, while the ground truth often includes the mask.

However, to an intelligent thermal imager, only the face area for temperature measurement needs to be determined. Those occluded parts of the face (such as the area covered by a mask) will not be used for parking spaces. Therefore, although Method 3 cannot detect a complete face in some cases, it can still be used in this scenario.

Therefore, if high precision is required, Method 4 is better; if low latency is required, Method 3 is better.

5   Conclusion

This paper mainly proposes two methods to solve the problem of face detection in infrared images. One (called Method 3) is to uses image processing methods and face detected from visible images to determine the position of the face in the infrared image, while the other (called Method 4) is to uses target detection algorithms on infrared images, including YOLOv3 and Faster R-CNN.

To be specific, Method 3 mainly consists of 4 steps:

Step 1: For each face box, expand it in the infrared image from the center
Step 2: In the expanded area, only keep the white pixel and set all the gray pixels to black
Step 3: Cut off the edge of the white region by one pixel
Step 4: Find the largest connected white region in the expanded area

The first step of Method 4 is the same as the one of Method 3, which is expanding each face box from the center. However, Method 4 directly uses target detection algorithms to detect a human face in the expanded area, while Method 3 uses 3 more steps to process the infrared image.

Experiments show that Method 3 can quickly find the positions of human faces in infrared images. However, Method 3 has weaker robustness than that of Method 4, which is the main reason why the performance of Method 3 is worse than Method 4's performance. Therefore, if high precision is required, Method 4 is better; if low latency is required, Method 3 is better.

Besides, the methods proposed in this paper still have room for improvement in the correlation between visible and infrared images. This paper uses the calibration method proposed in Sect. 2 to associate visible and infrared images. In the future, other association methods are also worth trying (such as Cross-Modal CNN [2]).

References

1. Bochkovskiy, A., Wang, C.Y., Liao, H.Y.M.: YOLOV4: optimal speed and accuracy of object detection. arXiv preprint arXiv:2004.10934 (2020)
2. Cangea, C., Veličković, P., Liò, P.: XFlow: cross-modal deep neural networks for audiovisual classification. IEEE Trans. Neural Netw. Learn. Syst. **31**(9), 3711–3720 (2019)
3. Dai, J., Li, Y., He, K., Sun, J.: R-FCN: object detection via region-based fully convolutional networks. In: Advances in Neural Information Processing Systems, pp. 379–387 (2016)
4. Girshick, R.: Fast R-CNN. In: Proceedings of the IEEE International Conference on Computer Vision, pp. 1440–1448 (2015)
5. Girshick, R., Donahue, J., Darrell, T., Malik, J.: Rich feature hierarchies for accurate object detection and semantic segmentation. In: Proceedings of the IEEE Conference on Computer Vision and Pattern Recognition, pp. 580–587 (2014)
6. He, K., Gkioxari, G., Dollár, P., Girshick, R.: Mask R-CNN. In: Proceedings of the IEEE International Conference on Computer Vision, pp. 2961–2969 (2017)
7. Kopaczka, M., Nestler, J., Merhof, D.: Face detection in thermal infrared images: a comparison of algorithm- and machine-learning-based approaches. In: Blanc-Talon, J., Penne, R., Philips, W., Popescu, D., Scheunders, P. (eds.) ACIVS 2017. LNCS, vol. 10617, pp. 518–529. Springer, Cham (2017). https://doi.org/10.1007/978-3-319-70353-4_44
8. Kopaczka, M., Schock, J., Nestler, J., Kielholz, K., Merhof, D.: A combined modular system for face detection, head pose estimation, face tracking and emotion recognition in thermal infrared images. In: 2018 IEEE International Conference on Imaging Systems and Techniques (IST), pp. 1–6. IEEE (2018)
9. Kowalski, M., Grudzień, A., Ciurapiński, W.: Detection of human faces in thermal infrared images. Metrol. Measure. Syst. **28**, 307–321 (2021)
10. Long, X., et al.: PP-YOLO: an effective and efficient implementation of object detector. arXiv preprint arXiv:2007.12099 (2020)
11. Redmon, J., Divvala, S., Girshick, R., Farhadi, A.: You only look once: unified, real-time object detection. In: Proceedings of the IEEE Conference on Computer Vision and Pattern Recognition, pp. 779–788 (2016)
12. Redmon, J., Farhadi, A.: YOLO9000: better, faster, stronger. In: Proceedings of the IEEE Conference on Computer Vision and Pattern Recognition, pp. 7263–7271 (2017)
13. Redmon, J., Farhadi, A.: YOLOV3: an incremental improvement. arXiv preprint arXiv:1804.02767 (2018)
14. Ren, S., He, K., Girshick, R., Sun, J.: Faster R-CNN: towards real-time object detection with region proposal networks. Adv. Neural. Inf. Process. Syst. **28**, 91–99 (2015)

15. Ribeiro, R.F., Fernandes, J.M., Neves, A.J.: Face detection on infrared thermal image. SIGNAL 2017 Editors, p. 45 (2017)
16. Wang, H., Bai, C., Wang, J., Yuan, Z., Li, J., Gao, W.: The application of intelligent thermal imagers in response to COVID-19. China Metrol. **5**, 119–132 (2020)
17. Wuhan Huazhong Numerical Control Co., Ltd. (HCNC): Infrared AI thermal imagimg camera thermometer sensor face recognition body temperature scanner with CCTV dual thermal imager. https://www.alibaba.com/product-detail/Infrared-AI-Thermal-Imagimg-Camera-Thermometer_62490883868.html? spm=a2700.galleryofferlist.normal_offer.d_title.706950c9Bn2BwU. Accessed 04 May 2021

Research on Control Algorithm of Unmanned Vessel Formation Based on Multi-agent

Wei Zhao[1], Xiaoqiang Wang[2], Rui Wu[4], Chang Liu[5], and Hao Zhou[3(⊠)]

[1] The 716th Research Institute of China Shipbuilding Industry Corporation,
Beijing, China
18936685616@189.cn
[2] Jiangsu Automation Research Institute, Jiangsu, China
[3] School of Naval Architecture, Ocean and Energy Power Engineering,
Wuhan University of Technology, Wuhan, China
zhzmq@whut.edu.cn
[4] School of Automation, Wuhan University of Technology, Wuhan, China
[5] Wuhan Digital Engineering Institute, Wuhan, China

Abstract. In order to improve the accuracy of the formation control of multiple unmanned vessels, reduce the construction and maintenance costs and the impact of the external environment, and improve the robustness of the formation control method. Based on the hierarchical formation control technology of the navigator method, the formation design and behavior control are carried out respectively. After the formation is formed, the artificial potential field method is used to maintain, and the gravitational field and repulsive field of the virtual navigator and other unmanned ships and the maximum communication distance are considered respectively, and an improved virtual navigator formation control algorithm is obtained. Finally, we conducted formation control experiments. The experimental results show that this paper uses the proposed improved virtual navigator algorithm to conduct formation control and obstacle avoidance experiments, and find that the algorithm has good performance. The formation control method has the characteristics of high accuracy, strong generalization ability, fast control speed, and strong environmental adaptability. It meets the needs of actual formation control of multiple unmanned ships, and the formation control method can be packaged into an intelligent control system. It has the characteristics of flexible deployment and application, strong adaptability, and has the application space for formation control in actual combat with multiple unmanned ships.

Supported by organizations of the National Natural Science Foundation of China (61572228 and 61572226),the Key Development Project of Jilin Province (20180201045GX and 20180201067GX),the Guangdong Key-Project for Applied Fundamental Research (2018KZDXM076),and the Guangdong Premier Key-Discipline Enhancement Scheme (2016GDYSZDXK036).

L. Pan et al. (Eds.): BIC-TA 2021, CCIS 1566, pp. 358–372, 2022.
https://doi.org/10.1007/978-981-19-1253-5_27

Keywords: Virtual navigator · Formation design · Behavior control · Gravitational field · Repulsion field · Maximum communication distance

1 Introduction

The multi-agent system is composed of a series of interacting agents. The internal agents communicate, cooperate, and compete with each other to complete a large number of and complex tasks that a single agent cannot complete. Therefore, how to quickly, accurately and effectively control the formation of multiple agents to complete complex and important tasks is an urgent problem to be solved [1]. At present, with the in-depth research of various countries, unmanned ships have become more and more intelligent, capable of completing some tasks that are difficult for humans to complete, and are becoming more and more popular with scientists.

In view of the problem that a single unmanned ship cannot effectively complete complex tasks, the system needs to control multiple agents in formation. At present, domestic research on formation control is mainly at the stage of theoretical simulation. Shenyang Institute of Automation, Harbin Engineering University, China Shipbuilding Industry Corporation and other units have a good research foundation in this field. Aiming at the problem of unstable formation of multiple unmanned ships due to positioning accuracy, a pilot-following formation control strategy combined with extended Kalman filtering is proposed to improve positioning accuracy and form a stable formation [2]. Aiming at the unmanned ship formation system based on the multi-agent collaborative model, Lu Yu proposed a multi-vessel distributed robust adaptive formation zoom control method based on azimuth, which can solve the unmanned ship formation under the input saturation constraints and uncertain conditions. Cluster formation zoom maneuver control problem [3]. Aiming at the problem of under-driven unmanned ship formation control with uncertain model parameters, unknown marine environmental disturbances and unknown input gains, Liu Yunjie proposed a single-path guided distributed time-varying formation control method with obstacle avoidance and connectivity maintenance functions [4]. Aiming at the unmanned ship pilot-following formation system, Li He adopts a cooperative trajectory tracking control method and introduces a fixed-time control algorithm to improve the tracking control convergence performance of the unmanned ship formation system; consider unmanned vehicles with unknown environmental disturbances and unmodeled dynamics For the tracking control problem of the ship formation system, by designing a limited time precise disturbance observer, the unknown information identification and compensation in the complex environment can be realized, and the rapid and accurate tracking control of the unmanned ship pilot-following the formation can be ensured [5]. Zheng Shuai proposed the MADDPG algorithm to solve the coordination problem in the tracking process, design the local environment state space, the action space and the global reward function, and train the algorithm based on the multi-ship rescue two-dimensional plane scene, and obtain the cooperative rescue strategy model [6]. Shen Wei analyzes the mathematical model of unmanned ships, and establishes a control model of multiple unmanned ships that lead and follow. After that, the formation controller was designed using the anti-step method to make each unmanned ship reach the predetermined speed and heading. At the same time, in response to the problem of unstable formation caused by low positioning accuracy in practical applications, a position estimation algorithm based on EKF technology under the same model is proposed [7]. Liu Chang, Du Wencai, and Ren Jia proposed a distributed topology control algorithm based on directional antennas in order to solve the problem of directivity constraints of directional antennas in the formation of unmanned ships. Fast network connection. Simulation experiments prove that the algorithm can maintain the network connectivity performance at a lower energy consumption cost [8]. Liu Chang proposed an improved topology control algorithm based on directional antennas. This algorithm considers the energy consumption problem of unmanned ship formation, in order to use the minimum power consumption to make it form a connected network more quickly. The experimental results show that the algorithm effectively solves the problems that arise in the topological structure of the unmanned ship formation in a dynamic situation, and reduces the energy consumption [9]. Xiang Xianbo uses a microcontroller to receive data from the GPS sensor to obtain latitude and longitude information, and to receive data from the attitude sensor to obtain heading angle information. The actuator adjusts the heading angle and speed of the unmanned ship in real time. Under the polling control of the host as the master node, multiple unmanned ships form a fleet of unmanned ships [10]. A new multi-unmanned vessel formation and path tracking control method uses a single unmanned vessel as the leader to track the required path; other unmanned vessels act as followers and only use the position of the leader to maintain the formation and track Navigator [11]. For multi-following ships, the outer loop is designed with a distributed time-varying formation tracking control law that only uses adjacent relative information, and the inner loop is designed with a robust attitude tracking law. In attitude tracking, the sliding mode control method is used to control the heading angle and sailing speed, which eliminates the influence of model parameter perturbation and external disturbances such as wind, waves and currents on the ship's motion [12]. The formation uses leader-follower architecture, the controller uses fuzzy control, and uses intelligent algorithms to optimize the entire controller [13]. The autonomous navigation control of the unmanned ship is realized by the deep reinforcement learning algorithm, which improves the adaptability of the unmanned ship under complex and changeable real-time simulation conditions. Through the continuous improvement and optimization of the machine reinforcement learning, it can successfully avoid obstacles and avoid obstacles in complex environments. Arrive at the destination [14]. The above-mentioned methods have problems such as high construction and maintenance costs, easy to be affected by the on-site environment, and poor adaptability. In order to improve the accuracy of formation control, reduce construction and maintenance costs and external environmental impact, and improve the adaptability of formation control methods. This paper proposes an improved virtual navigator formation control algorithm to control the formation. After the formation is formed, this article uses an improved artificial potential field method to maintain the formation, and finally analyzes it through field experiments.

2   Hierarchical Formation Control Technology Based on the Navigator Method

Since formation control is divided into three phases: formation change, formation maintenance and formation avoidance, it is necessary to design these three phases separately. First, we need to divide the entire formation system; then, we use ordered arrays and control matrices to achieve accurate formation of the formation; finally, we perform formation maintenance and formation avoidance separately.

2.1   Framework Diagram of Layered Formation System

The division of the entire formation system is shown in Fig. 1.

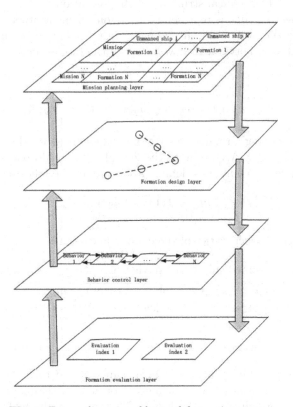

Fig. 1. Frame diagram of layered formation system.

2.2 Formation Design

Ordered array and control matrix to achieve accurate formation of formation. Among them, the four-element ordered array is used to determine the relationship between the connecting edges of the formation, and the control matrix is used to determine the hierarchical relationship between the unmanned ships in the entire formation system.

The characteristics of the formation system are as follows:

(1) There is one and only one leader in the formation system.
(2) For the navigator, its tracking degree is $d_{\overline{L}} = 0$, for the follower, its tracking degree is $d_{\overline{F}} = 1$, for the trailing person, its tracking degree is $d_{\overline{T}} = 0$, the tracking degree is defined as: whether a certain unmanned ship has a forward connection For an unmanned ship, if there is an unmanned ship before it, the tracking degree is 1, otherwise it is 0. The tracking degree is defined as: whether an unmanned ship has a follow-up unmanned ship, and if there is no follow-up unmanned ship, it will be The tracking degree is 0.
(3) In the formation system of N unmanned ships, there are N−1 connecting edges in the hierarchical structure of the formation.
(4) The connecting edge is represented by a four-element ordered array E_N, V_i represents the node, and, R_{ij} and σ_{ij} respectively represent the distance and orientation between the two nodes of the formation:

$$E_N = \{(V_1, V_2, R_{12}, \sigma_{12}), (V_2, V_3, R_{23}, \sigma_{23}), ..., (V_{N-1}, V_N, R_{N-1\,N}, \sigma_{N-1\,N})\} \tag{1}$$

The corresponding formation control matrix can be derived through the quaternary ordered array. According to the logical relationship between each node, the formation control matrix is defined according to the following ideas:

$$M_N = \begin{cases} m_{ij} = 1, \text{i is a follower of j}, \text{i} \neq \text{j} \\ 0, \qquad\qquad \text{others} \end{cases} \tag{2}$$

The element characteristics of the control matrix are:

(1) If the i-th unmanned ship is the navigator, then $\sum_{j}^{N} m_{ij} = 0$.
(2) If the j-th unmanned ship is a follower, then $\sum_{i}^{N} m_{ij} \geq 0$.
(3) If the j-th unmanned ship is a follower, then $\sum_{i}^{N} m_{ij} = 0$.

2.3 Behavior Control

For an unmanned ship, other unmanned ships in the team and obstacles in the environment will have a repulsive effect on it, and the real-time sub-target point will have a gravitational effect on it. There are mainly the following formation control behaviors: formation maintaining behavior, formation avoidance and obstacle avoidance behavior, and formation regeneration behavior. The safety of the formation system of the unmanned ship s is the most important. Therefore, under the constraints of the complex environment, the priority of the collision avoidance and obstacle avoidance behaviors of the formation is higher than other behaviors.

(1) Formation maintenance

During the entire formation operation, each unmanned ship needs to keep track of its corresponding sub-target point. Using the gravitational field of the artificial potential field method, the sub-target point is attractive to the unmanned ship and urges it to run to the sub-target point. , So as to achieve the expected formation geometry.

The formation remains as shown in Fig. 2. The gravity function is defined as a function of the relative distance and azimuth between the actual position of the unmanned ship and the sub-target point. The gravity function and the potential function are shown in the following formulas.

$$F_{PK} = -\sin\delta \cdot \nabla P_{PK} \tag{3}$$

$$P_{PK} = \frac{1}{2}\rho_{PK} \cdot \|d_{jj'}\|^2, \forall j = 1, 2, ..., N-1 \tag{4}$$

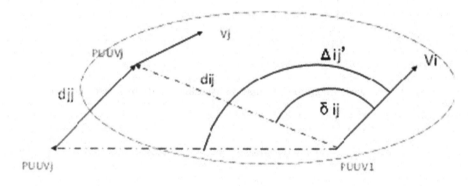

Fig. 2. Schematic diagram of formation keeping.

Where ρ_{PK} is the positive gain to keep track of the sub-target point; $\delta = |\delta_{ij'} - \delta_{ij}|$ represents the deviation between the actual position of the unmanned ship and the ideal position; $\|d_{jj'}\|$ represents the relative distance between the actual position of the first unmanned ship and the ideal position; σ_{ij}, $\sigma_{ij'}$ respectively represent the first unmanned ship The ideal and actual position between the ship and the first unmanned ship.

It can be known from the foregoing formula that when $\delta = 0$ or $\|d_{ij}\| = 0$, $F_{PK} = 0$. Therefore, when the unmanned ship reaches the corresponding sub-target point, it will maintain the same speed and orientation to complete the expected formation.

(2) Formation to avoid collision and obstacle

In the formation operation environment of unmanned ships, when the distance between the unmanned ships and the distance between the unmanned ships and obstacles is less than the maximum safe distance of the unmanned ships, there will be a danger of collision. When the distance is greater than a certain value, it can be considered that the unmanned ship is in a normal and safe state.

Figure 3 is a schematic diagram of formation avoidance and obstacle avoidance. The repulsion function is defined as the function of the relative distance and azimuth between the actual position of the unmanned ship and the obstacle or other unmanned ships. The repulsion function and the potential function are shown in the following equations.

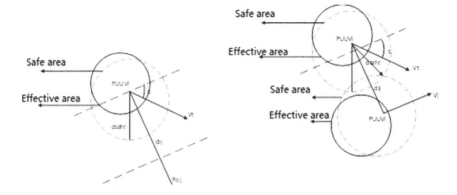

Fig. 3. Schematic diagram of formation avoidance and obstacle avoidance.

$$F_{CAi} = -\exp(\alpha) \cdot \sin\alpha \cdot \nabla P_{CAi} \tag{5}$$

$$P_{CAi} = \rho_{CA} \cdot \sum_{j=1}^{M} P_{CAi,j}, \forall i = 1, 2, ..., N \tag{6}$$

$$P_{CAi,j} \begin{cases} \frac{1}{2}(\frac{1}{d_{ij}} - \frac{1}{d_{safe}})^2, d_{ij} \le d_{safe}, \forall i, j = 1, ..., N \\ 0 \qquad\qquad\qquad d_{ij} > d_{safe} \end{cases} \tag{7}$$

Where d_{ij} is the distance between the unmanned ship and the obstacle or unmanned ship; d_{safe} is the maximum safety distance of the unmanned ship; ρ_{CA} is the positive collision avoidance gain) $\alpha = \cos^{-1}\frac{V_i \cdot V_j}{\|V_i\|\|V_j\|}$, is the angle of repulsion, that is, the angle between the current heading of the unmanned ship and the tangent plane of obstacles or other unmanned ships;

$$\sin\alpha = \begin{cases} \sin\alpha & \alpha \in [0, \frac{\pi}{2}] \\ 0 & others \end{cases} \tag{8}$$

This formula means that only when $\alpha \in \left[0\frac{\pi}{2}\right]$, Obstacles and other unmanned ships will pose a threat to the current unmanned ships. At this time, collision avoidance and obstacle avoidance are required. Under other circumstances, the unmanned ships do not need to perform collision avoidance and obstacle avoidance behaviors.

(3) Formation regeneration

When the formation runs into a complex environment, it will be disrupted. At this time, some or all of the unmanned ships will first complete collision avoidance and obstacle avoidance behaviors, and then enter a relaxed environment, the formation will be restored or converted to other formation types. During this period, because the position of some or all of the unmanned ships has a relatively large range, it is necessary to complete the task of regenerating the formation.

From this process, it can be seen that the nature of the formation regeneration behavior is different from the formation maintenance behavior:

1) When the formation maintenance is completed, the speed of the unmanned ship changes very little, and the orientation change is not too large, and the formation regeneration is completed. At that time, some or all of the unmanned ships will reach the new sub-target point at full speed, and the orientation adjustment will be large.
2) When the unmanned ship s is in the formation holding state, the overall shape is in a good state, and when in the formation regeneration state, the formation shape is in an irregular or completely disrupted state.

Figure 4 is a schematic diagram of formation regeneration. The gravity function is defined as a function of the relative distance and azimuth between the actual position of the unmanned ship and the new sub-target point. The gravity function and the potential function are as follows:

$$F_{PA} = -\exp(\sin\phi_{jj'}) \cdot \nabla P_{PA} \tag{9}$$

$$P_{PA} = \frac{1}{2}\rho_{PA} \cdot \|d_{jj'}\|^2, \forall j = 1, 2, ..., N-1 \tag{10}$$

Among them, $\|d_{jj'}\|$ is the relative distance between the actual position of the following unmanned vessel and the actual ideal position planned by the pilot unmanned vessel, $\|d_{jj'}\| = \sqrt{(x_j - x_{j'})^2 + (y_j - y_{j'})^2}$; $\phi_{jj'}$ is the azimuth difference between the actual heading of the unmanned vessel and the ideal heading, $\phi_{jj'} = |\alpha_j - \alpha_{j'}|$; ρ_{PA} is the sub-target point Positive gain; d is the motion vector of each unmanned ship, and α is the heading of each unmanned ship.

3   Improved Virtual Navigator Formation Control Algorithm

After the formation is formed, the gravitational field, repulsion field and communication distance will affect the formation of the unmanned ship. Therefore, the artificial potential field method in this chapter is improved to maintain the formation.

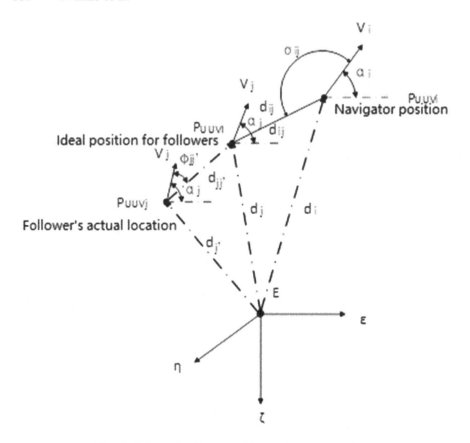

Fig. 4. Schematic diagram of formation regeneration.

3.1 The Gravitational Field or Repulsion Field of the Virtual Navigator

The force analysis of the unmanned ship is shown in Fig. 5.

The unmanned ship needs to maintain a proper distance and angle with the virtual navigator in order to maintain the formation. As shown in Fig. 5, the corresponding gravitational or repulsive force generated by the gravitational field or repulsion field provided for the virtual navigator is F_1. Gravity or repulsion is limited by the distance between the unmanned ship and the virtual navigator. Assuming that the theoretical value of the distance between the unmanned ship and the pilot is R_1, and the actual distance is R_0, the following model is available:

$$F_1 = \begin{cases} -\xi K_1 \sqrt{|R_1 - R_0|}, R_0 > R_1 \\ \xi K_1 \sqrt{|R_1 - R_0|}, R_0 < R_1 \end{cases} \tag{11}$$

Among them, $\sqrt{|R_1 - R_0|}$ represents the distance value between the theoretical position and actual position of the unmanned ship relative to the navigator; K_1 is the proportional coefficient; R_0 represents the constant of the potential field.

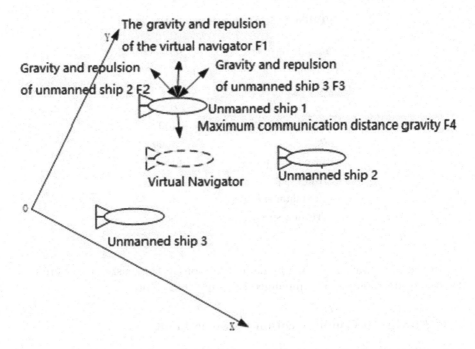

Fig. 5. Force analysis of unmanned ship.

By F_1 ensuring that the distance between the unmanned ship and the virtual navigator is stable, and then obtaining angle information through the sensor, the vector position of the unmanned ship and the virtual navigator can be kept consistent.

3.2 Gravitational Field or Repulsion Field of Other Unmanned Ships

When the unmanned ship is moving in the system, it is necessary not only to clarify its role in the entire formation, but also to ensure that it does not collide with other unmanned ships. This requires accurate relative positions between unmanned ships. Suppose the theoretical distance of the unmanned ship i to the unmanned ship is R_i, and the actual distance is R_{i0}, so the following model is obtained:

$$F_i = \begin{cases} -\xi K_2\sqrt{|R_i - R_{i0}|}, R_{i0} > R_i \\ \xi K_2\sqrt{|R_i - R_{i0}|}, R_{i0} < R_i \end{cases} \quad (12)$$

Among them, $\sqrt{|R_i - R_{i0}|}$ represents the distance value between the theoretical position and the actual position of the unmanned ship relative to the unmanned ship i; K_2 is the proportional coefficient; ξ is the constant of the potential field.

Table 1. Test parameter selection

Parameter	Value
Number of unmanned ships	5
K_1	1.5
K_2	0.2
K_3	150
$R_{\max}$	1000
Speed of sound	1500
Water depth	60
Maximum speed	12
Cruising speed	6

In the same way, obtaining angle information on this basis can ensure that the vector positions of the unmanned ships are consistent.

3.3   Maximum Communication Distance Limit

Due to the limited communication capability of the unmanned ship formation control system, it is necessary to add the communication distance constraint to the potential field model to prevent some unmanned ships from leaving the formation beyond the communication range. Assuming that the maximum communication distance is $R_{\max}$, and the distance between the unmanned ship and the nearest unmanned ship is R_s, the following model is available:

$$F_i = \begin{cases} -\xi K_3 R_{\max}, R_s > R_{\max} \\ 0, R_s < R_{\max} \end{cases} \tag{13}$$

Among them, K_3 is the proportional coefficient, ξ is the potential field constant.

When the unmanned vessel leaves the maximum communication distance, the unmanned vessel cannot receive the signal. This requires the unmanned vessel to record the direction of the adjacent unmanned vessel at the moment when it is about to leave the formation, and regard this direction as the direction of gravity.

4   Calculation and Analysis of Results

The details of the test parameters are as follows, as shown in Table 1:

Randomly deploy 5 unmanned ships at the starting position, randomly select one of the unmanned ships as the leader, and the remaining unmanned ships as the followers. After that, the five unmanned ships began to execute the formation algorithm, transform the formation into a triangle, and then maintain the formation to sail. If unmanned ships encounter obstacles (represented by black rectangles, 60 m long and 15 m wide) during navigation, they will trigger the execution of obstacle avoidance algorithms, passing between two relatively distant obstacles. After crossing the obstacle, they continue to execute the formation algorithm and change back to the triangular formation in time. The trajectory of the entire formation control process is shown in Fig. 6. During formation control, the relative distance between the four followers and the leader is shown in Fig. 7 below. The relative distance between the four followers is shown in Fig. 8 below.

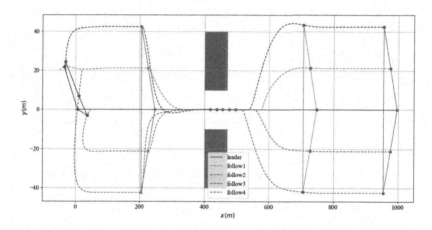

Fig. 6. Trajectory diagram of the whole process of unmanned ship formation control.

It can be seen from the trajectory of the entire formation control process in Fig. 6 that the formation algorithm can quickly transform multiple unmanned ships into a triangular formation. After encountering an obstacle, the obstacle avoidance algorithm can be executed in time to avoid the obstacle. At the same time, after passing through obstacles, it can revert to a triangular formation. It can be seen from Figs. 7 and 8 that the formation starts at 0 s and transforms into a triangle formation in about 20 s. During the period from 20 s to 50 s, the formation is in the holding phase. Since the formation is symmetric, the distance between the symmetrical unmanned ships is 0, and the relative distance to other unmanned ships remains unchanged. Obstacle avoidance starts at 50 s and ends at 120 s. Obstacle avoidance time is about 70 s. About 35 s after the obstacle avoidance is over, the formation can revert to the triangle formation, and then the formation is in the holding phase again.

From the above results, it can be concluded that the improved virtual leader formation control algorithm designed in this paper has good obstacle avoidance ability, and can quickly change to the corresponding formation after crossing obstacles, and has good robustness, rapidity and precision.

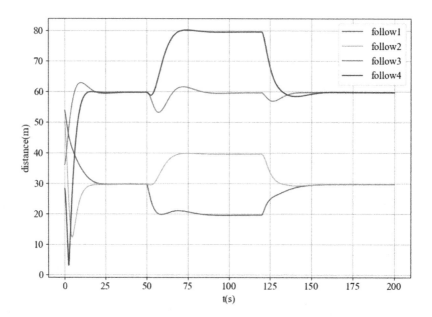

Fig. 7. The relative distance between the four followers and the leader.

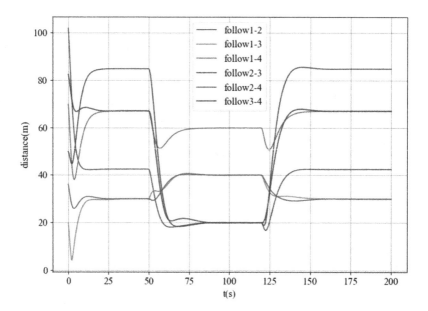

Fig. 8. The relative distance between the four followers.

5   Conclusion

Aiming at the formation and obstacle avoidance problems in the multi-formation control system, the formation control algorithm based on the navigator is adopted to carry out the formation design and behavior control respectively. Then, this article improves on this basis. After the formation is formed, the artificial potential field is used to maintain, and the gravitational field and repulsion field of the virtual navigator and other unmanned ships and the maximum communication distance are considered respectively, and the improved virtual navigator is obtained. Formation control algorithm, and then we conducted a formation maintaining experiment. The experimental results show that this paper uses the proposed improved virtual navigator algorithm to conduct formation control and obstacle avoidance experiments, and find that the algorithm has good performance.

The formation control method has the characteristics of high accuracy, strong generalization ability, fast control speed, strong environmental adaptability, etc., and the control method can be packaged into an intelligent control system. Use Java interface to provide third-party services, flexible deployment and application, and strong adaptability. In the future, we can continue to dig deeper into the artificial potential field to improve the robustness of formation control.

References

1. Wang, B., Li, B., Gao, M., Qin, L.: Summary of cooperative control strategies for unmanned ships. China Water Transp. **19**(02), 3–5 (2019)
2. Deng, Z., Wang, Z., Shen, W., Liu, Y.: Research on formation control and position estimation algorithm of multiple unmanned ships. Mech. Sci. Technol. 1–9 (2021). https://doi.org/10.13433/j.cnki.1003-8728.20200379
3. Lu, Y.: Research on Adaptive Formation Control Method for Multi-ship Coordination. Shanghai Jiaotong University (2020)
4. Liu, Y.: Anti-collision Time-Varying Formation Control of Unmanned Ships with Unknown Input Gain. Dalian Maritime University (2020)
5. Li, H.: Pilot-following the Fixed Time Control of the Unmanned Ship Formation on the Surface. Dalian Maritime University (2020)
6. Zheng, S.: Research on Target Tracking of Unmanned Rescue Vessel Based on Deep Reinforcement Learning. Dalian Maritime University (2020)
7. Shen, W.: Design and Implementation of Multiple Unmanned Ship Formation Control System. Nanjing University of Information Science and Technology (2020)
8. Liu, C., Du, W., Ren, J.: Topological control algorithm of unmanned ship formation based on directional antenna. J. Hainan Univ. **35**(02), 106–110 (2017)
9. Liu, C.: Research on the Topology Control Algorithm of Multi-unmanned Ship Formation Self-organizing Network Based on Directional Antenna. Hainan University (2017)
10. Xiang, X., et al.: Multi-unmanned-ship Formation System (2017)
11. Xia, L., Yan, W.: Formation & path tracking control for multiple unmanned ships. In: 2011 2nd International Conference on Intelligent Control and Information Processing, vol. 1, pp. 425–428 (2011)

12. Bai, W., Yu, J., Jiang, H., Dong, X., Ren, Z.: Robust time-varying formation tracking control of underactuated unmanned vessels. In: 2020 Chinese Automation Congress (CAC), pp. 5015–5020 (2020)
13. Zhang, L., Liu, Z., Papavassiliou, C., Liu, S.: Formation path control method for group coordination based on fuzzy logic control method. Clust. Comput. 1–14 (2017)
14. Yang, J., Liu, L., Zhang, Q., Liu, C.: Research on autonomous navigation control of unmanned ship based on unity 3D. In: 2019 5th International Conference on Control, Automation and Robotics (ICCAR), pp. 422–426 (2019)

Dynamic Path Planning Algorithm for Unmanned Ship Based on Deep Reinforcement Learning

Yue You[1], Ke Chen[1], Xuan Guo[2(✉)], Hao Zhou[3], Guangyu Luo[2], and Rui Wu[2]

[1] Naval Research Institute, Beijing, China
[2] School of Automation, Wuhan University of Technology, Wuhan, China
233980@whut.edu.cn
[3] School of Naval Architecture, Ocean and Energy Power Engineering, Wuhan University of Technology, Wuhan, China

Abstract. In order to enable the unmanned ship to have the ability of autonomous path planning in the complex marine environment, which can avoid obstacles and reach the destination accurately in the unknown environment, this paper combines the ability of deep learning to obtain information with the decision-making ability of reinforcement learning, and proposes an algorithm based on deep reinforcement learning. The simulation results show that after 3000 rounds of training in a given environment, the success rate of sailing to the end point in this environment is 100%. The path planning algorithm based on deep reinforcement learning performs well in the simulation experiment, achieves a very high accuracy after a large number of training times, and meets the needs of the operation and use of the unmanned ship on the water. This algorithm can be carried in the actual environment to realize the autonomous navigation of the unmanned ship on the water.

Keywords: Unmanned ship · Path planning · Deep learning · Reinforcement learning

1 Introduction

The exploration of marine resources promotes the application of path planning algorithm in unmanned ships. Path planning means that a ship finds the best or suboptimal path from the beginning to the target location in a complex environment with obstacles under certain constraints [10]. Compared to global static path planning, Local dynamic path planning is more suitable for the uncertain environment at sea, and it can realize real-time navigation more easily. At present, many scholars have developed different local dynamic path planning algorithms, including non-intelligent and intelligent algorithms:

Inspired by the concept of "field" in physics, Khatib et al. [6] proposed the concept of artificial potential field method in 1986. Chen Huiwei [2] applied the

L. Pan et al. (Eds.): BIC-TA 2021, CCIS 1566, pp. 373–384, 2022.
https://doi.org/10.1007/978-981-19-1253-5_28

artificial potential field method to the path navigation of unmanned ships by changing the models of gravitational potential field and repulsive potential field. Zadeh [8] and others put forward the concept of dynamic window method in 1997 and applied it to local obstacle avoidance of robots. Traditional non-intelligent algorithms also include A* algorithm [7], Theata* [1] algorithm and so on.

Non-intelligent algorithm is simple to apply, but it requires accurate modeling of agents, which leads to the fact that real-time and generalization cannot be well guaranteed. In contrast, the intelligent algorithm does not need an accurate model, and has a stronger sense of the environment and a stronger generalization ability. In 1991, DorigoM and others [4] put forward the ant colony algorithm to solve the travel agency problem. Zhao Feng [11] aims at combining traditional ant colony algorithm with greedy algorithm to meet the requirements of path planning in different dynamic environments. Chen Huiwei [3] applied ant colony algorithm to the path planning of unmanned ships by improving heuristic function and updating pheromones.

The aforementioned algorithm may encounter dimension disaster in complex environment, which makes the algorithm unable to converge. Combining deep learning with intensive learning can solve the problem. The deep neural network directly processes the high-dimensional original information, while the reinforcement learning algorithm interacts with environment.

At present, the commonly used deep reinforcement learning algorithms, such as DQN algorithm [9] and DDQN algorithm [5], are all proposed by combining neural network with Q-Learning algorithm. When these methods are iterative in strategy updating, agents only consider the influence of obtaining the reward values of two adjacent states on the Q value of state-action. Because the $Q(\lambda)$ algorithm can make the reward obtained by the agent affect the state-action Q value of the adjacent multi-step state. This is equivalent to making the agent gain the ability to perceive the development of the previous situation in advance. Therefore, we adopt the idea of $Q(\lambda)$ algorithm to improve DDQN algorithm, and propose a λ-Step DDQN mechanism-oriented DDQN algorithm (λS-DDQN).

2   Algorithm Design

2.1 λS-DDQN Algorithm

In the process of training, λS-DDQN enables the reward obtained by the unmanned ship to spread the estimated value of the state value of the λ-step interval state. In this way, it can better guide the unmanned ship to learn quickly, and at the same time, it can also make the unmanned ship aware of the changes in the future state in advance. The output of the λS-DDQN target value network is:

$$y_{t\,\text{arg}\,et}^{\lambda S-DDQN} = \sum_{i=0}^{i=\lambda-1} \gamma^i r_{i+1} + \gamma^\lambda Q_{t\,\text{arg}\,et}(s_{t+\gamma}, \arg\max_a Q(s_{t+\lambda}, a, \theta), \theta') \qquad (1)$$

The loss function of λS-DDQN network is:

$$L(\theta) = E[y_{t\,\text{arg}\,et}^{\lambda S-DDQN} - Q(s, a, \theta))^2]$$ (2)

For the training and learning using λS-DDQN algorithm, it is different from the conventional DDQN algorithm in that the data stored in the experience pool is different. In the conventional DDQN algorithm, the data stored in the experience pool is $[s_t, a_t, r_t, s_{t+1}]$, but it becomes $[s_t, a_t, \sum_{i=0}^{i=\lambda-1} \gamma^i r_{t+i}, s_{t+1}]$ in λS-DDQN, so the training methods of the λS-DDQN algorithm are as follows:

Algorithm 1. Training Steps of λS-DDQN

1: Randomly initialize the weight θ of the current network $Q(s_t, a; \theta)$ and the weight
   θ' of the target network $Q'(s_t, a; \theta)$;
2: Initialize experience pool D and set hyperparameters λ;
3: **For** *episode* = 1, M **Do**
4:     Reset the simulation environment and obtain the initial observation state
   $s_t, T \leftarrow \infty$
5:     Initialize three empty arrays S_t, A, R, S_{t+1}
6:     Select action $a_t = \arg\max Q(s_t, a; \theta)$ according to current policy
7:     Perform action a_t and return the reward value r_t and the new status s_{t+1}
8:     Put s_t into S_t, r_t into R, a_t into A, s_{t+1} into S_{t+1}
9:     **If** s_{t+1} is the terminal state **Then**
10:        $T \leftarrow t + 1$
11:        $\tau \leftarrow t - \lambda + 1$
12:     **If** $\tau \geq 0$ **Then**
13:        **If** $\tau + \lambda < T$ **Then**
14:           $r_t = \sum_{i=\tau}^{i=\tau+\lambda-1} \gamma^{i-\tau} r_i \quad r_i \in R_t$
15:        **Else**
16:           $r_t = \sum_{i=\tau}^{i=T} \gamma^{i-\tau} r_i \quad r_i \in R_t$
17:     Put $(s_\tau, a_\tau r_\tau s_{\tau+\lambda})$ into experience pool D
18:     Random sampling of sample data mini-batch from D
19:     Let $y_i = r_i + \gamma^\lambda Q_{t\,\text{arg}\,et}(s_{t+\lambda}, \arg\max_a Q(s_{t+\lambda}, a, \theta), \theta')$
20:     Update the weight θ of the current value network by gradient descent using
   the loss function $L(\theta) = E[(y_i - Q(s, a, \theta))^2]$
21:     **Util** $\tau = T - 1$
22: **End**

2.2   Reward Function

The reward function is the reward value that the unmanned ship takes one action in the current state and reaches the next state, indicating the good or bad degree of taking a certain action in the current state. Because the positive reward for unmanned ships is very sparse, a new continuous combined reward function is designed in order to speed up the convergence of the algorithm. Among them, one is the reward obtained after finishing a certain round of training, such as reaching the target point or colliding, which we call terminal reward. The other is the reward obtained when the training round is not finished, which we call non-terminal reward.

Terminal Reward Design

1. When the unmanned ship reaches the target point, it gets a positive reward:

$$r_{arr} = 100; if \ d_{r-t} \leq d_{win} \tag{3}$$

where d_{r-t} is the Euclidean distance from the unmanned ship to the target point, d_{win} is the threshold for the unmanned ship to reach the target point.
2. When the unmanned ship collides with an obstacle, it gets a negative reward:

$$r_{col} = -100; if \ d_{r-o} \leq d_{col} \tag{4}$$

where d_{r-o} is the Euclidean distance of the unmanned ship from the nearest obstacle, d_{col} is the threshold of collision between the unmanned ship and the obstacle.

Non-terminal Reward Design

1. When the unmanned ship moves towards the target point, it gets a positive reward, otherwise it gets a negative reward:

$$r_{t\_goal} = c_r[d_{r-t}(t) - d_{r-t}(t-1)] \tag{5}$$

where the coefficient $c_r \in (0, 1]$, is set to 1 in this paper. The unmanned ship is guided towards the target point by this reward.
2. When the minimum distance of an unmanned ship from an obstacle continuously decreases, so does the dangerous reward $r_{dang} \in [0, 1]$ earned:

$$r_{dang} = \beta * 2^{d_{min}} \ \ 0 \leq r_{dang} \leq 1 \tag{6}$$

where d_{min} is the minimum distance of an unmanned ship from an obstacle and β is the coefficient such that the space of values of r_{dang} is $(0, 1)$.

In addition, we designed a direction reward, which is to give the corresponding reward to the unmanned ship through the angle between the forward direction vector of the unmanned ship and the direction vector of the current coordinates of the unmanned ship. When the angle is less than $\pm 18°$, the reward is 1, when the reward is greater than $\pm 18°$ and less than $\pm 72°$, the reward is 0.3, and in other cases, the reward is 0.

$$r_{ori} = \begin{cases} 1 \ if \ a_{ori} \leq \ \pm 18° \\ 0.3 \ if \ 18° < a_{ori} \leq 72° \\ 0 \ otherwise \end{cases} \tag{7}$$

where a_{ori} is the angle between the forward direction vector of the unmanned ship and the direction vector of the unmanned ship reaching the target position in the current coordinates.

$r_{t\_goal} + r_{dang} + r_{ori}$ is defined as the final non-terminal award. This kind of reward combination solves the problem of sparse reward, so that the unmanned ship can get the corresponding reward at every step of the training process. Moving toward the target point, the unmanned ship will receive a positive reward, while away from the target point or in a collision it will receive a negative reward. In this way, the unmanned ship can better learn the corresponding strategies. On the other hand, the combined reward function enables the unmanned ship to learn strategies that can reach the target position more quickly in a shorter path.

2.3 Modular Neural Network

We divided the navigation task into two sub-tasks, namely the local obstacle avoidance module and the global navigation module. The local obstacle avoidance module is mainly used to guide the unmanned ship away from obstacles, and the global navigation is mainly used to guide the unmanned ship to a shorter path to the target position. The deep neural network module of local obstacle avoidance function and the deep neural network module of global navigation are designed respectively. The input state information of the local obstacle avoidance neural network includes the environment information detected by the distance sensor and the relative position information of the unmanned ship which becomes the control instructions output after propagating forward. The input state information of the global obstacle avoidance neural network is the relative position information of the unmanned ship, and the control command is output after the processing of the input information.

Because both the local obstacle avoidance deep neural network and the global navigation neural network output the corresponding instructions to control the unmanned ship, this paper designs an instruction selection module to determine which network's output action instructions to execute. We set a threshold $d_{to\_obs} = 40$ of distance from the ship to the nearest obstacle to determine which module's instructions to use. When the distance is less than 40, the instructions output by the local obstacle avoidance deep neural network will be executed, otherwise the instructions by the global navigation neural network should be carried out to reach the target position at a faster speed. Therefore, the system architecture of this deep learning method is shown in Fig. 1:

Based on the modular neural network framework, the unmanned ship can adopt different strategies in different environmental states. When the unmanned ship approaches the obstacle, the main task of the unmanned ship is to avoid the obstacle, and the global navigation task becomes a secondary task. When the unmanned ship is far away from the obstacle, the global navigation task becomes the main task to help the unmanned ship to reach the target position with a shorter path.

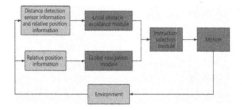

Fig. 1. The systematic framework of deep learning method.

3 Experiment

3.1 Dynamic Environment Implementation

A 500-inch 500 window size is defined as the simulation environment, and different obstacles, boundary walls and target locations are added in this window. The environment model established in this article is shown in Fig. 2.

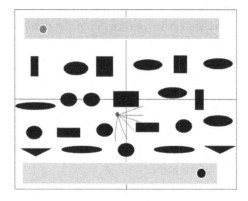

Fig. 2. Simulation environment model.

It is assumed that the starting position of the unmanned ship is P_{start} in the higher left corner of the simulation environment, the coordinate is (x_{start}, y_{start}), the moving speed is $v = 0.5$, and the current direction of the unmanned ship is $angle$. In the current state, the unmanned ship chooses an action to perform, that is, the unmanned ship chooses a steering action, the angle steering is $angle_{tran}$, the steering angle is $angle_{tran} \in (15°_{turn\_left}, 30°_{turn\_left}, 0°, 15°_{turn\_right}, 30°_{turn\_right})$, and formula (12) is the angle of the unmanned ship after performing the action:

$$angle \leftarrow angle + angle + angle_{train} \quad (8)$$

Combined with formula (12), the coordinates of the unmanned ship can be changed to:

$$x_{next} = x_{start} + \cos(angle) * v \quad (9)$$

$$y_{next} = y_{start} + \sin(angle) * v \qquad (10)$$

Before calculating the distance between the lidar simulator and the obstacle, the projection length of the x-axis and y-axis of each laser line in the unmanned ship as the center coordinate system is calculated, and then the projection length of each laser line segment in the environment model is calculated. The transformation from the unmanned ship as the center coordinate system to the environment model as the center coordinate system is based on the middle-two-dimensional coordinate system transformation process. Assuming that the coordinate of the unmanned ship is $(center\_x, center\_y)$, the code for solving the coordinates at the end of the laser segment centered on the environment model is shown in Fig. 3:

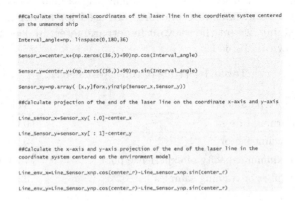

```
##Calculate the terminal coordinates of the laser line in the coordinate system centered
on the unmanned ship

Interval_angle=np. linspace(0,180,36)

Sensor_x=center_x+(np.zeros((36,))+90)np.cos(Interval_angle)

Sensor_y=center_y+(np.zeros((36,))+90)np.sin(Interval_angle)

Sensor_xy=np.array( [x,y]forx,yinzip(Sensor_x,Sensor_y))

##Calculate projection of the end of the laser line on the coordinate x-axis and y-axis

Line_sensor_x=Sensor_xy[ :,0]-center_x

Line_Sensor_y=Sensor_xy[ : 1]-center_y

##Calculate the x-axis and y-axis projection of the end of the laser line in the
coordinate system centered on the environment model

Line_env_x=Line_Sensor_xnp.cos(center_r)-Line_sensor_xnp.sin(center_r)

Line_env_y=Line_Sensor_ynp.cos(center_r)-Line_Sensor_ynp.sin(center_r)
```

Fig. 3. Coordinate conversion code.

The distance between the unmanned ship and the obstacle can be solved when the coordinate projection of the laser line segment in the coordinate system centered on the environment model is obtained. Then each edge vector of the obstacle, the laser line segment vector, and the vector from the position coordinates of the unmanned ship to each vertex of the obstacle are constructed. By solving a relative relationship between these vectors in real time, the position information between the unmanned ship and the obstacle can be obtained, and the length of each laser line detected by lidar can be obtained.

The rules for determining the collision of the unmanned ship: first, set d_{min} as the minimum safe distance between the unmanned ship and the obstacle, and when the minimum laser line detected by the lidar is less than the set d_{min}, it will be determined that the collision occurs and the training of this round ends, re-assign a new starting position to the unmanned ship. Otherwise, there is no collision, and the unmanned ship chooses the action to execute according to the relevant strategy.

The rules for determining the unmanned ship's arrival at the target position: first, $d_{Arrivals}$ is defined as the maximum distance for the unmanned ship to reach the target position. In the operation of the unmanned ship, the Euclidean distance between the current position coordinates of the unmanned ship and the target position coordinates is calculated. If the distance is less than or equal to $d_{Arrivals}$, it indicates that the unmanned ship reaches the target position.

3.2   Training of Unmanned Ship Navigation Model

The above simulation environment model is taken as the unmanned ship training environment, and the environment is set as the training environment 1(Env-1). In order to verify the effectiveness of the λS-DDQN method, we test the navigation ability of the unmanned ship in the training Env-1, and compare the λS-DDQN algorithm with the DDQN, PrioritizedDQN and PrioritizedDDQN algorithms. In order to ensure the fairness of the experiment, the same network structure and the same software and hardware platform are used for model training. Before starting the training, we set the relevant hyperparameters in deep reinforcement learning, as shown in Table 1:

Table 1. Setting of super parameter.

Hyper parameter	Value
Learning rate	0.001
Discount factor	0.9
Maximum capacity of experience pool	15000
Number of training samples	32
Number of steps λ	5
Number of steps between replication parameters θ	300

In order to evaluate the performance of each algorithm quantitatively, we use three indicators to evaluate the navigation model. The first is the success rate, which indicates the proportion of the unmanned ship's successful arrival at the target position to the total number of training from the beginning of the training; the second is the reward value curve, which represents the sum of the reward values received by the unmanned ship in each round during the training process. In order to smooth the reward curve, we use the moving average method to process the curve, and the sliding window size is 300. The third is the average value of the reward, which represents the sum of the rewards received by the unmanned ship during the training process and divided by the number of training rounds.

Based on λS-DDQN algorithm, DDQN algorithm, Prioritized DQN algorithm and Prioritized DDQN algorithm, the autonomous navigation ability of the unmanned ship in Env-1 is trained. The training results are shown in Fig. 4:

As shown in Fig. 4(a), we can see that the success rate curve of λS-DDQN rises faster than the other three methods, which indicates that the learning efficiency of λS-DDQN algorithm is higher. The reward curve in Fig. 4(b) also proves this view. After 3000 times of training, the success rate of λS-DDQN

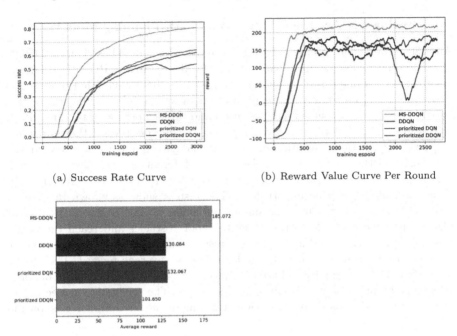

(a) Success Rate Curve   (b) Reward Value Curve Per Round

(c) Average Reward

Fig. 4. Training result.

reaching the target location is 80.133%, and the success rate of DDQN is 61.7%. The success rate of Prioritized DQN is 63.633%, and the success rate of Prioritized DDQN is 53.366%, we can see that the success rate of λS-DDQN is much higher than that of other algorithms. This shows that the unmanned ship based on λS-DDQN has carried out more collision-free and target-free training during the training process, indicating that it has stronger obstacle avoidance and navigation functions. In Fig. 4(b), we can see that the reward curve obtained through λS-DDQN is stable at more than 200 after 500 times' training, while the curves of the other three algorithms fluctuate greatly, which indicates that the navigation model based on λS-DDQN has higher stability. In Fig. 4(c), the average reward value of λS-DDQN is 185.072, that of DDQN is 130.064, that of Prioritized DQN is 132.067 and that of Prioritized DDQN is 101.650, which also proves that the unmanned ship based on λS-DDQN has stronger navigation ability. Because the lower reward value means a lot of negative reward, it means that the unmanned ship has more collisions.

By analyzing the success rate curve, reward value curve and average reward value curve of the navigation model based on different algorithms in the training process, it can be concluded that the unmanned ship based on λS-DDQN algorithm has stronger learning efficiency and higher stability than the other three algorithms in the training process.

3.3   Testing the Accuracy of Dynamic Path Planning Model

After 3000 rounds of training in Env-1, the navigation model based on λS-DDQN algorithm, DDQN algorithm, Prioritized DQN algorithm and Prioritized DDQN algorithm is obtained. In this section, we first test these navigation models 200 times in Env-1, and analyze the proportion of successful reaching the target location. In 200 tests, the starting position and target position of the unmanned ship were randomly assigned. By comparing the success rate of the unmanned ship reaching the target position in 200 tests and getting the average reward, the superiority of the navigation model based on different algorithms is measured. The higher the success rate, the higher the average reward, indicating that the navigation model is a better strategy. The results show as shown in Table 2: after 3000 times of training, the unmanned ships trained based on these four algorithms have basically learned how to avoid obstacles and reach the target position in Env-1. According to the test results, the λS-DDQN algorithm is the best, with a success rate of 100% and the highest average reward. The results show that the unmanned ship based on λS-DDQN algorithm has higher obstacle avoidance ability and better navigation strategy. The navigation trajectory of the unmanned ship based on λS-DDQN training in the environment is shown in Fig. 5.

Table 2. Setting of super parameter.

Environment	Algorithm	Success rate	Average reward value
Env-1	λS-DDQN	100.0%	243.996
Env-1	DDQN	88.0%	203.829
Env-1	Prioritized DQN	94.0%	228.829
Env-1	Prioritized DDQN	91.0%	215.293

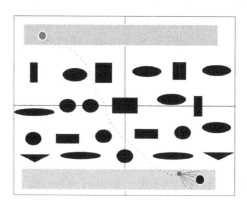

Fig. 5. Dynamic trajectory planning of underwater vehicle.

4 Conclusions

We divided the navigation task of the unmanned ship into two sub-tasks: global navigation and local obstacle avoidance. Through task decomposition, each neural network is more clear about the strategies and methods that need to be learned, so that the unmanned ship can better avoid obstacles and reach the target position with a shorter path.

By combining the idea of $Q(\lambda)$ algorithm with the traditional DDQN algorithm, a λ-step DDQN algorithm is proposed, which makes the current state of the unmanned ship obtain the influence of reward value to extend the action-state Q value of several states. This is equivalent to giving the unmanned ship the ability to perceive the future and facilitate it to evade obstacles in advance. In addition, in the process of training, we propose to use a continuous combined reward function to solve the problems of low accuracy and slow convergence caused by the sparse state of the unmanned ship.

Through the statistics of 3000 rounds of training data in a certain environment, we find that compared to the other three algorithms our algorithm have higher success rate and reward value, which shows that our algorithm has learned more information in the training process. Then the trained algorithm model is tested 200 times in this environment, and the test results show that the success rate of navigation is up to 100% under this model. The accuracy of this algorithm is enough to meet the autonomous navigation needs of unmanned ships in most marine environments, and can be encapsulated in the navigation system of unmanned ships.

References

1. Alexopoulos, C., Griffin, P.M.: Path planning for a mobile robot. IEEE Trans. Syst. Man Cybern. **22**(2), 318–322 (1992)
2. Chen, H., Chen, Y., Feng, F.: Research status of unmanned ship route planning based on artificial potential field method. Sci. Technol. Innov. **000**(17), 23–25 (2020)
3. Chen, H., Liu, P., Liu, S.: Research on path planning method of unmanned ship based on improved ant colony algorithm. Eng. Technol. Dev. **1**(8), 3 (2019)
4. Dorigo, M., Di Caro, G., Gambardella, L.M.: Ant algorithms for discrete optimization. Artif. Life **5**(2), 137–172 (1999)
5. Hasselt, H.V., Guez, A., Silver, D.: Deep reinforcement learning with double Q-learning. In: Proceedings of the Thirtieth AAAI Conference on Artificial Intelligence, AAAI 2016, pp. 2094–2100. AAAI Press (2016)
6. Khatib, O.: Real-time obstacle avoidance for manipulators and mobile robots. In: Autonomous Robot Vehicles, pp. 396–404. Springer, Cham (1986). https://doi.org/10.1007/978-1-4613-8997-2_29
7. Liu, H., Bao, Y.: Application of a* algorithm in searching optimal path of vector map. Comput. Simul. **25**(4), 253–257 (2008)
8. MahmoudZadeh, S., Powers, D., Sammut, K.: An autonomous reactive architecture for efficient AUV mission time management in realistic dynamic ocean environment. Robot. Auton. Syst. **87**, 81–103 (2017)

9. Mnih, V., et al.: Playing Atari with deep reinforcement learning. arXiv preprint arXiv:1312.5602 (2013)
10. Wu, H., Tian, G.H., Li, Y., Zhou, F.Y., Duan, P.: Spatial semantic hybrid map building and application of mobile service robot. Robot. Auton. Syst. **62**(6), 923–941 (2014)
11. Zhao, F.: Dynamic path planning based on ant colony algorithm and its simulation application in formation. Master's thesis, Kunming University of Science and Technology (2017)

Application of Bidirectional LSTM Neural Network in Grain Stack Temperature Prediction

Yongfu Wu[✉], Hua Yang[✉], Kang Zhou, Yang Wang, and Yongqing Zhu

Wuhan Polytechnic University, Dongxihu District, Wuhan 43040, China
2696968704@qq.com, 22669594@qq.com

Abstract. Food is a necessity for human survival, so it is particularly important to ensure the quality of food in the process of storage. Therefore, in the process of grain storage, the grain quality is extremely important. In the process of grain storage, the temperature of grain will change due to the accumulation of heat in the grain pile, which will eventually affect the quality of grain and thus affect the quality of grain. Therefore, it is necessary to accurately predict the temperature of grain pile. Based on this practical problem, this paper designs a bidirectional LSTM neural network structure, and trains and learns the existing temperature data through the neural network, so as to accurately predict the temperature at a certain time. The prediction results are compared with those of LSTM neural network. At the end of the experiment, a comprehensive comparative analysis is conducted with RNN neural network, bi-directional RNN neural network, GRU neural network and bi-directional GRU neural network. The experimental results show that the bi-directional LSTM neural network has a better temperature change trend than the LSTM neural network, RNN neural network, bi-directional RNN neural network, GRU neural network, bidirectional GRU neural network has better predictive ability. In this article the bidirectional LSTM neural network to predict the temperature of the grain heap experiments, so it can be applied to the actual process of grain storage, can through the grain heap more precise prediction of temperature, so the grain heap temperature can be precise adjustment, it ensures the quality of grain, which is of great significance for grain storage.

Keywords: Bidirectional LSTM neural network · LSTM neural network · Temperature prediction · Network training

1 The Introduction

Food relationship between the survival of human beings, the quality of the food relationship with human nutrition and health, focus on quality of food that has existed since ancient times, and one of the important indicators affecting the quality of grain storage is the temperature of the grain heap, for effective monitoring of the temperature of the grain heap can prevent the grain mildew occurred in the process of storage and so on the change of the quality. Therefore, the prediction of grain heap temperature has become a hot spot of intelligent temperature control. At present, some scholars at home and abroad have done a lot of research on temperature prediction, such as: Tian Xiaomei et al. predicted

© Springer Nature Singapore Pte Ltd. 2022
L. Pan et al. (Eds.): BIC-TA 2021, CCIS 1566, pp. 385–395, 2022.
https://doi.org/10.1007/978-981-19-1253-5_29

and controlled the temperature of grain drying tower based on information entropy [1], Wang Xiaomin et al. predicted hot metal temperature based on the image brightness of blast furnace tuyere [2], and Bin Lu et al. predicted and analyzed the air temperature inside the tunnel during operation period [3]. So temperature prediction has become a hot topic today.

The temperature prediction using LSTM neural network has become an important research content. Because the temperature is a kind of temporal data, the temperature forecast is a prediction based on time sequence, while the LSTM is a kind of neural network based on time sequence forecast, however the LSTM only on the basis of a moment before the moment of temporal information to predict the output of the next moment, at a certain moment can't focus on the future at a certain moment with the current relationship. Therefore, the LSTM neural network is improved to obtain the bidirectional LSTM neural network. It predicts the output based on the temporal sequence information of the time before and in the future, discovers more data features and obtains more accurate and sufficient prediction rules. In this paper, according to the implementation plan of shallow ground energy and air-cooled grain pile surface temperature control green grain storage technology research project of Wuhan National Rice Exchange Center Co., LTD., the grain pile temperature data at 8, 14 and 20 o'clock from June 29 to September 3 were collected, then the data is preprocessed. Based on the processed data, the bidirectional LSTM neural network to realize the grain heap temperature prediction, compared with the LSTM neural network, the results show that the prediction accuracy of the bidirectional LSTM neural network is higher than the LSTM neural network. At the end of the experiment, the bidirectional LSTM and RNN neural network, bidirectional RNN neural network, GRU neural network and bidirectional GRU neural network are comprehensively compared and analyzed. The results show that bidirectional LSTM is closer to the real value and has better prediction results than RNN, bidirectional RNN, GRU and bidirectional GRU. Therefore, we can take corresponding measures to adjust the temperature of the grain heap according to the more accurate prediction results of the bidirectional LSTM, so as to reduce the possibility of grain quality decline caused by high temperature storage problems, and ultimately effectively ensure the quality of grain.

2   Materials and Methods

2.1   Sample Collection and Preparation

The temperature data of the bottom and surface layer of grain stacks at 8, 14 and 20 o'clock from June 29 to September 3 collected by the implementation plan of shallow ground energy and air cooling process Grain stack Surface temperature control Green grain Storage Technology Research Project of Wuhan National Rice Exchange Center Co., LTD. Then the LSTM and bidirectional LSTM, RNN, bidirectional RNN, GRU, the bidirectional GRU neural network structure models are established respectively. Finally, the processed data are trained and predicted by the LSTM and bidirectional LSTM, RNN, bidirectional RNN, GRU, the bidirectional GRU neural network respectively.

2.2 Experimental Flow Analysis

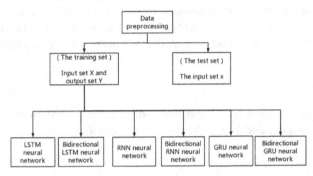

Fig. 1. Experimental processing flow of training set

By experiment flow Fig. 1, because the data contains null values, so, we need to preprocess the data, and then the processed data is divided into two parts, one part of the data is the training set of the neural network and the other part of the data is the test set of the neural network, the training set is divided into the input and output sets. Firstly, we need to train the LSTM and bidirectional LSTM, RNN, bidirectional RNN, GRU, the bidirectional GRU neural network model on the data in the training set. Its purpose is to make the results of the neural network trained by the input set better fit the output set.

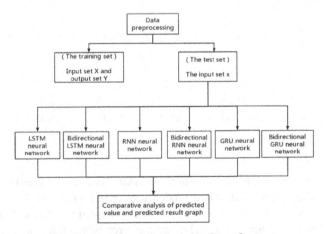

Fig. 2. Experimental processing flow of test set

As shown in experimental flow Fig. 2, the test set is input into trained the LSTM and bidirectional LSTM, RNN, bidirectional RNN, GRU and bidirectional GRU neural network models, and then the prediction is made. We compared the predicted result set of LSTM and bidirectional LSTM, RNN, bidirectional RNN, GRU, bidirectional GRU neural network model with the real result set. In order to be more intuitive, the graphs predicted by then LSTM and bidirectional LSTM, RNN, bidirectional RNN, GRU, bidirectional GRU neural network model are compared with those of real data more intuitively, through the comparison of the predicted value and the analysis of the numerical error and the trend comparison of the forecast graph, It is concluded that which of LSTM and bidirectional LSTM, bidirectional RNN, bidirectional RNN, GRU and bidirectional GRU neural network models has the best prediction effect.

3   Results

3.1   LSTM Neural Network Model and Bidirectional LSTM Neural Network Model Training and Error Comparative Analysis

Table 1. LSTM and bidirectional LSTM neural network models for grain pile bottom prediction results

Temperature value	8 o'clock on September 2nd	14 o'clock on September 2nd	20 o'clock on September 2nd	8 o'clock on September 3rd	14 o'clock on September 3rd	20 o'clock on September 3rd
The actual value	21.3	21.5	21.5	21.5	21.5	21.5
LSTM predicted value	19.97	19.96	19.98	20.02	20.02	20.03
Bidirectional LSTM predicted value	21.1	21.06	21.08	21.16	21.09	21.16
LSTM error	1.33	1.54	1.52	1.48	1.48	1.47
Bidirectional LSTM error	0.2	0.44	0.42	0.34	0.41	0.34

It can be seen from the predicted results in Table 1 that: The error between the actual value of 8 o'clock on September 2nd and the predicted value of LSTM neural network is 1.33, the error between the actual value of 14 o'clock on September 2nd and the predicted value of LSTM neural network is 1.54, and the error between the actual value of 20 o'clock on September 2nd and the predicted value of LSTM neural network is 1.52. The error between the actual value of 8 o'clock on September 3rd and the predicted value of LSTM neural network is 1.48, the error between the actual value of 14 o'clock on September 3rd and the predicted value of LSTM neural network is 1.48, the error between the actual value of 20 o'clock on September 3rd and the predicted value of LSTM neural network is 1.47.

The error between the actual value of 8 o'clock on September 2nd and the predicted value of bidirectional LSTM neural network is 0.2, the error between the actual value of 14 o'clock on September 2nd and the predicted value of bidirectional LSTM neural network is 0.44, the error between the actual value of 20 o'clock on September 2nd and the predicted value of bidirectional LSTM neural network is 0.42. The error between the actual value of 8 o'clock on September 3rd and the predicted value of bidirectional LSTM neural network is 0.34, the error between the actual value of 14 o'clock on September 3rd and the predicted value of bidirectional LSTM neural network is 0.41, and the error between the actual value of 20 o'clock on September 3rd and the predicted value of bidirectional LSTM neural network is 0.34. It can be seen from the above six results that the predicted value of the grain pile bottom of the bidirectional LSTM neural network is closer to the actual value than that of the LSTM neural network.

Table 2. Prediction results of grain pile surface based on LSTM and bidirectional LSTM neural network models

Temperature value	8 o'clock on September 2nd	14 o'clock on September 2nd	20 o'clock on September 2nd	8 o'clock on September 3rd	14 o'clock on September 3rd	20 o'clock on September 3rd
The actual value	29.1	29	29.1	28.8	28.8	29
LSTM predicted value	28.38	28.31	28.42	28.37	28.2	28.4
Bidirectional LSTM predicted value	29.13	28.96	29.07	29.01	28.95	29.17
LSTM error	0.72	0.69	0.68	0.43	0.6	0.6
Bidirectional LSTM error	0.03	0.04	0.03	0.21	0.15	0.17

It can be seen from the predicted results in Table 2 that: The error between the actual value of 8 o'clock on September 2nd and the predicted value of LSTM neural network is 0.72, the error between the actual value of 14 o'clock on September 2nd and the predicted value of LSTM neural network is 0.69, and the error between the actual value of 20 o'clock on September 2nd and the predicted value of LSTM neural network is 0.68. The error between the actual value of 8 o'clock on September 3rd and the predicted value of LSTM neural network is 0.43; the error between the actual value of 14 o'clock on September 3rd and the predicted value of LSTM neural network is 0.6; the error between the actual value of 20 o'clock on September 3rd and the predicted value of LSTM neural network is 0.6.

The error between the actual value of 8 o'clock on September 2nd and the predicted value of bidirectional LSTM neural network is 0.03, the error between the actual value of 14 o'clock on September 2nd and the predicted value of bidirectional LSTM neural network is 0.04, and the error between the actual value of 20 o'clock on September 2nd and the predicted value of bidirectional LSTM neural network is 0.03. The error between the actual value of 8 o'clock on September 3rd and the predicted value of bidirectional LSTM neural network is 0.21, the error between the actual value of 14 o'clock on September 3rd and the predicted value of bidirectional LSTM neural network is 0.15, and the error between the actual value of 20 o'clock on September 3rd and the predicted value of bidirectional LSTM neural network is 0.17. It can be seen from the above 6 results that the predicted value of grain pile surface of bidirectional LSTM neural network is closer to the actual value than that of LSTM neural network.

3.2 RNN, Bidirectional RNN, GRU, Comparative Analysis of Training and Error of Bidirectional GRU Network Models

Table 3. Prediction results of grain pile bottom based on RNN, bi-directional RNN, GRU and bi-directional GRU neural network

Temperature value	8 o'clock on September 2nd	14 o'clock on September 2nd	20 o'clock on September 2nd	8 o'clock on September 3rd	14 o'clock on September 3rd	20 o'clock on September 3rd
The actual value	21.3	21.5	21.5	21.5	21.5	21.5
GRU predicted value	19.99	19.99	20.01	20.05	20.05	20.06
Bidirectional GRU predicted value	19.98	19.98	19.99	20.03	20.03	20.04
RNN predicted value	20	19.99	20.02	20.05	20.05	20.06
Bidirectional RNN predicted value	19.97	19.97	19.99	20.03	20.02	20.04

(continued)

Table 3. (*continued*)

Temperature value	8 o'clock on September 2nd	14 o'clock on September 2nd	20 o'clock on September 2nd	8 o'clock on September 3rd	14 o'clock on September 3rd	20 o'clock on September 3rd
GRU error	1.31	1.51	1.49	1.45	1.45	1.44
Bidirectional GRU error	1.32	1.52	1.51	1.47	1.47	1.46
RNN error	1.3	1.51	1.48	1.45	1.45	1.44
Bidirectional RNN error	1.33	1.53	1.51	1.47	1.48	1.46

It can be seen from Table 1 that the error between the prediction result of the bidirectional LSTM neural network model and the actual value of grain pile bottom is within 0.45. Table 1 combined with Table 3 shows that the prediction result of bidirectional LSTM neural network is smaller than the prediction error of GRU, bidirectional GRU, RNN and bidirectional RNN at each time.

Table 4. Grain pile surface prediction results of RNN, bi-directional RNN, GRU, bi-directional GRU neural network

Temperature value	8 o'clock on September 2nd	14 o'clock on September 2nd	20 o'clock on September 2nd	8 o'clock on September 3rd	14 o'clock on September 3rd	20 o'clock on September 3rd
The actual value	21.3	21.5	21.5	21.5	21.5	21.5
GRU predicted value	28.44	28.33	28.44	28.43	28.29	28.45
Bidirectional GRU predicted value	28.37	28.34	28.41	28.38	28.27	28.37
RNN predicted value	28.45	28.35	28.48	28.44	28.31	28.42
Bidirectional RNN predicted value	28.33	28.28	28.43	28.37	28.29	28.42

(*continued*)

Table 4. (*continued*)

Temperature value	8 o'clock on September 2nd	14 o'clock on September 2nd	20 o'clock on September 2nd	8 o'clock on September 3rd	14 o'clock on September 3rd	20 o'clock on September 3rd
GRU error	7.14	6.83	6.94	6.93	6.79	6.95
Bidirectional GRU error	7.07	6.84	6.91	6.88	6.77	6.87
RNN error	7.15	6.85	6.98	6.94	6.81	6.92
Bidirectional RNN error	7.03	6.78	6.93	6.87	6.79	6.92

It can be seen from Table 2 that the error between the prediction result of grain pile surface and the actual value of the bidirectional LSTM neural network model is within 0.04. According to Table 2 and Table 4, the prediction result of bidirectional LSTM neural network is smaller than the prediction error of GRU, bidirectional GRU, RNN and bidirectional RNN at each time.

3.3 Comparison and Analysis of LSTM Neural Network Model and Bidirectional LSTM Neural Network Model

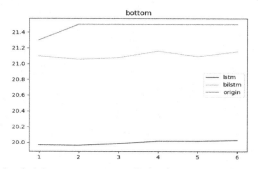

Fig. 5. Line graph of underlying temperature prediction for LSTM and bidirectional LSTM neural network models (Color figure online)

The abscissa 1, 2 and 3 in Fig. 5 and Fig. 6 respectively represent the three moments at 8:00 in the morning, 14 in the afternoon and 20 in the evening of the penultimate day. Abscissa 4, 5 and 6 in Fig. 5 and Fig. 6 respectively represent the three moments at 8:00 in the morning, 14:00 in the afternoon and 20:00 in the evening on the last day. The ordinate represents temperature. The green broken line is the actual value of grain heap temperature, the yellow broken line is the predicted value of grain heap temperature of bidirectional LSTM, and the blue broken line is the predicted value of grain heap

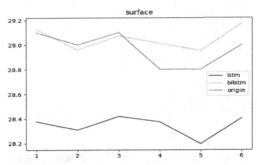

Fig. 6. Line graph of surface temperature prediction for LSTM and bidirectional LSTM neural network models (Color figure online)

temperature of LSTM. Figure 5 is the broken line diagram of the prediction of bottom temperature of LSTM and bidirectional LSTM. Figure 6 is the broken line diagram of the prediction of surface temperature of LSTM and bidirectional LSTM. Figure 6 shows intuitively that the predicted value of bidirectional LSTM neural network in grain heap temperature is closer to the actual value of grain heap temperature than the predicted value of LSTM neural network in grain heap temperature. Therefore, the error between the bidirectional LSTM and the actual value is smaller, and it has a better application prospect in grain stack temperature.

3.4 Comparison and Analysis of the Training Results of Bidirectional LSTM Neural Network Model and RNN, Bidirectional RNN, GRU, Bidirectional GRU Network Model

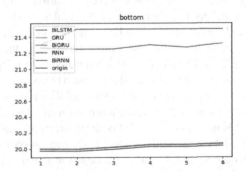

Fig. 7. Line diagram of bidirectional LSTM neural network model and underlying temperature prediction of GRU, bidirectional GRU, RNN and bidirectional RNN

The abscissa 1, 2 and 3 in Fig. 7 and Fig. 8 respectively represent the three moments at 8:00 in the morning, 14 in the afternoon and 20 in the evening of the penultimate day. Abscissa 4, 5 and 6 in Fig. 7 and Fig. 8 respectively represent the three moments at 8:00 in the morning, 14:00 in the afternoon and 20:00 in the evening on the last day. The ordinate represents temperature. The gray broken line is the actual value of grain

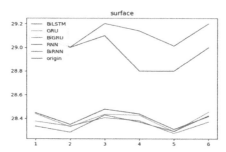

Fig. 8. The broken line diagram of bidirectional LSTM neural network model and surface temperature prediction of GRU, bidirectional GRU, RNN and bidirectional RNN

heap temperature, the blue broken line is the predicted value of grain heap temperature of bidirectional LSTM, the yellow broken line is the predicted value of grain heap temperature of GRU, the green broken line is the predicted value of grain heap temperature of bidirectional GRU, the red broken line is the predicted value of grain heap temperature of RNN, the purple broken line is the predicted value of grain heap temperature of bidirectional RNN, It can be seen intuitively from Fig. 7 and Fig. 8 that the predicted value of bidirectional LSTM neural network in grain heap temperature is closer to the actual value of grain heap temperature than that of other neural networks. Therefore, the error between the bidirectional LSTM and the actual value is smaller, and it has a better application prospect in grain stack temperature.

4   Conclusions

In this paper, a temperature prediction model based on bidirectional LSTM is proposed. Firstly, the advantages and disadvantages of LSTM neural network are introduced. Then, the bidirectional LSTM neural network prediction model is derived from the shortcomings of LSTM neural network. Firstly, the temperature data of the bottom and surface layer of the grain heap at 8, 14 and 20 o'clock from June 29 to September 3 collected by the shallow ground energy and air-cooled grain heap temperature control green grain storage technology research project of Wuhan National Rice Exchange Center Co., LTD were preprocessed. The simulated test was carried out using the LSTM neural network and the improved LSTM neural network, that is, the bidirectional LSTM neural network. It can be seen from the data results and line chart of the simulation test that the prediction results of LSTM and bidirectional LSTM are close to the actual value, but the predicted value of bidirectional LSTM is closer to the real value than that of LSTM, and has better prediction results. At the end of the experiment, the bidirectional LSTM and RNN neural network, bidirectional RNN neural network, GRU neural network and bidirectional GRU neural network are comprehensively compared and analyzed. The results show that bidirectional LSTM is closer to the real value and has better prediction results than RNN, bidirectional RNN, GRU and bidirectional GRU. Finally, the bidirectional LSTM has a better application prospect.

References

1. Can, H., Xiaomei, T.: Temperature Prediction control of grain drying tower based on information entropy. Comput. Measur. Control **22**(006), 1741–1744 (2014)
2. Wan, X., Zhu, G., Chen, Y., Zhang, T.: Metall. Autom. **201**, 45(S1), 67–73. (in Chinese)
3. Bin, L., Jiang, T., Wang, S., Liu, S., Yin, L., Zhai, K.: Prediction analysis of air temperature in tunnel during operation. Tunnel Constr. (English and Chinese) **40**(04), 597–602 (2020)
4. Ding, G., Zhong, S.: J. Astronaut. **03**, 489–492+545 (2006)
5. Chen, Q., Li, H., Xie, Z., Xie, J.: J. Ordnance Equip. Eng. **40**(06), 154–157 (2019)
6. Guangbin, Y., Gang, D., Wei, Y., et al.: Prediction of aero-engine exhaust temperature based on support process vector machine. Electr. Mach. Control **8**, 30–36 (2013)
7. Zhao, M., Wang, D., Fang, J., Li, Y., Mao, J.: Temperature prediction of subway station based on LSTM neural network. Beijing Jiaotong Univ. **44**(04), 94–101 (2020)
8. Qing, Y., Yan, Z., Yunsong, H.: Construction of indoor temperature prediction model based on lstm algorithm for office buildings in cold region during transition season. Cryogenic Build. Technol. **41**(03), 8–12 (2019)

Prediction Model of Gasoline Octane Number Based on GRNN

Bing Cai[✉], Hua Yang[✉], Kang Zhou, and Haikuan Yang

Wuhan Polytechnic University, Dongxihu District, Wuhan 43040, China
395258541@qq.com, 22669594@qq.com

Abstract. The process affects the most valuable octane number in gasoline, which in turn hurts profits. In this paper, through data cleaning, PauTa was used to output processing samples, and principal component analysis (PCA) algorithm was used to screen several operating variables of gasoline processing, so as to obtain the operating variables with high correlation with the octane number loss of gasoline. Based on the above work, the octane number prediction model based on GRNN is established. According to the test results, the prediction efficiency reaches 99.57%. The fitting effect of the model is close to the real octane number loss, which is helpful to optimize the operating conditions, reduce the octane number loss of gasoline and improve the economic benefit of production. The model is highly fitting to the prediction of the target value, which is helpful to optimize the operating conditions and reduce the octane number loss of gasoline in actual production, thus improving the economic benefit.

Keywords: Octane number · Prediction model · Generalized regression neural network · Principal component analysis

1 Introduction

As the main source of automobile energy, the waste gas from gasoline combustion seriously affects the ecological environment. Therefore, the requirements for gasoline quality standards become extremely stringent. Octane number (RON) is a key index that determines the efficiency of gasoline combustion and becomes the symbolic attribute of gasoline products. The octane number is reduced to a certain extent because of the contradiction between ensuring octane number and sulphur reduction. One unit octane reduction is equivalent to a loss of about 150 CNY/t. Therefore, studying the octane number of gasoline is of great significance to protecting the atmospheric environment and improving the economic benefits of factories [1].

RON can represent an important parameter of steam quality and function rate, and can generally measure the knock suppression ability of gasoline. A low RON value in the oil will greatly reduce the thermal efficiency of the automobile engine, which may result in component loss, and in extreme cases directly lead to engine knock. When this happens, the cylinder will sound and smoke will appear in the gas pipe, accompanied by a sudden rise in the temperature of the combustion chamber. If the gasoline RON

© Springer Nature Singapore Pte Ltd. 2022
L. Pan et al. (Eds.): BIC-TA 2021, CCIS 1566, pp. 396–404, 2022.
https://doi.org/10.1007/978-981-19-1253-5_30

value is high enough, it will have certain inhibition ability, which will largely avoid the damage of automobile parts and maintain the life of the automobile. Therefore, RON has a direct impact on the safety of automobile components. For refineries, RON is a symbol of profit, and the content of RON directly determines the price.The current situation is that the technical means and equipment tools of refining are not consistent, and there is no integrated exploration to improve quality, making it difficult to complete the production optimization. According to this situation, how to improve RON content under the premise of low sulfur and alkene has become a problem that the field needs to face and customer service.

Nowadays, neural network technology is widely used in image recognition [2], flow prediction [3] and other aspects, causing more and more researchers to consider using neural network [4, 5] to predict octane number. The most commonly used BP neural network needs manual testing and tuning, and has the possibility of falling into local optimal, and is relatively dependent on data, so it needs to have. Compared with the former, the generalized regression neural network does not need to adjust parameters, so the generalized regression neural network is considered here to build the model.

There are a lot of parameter information in the data set, and the data dimension is too high, so it is difficult to carry out prediction analysis. It is necessary to screen variables and extract some indicators with the highest correlation. Here, principal component analysis is used to reduce the dimension of data, and then generalized regression neural network is used to establish the octane number prediction model. The obtained gasoline data was analyzed, and the redundant variables were filtered, including the deletion of irrelevant variables, the completion of variable values, and the cleaning of bad values of variables. After that, 336 operational variables were obtained. Then, 20 variables with the highest score and the most relevant variables were obtained through dimension reduction, and some of the most important variables affecting octane number were obtained. On this basis, the model training and detection, get the optimal model, and prediction, analysis to improve the quality of gasoline.

2   Introduction to Relevant Theories

2.1   Principal Component Analysis Method

There are many factors affecting octane number, and the information contained in each factor is also very complex [6, 7]. How to extract the key information from the complex information is the top priority of model construction. The purpose of data dimension reduction is to reduce the dimension of data and extract some indicators that have the greatest impact on the target value, so as to facilitate subsequent operation analysis. In essence, it is a mapping relationship, which means to map data points from the original high-dimensional space to low-dimensional space. The characteristics of the data are proposed through principal component analysis, and the data dimension is reduced as much as possible on the premise of ensuring the nature of the data. According to the idea of principal component analysis, this paper explores and finds some variables with the highest correlation. These newly generated variable data are independent and do not interfere with each other, and can directly reflect the nature of the overall data.

2.2 An Overview of Generalized Regression Neural Networks

General Regression Neural Network (GRNN), whose overall structure is similar to RBF, mainly includes four layers of input, output, hidden and sum, which is a variant form of RBF.GRNN has a unique summation layer, and the neurons with two summation modes sum the transfer function of the pattern layer. Removed the weight connection between the hidden layer and the output layer. It is generated based on mathematical statistics and based on radial basis network. It has the advantages of small computation, can cope with the scene with small sample number, excellent convergence speed, and does not need to manually set parameters such as network layer number and neuron number. It is easy to operate and has good nonlinear approximation ability (Fig. 1).

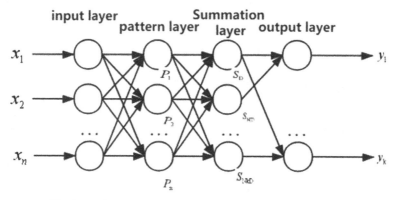

Fig. 1. Basic structure of generalized regression neural network

N neurons in the mode layer correspond to N training samples, and the transfer function of neurons in this layer is:

$$pi = \exp[-\frac{(X - Xi)}{2\sigma^2}]i = 1, 2, ..., n \tag{1}$$

The number of neurons in the input layer directly depends on the vector dimension of the sample, and the neurons will transmit the input vector directly to the pattern layer.

Where x is the input vector, and Xi is the ith training sample corresponding to the ith neuron.

In the summation layer, the connection weight of each neuron of the first type and the mode layer is 1, and the transfer function is:

$$S_D = \sum_{i=1}^{n} Pi \tag{2}$$

The number of neurons in the output layer is the same as the dimension k of the output vector in the learning sample. The output of the ith neuron corresponds to the ith = 1 element in the synthesis layer divided by the ith element:

$$yi = \frac{Sni}{S_D}, i = 1, 2, ..., k \tag{3}$$

The structure of the network is simple, the prediction effect is good under a small number of samples, and it is suitable for dealing with unstable data.

3   The Experimental Operation

3.1   Data Preparation

Most of the variables in the raw data collected are normal, but some variables contain only partial time data, and some variables have null values, so the data can only be used after processing. Different data exceptions need to be handled in different ways:

1. If the index column data in the data set is seriously missing, the index can be deleted directly.
2. Indicators with serious data loss are directly deleted for processing;
3. Some null and wrong values, demand sampling should be the average of the index, data filling; According to the nature of gasoline itself, as well as some data statistics obtained from industrial production, gasoline related index values have a normal range. For data not in the normal range, it is necessary to remove and fill with the average value of this index.
4. The outliers were removed according to The PauTa.

PauTa: suppose that the observed variables are measured with the same precision, and the initial data $x1, x2, ..., xn$, first calculate the arithmetic mean value $\bar{x}$ of the observed variable, and then calculate the residual error $vi = xi - \bar{x}(i = 1, 2, ..., n)$. Based on the above, standard error σ is obtained according to Bessel formula (4). Judge whether residual error vm of data xm is within the range of 3σ. If vm is within the range of 3σ, the data is considered normal; otherwise $|vm| = |xm - \bar{x}| > 3\sigma$, data xm contains a large error and should be deleted [8].

$$\sigma = [\frac{1}{n-1} \sum_{i=1}^{n} vi^2]^{1/2} = [\frac{\sum_{i=1}^{n} xi^2 - (\sum_{i=1}^{n} xi^2)^2/n}{(n-1)}]^{1/2} \tag{4}$$

3.2   Data Dimension Reduction

There are many operating parameters that affect octane number. Direct prediction will seriously affect the prediction efficiency, and irrelevant variables will directly lead to the instability of the results. Should be normalized data processing first, and then to the correlation between indicators, solving the covariance matrix, the calculation of the covariance matrix eigenvalue and eigenvector, determine the number of principal components, get the several characteristics of the corresponding principal component number biggest value, use the corresponding eigenvalue of the corresponding eigenvectors constitute a new matrix; In this paper, the variance contribution rate corresponding to each feature is calculated. Based on the cumulative contribution rate exceeding the given value, these features are obtained to obtain the corresponding index, that is, the index with the greatest influence. It is generally believed that when set to 80%, these indicator information can basically retain the essence of data. To make the experiment more convincing, set the contribution rate at 85% (Fig. 2).

$$xi = \frac{xi - \bar{x}}{S} \tag{5}$$

$$\bar{x} = \frac{1}{n} \sum_{i=1}^{n} xi \tag{6}$$

$$s = \sqrt{\frac{1}{n-1} \sum_{i=1}^{n} (xi - \bar{x})^2} \tag{7}$$

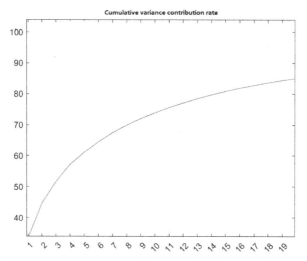

Fig. 2. Relationship between cumulative variance contribution rate and number of principal components

Establish a visual graph of the relationship between variance contribution rate and the number of indicators. Indicators here are in descending order from the maximum eigenvalue. It can be clearly seen that with the increase of indicators, the cumulative variance contribution rate keeps increasing until it reaches 85% near the 20th indicator. The first 20 principal components are selected as input variables of the multilayer sensory neural network. Through principal component analysis, more than 300 variables were selected into the current 20 variables, the data dimension was greatly reduced, and some indicators most related to octane number were obtained, which laid a good foundation for subsequent model training and prediction.

3.3 Build Training Sets and Test Sets

In the sample data of pre-processing and dimension reduction, 280 data were randomly selected for training, and the other 45 samples were used as test sets to test the model performance and analyze the results, so as to continuously adjust and obtain the optimal model.

4 Predicting Octane Number Loss Rate Based on Generalized Regression Neural Network Model

4.1 The Construction Method of Prediction Model

1. Select training set and test set
2. Create GRNN model group
3. Perform training and prediction

4.2 Algorithmic Process

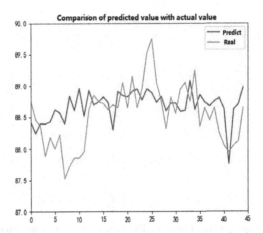

Fig. 3. Comparison between forecast and actual value

The data set consisted of 325 data samples, of which 280 were used as training sets for model training and 45 were used as test sets for model. RON value was selected as the research object, the model was built by software code, and the model was predicted. The comparison diagram of the analysis results was obtained. Fig. 3 shows the result curve where the data are the real value and the predicted value. The variation trend between the curves is relatively consistent, and it can be seen that the predicted result has a high fitting degree with the actual result.

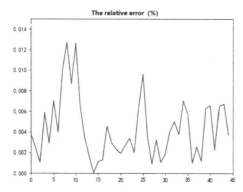

Fig. 4. Relative error between RON predicted value and actual value

In order to make the result more convincing, the relative error graph of predicted value and real value is drawn by the function, as shown in Fig. 4. The average relative error rate was about 0.43%, and only a few values exceeded 1%. The error is in a very small range, it can be seen that the model itself has a very small deviation from the real situation.

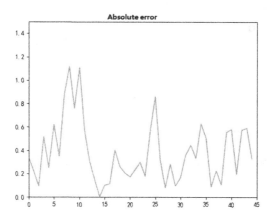

Fig. 5. Absolute error between RON predicted value and actual value

The absolute error curve between the predicted value and the real value is shown in Fig. 5, and the absolute error is less than 1.2.

5 Conclusion

Table 1. The relative errors of several different prediction methods are compared

Algorithm	Traditional SVR	Traditional AST -NRAX	A two-stage SVR	AST -NRAX second stage	Two-stage heterogeneous random forest	PCA-GRNN
Accuracy	0.8345	0.8753	0.8895	0.9134	0.9667	0.9957

The Table 1 above shows the octane number prediction model based on PCA and GRNN after results from other methods to predict the accuracy of [10], comparative analysis, clearly see the proposed method has certain advantages and accuracy, under the influence of a large amount of data index, a lot of methods of prediction accuracy is not high, but by PCA dimension reduction and GRNN prediction after processing, Accuracy rate further improved; Through principal component analysis (PCA) dimension reduction according to according to pull up to remove outliers, complete the dimension of data cleaning, using generalized regression neural network to forecast, its main characteristic is a structure easy to understand, without having to test to get the best parameters for many times, save a lot of time needed for the experiment, conducive to rapid modeling, rapid access to high quality model, Moreover, the accuracy is further improved by dimension reduction of data, and finally reaches 0.9957 algorithm accuracy. This shows that GRNN itself has significantly better application effect than other algorithms in complex nonlinear scenarios, and the model proposed in this paper has advantages over traditional algorithms in RON prediction model.

References

1. Du, M., Zhang, T., Bo, Q., Xu, W.: Prediction model of octane number loss in gasoline refining process. J. Qilu Univ. Technol. **35**(01), 73–80 (2021)
2. Wang, P.T., Wang, Z.W.: Face recognition algorithm based on PSO-LDA. J. Guangxi Univ. Sci. Technol. **28**(1), 85–90 (2017)
3. Hao, C.: Research on mobile network traffic prediction based on wavelet neural network. Electron. World **15**, 81–82 (2020)
4. Chen, X., Liu, D., Sun, X.: Reduction of octane number Loss in refining process based on neural network. Sci. Technol. Innovat. Appl. **5**, 25–27, 31 (2021)
5. Dan-hua, L.: Octane Infrared Spectral Data Analysis Based on Neural Network. Henan University, Zhengzhou (2018)
6. Badra, J., AlRamadan, A.S., Mani Sarathy, S.: Optimization of the octane response of gasoline/ethanol blends. Appl. Energy **203**, 778–793 (2017). https://doi.org/10.1016/j.apenergy.2017.06.084
7. Laurgeau, C., Espiau, B., Barras, F.: de Termina -tion de l'indice d 'Octane par chromatographie gazeuse de-termining the octane number by gas Chromatography-acetic acid chromatography. Chin. J. Chromatogr. **5**(4), 251–258 (2006)

8. Wen, M., et al.: Effects of gasoline octane number on fuel consumption and emissions in two vehicles equipped with GDI and PFI spark-ignition engine. J. Energy Eng. **146**(6), 04020069 (2020). https://doi.org/10.1061/(ASCE)EY.1943-7897.0000722
9. Liu, C., Xia, T., Tian, J., et al.: Shandong Chem. Ind. **49** (19), 106,109 (2020)
10. Xie, X., Wang, S., Yan, T., Wang, X.: Gasoline octane number prediction based on two-stage heterogeneous random forest. Math. Model. Appl. **10**(01), 39–44 (2012)

Research on Ship Speed Prediction Model Based on BP Neural Network

Weigang Xu[1](✉), Zhongwen Li[1], Qiong Hu[2], Chuanliang Zhao[2],
and Hongtao Zhou[1]

[1] Huazhong University of Science and Technology,
Wuhan 430074, People's Republic of China
524545375@qq.com, 18674075322@163.com
[2] China Ship Scientific Research Center, Wuxi 214026, People's Republic of China

Abstract. In order to predict the speed of ships, an prediction model is proposed according to the principal component analysis and BP neural network. Aimed at Changhang Yangshan ship 2, five main factors affecting speed are extracted through principal component analysis (PCA). Furthermore, the input and output of the BP neural network is designed by five main factors and predicted speed respectively. The initial parameters are selected to reduce the mean square error and the prediction error of the model. Finally, the prediction results show that the real speed is consistent with the predicted speed in trend, and the prediction accuracy is accurate. An effective way of speed prediction is provided by principal component analysis and BP neural network.

Keywords: Intelligent navigation · Ship speed prediction · Principal component analysis · BP neural network

1 Introduction

In recent years, due to the development of intelligent navigation optimization technology, ship intelligence has become the general trend of global shipping. Ship intelligence is inseparable from the support of economic speed. The forecast of economic speed can not only cut costs for the shipping industry, but also contribute to low-carbon and environmentally friendly construction [1].

The ocean is a relatively complex environment, which leads to the fact that the speed of ships sailing on the sea will be affected by many factors [2]. It is not accurate to predict the speed by simple linear regression, so an effective nonlinear model is the key to solving the speed prediction. Due to the complexity of ship navigation, it is extremely complicated to establish a strict mathematical model. However, BP neural network can overcome this shortcoming and realize the prediction of ship speed based on data [3]. As for the input data to the neural network, it needs to be preprocessed, and the principal component analysis method can effectively reduce the dimensionality of the data factors and eliminate the correlation between the factors [4]. Therefore, this paper proposes a ship speed prediction model based on the combination of principal component

ⓒ Springer Nature Singapore Pte Ltd. 2022
L. Pan et al. (Eds.): BIC-TA 2021, CCIS 1566, pp. 405–411, 2022.
https://doi.org/10.1007/978-981-19-1253-5_31

analysis and BP neural network. The principal component analysis is used to select the main factors affecting the ship speed, then the ship speed is predicted by BP neural network. Finally, the network parameters are set to reduce the prediction error.

2 Dimensionality Reduction of Speed Influencing Factors Based on Principal Component Analysis

2.1 The Basic Idea of Principal Component Analysis

The basic idea of principal component analysis is to use the method of dimensionality reduction to convert multiple related input variables into several comprehensive input variables [5,6]. It mainly performs linear transformation on the data set, and projects the variance of the data sample into a new coordinate system. Then it calculates the variance of all input variables and arranges them in descending order.

The principal component analysis method ensures that the linearly transformed data contains the information of the original data to the greatest extent and achieves the purpose of reducing input variables at the same time [7,8]. This method selects the low-order components of the principal components and discards the high-order components, because in general, the low-order components of the principal components can well retain most of the information in the original data [9,10].

2.2 Dimensionality Reduction Analysis

The data used in this article is from the voyage data of Changhang Yangshan 2. The collected data is composed of environmental and ship's factors. Environmental factors include wind speed (m/s) and wind direction (°). Ship's own factors include course (°), speed (kn), rotation speed (rpm), torque (kNm), power (kW), fuel consumption (m^3). Since speed is the factor that we want to optimize and predict, we will use it as the dependent variable and the remaining 7 factors as independent variables. Our goal is to reduce repetitive effects and dimensionality reduction through PCA. Due to the large amount of data, Table 1 only lists part of sample data.

Table 1. Partial sample data table

Wind speed (m/s)	Wind direction (°)	Course (°)	Ship speed (kn)	Rotating speed (rpm)	Torque (kNm)	Power (kW)	Fuel consumption (m^3)
7.77	69.0	0.00	0.03	1.00	−4.71	24.44	0.000941
6.38	59.00	0.00	0.03	1.88	−4.72	24.60	0.030112
7.47	63.00	0.00	0.01	1.00	−4.68	24.77	0.030112
8.18	83.68	35.10	0.14	34.66	−12.91	−53.35	0.031053

Before the PCA process, the data needs to be preprocessed:

(1) Eliminating missing data.
(2) Taking the absolute value of the power data, and turning it into a positive number.
(3) Excluding the data of the ship in the stopped state, the standard of the ship in the stopped state is: the fuel consumption is 0, the speed is 0.

In this paper, the comprehensive indicators obtained by principal component analysis are used as the principal components of the sample data. They are not relative, and contain the main information of the original sample. The variance of the principal components is used to represent the coverage of the original sample information, and the index with the cumulative coverage exceeding 85% is used as the principal component of the sample data.

Table 2. Contribution rate of various factors

	Fuel consumption	Power	Torque	Rotating speed	Course	Wind speed	Wind direction
Coverage	0.4859	0.1763	0.1290	0.1129	0.0880	0.0069	0.0011
Cumulative coverage	0.4859	0.6622	0.7912	0.9041	0.9921	0.9990	1.0000

The contribution rate of each factor as shown in Table 2 is calculated by Matlab. The cumulative variance contribution rate of the first 4 components has reached 90%, exceeding the requirement of 85%. But we do not need to be limited to the 85% standard. In order to better cover the information of the original sample data, we have selected 5 components as the final principal components, which are the linear combination of 7 factors.

Table 3. Principal component coefficient table

	Component 1	Component 2	Component 3	Component 4	Component 5
Wind speed	0.2644	0.7185	0.3349	0.3846	−0.3920
Wind direction	−0.2017	−0.7784	0.3852	0.0895	−0.4437
Course	0.4541	−0.1460	−0.7723	0.2624	−0.3273
Rotation speed	0.9662	−0.0138	0.0569	−0.1952	−0.0079
Torque	−0.9705	0.0469	−0.1010	0.2014	0.0191
Power	0.9592	−0.0697	0.1173	−0.1879	−0.0253
Fuel consumption	0.5380	−0.2882	0.1382	0.6718	0.3963

The data in Table 3 represents the coefficients obtained after principal component analysis of each sample variable. Five input variables are finally selected as principal components, which not only contain most of the information of the original sample data, but also reduce the dimensionality of the input variables.

3   Prediction of Ship Speed Based on BP Neural Network

3.1   Construction of Neural Network for Ship Speed Prediction

Artificial neural network is composed of a large number of neurons which are connected to each other [11,12]. It is inspired by exploring the perception and processing of information by human brain nerves, so as to perform non-linear conversion of information and parallel processing of information [13,14].

BP neural network construction steps are as follows [15]:

(1) Initializing neural network.
(2) Selecting some training samples as the input of the neural network and training the network.
(3) Calculating the error between the actual output value of the neural network and the expected output value. If the error does not reach the preset accuracy, process backward propagation of errors.
(4) Through the back propagation of errors, iterative calculations are continuously carried out to correct the connection weight of the network. Step (3) is repeated until the preset error accuracy requirement is reached.

The above algorithm steps are represented as a flowchart as shown in Fig. 1:

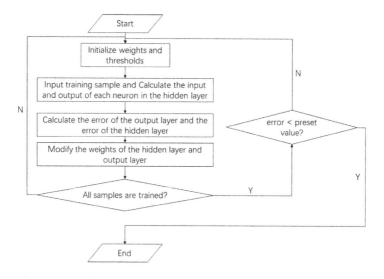

Fig. 1. Back propagation algorithm flow.

3.2   Predicting Results

The original sample data used in this article is taken from the voyage data of Changhang Yangshan 2 from May 5 to May 22. The initial parameters selected in this paper are represented as shown in Table 4. Neural network predicted value and expected value results as shown in Fig. 2. The green circle and the blue asterisk in Fig. 2 represents the expected value and the predicted results respectively. The test set error is shown in Fig. 3.

Table 4. The initial parameters in neural network

Layers	Learning rate	Hidden layer nodes	Input layer nodes	Output layer nodes
3	0.1	10	5	1

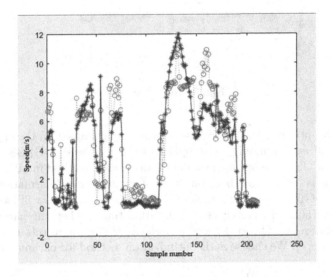

Fig. 2. Comparison between expected value and output value predicted by neural network.

In order to reduce the error of nerural network, the parameters of BP neural network need to be optimized. First, we need to select an appropriate activation function. The commonly used activation functions are sigmoid, tanh and relu.

Sigmoid function has been used widely, but in recent years, fewer and fewer people use it. This is mainly because when the input is very large or very small, the gradient of these neurons is close to 0, and the mean of output combined with sigmod is not 0.

Tanh is a deformation of sigmoid. The mean of output combined with tanh is 0. Therefore, tanh is better than sigmoid in practical application.

The convergence rate of SGD obtained by relu is much faster than sigmoid/tanh. Compared with sigmoid/tanh, relu only needs a threshold to get the activation value without a lot of complex operations. Therefore, we choose relu as our activation function.

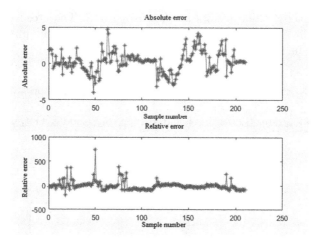

Fig. 3. Test set error.

Different optimization methods also have a great impact on the error results. There are three commonly used optimization methods: L-BFGS, SGD and ADAM. L-BFGS is the optimization of quasi Newton method family. The essential principle is Newton method, but a lot of optimization deformation has been carried out. SGD is a random gradient descent method, which will have the best performance (classification effect and iteration times) when the parameters are adjusted better. ADAM works well on relatively large data sets (thousands of samples or more). We choose SGD optimization method for parameter optimization.

Comparing the two BP neural networks in Python, it is found that the error after parameter optimization is smaller, and the results are shown in Table 5.

Table 5. Mean square error table

MSE	Train error (%)	Test error (%)
Before parameter optimization	2.4832	2.8975
After parameter optimization	1.4937	1.9718

4   Conclusion

In this paper, the principal component analysis method is incorporated to calculate the variance contribution rate of these factors and the top five factors with the most contribution are selected for dimensionality reduction. Then we establish a speed prediction optimization model based on BP neural network, which can better predict the speed at the next time. By introducing principal component analysis, BP neural network and parameter optimization into speed prediction can play a good guiding role in understanding the law of speed change, and correctly guide navigators to make navigation decisions. The BP neural network can been used as a redundant system in case of failure of a sensor providing the foreseen information for the controllers. Therefore, the BP neural network can help in anticipating some ship speed deviation from predefined target conditions, and optimizing the ship operation.

Acknowledgment. This work is supported by China Ship Scientific Research Center.

References

1. Harilaos, N., Christos, A.: Ship speed optimization: concepts, models and combined speed-routing scenarios. Transp. Res. Part C Emerg. Technol. **44**(01), 52–69 (2014)
2. Li, Q.: Research on the non-linear mathematical model of ship sailing speed prediction. Ship Sci. Technol. **42**(06), 34–36 (2020)
3. Xu, T., Liu, X., Yang, X.: Real-time prediction of ship track based on BP neural network. J. Dalian Marit. Univ. **38**(01), 9–11 (2012)
4. Zhang, Y., Zhu, Y.: Prediction of welding quality of strip steel based on principal component analysis and GA-BP neural network. Thermal Process. Technol. **49**(17), 128–132 (2020)
5. Huang, Y.L., Wang, T., Wang, J., Peng, H.: Reliability evaluation of distribution network based on fuzzy spiking neural P system with self-synapse. J. Membr. Comput. **3**(1), 51–62 (2020). https://doi.org/10.1007/s41965-020-00035-1
6. Alhazov, A., Freund, R., Ivanov, S., Verlan, S.: Variants of derivation modes for which catalytic P systems with one catalyst are computationally complete. J. Membr. Comput. **1**, 1–13 (2021). https://doi.org/10.1007/s41965-021-00085-z
7. Wold, S., Kim, E., Paul, G.: Principal component analysis. Chemom. Intell. Lab. Syst. **2**(1–3), 37–52 (1987)
8. A Tutorial on Principal Component Analysis. http://www.cs.cmu.edu/~elaw/papers/pca.pdf. Accessed 4 Nov 2021
9. Bao, T., Zhou, N., Lv, Z., Peng, H., Wang, J.: Sequential dynamic threshold neural P systems. J. Membr. Comput. **2**(4), 255–268 (2020). https://doi.org/10.1007/s41965-020-00060-0
10. Jiang, Y., Su, Y., Luo, F.: An improved universal spiking neural P system with generalized use of rules. J. Membr. Comput. **1**, 270–278 (2019). https://doi.org/10.1007/s41965-019-00025-y
11. Mi, S., Zhang, L., Peng, H., Wang, J.: Medical image fusion based on DTNP systems and Laplacian pyramid. J. Membr. Comput. **3**, 284–295 (2021). https://doi.org/10.1007/s41965-021-00087-x
12. Oludare, I., Aman, J., Abiodun, E.: Comprehensive review of artificial neural network applications to pattern recognition. IEEE Access **7**(01), 158820–158846 (2019)
13. Wang, S.: Artificial neural network. Interdiscip. Comput. Java Program. **743**(01), 81–100 (2003)
14. Zhang, D.: Image presentation. In: Fundamentals of Image Data Mining. TCS, pp. 335–352. Springer, Cham (2021). https://doi.org/10.1007/978-3-030-69251-3_13
15. Al-Yousef, A., Samarasinghe, S.: A novel computational approach for biomarker detection for gene expression-based computer-aided diagnostic systems for breast cancer. In: Cartwright, H. (ed.) Artificial Neural Networks. MMB, vol. 2190, pp. 195–208. Springer, New York (2021). https://doi.org/10.1007/978-1-0716-0826-5_9

Real-Time Maritime Obstacle Detection Based on YOLOv5 for Autonomous Berthing

Guotong Chen[1]($\boxtimes$) (iD), Jiangtao Qi[2], and Zeyu Dai[2]

[1] Key Laboratory of Image Information Processing and Intelligent Control of Education Ministry of China, School of Artificial Intelligence and Automation, Huazhong University of Science and Technology, Wuhan 430074, China
`gtchen@hust.edu.cn`
[2] China Ship Scientific Research Center, No. 222 Shanshui East Road, Binhu District, Wuxi 214082, China

Abstract. The shipping industry is developing towards intelligence, in which autonomous berthing and docking systems play an important role. Real-time maritime obstacle detection is essential for autonomous berthing, which can protect ships from collisions. In the field of real-time objection detection, YOLOv5s is one of the most effective networks. To solve the real-time maritime obstacle detection for autonomous berthing, we propose an improved network, named YOLOv5s-CBAM, which employs the convolutional block attention module to boost the representation power of YOLOv5s. In addition, we propose another network, named YOLOv5-SE, in which a squeeze-and-excitation block is introduced to recalibrate the channel-wise features adaptively. The experimental results demonstrate that YOLOv5s-CBAM outperforms YOLOv5s in the detection of large obstacles. Both YOLOv5s-CBAM and YOLOv5s-SE achieve state-of-the-art performance in various metrics compared with previous related work for maritime obstacle detection.

Keywords: Autonomous berthing · Maritime obstacle detection · Deep learning · Attention module

1 Introduction

In recent years, the shipping industry is rapidly developing towards intelligence. The autonomous berthing and docking system is an essential part of intelligent ships [1], which uses computer technology and control technology to design the ship's route and speed in various maritime environment conditions, such as open water and narrow waterways. Automatic collision avoidance planning is an important technology in the field of autonomous berthing and docking, which requires the ship to quickly and effectively recognize nearby floating obstacles

Supported by Jiangsu Key Laboratory of Green Ship Technology (No. 2019Z04).

L. Pan et al. (Eds.): BIC-TA 2021, CCIS 1566, pp. 412–427, 2022.
https://doi.org/10.1007/978-981-19-1253-5_32

on the water, and adjust the speed and course for automatic collision avoidance. Since collision avoidance planning requires the information about surrounding obstacles in advance, an efficient and reliable approach to maritime obstacles detection is the first and key step.

To acquire maritime obstacles information around the ship, several methods based on different devices have been proposed. Some researchers applied remote sensing images to detect the obstacles nearby ships [2], which relatively achieved a high recognition accuracy, but with high time delay and expensive cost. Another approach was to send an unmanned air vehicle (UAV) to follow the ship, taking photos of the maritime environment nearby the ship and then transferring photos [24]. Due to the limited endurance of UAV, it is not reliable to perform obstacles detection in this way. A more feasible and adaptable approach is to use LiDAR sensors to generate 3-D point clouds for environment representation, which can be further processed to obtain information about the distance and size of obstacles. Despite the relatively high cost, there are several advantages of LiDARs. First, LiDAR sensors are less sensitive to poor weather and illumination conditions. Second, LiDAR sensors are capable of getting data with low delay. Finally, this type of sensor has been equipped on many autonomous vehicles for obstacle avoidance and proven to work well for this purpose [5].

The LiDAR sensors equipped on ships have blind areas, which leads to a blind zone in the close range area of the ship, where no echo data reflects from obstacles or the reliability is very low. As a result, obstacles in the blind zone are unable to be effectively detected, which may cause potential hazards. Therefore, there is a demand to develop the method of real-time maritime obstacle detection in case that obstacles exist in the blind zone.

In this work, we introduce YOLOv5s network to perform the real-time maritime obstacles detection task. We adopt two attention modules, squeeze-and-excitation (SE) block and convolutional block attention module (CBAM), to design YOLOv5s based networks, named YOLOv5s-SE and YOLOv5s-CBAM. We evaluate our networks on a novel image based benchmark dataset for water surface object detection, named Water Surface Object Detection Dataset (WSODD). The results show that our networks outperform the previous obstacle detection methods on WSODD. In addition, the SE block and CBAM can improve the feature representation power for specific obstacles.

2 Related Work

2.1 Object Detection Methods

Object Detection is one of the fundamental tasks in the field of computer vision and has been studied in academia for nearly two decades. The progress in object detection has generally experienced two historical periods: the traditional object detection period (before 2014) and the deep learning based object detection period (after 2014) [28].

In the traditional object detection period, most object detection methods were developed based on handcrafted features, such as Viola-Jones detectors [20],

HOG detectors [4], and DPM [6]. The early object detection methods required researchers to expertly design sophisticated feature representations to perform object detection. Due to the limitation of handcrafted features and computing resources, the precision and speed of traditional object detection methods were relatively limited.

The object detection methods in the deep learning based object detection period can be mainly divided into two categories: two-stage detectors and one-stage detectors. The first deep learning based two-stage object detection method was the R-CNN [8], which significantly improved the mean average precision (mAP) compared with the traditional method. Since then, other improved two-stage object detection methods were proposed, such as Fast R-CNN [7], Faster R-CNN [19], and Mask R-CNN [10]. Although the two-stage detectors could reach relatively high precision, the speed failed to meet the demand of real-time object detection tasks. To solve this problem, one-stage detectors were proposed, which enabled end-to-end training and real-time speed. YOLO [18] was the first one-stage detector in the deep learning era, followed by its improvements YOLOv2 and YOLOv3. Other famous one-stage detectors included SSD [16], RetinaNet [15], etc. One-stage detectors can reach high detection accuracy while keeping a very high detection speed, which is suitable for real-time object detection tasks.

2.2 Maritime Object Detection Based on Deep Learning

The technology of deep learning has greatly promoted the development of maritime object detection. Yang et al. employed Faster R-CNN to locate the object more accurately for USVs [25]. Qin et al. proposed a robust vision-based obstacle detection method for USVs, which adopted FCN for obstacle detection [17]. Zhang et al. presented a ship tracking algorithm based on YOLO, which reached higher accuracy, stronger robustness, and better real-time [26]. Chen et al. used an improved YOLOv2 algorithm for small ship detection, which can also be utilized for identification of various maritime obstacles [3]. Jie et al. performed ship detection and tracking of ships using the improved YOLOv3 and Deep SORT tracking algorithm [13]. Recently, Han et al. proposed ShipYOLO [9], which is an improved YOLOv4 detection model with faster speed and higher accuracy.

3   Methodology

The LiDAR based obstacle detection fails to work well when obstacles exist in the blind zone. Therefore, it is very necessary to develop obstacle detection methods using cameras equipped on the ship. The requirement of real-time and high accuracy must be taken into account when designing obstacle detection methods. Therefore, the one-stage detectors have become the first choice, among which YOLOv5, the fifth version of YOLO proposed by Utralytics, has achieved outstanding performance and surpassed all previous versions in speed and accuracy [12]. YOLOv5 includes four versions, YOLOv5s, YOLOv5m YOLOv5l, YOLOv5x, respectively. YOLOv5 is the simplest with the least number of model parameters and the fastest speed. Hence we choose YOLOv5s to perform maritime obstacle detection. In addition, two modules, squeeze-and-excitation block (SE block) and convolutional block attention module (CBAM), are introduced to design two modified networks, named YOLOv5s-SE and YOLOv5s-CBAM. The details of the three networks are described as follows.

3.1 YOLOv5s

The network structure of YOLOv5s is shown in Fig. 1, which is mainly composed of three parts: the backbone part, the neck part and the prediction part. Moreover, the details of function blocks are also shown in the top, including Focus, CBL, CSP1_X, and CSP2_X.

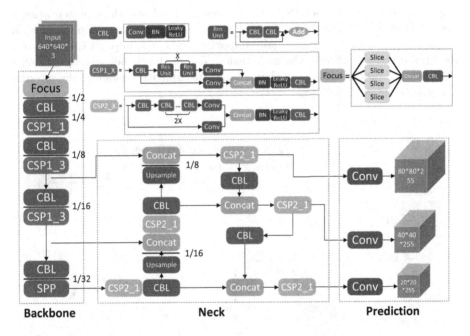

Fig. 1. YOLOv5s network structure and details of different function blocks

The backbone part is used to extract features. First, the Focus block is designed to transform the feature maps from high resolution to low resolution, which samples every two pixels periodically to generate low-resolution images. It aims to reduce the amount of calculation and speed up. Second, CBL, CSP1_1, and CSP1_3 are used to extract features of different levels. Lastly, the SPP network uses pooling layers of different sizes to fuse features of different scales to amplify the receptive field.

The neck part is used to further enhance the ability of feature extraction, which includes the structure of FPN+PAN [14,21]. The FPN structure can pass the strong semantic features from deep layers to shallow layers, whereas the localization information is not considered. To address this problem, The PAN structure is implemented after FPN, passing up the strong localization features of the lower layers. In this way, features from different layers can be fused.

The prediction part (or head part) has three branches, which are designed to detect objects with different sizes. The output information of prediction consists of object coordinates, category, and confidence. By further post-processing, the detection results can be displayed on the image.

3.2   YOLOv5s with SE Block

The Squeeze-and-Excitation (SE) block is designed to boost the representational power of the network. In the traditional process of convolution and pooling, each channel of the feature map is equally important, whereas, in practical problems, the importance of different channels varies. The SE block can adaptively refine the feature responses along the channel axis by explicitly modeling the interdependencies between them [11].

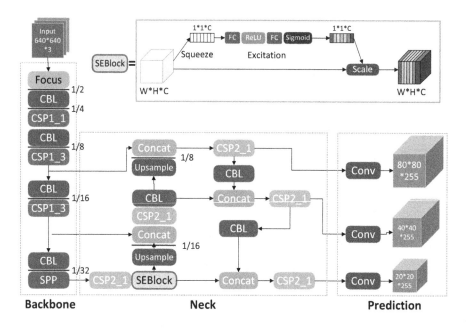

Fig. 2. YOLOv5s-SE network structure. SE block (yellow) is implemented in the neck part, replacing the original CBL block. (Color figure online)

As shown in Fig. 2, the SE block consists of two parts: a squeeze operation and an excitation operation. First, the squeeze operation uses global average pooling to generate a channel-wise vector $\mathbf{v} \in \mathbb{R}^C$, and the c-th element of $\mathbf{v}$ is calculated by

$$\mathbf{v}_c = \mathbf{F}_{sq}\left(\mathbf{u}_c\right) = \frac{1}{H \times W} \sum_{i=1}^{H} \sum_{j=1}^{W} u_c(i, j), \tag{1}$$

where u_c is the c-th feature map. Then the excitation operation is conducted by

$$\mathbf{s} = \mathbf{F}_{ex}(\mathbf{v}, \mathbf{W}) = \sigma(g(\mathbf{v}, \mathbf{W})) = \sigma\left(\mathbf{W}_2 \delta\left(\mathbf{W}_1 \mathbf{v}\right)\right), \tag{2}$$

where σ, δ denote the sigmoid and ReLU function, respectively, $\mathbf{W}_1 \in \mathbb{R}^{\frac{C}{r} \times C}$, $\mathbf{W}_2 \in \mathbb{R}^{C \times \frac{C}{r}}$ and the reduction ratio r is set to 16 in this work. The output $\mathbf{s}$ is used to scale the input feature maps $\mathbf{u}$ by channel-wise multiplication. Through the SE block, the reweighted feature maps are generated, which can be directly fed into subsequent layers of the network.

SE blocks are lightweight which only slightly increase the computational cost, therefore they can be used to replace the original block of the network, or placed in any depth in the architecture. It is conceivable that different network structures with SE blocks will lead to different experimental results, but we are not concerned with finding out the best model design. In this work, we just use one SE block to replace the original CBL in the neck part to see how much one SE block can affect the final results.

3.3 YOLOv5s with CBAM

Convolutional Block Attention Module (CBAM) is a simple but effective attention module, like SE blocks, which can improve the representational power of convolutional neural networks [23]. There are two main dimensions in the process of feature extraction: channel and spatial axes. The traditional convolution neural networks extract the informative features by fusing spatial and channel-wide information together. However, the information in different spatial and channel features is not equally important. To increase the representational power, CBAM is proposed to effectively help the network to focus on important features and suppress the unimportant ones.

As shown in Fig. 3, a channel attention module and a spatial attention model are sequentially applied to emphasize important informative features. First, the channel attention module uses average-pooling and max-pooling to squeeze the spatial dimension of the input feature maps, generating two different spatial context descriptors, $\mathbf{F}_{avg}^c$ and $\mathbf{F}_{max}^c$, which are then forwarded to a shared network to produce the channel attention map. The shared network includes two fully connected layers. In brief, the channel attention is calculated by

$$\mathbf{M_c}(\mathbf{F}) = \sigma\left(\mathbf{W_2}\left(\mathbf{W_1}\left(\mathbf{F}_{avg}^c\right)\right) + \mathbf{W_2}\left(\mathbf{W_1}\left(\mathbf{F}_{max}^c\right)\right)\right), \tag{3}$$

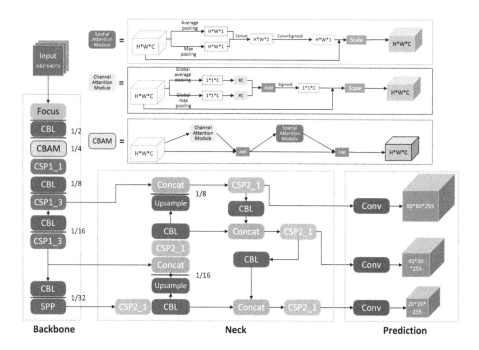

Fig. 3. YOLOv5s-CBAM network structure. CBAM is placed after the first CBL in the backbone part.

where σ denotes sigmoid function, $\mathbf{W}_1 \in \mathbb{R}^{\frac{C}{r} \times C}$ and $\mathbf{W}_2 \in \mathbb{R}^{C \times \frac{C}{r}}$ are transformation matrices for two fully connected layers in the shared network. The channel attention map is used to reweight the input feature maps by multiplication to capture meaningful channel informative features, which tells the network "what" to focus.

Furthermore, the reweighted feature maps are processed by the following spatial attention module to emphasize the important spatial informative features. First, the input feature maps are squeezed along the channel axis by applying average-pooling and max-pooling. Then the outputs of the two pooling operations, $\mathbf{F}_{avg}^s$ and $\mathbf{F}_{max}^s$, are concatenated to generate a spatial feature descriptor. Next, the spatial attention map $\mathbf{M}_s(\mathbf{F}) \in \mathbf{R}^{H \times W}$ is generated by applying a convolutional layer with sigmoid function on the spatial feature descriptor. In short, the spatial attention map is calculated by

$$\mathbf{M}_s(F) = \sigma\left(f^{7 \times 7}\left(\left[\mathbf{F}_{avg}^s; \mathbf{F}_{max}^s\right]\right)\right), \tag{4}$$

where $f^{7 \times 7}$ represents the convolutional operation with a kernel size of 7×7, and $[\cdot]$ represents the concat operation. Finally, by element-wise multiplication, the spatial attention module helps the network to learn "where" to focus, generating the refined feature maps, which can be fed into the further layers and improve the representational power of the network. The overall calculation of CBAM can be summarized as

$$\mathbf{F}' = \mathbf{M}_c\left(\mathbf{F}\right) \otimes \mathbf{F},$$
$$\mathbf{F}'' = \mathbf{M}_s\left(\mathbf{F}\right) \otimes \mathbf{F}', \tag{5}$$

where $\otimes$ denotes the element-wise multiplication.

Since CBAM is also a lightweight block, the overhead of parameters and burden for computation are negligible in most cases. The different arrangements of CBAMs in the architecture can lead to different results. In this work, we just place one CBAM after the first CBL in the backbone part. The experimental results of YOLOv5 and YOLOv5s-CBAM will show how this arrangement can affect the performance of object detection.

4 Experiment

4.1 Dataset

We evaluated the three networks on a novel image based benchmark dataset for water surface object detection, named Water Surface Object Dataset (WSODD) [27]. This dataset consists of 7467 water surface images in different water environments (oceans, lakes, and rivers), climate conditions (sunny, cloudy, and foggy days), and shooting times (daytime, twilight, and night). There are 14 categories and 21911 instances of common obstacles on the water surface (see Fig. 4). We divided WSODD with the ratio of 8:2 to generate a training dataset (5929 images) and a validation dataset (1538 images). The statistical results for instances of each category are shown in Fig. 5.

Fig. 4. WSODD includes 14 categories of water surface obstacles, namely, boat, ship, ball, bridge, rock, person, rubbish, mast, buoy, platform, harbor, tree, grass, and animal.

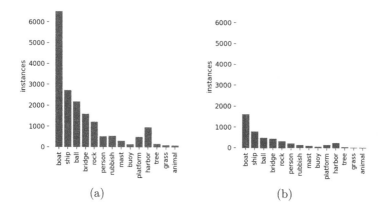

Fig. 5. Instances of each category in (a) training dataset and (b) validation dataset.

4.2   Implementation Details

The experiment is carried out on a platform of Ubuntu 16.04 operating system, which is equipped with 64 GB memory, an Intel Core i9-9700X CPU, and an Nvidia TITAN Xp GPU (11 GB memory). The three networks are implemented based on the PyTorch framework. The optimization algorithm adopts the stochastic gradient descent with the initial learning rate of 0.01 and the momentum of 0.9. The batch size is set to 16 and the training iteration is 100 epochs.

In the training phase, since the randomly initialized model parameters may spend more time to make the network converge, we used the model parameters pretrained on the MS COCO for initialization. In addition, the pretrained YOLOv5s network is designed to detect 80 classes of objects, whereas WSODD is composed of 14 categories of maritime obstacles. Therefore, we adjust the prediction part to fit the maritime obstacle detection task.

To evaluate the performance of each network, we adopt three evaluation indexes: precision (P), recall (R), and mean average precision (mAP). P and R are calculated by

$$P = \frac{TP}{TP + FP}, \tag{6}$$

$$R = \frac{TP}{TP + FN}, \tag{7}$$

where TP (true positive) represents the correctly detected obstacle, FP (false positive) indicates the wrongly detected obstacle, and FN (false negative) refers to the obstacle that fails to be detected. In addition, the intersection over union (IOU) is used to determine whether a detection result is positive or negative, which is defined as

$$IOU = \frac{\text{area}\left(B_p \cap B_{gt}\right)}{\text{area}\left(B_p \cup B_{gt}\right)}, \tag{8}$$

where B_p, B_{gt} denote the bounding boxes of the prediction and the ground truth. The IOU indicates the overlap of the prediction bounding box and the ground truth. The threshold of the IOU determines the detection result. For example, if the threshold of IOU is set to 0.5, detection results with an IOU over 0.5 are considered positive, while those with an IOU below 0.5 are considered negative. Each value of the threshold of IOU (from 0 to 1) corresponds to a pair of P and R values. The precision-recall curve (P-R curve) is generated based on all pairs of P and R values. Furthermore, the AP and mAP are calculated by

$$mAP = \frac{\sum_{i=1}^{n} AP_i}{n}, \tag{9}$$

$$AP = \int_0^1 P(r)dr, \tag{10}$$

where n is the number of categories and AP_i denotes the average precision (AP) of the i-th category. $P(r)$ represents the P-R curve, in which the area under the curve indicates the AP. The mAP is the mean of APs of all categories, which shows the performance of the detector.

5   Results

The P-R curves of YOLOv5s, YOLOv5s-SE, and YOLOv5s-CBAM are shown in Fig. 6. In each subfigure, the AP of each category and the mAP are given. The area under the blue curve represents the mAP. The mAPs of YOLOv5s, YOLOv5s-SE, and YOLOv5s-CBAM are 0.846, 0.820, and 0.844, respectively. YOLOv5s and YOLOv5s-CBAM perform comparably whereas YOLOv5s-SE performs with the lowest mAP, which indicates that the SE block and CBAM implemented in YOLOv5s do not lead to significant improvements in terms of mAP. Nevertheless, the mAP represents the mean average precision of 14 categories of obstacles, which include large obstacles and small ones. Generally, large obstacles are more dangerous than small ones in the event of a collision. Therefore, we should pay more attention to the detection of large obstacles. YOLOv5-SE and YOLOv5-CBAM reach higher APs in the detection for several specific categories, which indicates that SE block and CBAM have the ability to enhance the representation power of YOLOv5s.

In order to find out the specific effects of the SE block and CBAM, we make a comparison of precision, recall, and mAP for the three networks, which is shown in Table 3. The results show that the SE block only contributes to the precision of the grass with 0.899 and the recall of the buoy with 0.690. In addition, the CBAM enhances YOLOv5s in many ways. Specifically, YOLOv5s-CBAM has improvements in the precision of 6 categories, the recall of 10 categories, and the mAP of 7 categories. Especially, for the detection of large objects such as the boat, ship, bridge, and platform, YOLOv5s-CBAM has a better performance compared with YOLOv5s. Since large obstacles are more dangerous than small obstacles if the collision occurs, the accuracy of large obstacles is more important and should be mainly taken into account when designing a maritime obstacle detection method. Moreover, the detection performance of small objects, such as the ball, rock, person, and rubbish, is relatively poor with mAPs lower than 0.8. The reason is that the small object covers fewer pixels in the image, which leads to the deficiency of useful features and the weakness of feature representation in the process of feature extraction. Fortunately, the small obstacles do not cause severe damage as larges ones do. It is acceptable that the detection performance of small obstacles is relatively unsatisfactory.

Furthermore, we compare the performance of YOLOv5s, YOLOv5s-SE, and YOLOv5s-CBAM with other object detection networks applied in the WSODD, namely, YOLOv4 [22], ShipYOLO [9], and CRB-Net [27]. In Table 1, we summarize the performance of the six networks, including the mAP and AP for each category. The result indicates that the three networks evaluated in this work outperform the previous three networks significantly. The mAPs of YOLOv5s, YOLOv5s-SE, and YOLOv5s-CBAM are 0.846, 0.820, and 0.844, respectively, whereas the mAP of CRB-Net is 0.654, which is the highest in previous related work for maritime obstacle detection.

As shown in Table 2, the SE block and CBAM increase the parameters very slightly, which indicates that we can implement more blocks in any depth of the network without increasing a significant computation burden. It is worthwhile to further investigate how to implement the blocks in the network, including how many blocks we should use and where to place the blocks. There are three parts in YOLOv5s network, namely, the backbone part, the neck part, and the prediction part. In this work, we placed one SE block in the neck part and one CBAM in the backbone part, the latter has proven to be helpful to enhance the feature representation power, which indicates that the modification in the backbone part works better than that in the neck part. Since the prediction part has three branches to fuse features maps from different layers, it is a feasible design to place blocks in each branch.

In addition, the speeds of the three networks are 24.2 ms, 24.2 ms, and 25.8 ms, respectively. YOLOv5s-SE is as fast as YOLOv5s and YOLOv5s-CBAM is the slowest. The CBAM slightly increases the computational burden. However, it is accepted that when the frame per second (FPS) is over 30, the network can meet the real-time requirement. Therefore, YOLOv5s-CABM can also be used in the real-time maritime obstacle detection task with an FPS of 38.7.

The above results show that YOLOv5s, YOLOv5s-CBAM, and YOLOv5s-SE achieve state-of-the-art performance in the real-time maritime obstacle detection task. The CBAM contributes to the detection performance of the original network, especially the detection for large obstacles, which reveals that the modified block can boost the representation power of YOLOv5s to some extent (Fig. 7).

Table 1. Detection performance of different networks.

Method	mAP	AP_{50}													
		Boat	Ship	Ball	Bridge	Rock	Person	Rubbish	Mast	Buoy	Platform	Harbor	Tree	Grass	Animal
YOLOv4	57.2	85.5	84.7	25.4	92.7	47.8	62.5	56.8	57.1	55.7	69.3	88.4	73.9	44.8	54.4
ShipYOLO	58.4	88.1	87.1	41.5	93.2	52.7	66.7	45.2	63.8	59.1	71.8	78.6	59.5	57.9	56.7
CRB-Net	65.4	89.0	90.1	69.5	96.4	70.2	71.8	49.5	49.7	59.3	75.4	88.3	72.1	47.5	74.3
YOLOv5s	84.6	90	92.9	71.7	98.6	**81.4**	78.4	62.9	**89.4**	**83.2**	85.0	**93.1**	87.2	**70.1**	**99.3**
YOLOv5s-SE	82.0	89.6	92.3	67.2	97.8	75.3	72.0	65.3	84.4	78.5	86.2	89.9	**87.9**	62.7	99.0
YOLOve5-CBAM	84.4	**90.9**	**93.2**	**71.8**	**98.9**	78.5	**79.9**	**68.5**	86.3	78.6	**87.6**	92.3	86.7	69.0	98.9

Table 2. The speed and parameters of detection for three networks.

	Speed (ms)	FPS	Parameters (M)
YOLOv5s	24.2	41.3	14.1
YOLOv5s-SE	24.2	41.3	14.6
YOLOv5s-CBAM	25.8	38.7	14.1

Table 3. Details of precision, recall, and mAP for YOLOv5s, YOLOv5s-SE, and YOLOv5s-CBAM.

	P			R			mAP		
	v5s	v5s-SE	v5s-CBAM	v5s	v5s-SE	v5s-CBAM	v5s	v5s-SE	v5s-CBAM
All	**87.5**	84.9	87.3	76.7	76.3	**78.7**	**84.6**	82.0	84.4
Boat	**89.2**	87.4	89.0	85.9	**86.0**	85.8	**90.8**	89.6	**90.8**
Ship	91.8	91.9	**94.2**	89.4	88.3	**89.7**	92.9	92.3	**93.2**
Ball	73.9	69.6	**74.9**	62.7	63.9	**65.3**	71.7	67.2	**71.8**
Bridge	96.0	95.3	**96.2**	95.5	93.8	**96.2**	98.6	97.8	**98.9**
Rock	**86.7**	85.2	86.6	**68.2**	64.6	67.8	**81.4**	75.3	78.5
Person	**88.2**	77.5	84.7	**71.0**	69.9	76.5	78.4	72.0	**79.9**
Rubbish	78.4	70.8	**80.6**	58.0	62.5	**64.4**	62.9	65.3	**68.5**
Mast	**85.9**	81.9	83.0	83.1	79.7	**84.7**	**89.4**	84.4	86.3
Buoy	**94.5**	84.0	85.6	58.7	**69.0**	62.1	**83.2**	78.5	78.6
Platform	**84.4**	80.3	83.8	83.6	82.2	**84.5**	85.0	86.2	**87.6**
Harbor	**92.6**	89.7	92.4	79.9	74.3	**81.8**	**93.1**	89.9	92.3
Tree	89.3	91.9	**96.7**	79.4	82.4	**92.4**	87.2	**87.9**	86.7
Grass	89.2	**89.9**	89.6	57.9	57.9	**63.2**	**70.1**	62.7	69.0
Animal	85.5	93.7	**94.6**	**100**	94.4	97.0	**99.3**	99.0	98.9

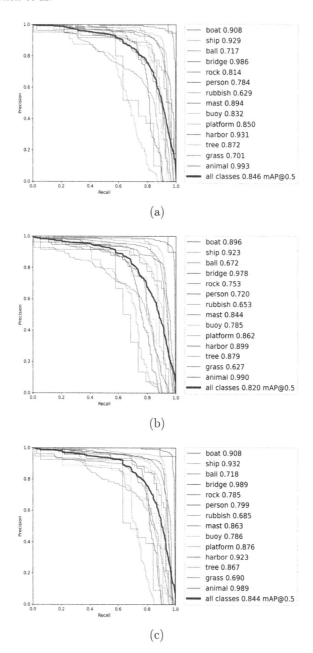

Fig. 6. P-R curves of (a) YOLOv5s, (b) YOLOv5s-SE, and (c) YOLOv5s-CBAM.

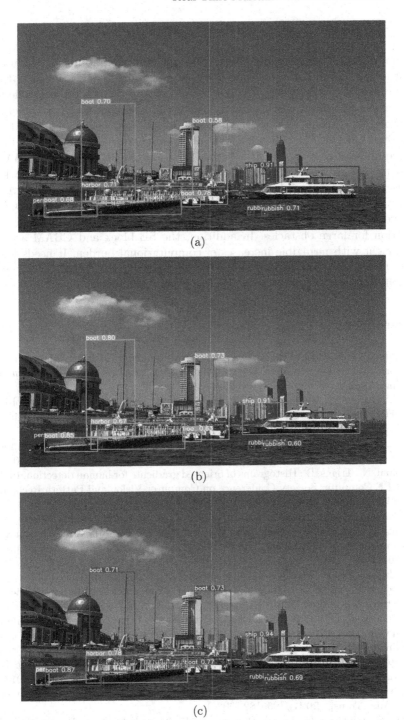

(a)

(b)

(c)

Fig. 7. Detection results of (a) YOLOv5s (b) YOLOv5s-SE (c) YOLOv5s-CBAM.

6   Conclusion

The autonomous berthing and docking system plays an important role in intelligent ships, in which the collision avoidance planning is essential. Due to the limitation of the LiDAR sensor based obstacle detection method, it is a demand to develop a real-time maritime obstacle detection approach based on cameras. In this work, we introduced three networks, namely YOLOv5s, YOLOv5s-SE, and YOLOv5s-CBAM. They all reach state-of-the-art performance on WSODD with the requirement of real-time. It is turned out that the SE block and CBAM can boost the feature representation power in case that we implement the block in a practicable way. We conclude that YOLOv5s-CBAM can meet the requirement of the real-time maritime obstacle detection task. Although YOLOv5s-CBAM achieves an mAP slightly lower than YOLOv5s, it outperforms the latter in the detection for large obstacles. In addition, the SE block and CBAM are both lightweight with negligible increases of computational burden. It needs further study to find out how to implement the SE blocks and CBAM since they can help the network to perform obstacle detection tasks better.

References

1. Ahmed, Y.A., Hasegawa, K.: Automatic ship berthing using artificial neural network trained by consistent teaching data using nonlinear programming method. Eng. Appl. Artif. Intell. **26**(10), 2287–2304 (2013)
2. Bi, F., Chen, J., Zhuang, Y., Bian, M., Zhang, Q.: A decision mixture model-based method for inshore ship detection using high-resolution remote sensing images. Sensors **17**(7), 1470 (2017)
3. Chen, Z., Chen, D., Zhang, Y., Cheng, X., Zhang, M., Wu, C.: Deep learning for autonomous ship-oriented small ship detection. Saf. Sci. **130**, 104812 (2020)
4. Dalal, N., Triggs, B.: Histograms of oriented gradients for human detection. In: 2005 IEEE Computer Society Conference on Computer Vision and Pattern Recognition (CVPR 2005), vol. 1, pp. 886–893 (2005)
5. Esposito, J.M., Graves, M.: An algorithm to identify docking locations for autonomous surface vessels from 3-D lidar scans. In: 2014 IEEE International Conference on Technologies for Practical Robot Applications (TePRA), pp. 1–6 (2014)
6. Felzenszwalb, P., McAllester, D., Ramanan, D.: A discriminatively trained, multi-scale, deformable part model. In: 2008 IEEE Conference on Computer Vision and Pattern Recognition (CVPR), pp. 1–8 (2008)
7. Girshick, R.: Fast R-CNN. In: Proceedings of the IEEE International Conference on Computer Vision (ICCV), pp. 1440–1448, December 2015
8. Girshick, R., Donahue, J., Darrell, T., Malik, J.: Rich feature hierarchies for accurate object detection and semantic segmentation. In: Proceedings of the IEEE Conference on Computer Vision and Pattern Recognition, pp. 580–587 (2014)
9. Han, X., Zhao, L., Ning, Y., Hu, J.: ShipYolo: an enhanced model for ship detection. J. Adv. Transp. **2021**, 1060182 (2021)
10. He, K., Gkioxari, G., Dollar, P., Girshick, R.: Mask R-CNN. In: Proceedings of the IEEE International Conference on Computer Vision, pp. 2961–2969, October 2017

11. Hu, J., Shen, L., Sun, G.: Squeeze-and-excitation networks. In: Proceedings of the IEEE Conference on Computer Vision and Pattern Recognition (CVPR), pp. 7132–7141, June 2018

12. Jia, W., et al.: Real-time automatic helmet detection of motorcyclists in urban traffic using improved YOLOv5 detector. IET Image Proc. **15**, 3623–3637 (2021)

13. Jie, Y., Leonidas, L., Mumtaz, F., Ali, M.: Ship detection and tracking in inland waterways using improved YOLOv3 and Deep SORT. Symmetry **13**(2), 308 (2021)

14. Lin, T.Y., Dollár, P., Girshick, R., He, K., Hariharan, B., Belongie, S.: Feature pyramid networks for object detection. In: Proceedings of the IEEE Conference on Computer Vision and Pattern Recognition (CVPR), pp. 2117–2125, July 2017

15. Lin, T.Y., Goyal, P., Girshick, R., He, K., Dollár, P.: Focal loss for dense object detection. In: Proceedings of the IEEE International Conference on Computer Vision (ICCV), pp. 2980–2988, October 2017

16. Liu, W., et al.: SSD: single shot MultiBox detector. In: Leibe, B., Matas, J., Sebe, N., Welling, M. (eds.) ECCV 2016. LNCS, vol. 9905, pp. 21–37. Springer, Cham (2016). https://doi.org/10.1007/978-3-319-46448-0_2

17. Qin, Y., Zhang, X.: Robust obstacle detection for unmanned surface vehicles. In: MIPPR 2017: Remote Sensing Image Processing, Geographic Information Systems, and Other Applications, vol. 10611, pp. 340–345 (2018)

18. Redmon, J., Divvala, S., Girshick, R., Farhadi, A.: You only look once: unified, real-time object detection. In: Proceedings of the IEEE Conference on Computer Vision and Pattern Recognition (CVPR), pp. 779–788, June 2016

19. Ren, S., He, K., Girshick, R., Sun, J.: Faster R-CNN: towards real-time object detection with region proposal networks. IEEE Trans. Pattern Anal. Mach. Intell. **39**(6), 1137–1149 (2017)

20. Viola, P., Jones, M.: Rapid object detection using a boosted cascade of simple features. In: Proceedings of the 2001 IEEE Computer Society Conference on Computer Vision and Pattern Recognition (CVPR), vol. 1, pp. I-511–I-518 (2001)

21. Wang, K., Liew, J.H., Zou, Y., Zhou, D., Feng, J.: PANet: few-shot image semantic segmentation with prototype alignment. In: Proceedings of the IEEE/CVF International Conference on Computer Vision, pp. 9197–9206 (2019)

22. Wang, Y., Wang, L., Jiang, Y., Li, T.: Detection of self-build dataset based on YOLOv4 network. In: 2020 IEEE 3rd International Conference on Information Systems and Computer Aided Education (ICISCAE), pp. 640–642 (2020)

23. Woo, S., Park, J., Lee, J.Y., Kweon, I.S.: CBAM: convolutional block attention module. In: Proceedings of the European Conference on Computer Vision (ECCV), pp. 3–19 (2018)

24. Xiao, X., Dufek, J., Woodbury, T., Murphy, R.: UAV assisted USV visual navigation for marine mass casualty incident response. In: 2017 IEEE/RSJ International Conference on Intelligent Robots and Systems (IROS), pp. 6105–6110 (2017)

25. Yang, J., Xiao, Y., Fang, Z., Zhang, N., Wang, L., Li, T.: An object detection and tracking system for unmanned surface vehicles. In: Target and Background Signatures III, vol. 10432, pp. 244–251 (2017)

26. Zhang, Y., Shu, J., Hu, L., Zhou, Q., Du, Z.: A ship target tracking algorithm based on deep learning and multiple features. In: Twelfth International Conference on Machine Vision (ICMV 2019), vol. 11433, pp. 19–26 (2020)

27. Zhou, Z., et al.: An image-based benchmark dataset and a novel object detector for water surface object detection. Front. Neurorobot. **15**, 127 (2021)

28. Zou, Z., Shi, Z., Guo, Y., Ye, J.: Object detection in 20 years: a survey. arXiv preprint arXiv:1905.05055 (2019)

Author Index